W9-CBD-739

The Flowering of
Old Testament Theology

Sources for Biblical and Theological Study

General Editor:
David W. Baker
Ashland Theological Seminary

1. *The Flowering of Old Testament Theology: A Reader in Twentieth-Century Old Testament Theology, 1930–1990*
   edited by Ben C. Ollenburger, Elmer A. Martens, and Gerhard F. Hasel

2. *Beyond Form Criticism: Essays in Old Testament Literary Criticism*
   edited by Paul R. House

3. *A Song of Power and the Power of Song: Essays on the Book of Deuteronomy*
   edited by Duane L. Christensen

The Flowering of Old Testament Theology

A Reader in Twentieth-Century
Old Testament Theology, 1930–1990

edited by
Ben C. Ollenburger
Elmer A. Martens
Gerhard F. Hasel

Eisenbrauns
Winona Lake, Indiana
1992

Library of Congress Cataloging-in-Publication Data

The Flowering of Old Testament theology : a reader in twentieth-century Old
    Testament theology, 1930–1990 / edited by Ben C. Ollenburger, Elmer A.
    Martens, Gerhard F. Hasel.
        p.   cm.—(Sources for biblical and theological study ; 1)
    Includes bibliographical references and indexes.
    ISBN 0-931464-62-5
    1. Bible. O.T.—Theology—History—20th century.   2. Bible. O.T.—
Theology.   I. Ollenburger, Ben C.   II. Martens, E. A.   III. Hasel,
Gerhard F.   IV. Series.
BS1192.5.F564   1991
230—dc20   91-24963

96 97 99
10 9 8 7 6 5 4 3

The paper used in this publication meets the minimum requirements of the
American National Standard for Information Sciences—Permanence of Paper
for Printed Library Materials, ANSI Z39.48-1984.∞™

CONTENTS

Part 3: The Way Forward:
Old Testament Theology in the Twenty-first Century

Appendix

SERIES PREFACE

Old Testament scholarship is well served by several recent works which detail, to a greater or lesser extent, the progress made in the study of the Old Testament. Some survey the range of interpretation over long stretches of time, while others concern themselves with a smaller chronological or geographical segment of the field. There are also brief *entrés* into the various subdisciplines of Old Testament study included in the standard introductions as well as in several useful series. All of these provide secondary syntheses of various aspects of Old Testament research. All refer to, and base their discussions upon, various seminal works by Old Testament scholars which have proven pivotal in the development and flourishing of the various aspects of the discipline.

The main avenue into the various areas of Old Testament inquiry, especially for the beginner, has been until now mainly through the filter of these interpreters. Even on a pedagogical level, however, it is beneficial for a student to be able to interact with foundational works firsthand. This contact will not only provide insight into the content of an area, but hopefully will also lead to the sharpening of critical abilities through interaction with various viewpoints. This series seeks to address this need by including not only key, ground-breaking works, but also significant responses to these. This allows the student to appreciate the process of scholarly development through interaction.

The series is also directed toward scholars. In a period of burgeoning knowledge and significant publication in many places and languages around the world, this series will endeavor to make easily accessible significant, but at times hard to find, contributions. Each volume will contain essays, articles, extracts, and the like, presenting in a manageable scope the growth and development of one of a number of different aspects of Old Testament studies. Most volumes will contain previously published material, with synthetic essays by the editor(s) of the individual volume. Some volumes, however, are expected to contain significant, previously unpublished works. To facilitate access to students and schol-ars, all entries will appear in English and will be newly typeset. If students are excited by the study of Scripture and scholars are encouraged in ami-cable dialogue, this series would have fulfilled its purpose.

DAVID W. BAKER, *series editor*
Ashland Theological Seminary

EDITORS' FOREWORD

Old Testament Theology as a scholarly discipline has had a lively history in the twentieth century. Magisterial volumes appeared prior to mid-century; debate on methodology and the publication of scores of Old Testament theologies followed. At intervals the entire enterprise of setting out a theology of the Old Testament was lamented and described as being in crisis. Still, after some six decades the scholarly deposit is extensive.

This volume is especially an attempt to orient the student. By sampling the writing, the reader will better understand not only the issues but the progress and the achievements. The book attempts something of a grand sweep through the century. An introductory essay in part 1 surveys the developments in former centuries that led to the issues addressed in the classic essays by Otto Eissfeldt and Walther Eichrodt in the 1920s. These essays, now for the first time made available in English, set the stage for further developments. In part 2 excerpts from selected authors should give readers a feel, not only for variations in style, but, more important, for varieties of perspectives. Some most insightful syntheses have been put forward. There is not, it must be said, unanimity on either method or structure of the discipline. In part 3 a glimpse into fresh proposals is given. These, in one way or another, will shape the discussion for the twenty-first century. So beyond an orientation for the student, this volume, so the editors hope, will foster scholarly discussion.

For each of the fourteen authors in part 2, there are two types of excerpts. The first focuses on the author's programmatic statement; the second offers a sample of the content of an Old Testament theology from that author's point of view. Granted that Old Testament theology is occupied to see the "whole" Old Testament, excerpts will not do justice to an author's larger conceptualization. But the justification for an excerpt is in part to whet the student's appetite to consult the primary source. An interpretive overview by one of the editors introduces the author, presents the setting, and highlights the nature of his contribution.

The editors attempted a balance in their choices of excerpts according to criteria such as geographical balance (European/North American), temporal balance (early/late in the century), and theological orientation.

Different editors would have made different selections; the subjective element is ever present. To keep the volume affordable for students, the editors and publisher agreed to a selection of approximately twenty pages per author, despite the greater influence of some scholars compared to others. Representations from Asia or other continents, or from liberation or feminist perspectives, were seriously considered, but could not be included because of space limitations and other factors. At the outset large numbers of periodical articles were reviewed as candidates for inclusion. It was then thought preferable in part 2 to provide excerpts only from complete monographs. Even so the project, stretching over four years, was more demanding than at first envisioned.

The excerpts have not been edited for gender-inclusive language, nor have the editors changed "Old Testament" to "Hebrew Scripture," a designation now current in academic circles. Clarifications or additions supplied by the editors are enclosed in double square brackets, as are original page numbers. A long omission is indicated by a line of spaced dots.

Aside from the general use of this reader to supplement class texts, the following are specific suggestions for its use in teaching. Students might read selectively on methodology from the "approach" excerpts, write an initial summary, and follow that with a "supplement" from readings (say in Hasel 1991, Reventlow 1985, or Høgenhaven 1988). Students might choose a "content" excerpt and develop or critique the relevant topic. Or, as various themes are broached in class lectures, appropriate readings by content might be assigned. Experience shows that students highly value the orientation essays.

Grateful acknowledgement is given to the publishers who gave permission to excerpt. David Baker, series editor, and Jim Eisenbraun from the publishing firm have been helpful coaches and allies. David Aiken, editor at Eisenbrauns, has been meticulous with detail, creative in design, and helpful in numerous ways. Hans Kasdorf and Gordon Zerbe assisted with the translation of the essays by Eissfeldt and Eichrodt. In her work at the word-processor, Donna Sullivan was patient and cheerful, as well as efficient. Douglas Heidebrecht, a teaching assistant, made the task easier and the product better.

April 1990   BEN C. OLLENBURGER
                                    Associated Mennonite Biblical Seminaries

                                    ELMER A. MARTENS
                                    Mennonite Brethren Biblical Seminary

                                    GERHARD F. HASEL
                                    Theological Seminary, Andrews University

ABBREVIATIONS

General

A.T.	Altes Testament
E	Elohist writings
ET	English translation
J	Jahwist writings
LXX	Septuagint
MT	Masoretic Text
NF	Neue Folge (New Series)
NJV	New Jewish Version
NT	New Testament
OT	Old Testament
P	Priestly writings
RSV	Revised Standard Version
R.V.	Revised Version

Books and Periodicals

AnBib	Analecta Biblica
ANEP	J. B. Pritchard (ed.), *Ancient Near East in Pictures*
ANET	J. B. Pritchard (ed.), *Ancient Near Eastern Texts Relating to the Old Testament*
BASOR	*Bulletin of the American Schools of Oriental Research*
BK	Biblischer Kommentar
BSt	Biblische Studien
BZ	*Biblische Zeitschrift*
CBQ	*Catholic Biblical Quarterly*
CJ	*Conservative Judaism*
CJT	*Canadian Journal of Theology*
DBS	*Dictionnaire de la Bible, Supplément*
ET	*Expository Times*

Ev. Quarterly	*Evangelical Quarterly*
Ev. Th./EvTh	*Evangelische Theologie*
FRLANT	Forschungen zur Religion und Literatur des Alten und Neuen Testaments
HSM	Harvard Semitic Monographs
HSS	Harvard Semitic Studies
IDB	*Interpreter's Dictionary of the Bible*
IDB, Suppl. Vol.	*Interpreter's Dictionary of the Bible: Supplementary Volume*
In./Int/Interp	*Interpretation*
JAOS	*Journal of the American Oriental Society*
JBL	*Journal of Biblical Literature*
JJS	*Journal of Jewish Studies*
JQR	*Jewish Quarterly Review*
JSOT	*Journal for the Study of the Old Testament*
JT(h)S	*Journal of Theological Studies*
MSL	Materials for the Sumerian Lexicon
OTS	*Oudtestamentische Studiën*
RHPR	*Revue d'histoire et de philosophie religieuses*
RTP	*Revue de théologie et de philosophie*
SJT	*Scottish Journal of Theology*
StBib	*Studia Biblica et Theologica* (Pasadena)
ThB	*Theologische Bücherei*
Theol. Lit. Zt./ThLZ	*Theologische Literaturzeitung*
ThR	*Theologische Rundschau*
ThSt	*Theologische Studien*
TS	*Theological Studies*
TWNT	Gerhard Kittel and Gerhard Friedrich (eds.), *Theologisches Wörterbuch zum Neuen Testament*
TZ	*Theologische Zeitschrift*
VT	*Vetus Testamentum*
ZATWiss/ZAW	*Zeitschrift für die Alttestamentliche Wissenschaft*
ZT(h)K	*Zeitschrift für Theologie und Kirche*

Part 1

Setting the Stage

From Timeless Ideas to the Essence of Religion

Method in Old Testament Theology before 1930

BEN C. OLLENBURGER

In the Beginning

Biblical theology, including Old Testament theology, is marked by diversity and debate. That should not surprise us. In the course of two centuries disagreements are bound to emerge regarding the nature and task of any academic discipline, as they have in our case. In our case, as with other disciplines, the reasons for disagreement are not only academic. One biblical theologian has suggested that it is because of "the current crisis in church and theology" that biblical theology commands a special interest. In such a situation, he says, "many different attempts at biblical theology will have their place." In fact, he reports that scholars use the term *biblical theology* to mean six quite different things, and he tries to chart his own course through this diversity.

One might expect that an account of Old Testament theology's earlier history, such as I will offer in this chapter, would show how its current

---

BEN C. OLLENBURGER was born in Kansas in 1948 and graduated from California State University (Long Beach) and Mennonite Brethren Biblical Seminary (Fresno, California). He taught at Tabor College (Hillsboro, Kansas) before studying for his doctorate in Old Testament at Princeton Theological Seminary. Upon graduation in 1982 he continued as assistant professor at Princeton until 1987, teaching, among other courses, several on Old Testament Theology. Since 1987 he has been associate professor of Old Testament at Associated Mennonite Biblical Seminaries in Elkhart, Indiana. His dissertation was published under the title *Zion, the City of the Great King: A Theological Symbol of the Jerusalem Cult* (1987). His translations of articles by Claus Westermann and Walther Zimmerli appeared in *Understanding the Word: Essays in Honor of Bernhard W. Anderson,* of which he was also coeditor.

3

diversity emerged over time. It seems, however, that the diversity was already there at the beginning. The challenge to come to terms with that diversity is a continuing one. Even though the quotations in the previous paragraph seem quite up to date, they are from the preface of a book by Ludwig Friedrich Otto Baumgarten-Crusius, late professor of dogmatic theology in the University of Jena. His book, on "The Basic Characteristics of Biblical Theology," was published in 1828. It is somewhat disheartening to realize that by the time biblical theology had come to be acknowledged as a distinct area of study, about the time of Baumgarten-Crusius, its diversity was already confusing. It also means that we cannot look back to a time when everyone agreed what biblical theology was and what it should do.

In alluding to "the current crisis in church and theology," Baumgarten-Crusius already gave some hint why there was so much disagreement about biblical and Old Testament theology. From the beginning, biblical theologians saw themselves addressing significant theological issues on behalf of the church. While they may have agreed that the church was in crisis, they differed about what the crisis was or how it should be resolved. And while they may have agreed that theology was in crisis, they differed about how theology should use the Bible in resolving its crises. Those disagreements made it inevitable, right from the start, that biblical theology would be conceived in different ways. But despite these disagreements and the various approaches to biblical theology resulting from them, Baumgarten-Crusius was able to cite one unifying factor: biblical theology emerged together with historical interpretation of the Bible. "The idea and the execution of biblical theology," he says, "are joined essentially with historical interpretation, and each of them has developed in recent times in relation to the other" (1828: 4).

One of the eighteenth century's most important intellectual contributions was its emphasis on historical understanding. That emphasis had a significant impact on arts and letters generally, and it was crucial for theology (Shaffer 1975). By the end of the eighteenth century it had become clear that historical interpretation—more precisely, historical-*critical* interpretation—offered a fresh and different understanding of the Bible. More specifically, some Protestant theologians were convinced that historical interpretation of the Bible provided new and much more adequate foundations for dogmatic (or systematic) theology. However, it remained a matter of controversy exactly how those two, historical interpretation and dogmatic theology, should be related to each other. Biblical theology emerged as a consequence of this controversy. In fact, it would not be too strong to say that, at its beginning, biblical theology *was* this controversy; it was an inquiry into the question how historical study of the Bible should relate itself to dogmatic theology. Historical interpretation made biblical theology possible, and it posed at the same time the particular problems that biblical theology had to confront.

Baumgarten-Crusius was right: historical interpretation and biblical theology developed in relation to each other. Scholars often locate the beginning of that development in 1787, when Johann Philipp Gabler gave his inaugural address as professor of theology in the University of Altdorf, Germany. In his address (reprinted below, pp. 489–502), and in later publications, Gabler proposed that biblical and dogmatic theology are different tasks requiring different procedures. *Biblical* theology, he said, must come first. It consists of historical exposition of the Bible, which treats each biblical statement in terms of its author's historical setting, followed by a philosophically informed explanation of those biblical statements; this explanation seeks to determine which of the biblical ideas or concepts are abidingly true. The biblical ideas that pass the test of reason, those that are not merely historical or local, then provide the foundation for dogmatic theology (Ollenburger 1985).

This brief outline of Gabler's proposal is sufficient to show that, for Gabler, biblical theology's problem consisted in determining what in the Bible was of abiding validity, and how to present it in a way appropriate to the Bible's historical character. Gabler's own solution was to combine the "grammatical-historical" interpretation of scripture with a theory of historical "development by stages" (Hartlich and Sachs 1952: 46). According to this theory, which Gabler borrowed from the classical and biblical scholars Heyne and Eichhorn, people in more primitive stages of development expressed themselves in ways suited to their limited rational powers, namely, in mythical images. Interpretation has the task, then, of separating the unchanging truth from the changing mythical imagery that shrouds it. In the Bible's case, it is important to determine where the authors of its various texts stand on the ladder of rational development. Once we see that its authors were using various mythical images, rather than writing like philosophers, we can extract the timeless truths from the images and elaborate them in dogmatic theology. And then, according to Gabler, we will have a sure foundation on which to resolve the crises of church and theology.

One possible implication of Gabler's proposal is that the Old Testament occupies a lower rung on the ladder of reason than does the New; after all, it is from an earlier era. Georg Lorenz Bauer was the first to draw this implication, in the first published Old Testament theology, in 1796. His book carried the subtitle, "A Summary of the Religious Concepts of the Hebrews." Bauer, who was for a time Gabler's colleague in Altdorf, argued that the differences between the two testaments are decisive; a separate theology would have to be written for each of them. In his decision to

make Old Testament theology an undertaking of its own, Bauer anticipated later nineteenth- and twentieth-century scholars. He anticipated
many of them in at least three other respects as well. (1) For Bauer, Old
Testament theology focused primarily on religious ideas or concepts.
(2) He claimed that historical interpretation must trace the development
of those ideas and interpret them in independence from dogmatic theology's definitions. Only in that way would Old Testament (and then New
Testament) theology be able to reform dogmatics. (3) In the course of
their development, in the Old Testament as in history generally, ideas
move from particular to universal, and it is these universal religious ideas
that are most important for the present. Bauer says that in the Old Testament these universal ideas are to be found principally in Proverbs and
Job, because their authors are the least concerned with *particulars*—with
their own time, their own people, their own situation. (The same view appears later, in Ludwig Noack 1853: 89–90.) Still, the Old Testament is
everywhere inferior to the New.

Bauer anticipated his nineteenth-century successors in still another respect: despite his insistence on the historical character of Old Testament
theology, he arranges the ideas in strictly doctrinal categories. His two major categories are "theology, or the doctrine of God and his relation to humankind," and "anthropology, or the doctrine of humankind and its
relation to God," with an appendix on "Christology, or the doctrine of the
ancient Hebrews concerning the Messiah" (Bauer 1796). To deal with this
inconsistency between method and presentation, later editions of his book
included Bauer's *Beilagen* ("supplements"), which trace the Old Testament's religious ideas historically through the canonical books.

Philosophy and History

While Bauer set the tone for what followed, his successors tended to agree
that one of two problems afflicted Bauer's Old Testament theology: either
it was insufficiently historical, or it was theologically inadequate; some
even said it was both. They disagreed, however, about how to resolve these
problems. His immediate successors tried to deal with Bauer's theological
inadequacy by placing Old Testament (or more often, biblical) theology
within a comprehensive philosophical framework. The purpose of such a
framework was hermeneutical: it served as a theory for the interpretation
of the Bible.

Christoph Friedrich von Ammon set his *Biblische Theologie* (published
in 1801–2, as the revised version of an earlier attempt in 1792) within the
framework of Immanuel Kant's moral philosophy, and specifically of
"Kantian hermeneutics" (1801: xii). He did so cautiously, however, admit-

ting that Kantian interpretation, on the basis of "pure practical reason," was a "philosophical midrash" and a version of allegorical interpretation, as Gabler also argued. It tended to confer equal value, he said, on a theology of the Qurʾān, the Mishnah, and the I Ching, and "my hermeneutical principles do not permit me to share in this multiplication of theological profit" (1801: xii–xiii). Ammon's goal was to provide a more adequate account of the biblical foundations of dogmatic theology through a critical study of the Bible. This would free it, he says, from the "nimbus of illusory ideas" with which previous dogmatic interpretation had surrounded it (1801: 8). Ammon also recognized that there is a history of development within the Old Testament, and thus a history of revelation, but he took almost no account of it. Instead, he treated individual doctrines, citing the traditional proof texts and testing them against the criterion of rationality. That criterion, understood in a Kantian moral sense, was crucial for Ammon, because only what is rational can be judged revelation and carried over into dogmatics.

Wilhelm Martin Leberecht de Wette was much more self-conscious about method than were either Bauer or Ammon. He opens his *Biblische Dogmatik* (1813; third edition, 1831) with a lengthy discussion of the nature of religion and the requirements for understanding its historical expression in the Old Testament. He borrowed the terms of this discussion from the philosophical anthropology of Jakob F. Fries, another Kantian. De Wette was no less adamant than was Bauer that the Bible is a historical document, but he argued that it is necessary to lay out a careful strategy, a method, in order to grasp correctly the Bible's religious ideas in their purity. Anthropology, in a strictly philosophical sense, provided such a method. The subject matter of dogmatics is religion, said de Wette, and religion is a part of human spiritual life. This anthropological starting point is grounded in the immediate "fact" of self-consciousness, which includes a religious component. Self-consciousness itself thus yields "the pure idea of religion." A theology, or a dogmatics, of the Old Testament must begin, then, with the "internal organization of the human spirit as such" (de Wette 1831: 1). However, it must also include an investigation of the laws and conditions under which the inner manifestation of religion is expressed externally. These religious expressions stem from the convictions, feelings, and faith of the Old Testament authors themselves. This anthropological foundation then provided de Wette with a critical tool for recognizing the Old Testament's pure religious ideas, and for distinguishing them from the mixed historical forms in which they are clothed (1831: 30). This two-pronged strategy, which de Wette called biblical theology's anthropological and critical operations, uses "inner revelation"—the pure idea of religion given in self-consciousness—as a critical principle in the study of "external revelation." Historical interpretation is then an active effort to correct, by the criteria of internal revelation, the historical revelation of the Old Testament's authors. De Wette's goal was exactly the same as Gabler's, pursued according to a different strategy.

In pursuing Old Testament theology itself, de Wette begins by identifying the "fundamental idea on which everything depends," and around which everything must be ordered (1831: 38). It is, he says, "the moral idea, free of myth, of one God as a holy will" (1831: 63). This decision determines the way de Wette presents the theology of the Old Testament. He first differentiates Hebraism from Judaism, which represents a religious decline, and then distinguishes within Hebraism between its "ideal universalism" and its "symbolic particularism." Universal are the doctrines of God and humankind, while particularism is identified with the theocracy: God's particular relation to Israel. De Wette claimed that Israel showed its tendency to misunderstand this particularism by reducing the universal character of God's rule to nationalism, thus preparing the way for Judaism. In his discussion of the philosophical or hermeneutical framework that guides his biblical theology, and in the execution of his interpretive strategy on the Old Testament, de Wette reflects idealism's characteristic interest in the abstract and universal, rather than the concrete and particular. Idealism provided him a way to merge historical and theological interpretation on behalf of dogmatics. It was also—and not only in de Wette's hands, lamentably—a weapon to wield against Judaism.

Gottlieb Philipp Christian Kaiser published the first volume of his *Biblische Theologie* in the same year as de Wette's first edition, 1813. It is a thoroughly eccentric book—Ludwig Diestel called it a "frightening caricature" (1869: 713; Hayes and Prussner 1985: 92)—but it casts in bold relief the effort of these early Old Testament theologians to find behind or above the Old Testament, or within its authors, something more universal and thus, they thought, more purely religious. Kaiser did not borrow a philosophy with which to devise a hermeneutical framework for interpreting the Old Testament; instead, he used religion itself. He subsumed the Old Testament under "the universal history of religion," and then ultimately under "the universal religion." The particularity of Old Testament religion, which Kaiser refers to as Judaism, can only be understood in relation to religion in general. It is then taken up, together with Christianity and all other particular religions, into what Kaiser calls a genuine "catholicism" (1813: 12). Like de Wette, Kaiser's method relies on a relation and a distinction between internal and external. Revelation, he says, is grounded in external facts, though not those of any one religion; but revelation is grounded preeminently in internal facts, and thus in humanity itself (1813: vii). By describing the "principal moments" of religion, putting particular religions in a critical, dialectical relation to each other, and drawing random insights from philosophy, Kaiser goes on to pare from the Old Testament the temporal ideas that must be left behind in the universal religion of humanity.

Kaiser was the first to make comparative religion an essential part of biblical theology's method. He drew on the features of various religions to arrive at a description of religion itself, and he set the Old Testament within that universal religion. To do so, Kaiser required new categories, and he invented his own. Thus, he speaks of geofetishology, anthropotheology, cosmocraty, demonophany, and so on. He used this grotesque vocabulary, much as Ammon and de Wette used the vocabulary of philosophy and dogmatics, to get beyond the Old Testament's particularity to what is universal, and thus valid in the present. Kaiser moved further than either of the other two, however, into a vacant universalism that even he could not abide. In the preface to the third part of his work, published eight years later, he abandoned his earlier views and announced his commitment to "the word revealed in the Bible" (1821: iv).

It was a common complaint of Old Testament theologians in the nineteenth century, and even later, that previous Old Testament and biblical theologies were insufficiently historical in character. The idealism of Bauer, Ammon, de Wette, and Kaiser, and the dogmatic interests of Ammon and de Wette, did tend to deny history any real importance. Toward the end of his career, de Wette wrote a popular book whose title is, in English, "Biblical History as the History of God's Revelation" (1846). But biblical theologians continued to search for a genuinely historical approach to the Old Testament, by which they usually meant one that was not decisively influenced by dogmatics. Baumgarten-Crusius, whom we already encountered, made the first attempt in 1828, followed immediately by Carl Peter Wilhelm Gramberg (1829–30). These two were overshadowed, however, in both methodological clarity and influence, by Daniel George Conrad von Cölln; his *Biblische Theologie* was published posthumously in 1836. Cölln modeled his presentation on de Wette, but he claimed that neither de Wette nor anyone else had yet fulfilled the strictly historical requirements of Old Testament theology, requirements he believed had been laid down by Gabler. From Cölln's own work it is clear, however, that what he really opposed was the use of philosophical categories. His understanding of Old Testament theology's task—to differentiate the universal from the particular, or the "inexact forms of representation" from the "pure concepts" hidden in them (1836: 11)—otherwise hardly differed from de Wette's. As Bauer had done, Cölln argued that these judgments can and must be made by historical criticism itself, and not by means of philosophical or dogmatic categories, or on the basis of their criteria. Historical criticism, Cölln says, follows the Old Testament's religious concepts, through the process of their formation and development, into the New Testament. It is only *in* the New Testament, however, that these religious concepts are deepened and broadened to form the basis of a "universal religion" (1836: 4).

Old Testament theology was for Cölln, as also for de Wette and Baumgarten-Crusius, the first chapter of historical theology (Dentan 1963: 33) and part of the foundation of dogmatics—or, as Cölln preferred to say—of systematic theology. As part of historical theology, or the history of dogma (Cölln 1836: 4), biblical theology determines which of the Old Testament's religious concepts actually belonged, originally, to Christianity, and how they developed historically (1836: 7). As the foundation of systematic theology, biblical theology tries to derive the Old Testament's concept of religion from the textual sources in which it lies hidden. Since the biblical sources clothe their religious concepts in images, it is crucial to "illumine these inexact forms of representation (symbol, myth, accommodation) according to their essence," and thus to determine their meaning (1836: 11). But biblical theology stops there. "Any attempt to further develop the meaning determined in this way, to apply it, to confirm the notion itself according to its inner truth, to establish its harmony with other kinds of philosophical or dogmatic-ecclesiastical concepts, lies outside the sphere of genuine interpretation and cannot be designated as such" (1836: 11).

It would seem that by 1836, biblical theology had made little progress beyond Gabler's programmatic description of its task in 1787. In particular, it had failed to resolve the issue of its relation to history on the one side, and philosophy or theology on the other. The result was a methodological tension between historical approaches, such as those of Bauer and Cölln, and more philosophical or theological approaches, such as those of Ammon and de Wette. This tension was resolved or sublated in a higher unity—*aufgehoben*, as he put it—by Johann Karl Wilhelm Vatke in *Religion des Alten Testamentes*, the only volume of a proposed six-part biblical theology he was able to publish. It was published in 1835, the year before Cölln's. If Baumgarten-Crusius thought the crisis in church and theology made biblical theology especially interesting, Vatke proved that the church may not be at all interested in what biblical theologians produce. Ernst Wilhelm Hengstenberg, Vatke's conservative Old Testament colleague at the University of Berlin and an influential church leader, saw to it that Vatke would retain his teaching post only on condition that he publish nothing more on biblical theology (Brömse 1984). Hengstenberg himself had come to Berlin after de Wette was dismissed for expressing sympathy to the mother of a political assassin (Plümacher 1987). Old Testament theology has not always been just a staid academic discipline.

A close friend of Vatke wrote concerning the "standpoint" of Friedrich Schleiermacher, another Berlin faculty member, that "nowadays one hears even ecclesiastical authorities speak from this perspective—certainly the surest proof that it has been superseded." Vatke believed that his Old Testament theology genuinely superseded its predecessors, and he was right. Unfortunately for Vatke, this supersession depended on a radical historical criticism and a philosophy inspired by Hegel. On both counts, Vatke and his friend—David Friedrich Strauss—earned the wrath of ecclesiastical authorities (Strauss 1977: 4). Old Testament theology must be historical, Vatke argued, because it pursues the idea of Old Testament religion through the "principal moments" of its historical development, and because this development occurs in and through historical, religious representations. But historical criticism by itself is subjective; it is not concerned with truth, because it is not properly scientific (1835: 156). Only relative objectivity is possible, Vatke argued, sounding a decidedly modern note, since objectivity is "restricted by the period's stage of consciousness" (1835: 14). We can only attain *relative* objectivity, because our objectivity is limited by our situation in history. Even at that, historical criticism can only achieve scientific status (and relative objectivity) if it is taken up into a philosophically grounded conceptual analysis. Hegel provides the tools for such an analysis, which is scientific because it comprehends the most universal horizon possible, which is to say, history as a completed whole. Conceptual analysis will necessarily be historical, because the concept of a religion is unfolded in a historical dialectic: the subjectivity of the concept itself and the objectivity of its manifestations are *aufgehoben*—sublated—in the idea (the unity of subject and object) of Israel's religion. Since the same dialectic occurs in the "knowing subject"—the biblical theologian, in this case—the subjectivism of historical criticism is overcome. And since the pursuit of this dialectic simply *is* the scientific form of understanding, the formal differences among biblical, historical, and systematic theology are themselves overcome. In this way, Hegelian philosophy provided Vatke's hermeneutical framework for understanding the history of Old Testament religion theologically.

While Vatke's Old Testament theology has the longest philosophical preface in the history of the discipline, it was also the first to have a thoroughly historical character. He thus achieved a greater harmony between method and presentation than anyone before him—and perhaps after him. Furthermore, he was the first to determine that the system of legislation in the Pentateuch came after, rather than before, the prophets (1835: 204). Apart from that landmark observation, he generally followed the historical reconstructions of his predecessors, particularly de Wette. However, he was better able than they to place these reconstructions unforced within a comprehensive framework, without losing sight of the theological work he was doing. In arguing that Israel's religion reached its zenith in the postexilic period, Vatke disagreed with those—including Hegel and most everyone else—who characterized this period as one of religious decline (into Judaism). And, in emphasizing the need to understand Israel's religion from the perspective of its completed history, he paved the way for many who came later. His Hegelian language is dense and in many respects as forbidding as Kaiser's, as this summary will have demonstrated, but Vatke's brilliance and the synthesis he achieved between philosophy (or hermeneutics) and historical criticism have not been exceeded in the discipline from which he was banned.

Salvation History and History of Religion

Vatke's synthesis did not survive him—Bruno Bauer's similarly Hegelian work took no account of historical criticism—but his view of history's theological importance reappeared, without an explicitly Hegelian framework, among a series of conservative scholars oriented to "salvation history": Steudel, Hävernick, Oehler, Hofmann, and Schultz (in the first edition, 1869). This group was influenced, to varying degrees, by a mixture of mystical pietism and historical speculation drawn from Cocceius, Böhme, Oetinger, and Bengel (Diestel 1869: 698–708). Since this influence was rooted in Württemberg and Tübingen, it is not entirely surprising that Hegel and Schelling absorbed it as well (Toews 1980: 13–26; Benz 1983), or that Steudel, Oehler, and especially Hofmann sound very much like Hegel and Schelling even while opposing them (or without having read them).

Central to these "salvation historians"—the term *salvation history* appears for the first time in Hofmann's *Weissagung und Erfüllung* (1841–44: 1:8)—are the origin of the history of Israel and of the world in the activity and decree of God; the importance of the "facts" of God's activity in Israel's history, which forms an organic whole; the consequent conception of Old Testament theology as historical in nature; the actual or virtual correspondence between the Old Testament narrative and history; and, finally, participation in the spirit of revelation—or God's spirit rather than the human spirit, as in de Wette (Steudel 1840: 2)—as the condition for understanding the history of revelation (Oehler 1845: 32–34; Schultz 1869: 72). Despite their emphasis on history, and even on the narrative and canonical form of the Old Testament (Steudel 1840: 11–19), Steudel, Hävernick, and Oehler were unable to achieve consistency between that methodological emphasis and their actual presentation of Old Testament theology. As we have seen, that inconsistency afflicted Old Testament theology since G. L. Bauer, with the exception of Vatke.

Hofmann was another exception. Johann Christian Konrad von Hofmann wrote no separate Old Testament theology. He regarded all of theology, like history, to be one organic whole. Its starting point is the one "fact" of which every Christian—but only every Protestant Christian!—is immediately and thus indubitably certain: reconciliation with God, mediated in Christ. Theology, then, has a threefold task. Systematic theology consists in an exposition of the one fact of which a Christian is certain. Biblical interpretation is the scientific proof of systematic theology's exposition, and it provides a critical norm for judging the history of the church. In the mutual agreement among these three—systematic theology, biblical interpretation, and church history—Christian self-certainty becomes scientific certainty (Hofmann 1879: 33).

According to Hofmann, the necessary presupposition of Christian self-certainty (communion with God mediated in Christ) is a relation within the Trinity, among the Father, Son, and Spirit, that involves both unity and differentiation—or objectification. All of history, from the world's creation to its consummation, is a historical manifestation of the divine self-differentiation (1852–56: 1:36, 234). Within universal history there occurs salvation history, a set of events that achieves the Son's reconciliation with the Father and humankind's reconciliation with God. Salvation history is the meaning of universal history, and each of its discrete events, narrated in the Bible, occupies its own necessary place. Thus, the whole of salvation history is the essential framework for understanding any particular text. Hofmann was not a fundamentalist; he acknowledged that the Bible contains errors, and that what it says about some historical event may not be literally true. What is and must be true, at a symbolic level, is what the Bible *says* about the relation of certain events to salvation history. Faith is able to determine the truth of what the Bible says, because faith knows what it is certain of (Hofmann 1959). Faith's certainty is immediate, and thus absolute.

In Hofmann's theology, then, there is a perfect symmetry among (*a*) that of which Christians are certain, (*b*) the presuppositions of that certainty spelled out by systematic theology, and (*c*) the salvation history narrated in the Bible. The historical form of the Bible is not accidental; it is necessarily analogous to God's trinitarian history, which expands and unfolds itself into the world's history and then Israel's. For Hofmann, biblical theology is thinking *in* our relation to God, not *about* it; hence, its relation to systematic theology is organic, not something to be considered separately. No one before or after Hofmann achieved such a thorough integration of historical interpretation of the Bible and systematic theology. Whether he brought Gabler's programmatic distinctions to fruition, or simply betrayed them, is a matter of judgment.

Hofmann and the salvation historians were soon overshadowed by the historians of religion—in the first place, by Julius Wellhausen. The career of Hermann Schultz illustrates this development. In 1863, Schultz edited Hävernick's work, which was firmly within the salvation-history school, and the first edition of his own Old Testament theology (1869) reflects Schultz's relation to the salvation historians. In the second edition (1878), however, he accepted Wellhausen's (and Vatke's) late dating of the law, and in subsequent editions he moved still further toward history of religion (which is the name of a method or approach, *Religionsgeschichte*, and not just of a field of study). The first to conceive Old Testament theology purely as the history of Israel's religion was August Kayser, in 1886; the second and subsequent editions of his work were written by Karl Marti, who changed the title of the third edition from "The Theology of the Old Testament" (Kayser 1886) to "The History of Israelite Religion" (Marti 1897).

After the turn of the century, the term *history of religion* was associated with a group of younger scholars whose chief Old Testament representative was Hermann Gunkel. The history-of-religion school, which was associated with the University of Göttingen, raised fundamental questions about Old Testament theology. Gunkel was not opposed to theology; in fact, he said explicitly that "biblical exegesis is theological exegesis" (1913: 24). But theology, according to Gunkel, is concerned with religion and not with doctrine or dogmatics. Since Gabler the task of Old Testament theology had been defined in some kind of relation to dogmatics. If dogmatics is no longer a proper concern of theology, then Old Testament theology has lost much of its rationale. For Gunkel, a genuinely theological interpretation of the Old Testament will avoid dogmatics in favor of religion, and religion is fundamentally piety. Interpretation of the Old Testament will thus seek to penetrate to the "inner life" of its authors (1913: 25).

This marks a radical departure in the history of Old Testament theology. Beginning with Gabler and G. L. Bauer, Old Testament theology had been concerned above all with ideas. Even for Vatke, the most radically historical of Old Testament theologians, historical study is *conceptual* analysis. And Hofmann, the preeminent salvation historian, acknowledged that in the Bible history becomes doctrine. Historical interpretation and biblical theology belong together, in Baumgarten-Crusius's terms, because historical interpretation makes it possible to understand the Bible's concepts. Gunkel reverses all of this. The goal of interpretation is not just to understand the ideas of a text, he says, but to understand them as the "expressions of a living, vital soul. . . . It is thus the living person, in its willing and thinking, in the variety of its whole spiritual being, which is the real object of all exegesis" (1913: 12–13). With respect to the religion of the Bible, says Gunkel, the task is "to understand this religion in its depth and breadth, to trace it through its winding course, to be present at the birth of its deepest thoughts" (1926–27: 533). Those thoughts mattered less to Gunkel than did the "inner life," the piety, that produced them.

The Renewal of Old Testament Theology

Wellhausen and Gunkel helped bring Old Testament theology to a stalemate. Bernhard Stade, a friend and follower of Wellhausen, wrote an Old Testament theology as late as 1905, but it served more to illustrate than to resolve the problems Old Testament theology faced. According to Stade, Old Testament theology is nothing more nor less than "the history of religion under the Old Covenant" (1905: 1). Its task is to determine the origin and content, as well as the conceptual structure, of the faith of Judaism, which is "the historical presupposition of Christianity" (1905: 2). He also wanted to distinguish those dimensions of Israel's faith whose development can be traced into Judaism but were not taken up by Jesus and the apostles. On either account, "the New Testament is the best source for the theology of the Old Testament" (1893: 93). In his emphasis on faith and religion over against doctrine, and in his insistence that Old Testament theology is identical with the particular history of the religion that precedes Christianity, Stade reflected the influence of Wellhausen and, to a lesser degree, Gunkel.

At the same time, other scholars were asking whether Old Testament theology, pursued along lines laid down by Wellhausen and Gunkel, was adequate to its task. Once more, this was not only an academic issue. Stade himself felt it necessary to insist on the importance, to Christianity, of affirming that the Old Testament "contains revelation" (1905: 15). Other Christians were denying just that. A few years later, Adolf von Harnack urged that the Old Testament be removed from the Christian canon (Hayes and Prussner 1985: 153). In such an environment it was unclear how, or whether, Old Testament theology as the history of Israelite religion could respond to "the current crisis in church and theology." The result was a renewed debate about how to proceed.

Justus Köberle (1906) argued that the presuppositions of the history-of-religion school were at odds with Christian faith. Old Testament theology, he said, must deal with the Old Testament as the revelation of God, and not just as a series of preliminary steps to the New Testament. Thus, he advocated a turn from history of religion to a revised form of salvation history, one that takes modern historical scholarship seriously without making it the measure of Christian faith. Rudolf Kittel (1921) complained that the history-of-religion scholars, with their emphasis on comparative material, made it seem as if *extra babylonem nulla salus* (outside of Babylon there is no salvation; 1921: 96). What is needed, he said, is a systematic Old Testament theology that employs a philosophy or dogmatics of religion to penetrate to the essence of religion and its truth. "It must finally seek to fathom the secret of its divine power" (Kittel 1921: 96). Köberle is as reminiscent of Hofmann as Kittel is of de Wette.

Willy Staerk (1923) saw the flaw in history of religion's approach to Old Testament theology as consisting in its concentration on factual matters, and its failure to arrive at the essentials of Old Testament religion. It could only achieve this if it were to relate "the religious object, grasped phenomenologically, to the totality of the religious idea" (1923: 290). The religious object has to be "thought through" philosophically, which can only happen if Old Testament theology is a component of systematic theology, "which it was from the beginning and which it must remain" (1923: 290). While Staerk urges a combination of historical and philosophical study, philosophy has precedence: inquiry begins with the phenomenon of religion and then follows the unfolding of its rational structure in history. What this means, concretely, is that Old Testament theology grasps the basic religious experience of Moses and follows its unfolding in Israel's history. By "unfolding" Staerk means a combination of historical development and revelation: God's self-mediation through the instrument of (usually prophetic) personality. Israel's religious history thus developed intrinsically, and not by force of external causes, to higher degrees of purity from the founding religious idea. As Staerk inelegantly put it, "Religion is the transcendental unity of apperception in the experience of the unconditioned-personal as a synthetic *a priori*" (1923: 292).

Staerk's convoluted language obscures a very simple notion: Moses was the founder of Israel's religion because he had a uniquely immediate experience of God, and Israel's religion is the progressive unfolding of its founder's experience. That simple notion later became the basis of Walther Eichrodt's theology. Perhaps having read Staerk, Carl Steuernagel (1925) suggested that, while Old Testament theology should offer a systematic presentation of Israelite religion, it should do so strictly in categories drawn from historical analysis of the Old Testament. Neither Old Testament theology's categories nor its methods should be borrowed from philosophy, or from dogmatics.

In the early years of this century, Old Testament theology's problems were often credited to the history-of-religion approach that dominated biblical studies. Steuernagel says, with reference to Gabler, that "If it was then necessary to free biblical theology from the shackles of dogmatics, so it is time now . . . to free Old Testament theology from the shackles of Old

Testament history-of-religion" (1925: 266). Whether or not Steuernagel was right in this judgment, he reflects a common point of view. What Steuernagel and his peers did not entirely recognize was the degree to which assumptions about Old Testament theology's very task had changed since Gabler's programmatic essay. For Gabler, and for many who followed him, the task of biblical theology consisted in determining which of the Bible's ideas were universal and had abiding validity, and in distinguishing them from those ideas that were merely particular or historical. By the time of Steuernagel, the task of Old Testament theology was thought to consist much more in penetrating to, or grasping, the essence of Israel's religion. Rather than causing this change in definition, history of religion was a reflection of it. This change in assumptions about Old Testament theology's task was a product of the coordination between biblical theology and historical interpretation that Baumgarten-Crusius noted in 1828. However, it was not until Old Testament theologians attended to the subjective dimension of history that the change occurred. The most liberal (Vatke 1835) and the most conservative or confessional (Hävernick 1848; Hofmann 1852–56) theologians agreed on this subjective dimension, but they construed it differently. For Vatke, it involves the location of both the interpreted object (the texts) and the interpreting subject (the theologian) within the dialectical history of the Spirit (*Geist*). For Hofmann, it involves the certainty of the interpreting subject (the theologian) regarding her or his participation in the trinitarian history of reconciliation. For both liberals and conservatives, an emphasis on history served to divert attention from timeless or abiding concepts to the web of history, and thus to historical subjects. For a conservative like Hävernick, it became important to emphasize the "acts of God" and not just doctrines, and specifically to emphasize the subjective effects of these acts, which reflect different stages of "religious consciousness" (1848: 17). For another conservative, Steudel, the "facts" of revelation in the Old Testament are more important than its religious concepts, or the religious consciousness that lies behind them, because the facts of revelation are the source of both concepts and consciousness (1840: 18–19; cf. Riehm 1889: 8–10).

Whether working from the most liberal or the most conservative standpoint, Old Testament theologians gradually undermined Gabler's program and made history of religion both possible and sensible. Even when Walther Eichrodt casts his *Theology of the Old Testament* explicitly as a repudiation of history of religion, he proceeds on assumptions that square exactly with those of his opponents. Ernst Troeltsch, in his essay of 1913 on the dogmatics of the history-of-religion school, says that this school regards "the entire territory of Christian life and thought as a gradual unfolding of an immanent impelling power or fundamental ideal, realizing itself in historical Christianity. This ideal, or this 'essence' persisting in all specific manifestations, might then be taken as the subject-matter and the normative principle of dogmatics" (1913: 11–12). Eichrodt would later talk in virtually the same terms about Old Testament theology (see below, pp. 71–78). There were disagreements of course, but these turned on how the interpreter or theologian could get in a position to grasp the religious essence, not whether religious essence was the proper goal of theology. More specifically, the parties disagreed about whether grasping the religious essence of the Old Testament's historical content is itself a matter of historical interpretation, or whether it requires a separate, theological operation apart from historical interpretation. Without the philosophical hermeneutics of someone like Vatke, or the theological hermeneutics of someone like Hofmann, it seemed impossible that historical interpretation or inquiry could itself grasp the sought-for essence. If that is the case, and if Old Testament theology does seek the religious essence of Israelite religion, then Old Testament theology cannot be a historical discipline.

This, then, was the state of the question by 1930. It is the question that Walther Eichrodt debated with Otto Eissfeldt. (See the translations of their *ZAW* articles below, pp. 20–39.) Eissfeldt, the historian, urged a sharp distinction between the history of Israelite (and Jewish) religion and Old Testament theology (1926). They employ two different approaches, he says, which correspond to different functions of the human spirit: active knowing and passive believing. History of religion is objective, although it depends on an "empathetic reliving" of its object (p. 27 below), and it makes no judgments about validity or truth. Old Testament theology, on the other hand, cannot be a historical inquiry, because it is concerned with what is timelessly or abidingly true, as determined by a particular (Christian) confession. Eissfeldt bases this argument on the assumption that historical-critical research cannot penetrate to the "proper essence" of Old Testament religion, and is thus unable to answer the questions of faith assigned to Old Testament theology.

Eichrodt, the theologian, answered that Eissfeldt's view, while preserving the integrity of history of religion, compromises that of Old Testament theology by removing it from the framework of Old Testament and historical inquiry generally (1929). In opposition to Eissfeldt, Eichrodt claimed that historical investigation *can* get to the essence of Old Testament religion. But Eichrodt redefined the "essence" of the Old Testament as the "deepest meaning of its religious thought world that historical investigation can recover" through an analysis that cuts across the various historical levels in the Old Testament (see p. 33 below). In other words, since "essence" is whatever historical inquiry can recover, historical inquiry, as a matter of definition, can recover the essence of Old Testament religion. Much of what Eissfeldt included within Old Testament the-ology—questions of truth and faith—Eichrodt assigned to dogmatics. On the other hand, however, he ascribed to historical investigation a distinctly theological character: all historical research presupposes a subjective mo-ment, he claims, and the interpreter's Christian confession provides the content of that moment in Old Testament theology—thus, it must be considered a legitimate part of historical scholarship.

The debate between Eissfeldt and Eichrodt shows the extent to which the historical and subjective emphases of previous theologians, the most conservative and the most radical, came together by 1930. It may be that Eichrodt is responsible for keeping Old Testament theology within the sphere of historical scholarship. On the other hand, we may wonder whether he has done so by infusing history with too heavy a dose of the-ology. However we decide those questions, it should help us in reading these essays to recall that the debate took place amid great theological controversy—some of which Eissfeldt discusses in his very lengthy first footnote—and in the troubled years of the Weimar Republic, just prior to the most strenuous and murderous efforts to eliminate the Jews, and with them the "Old Testament." The debate was not only academic.

OTTO EISSFELDT

The History of Israelite-Jewish Religion and Old Testament Theology

⟦1⟧ The tension between absolute and relative, between transcendence and immanence, is the current problem of theology. For biblical scholarship, this general problem is reduced to a particular one: history and revelation. It is with this problem that the study of both Testaments, of the New just as of the Old, has to grapple, and a new solution must be found that applies fundamentally to both. However, particular matters in the Old Testament differ from those in the New, so that a treatment restricted to the Old Testament is legitimate. The question, then, is whether the religion of the Old Testament is to be understood and presented as a historical entity like other religions of antiquity, and thus in terms of the history of Israelite-Jewish religion, or as a religion which is, even if in some limited way, the true religion, the revelation of God, and thus—so the term will be understood here—as "Old Testament theology."

In the last three decades, the question has been debated repeatedly. Even if that has taken place most often in a way that has gone beyond the Old Testament and put the Bible as a whole or Christianity at the center, from the general answers given here those that apply particularly to the Old Testament can be immediately derived. Two conceptions stand over against each other. The one, the *historical* or the *scientific study of religion*, requires that the religion of the Old Testament be investigated by the same means with which historical scholarship otherwise works: linguistic and historical-critical mastery of the sources, and analysis of their content on the basis of

Translated and reprinted with permission from Otto Eissfeldt, "Israelitisch-jüdische Religionsgeschichte und Alttestamentliche Theologie," *Zeitschrift für die Alttestamentliche Wissenschaft* 44 (1926) 1–12. Translated by Ben C. Ollenburger.

an empathetic personal reliving. However, this conception understands the valuation of Old Testament religion, and the question of its truth altogether, as matters [[2]] of personal conviction; science does not proceed that far. The other conception, the *theological* (in the narrow sense of the term) or *churchly*, claims on the other hand that perception of the true essence of Old Testament religion merely by application of the otherwise typical methods of historical investigation is impossible. Rather, it discloses itself only to faith, and that is something different from empathetic reliving; it consists, namely, in being overwhelmed and humbled in inner obedience to that which has taken hold of oneself. Accordingly, in Christian theology the decisive contents of the Old Testament will be determined on the basis of Christianity, while the Old Testament will be joined to the New, and the Bible will be interpreted from a foundational experience, naturally of a Christian sort, whether this be called religious-moral renewal or justification by faith or the revelation of God in Jesus or something else. Whatever has gone into belief in the Old Testament as the revelation of God is precisely what has to be treated by Old Testament theology.

Prior to the [[First]] World War these two conceptions, the historical and the theological, somewhat counterbalanced each other, but in such a way that the historical appeared to be "modern." But after the war, the situation has changed completely. Among those who have since expressed themselves on these matters, the overwhelming majority have declared the historical study of the Bible, and thus also of the Old Testament, to be antiquated and outmoded, and they enlist on the side of the theological conception, to which the present and the future belong. Weary of the historicism, the psychologism, and the relativism of the scientific-study-of-religion method, one yearns for revelation and demands a scientific treatment of the Bible that does justice to its claim to be revelation of absolute worth—namely, the theological. Especially the representatives of dialectical theology have expressed this demand. But they have not yet gone much beyond criticism of the old and the basic demand for something new. More precise expositions of how the scientific presentation of the religion of the Bible or of the Old Testament should now be done have not yet appeared.[1] Alongside the representatives of dialectical theology it has been

---

1. Worth noting are the statements in Eduard Thurneysen's article on "Schrift und Offenbarung" (*Zwischen den Zeiten* 2 [1924] 1–30), and in Karl Barth's article on "Das Schriftprinzip der reformierten Kirche" (*Zwischen den Zeiten* 3 [1925] 215–45). I can agree with a whole series of Thurneysen's propositions, since they are congruent in their intention with those I will set out. Propositions such as these:

> It is characteristic of the so-called historical-critical school of the past decade that it has at least made a point of putting into practice the method of historical-psychological interpretation, which during the course of the past century has

[[3]] theologians of a conservative bent like Girgensohn and Procksch who have recently taken up the struggle against the scientific-study-of-religion treatment of the Bible. In its place they propose treating it pneumatically, wherein the concept pneumatic is nearly identical with what has been identified previously as theological in the narrower sense. One of the two, Procksch, has also shown how this proposal is to be worked out when ap-

> universally prevailed in the treatment of historical problems. . . . None of us can any longer retreat behind this historical-psychological view. . . . What has to be asserted against liberal theology is this: that it has never taken up . . . the question posed to it in the biblical claim of revelation. And yet, precisely this theology would have been in a unique position to approach the problem of revelation, based on the only correct assumption; namely, that revelation as such can never be established in the domain of historical events. . . . A revelation that must be defended on rational grounds—that, indeed, can really only ever be so defended— is no revelation. This attempted defense has always been made, however, and always will be made. It is the essential characteristic of that which is called orthodoxy. Orthodoxy is precisely the attempt . . . to confirm revelation. The understanding of revelation marks a transcendence of liberalism and orthodoxy; it is the crisis of them both.

And very similar expressions are found in Barth's article. But since revelation is then equated with the canon, and thus with a historical entity, and the correlative relation of the twin concepts, revelation and faith, is thereby sundered, the promising beginning is nipped in the bud. This can already be seen in Thurneysen, when he says:

> The same claim of revelation is also the secret of the New Testament, the meaning of the prophets and that of the Psalms, of Job, and of the historical books. And even if often so dimmed as to be unrecognizable, it extends to the farthest margins of the Bible. . . . This claim has found its unequivocal and powerful expression in the fact of the canon.

But this is much clearer in Barth:

> Even if the individual reader is able, in light of his own understanding, to distinguish between the center and the periphery of the Bible, between what he "experiences" and something else that he has not "experienced," between what in his judgment "promotes Christ," as Luther put it, and something else where he judges such to be missing, the distinctions that result from such considerations may in no way have the character of distinctions in principle. With God it is not a matter of more or less, but of either-or. The Reformed Church has long since laid special emphasis on this determination. It has fundamentally disapproved Luther's imperious way of arranging, on the basis of a most individually conditioned dogmatics, a kind of selected Bible. And we believe that in so doing, it has done well.

Here the bond between faith and revelation is completely sundered, because what Barth calls Luther's most individually conditioned dogmatics is, in truth, faith. Thus, also among the representatives of dialectical theology the two different modes of consideration, that from the outside (the historical) and that from within (from faith), are not held strictly apart. Moreover, it is significant that in Barth the Reformed confession is played off against Luther. But here, if anywhere, evangelical theology must follow the path indicated by Luther, and not that of the Reformed confession.

plied to [[4]] the study of the Old Testament, so that his exposition must be investigated somewhat more thoroughly as the more important contribution to our question.[2]

Procksch proposes as the ultimate task of biblical exegesis that it must expound divine revelation, whose validity is eternal, in human forms. To this end it must apply with complete thoroughness those means at the disposal of the historian in the interpretation of other literary works: philology, historical criticism, empathy. However, investigation that works only with these tools is unable to fathom precisely the decisive elements of the Old Testaments—words, historical events, the notion of God. Words like the first sentence of the Bible, events like the crossing of the Red Sea and the Sinai covenant, and most especially the notion of the transcendent, personal God, are irrational, paradoxical, and contradict any merely historical understanding. Here it is a matter of pneumatic entities that can only be understood from within, from faith.

> Faith is the organ of perception for the pneumatic world. Exegesis, historical understanding, and esthetic empathy continually come up against the world of the Bible, which discloses itself to faith as God's miracle, and which contains at the same time God's revelation.

Nonetheless, it is not the case that the pneumatic subjects pointed to in the Old Testament are by themselves able to awaken the faith which can now penetrate to their mystery. Rather, they become clear only from the perspective of faith in Christ.

> Christ is the central figure of the Bible from whom all effects of the New Testament proceed, in whom all effects of the Old Testament are comprehended. . . . In Christ [[5]] the Bible becomes a seamless whole. One can sever no member from this organism without wounding the entire organism. . . . As the Father of Jesus Christ, the God of the Old Testament is our God. Whoever denies this proposition puts himself outside the fundamental certainty of biblical religion.

It is clear from all this that Procksch is talking about a presentation of Old Testament religion drawn on the basis of faith, and even from a distinctly Christian faith. The otherwise typical methods of historical investigation are not thereby scorned, but they are nonetheless—despite every insistence on their importance—finally valued only as *ancillae theologiae*. All decisive statements about the essence of Old Testament religion are

---

2. "Über pneumatische Exegese," *Christentum und Wissenschaft* 1 (1925) 145–58; "Die Geschichte als Glaubensinhalt," *Neue Kirchliche Zeitschrift* 36 (1925) 485–99; "Ziele und Grenzen der Exegese," *Neue Kirchliche Zeitschrift* 36 (1925) 715–30. This last essay concludes with a brief debate with Barth.

made from faith, and it is emphatically determined that faith remains the organ of historical reflection for the Christian.

If the historical approach to the Old Testament and its religion is here robbed of its independence and made subservient to the theological, as alone able to grasp the essence of the subject completely, there is on the other hand no lack of attempts to treat the theological as an appendix to the historical, and to see the former as a direct continuation of the latter. The efforts of Schleiermacher and Hegel, by means of a historical-philosophical comparison of religions to show Christianity and thereby, at least indirectly, Old Testament religion to be the highest and absolute religion, have continued to find followers in the present.[3] And there is no lack of those who—like Hermann Schultz—are of the opinion that Old Testament religion "discloses itself in all its truth," as does any other spiritual development, "only to one who has an intrinsic appreciation of its essence, who has a love for it, and who takes delight in its specific character,"[4] but reject a particular theological method for comprehending it. Thus, they suppose that they can treat the claims of faith satisfactorily by means of a historical presentation. Over against this very [[6]] widespread inclination to tie these two approaches in one way or another, it must be emphasized that such a blending can only be harmful. Historical understanding of the Old Testament may never go beyond the relative and the immanent, while on the other hand, faith grasped by the absolute and transcendent is not the instrument that could comprehend the Old Testament as a historical entity. The theological approach reduces the diversity of historical phenomena, since it seeks to interpret them on the basis of the decisive experience of faith, and the historical approach flattens the depth of revelation that faith experiences in the Old Testament, since it arranges it alongside these other phenomena.

The historical approach on the one hand and the theological on the other belong on two different planes. They correspond to two differently constituted functions of our spirit, to knowing and to believing. Knowing consists in intensely engaged activity; as historical knowing, it is a tireless effort to inquire after what has taken place. The manner of religious believing is passivity, which allows itself to be grasped by something higher and purer, in order to surrender itself freely to it. Knowledge is aware that

3. Willy Staerk, "Religionsgeschichte und Religionsphilosophie in ihrer Bedeutung für die biblische Theologie des Alten Testaments," *Zeitschrift für Theologie und Kirche* 21 (1923) 289–300; C. Stange, "Die Absolutheit des Christentums," *Zeitschrift für systematische Theologie* 1 (1923/24) 44–68; "Die Aufgabe der Religionsgeschichte," *Zeitschrift für systematische Theologie* 1 (1923/24) 301–13; "Stimmungsreligion, Stifterreligion und Christentum," *Zeitschrift für systematische Theologie* 1 (1923/24) 427–37; and etc.

4. *Alttestamentliche Theologie* (5th ed.; Göttingen: Vandenhoeck & Ruprecht, 1896), 1:8.

despite all its efforts it cannot get beyond the world limited to space and time, while faith knows that it has been laid hold of by the eternal. Knowledge strives for certain, clear evidence that will convince others even against their will, while faith always remains a completely personal venture to be undertaken anew by each individual, which is at its greatest when it signifies a not-seeing but yet believing. With this twofold intellectual function we approach Old Testament religion. Knowledge subordinates this entity to itself, since it masters it; yet, at the same time, it is stronger than we are, since it submits itself to us as believers. Thus, the necessity of both approaches is given in our intellectual being, and we have only to choose either to effect a compromise between them, or to recognize and attend to each in its own character and integrity.

As we have seen, compromises prove in the long run to be unsatisfactory, so it is worth leaving both approaches in their unrestricted independence and tolerating the tension that arises between them, ⟦7⟧ even should this occasionally become—and perhaps it must become—torment and temptation to the pious. But in the long run this is not fate but fortune, because the more purely the two approaches are distinguished from each other, the more they will be able to enrich each other. Powers of faith, and not of knowledge, have formed the Old Testament, and if in the successive generations of theologians knowledge turns first to one and then to another portion of Old Testament religion, this is grounded not only in the internal movement of knowledge itself but also and above all in this, that new dimensions of the religious treasure transmitted from the past always assume importance in the life of faith of individual epochs, and that knowledge then takes hold of these dimensions. If investigation now emphasizes particularly the demonic, irrational, and unfathomable with respect to Yahweh, this can be explained on the basis of the religious experience of our generation, in which this side of God has become newly apparent. And it is no accident that, at the same time, work in church history and systematics has learned anew to understand Luther's *deus absconditus.* So it is faith that has provided knowledge with its object and continually sheds new light on it.

On the other hand, knowledge can be useful for faith by enriching and relieving it. The life of faith of individuals and even of an entire generation can never appropriate more than a part of Old Testament religion; the remainder remains foreign to it. The Old Testament is too rich and too diverse for it to be otherwise. Thus, the prophets as religious personalities, that is, as heroes, remained unknown to Christianity for eighteen centuries. They supposedly lived and worked—one need only recall the paintings on the ceiling of the Sistine Chapel—as those who had predicted the Christ. Accordingly, only their isolated words were important; as personalities, they remained unknown and without effect. It was nineteenth-century historical research that taught us to understand the grand prophetic characters, since it had empathetically relived their proclamation. And who would deny that these valuable discoveries of knowledge have not also enriched the life of faith? The other side of it is that the historical consideration of the Old Testament is able to prove of ⟦8⟧ service to faith in relieving it of the burden of such elements in the Old Testament that appear to us, and must appear, as sub-Christian and immoral. Thus, it shows that the narratives of Jacob's cunning and deceitful behavior toward Esau and Laban, and the passages that attribute the ruthless and horrible extermination of the Canaanites to Yahweh's command, are emanations from a nationally restricted religiosity, which is also to be found elsewhere in history and in the present. With naive and subjective sincerity, God and nation are equated—a kind of piety that can be shared, however, only by those who feel themselves to be part of the nation concerned. Already for that reason those elements of the Old Testament are meaningless for the faith of Christians. But historical consideration shows, further, that this nationally restricted piety represents a form of religion that is overcome in the course of the history of Israelite religion itself. Prophecy severs the bond that unites God and the nation, and thereby creates space for a piety that leaves everything earthly behind and can say to God: "If I have only you, then I care nothing of heaven and earth"—a word that corresponds completely to the loftiness of Christianity. In this way, historical knowledge frees faith from sub-Christian religious forms of the Old Testament and does justice to them at the same time, since it teaches us to consider them as historically conditioned.

How dangerous it is to combine the two approaches can be shown with particular clarity from the Old Testament. It is here especially clear that Procksch's statement—that faith remains the organ even of historical reflection for the Christian—is to be questioned. We have examples in the Old Testament of historical reflection and of historical description in which faith was the decisive factor. It is what has been called religious or theological pragmatism in Judges and in the books of Kings and the Chronicler: the depiction of the period of the judges according to which Yahweh's punishment (oppression by enemies) follows on the apostasy of the nation, and then Yahweh's help (the sending of a savior or a judge) follows on the nation's conversion; and in the books of Kings and the Chronicler, the schema of the kings' success and failure, fortune and misfortune, which depends on their religious-cultic actions. ⟦9⟧ That this religious-pragmatic understanding of history has distorted and falsified reality will be universally admitted; however, it not only hinders historical knowledge but also endangers the purity of faith. The view underlying this understanding of history, that the way of the world can be evenly calculated in such a way that piety and fortune, conduct pleasing to God and success—or the reverse, sin and suffering—always go together, corresponds in no way at all to what can be recognized at the high points of Old Testament religion as the nature of faith. There, faith always entails struggle and daring, and precisely where an incongruity between piety and fortune is discovered and must be overcome, faith displays itself in its full power: "Nevertheless, I abide with you." What is clear from this example applies generally: on behalf of knowledge, just as on behalf of faith, one must guard against confusing the historical treatment of the Old Testament with the theological.

On this basis it becomes clear that the development traversed by our discipline—now usually, and significantly, designated by the double name of "history of Israelite-Jewish religion (Old Testament theology)"—from the *dicta probantia* of orthodoxy and the Bible doctrines of pietism on the one hand, to the history of religion of the nineteenth century on the other, was not accidental but necessary. In each of the two phases two modes of consideration came into view: that of faith and that of historical knowledge. To the first, the Old Testament means God's revelation, while to the second it offers itself as a historical entity. Orthodoxy and pietism allowed history to be submerged into revelation, while the historical understanding of the nineteenth century threatened to dissolve revelation into history. It is important to avoid the errors of both phases, and to carry further the appropriate starting points of each; that is, to acknowledge and to practice both approaches: history of Israelite-Jewish religion and Old Testament theology.

The first is, as the name implies, a historical discipline. It presents Old Testament religion as an entity having undergone historical development, and treats it with the [[10]] usual philological-historical tools, as has already been mentioned. To it belongs the instrument of empathy with the subject, which is especially important in this particular field. But this is then sufficient for accomplishing the historical task; it requires no other means. The historian does not answer the question of absolute value, of the "truth" of the subject. He must remain satisfied with establishing that he has to do with an entity that makes the claim to be revelation and the word of God; he does not decide whether this claim is justified. It is his responsibility to show that here men appear who assert that they have been called and commissioned in miraculous fashion by a personal power outside of and over the world, by Yahweh, and he must acknowledge that it is here doubtless a matter of a subjectively truthful assertion. Whether this assertion is also true objectively remains undecided. With respect to Old Testament religion, the historian is aware that he can never go beyond the world of space and time. Insofar as value judgments are made in the presentation of the history of Israelite-Jewish religion, in speaking of its rise and fall or its flowering and withering, they are of a relative kind, and the criterion of judgment must be derived from the history of Jewish-Israelite religion itself. It is therewith assumed that the historian must omit any forward reference to the New Testament. He may and must look beyond the historical development he has to treat only insofar as it makes its own reference beyond itself, but he leaves undecided whether the New Testament and Christianity represent its fulfillment. It goes together with this kind of history of Jewish-Israelite religion that its treatment is fundamentally independent of the scholar's form of religion, and that in this field those who belong to diverse Christian confessions, and even those of non-Christian religions, can work hand in hand, as indeed actually happens.

Quite different the theological consideration of the Old Testament! Here it is a matter of presenting that which, with respect to the Old Testament, has become revelation, God's word, for the interpreter and his religious community—because he will always be in some way the organ of his religious community. It will thus bear the character of witness, even though of a thoroughly scientific ⟦11⟧ kind, and its validity will be restricted to the circle of those whose piety is the same as, or similar to, that of the interpreter; in other words, it is relative to church and confession. There is, therefore, no possibility here of cooperation among members of different religious communities who could further their knowledge through cooperative investigation and argument; rather, here one community can convince the other only by the more powerful demonstration "of spirit and of power."

In Old Testament theology it is a question of describing the revelation of God as it has occurred and occurs ever anew for faith in relation to the Old Testament. For that reason, it can never take the form of a historical presentation, because faith has not to do with things past but with the timeless present; revelation is exalted above the category of time. Thus, a systematic form of presentation is appropriate for Old Testament theology—if systematic is understood to mean not the methodological development of everything from a first principle but, rather, the sequential arrangement of propositions in the manner of *loci*. The "attributes" of Yahweh, which have come to be, for the interpreter, revelations concerning the essence and will of his God (God the Lord, God the Holy, etc.); the estimation of the world and of humankind, which is truth for the interpreter (the world of God's creation, and the God who abides with humankind despite its insignificance in comparison with this vast creation [Psalm 8], etc.); these and others must be so treated.

Of course, this kind of Old Testament theology, structured on the basis of faith, is influenced throughout by the central faith experience of its author and his religious community, but it is not required that every assertion must be expressly related to this. In other words, Old Testament theology does not always require "fulfillment" in New Testament theology. There are elements in the Old Testament—for example, the psalms that praise God's majesty as it is unfolded in creation—that can also be direct revelation to the Christian, all the more since such are almost wanting in the New Testament. In this case, the otherwise self-evident schema of placing the religion [[12]] of the New Testament above that of the Old[5] must be replaced by a schema that sets them alongside each other. Here the Old Testament serves to complement the New.

Despite every distinction between the two approaches, the historical and the theological, it is nonetheless finally the case that, seen from a higher vantage point, they form a unity—and they do so not just to the extent that its importance to us as the source of revelation, rather than only or even primarily as the object of historical knowledge, accounts for the extraordinarily urgent historical investigation of Old Testament religion. Rather, beyond all this, we are confident that it is the one identical truth for which knowledge strives and by which faith is grasped. Knowing and believing belong, as we have seen, to two parallel planes, and they must meet each other in infinity—but only in infinity. Within the finite realm the two approaches form a unity only to the extent that one person can master them.

---

5. This applies above all, as Karl Holl has justifiably stressed ("Urchristentum und Religionsgeschichte," *Zeitschrift für systematische Theologie* 2 [1924/25] 387–430), to conceptions regarding the relation of God to sin and the sinner. The New Testament idea of a God who offers himself to the sinner is actually foreign to the Old Testament. But it is equally correct and worth noting when Holl adds this conclusion: "Indeed, in the question of evil, Judaism came to a similar recognition never attained elsewhere among humankind. Recalling only Isaiah 53 and the *anawim* in the Psalms—Judaism broke through the conventional wisdom which held that the best person must also be the most fortunate. Just the reverse: precisely the most pious can suffer the harshest troubles. The unfortunate one does not necessarily despise God; he may stand closer to God than the one who gains everything." With respect to overcoming evil, the Old Testament must here be placed *alongside* the New. In addition, compare Holl's statements with what was said above concerning the religious pragmatism of the Old Testament's historical books.

WALTHER EICHRODT

Does Old Testament Theology Still Have Independent Significance within Old Testament Scholarship?

[[83]] In the *Festschrift* for Karl Marti in 1925, Steuernagel still interceded, with noteworthy arguments, on behalf of retaining Old Testament theology as an independent discipline within Old Testament scholarship.[1] He showed that from the standpoint of the general history of religion as well as of theological scholarship, but also in the interests of research into Old Testament religion itself, an Old Testament theology in the sense of a systematic overview of Old Testament religion is indispensable. In observing the prevailing uncertainty regarding the task and method of Old Testament theology, which is leading toward the complete displacement of systematic presentations by historical-genetic ones, one can only wish that the arguments Steuernagel brought forward would gain a wider hearing.

But the justification of Old Testament theology as a historical discipline related to the history of Israelite religion, and distinguished from it only by the means of analysis and selection of material, has been most vehemently disputed in the most recent phase of theological discussion. By the dialectical theologians on the one side, and the proponents of pneumatic

Translated and reprinted with permission from Walther Eichrodt, "Hat die Alttestamentliche Theologie noch selbständige Bedeutung innerhalb der Alttestamentlichen Wissenschaft?" *Zeitschrift für die Alttestamentliche Wissenschaft* 47 (1929) 83–91. Translated by Ben C. Ollenburger. The footnotes have been supplied, in large part, by the translator.

1. Carl Steuernagel, "Alttestamentliche Theologie und Alttestamentliche Religionsgeschichte," in *Vom Alten Testament: Karl Marti zum siebzigsten Geburtstage* (ed. Karl Budde; Beiheft zur Zeitschrift für die Alttestamentliche Wissenschaft 41; Giessen: Töpelmann, 1925) 266–73.

exegesis on the other, Old Testament theology has been assigned a completely different purpose. Precisely the historical character of the discipline elicits opposition, because one is purportedly unable by means of the usual methods of historical research to perceive the true essence of Old Testament religion. This latter is said to reside in the reality of revelation to which the Old Testament bears witness. However, if one wants to penetrate to this center of the Old Testament, rather than to remain on its periphery, then an approach wholly different from the historical is said to be in order, either the pneumatic or one moving within the category of existential judgment, or whatever name one may choose. By their very nature, the means of historical research extend only to the understanding of the conditional, the finite; in order to attain to the unconditional, to what is of absolute value, we are said to require a new disposition toward reality—in short, that of faith, which, as the organ for knowing the pneumatic world, is alone able to disclose the world of the Bible. A new function of our spirit thus becomes active, a new method of understanding reality is to come into play, and thereby we purportedly achieve a new discipline that is differentiated from the rest of Old Testament scholarship by its own wholly distinct character.

If one wants to do justice to the new state of affairs thus brought about, then it is appropriate first of all to admit candidly that in these new demands a completely justified requirement of our current theological situation has asserted itself. One [[84]] can take whatever position one wants regarding dialectical theology, but everyone will have to admit that it has urgently drawn theology's own attention once again to its foundation and, at the same time, to its central problem, that of the reality of revelation. It has become impossible henceforth to remain content with a historicizing approach. After Rudolf Kittel referred emphatically to this point, at the Leipziger Alttestamentlertag in 1921,[2] and to the important task of Old Testament theology that follows from it, Old Testament research of the last few years has also moved increasingly in this direction. I mention only the fine study by Hempel, *Gott und Mensch im Alten Testament,*[3] or call attention to the debates at the first Deutschen Theologentag.

However, even if the goal of achieving a deeper understanding of the religious life attested in the Old Testament is clearly before us, the question is not yet answered how this goal can be attained. In fact, it is precisely this question that seems inevitably to threaten the place of Old Testament theology within the framework of Old Testament scholarship,

2. Kittel's lecture was published as "Die Zukunft der Alttestamentlichen Wissenschaft," *ZAW* 39 (1921) 84–99.

3. Published as volume 38 in the series Beiträge zur Wissenschaft vom Alten und Neuen Testament (Stuttgart: Kohlhammer, 1926).

since Old Testament theology as a historical discipline, in Steuernagel's sense, is repudiated. It must now pose the question of truth, and must thus go beyond the phenomenology of religious life to a religio-dogmatic presentation of the essence of Old Testament religion. But thereby it doubtless leaves the ranks of empirical-historical scholarship and enters the circle of normative science. So also Staerk, in an interesting exposition of the significance of history of religion and philosophy of religion for Old Testament theology, vigorously claims the latter as part of systematic theology.[4] In a penetrating study, Eissfeldt has attempted to formulate theoretically the opposition this conception entails to the previously typical definition of the task of Old Testament research. In his presentation, "The History of Israelite-Jewish Religion and Old Testament Theology,"[5] he ultimately fixes the contrast between these two disciplines as that between history and revelation, knowing and believing. Only if these are cleanly separated and developed according to the laws internal to each does he see the possibility of preserving the legitimate interests of the historian and the theologian. Any compromise would only lead to intolerable tensions. But then we confront a momentous decision, because this new definition of Old Testament theology's task means a burden for Old Testament scholarship that not a few will think unbearable. If there were already serious reservations about the task of presenting Old Testament religion in a cross section—that is, in a systematic outline but still entirely within the boundaries of the historical discipline—then the introduction of a religio-dogmatic discipline will, it seems to me, encounter far more decisive repudiation. The feeling will not be entirely unjustified that here a task has been imposed on the Old Testament scholar which [[85]] really belongs to the dogmatician, and which only he with his particular education can satisfactorily undertake. Do we not still have the obligation to preserve Gabler's legacy and to insist on the clear distinction of Old Testament theology from dogmatics? We are thus confronted with a methodological question whose significance, not only for Old Testament scholarship but also for theological inquiry in general, demands the most serious consideration and fundamental reflection. Here are offered only a few indications of where I see the decisive point of the problem to lie, and the direction in which its solution must be sought.

I would like to begin, then, with history and its investigation, because the proposition, "We are unable by historical means to penetrate to the

4. Willy Staerk, "Religionsgeschichte und Religionsphilosophie in ihrer Bedeutung für die biblische Theologie des Alten Testamentes," *Zeitschrift für Theologie und Kirche* 21 (1923) 389–400.

5. Otto Eissfeldt, "Israelitisch-jüdische Religionsgeschichte und Alttestamentliche Theologie," *ZAW* 44 (1926) 1–12; English translation on pp. 20–29 above.

essence of Old Testament religion," is actually the general assumption ly-ing at the basis of all the challenges to refashion our discipline, however opinions regarding the ways and means of this refashioning may otherwise diverge. Now certainly, this proposition contains an incontestable truth, insofar as history can say nothing about the final truth of a matter; that is, it is unable to make any claims concerning its validity for our current ex-istence or its significance for our world view. To the extent that historical research is able to view and to describe more precisely any event—also anything of an intellectual scope—only within a system of relations, its as-sertions about a historical entity always remain relative; that is, they have meaning only in relation to other entities and only in this sense command assent. To judge regarding what is true and what is false, what has an ab-solute claim to validity and what is worthless, continues to be reserved fun-damentally to the science of values, to philosophy or to dogmatics. If one takes a proper understanding of the essence of Old Testament religion to mean a judgment concerning its truth and validity claims, then this falls out-side the boundaries of Old Testament scholarship as empirical-historical research, and requires a discipline related to dogmatics.

It is quite otherwise if we understand "the essence of Old Testament religion" to be, very simply, what the Old Testament means, what the es-sentials of its history really consist in, what constitutes the deepest mean-ing of its religious thought world. Historical investigation of the Old Testament will never be able to renounce the explication of "essence" in this sense if it wishes to carry out its task completely. Historical research must insist on the fullest possible understanding of the meaningful con-tent, and the comprehending reconstruction of the actions in which this meaningful content is given—what is also called the "interpretation" of phenomena—if it does not want to forfeit its noblest task. But precisely this task entails that research may not remain content with a genetic analysis but has a vast systematic assignment to carry out: It must lay a cross section through the developed whole in order to demonstrate the inner structure of a religion ⟦86⟧ in the mutual relation of its various contents. It would be wrong to see in this systematic task an opposition to historical method. It is an impermissible restriction of the concept "his-torical" to relate it, as if self-evidently, only to observation of the growth process, to the genetic method; rather, "historical" may be understood as the opposite only of anything normative. Thus, the systematic consider-ation is to be comprehended completely within the historical.

This explicit inclusion of the systematic task within the sphere of his-torical research has as it consequence, of course, that there appears more sharply an epistemological problem of historical scholarship normally overlooked in such a restriction to genetic analysis: the subjective moment included within historical research. With respect to its extent and its significance there are, for the most part, only very imprecise notions. On few points is one more painfully aware of the lack of rigorous reflection, because the most precise grasp of the subjective moment bound up with it is indispensable for the correct determination of historical method and its general scientific character. Historicism's mistake is the suggestion that one can, by historical-empirical means, advance to norms or to universally valid propositions. The error of positivism is certainly no better—that a particular discipline must renounce any philosophical grounding if it is to be "objective." Today, the renewed permeation of the particular disciplinary specializations with a philosophical spirit is perceived as essential, and we recognize that the historian cannot even investigate and present discrete historical developments without the support of general concepts and notions provided by the philosophy of history.

The discussion among secular historians on this point has made it sufficiently clear that, to a certain degree, a subjective moment already plays into the determination of the *object of historical research*, insofar as the work of historical scholarship has as its presupposition that one knows what historical life is.

The subjective moment appears even more clearly if one inquires concerning the *principle of selection* by means of which the historian orders the vast quantity of individual phenomena and arranges their broad inner connections. Is there a universally valid principle of selection? Work in logic and methodology, in any event, has been unable to establish one. Presumably, it will not be able to do so in the future, either, to the extent that even here the influence of our basic value orientation, our individual world view, cannot be eliminated. Indeed, even a comparison of significant contemporary historical achievements shows that the governing category under which particular events are subsumed is not only a neutral, comprehensive key concept, but is obviously also ⟦87⟧ a value concept. All that can here be required is that the scholar, with methodological self-consciousness, be clear about his guiding conception and its standing in the world of values, and not set to work in the cheery optimism of absolute objectivity.

Closely related to the principle of selection is the *perspectival concept of purpose* under which a historical development is placed. This, too, is a particular guiding conception, determined in its content by the object in question; thus, it stands in the closest connection with the historical material. It is not determined only by the requirements immanent in this material, however, but receives its decisive character from the subjectivity of the scholar.

Let us then set these general presuppositions of a subjective kind, from which every scholar's work must proceed, alongside the particular intellectual preparation that a scholar must bring along in order to do the material justice! The current inclination is to pursue this factor more precisely, and to determine more carefully the often-used but somewhat vague notion of "congeniality." In this case it is evident that the scholar must have an internal affinity with his object, in order to overcome the distance to the unfamiliar phenomenon, and in order to comprehend its essence correctly. By no means can anyone understand everything, but only the circle of phenomena and human beings with whom one possesses an affinity.[6] For genuine understanding goes beyond empathetic reliving; genuine understanding requires a spontaneous productive action, a release of the plenitude of spiritual powers, in order to absorb the unfamiliar reality into oneself, so to speak, and then to place it once more outside oneself. But only in the encounter with a related life are these powers awakened: one comprehends only that in which one shares in some way— which one is like—and not more.

One can view this psychological conditionedness of historical work as a deficiency and fear the dangers given therein: prejudice, lack of discrimination, evident bias. And one should certainly not take these lightly, but should oppose them with every weapon that a scrupulous methodology makes available. But even so, one may not on that account evaluate it only negatively, seeing the ideal to consist in somehow extinguishing one's own identity. That would be to misunderstand that just in this psychological moment resides the possibility of entering into the historical event, of giving it blood and life, and thus of constructing that third [[88]] element that goes beyond the mere subject and the pure object: history elevated to a new present.

In light of these conclusions, it will come as no surprise if Eduard Spranger claims, "These days, it is simply common knowledge among all reflective historians that there is no discipline of history without a philosophy of history." And that is only one among many similar statements by recognized historical scholars. The wide-ranging consequences this has for the evaluation of historical scholarship, and for its task generally, have been drawn by C. H. Becker, in an essay on the "Change in Historical Consciousness,"[7] although we are unable here to take up his exposition in detail or to identify ourselves with it.

6. Eichrodt refers "above all" to Joachim Wach, *Religionswissenschaft: Prolegomena zu ihrer wissenschaftstheoretischen Grundlagen* (Veröffentlichen des Forschungsinstitut an der Universität Leipzig 10; Leipzig: Hinrichs, 1924). He also mentions works by Spranger, Litt, and Bächtold. See Eduard Spranger, *Der Sinn der Voraussetzungslosigkeit in den Geisteswissenchaften* (Darmstadt: Wissenschaftliche Buchgesellschaft, 1963); Theodor Litt, *Die Wiederweckung des geschichtlichen Bewusstseins* (Heidelberg: Quelle & Meyer, 1956).

7. "Wandel im geschichtlichen Bewusstsein." As a reference, Eichrodt gives only *Die neue Rundschau* 38 (1927) 113ff.

What, then, can this more precise conception of the subjective moment in all historical scholarship teach us regarding our particular problem? Above all, it may deter us from a fruitless opposition between history
and faith's intuitive knowledge, which would be the basis for requiring, on
the one hand, a dogmatic discipline of Old Testament theology and, on
the other hand, an objective history of Israelite-Jewish religion chemically
pure of any valuation. In reality, history and intuitive knowledge do not
stand in any relation of opposition to each other, but one of mutual fulfillment. The discussion about historical scholarship in general teaches us
that there just is no history of Israelite religion independent of all subjective presuppositions. In its case, as with every historical presentation, the
concept of purpose and understanding's governing category, the principle
of selection, are derived from considerations that stem not from empirical
scholarship but from our basic value orientation. In other words, the pursuit of its lines of development must find its goal, at least for the theologian, in the thought world of the New Testament. And the selection of
particular material can only occur from the perspective of the extent to
which this serves to make clear and comprehensible the preparation of the
historical basis of revelation in Christ, acknowledged as the supreme value.
Thereby, however, we are only comprehending with fundamental clarity
what was already commonly recognized among earlier historians. None
other than Bernhard Stade expressed this in 1892, in his university address
on "The Task of Biblical Theology of the Old Testament,"[8] saying that if
the presentation of Israelite religion wants to find a center of gravity, it will
have to offer as a conclusion a brief outline of the whole course of development of Jesus' preaching.

Naturally, this is not at all to deny that the history of Israelite-Jewish
religion can also be portrayed from another standpoint, just as long as
there, too, methodological reflection and clarification regarding this
standpoint has preceded. But, of course, [[89]] a theological presentation
can be given on no other presupposition than marked out above.

On this basis the task and character of Old Testament theology can be
determined more precisely. If the history of Israelite-Jewish religion is a
matter of the genetic understanding of Old Testament religion in the in-
terplay of historical forces, then Old Testament theology has to do, as was
already stated, with the systematic task of a cross section through the developed whole, which should illumine the entire dynamic content of the
religion according to its internal structure, and which should perceive its

8. Published as "Über die Aufgabe der biblischen Theologie des Alten Testaments,"
Zeitschrift für Theologie und Kirche 3 (1893) 31–51; also in *Ausgewählte Akademische Reden und
Abhandlungen* (Giessen: Töpelmann, 1907) 77–96.

uniqueness over against the religious environment—that is, over against the typology of the history of religion generally. For the fulfillment of this task, Old Testament theology has no tools other than history of religion; that is, it proceeds from the same subjective presuppositions, in order to arrange matters of empirical fact, and to bring them to a conclusive understanding. Thus, according to both its object and its method, Old Testament theology has its place entirely within empirical-historical Old Testament scholarship.

I would like to believe that this also meets the legitimate concern of those who would require a dogmatic discipline for perceiving the essence of Old Testament religion. Those who represent this demand are entirely right in referring to the internal relation of the scholar to his material as the presupposition of a genuine understanding, and in defining this internal relation more precisely as a basic value orientation—theologically expressed, as a relation of faith. Except that this presupposition also applies to *historical* work, if the interpretation of phenomena according to their deepest meaning is kept in mind as its goal, rather than the "drayman's work" of chronistically determining facts whose inner connection remains in the dark. Just as historical research in every regional specialization recognizes with increasing clarity that among the most important presuppositions of any significant work is fruitful cooperation between philosophy and individual empirical disciplines, so the theological treatment of history must become clear that it can proceed to the meaningfulness of Old Testament history in no other way than from a supraempirical fundamental presupposition, namely, the viewpoint gained from the reality of New Testament revelation.

To comprehend the essence of Old Testament religion in this way would certainly not involve the explicit faith statements of a *kerygma*, of a direct testimony; if that should be what is meant by the demand for a religio-dogmatic discipline of Old Testament theology, we would have to reject it. Comprehending the essence of Old Testament religion under the viewpoint of the reality of revelation can indeed occur only in such a way that one makes explicit its thoroughgoing relation to the supreme value. But once again, that can only occur on historical bases, and by historical means.

It is really superfluous to say that this demonstration of [[90]] relatedness is still no proof for the reality of revelation. Relatedness to the supreme value will say nothing to anyone who does not share the same fundamental presupposition. But for someone who is internally convinced of the reality of revelation, it is certainly essential whether historical matters of fact attested in the records of revelation stand in a demonstrable outer and inner connection to the center of revelation, for only if they do can one appropriate their intellectual content.

Admittedly, one could here raise the objection that, with everything that has been said, the specific character of theological knowledge has not yet been taken into account, to the extent that in its case it is, supposedly, not a matter of the usual kind of intuitive knowledge that is also indispensable to other disciplines. Rather, here there is said to loom the sphere of decision, in which there are only existential judgments. For that reason as well, the relation of the Old Testament scholar to his material is said to differ from that of the literary historian, in spite of all they hold in common regarding their subjective presuppositions.

However, such an objection would not have considered that proof of similarity in methodological definition cannot be a question of identity in the content of the postulated fundamental presupposition. It is self-evident that any material will once again require distinctive criteria for its own evaluation, and will disclose itself fully only to an interpreter who brings with him this requisite affinity to the object. This, then, in no way implies an alteration of theology's scientific character, but only indicates its special distinction; namely, that in its case the subjective presupposition falls in the sphere of existential decision.

However, even the recognition of this distinctiveness in no way grants that the Old Testament scholar in his biblical-theological work generally would be constrained toward existential judgments. To be sure, such a scholar makes his statements under the presupposition of an existential judgment; however, he is otherwise involved in the presentation of historical states of affairs and their inner connections. Whatever connections he shows there to be in the Old Testament between God and humankind he leaves to the dogmatician, as the representative of regulative science, to utilize in the system of Christian faith as normative knowledge.

Naturally, these claims are only intended as an attempt to establish theoretical boundaries between the individual theological disciplines. In practice, it may happen more than once that an Old Testament scholar will feel constrained at this or that point to transcend the boundaries of historical-empirical scholarship, and to state explicitly that New Testament revelation as the point of departure does not mean for him only a heuristic principle, which he applies to serve some external purpose or with reference to the common basis of the Christian church's faith; but rather, that it corresponds to a living reality which recognizes the Old Testament as normative foundation that he himself applies. The inner, living connection within which all the theological disciplines [[91]] stand may dispose them more to such a transgression of boundaries than is the case with other disciplines. But one thing would need to be stressed by way of methodological clarity: that rendering a verdict and offering proof, as is appropriate to normative science, is not thereby to be carried into Old Testament scholarship as an essential component.

It may seem desirable to consider many points further in explanation of what has been said. Nonetheless, it can only be a question here of offering a few indications of the problem, not of pursuing it in its entire scope. If I have been successful in gaining the active interest of my colleagues in the significance of our question just now, and in view of the situation of the human sciences in general, then this lecture has achieved its goal.[9]

9. Presented at the fifth Orientalistentag, Bonn, 1928.

Part 2

Sampling Old Testament Theology

The Multicolored Landscape of Old Testament Theology

ELMER A. MARTENS

The vitality in the discipline of Old Testament theology during most of the twentieth century has been due in part to the debate about how one goes about formulating a theology of the Old Testament. But preoccupation with method can blind one to the outcome, the substantive formulations of Old Testament theology. These formulations, which usually turn on particular themes or features, are not unlike a variegated landscape aburst with color.

In this six-decade overview (1930–1990), attention is minimally on method and primarily on the product. (For method, see Ben Ollenburger's essay, pp. 3–19 above.) Our questions are two: What have biblical theologians offered as the results of their research? What are the noticeable shifts in setting forth the results of an Old Testament theology? In answering the second question, we will find a convenient way to address the first. By means of six observations that characterize Old Testament theology in this sixty-year period, we will chronicle the shifts in nuance. Like much of biblical theology itself, our method is descriptive rather than evaluative. Our data is drawn primarily, but not only from the authors whose works have been excerpted.

Capturing the Sense of the Dynamic, but in Different Ways

The Old Testament by its very arrangement is not a catalog of ideas or doctrines, but, as in a story, embodies movement. God takes the initiative. Individuals and communities respond. There is both action and reaction.

For biographical data on Elmer A. Martens see pp. 298–99.

That dynamism has been expressed by different theologians in different ways.

Walther Eichrodt focused on God's covenant as the theme within which one could incorporate the variety of Old Testament material. Though there are numerous divinely originated covenants, Eichrodt held up primarily the Sinaitic covenant as the lens through which to view the Old Testament. In grace God disclosed his will. Contrary to the gods of the surrounding cultures, Yahweh was not capricious. Israel, in responding, was bonded to God as his people. A covenant now existed between the two.

Eichrodt wrote prior to the explosion of essays generated by the observations of George Mendenhall and others that biblical covenants had a form similar to that of ancient Near East vassal treaties (Mendenhall 1955). Now the historical reviews within biblical covenants made greater sense. More important, now the place of law within covenant could be better understood and appreciated. Covenant-making was an ancient institution.

Though an ancient institution, covenant, Eichrodt insisted, was not to be understood as a static idea, a given piece, like furniture, set up as part of Israel's world view. Critics charged that covenant was both static and abstract, but Eichrodt saw it as "living process." He answered his critics:

> For in the systematic presentation of Israel's faith we are not concerned with framing a system of religious concepts capable . . . of a consistent and harmonious intellectual structure. Our purpose is to examine the content for faith of a particular relationship with God, a relationship which has always to be seen as a dynamic process, expressing itself in history in many ways, and fluctuating between periods of rich and profound insight and periods of stunting and impoverishment, but which for all that exhibits a marvelous consistency in fundamental features which marks it out from its religious environment as an entity *sui generis* (1961: 517).

For Eichrodt, interaction, motion, and dynamic were most notable features of the Old Testament message.

Later theologians subsequently singled out features other than covenant, but common to most was the stress on a certain dynamism present in the Old Testament. Theodorus C. Vriezen elaborated on communion, a category which for him was more encompassing than covenant, though it could include covenant. Communion between God and people was essentially a matter of exchange/interchange. Such intercourse by its very definition assumed an activity, an ongoing dynamic: "In the Old Testament knowledge is living in a close relationship with something or somebody, such a relationship as to cause what may be called communion" (1970: 154). Vriezen spoke about radiations from God. He warned against arriving "at a closely reasoned whole, a rationally justified doctrine" (1970: 156). He too wanted to preserve the sense of the dynamic.

G. Ernest Wright encapsulated the same point about movement, something transpiring or happening, in the title of his book, *God Who Acts* (1952). The plot of the story began with God's promises to the patriarchs, thickened with Israel's detainment and oppression in Egypt, but eventually climaxed in a conquest—not only of the land of Canaan, but of other territories, as later through David. Edmond Jacob stated: "The Old Testament does not bring us ideas about God, but acts of God, a God who leaves his transcendence to link his own destiny with the destiny of a people and through that people with the whole of humanity" (1958: 32).

The dynamic nature of the Old Testament could be laid bare, however, in ways other than by pointing to an active deity. Gerhard von Rad identified a series of Israelite traditions which were transmitted from generation to generation, and not only transmitted but adapted. In this process elements of the exodus tradition, for example, were expanded, when the Sinai component was inserted. Between the simple formulation of the old credo (Deut 26:5–9) and "the form in which the history of the patriarchs now appears in Genesis, there lies a very long road in the history of tradition, the main stages of which can, however, be approximately reconstructed" (1962: 166). This building up of units of traditions was "of great significance for Biblical theology" (1962: 166).

Georg Fohrer's schema for Old Testament theology was constituted by two poles, God's rulership and the communion between God and people, around which, as in a cassette, the Old Testament material moved (1972). Similarly Samuel Terrien, by calling attention to God's elusive presence, namely his coming and his withdrawal, as sketched, for example in the psalms of confidence and lament, showed that a dynamic was operative (1978). Paul Hanson depicted the continuing engagement of a community like Israel with its tradition: "According to this model, a contemporary community of faith is thus not primarily an archive where members can study records about ancient happenings, or an institution committed to perpetuating structures of a bygone age, but rather a community called by God to participate in an *ongoing* drama" (1986: 533; italics his).

So the concern to highlight the dynamism present in the Old Testament record has surfaced, though in various ways, whether the focus be on covenant (Eichrodt), communion (Vriezen), God's action (Wright), rulership and communion (Fohrer), God's presence (Terrien), or God's people (Hanson).

Awareness of Culture Contexts—Theirs and Ours

A body of literature like the Old Testament cannot be properly interpreted without attention to context. In the early days of the period under review, the context was Israel's neighbors of the Near East. Half a century later, the theologian's eye was more sharply trained on the contemporary culture.

To elaborate on this shift we begin again with the German scholar Walther Eichrodt, who along with others was much occupied with the history of religions. He made clear at the outset that to illumine the profoundest meaning of the Old Testament he would examine Israel's religious environment. And so he did. Canaanite thought imperiled a correct understanding of covenant (1961: 45ff.). Theistic religions with demonistic practices were now opposed by a unique deity (1961: 159). Eschatological thinking was peculiarly Israelite: "In all those religions of the Near East which are fairly well known to us there is not a single instance of unquestionably eschatological thought to be found" (1961: 495).

The mood of the scholars in making comparisons between Israel and others was caught in the title of Norman Snaith's book, *Distinctive Ideas in the Old Testament* (1944). G. Ernest Wright, for example, in emphasizing a God who acts, stressed that the idea of linear history found in the Bible differed from the cyclical notions of history found in the non-Israelite world. As the seasons follow each other routinely, so, rhythmically, events in history were cyclical. Newness was basically absent. Such a pagan view, however, was in sharp contrast to that spelled out by Paul in Acts 13 or found in Psalms (78, 105, 106) or in the historical books. Here life was analyzed, not over against nature, but in terms of the will and purpose of God worked out historically toward a goal (Wright 1952). Ludwig Köhler's judgment, when comparing Hebrew religion with neighboring religions, was, "There is hardly a word so characteristic of the Old Testament as the word joy" (1957: 151).

Recent theologies have tended to place the emphasis elsewhere. Accent now falls heavily on the *current* community of faith. Brevard S. Childs and Paul Hanson can serve as examples. Childs stresses Scripture as the canon for the community of faith, then and now. His chapter on "Male and Female as a Theological Problem" not only illustrates in greater detail the forms of Israel's institutions, but self-consciously takes account of the current debate about the role of women (1985: 188). From one perspective, the Bible's witness is to equality, says Childs. But since biblically there are varying roles assigned to men and women, an egalitarian ideology in the modern idiom of identifying the sexes in every respect with the same roles is in danger of going beyond the biblical witness (1985: 192). Paul Hanson concludes his theology of the Old Testament with a chapter on "The Biblical Notion of Community: Contemporary Implications" (1986: 467–518). One of these implications is to accept the vision of the entire creation as an intricate organism in which humans find a place to experience life's highest purpose in praising God. To follow such a vision is for *the contemporary community* to be involved in struggle.

It is precisely in the mood and tone that the implications of the shift from comparative ancient Near Eastern religions, to the application to modern communities, lie. The shift is a move from the mere descriptive to the present-day relevance. At the midpoint of the century, and in successive decades, the concern was to describe the theological dimensions of the Old Testament. But something more than detached description characterized the later theologies, for these were exercised to address the contemporary community. Georg Fohrer is a good illustration. His final chapter entitled "Applications" stretches almost a hundred pages and covers such topics as the state and politics, culture and technique. On the latter subject, after tracing various perspectives on culture within the Old Testament, Fohrer concludes that humankind is summoned to develop culture and technique in obedience to the assignment to be God's vicegerent (1972: 259–60). Fohrer is not only concerned with a descriptive account but outlines the application of this theology to modern life.

To be sure, the enterprise of formulating a theology of the Old Testament is primarily an enterprise in the service of the faith community. Theologies guide the orientation and direction of church and synagogue. Still, the tone of theologies written toward the end of the twentieth century was louder than earlier attempts in stressing the relevance of their findings for their contemporaries.

Sensitive to Old Testament Sequels: The New Testament and the Talmud

Good arguments have been advanced concerning why it is proper to isolate the Old Testament for theologizing (Childs 1985: 17). The first such isolated treatment of the Old Testament was by Georg L. Bauer in 1796. The majority of the twentieth-century biblical theologians, however, even when concentrating on the Old Testament, have specifically noted the theological continuity between it and its sequel, the New Testament. An exception was John L. McKenzie who claimed to write his Old Testament theology as though the New Testament did not exist (1974). In this concern for continuity, one can observe a shift, however, for several writers later in the century show greater sensitivity to the tie of the Old Testament with Judaism as well as with Christianity.

Once more Walther Eichrodt is an obvious starting point for an elaboration of this shift. Part of the task of Old Testament theology, he noted, was to tie in the Old with the New Testament (1961: 27). Once he had laid bare the importance of covenant as being the key pillar in the structure of

Israel's faith, he could with a little extension make a bridge into the New Testament. Eichrodt spoke of the Old Testament hope of salvation represented in the figure of the Savior-king. He was critical of the "mechanical transference of OT statements about the coming age of salvation to the Person and Work of Christ" (1961: 502). Still, he discussed prediction and fulfillment, though on a grand order, and, it should be noted, with reference to Jesus Christ. G. Ernest Wright, after cataloging the acts of God in Hebrew Scripture, could point to Jesus Christ as God's magnificent action of incarnation (1952: 84). Edmond Jacob stated, "A line not always straight, but none the less continuous, leads from the anthropomorphism of the earliest pages of the Bible, to the incarnation of God in Jesus Christ" (1958: 32).

So also Gerhard von Rad had no difficulty, after showing how traditions were repeatedly appropriated and changed, to show that the New Testament was but one more, and that a singularly grand illustration, of readaptation of tradition. He devoted almost one hundred pages to the linkage of the Old and the New, noting how the Old Testament can only be read as a book of ever-increasing anticipation, and how the New Testament then absorbs the Old, in a manner akin to the actualization of traditions within the Old Testament, namely by an "eclective process based on *charisma*" (1965: 324). Like others, von Rad concentrated on the New Testament as sequel to the Old (Oeming 1985).

Illustrations of Old Testament theologies which even more painstakingly linked the Old with the New are not hard to find. George A. F. Knight, by the very title of his book, *A Christian Theology of the Old Testament* (1959), highlighted the connection between the Old and the New Testaments. The chapter heading for his discussion of Isaiah's "servant," is "The 'Crucifixion' of Israel." The five "moments" in the life of Israel are birth (exodus), marriage (Sinai), death (exile of 587), restoration (Ezekiel 37), and the eschatological hope. These correspond to the work of Christ: birth, marriage (the giving of a new Tora), death, resurrection and exaltation (1959: 202–17). Earlier, Wilhelm Vischer's summary of the Old Testament under the title *The Witness of the Old Testament to Christ* (1949) made the same point of the New Testament's continuity with the Old. J. Barton Payne, also by means of his title, *The Theology of the Older Testament* (1962), left no doubt about the premium he placed on connecting the two. Indeed, Payne centered the Old Testament material around the word *covenant* but construed this in terms of testament with subheadings such as "The Testator: God," "The Heir: Man," and "The Inheritance: Reconciliation."

Walter C. Kaiser Jr. pursued the subject of *promise* into the New Testament. Promise marked the era of the patriarchs theologically speaking; it figured prominently in the Mosaic era; it emerged in the Davidic period;

it was renewed in the seventh century; and it was the subject of the prophets' message. Kaiser quoted Willis Beecher to summarize the connection of Old and New: "God gave a promise to Abraham, and through him to all mankind; a promise eternally fulfilled and fulfilling in the history of Israel; and chiefly fulfilled in Jesus Christ, he being that which is principal in the history of Israel" (1978: 263). Elmer A. Martens (1981) also, by describing God's design as embracing activities of deliverance and covenant-making and as fostering knowledge of God and the bestowal of blessing (e.g., land), was in a position in his final chapter to sketch how these components reappeared in the New Testament.

Samuel Terrien, in *The Elusive Presence* (1978), was one of a few during this period who attempted a biblical theology which incorporated both Testaments (compare Millar Burrows [1946], Geerhardus Vos [1948], Chester Lehman [1971]). The name of Yahweh, "at once revelatory and reticent," was disclosed in the Sinai theophany (Terrien 1978: 151). In revelatory fashion, the name linked God's presence with the people of Israel. Still, it was "reticent because it preserves the freedom of the divine" (Terrien 1978: 151). The story of God's presence in theophany culminated in the person of Jesus Christ who claimed and was acclaimed as "the bearer of the presence." The New Testament evangelist interpreted Jesus, especially at the pivotal moments of the annunciation, the transfiguration, and resurrection. The motifs of theophany, epiphany, and divine manifestation were brought together in the person of Christ (Terrien 1978: 411).

But the same body of literature was Scripture not only for the Christians, but also for the Jews. In the closing decades of the twentieth century, Christian theologians began to give greater attention to the Jewish sequel of the Old Testament.

Paul Hanson traced the theme of "the people called" through apocryphal literature as well as into Qumran times. He acknowledged,

> Two major religious communities stem from the history we have traced thus far in our study. Modern Judaism is the child of Pharisaism, its canon of authoritative writings being the Hebrew Bible, the Mishnah, the Palestinian and Babylonian Talmuds, and the rabbinical biblical commentaries (Midrashim). Modern Christianity is the child of the movement arising from the life and teachings of Jesus of Nazareth. . . . One of the most fascinating challenges facing Jews and Christians in our own day is the clarification of the relationship between these two religious communities (1986: 383).

Ronald E. Clements already earlier was sensitive to that challenge. The "fresh approach" signaled in the subtitle of his work was to search out the implications of the Hebrew Scriptures having two communities, the Jewish and the Christian, for its sequel. For Judaism that Scripture was designated as Torah; for Christianity it was characterized as promise. Law (*torah*), defined in Deut 4:44–45, brought together "words denoting laws, decrees, and admonitions under one all-embracing category. . . . To obey *tôrâh* was to satisfy the demands of religious, social and family life in the broadest possible compass. . . . *Tôrâh* is the comprehensive list of instructions and stipulations by which Israel's covenant with God is controlled" (1978: 108, 110). As for promise, its recurring themes were return from the exile, Israel's reconstitution as a nation, the restoration of the Davidic line, and the glorification of Zion. The message of hope entered the mainstream of Israelite prophecy in the seventh century according to Clements, but in Isaiah 40–55 it was given a central place. In expounding how the same material received different accents from two different communities, Clements was able not only to open up the Old Testament message, but to facilitate communication between Christians and Jews.

Similarly Brevard S. Childs's canonical approach had the advantage of gaining a hearing from adherents to Judaism who share with Christians the thirty-nine books as Scripture. So the shift was from doing an Old Testament theology within the confines of the Christian community, to an approach which recognized that the sequel to the Old Testament was not alone the New Testament, but also Jewish canonical literature.

Wrestling with Revelation: How Important was History?

Never far from the task of summarizing the theological dimensions of the Old Testament was the spoken or unspoken issue of its authority. The Dutch theologian Theodorus C. Vriezen devoted one-third of his book to the subject of the Old Testament's authority for the church (1970). The American Otto Baab addressed the subject in his final chapter, "The Validity of Old Testament Theology" (1949: 250–72). Closely allied to the question of authority was the issue of divine revelation. Here the shape of the agenda kept changing over a sixty-year period.

Though he did not prepare a full-orbed Old Testament theology, the British scholar H. Wheeler Robinson presented lectures in the 1940s which were to be prolegomena to such a theology. In these he examined the inspiration of the prophet, especially the psychology of inspiration, which was the counterpart, or even the necessary constituent for the theology of revelation. But revelation also came through the priests, "the guardians of tradition." The priestly formula "Yahweh spoke to Moses" was in many ways parallel to the prophetic revelatory formula "Thus says the Lord" (1946:

210). Geerhardus Vos, whose work was published two years later, arranged his material for a biblical theology around the subject of progressive revelation (e.g., in the Mosaic era, in the prophetic era, in the New Testament).

Theologians within the so-called Biblical Theology movement in the 1950s gave marked accent to "divine revelation" by insisting on the importance of God's acts. History, it was said, was the medium of revelation. Events in the life of Israel were conveyors of knowledge about God. Whether by a more traditional *Heilsgeschichte* (as G. Ernest Wright) or by a nonconventional *Heilsgeschichte* (as Gerhard von Rad), common to both was attention to history. That deeds were not the only vehicle of revelation was soon pointed out. A debate ensued in which arguments turned on the relative revelatory value of deeds and speech (e.g., James Barr 1963: 193–205). Clearly, events, as naked uninterpreted happenings, had no revelatory value. Words, along with events, were constitutive of revelation.

Walther Zimmerli stressed that the knowledge of God was not to be attained by philosophical reflection but through "event-interpreted-through word," a result of his thorough work on the recognition formula in Ezekiel, "And you shall know that I am Yahweh." The name *Yahweh*, Zimmerli proposed, held within it the theology of the Old Testament. Hence his *Old Testament Theology in Outline* (1978) begins with the fundamentals, namely the revealed name of Yahweh. This Yahweh is the God of Israel, but also the God of the fathers, and in fact creator and universal king. The point of departure for him was "that focal point where the faith of the Old Testament specifically confesses the God of Israel under the name of Yahweh" (1978: 14). Even though in the confession of this name there is an intimate association with a historical event, "we must still avoid the mistaken assumption that for Israel history as such became the revelatory word of Yahweh" (1978: 25). The commandments, along with other divine speeches, so Zimmerli insisted, offer primary insight into Yahwism.

By the time Zimmerli's *Old Testament Theology in Outline* appeared in English translation (1978), the avid discussions about revelation had waned. Brevard S. Childs, however, in his 1985 volume returned to the theme: "The term revelation is integral to the task of Old Testament theology, but only as a shorthand formula pointing to the whole enterprise of theological reflection on the reality of God" (1985: 25–26). "How is God known?" he asked, and then answered: through creation, wisdom, history, and the name (1985: 30–39). The recipients of God's revelation were Israel, God's chosen people, individuals, and the nations (1985: 93–107). Specifically, Childs tied revelation to the canon, so that, while a given narrative might not in itself disclose hitherto unknown information about God, the canonical corpus, which included the narrative, became a vehicle by which Israel could learn about its God (1985: 23).

It should be noted that in the flowering of Old Testament theology a
theme such as revelation, while still a usable theme in the mid-1980s, had
a more nuanced and refined meaning than in the days of Theodorus C.
Vriezen and G. Ernest Wright at mid-century.

Exploring the Options:
Increased Freedom of Form

The reader of Old Testament theology, if confused by the varieties of attempted summaries of the Old Testament, might be excused. The range
of proposals is understandably bewildering. Still, the limitations of one approach have led scholars over the years to fresh probes.

In the course of years, the discipline was increasingly cut free from
dogmatic systems—a point to which Johann Gabler spoke (see appendix,
pp. 489–502 below). However, the first English Old Testament theology
to appear in the twentieth century, Andrew B. Davidson's *Theology of the
Old Testament* (1904), essentially returned to the venerable dogmatic
scheme of treating the subjects: God, man, and salvation. Basically a similar scheme was also followed in mid-century by Paul Heinisch (1950) and
Paul van Imschoot (1965), both Catholic theologians. That deference to
dogmatic theology was broken by Walther Eichrodt and Gerhard von Rad;
since then greater and greater freedom from the hallowed schema has
been evident (cf. Ollenburger 1991).

John McKenzie, a Catholic theologian, is an example of one of many
who broke with the dogmatic scheme. Systematization cannot be avoided,
of course. But, as McKenzie noted, "what emerges in the Old Testament is
not a rational system but a basic personal reality, Yahweh, who is consistent as a person is, not as a rational system" (1974: 23). So McKenzie set
out to analyze an experience, to set forth insights which arose out of the
totality of Old Testament utterances. Where did Israel experience Yahweh? In the cult. A discussion of the cult—festivals, sacrifices, temple and
sanctuary, priesthood—became the starting point for McKenzie. Israel
also experienced Yahweh in revelational settings, as for example through
prophecy (cult prophets, court prophets, the writing prophets). History,
as contrasted to myth, was another arena in which Israel experienced Yahweh. Thus McKenzie gave attention to promise and fulfillment and the
saving/judging acts of Yahweh. "Nature" and "wisdom" received treatment, for these too fell within Israel's experience of Yahweh. William Dyrness was similar to McKenzie in treating disparate topics, but for Dyrness
these topics were more aligned with topics from dogmatic theology
(1979). McKenzie, however, floated free of old strictures in which the Old
Testament was approached as a set of ideas for doctrine.

Theologians also departed increasingly from the notion that Old Testament theology can be rendered under a single theme. Single themes

were put forward as organizing themes: covenant (Eichrodt), communion (Vriezen), God's sovereignty (Jacob), and promise (Kaiser). Despite these valiant attempts it was argued, more and more compellingly, that no one single theme was a sufficiently large umbrella. Georg Fohrer proposed the dual theme of God's rulership and communion between God and humanity. Walther Zimmerli and Brevard Childs opted for a multiplicity of themes. A dialectical approach was followed by Samuel Terrien (God's presence/absence) and by Ronald Clements (law/promise). The sheer diversity was itself a problem.

Claus Westermann was another theologian who basically followed a dialectical schema. He held that "the theology of the Old Testament thus remains determined in every aspect by the outline of a story entrusted to us which includes the occurrence of God speaking and the response of those who experience these events" (1982: 11). Here was already one dialectic: God's acts/human response. Another prominent dialectic was God acts/God speaks. The prophets offered oracles of salvation but also oracles of judgment. The psalms could be summarized around a dialectic: praise/lament. But for Westermann it was the blessing/deliverance dialectic that was dominant. "Blessing" represented God's activities of provision and sustenance. Not only the creation account but also the entire Book of Genesis moved on this note. "Deliverance" or "salvation" represented God's activities of intervention, as in the exodus. Fond of pointing out structural aspects, Westermann pointed to the Pentateuch, where the deliverance motif in Exodus–Numbers was bracketed by the blessing motif of Genesis and Deuteronomy.

So complex, even confusing, have become these various proposals for organizing an Old Testament theology that one can understand the reason for launching a series entitled "Overtures to Biblical Theology" in 1977. In this series of monographs single topics such as *Israel in Exile* (Ralph W. Klein, 1979), *The Land* (Walter Brueggemann, 1977), and *The Suffering of God* (Terence E. Fretheim, 1984), were treated. Sorting out the complexity—which has come with the increased freedom and experimentation—may well be part of the agenda for the next era of the discipline. In the meanwhile, it is as though one were hesitant about putting together a bouquet, but found satisfaction in selecting corsages.

Balancing Old Testament Themes: Highlighting Neglected Subjects

Old Testament theology may be thought of as a science, a science which is self-correcting. Sooner or later an area of neglect will be addressed to bring about a more balanced understanding of a phenomenon. An overview of the parade of themes in theologizing on the Old Testament displays examples of compensative corrections.

One example of bringing matters into balance is the shift from examining ideas to examining process. Some consensus prevailed early on in our period that the mother lode of Old Testament theology was the vein of religious ideas. Various ideas would be "excavated" and examined. Otto Baab's chapter on "The Idea of Sin" can serve as an example. In the process of analyzing the idea, a range of Hebrew words, some seventeen of them—"not a complete list"—were cited and explained (1949: 84–113). Edmond Jacob's opening sentence was, "The theology of the Old Testament may be defined as the systematic account of the specific religious ideas which can be found throughout the Old Testament and which form its profound unity" (1958: 11). Accordingly, Jacob elaborated on the nature of God's holiness. He asserted that "the essential aspect of holiness is that of power, but of power in the service of a God who uses all things to make his kingdom triumph" (1958: 87). Israel's history was an outworking of God's holiness, as the psalmist said, "Your way, O God, is in holiness" (Ps 77:14, 68:25).

One cannot discuss theology apart from concepts, of course. One theologian, however, who offset the one-sidedness of ideas, was Hartmut Gese. He shifted attention away from ideas to "process," specifically the process of tradition building (1981a). For example, on the subject of death, Gese focused not on the idea of death, but on the experience of death and the way this experience was handed down through the generations. With the strong sense of family in the Old Testament, death, though it comes to the individual, was an experience of being placed, or gathered, with the ancestors. The dead person was not considered nonexistent but had "entered a non-living existence" (1981a: 37). Further, by examining Israelite teaching about sacrifice to the dead, Gese provided an understanding, not of the concept of death, but of the way Israel experienced death. In Israelite thought, in contrast to other myths, there was not an independent power of death alongside God, but the dead as well as the world of the dead belonged to Yahweh. Gese explained the contribution of wisdom so that in another stage in the tradition assurances of eternal life become pronounced: "You guided me with your counsel, and afterward you will receive me to glory" (Ps 73:24). More than that. With apocalyptic, there was talk of resurrection. Gese kept his finger on the process of tradition formation and transmission. To single out ideas from the mother lode was a theological activity, but, on balance, so was the tracing of the formation of the mineral vein.

Other examples of "correctives" introduced to balance right but one-sided emphases can be adduced. The earlier theologies with their stress on God and his actions (e.g., Wright, Jacob) did not incorporate discussions about the human response, as did Zimmerli (cf. his chapter on "Life before God"; 1978: 141–66) or Westermann (cf. the chapter entitled "The Response"; 1982: 153–216). Human response, as a theological item, had been given high visibility in von Rad who, after delineating Yahweh's deliverance of Israel from Egypt, the divine revelation at Sinai, and God's grant of the land of Canaan, concluded his first volume with a section entitled "Israel before Jahweh (Israel's Answer)" (1962: 355–459). Here von Rad elaborated on the praises of Israel which included the psalms but also such credos as Deut 26:5–11 or Josh 24:2ff. Along with the saving history, Israel extolled the great theme of Yahweh's action in nature. The proper human response is praise: "Praise is man's most characteristic mode of existence" (von Rad 1962: 369–70). It was also in this "response section" that von Rad treated "righteousness"—Yahweh's and Israel's.

The subject of wisdom was not only omitted in earlier theologies (e.g., Sellin) but disparaged, as by G. Ernest Wright as a cul-de-sac. Redress came from Samuel Terrien, whose theology incorporated wisdom under the title "The Play of Wisdom." Terrien held that in Hebrew thought wisdom became personified. From Job 28 Terrien showed how wisdom was God's playful partner, and how in the final verse of that hymn wisdom was made available to Job. So also in Prov 8:22–31 wisdom's ambience was with the Creator, but not only. She also found her delight with "the sons of men" (Prov 8:31b). So "playful Wisdom is the mediatrix of presence" (Terrien 1978: 357). Wisdom, as God's companion, asserted Terrien, was not alien but integral to the Old Testament's theme of God's presence: "Although Amos and his successors had hailed Yahweh as the creator of heaven and earth, the sages shifted their attention from history—a stage now empty of God—to the theater of the universe, where they detected his presence" (1978: 380). Wisdom, then, was not a cul-de-sac.

A final example of redressing an imbalance turns on the polarity of the spiritual and material. The very designation is hardly appropriate in talking about Hebrew religious literature. Still, Walther Eichrodt's covenant theme, and certainly Paul Heinisch's treatment, tended to underplay the subject of nature. These tended to minimize the "this-worldly"; for any significant theological discussion about "land" was omitted. Yet land was a dominant topic. Walther Zimmerli, among others, restored the balance. In the second of his five sections ("The Gifts Bestowed by Yahweh"), "land and its blessings" figured prominently, standing alongside war and victory, God's presence, and charismatic leadership (1978: 59–108). Martens's volume was distinguished in assigning to land and the blessings which it came to symbolize a major role in "God's Design" (1981: chaps. 6, 10, 14; cf. Walter Brueggemann's *The Land,* 1977). Old Testament spirituality could not be described alone on the God–Israel axis, or people–people axis, but, if a balance was to be observed, must also include the God–people–land axes.

In summary, the shifts I have sketched underline the vibrancy of biblical theology in a sixty-year period, and that despite the several unresolved issues about method. Commonalities there have been—such as, highlighting the dynamism of the Old Testament, connecting the Old Testament with its sequel, observing a cultural context for the message, dealing with the theme of revelation, looking for fresh ways of treating the subject, and working toward a balance in representing the Old Testament. But shifts within these commonalities there have been also. The hues of color have flashed abundantly and sometimes brilliantly in this landscape of Old Testament theology.[1]

1. For a complementary article see John R. Donahue, "The Changing Shape of New Testament Theology," *TS* 50 (1989) 314–35.

Chronological List of Some "Old Testament Theologies" 1930–1990 (Detailed bibliography on pp. 503–20)

The First Wave

1933	Ernst Sellin, *Old Testament Theology on a History-of-Religion Basis*
1933–39	Walther Eichrodt, *Theology of the Old Testament*
1935	Ludwig Köhler, *Old Testament Theology*
1938	Wilhelm Möller and Hans Möller, *Biblical Theology of the Old Testament in Its Development of Salvation History*
1940	Paul Heinisch, *Theology of the Old Testament*
1946	Millar Burrows, *An Outline of Biblical Theology*
1948	Albert Gelin, *The Key Concepts of the Old Testament*
1948	Geerhardus Vos, *Biblical Theology*

The Second Wave

1949	Otto Baab, *The Theology of the Old Testament*
1949	Theodorus C. Vriezen, *An Outline of Old Testament Theology*
1950	Robert C. Dentan, *Preface of Old Testament Theology*

1950	Otto Procksch, *Theology of the Old Testament*
1952	George Ernest Wright, *God Who Acts: Biblical Theology as Recital*
1954–56	Paul van Imschoot, *Theology of the Old Testament*
1955	Edmond Jacob, *Theology of the Old Testament*
1956	H. H. Rowley, *The Faith of Israel*
1957–61	Gerhard von Rad, *Old Testament Theology*
1959	George Knight, *A Christian Theology of the Old Testament*
1961	James Muilenburg, *The Way Of Israel*
1962	J. Barton Payne, *The Theology of the Older Testament*
1962–65	Abraham J. Heschel, *Theology of Ancient Judaism*
1968	Werner H. Schmidt, *The Faith of the Old Testament: A History*

The Third Wave

1970	Maximiliano Garcia Cordero, *Theology of the Bible: Old Testament*
1971	Chester K. Lehman, *Biblical Theology: Old Testament*
1972	Alfons Deissler, *The Fundamental Message of the Old Testament*
1972	Georg Fohrer, *Basic Theological Outlines of the Old Testament*
1972	Walther Zimmerli, *Old Testament Theology in Outline*
1974	John L. McKenzie, *A Theology of the Old Testament*
1976	David Hinson, *Theology of the Old Testament*
1978	Ronald E. Clements, *Old Testament Theology: A Fresh Approach*
1978	Walter C. Kaiser Jr., *Toward an Old Testament Theology*
1978	Samuel L. Terrien, *The Elusive Presence: Toward a New Biblical Theology*
1978	Claus Westermann, *Elements of Old Testament Theology*
1979	William A. Dyrness, *Themes in Old Testament Theology*
1981	Elmer A. Martens, *God's Design: A Focus on Old Testament Theology*
1986	Brevard S. Childs, *Old Testament Theology in a Canonical Context*
1986	Paul D. Hanson, *The People Called: The Growth of Community in the Bible*

WALTHER EICHRODT

b. 1890   d. 1978

Covenant

Theological Synopsis

In the decades surrounding World War I, the discussion of Old Testament theology in Germany was remarkably intense. On one side of the debate were those who insisted that Israel's religion could be presented only in terms of its historical development. Others argued, just as insistently, that such "genetic" accounts of Israel's religion could not penetrate to its life and spirit. Walther Eichrodt was anxious to preserve Old Testament theology as a historical discipline, one that treated the essence of Israel's religion instead of only its development. He believed that, if it followed "a new concept of the essential nature of true historical study" (1961: 13), Old Testament theology could be genuinely historical, without falling into "the tyranny of historicism" (1961: 31).

Eichrodt had already put forward his ideas on "the essential nature of true historical study" in his article. "Hat die Alttestamentliche Theologie noch selbständige Bedeutung innerhalb der Alttestamentlichen Wissenschaft?" (1929; "Does Old Testament Theology Still Have Independent Significance within Old Testament Scholarship?"; English translation on pp. 30–39 above). In his *Theology of the Old Testament,* published in 1933, just prior to another war, he put these ideas into practice. His aim was to interpret the religion recorded in the Old Testament "as a self-contained entity exhibiting, despite ever-changing historical conditions, a constant basic tendency and character" (1961: 11). Eichrodt argued that the constant basic tendency of Israel's religion was best expressed in the Old Testament concept of covenant: It "enshrines Israel's most fundamental conviction, namely its sense of a unique relationship with God" (1961: 17). Old Testament theology must then undertake a systematic analysis of the Old Testament, in order to make visible "the structural unity of the

OT message." (1961: 17). For Eichrodt, systematic analysis was not opposed to historical-critical inquiry. In fact, the "complementary role" of each was essential to the true historical study of the Old Testament that he recommended (1961: 32). Since the terms of Old Testament theology were given and defined by the Old Testament itself, covenant was a dynamic concept, not a static or dogmatic one: It is "the typical description of a living process" (1961: 18).

Eichrodt did not investigate only those texts that speak explicitly of covenant. Instead, he examined a cross section of Israel's life, history, and literature to discover the living process that covenant describes. In this way, Eichrodt attempted to avoid both historicism and the imposition on the Old Testament of static theological categories, and at the same time to show the Old Testament's necessary relation to the New. His concern for that relation led him to characterize Judaism as having a "torso-like appearance," thereby implicitly denying its continuity with Israel and, hence, its legitimacy.

The organization of Walther Eichrodt's *Theology of the Old Testament* (around God's relation to the people, the world, and the individual) was influenced by his teacher, Otto Procksch. Eichrodt studied under Procksch at the University of Erlangen, where he completed his Habilitation (1915–22). He had previously studied philosophy and theology at Bethel, Greifswald, and Heidelberg. In 1921, he was called to the faculty of the University of Basel, where he taught Old Testament and the history of religion until 1966. He wrote numerous commentaries (e.g., Ezekiel) and exegetical articles on biblical books and themes, as well as a history of Israelite religion.

B.C.O.

Writings by Eichrodt

1929   Hat die Alttestamentliche Theologie noch selbständige Bedeutung innerhalb der Alttestamentlichen Wissenschaft? *Zeitschrift für die Alttestamentliche Wissenschaft* 47:83–91. [English translation on pp. 30–39 above.]

1933   *Theologie des Alten Testaments.* Volume 1: *Gott und Volk.* Leipzig: Hinrichs.
1935   *Theologie des Alten Testaments.* Volume 2: *Gott und Welt.* Leipzig: Hinrichs.

1939   *Theologie des Alten Testaments.* Volume 3: *Gott und Mensch.* Leipzig: Hinrichs.

1959   *Theologie des Alten Testaments.* Volume 1: *Gott und Volk.* 6th edition. Stuttgart: Klotz/Göttingen: Vandenhoeck & Ruprecht.

1961   *Theology of the Old Testament.* Volume 1. Translated by John A. Baker. London: SCM/Philadelphia: Westminster.

1964   *Theologie des Alten Testaments.* Volume 2/3: *Gott und Welt/Gott und Mensch.* 5th edition. Stuttgart: Klotz/Göttingen: Vandenhoeck & Ruprecht.
1967   *Theology of the Old Testament.* Volume 2. Translated by John A. Baker. London: SCM/Philadelphia: Westminster.
1969   *Religionsgeschichte Israels.* Bern: Francke.
1970   *Ezekiel: A Commentary.* Old Testament Library. Translated by Cosslett Quin. London: SCM/Philadelphia: Westminster.

Writings about Eichrodt

Gottwald, Norman K.
1970   W. Eichrodt: *Theology of the Old Testament.* Pp. 23–62 in *Contemporary Old Testament Theologians.* Edited by Robert B. Laurin. Valley Forge, Pennsylvania: Judson.
Saebø, Magne
1982   Eichrodt, Walther. Volume 9: pp. 371–73 in *Theologische Realenzyklopädie.* Berlin: de Gruyter.
Spriggs, David G.
1974   *Two Old Testament Theologies: A Comparative Evaluation of the Contributions of Eichrodt and von Rad to Our Understanding of the Nature of Old Testament Theology.* Studies in Biblical Theology 2/30. London: SCM/Naperville, Illinois: Allenson.
Stoebe, Hans J., Johann J. Stamm, and Ernst Jenni (editors)
1970   *Wort–Gebot–Glaube: Beiträge zur Theologie des Alten Testaments: Walther Eichrodt zum 80. Geburtstag.* Abhandlungen zur Theologie des Alten und Neuen Testaments 59. Zurich: Zwingli.

Walther Eichrodt's
Approach to Old Testament Theology

Excerpted with permission from Walther Eichrodt, *Theology of Old Testament* (Philadelphia: Westminister, 1961), vol. 1: pp. 25–33.

Old Testament Theology:
The Problem and the Method

[[25]] Among all the problems known to OT studies, one of the most far-reaching in its importance is that of the theology of the OT: for its concern is to construct a *complete picture of the OT realm of belief,* in other words to comprehend in all its uniqueness and immensity what is, strictly speaking, the proper object of OT study. The tasks of this science are very various in character, but this is the crown of them all; and to this, therefore, the other disciplines involved are ancillary.

But though the domain of OT theology proper is comparatively restricted, yet it is closely linked both to the prolific variety of pagan religions and to the exclusive realm of NT belief. Thus it exhibits a *double aspect.*

On the one side it faces on to the *comparative study of religions.* To adapt a well-known dictum of Harnack[1] (which he coined in opposition to the thesis of Max Müller that 'The man who knows only one religion knows none') one might say, 'The man who knows the religion of the OT knows many.' For in the course of its long history it has not only firmly consolidated its own unique contribution, but also, by a process of absorption and rejection, has forged links with the most varied forms of paganism. Hence the study of it can become at the same time a course in the comparative study of religions. *No presentation of OT theology can properly be made without constant reference to its connections with the whole world of Near Eastern religion.* Indeed it is in its commanding such a wide panorama of the rich domain of man's [[26]] religious activity that many will prefer to see the special significance of the faith of the OT.

And yet there is this *second aspect,* looking on towards the New Testament. Anyone who studies the historical development of the OT finds that throughout there is a powerful and purposive movement which forces itself on his attention. It is true that there are also times when the religion seems to become static, to harden into a rigid system; but every time this occurs the forward drive breaks through once more, reaching out to a

1. *Die Aufgabe der theologischen Fakultäten und die allgemeine Religionsgeschichte,* 1901, p. 10.

higher form of life and making everything that has gone before seem inadequate and incomplete. This movement does not come to rest until the manifestation of Christ, in whom the noblest powers of the OT find their fulfilment. Negative evidence in support of this statement is afforded by the torso-like appearance of Judaism in separation from Christianity.

The affinity with the NT is not, however, exhausted by a bare historical connection, such as might afford material for the historian's examination but no more. It rather confronts us with an essential characteristic, which must be taken into account if the OT is to be understood. Moreover this is an impression which is confirmed over and over again when we enter the unique spiritual realm of the NT. For in the encounter with the Christ of the Gospels there is the assertion of a mighty living reality as inseparably bound up with the OT past as pointing forward into the future. *That which binds together indivisibly the two realms of the Old and New Testaments—different in externals though they may be—is the irruption of the Kingship of God into this world and its establishment here.* This is the unitive fact because it rests on the action of one and the same God in each case; that God who in promise and performance, in Gospel and Law, pursues one and the selfsame great purpose, the building of his Kingdom. This is why the central message of the NT leads us back to the testimony of God in the old covenant.

But in addition to this historical movement from the Old Testament to the New there is a current of life flowing in the reverse direction from the New Testament to the Old. This reverse relationship also elucidates the full significance of the realm of OT thought. Only where this two-way relationship between the Old and New Testaments is understood do we find a correct definition of the problem of OT theology and of the method by which it is possible to solve it.

⟦27⟧ Hence to our general aim of obtaining a comprehensive picture of the realm of OT belief we must add a second and closely related purpose—*to see that this comprehensive picture does justice to the essential relationship with the NT* and does not merely ignore it. Naturally this does not mean that the language of the OT must be artificially screwed up to the pitch of the New in order that both Testaments may be on the same spiritual plane. To seek to do this would merely betray a very poor idea of the difference between a process in real life and a process in logical thought. It was just at this point that the old orthodoxy, in spite of having a sound idea of the correct course, had the misfortune to lose its grasp of the living reality and to slip back into the procedures of logical demonstration, thereby concealing rather than clarifying the actual relation between the Old and New Testaments. The reaction to this was rationalism with its root-and-branch rejection of the OT.

This then is the problem that confronts us. In expounding the realm of OT thought and belief we must never lose sight of the fact that the OT religion, ineffaceably individual though it may be, can yet be grasped in this essential uniqueness only when it is seen as completed in Christ. None other than B. Stade, well known for the radical nature of his criticism, emphasized this 'homogeneity and similarity of the Old and New Testament revelations' in his own theology of the OT; and he saw in this fact the premiss from which this branch of OT studies could be proved to be a necessary part of Christian theology.[2]

The more clearly the shape of this problem is seen, the more apparent it becomes that it is not to be solved along the lines which OT studies have so far taken, namely the consideration of the process of historical development only. It is not just a matter of describing the all-round expansion of OT religion, or the phases through which it passed, but of determining to what extent—as B. Stade remarked—it ties up with the NT revelation and is analogous to it. But this can only be done by taking a cross-section of the realm of OT thought, thus making possible both a comprehensive survey and a sifting of what is essential from what is not. In this way both the total structure of the system and the basic principles on which it rests can be exposed to view. In other words we have to undertake a *systematic examination* with objective classification and rational arrangement of the varied material. This does not in any way imply that the historical method [[28]] of investigation is worthless, nor that it should be set aside. We ought rather to build deliberately on its conclusions and make use of its procedures. Nevertheless developmental analysis must be replaced by systematic synthesis, if we are to make more progress toward an interpretation of the outstanding religious phenomena of the OT in their deepest significance.[3]

A glance at the history of our particular discipline will abundantly confirm that this method, deriving as it does from the nature of the material, is the proper one. As we have already stated, rationalism tore to shreds the inadequate attempts of orthodoxy to demonstrate the inner coherence of the Old and New Testaments by the collation of proof-texts and an extensive system of typology.[4] It proved that it was impossible to reduce the whole realm of OT thought, conditioned as it is by such an immense

---

2. *Biblische Theologie des Alten Testaments*, 1905, p. 15.

3. I have given the main outlines of the relationship between this task and the dogmatic religious presentation, properly so called, of OT religion in my lecture, 'Hat die alttestamentliche Theologie noch selbständige Bedeutung innerhalb der alttestamentlichen Wissenschaft?', *ZAW* 47, 1929, pp. 83ff. [[See pp. 30–39 above for an English translation.]]

4. It is not possible to take into consideration in this work such exceptional cases as G. Calixt and J. Cocceius.

variety of ages and individuals, to a handbook of dogmatic instruction without doing violence to it. Rationalism itself, however, was quite unable to offer any substitute; for in its delight in critical analysis it lost its feeling for the vital synthesis in the OT and could only see the differing teachings of individual biblical writers.[5]

Into the meaningless confusion of *disjecta membra*, into which the OT on such a view degenerated, the new approach to history which began to flower with the age of romanticism brought a unifying principle. It dismissed once for all the 'intellectualist' approach, which looked only for doctrine, and sought by an all-inclusive survey to grasp the totality of religious life in all its richness of expression. Furthermore it brought this unexpected expansion of the field of study under control with the magic formula of 'historical development', allowing all the individual elements to be arranged in one historical process and thus enabling the meaning of the whole to be demonstrated in its final achievement.

This method of treatment, which began with Herder[6] and de [[29]] Wette,[7] reached its high-water mark with Wellhausen[8] and his school, and for decades diverted work on OT theology into historical channels. Of what avail was it that a Beck[9] or a Hofmann[10] should attempt, about the middle of the last century, to develop a system of biblical doctrine? By making use of the OT for this purpose they were indeed standing up for its vital importance for the Christian faith, but they made no headway against the rising stream of historical investigation—to say nothing of the fact that the dogmatic system to which they harnessed the thought of the OT was seriously defective.

All the more deserving of notice, therefore, are three men who in the second half of the nineteenth century, right in the thick of the triumphal progress of historical criticism, attempted to expound the essential content of the OT in systematic form, while at the same time giving full consideration to the newly emergent problems connected with it. These were G. F. Oehler,[11] A. Dillmann,[12] and H. Schultz.[13] All three took account of

5. Cf. C. F. Ammon, *Biblische Theologie*, 1792; G. L. Bauer, *Theologie des Alten Testaments*, 1796, and others.

6. *The Spirit of Hebrew Poetry, Letters on Theology, The Oldest Documents of the Human Race*, etc.

7. *Beiträge zur Geschichte des Alten Testaments*, 1806–7; *Biblische Dogmatik*, 1813, 3rd edn, 1831.

8. *Prolegomena to the History of Israel*, ET, 1885; originally 1878; *History of Israel*, ET, 1894; *Die israelitische-jüdische Religion*, 1906 (Kultur der Gegenwart I, 4).

9. *Die christliche Lehrwissenschaft nach den biblischen Urkunden*, 1841.

10. *Der Schriftbeweis*, 1852–55.

11. *Theologie des Alten Testaments*, 1873; 3rd edn, 1891.

12. *Handbuch der alttestamentlichen Theologie*, ed. R. Kittel, 1895.

13. *Old Testament Theology*: ET in 2 vols., 2nd edn, 1898; 5th German edn, 1896.

the new movement by prefacing their exposition with a historical summary of OT religion. They then went on, however, to contend earnestly for a systematic correlation of the elements which had so far been examined only as they occurred in the course of the historical process. It was unfortunate that the two first-named works did not appear until after the deaths of their authors and so were already at the time of their publication no longer defensible in many details.[14] Nevertheless, repeated new editions witness to their having met a pressing need. Even today they still provide the most thorough treatment of the realm of OT belief from the systematic standpoint; and even though since that time research has brought to light much new relevant material and has introduced different ways of framing the problems, so materially altering the total picture, one can turn to them again and again. It is significant that for twenty-five years after the last edition of Schultz's *Theology* no one ventured on a further attempt to provide an exposition of this kind in the realm of OT belief. The historical approach had triumphed on every side.

[[30]] To say this is of course not to attempt to deny that this method accomplished an immense amount for the historical understanding of OT religion. It is impossible even to conceive of a historical picture that does not make use of its findings, and to that extent not one of us can help being in its debt. For this very reason, however, the method had a particularly fatal influence both on OT theology and on the understanding of the OT in every other aspect, because it fostered the idea that once the historical problems were clarified everything had been done. The essential inner coherence of the Old and New Testaments was reduced, so to speak, to a thin thread of historical connection and causal sequence between the two, with the result that an external causality—not even susceptible in every case of secure demonstration—was substituted for a homogeneity that was real because it rested on the similar content of their experience of life. How appallingly this impoverished the conception of the relationship of the two Testaments strikes one at once; but it is also clear that the OT itself, if valued only as the historical foundation or forerunner of the New, was bound to lose its own specific value as revelation, even though from the historical angle it might be assessed as highly as ever. One consequence of this is the fact that the OT has completely lost any effective place in the structure of Christian doctrine. Indeed, in the circumstances, it sometimes seems more from academic politeness than from any real conviction of its indispensability that it is so seldom denied all value as canonical Scripture[15]—a step which would enable the whole

14. This applies also to the less important OT Theology of E. Riehm, 1889.
15. Harnack (*Marcion*, 1921, pp. 247ff.) was one notable exception.

subject to be transferred from the sphere of theology to that of the comparative study of religions.

That OT theologians for their part were content to put up with this development, and thought that the value of the OT could be safeguarded even along these lines, can only be understood if we remember that the full flood of historicism, which overflowed every academic discipline, had blinded them to the fact that historical investigation, for all its glittering achievements, could yet offer no serious substitute for the concept of the essential coherence of the Old and New Testaments. The little still left to OT theology to do, viz., the historical presentation of the Israelite and Judaistic religion, was quite insufficient to conceal, even with the help of the magic word 'development', how serious the loss had been. There was no longer any unity to be found in the OT, only a collection of detached periods which were simply the reflections of as many different [[31]] religions. In such circumstances it was only a logical development that the designation 'OT Theology', which had formerly had quite a different connotation, should frequently be abandoned and the title 'the History of Israelite Religion' substituted for it.[16] Even where scholars still clung to the old name,[17] they were neither desirous nor capable of offering anything more than an exposition of the historical process.

When, therefore, in 1922 E. König ventured to publish a Theology of the OT which attempted to take its title seriously, it was a real act of courage which deserves to be recorded. It is true that to some extent a hybrid form is still noticeable in the book. The historical-developmental method of examination, carrying over from the opening historical section into the systematic part, never allows the synthesis its rightful scope. Furthermore, the recalcitrant material is forced into a Procrustes' bed, because it has been made to fit a dogmatic arrangement foreign to the subject. Nevertheless, that the author had rightly sensed the need of the contemporary situation was proved by the grateful reception accorded to his work.

It is high time that the tyranny of historicism in OT studies was broken and the proper approach to our task re-discovered. This is no new problem, certainly, but it is one that needs to be solved anew in every epoch of knowledge—*the problem of how to understand the realm of OT belief in*

16. So R. Smend in his widely-used *Lehrbuch der alttestamentlichen Religionsgeschichte*[2], 1899; F. Giesebrecht, *Grundzüge der israelitischen Religionsgeschichte*, 1904; K. Marti, *Geschichte der israelitischen Religion*[5], 1907; K. Budde, *Die Religion des Volkes Israel bis zur Verbannung*[3], 1912; E. König, *Geschichte der alttestamentlichen Religion*[2], 1915; R. Kittel, *The Religion of the People of Israel*, ET, 1925; G. Hölscher, *Geschichte der israelitischen und jüdischen Religion*, 1922.

17. B. Stade, *Biblische Theologie des Alten Testaments*, E. Kautzsch, *Biblische Theologie des Alten Testaments*, 1911. So also A. Kuenen, *De godsdienst van Israel*, 1869ff., and the work of the same name by B. D. Eerdmans, 1930.

its structural unity and how, by examining on the one hand its religious environ-
ment and on the other its essential coherence with the NT, to illuminate its pro-
foundest meaning.[18] Only so shall we succeed in winning back for OT
studies in general and for OT theology in particular that place in Christian theology which at present has been surrendered to the comparative
study of religions.

We are not for one moment trying to make light of the difficulties that
stand in the way of this undertaking. It is a fact that the unique [[32]] quality
of Israelite religion obstinately resists all efforts to subject it completely to
systematic treatment. For if there is one feature that it exhibits more than
any other religion, it is an abundance of creative religious personalities,
who are closely involved in the historical experiences of the people. In any
religion where this is not so the main content of the thought is usually
present at its foundation and changes but little in the course of time, being
rather worn away and levelled down than made more profound or fashioned afresh. In the OT, however, we find both a stock of spiritual values
firmly established at the outset and also an incessant process of growth
which is continually enriching the religion by drawing into its sphere new
content from without. At the same time the internal shape of the religion
becomes increasingly well-defined. It is *this prominence of the personal and
historical factors* in Israelite religion which constitutes a constant temptation
to the writer to resort to an exposition along the historical line of
development.

But though such a motive may be justifiable, it should not be overriding. A picture of the historical development of Israelite religion can
equally well be conveyed by means of a History of Israel, so long as the religious life is allowed that place in the work which its close contact and interaction with the political history merits. It is true that to this extent OT
theology presupposes the history of Israel. Nevertheless, in so far as the
spiritual history of Israel has brought about a drastic remodelling of many
religious ideas, the right way to make allowance for this is *to have the histori-*
cal principle operating side by side with the systematic in a complementary role. In
treating individual religious concepts the major elements of their historical background must be taken into account. Only so can we hope to do
justice to the great unitive tendency that runs through the whole religious
history of Israel and makes it with all its variety a self-consistent entity.

One thing, however, must be guarded against and that is any *arrange-*
ment of the whole body of material which derives not from the laws of its own
nature but from some dogmatic scheme. It is impossible to use a system

18. In this connection cf. the examination by R. Kittel of the importance of OT theology
in his essay, 'Die Zukunft der alttestamentlichen Wissenschaft', *ZAW* 39, 1921, pp. 94ff.

which has been developed on a basis quite different from that of the realm of OT thought to arrive at the OT belief about God. All that results is a grave danger of intruding alien ideas and of barring the way to understanding.

It has often been observed that the OT contains very little actual 'doctrine'. Nowhere are formal 'instructions' about the Being of God [[33]] or his attributes delivered to the Israelite. His knowledge of God comes to him from the realities of his own life. He learns about the nature of God by reasoning *a posteriori* from the standards and usages of Law and Cult, which rule his personal life with divine authority, from the events of history and their interpretation by his spiritual leaders, in short, from his daily experience of the rule of God. By this means he comprehends the divine essence much more accurately than he would from any number of abstract concepts. The result is that the formation of such concepts in the OT lags far behind, while the same spiritual values which they are normally the means of conveying to us are yet uncompromisingly real and effective.

In deciding, therefore, on our procedure for the treatment of the realm of OT thought, we must avoid all schemes which derive from Christian dogmatics—such, for example, as 'Theology—Anthropology—Soteriology', '*ordo salutis*' and so on. Instead we must plot our course as best we can along the lines of the OT's own dialectic. This speaks of a revelation of the God of the People, who in his rule proves himself to be also the God of the World and the God of the Individual. We are therefore presented with three principal categories, within which to study the special nature of the Israelite faith in God: *God and the People, God and the World* and *God and Man.*[19]

Synopsis of Eichrodt's *Theology of the Old Testament* (1961, 1967)

19. I owe this pregnant formulation of the three major categories to the outline by O. Procksch, which formed the basis of his university lectures on OT theology and which has provided me with many stimulating ideas. The division of the material here suggested had already been anticipated by H. Schultz in the arrangement of the second part of his *OT Theology*, except that in a way characteristic of him he treated Hope separately in a special section. . . .

he's a reformed theologian:

covenant is to reform
what peace is to Mennos —>
no surprise that covenant is
the axis of the OT

Walther Eichrodt on Covenant

Excerpted with permission from Walther Eichrodt, *Theology of Old Testament* (Philadelphia: Westminister, 1961), vol. 1: pp. 286–96.

Affirmations about the Divine Activity: Synthesis

⟦286⟧ The unique character of the picture of God in ancient Israel is derived in essence from the attempt to hold together the ideas of a ⟦287⟧ divine *power without limitation* and of a divine *act of self-limitation* in the establishment of a *bᵉrīt* ⟦'covenant'⟧—an act where God makes himself known as *sovereign and personal will.* The conception of God's power is given its special character by its association with first the idea of the divine *holiness,* that which is annihilating and inaccessible and utterly distinct from every created thing, and secondly the divine *wrath,* God being, in his sovereign freedom, inscrutable to men. Contrasted with this is God's voluntary engagement of his sovereignty to the covenant fellowship with Israel, by virtue of which he grants men to know his *lovingkindness* as Father and Shepherd and demonstrates his *righteousness* by victoriously defending them against their enemies. Since these dealings of God with his people have as their object the establishment of his dominion in the holy land, the divine will is revealed as *power directing history;* and this implies a *fullness of personal life* which not only is different in principle from mere natural forces, but rejects as utterly alien the primitive conceptions of God attaching to the beliefs in spirits, 'power' and magic.

This unique attempt to combine the ideas of the manifest and the hidden God by way of the claim which he made upon men established itself in the succeeding period in opposition to an understanding of the world and of life which had been enriched by foreign elements, and in the process gained in force both in comprehensiveness and profundity. No longer was it simply exceptional incidents and occasions which were seen in the light of the divine presence, but every detail of life was now interpreted with increasing logical consistency in this way. As a result the *wrath of God* was ever more closely connected with his *punitive righteousness* and with *individual retribution,* while his *holiness* was understood as the *perfection of the divine being,* reflected in the Law as the pattern of life or the holy people and annihilating everything which resisted the purposes of that law. That all this was the work not of some impersonal world-order, but of the *will of a personal Lord,* was newly comprehended and expressed in the recognition of *love* as the deepest meaning of election and of *righteousness* as the power educating the pious in the attainment of their own righteous conduct. Holiness was now understood as God's supremacy over the heathen; the idea of him as Father was extended to cover the whole Creation; the concept of love now applied to God's relations with each individual member of the nation; and consequently men came to a new vision of how far-reaching might be the scope of their covenant God in his operations.

[[288]] This line of thought presented the divine activity as matched to human understanding and attuned to human needs, with the result that the 'absolute' quality of the divine, God's being by nature 'unintelligible', receded in importance. But in the prophetic preaching the superhuman and enigmatic, nay irrational liberty and superiority of God returned in force. This came about not by a revival of the ancient Israelite way of looking at the matter, but by the ascription of a superhuman character even to God's self-involvement. Indeed, *God's sovereignty* appears to be raised to the highest possible power in the proclamation of the *eschatological doom of wrath*, which reveals the ultimate depth of the abyss between God and man and characterizes the whole of this world as a temporary and provisional order incapable of standing in the presence of the Holy One. But this very act of concluding every element of earthly existence in one vast community of guilt, breaking man's link with God and hurling humanity far from his presence, becomes the means whereby *God's voluntary self-involvement* is revealed as something transcending all human standards and shattering all men's categories of retribution. It means that God's *covenant lovingkindness* now becomes the free gift of mercy; his *righteousness* becomes that redeeming activity, which pleads even for the godless and restores not only Israel but the world; his *holiness* acquires its deepest meaning as the moral governance of the universe or the inconceivable power of love which suffers for the sake of the condemned, until it has achieved his salvation. Thus the ultimate secret of the *divine personhood* is manifested as *love concealed in wrath*, redeeming righteousness, the lovingkindness that remains constant despite the instability of the covenant. The antinomies that must for human thought remain for ever insoluble are fused in the amazing truth that God is a living person; but this truth is manifested as a living reality only to the man who can apprehend by faith the breaking into this present aeon of God's new world. [[289]]

The Instruments of the Covenant: The Charismatic Leaders

The Founder of the Religion

In the opinion of J. Burckhardt the forces at work in the emergence of a religion also determine its whole succeeding history.[1] If this is true, then

---

1. Cf. *Weltgeschichtliche Betrachtungen*, ed. J. Oeri, 1905, p. 42.

the figure dominant at the outset of Israelite religion must be of decisive importance for the interpretation of the spiritual mediators of the concept of Yahweh in later times.

Now it is characteristic of Moses that it should be impossible to classify him in any of the ordinary categories applicable to a leader of a nation; he is neither a king, nor a commander of an army, nor a tribal chieftain, nor a priest,[2] nor an inspired seer and medicine man. To some extent he belongs to all these categories; but none of them adequately explains his position. In many respects he gives the impression of exercising kingly authority; he determines the direction of the line of march and appoints its destination; he gives laws and administers justice and orders the external details of the common life of the tribes. But that which is specifically characteristic of a king, prowess in war and leadership in battle, is just what is lacking in Moses. Similarly nothing is heard of his having made any arrangements for a son and successor to inherit his position. His giving of *tōrā*, that is to say his instructions at the sanctuary and the organization of the cultus attributed to him, suggest the priest; but on the other hand his office of supreme judge is not to be regarded simply [[290]] as a priestly function, and we are told nothing of his offering sacrifice, a task which seems to have been reserved to Aaron and the Levites, or to specially chosen laymen such as the young men of Exodus 24:5. The seer seems to be suggested by many individual traits, such as the theophanies, his remaining forty days on the mount of God, his delivery of the divine decisions; but there is no tradition in the case of Moses of the one feature especially celebrated in other seers, miraculous foreknowledge of the future or clairvoyant explication of puzzling situations. Attempts have been made to explain him as a medicine man or magician;[3] but even if isolated features can be made to support this view, in particular the various miracle stories, it is manifestly quite inadequate to cover the whole of this man's life work and the traditions that have been connected with him.

For these reasons, and from a perfectly correct feeling that his most important work lay in the field of religion, the title of Prophet has often been conferred on him, in support of which a number of Old Testament passages from the later monarchy may certainly be quoted (Deut 34:10; 18:15, 18; Hos 12:14). Nevertheless, it should be noted that the tradition of Israel taken as a whole does not regard Moses as the prophet κατ᾿ ἐξοχήν [['par excellence']], but portrays him, in accordance with his various

2. The points which P. Volz (*Mose*[1], p. 100) enumerates as marks of his priestly character are not sufficient to justify this as an exclusive classification. (In the 2nd ed. of his work, pp. 57, 91ff., 125f., Volz advances a quite different opinion.) A similar view of Moses as priest may be found in E. Meyer, *Die Israeliten*, p. 72.

3. The view of Beer in his study *Mose*, 1912.

achievements, as intercessor, miracle worker or lawgiver; it is only where there has been time to reflect on the analogy between Moses and prophetism, that he is explicitly displayed as the supreme preacher of the divine will, towering above all the prophets of later days (cf. Exod 4:16; 7:1; 33:11 and Num 11:24–30; 12:1–8). It is in keeping with this that Deuteronomy characterizes him as *the mediator between God and his people* (5:24–28).

Justice, then, can never be done to the full historical reality, if the attempt is made to imprison this outstanding figure in any one of the ordinary categories of 'holy men,' *homines religiosi*. It is precisely the secret of this man's greatness that he unites in himself gifts not normally found in combination, and is therefore able to work with lasting effect in the most diverse fields. If we ask, however, what is *the master key to the career* of this rarely endowed personality, the common factor which saves it from being a jumble of dissociated elements, the answer lies in *the concrete historical task* which was entrusted to him in the very hour in which he was seized of a new understanding of the whole nature of God. To bring a nation to Yahweh, the mighty Lord, a nation in which his sovereignty could ⟦291⟧ be established and his nature expressed, which furthermore he could forge into an instrument for the execution of his judgment upon the nations and the founding of a new world order[4]—that was the goal which dominated the life of this man whom Yahweh had conquered. To the service of this calling he dedicated all his wealth of gifts and became *the messenger who should proclaim God's will for social, political and cultic life*, whether in the summons to escape from Egypt and in the holy war or in the marvellous redeeming acts of the perilous wandering in the wilderness. Only such personalities as Zoroaster or Mohammed, who were themselves founders of religions, and who likewise closely combined political and national activity with their religious work, can be compared with him; and it is just the fact that it is only such leader-figures who are at all comparable that should warn us not to try to bring Moses down to the level of those more ordinary servants of God or consecrated men whose operations were confined to a restricted sphere.[5]

4. Cf. the view, long predominant in Israel, that Yahweh's battles were the execution of his judgment upon his enemies: Num 23:22ff.; 24:8ff.; 10:35; Judg 5:20, 23, 31; Gen 15:16; 1 Sam 15:2, 33; Ps 2; 45:4ff.; 110 etc. It is possible to argue about how far the dominion of the new world order was thought to extend; but at least there can be no doubt that from the very beginning it was seen as extending beyond Israel, since it clearly applies to the nations overthrown by her.

5. An enterprising and most effective attempt to present this comprehensive interpretation of the figure of Moses has been made by M. Buber (*Moses*) with complete disregard for prevailing source-criticism. His penetrating religious exposition will always be of value even for those who cannot follow him in his method or in many details. E. Auerbach in his book of the

One thing, however, is clear at the start. This organizer who enjoyed no proper political power, this national leader who boasted no prowess in war, this man who directed the worship of God without ever having received the status of priest, who established and mediated a new understanding of God without any of the credentials of prophetic powers of prediction, this wonder-worker who was yet far above the domain of mere magic, confronts us from the very outset with one ineluctable fact: Israelite religion is not the product of a scrupulously guarded tradition, swollen with the accretions of history, nor does it rest on any sort of organization, [[292]] however cleverly or successfully devised, but is *a creation of that spirit* which bloweth where it listeth, and which in mockery of our neat arrangements unites in the richness of marvellously equipped personalities things patently incompatible, in order that it may forward its own mighty and life-giving work. *At the very beginning of Israelite religion we find the charisma*, the special individual endowment of a person; and to such an extent is the whole structure based on it, that without it it would be inconceivable.

1. *That men's relationship with God should be founded on the activity of one specially called and equipped mediator* is of abiding significance for the whole character of their understanding and worship of God. The single historical event in which God encountered the nation becomes what the mediator declared it to be, *the point of alignment for their belief in God*; the redemption from Egypt received its definitive interpretation at the covenant-making on Sinai—and thus became *the foundation and the orientation of all the mutual relations of Yahweh and his people*. It has already been explained[6] how this meant that man's relationship with God was based on revelation in the strict sense of the word—that is to say, on God's imparting of himself through the contingency of historical circumstance—and required submission to the will of God simply as that was made known here and now; and further how this excluded any attempt to base a doctrine of God on general concepts or principles derived from human experience. It was also pointed out that this makes explicit the principle of God's being undetermined by any involvement with Nature. It remains to add here, that the very fact of the emergence of a mediator supplied further confirmation of these basic features of the new relationship with God; for the activity of the

---

same title has adhered more closely to contemporary scholarship in his attempt to portray Israel's 'mightiest genius'; on occasion his simplifications and strongly rationalist interpretation do violence to the material, but he has a sound feeling for the untenable nature of most criticism of Moses hitherto. Each of these authors has in his own way made abundantly clear the need for a new understanding of the accounts relating to the first preacher of the faith of Yahweh.

6. Cf. ch. II, The Covenant Relationship, [[Eichrodt 1961:]] pp. 37ff.

mediator was an emphatic reminder of *the distance between God and man,* a distance not in any way lessened for the chosen people. That this was indeed felt to be the significance of the mediator is indicated by the many interpretations of his work along these lines,[7] but also by the sense, which loomed so large in Israel's religion, that Yahweh was terrible and unapproachable, and that to draw near to him without such mediation was to court destruction. The frequent references to the fact that Moses' own intercourse with God was unique precisely [[293]] because it was unmediated, and that this constituted the special character of his position,[8] prove that men never ceased to meditate on the gulf between God and man which he had bridged.

2. Moreover, the way in which Moses brought God near to his people became an important model for the future. For it made clear that *the demands of God in the Law*, which strove to order every detail of the national life and to conform it to the mind of God himself, *were those of a personal will.* From thenceforward the legal regulation of the people's conduct was not only raised to the status of a religious obligation, and distinguished definitely from all merely human opinions,[9] but it was also bound up with the type of lawgiving mediated by Moses. In the Torah of Moses, regardless of whether this is held to be simply oral tradition or to have been fixed in writing, is to be found the source of all law, public and private. Deuteronomy may have derived its distinctive form, the presentation of the law as an address from the founder of the religion, from the traditional practice of having a reader of the law at local assemblies,[10] but it was a real dependence which made this established form the most fitting mode of expression. Again, the constantly recurring formula of the Priestly Law—'And the Lord spake unto Moses'—in both early and late passages, bears witness to the feeling that the regulation of cultic life could only be carried out by associating it with the original giver of the Law. This means, however, that from the time of Moses onwards the will of God, as this applied to the nation, was conceived as being *normative for all human relations and remaining ideally the same for ever,* it was his proclamation of this will, and his application of it to the new problems that were arising, which brought about the submission of the people and caused the rule of God to be accepted. The whole intensity of Israel's devotion to the Law, which arises from her knowledge that she is carrying out God's unchanging will, rests ultimately on this foundation.

7. Exod 20:18ff.; 33:5; 33:7ff.; 34:9; 34:29ff.; Num 11:2; 11:25ff.; 12:2ff.; 17:27f.; 21:7; Deut 5:5, 22ff. Cf. also the way in which Moses is in general portrayed as an intercessor.

8. Exod 4:16; 7:1; Num 11:24–30; 12:1–8; Deut 5:24, 28.

9. Cf. chs. III and IV, The Covenant Statutes.

10. Cf. A. Klostermann, *Der Pentateuch* N. F., 1907.

Combined with this, however, is a renewed sense of *the Word of God* addressed to the will as the true basis of man's association with him; it is from this, and not from any naturalistic or mystical significance it may possess, that every sacred act derives its sanction; and the obedience of the pious comes to the forefront as the only justification of the sacramental. The person of the mediator [[294]] determined for ever the personal character of man's relations with God.

3. This divine will, which was normative for the whole of life, also indicated the role of the nation in men's relationship with God, giving it on the one hand an undeniable importance, but on the other taking care that this importance should be clearly limited. Because the divine covenant did not embrace simply the Israelites as individuals or the tribes as separate entities, but the people as a whole, it was possible to recognize *the existence of the nation as rooted in the will of God.* National feeling was given an out-and-out religious colouring; under Moses' leadership the tribes learnt that they had a duty of mutual support not, primarily, because they were all Israelites, but because they were all followers of Yahweh. Loyalty to the nation was made an explicitly religious obligation.[11]

There can be no question but that this subordination of the nation to the aims of the theocracy was achieved more easily in an age which knew none but a charismatic leader, and which was learning to make national unity an effective reality under his direction, than in the period in which the Israelite nation-state was emerging. Conflict only broke out in all its fierceness when nationalist ideals were confirmed and given independent validity under a strong monarchy, and Israel awoke with pride to the fact of her national coherence and power. It must, however, have been of the most essential importance for the clashes which at this stage had to come, that the work of the founder of the religion should already have included among its principal features a definite evaluation both of the importance and of the limitations of the nation, and that this should have become the common inheritance of a wide circle.

4. These considerations may have helped to clarify the underlying importance of the activity of the founder and mediator for the whole structure of Israelite faith and worship. But they should not be allowed to obscure the fact that *the continued influence of Moses* was essentially different from that of other great founder-personalities. The revelation of God which Moses mediated did not acquire its final form in his own lifetime; his work only laid the initial foundation. From those beginnings was to develop a permanent intercourse between God and the nation, with all the

---

11. That this does not imply that Yahweh was included among the purely national deities, has already been explained in ch. II: The Covenant Relationship.

possibilities which that implied of further self-imparting by God. However highly the ⟦295⟧ Mosaic interpretation of God's will was valued as determining the line of development for all succeeding ages, *it was never accorded the character of a final and definitive communication concerning God's nature and operation*; it pointed categorically to the future. It is significant in this connection that not one saying of the founder of the religion, not one λόγιον ⟦'quotation'⟧ of Moses, has been preserved as part of the content of the revelation; there is nothing to compare with the Gathas of Zoroaster or the Suras of Mohammed. Even the transmission of Moses' law was carried out in a spirit of freedom, as the frequent additions, transpositions and expansions of the Book of the Covenant and the various forms of the Decalogue and other basic laws make clear. *An incessant process of expanding and adapting the law* to meet the demands of changing situations was perfectly compatible with loyalty to the religious and social spirit of the Mosaic legislation. Just as little was it supposed that after Moses there would be no need of any further prophetic souls to interpret or reveal the divine will; on the contrary, an abundant provision of new men of God was regarded as the guarantee that Yahweh's favour was still guiding the destinies of his people. The figure of the mediator was never 'improved' into a hagiological portrait, even though devout and thankful minds may have taken a delight in adding a good many decorative—but non-essential—details to the traditional account of his doings. In complete contrast to the case of the Patriarchs, there is no trace of any cultus of his tomb or relics; the tradition lays particular stress on the fact that no man knew his grave. It is this, among other things, which distinguishes him sharply from the ordinary chieftain and medicine-man endowed with power, a well-known figure in the realm of primitive religion, even though certain stories, such as those of the miraculous demonstrations in the presence of Pharaoh, of his prayer prevailing in the battle with the Amalekites, or of the healing of the serpent-bites by means of a wonder-working idol,[12] might seem to suggest such an identification. It is precisely the fact that the powerful fascination of this mysterious personality did not lead popular tradition, always particularly susceptible to phenomena of this kind, to exalt Moses into a wonder-working magician or *tabu*-man which is the most striking testimony to his belonging to a completely different sphere. Moreover, in his case magical power was quite distinct in character from that of the primitive sorcerer, for it was entirely subordinated to the activity of the Deity; hence, ⟦296⟧ even when similar in external appearance, there was no similarity whatever in significance. Furthermore, the death of the founder of the religion before the conquest of the Promised Land for which he

12. Cf. on this point ⟦Eichrodt 1961:⟧ pp. 112f.

had paved the way seemed to the Israelite historians on reflection to mean that Yahweh's first servant had been sternly recalled by his heavenly Lord, precisely because that Lord wished to crown his work of liberation without him. At no stage is there any mention of a return of Moses in the future such as was envisaged for Zoroaster or Mohammed. The God who sends his servant safeguards his own supreme sovereignty by refusing to associate his work throughout with the person of the mediator. With unconditional authority he recalls him and discharges him from his service at the very moment when, in human eyes, he would seem to have been most indispensable. The work of the founder of the religion seemed after his death to have been scattered to the winds; in fact, it was firmly established on the *charisma*, the free activity of God-inspired personalities—which is to say, on God himself.

THEODORUS C. VRIEZEN

b. 1899   d. 1981

The Nature of the Knowledge of God

Theological Synopsis

Vriezen's book, *An Outline of Old Testament Theology*, published in the Netherlands in 1949, had a pastoral intent. It was intended to meet the need of post–World War II clergy and young theological students for a theological introduction to the Old Testament. The book was revised and enlarged in 1954, and again in 1966, with additional arrangement of the material. Aside from numerous reprints in English, translations have been made into German, Spanish, and Japanese.

Two topics dominate that book in accord with its two parts. One topic is the unity of the Old Testament, a unity focused in the communion between God and people. That communion is highlighted, for example, in the sacrifices and festivals. The personal character of Israel's religious life and the emphasis on community with its social forms and its ethical standard underscore the pervasive theme of community.

For Vriezen, communion or "intercourse" between God and humankind is the purpose of revelation. It is classically illustrated in God's covenant with Israel, but covenant is only one of several illustrations: communion is also expressed in such relationships as "father and child, husband and wife, lord and servant, king and people" (1970: 170). Growing out of communion with God is the "community of God," a term Vriezen prefers to "covenant community" or "people of God." The God of that community is above all else holy, a fact which makes the possibility of communion—given human sinfulness—all the more remarkable.

A second topic, one which occupies the first 150 pages of the latest edition, is the appropriation of the Old Testament by the Christian church. Vriezen is at pains to show how important and relevant the earlier part of the canon is for the present-day church. He discusses the authority of the Old Testament as well as its use. The Old Testament's authority arises from its theological truth, as measured by the revelation of Jesus Christ, and not from the accuracy of its historical statements (1970: 99): "Fundamentally, when we make the New Testament our starting-point, we cannot deny the fact that the message of the Old Testament is derived from the Spirit of God, and we must admit that the Old Testament is authoritative in its preaching, even if this message is wrapped up to a great extent in ancient Oriental material" (1970: 115). The theological assessment of the Old Testament is made with the gospel of Jesus Christ as the starting point. Those for whom labels are important can place Vriezen in the general camp of the Neo-orthodox, with such theologians as Barth and Brunner.

Vriezen's agenda was that pinpointed by Eissfeldt and Eichrodt (see pp. 20–39). Was theology descriptive or confessional? How should one address the issue of divine revelation, history, and historical criticism? Vriezen rewrote and reorganized major sections of part 2 (1966) in order to stress—against von Rad and his multiple "theologies"—the theological unity of the whole.

Theodore C. Vriezen was born at Dinxperlo, Netherlands, in 1899. He studied at the universities of Utrecht, Leiden, and Groningen, and later taught at two of these: Groningen (1941–57) and Utrecht (from 1958 until his retirement). Earlier he was professor at The Hague (1929–41), and earlier still he was a minister in the Dutch Reformed Church at Tubbergen en Sittard (1925–29). A Festschrift for him was prepared with the title *Studia Biblica et Semitica*.

E.A.M.

Writings by Vriezen

1949   *Hoofdlijnen der Theologie van het Oude Testament.* Wageningen: Veenman & Zonen.

1954   *Hoofdlijnen der Theologie van het Oude Testament.* 2d edition. Wageningen: Veenman & Zonen.

1958   *An Outline of Old Testament Theology.* Translated by S. Neuijen. Boston: Branford/Oxford: Blackwell.

1966   *Hoofdlijnen der Theologie van het Oude Testament.* 3d edition. Wageningen: Veenman & Zonen.

1970   *An Outline of Old Testament Theology.* 2d edition. Translated by S. Neuijen. Newton, Massachusetts: Branford/Oxford: Blackwell.

Writings about Vriezen

Clements, Ronald E.
  1970   Theodorus C. Vriezen: *An Outline of Old Testament Theology.* Pp. 121–40
            in *Contemporary Old Testament Theologians.* Edited by Robert B. Laurin.
            Valley Forge, Pennsylvania: Judson.
van Unnik, W. C., and A. S. van der Woude (editors)
  1966   *Studia Biblica et Semitica: Theodoro Christiano Vriezen . . . Dedicata.* Wa-
            geningen: Veenman & Zonen.

Theodorus C. Vriezen's
Approach to Old Testament Theology

Excerpted with permission from Theodorus C. Vriezen, *Outline of Old Testament Theology* (2d ed.; Newton, Massachusetts: Branford, 1970), pp. 147–52. Some footnotes have been omitted.

Basis, Task and Method of Old Testament Theology

[[147]] In this book we start from the view that *both as to its object and its method Old Testament theology is and must be a Christian theological science.*[1] That does not mean that it denies the empirico-historical, phenomenological or any other results of the other branches of Old Testament study, but that it performs its task independently while taking account of and assimilating the results attained by Old Testament scholarship in all its various aspects—the results, therefore, not only in research in the fields of phenomenology and the history of religion, but also those of archaeology, philology, literature, history, exegesis, etc. It is [[148]] not correct, therefore, to incorporate the science of religion as such into theology itself, as was done by Procksch in his *Theologie des A.T.*, for in that case the same procedure should be applied in the other branches of scholarship.[2]

It would be preferable to treat the history of religion as an independent parallel science, as was done by E. Sellin in his *Alttestamentliche Theologie auf religionsgeschichtlicher Grundlage*, the first part of which deals with the *Israelitisch-Jüdische Religionsgeschichte* and the second with the *Theologie des A.T.* It is hardly possible, though, to look upon the history of the religion of Israel as the twin brother of Old Testament theology, for the two are indeed too far apart, even if this view is understandable from a historical point of view. Old Testament theology is a form of scholarship differing from the history of Israel's religion in its object as well as in its method. In its object, *because its object is not the religion of Israel but the Old Testament;*[3] in its method *because it is a study of the message of the Old Testament both in itself and in its relation to the New Testament.*[4]

---

1. Also O. Procksch, *Theologie des A.T.*, 1950. . . .

2. Nowadays several scholars propose to incorporate the Introduction to the Old Testament into theology, as was already done to a large extent by Von Rad.

3. On what grounds this distinction can be made is evident from what has been said above on [[Vriezen 1970:]] pp. 24ff. and 51ff.

4. The English works on the theology of the O.T. (A. B. Davidson, *The Theology of the O.T.*, 1911, and H. Wheeler Robinson, [[p. 86 n. 13 below]]) give us particularly the impression that

About both these aspects we shall go into more detail. Only when Eissfeldt's line of thought is followed out consistently can we arrive at a definition of Old Testament theology which guarantees a science independent in name and content. Old Testament theology is concerned with the Old Testament; that is to say it is not the religion of Israel in its historical growth and origin, in its development and formation, that is of central importance (so that e.g. Israelite Baalism has as much right to our attention as Yahwism), but it is concerned with the Old Testament as the Holy Scriptures of the Jews, and more especially of the Christians; its task is to define the characteristic features of *the message of the Old Testament,* and for that reason many things can be left out of account which are of more importance in the study of the religions of Israel; as a theological branch of scholarship the theology of the Old Testament seeks *particularly the element of revelation in the message of the Old Testament;* it must work, therefore, with *theological standards* and must give *its own evaluation of the Old Testament message on the ground of its Christian theological starting-point.* In doing so it must guard against the error of tearing apart the *correlation between faith* [[149]] *and revelation* by identifying revelation and canon.[5] From the Christian theological point of view the canon, too, must be submitted to the judgement of the preaching of Jesus Christ. This implies that the method of Old Testament theology is not only purely phenomenological (a reproduction of the Old Testament message in context), but it also gives the connection with the New Testament message and a judgement from the point of view of that message.[6] So, as a part of Christian theology, Old

---

they start from a synthesis of the theological and the religio-historical methods (e.g. Davidson, p. 6) and that it is this which makes their work so fascinating; cf. also the books by Rowley [[*The Unity of the Bible,* 1953; *The Faith of Israel,* 1956]] and North [[*The Thought of the Old Testament,* 1948]].

5. Cf. Eissfeldt, *op. cit.* p. 3n. (continuation of p. 2, n. 1), who reproaches Barthian theology with this.

6. The programme unfolded above is an ideal objective, which could only be realized by the close co-operation of theologians in the fields of both the Old and the New Testament. Therefore any Old Testament scholar who devotes himself to this task can achieve no more than patch-work. Von Rad thinks the application of standards so problematical that he prefers to refrain from using them completely, for the present at any rate, and to go no further than allowing the Old Testament authors to proclaim their message as objectively as possible (see Th.L.Z. 1963, pp. 407f.). Meanwhile in the latter part of the second volume of his Theology he meets the problem of the relationship between the two Testaments in such a way as to relate the Old Testament typologically to the New Testament. It remains to be seen if in doing so he pays sufficient attention to the critical relationship between the two Testaments and if this kind of methodical search for a solution does not imply a theological conception which does identify canon and revelation after all.

Testament theology in the full sense of the word gives an insight into the
Old Testament message and a judgement of this message from the point
of view of the Christian faith. It includes the theological motives found in
the Old Testament,[7] but it is also concerned with the whole reality of the
revelation of God, as described to us in the historical conceptions and the
literary testimony of the Old Testament. In doing this it is not enough to
give a general survey of 'sacred history', with a simple rendering of the
biblical narrative in the order in which it is given to us in the Canon,[8] but
it must express the message of God of the Old Testament (using the results of critical research) as it took shape in the various books and sources
of the Old Testament during the history which God made Israel pass
through until Jesus Christ. All this means complete absorption in the
voices which bear witness in the Old Testament to the work of God and so
to Him in the course of history and this is not ⟦150⟧ merely a philological
and historical exercise but also a personal exercise in listening and spiritual understanding.

When the question of method is raised we must say first of all that Old
Testament theology must first and foremost inquire into the kerugmatic
nature[9] of the Old Testament as a whole and of its parts.[10] This should
really be looked upon as a necessary preliminary. For this reason the outline of the message of the separate writings has been given in the prolegomena (Ch. III). This study must always be continued.

On the ground of the understanding of the message of the books and
their authors we can expound the whole body of their testimony concerning God, His work and His relations with man and the world. Fundamen-

---

7. See ⟦Vriezen 1970:⟧ p. 153.

8. As given e.g. by A. C. Welch in his book for religious instruction, *The preparation for Christ*,
1933, or by O. Weber, *Bibelkunde des A.T.*, I, II, 1935, or by P. Heinisch, *Geschichte des A.T.*,
1950, however important this sacred history may be; (cf. that already A. J. C. Vilmar, *Theologie
der Tatsachen*, 3rd printing, 1938, p. 33 emphasizes the necessity of a 'special acquaintance
with the contents of the whole Bible, which has long since been lost'); the sacred history is an
indispensable and *basic* element of all theological study, though one which is all too often
lacking. If, however, theology were to stop short here, it would mainly bear witness to only
one type of preaching in O.T. viz. that of the last editors of the books, and give us too little
insight into the various forms of the message and its spiritual development in Israel.

9. See G. von Rad, 'Grundprobleme einer biblischen Theologie des A.T.', *Theol. Lit. Zt.*,
Sept./Oct. 1943, pp. 225ff.

10. Essentially Von Rad would restrict the task of Old Testament theology to this latter
inquiry, for the present anyway. Actually he does not, because he also raises the subject of the
relationship between the two Testaments in his *O.T. Theology* (II, pp. 319ff.), where he gives
theological directives which make us wonder if they sprang from the study of the tradition-
theology, or rather dominate the latter (cf. also the closing remarks of von Rad's article in
ThLZ, 1963, p. 416). This does not mean that all the historical sources of the Old Testament
conform to a certain kerygmatic ground-plan (creed), as Von Rad thinks.

tally the witness of the God of Israel, Yahweh, is the central element of the words of the Old Testament authors. There are many voices to be heard in the various writings, but the speakers and singers all want to proclaim one and the same God. He is the one focal point of all the Old Testament writings, whatever their literary character, whatever their period of origin.[11] This leads me to the conclusion that Old Testament theology must centre upon Israel's God as the God of the Old Testament in His relations to the people, man, and the world, and that it must be dependent upon this central element for its structure.

The attempt to understand the Old Testament in this respect demands a continuous intensive contact with the whole of Old Testament scholarship, with its philological and literary aspects as well as [[151]] with its aspects in the field of general history and the history of religion. To demonstrate this connection, this last question was expressly put in Ch. II.

It is, however, neither possible nor necessary in a theology of the Old Testament to deal with all questions concerning the '*religionsgeschichtliche*' and phenomenological background of the message of the Old Testament. It can only lightly touch on a few very important points, so that the true nature of certain elements can be understood more clearly by a comparison with this background. A synthesis of the material obtained in this way cannot be given without more ado, for the content of the message of several books, even concerning one special aspect, is not always the same; these books will have to be confronted with each other and then with the message of the New Testament, in order that we may form an idea of the deepening or decay of spiritual knowledge by seeing the mutual relations between these different elements, and in order that an impression may be obtained of the guidance of the Spirit in the history of revelation.

It is not really possible to press Old Testament theology into a complete systematical survey, though many have attempted this, including Ludwig Köhler in his well-known *Theologie des A.T.*[12] Porteous is probably

11. Von Rad, too, accepts Yahweh as the element in the Old Testament common to all efforts in the field of historical theology (ThLZ, 1963, p. 409); he could hardly do anything else. It is a mystery to me, however, why he should deny that Yahweh is to be looked upon as the central element of the Old Testament. Does this imply a theological conception that makes Christ the 'centre' of the Old Testament? (cf. *O.T. Theology* II, pp. 362ff.). However that may be, I am of the opinion that he lays too much stress upon the divergence between the various testimonies concerning Yahweh to be found in the books of the Old Testament. His point of view is theologically unrealistic when considered in the light of the unity that is a characteristic of the Old Testament witness to God in all its divergent traditions. In *The Meaning of Biblical Theology* (JThS 1955, pp. 21off.) G. Ebeling expresses the view that its task consists in the inquiry into the relations between the variety of testimony and the inner unity of the New Testament.

12. Third ed. 1953.

right when he remarks that owing to this procedure Köhler has failed to find a satisfactory place in his scheme for the cult so that he came to relegate it to anthropology. At any rate the subjects of the Old Testament always interlock in such a way that a systematic classification of the material implies some measure of arbitrariness. A classification which expresses an existential relationship, such as that between God and people, God and the world, or God and man, attempted by Eichrodt and Procksch, has many advantages but is not wholly satisfactory either.

In view of what we said on ⟦pp. 84–85⟧ we shall have to divide up our subject as follows: communion as a relationship and the communion between God and man, communion with Yahweh in history, and the prospects for man and the world. We have always considered these subjects in their connection with each other; this feature is emphasized especially by the first chapter on the content of Old Testament theology—the nature of the Old Testament knowledge of God as a relationship between the holy God and man—in which we have tried to keep the essential characteristic of the Old Testament message to its existential plane; the chapter anticipates the next three: communion between God and man, the communion of faith and the prospects for man and the world and was intended as a summarizing introduction to these chapters.

⟦152⟧ In this procedure repetition could not always be avoided. If the various subjects are to be considered in their true connection, certain matters must come up for discussion more than once, though from different points of view.

One thing is certain, though, that the attempt to give a living and true picture of the Old Testament message, on the one hand in its connection with the history of Israel,[13] on the other hand in its perspective in revelation in Jesus Christ, can never succeed fully, not only because our understanding of the Old Testament and the New Testament and of their mutual coherence will always remain imperfect, but above all because God's activity in the history of Israel, the history of salvation (and there is no better name to be found for it), can never be made completely perspi-

---

13. This is emphasized by H. Wheeler Robinson in his contributions to the theology of the O.T. in *Record and Revelation,* and in his *Inspiration and Revelation in the O.T.,* 1946. This is done even more strongly by Von Rad, who ranks history, in the form of the traditions concerning God's activity so highly that it becomes the *source* of the knowledge of God and a separate, independent element in Israel's religious life, an element, even, of central importance. Here various objections make themselves felt, i.a. that this view is too one-sided, that it systematizes and abstracts too much ("history" is detached almost completely from the historical facts and, as the central element of the Old Testament message, it is, in fact, as much of a concept as the terms formerly derived from Christian theology). Has 'history' in the Old Testament any other aim than leading man to God and to belief in Him (Exod 14:31)? On this question see also ⟦Vriezen 1970:⟧ pp. 188ff.

cacious to the depths of God Himself, for if we compare this history with a line, there are only certain points of this line that are visible, the line itself cannot be copied by any man, because it is God's secret[14] and He Himself, too, remains a miraculous and essentially hidden God, also in the Old Testament, however much He reveals Himself again and again in history, personal relationship or otherwise.

Synopsis of Vriezen's *Outline of Old Testament Theology* (1970)

14. For that reason one must be careful in using the name *historia Revelationis*, which Kuyper (*Encyclopaedie* III, p. 166) wished to give to this subject and especially in using the definition of its task: 'to describe the process of the Revelation of God to mankind and to throw light upon this process both in its parts and in the whole of its progress'. Kraemer rightly remarks (op. cit., p. 23) that the word 'process' is entirely out of place beside the word 'revelation'. On the other hand a Christian need not shrink back from the idea of a line of development which is implicit in the idea of history—for a Christian believes that God has a plan, and he may try to trace this plan, if only he realizes that this plan is fully known only to God.

Theodorus C. Vriezen
On the Nature of the Knowledge of God

Excerpted with permission from Theodorus C. Vriezen, *Outline of Old Testament Theology* (2d ed.; Newton, Massachusetts: Bradford, 1970), pp. 157–58, 160–66, 168–72, 174–75. Some footnotes have been omitted.

The Nature of the Knowledge of God in the Old Testament as an Intimate Relationship between the Holy God and Man

[[157]] We saw that the Old Testament esteems the knowledge of God as the real, decisive element of religion, and that this knowledge can be defined as communion with God, whose Being as such remains a secret and who is holy. *The basis of Israel's conception of God is the reality of an immediate spiritual communion between God, the Holy One, and man and the world.* God is *directly* and personally concerned with the things of this world, first and foremost with Israel as a people, but *by implication* also with the individual Israelite, with the world of nations, and even with man in general and with the world at large. The experience of communion with the Holy One always implies a sense of distance between God and man, which finds expression either in the form of a confession of guilt (Isaiah 6) or of fear (Gen 28:17, Exod 20:18ff.) or of wonder (Psalm 8, Isaiah 28f.).

This certainty of the immediate communion between the Holy God and weak, sinful man may be called the underlying idea of the whole of the Biblical testimony, for in its essence this basic idea is also found in the New Testament.

It is most surprising that this has been denied again and again and that the conception of God in the Old Testament has been set against that of the New Testament, as if the Old Testament spoke of God as a hard despot and the New Testament of a merciful Father in heaven. In this way neither the Old Testament nor the New Testament was done justice: the God and Father revealed in Jesus Christ, who is love (1 John 4:8b) did not have justice done to His holiness—and Yahweh, who is the God of communion, was denied in His *chesed*, His love. The attempt of M. Buber in his book *Two Types of Faith*, to represent the *relationship to God* in the Old Testament as quite unlike that in the New Testament (in the Old Testament the relation to God rests on an immediate faith, in the New Testament on an intellectual act of faith, namely the affirmation of faith in Jesus Christ) is a misconception, too, for the Old Testament as well as the New Testament demands faith in God's work of salvation to which the prophets revert again and again, and conversely the New Testament also knows the intimate immediate relationship with God based on His work of salvation.

This communion between God and man is given a central position in the historical narratives, prophecies, the psalms and the wisdom-literature as a basic hypothesis or as an explicit testimony and may ⟦158⟧ be called the A-B-C of the Biblical religion and message. It is the spiritual presupposition and the purpose of the cult and of the other institutions of salvation (the monarchy, prophetism), the foundation-stone of creed and hymn, the starting-point of faith, ethics and expectations; it dominates the whole field of Israel's religious life and thought. For a theological interpretation of the Old Testament, not only in its historical and prophetical traditions, but also regarding its inward vital principle that integrates all the expressions of Israel's faith, we shall have to deal with this fundamental category of the communion between *this* God Yahweh and *this* people of Israel. Here we find the factual content of the Old Testament expressed most profoundly. Times without number the words: "I am Yahweh, thy God" are repeated in the historical and prophetical writings; in the latter it becomes a guiding principle for a hope of salvation in the future.[1]

· ·

⟦160⟧ It must remain an established fact that communion between the Holy One and man is the essential root-idea of the Old Testament message, but equally, that the knowledge concerning this relation is only the effect of God's work of revelation and the relation itself was only ordained by God in His grace (Deuteronomy 7; 9)! In this communion man may, on the one hand, realize that he does indeed stand in a personal relationship to God and may speak to God as God speaks to him;[2] on the other hand this should never make him think that his relation to God is a true "dialogue-situation."[3] Man cannot keep quarreling with God to the end: even if God does allow man to dispute with Him (cf. Job, Jeremiah 15),[4] ultimately disputing man is always silenced and condemned (Job 42, Jer 15:19). The discussion between God and man is never a dialogue pure and simple; the man who speaks must always realize and experience that he is addressing himself to the *Holy One,* and his word or answer spoken to God can fundamentally be a prayer only.

1. Cf. Jer 31:33 and elsewhere, Ezek 11:20, 26:28, 27:27; Zech 8:9. No wonder that F. Baumgärtel considered these words to be the content of the whole of the Old Testament message (cf. *Verheissung,* 1952).

2. J. Muilenburg, *The way of Israel,* 1961, pp. 18ff. rightly points to the frequent use of the vocative where God speaks to man and conversely.

3. Buber, *Kampf um Israel,* p. 32. This view is connected with the one quoted above, ⟦Vriezen 1970:⟧ p. 158.

4. Cf. also M. A. Beek, *Het twistgesprek van de mens met zijn God,* 1946.

The last word, therefore, never rests with man; even in Gen 18:33 God terminates the discussion with Abraham more or less abruptly; and even Israel's prayers of penitence are not always answered by Yahweh (Jeremiah 15; Hosea 6).[5] It is for Him to take *the decision* whether or not to accept man's words. Therefore Buber just oversteps the mark when he says that in the dialogue between God and His creature man is a real partner in his own right who can speak his own word independently and of his own free will.[6] This view smacks too much of modern individualism and humanism.

When the communion between the Holy God and man is taken to be the underlying idea of the Old Testament witness concerning God we must always keep in view that there is in this message a strong tension, which for the sake of truth must never be relaxed, between these two elements: the Holiness of God and His communion with man. The fact, already pointed out, that the most fundamental expression for faith or religion in the Old Testament is *yir°ath Yahweh*, the fear of the Lord, speaks for itself;[7] this need not be taken to mean, [[161]] as some commentators think, that Israel never managed to rise above the terror of God, for the word fear also occurs as a synonym for faith and expectation; but the presupposition of the glory and holiness of God is always implicit in the word. When God appears to Israel or to a prophet, the first reaction felt is always that of fear (Exodus 19f.; Isaiah 6; Ezekiel 1ff.).

All through the Old Testament we find that man cannot behold God, that man must die after having seen God or one of His messengers. God cannot, therefore, really be seen or described. There are a few exceptions to the former, where God is actually seen, so e.g. Exod 24:10f., where the elders of Israel see God but the appearance itself is not described; it is, however, stated emphatically that God did not lay His hand upon the 'nobles of the children of Israel', those who had been specially elected for this purpose. In connection with the concluding of the Covenant we are here informed of a most peculiar event (to a certain extent comparable with St. Paul's 'mystical' experience in 2 Corinthians 12). Also in connection with the concluding of the Covenant God is said to have spoken to Moses face to face (Exod 33:11; Num 12:8; Deut 34:10) and the appearance of God to Moses is assumed (Exod 34:5ff., 29ff.), but on the other hand Exod 33:18ff. expressly states that even Moses could not bear to see Yahweh in all His glory; God's face could not be seen, only His back.[8] In

---

5. Neither does He accept sacrifice—Amos 5, Isaiah 1, Psalm 1, Genesis 4, etc.

6. Buber, op. cit., p. 33. . . .

7. Cf., for instance, Isa 29:13c: 'their fear toward me is taught by the precept of men'; another possible translation would be: 'their religion is a lesson learnt by heart'.

8. The end of Exodus 33, from vs. 12 onwards, looks like a discussion on the question of the reality of knowing God face to face (vs. 11) and reminds of a later collection like the midrash; see [[Vriezen 1970:]] pp. 186ff.

later times the appearance of God is beheld, by prophets such as Isaiah (ch. 6) and Ezekiel, but they cannot see, let alone describe, God properly speaking; for in Isaiah's case even the seraphim shroud their faces and figures and encircle the throne of God, while in Ezekiel 1 the prophet can only describe the appearance approximately ('I saw as it were . . . ').

On the other hand the anthropomorphical appearances of God, taking place especially in the stories of the patriarchs, show the other aspect: the communion between God and man. This representation of the appearance of God may be partially due to a more primitive aesthetic way of expression, going back to oral folk-tales, on which the authors draw, it is at any rate also partly due to the tendency of the authors to make the people of Israel participate in the experience of [[162]] the original intimacy of the relationship between God and man; this tendency is not primitive, but originates purely in religious Yahwism.

Finally we shall point out a few main ideas that dominate Old Testament religion and give expression to various aspects of the leading motif of Israel's religion, namely the direct relationship between the Holy God and man.

a. One of the most fundamental elements of the Old Testament teaching is the great stress laid on *God's activity in history.*[9] The belief in God seems to be wholly based on the experience of this activity. The background against which the image of God stands out in the Old Testament is history.[10] Yahweh is in the Old Testament rather the God of history than the Creator or the God of Nature, though these latter elements are not lacking (cf. [[Vriezen 1970:]] pp. 331ff.). This thought was expressed by Pascal in his well-known words: 'Dieu! Dieu d'Abraham, d'Isaac et de Jacob! Dieu de Jésus Christ, non des philosophes et des savants.' Israel derives its knowledge of God from His activity in history on behalf of His people, particularly in Egypt and in the desert. He has intervened in behalf of the oppressed and the forsaken and has thus called Israel into being. This is pointed out continually with great emphasis by the prophets. In history, by His activity for the good of His people, God has revealed Himself as the living God who is near, but who is holy, too.[11] And throughout the course of history God intervenes at critical moments; He

9. See [[Vriezen 1970:]] pp. 26ff. and pp. 190ff.

10. A. Weiser, *Glaube und Geschichte im A.T.*, 1931; C. R. North, *The O.T. interpretation of history*, 1946, pp. 141ff.; H. Wheeler Robinson, 'The Theology of the O.T.', *Record and Revelation*, 1938, pp. 303ff.; id., *Inspiration and Revelation*, 1946, pp. 106ff.; Köhler, *Theologie des A.T.*[3], pp. 77ff.; J. deGroot and A. R. Hulst, [[*Macht en Wil*, 1952,]] pp. 213ff.; R. C. Dentan, *The idea of history in the Ancient Near East*, 1955, see the contribution on Ancient Israel by Millar Burrows, pp. 99ff.

11. Cf. for example W. J. Phythian-Adams, *The call of Israel*, 1934.

follows His people, saving as well as judging them, and He controls their destiny. The whole life of the people passes under His eyes in times of disaster and of prosperity; both are signs of His activity. There are always these two aspects to His activity: it is majestic and inspires confidence, for it is the Supreme God who intervenes, who does as He pleases and who is terrible [[163]] even when He intervenes in behalf of His people; cf. e.g. Exodus 15; Psalm 68, 111, 114; Isaiah 45. The works of Yahweh are performed to make His people glorify Him, but also give Israel reason to extol Him because they have thus experienced His faithfulness and love (many Psalms, Deuteronomy, Deutero-Isaiah and Ezekiel).

    b. Whereas God's saving activity in history is the general basis for the certainty of the direct relationship between God and man, *prophecy* is the deepest and strongest revelation of the communion between the Holy One and man. It is found throughout the history of Israel and is the most characteristic element of the structure of the Israelite religion. God is not only the God of history, who acts with and on behalf of man, but He is also the God who allows the man whom He has called to share in His activity by His Spirit or Word. God performs nothing without revealing His decree to His servants, the prophets (Amos 3:7), the prophet is allowed to be a witness to God's work in history and, as it were, "sees reality through God's eyes" (Heschel); that is why he is called a "seer".

    It is even possible to speak of a 'pathetic' theology.[12] God's work in history is accompanied by the prophetic revelation, God reveals His mind to man. *There must be an original connection between Israel's belief in God who acts in history and the prophetic experience* expressed so strongly by Amos; for this word is not merely *his* conviction, but it is the testimony of the Old Testament generally.[13] The prophets did not only explain God's work in history, but revealed it, too (often also by foretelling it).

    That this certainty is found again and again through the course of the centuries can only be attributed to the fact that this connection between prophetic revelation and God's work in the history of His people formed part of Israel's religious conceptions from the very beginning: the figure of Moses must therefore have been prophetic; it is to him that the religious relationship dates back.[14] For this reason [[164]] prophecy and his-

---

12. A. J. Heschel, *Die Prophetie*, Krakow, 1936; *The Prophets*, 1962. It is this reality of the knowledge of God that is denied to man by Ecclesiastes.

13. Cf. e.g. J. Bright, *Jeremiah*, 1965, pp. xxviiff.

14. The use of the word 'prophetic' in this book to denote the personal and moral character of Israel's religion, is based upon this conviction that the religion of Israel dates back in the first instance to the prophetic work of Moses; besides this general broad use of the word prophetic there is the more limited sense of the word denoting the religious conviction of the classical prophets.

tory are not to be separated, as some theologians are inclined to do, for that would make the prophets mere interpreters of what has already happened, and history itself would become the medium of revelation.[15]

Hempel rightly says:[16] 'In the origin of the religion of Israel two elements cooperate: the miracle, the exceptional event in nature or history, experienced as a miracle, and the extraordinary man who explains this miracle; revelation and inspiration, to use dogmatic terminology.'

And it is exactly in this prophetic experience focused on the history of today and tomorrow that the two elements of the knowledge of God, the Holy One, *and* of communion with Him are most closely linked; we mention here the figure of Isaiah who comes to know God as the Holy One in the vision of his vocation and announces His judgment with great force, but who on the other hand is the very proclaimer of confidence, or faith, almost more so than any other prophet (cf. Isa 7:9: 'believe', 30:15: 'quietness and confidence'); another such prophetical figure is Deutero-Isaiah, in whose message both elements are found very strongly supplementing each other, compare Isaiah 40 and 45 with Isaiah 55. But with Hosea, too, the preacher of God's love, the element of dreadfulness in the Nature of God stands out clearly. He depicts Yahweh as a lion (5:14), or even as a consuming disease (5:12), a lion or a leopard by the way (13:7ff.). The same applies to the earliest prophet Amos, who sees God as a destroyer (7:7ff., 8:1ff., 9:1ff.), and as a roaring lion (1:2, 3:8), but also as saving righteousness. To this experience of communion by the prophets clearly corresponds the message they teach, always ending in the proclamation that Yahweh shall be Israel's God and Israel Yahweh's people (e.g. Hosea 2, 14; Isaiah 2; Jeremiah 31; Ezekiel 36f; Isaiah 45, 51f; Zechariah 8, etc., see [[p. 89 above]]). The keystone of the message of salvation is always the proclamation of the actualization of communion with God.

c. A third typical characteristic of Israel's religion, connected with the preceding, is *the personal character of religious life.* Like the belief [[165]] in Yahweh as the God who acts in history, this element of Israel's religion may also be looked upon as closely connected with its prophetic character. Like the two preceding elements this characteristic, too, is of a very early date and it is, as it were, the product of the first two; it stands out clearly in the Yahwistic narratives of the patriarchs in the calling of Abraham and his faithful obedience in the Word of God. We may agree here with A. Alt who discovers evidence of the personal character of the relationship between the patriarchs and their God in names such as "the God

15. Cf. W. Pannenberg c.s., *Offenbarung als Geschichte*, 1961, particularly the contribution of R. Rendtorff, *Die Offenbarungsvorstellungen im A.T.* and the discussion between W. Zimmerli and R[[endtorff]] in *Ev. Th.* 1962, pp. 15ff and 62ff. . . .

16. J. Hempel, *Gott und Mensch im A.T.*[2], 1936, p. 2 n. 2 now also *Geschichten*, p. 232. . . .

of the fathers", "the God of Abraham", "the fear (relation?) of Isaac", "the Mighty One (?) of Jacob".[17] As to the stories concerning Moses, which are highly coloured by later religious conceptions, as are the patriarchal narratives, we may be brief. In Exodus 33f., Numbers 12 and Deuteronomy 34 the personal relationship is emphasized so strongly, that any sense of distance seems to have disappeared altogether. The same is true of the earliest historical work that has come down to us, the history of David and his succession; for in 2 Sam 12:16 we already find how David very personally 'besought God for the child' to which Bathsheba had given birth; this chapter is a profound account of David's spiritual struggle with God to save the child's life. In 1 Sam 30:6 we read that David, in one of the most difficult moments of his life, when he stood all alone during a catastrophic event, 'encouraged himself in the Lord his God'. In the Psalms God is invoked again and again with the simple, direct exclamation: '*Elohai,* my God,'[18] and on comparing this appellation with the many titles and names of deities that we meet with in the initial verses of Accadian psalms it becomes quite apparent that there is a vast difference in distance between gods and men in Babylon and God and man in Israel;[19] the word 'my God' bear witness to the intimacy of the communion between man and God. Many other Psalms (Psalm 33, 16, the final vss of 73, etc.) testify to the reality of the communion and to the spiritual strength radiating from it. In the prophetic type of piety, especially in Jeremiah's confessions, we are struck by the directness of the relationship between man and God, which is perhaps brought out even more clearly by the way in which Micah (6:8) defines religion: 'He hath shewed thee, [[166]] O man, what is good; and what doth the Lord require of thee but to do justly, and to love mercy, and to walk humbly with thy God?' The simple farmer of Moresheth near Gath must have known a very direct contact with God. The personal relationship to God as the God of history brings with it *faith,* complete reliance on God; this is stressed by the prophet Isaiah, and it is by this faith that Abraham's life is judged in Gen 15:6.

The other side to this personal relationship between God and man is the consciousness that all lies exposed before the Holy God, who knows man in all his ways (Psalm 139; Isa 29:15ff.), and calls him to account for all his acts (Amos 3:2). Moreover, communion with God also leads to the experience of the terribly severe demand which serving God involves. It is

17. See A. Alt, *Der Gott der Väter,* 1929, pp. 42ff. and 62ff.

18. See also Hempel, op. cit., pp. 185–86; O. Eissfeldt, '"My God" in the O.T.', *Ev. Quarterly,* XIX, 1947, pp. 7ff. (cf. p. 83, n. 2).

19. An exception to this in Mesopotamia is the relationship to the personal tutelary deity, a lower deity who must intercede with the mighty gods as an intermediary; see H. Frankfort, *Intellectual adventure,* 1946, pp. 203ff. . . .

precisely the man who has been called personally by God who is led into the fight by Yahweh (Mic 3:8; Jeremiah 1; 8:18ff.; 9:1ff.; 11:18ff.; 15:15ff.; 16; 17:14ff.; 20:14ff.; 36ff.). The prophet of the exile who experienced this personally (Isaiah 1) realized most profoundly how the true Servant of the Lord, the ᶜ*ebed Yahweh*, would have to suffer and die for God's people, according to God's will.

d. In the preceding more *general structure forms* of Israel's religion, as depicted in the Old Testament, it becomes quite clear that the relationship between God and man is a communion. The same holds good for the two following important *theological conceptions: the idea of the Covenant* and the doctrine of *man as the image of God.* On closer examination, however, we also see that these, too, are based on the recognition of the fundamental distinction between God and man.

We shall first deal with the *conception of the Covenant*, as this idea was the most influential in the Old Testament writings, especially in and influenced by Deuteronomistic theology.

. . . .

[[168]] The doctrine of the Covenant presupposes a relationship between Yahweh and Israel which arose in history, not a natural relationship. The Covenant relation was established by Yahweh alone—in the Old Testament Yahweh is always the subject of the verb used to indicate the concluding of the Covenant. This clearly shows that Yahweh and Israel are not co-equal partners: everything originates with Yahweh, it is He who states the terms of the Covenant. The Judaic theological notion of a bilateral covenant is hardly supported by the Old Testament data, but rather by a later theological interpretation of these data. It is true, though, that especially in the Deuteronomic works such a tendency is, indeed, to be observed: we see how Israel as a partner to the Covenant confirms it and agrees with it; in this way Israel acknowledges its responsibility for adhering to the rules of the Covenant decreed by Yahweh (e.g. Deut 26:16–19; Exod 19:7, 24:2ff.)[20]

By concluding the Covenant with Israel Yahweh enters into communion with this people. The Hebrew word *berith* (covenant) means something like 'bond of communion'; by concluding a covenant a connective

---

20. Especially in Joshua 24 the bilateral aspect seems to be emphasized, but the situation is different; this appears to be a description of the historical formation of the Yahweh-amphictyony, in which the ancient pre-Mosaic tribes enter into the Yahweh-religion and join the Yahweh-league. Even here, though, those who enter into the Covenant do not decide on the condition of entering.

link is effected[21] (by means of a sacrifice or a meal or both) between the two partners, who thereby enter into an intimate relationship.

Yahweh entered into such a relationship with Israel. To that end he has drawn up the rules that are to obtain, rules which Israel could not but accept if it wanted to be accepted or remain within this circle. Thus Israel was admitted to God's Covenant and thus it was sanctified. By allowing Israel to enter into this Covenant God by no means gives up His holiness, but Israel is admitted to His holy sphere of life (cf. Leviticus 19).

The Covenant may be 'transgressed' (ᶜabar), 'left' (ᶜazab), 'broken' (hefer), but Israel cannot meddle with its laws. We must, therefore, [[169]] certainly not represent the Covenant as a 'voluntary agreement' between the two parties.[22] As we said above, and Köhler himself admits (p. 45) God is always the subject when the Covenant is concluded, and in later times He is always said to 'cause the Covenant to exist', 'to establish' (heqim), 'found' (sim) or 'give' (nathan) it.

The Covenant is, therefore, 'unilateral', not bilateral in origin: Israel is expected to obey the rules of the Covenant drawn up by God and by Him alone. After the Deuteronomic reformation Israel was called God's heritage, His own, to the glory of God in the world. Israel is elected by God, and therefore the object of His electing will, committed to this will. As the elected people Israel is the ᶜebed, the *servant*, as Deutero-Isaiah has it.

Though the Covenant is broken by Israel and God punishes His headstrong and wilful people, the Covenant itself is not set aside by God. Even if God rejects the empirical Israel in its entirety for some time, that does not mean that Israel as such is rejected. None of the prophets taught that the judgment of the people in their days implied the lasting rejection of the people as such! Each prophet was, somehow, a prophet of salvation as well as a prophet of evil and hoped that God's Covenant, which owed its existence to His love would also be restored by Him. Israel was never rejected absolutely, a conception which is found with the ancient Orientals, e.g. the Babylonians, who in their Creation-narratives supposed that the wrath of the gods had in view the complete destruction of mankind.[23]

21. According to Buber, *Königtum Gottes*, 1932, pp. 113, 231, *Berith* means 'Umschränkung' ('circumscription', 'confinement'). The word cannot be divorced from the Assyrian *biritu*, intervening space, in the sense of what is common, and unites (*ina birit* = between); cf. B. Landsberger, *Ana ittišu*, MSL [[1]] 1937, p. 89; W. von Soden, *Akkadisches Handwörterbuch*, *s.v.* and M. Noth, *Das alttest. Bundschliessen im Licht eines Mari-textes* [[in *Gesammelte Studien zum Alten Testament*, 1960]], pp. 142ff.

22. Köhler, *Theologie*, p. 52.

23. The view that the counterpart of the election of Israel in the O.T. is the rejection of Israel (Köhler, *Theologie*, p. 66) cannot be maintained in this general form. It is true that in Ps 78:67 the rejection of the northern tribes—because of their idolatry—is mentioned, and in Isa 14:1 and Zech 1:17, 2:6 (R.V.12) we read of the '*further*' (Hebr. ᶜod is 'anew', or 'further')

All this points the same way: the *Covenant* between God and the people *did not bring these two 'partners' into a contract-relation, but into a communion, originating with God, in which Israel was bound to Him completely and made dependent on Him.*

The Covenant absolutely obliges Israel to do God's will. Israel cannot remain itself but must let itself be sanctified. Particularly the book of Deuteronomy emphasizes strongly the spiritual obligations while the Priestly Code stresses the fact that God has *made* the Covenant and that Israel is sanctified to the Lord.

[[170]] The priestly author considers all communion between God and man from the angle of the Covenant. In his conception of history (see [[Vriezen 1970:]] pp. 62ff.) there are three kinds of covenant: besides the Mosaic Covenant there is the Covenant with Abraham (Genesis 17) sealed by circumcision, and before that the Covenant with the whole of mankind and, indeed, with all creation—the Noachian Covenant (Gen 9:9ff.).

The doctrine of the Covenant implies, therefore (1) the absolute recognition of the reality of a true *communion* between God and people (man); (2) the absolute recognition of God, the Holy One, the Supreme, who has established and guides this relationship; (3) the absolute acknowledgment of the rules of the Covenant, given by God. Thus the doctrine of the Covenant is the clearest illustration of communion with God, the fundamental idea of the Old Testament message.

The Covenant-relationship is one of the most important forms in which the communion between God and man reveals itself in Israel's religion, but this communion is also expressed by quite different relations, such as those between father and child, husband and wife, lord and servant, king and people. For that reason the present author thinks it preferable, for various reasons, to use the much wider term 'communion' in a theological exposition to denote the relationship between God and man rather than the more definite notion of the 'Covenant'.

e. Finally: *the doctrine of man as the Image of God.*

. . . .

[[171]] The outstanding feature of the conception of man in the Old Testament is the pronouncement of the Priestly Code that man is created *in God's image, after His likeness* (Gen 1:26f., cf. 5:1, 9:6; Psalm 8). Like

---

election of Jerusalem. This implies the continuous faithfulness of the electing God rather than the possibility of definite rejection by God of what He has once elected. In any case rejection is a judgment based on the inconvertibility of man and never founded on the unwillingness of God, as may be found elsewhere, as far as Israel is concerned rejection only exists partially and temporarily as punishment. Cf. my *Die Erwählung Israels*, pp. 98ff.

other elements in Genesis 1 this wording must be considered in the light of the ancient oriental range of ideas: there man is often placed in a directly physical relationship with the deity: man is frequently represented as both from the mother-goddess or as created by the deity from divine blood (partially at least). This view is the expression of an 'idealistic' anthropology namely the conception that man is essentially of divine origin, an idea well-known from Greece (cf. Acts 17) and inherent in naturalistic paganism which puts cosmogony on a level with theogony. According to Babylonian theory, e.g. man distinguishes himself from the gods by weakness and mortality, but otherwise man and the gods spring from the same stock (men can also be looked upon as deities, as is proved by the Mesopotamian and especially the Egyptian ideology concerning the monarch).

[172]] This notion is utterly unknown to the Old Testament and this constitutes the essential difference between the Biblical and non-Biblical conceptions of God. In the Bible God and man are absolutely distinct, because God essentially precedes nature and is superior to it,[24] however much He may reveal His power in nature.

In spite of the fact that this absolute difference is clearly recognized in the Old Testament, the Old Testament is by no means behind any of the non-Biblical philosophies in its spiritual appreciation of man, as appears from the recognition of the communion between God and man. Whereas there is a great ideological tension in the ancient oriental world concerning the relationship between God and man (on the one hand man is the child of God, or at any rate he shares in the same life with the deity, and on the other hand he is merely a slave used by the deity) which gives rise to the typically naturalistic (ancient oriental and Greek) and tragic view of life, the Old Testament religion is founded upon the certainty of the relationship between the holy God and man.

The representation of man as the *imago Dei* is the symbol of this certainty of the communion of the Holy God who is 'wholly different', with man, the creature of God. This term may be called a 'critico-theological' idea which on the one hand indicates a direct, positive communion, but on the other hand excludes any equality. By this wording, the actual terms of the Father-child relationship are avoided, but the relation itself is meant, as also in the whole of the Old Testament, to denote the relationship between God and man.

. . . .

[174]] It would be possible to add many important points to the five already mentioned; we indicate the following, without pursuing the sub-

---

24. In fact, the *ruach³ Elohim* is said to circle over the waters of the chaos before the creation of the world (Gen 1:2, see [[Vriezen 1970:]] p. 215.

ject further, because they are discussed more or less fully in the factual part of the book; the *cult*, whose main object is the strengthening or restoration of the communion between God and the people (see especially ⟦Vriezen 1970:⟧ pp. 255ff.); *wisdom* which in its Israelite form fully aims at keeping peace with God and leads to the proclamation of communion with Him, as we see particularly clearly at the end of the book Job;[25] *eschatology*, which proclaims the message of the kingdom of peace between God and man with God as the focal point of this communion (cf. ⟦Vriezen 1970:⟧ p. 204f.); the *Spirit of God* which operates in history and dominates the kingdom of God (cf. ⟦Vriezen 1970:⟧ p. 211f.), and last but not least the very *name of God* in Israel, *Yahweh*, in which both the idea of nearness, of being present and the idea of mystery are found (cf. ⟦Vriezen 1970:⟧ pp. 180f.).

Thus the Old Testament is pervaded throughout by the security contained in the name which Isaiah held up to his people: Immanuel, God with us. Right from the start, Gen 1–3 tells us, God had in view life in communion with man. The historians bear testimony to the fact that throughout history, in spite of sin and guilt, transgression and unbelief, God went with His people, to which He revealed His communion. To this the prophets add the message that at the end of time there shall be full *shalom* between God and man. And in the face of death one of the Psalmists sings; 'My flesh and my heart faileth: but God is the strength of my heart and my portion for ever'.

This communion is always experienced in the Old Testament as something miraculous, for God is God and no man; man is on earth, God is in heaven. Yet they belong together, because He willed ⟦175⟧ it so in His incomprehensible goodness (Psalm 8).[26] In this fundamental point of faith the New Testament is in complete agreement with the Old. And for that reason the communion between God and man is the best starting-point for a Biblical theology of the Old Testament, and the following chapters will, therefore, be arranged with this aspect in view.

---

25. See ⟦Vriezen 1970:⟧ p. 84 n. 3.

26. This relationship should never be denoted by the word 'kinship', a supposition which we find all through Pedersen's *Israel*, and in H. Wheeler Robinson's well-considered work, *Inspiration and Revelation in the O.T.*, 1946, p. 190 ('there is a real kinship between God and man. Man is presented in the O.T. as a spiritual being and as such he is, notwithstanding all limitations, akin to God who is Spirit'). The former places God and man too much in a relationship of natural mysticism, the latter spiritualizes man too much.

GEORGE ERNEST WRIGHT

b. 1909   d. 1974

God the Warrior

Theological Synopsis

At the end of World War II, in North America, as elsewhere, Dachau and Hiroshima were large in people's memories. In North America's religious world a certain sterility and malaise were noticeable. The Bible was often expounded as so many propositions or ideas which could be set alongside the ancient Near East or modern religions. At the same time, however, the subject of divine revelation, thrust to the forefront by Barth and Brunner, was alive in the discussion.

A change was in the making, evidenced by what has come to be known as the Biblical Theology movement. Strong in the 1950s, the movement emphasized the Bible: its unity, its history as a medium of divine revelation, its religion as distinctive over against Near Eastern religion, its vocabulary in Hebrew and Greek word studies, its message more than its sources, and its relevance to the modern world. Buttressed by archeology, the theological significance of history in the form of *Heilsgeschichte*, "salvation history," was underlined. Of the scholars of this era (H. H. Rowley, William F. Albright, John Bright, Alan Richardson, James Smart, Millar Burrows, James Muilenburg), G. Ernest Wright was decidedly the most aggressive advocate of the movement.

Wright, in reviews of Old Testament theologies by European theologians (Ludwig Köhler, Edmond Jacob, Theodorus Vriezen), commented that, as valuable as these theologies were, they did not capture a certain dynamic present in the Old Testament (1959, 1960). Wright (1950) was also critical of R. C. Dentan, who defined biblical theology as "that Christian theological discipline which treats of the religious ideas of the Old Testament *systematically*, i.e., not from the point of view of historical development, but from that of the structural unity of Old Testament religion, and

100

which gives due regard to the historical and ideological relationship of that religion to the religion of the New Testament" (Dentan 1950: 94–95). More attention should be given, noted Wright, to *Heilsgeschichte*, for surely the Bible was more than "ideas."

Wright's slim volume, *God Who Acts*, highlighted the category of history, a category he found in the apostle's rehearsals of the Old Testament (e.g., Acts 13) and one which, he claimed, differentiated the Bible from ancient Near East religions with their stress on nature. He wrote: "Another ingredient in my attempt during the years 1948–1952 to reconceive the nature of Old Testament theology was Gerhard von Rad's highly original and now basic monograph, *The Problem of the Hexateuch*" (1969: 42). Wright agreed with von Rad: "Israel's epic tradition in both prose and poetry is a confessional history" (1969: 43). The great acts of God began with creation and continued in the promises to Abraham, the deliverance from Egyptian slavery, the gift of the good land, and the Davidic conquests. In his articles and books, Wright repeatedly stressed the unity of the Old Testament.

More than many other theologies, Wright's expositions filtered into the churches. At the heart of his later book, *The Old Testament and Theology*, were chapters on God as creator, God as Lord (a shift here toward covenant), and God as warrior. Thus, modes of God's action as well as certain images of God shaped Israel's theology.

In the preface to his 1952 book Wright expressed gratitude to two readers who kept "me from over-stating my thesis" (pp. 13–14). But perhaps he did overstate it, for some seventeen years later he was prepared to give more weight to election and covenant than did von Rad, and so Wright later aligned himself (1969: 61–69) with Eichrodt instead.

G. Ernest Wright's interests were in archeology and theology. As an archeologist he was trained by W. F. Albright. Wright published on Palestinian pottery in 1937; he conducted excavations at Shechem (Israel) and Idalion (Cyprus). He was founder and for twenty-five years editor of *The Biblical Archeologist.* He also worked as an exegete and theologian; half of his eighteen books fall in this category. He taught at McCormick Theological Seminary beginning in 1939 and later at Harvard University. He died of a heart attack in 1974, one week before his sixty-fifth birthday.

E.A.M.

Writings by Wright

1950   Review of *Preface to Old Testament Theology*, by Robert C. Dentan. *Journal of Biblical Literature* 69:393–97.

1952   *God Who Acts: Biblical Theology as Recital.* Studies in Biblical Theology, vol. 8. London: SCM/Chicago: Regnery.

1957   *The Book of the Acts of God: Christian Scholarship Interprets the Bible.* Garden City, New York: Doubleday. [With Reginald H. Fuller.]

1959   Review of *Old Testament Theology,* by Ludwig Köhler. *Religious Education* 54:386–87.

1960   Review of *Theology of the Old Testament,* by Edmond Jacob. *Journal of Biblical Literature* 79:78–81.

1969   *The Old Testament and Theology.* New York: Harper & Row.

Writings about Wright

Cross, Frank M., Werner E. Lemke, and Patrick D. Miller Jr. (editors)

1976   *Magnalia Dei, The Mighty Acts of God: Essays on the Bible and Archaeology in Memory of G. Ernest Wright.* Garden City, New York: Doubleday.

G. Ernest Wright's
Approach to Old Testament Theology

Excerpted with permission from G. Ernest Wright, *God Who Acts:
Biblical Theology as Recital* (London: SCM, 1952), pp. 33–35, 55–
58; and G. Ernest Wright, *The Old Testament and Theology* (New
York: Harper & Row, 1969), pp. 61–63.

Theology as Recital
[from *God Who Acts*]

[[33]] Biblical theology has long been dominated by the interests of dogmatic or systematic theology. Indeed, throughout the first three centuries
of Protestantism the two disciplines were scarcely distinguished, at least
among conservative churchmen. All theology was Biblical theology in the
sense that it was a system of doctrine drawn from the Bible and supported
by collections of proof-texts. While the fact of the Reformation is illustra-
tive of the perennial tension which has always existed between the Bible
and theology, nevertheless the separation of Biblical theology as an independent subject of study occurred in a new form within pietism and eighteenth century rationalism, when the Bible was used to criticize orthodox
dogma. Johann Philipp Gabler in 1787 seems to have been the first in
modern times formally to advocate a distinction between the two disciplines. To him Biblical theology is an objective, historical discipline which
attempts to describe what the Biblical writers thought about divine matters. Dogmatic theology on the other hand, is didactic in character and
sets forth what a theologian philosophically and rationally decides about
divine matters in accordance with his time and situation.[1] Nevertheless, in
organizing the data of Biblical faith the rubrics of systematic theology continued in use, the chief of these being the doctrine of God, the doctrine
of man, and the doctrine of salvation.

During the nineteenth century, however, the historical nature of the
Bible was more clearly seen than ever before. As a result, men came to believe that Biblical theology must concern itself primarily with the development of religious ideas. This point of view made the task of the Biblical
theologian so difficult that few scholars attempted anything other than a
history of religion in the Old and New Testaments. Perhaps the greatest
work in Old Testament theology produced during the last century was

---

1. So Robert C. Dentan, *Preface to Old Testament Theology* (New Haven, 1950), p. 8.

⟦34⟧ that by the German scholar Hermann Schultz.[2] He tried to solve the problem by presenting first a historical account of the development of Israel's religion and then by giving a topical treatment in which theological concepts were traced through the various historical periods. In other words, no attempt was made to present a systematic theology of the Old Testament as a whole. The growth of religious concepts through the history was thought to be too great to permit a systematic survey. A different type of treatment is illustrated by the work of the French pastor, Ch. Piepenbring, first published in 1886.[3] He presented three cross sections through Israel's history, the first being the pre-prophetic period beginning with Moses, the second the age of prophecy, and the third the Exilic and post-Exilic age. In each period he systematically treated the doctrines of God, man, worship and salvation under a variety of chapter headings.

the work of older theologians?   It will be noted that these works are based upon two presuppositions. The first is that the evolution of religious concepts in the Bible is so great that there are virtually different theologies in different periods. The second is that the procedure of dogmatic theology is normative for all theology, including that of the Bible. If both these presuppositions are correct, then the task of Biblical theology is quite clear. It is either to trace the evolving history of religious concepts through the various Biblical periods, as did Schultz, or else it is to take a cross section through the Bible at one period and treat that as systematically as possible.

With regard to the first presupposition there is an increasingly widespread belief today that while historical development is indeed a very important factor in the Bible yet it is one which has been overemphasized. A living organism is not a blank tablet on which all writing is done by environmental, geographical and historical conditioning. If it were, then a description of a historical process might be sufficient to enable us to comprehend its inner significance. But in every organism there is something given which determines what it is and what it will become. Environment and geography can explain many things in ancient ⟦35⟧ Israel, but they cannot explain why Israel did not undergo the same type of evolution as did her pagan neighbours, nor why the early Church did not become another Jewish purist sect or Hellenistic mystery religion. One explanation for this difference in evolution which positivist scholars have been wont to give is the presence in Biblical history of remarkable series of religious geniuses: Moses, the prophets, Jesus, Paul. Yet every genius is in part a product of his historical situation in a given social context. He cannot be

---

2. See his *Old Testament Theology* (translated from the 4th German ed. by J. A. Paterson, in 2 vols., Edinburgh, 1892).

3. *Theology of the Old Testament* (translated from the French by H. G. Mitchell, Boston, 1893).

explained apart from certain inner, spiritual factors which are a vital part of the cultural situation in which he arose. In other words, there is in the Bible something far more basic than the conceptions of environment, growth and genius are able to depict. It is this 'given' which provided the Bible's basic unity in the midst of its variety and which sets Biblical faith apart as something radically different from all other faiths of mankind.[4]

. . . .

[55] From the above survey we are now in possession of the chief clues to the theological understanding of the whole Bible. There is, first, the peculiar attention to history and to historical traditions as the primary sphere in which God reveals himself. To be sure, God also reveals himself and his will in various ways to the inner consciousness of man, as in other religions. Yet the nature and content of this inner revelation is determined by the outward, objective happenings of history in which individuals are called to participate. It is, therefore, the objectivity of God's historical acts which are the focus of attention, not the subjectivity of inner, emotional, diffuse and mystical experience. Inner revelation is thus concrete and definite, since it is always correlated with a historical act of God which is the primary locus of concentration. Mysticism in its typical forms, on the other hand, subtly turns this concentration around, so that the focus of attention is on the inner revelation, while the objectivity of God's historical acts is either denied altogether or left on the periphery of one's vision. Important as Christian pietism has been in the Church, it has not escaped this subtle inversion with the result that the central Biblical perspective has been lost.

Secondly, the chief inference from this view of history as revelation was the mediate nature of God's action in history: that is, his election of a special people through whom he would accomplish his purposes. This was a proper inference from the Exodus deliverance; and the migration of Abraham to Canaan was believed to have been occasioned by a Divine call which involved election. In Genesis the election is portrayed as the goal of history and the Divine answer to the human problem. After the Exodus, it formed the background for the interpretation of Israel's life in Palestine and a central element in prophetic [56] eschatology and in the apocalyptic presentation of the Book of Daniel.

Thirdly, the election and its implications were confirmed and clarified in the event of the covenant ceremony at Sinai. Israel's sin was the breach of this covenant, which, therefore, enabled the faithful to see that election was not unalterable. It could be annulled by Israel herself. Consequently,

4. See further the monograph by the writer, *The Old Testament Against its Environment*, and that by Floyd V. Filson, *The New Testament Against its Environment* (London and Chicago, 1950).

covenant was something that had to be periodically renewed by ceremonies of rededication.[5] It involved the interpretation of the whole life of the people, in the social, economic, political and cultic spheres. The law of the society was the law of the covenant, given by God with the promise of justice and security within the promised land. Consequently, the central problem of Israel was envisaged as the problem of true security in the midst of covenant violation and international upheaval. This security was seen by the prophets as only to be found beyond the suffering and judgment of the Day of Yahweh. There would be a revival of the community, but only after the elect people had become scattered and dry bones (Ezekiel 37).

These three elements are together the core of Israelite faith and the unifying factor within it.[6] They have little abstract or propositional theology within them. They are based on historical events and the inferences drawn from them. They cannot be grasped by the abstract rubrics of dogmatic theology. And these very same elements are the centre and core of the faith of the early church. For this reason the advent of Jesus Christ could not be understood solely or chiefly as the coming of a teacher of moral and spiritual truths. His coming was a historical event which was the climax of God's working since the creation. All former history had its goal in him because God had so directed it. All subsequent history will be directed by him because God has exalted him as Lord. In so doing he will fulfill the promises [[57]] of God in the government of Israel, assuming the royal office of David at the right hand of God and providing the security which the sin of Israel made impossible of achievement. The election of Israel as the agent of God in universal redemption is reaffirmed in the New Israel (e.g. 1 Pet 2:9–10), the Body of Christ, which is the partaker of the New Covenant of Christ's blood. In Christ God has inaugurated the new age, foreseen of old; entrance into it is by faith and by the sharing of Christ's cross, for in him our sins are forgiven and our alienation from God done away. Thus God in Christ has completed the history of Israel; he has reversed the work of Adam, fulfilled the promises to Abraham, repeated the deliverance from bondage, not indeed from Pharaoh but from sin and Satan, and inaugurated the new age and the new covenant. To be sure, the world is unredeemed and the final consummation is yet to appear. Yet Christ is the sign and seal of its coming. Hence he is the climactic event in a unique series of events, to be comprehended only by what

5. For a brief review of these ceremonies, see the writer in *The Old Testament Against its Environment*, Chap. II. Form criticism has led some scholars to the highly probable view that in early Israel, at least, the ceremony of covenant renewal was a yearly affair: see Gerhard von Rad, *Das formgeschichtliche Problem des Hexateuchs* (Giessen, 1938), and Martin Noth, *Überlieferungsgeschichte des Pentateuch* (Stuttgart, 1948), pp. 63f.

6. For the problem of the wisdom literature in this connection, particularly Job, Proverbs and Ecclesiastes, see the treatment in Chap. IV.

has happened before him, but at the same time the new event which marks a fresh beginning in human history.

This, then, is the basic substance of Biblical theology. It is true that we simply cannot communicate it without dealing with the *ideas* of which it is composed. Yet to conceive of it primarily as a series of ideas which we must arrange either systematically or according to their historical development is to miss the point of it all. It is fundamentally an interpretation of history, a confessional recital of historical events as the acts of God, events which lead backward to the beginning of history and forward to its end. Inferences are constantly made from the acts and are interpreted as integral parts of the acts themselves which furnish the clue to understanding not only of contemporary happenings but of those which subsequently occurred. The being and attributes of God are nowhere systematically presented but are inferences from events. Biblical man did not possess a philosophical notion of deity whence he could argue in safety and 'objectivity' as to whether this or that was of God. This ubiquitous modern habit of mind which reasons from axioms and principles of universals to the concrete would have been considered as faithless rebellion against the Lord of history who used [[58]] history to reveal his will and purpose. Hence the nearest approach to atheism which the Old Testament possesses is the fool who says in his heart there is no God (Ps 14:1; 53:1). Yet the Psalmist means by this, not a theoretical atheism, but rather the practical atheism of a sinner who calls God's works, not his being, into question.[7] Jeremiah clarifies the point when he speaks of people in his day who refuse to believe that the great events which then are happening are the work of God. They thus 'have denied Yahweh and said: "It is not he; neither shall evil come upon us; neither shall we see sword nor famine"' (5:12). To refuse to take history seriously as the revelation of the will, purpose and nature of God is the simplest escape from the Biblical God and one which leaves us with an idol of our own imagining.

Consequently, not even the nature of God can be portrayed abstractly. He can only be described *in relation to* the historical process, to his chosen agents and to his enemies. Biblical theology must begin, therefore, with the primary question as to why the Bible possesses the historical nature that it does. It thus must point in the first instance to this confessional recital of traditional and historical events, and proceed to the inferences which accompanied those events, became an integral part of them, and served as the guides to the comprehension of both past and future. Biblical theology, then, is primarily a confessional recital in which history is seen as a problem of faith, and faith a problem of history.[8]

---

7. Cf. Ludwig Köhler, *Theologie des Alten Testaments* (Zweite Auflage; Tübingen, 1947), p. 1.

8. An affirmation of Artur Weiser, *Glaube und Geschichte im Alten Testament*, p. 19, here used in a somewhat different context.

Revelation and Theology
[[from *Old Testament and Theology*]]

[[61]] Here all too briefly is the direction in which I have been moving.

By 1950 I had independently come to a position similar to that of von Rad with regard to revelation by event, the interrelation of word, event, and history (see section I of this chapter [[not reprinted here]]). In my monograph of lectures, *God Who Acts: Biblical Theology as Recital* (1952), I found von Rad's theological views, so far as they were then published, most stimulating and helpful. However, with the publication of von Rad's *Theology*, I discovered certain differences of viewpoint:

1. While I agree completely with the confessional center of revelation to Israel, it appears that von Rad, like Bultmann,[1] has carried the Lutheran separation of law and gospel back into his Old Testament scholarship so that Israel's recitals of the *magnalia Dei* are interpreted as having nothing to do originally with the Sinai covenant tradition. The welding of the two is a secondary phenomenon, which marked the beginning of the law-gospel tension in the Bible. This viewpoint from a scholarly standpoint has been rendered highly unlikely by George E. Mendenhall's basic work, *Law and Covenant in Israel and the Ancient Near East* (1954–1955), and by the dissertation of one of von Rad's own students, Klaus Baltzer, [[62]] *Das Bundesformular* (1960),[2] the implications of which von Rad evidently cannot face. The pioneering work of Mendenhall and Baltzer means that the two forms, *magnalia Dei* and Sinai covenant tradition, are inseparable and that the covenant is the setting for the recitation of the acts.

2. This means that Eichrodt is right in insisting that Israel's testimonies find their setting and particularity only in the framework of the Sinai covenant. Von Rad's existentialist interpretation of Israel's theology has no *Sitz im Leben* apart from a people dominated by the conception of a world empire whose Suzerain has created a people, Israel, whose identity is one of vassalage by treaty in the cosmic empire. Hence Old Testament theology without a sense of this cosmic structure, which informs Israel's every testimony, is simply impossible.[3]

---

1. Cf. my analysis in "History and Reality . . . ," Chap. 10 in B. W. Anderson, ed., *The Old Testament and Christian Faith.*

2. Mendenhall's work originally appeared as Vol. XVII.2 and 3 (May and Sept., 1954) of *The Biblical Archaeologist*, and reprinted as a monograph in 1955 from the same plates. . . . The Baltzer volume was published by Neukirchen Verlag in Neukirchen-Vluyn, Germany.

3. For a proper discussion of the political form of the Bible, which so many today want to "demythologize," see, e.g., Paul Lehmann, *Ethics in a Christian Context* (New York: Harper & Row, 1963), Chap. III, entitled "What God is Doing in the World."

3. What, then, is theology? I must side with Eichrodt that it is impossible to separate testimonies to God's saving activity, reactualized in succeeding periods, from conceptual and structural elements provided by the Sinai covenant tradition. On the other hand, Eichrodt is much too wedded to older terms like "system," "systematic," which are unnecessary. "Coherence" and *sui generis* seem to me more appropriate.

In other words, theology is the effort of a man to explicate his own or someone else's tradition meaningfully in his conceptual world, so that he can understand it. To restrict theology to the proclamation of Israel's or the Christian's kerygma is too confining. What is kerygma without exposition and application? What is [[63]] the proclamation of the Word apart from the structure of "the people of God" whom it has created and whom it recreates?

Synopsis of Wright's *God Who Acts* (1952)

Synopsis of Wright's *Old Testament and Theology* (1969)

G. Ernest Wright on God the Warrior

Excerpted with permission from G. Ernest Wright, *The Old Testament and Theology* (New York: Harper & Row, 1969), pp. 121–26, 129–31, 145–50.

[[121]] A most pervasive Biblical motif is the interpretation of conflict in history as owing to the sin of man, against which the cosmic government and its Suzerain take vigorous action. Since so much of history is concerned with warfare, it therefore must be expected that one major activity of the Suzerain will be the direction of war for both redemptive and judgmental ends. That is, a major function of the Suzerain will be understood to be his work as Warrior.

Yet in our time no attribute of the Biblical God is more consciously and almost universally rejected than this one. The reason is that theologically we are unable to keep up with our emotional attitudes toward war. The latter are so shocked by the savage horror of war that it is most difficult to see any positive good in this type of conflict. As the weapons of war become more efficiently destructive, the harm caused is surely greater than the good brought by success. As a result, the Bible on this subject is simply dismissed, or at best treated in the most simplistic and superficial manner. Jesus and the New Testament portray love and the God of love, while the God of the Old Testament, especially the God of Joshua, is another deity altogether, or at least a lower, more primitive understanding of deity.

Such an attitude is more a derivative from idealism than it is from a faith that struggles with history, with the way men actually act in time and space, and seeks there the evidence of Providence. Idealism predetermines its conception of The Good, and thus ends with a "philosophy" unable to deal with human life as it is actually lived.[1] Hence, the sermons and contemporary prayers in the typical [[122]] synagogue or church have generally dealt with the inner resources of faith, though the recent civil rights and poverty problems are now receiving attention, primarily because the safety of law and order is threatened. One can see the truth in the statement attributed to Harry Golden to the effect that in his town he as a Jew can go to church for six months without hearing anything to offend him.

It is the intent of this chapter to suggest that if the conception of the Divine Warrior cannot be used theologically, then the central core of the

1. See Chap. 1, and esp. the quotations from Kierkegaard and William James about the classical philosophers being unable to live in the marble palaces which they had created.

Biblical understanding of reality is dissolved with drastic consequences for any theology which would maintain a connection with what most distinguishes and characterizes the Bible in the world of religious literature.

We begin by recalling a simple and obvious fact about the Book of Joshua. It cannot be considered to contain a "primitive" theology of God and war which later books replace with a God of love. The book in its completed form is an indispensable and climactic part of Israel's epic of her formation as a nation by the great providential acts of God in western Asia during the second millennium B.C. Formally, it stands at the beginning of the Deuteronomistic history of the ways of God with Israel in the Promised Land (Deuteronomy–2 Kings). It is a creation of the Deuteronomic historian from old sources, perhaps during the reign of Josiah at the end of the seventh century B.C., or else after the fall of Jerusalem, *ca.* 550 B.C.[2] Theologically, [[123]] it furnishes traditional details about how the initial wars of conquest were won by Joshua. Israel was victorious, not because they were marvelous fighters under a brilliant general, but because God went before Israel, threw fear into the hearts of the opposition, and wrought the victory for his own purposes.

In Israel's confessions of faith and praise to God for his marvelous works, the Conquest is closely associated with the Exodus. The slaves who were freed from Egyptian bondage are given a land. The outcasts, the powerless, the slaves of the greatest world power of the day, are now a nation with "a land of milk and honey" as a gift of God (Deut 26:9). It is the Promised Land, promised by God to Abraham, Isaac, and Jacob (Gen 12:7; Deut 6:23). The victories in the Conquest were "not by your sword or by your bow. I gave you a land on which you had not labored" (Josh 24:12–13).

Biblical references to the conquest generally omit all mention of specific battles and human activity. It is God's deed; he is the sole actor; there are no human heroes.[3] A few citations will suffice:

2. Most scholars have concluded that the history was completed at the end of the seventh century and that 2 Kings 24–25 are a subsequent addition to bring the story up to date *ca.* 550 B.C. A decision between the two views is difficult. Granted that nearly all the material used is preexilic, the period when the chief historian drew it together depends so much on one's understanding of the theological purpose of the historian.

3. In spite of the number of Biblical theologies which have been written, the task of preparing such a work, in the view of this writer, is very difficult because the basic research work has either not been done or must be redone because of the advance in research. A definitive study of the theology of the conquest theme in Biblical literature is an example; it simply has not been made—or at least not published. It is interesting that whereas Sihon and Og whom Moses conquered in Transjordan are occasionally mentioned (a tradition surviving from the liturgy of celebration once used at Gilgal?), no specifies are ever given in prophecy or psalms of battles west of the Jordan, except on a very rare occasion, Jericho. All activity is Yahweh's.

The prophet Amos, speaking for God, exclaimed:

> It was I who destroyed the Amorite before them
> Whose height was like the height of cedars
> and whose strength was that of oaks.
> I destroyed his fruit above
> and his roots below.   (2:9)

[124] An early psalm has the following reference to God's work as Warrior:

> He led them in safety and they were not terrified;
> their enemies, the sea covered over!
> He brought them into his holy boundary,
> this mountain which his right hand had acquired.[4]
> He expelled nations before them;
> he assigned them a measured allotment.[5]
> he made the tribes of Israel to dwell[6] in their tents.
> (78:53–55)

Another psalm refers to the Conquest as God's planting of a vine:

> A vine out of Egypt you removed;
> You expelled nations and planted it.
> You cleared [the ground] for it;
> its root took root;
> it filled the land. . . .
> Its shade covered the hills,
> its branches mighty cedars.
> It sent its branches to the Sea [the Mediterranean],
> to the River [the Euphrates] its shoots.
> (80:8–11 [Heb. 9–12])

Nowhere in the Bible is this interpretation of the Conquest challenged or corrected. Paul is cited as using the old confession in his preaching:

4. Or "this mountain which his power had created."
5. This colon is not clear. It could mean that he gave Israel property which had been measured out by lot for the tribes, or that he had destroyed the nations by means of a determined penalty. It can thus be interpreted as going either with the colon before it or the one after it. ("Colon" here is a technical term for one part of a Hebrew poetic line.)
6. Literally, "to tent."

Men of Israel and you who reverence God, listen: The God of this people
Israel chose our Fathers and made the people great in the sojourn in the
land of Egypt, and with uplifted arm [great strength] he led them out of
it. . . . And having [[125]] destroyed seven nations in the land of Canaan,
he gave them their land as an inheritance. . . . [7] (Acts 13:16–19)

Stephen in his defense carefully and in detail reviews the same epic
story, doing so, however, from the standpoint of Israel's faithless response
to God's beneficence.[8] Speaking of the tabernacle in the wilderness, he is
recorded as saying: "This our fathers in turn brought in with Joshua [at
the time of] the dispossession of the nations whom God thrust out before
the presence of our fathers" (Acts 7:45).

More generalized and oblique but nevertheless referring to the interpretation of the Exodus-Conquest events as God's mercy and salvation is
such a passage as the following:

Indeed you are an elect race, a royal priesthood, a holy nation, God's
own possession,[9] in order that you may proclaim the wondrous deeds of
him who called you out of darkness into his marvelous light, [you who]
once were no people but now are God's people, [you who] had not received mercy but now have received mercy. (1 Pet 2:9–10)

In other words, the Conquest as God's gracious gift to those who had
been outcast—this is the unanimous account of Biblical authors. In only
one place is there a more rationalizing and broad perspective presented
from the standpoint of the whole divine purpose in the world. That is
Deut 9:4–7:

Do not say in your heart when the Lord your God drives them [the na-
tions] out before you: "Because of my righteousness the Lord has brought
me in to possess this land." It is because [[126]] of the evil of these nations
that the Lord is dispossessing them before you. Not because of your righteousness nor because of the uprightness of your heart are you entering
to possess their land. Instead it is because of the evil of these nations that
the Lord your God is dispossessing them before you, and [also] to the
end that he confirm the thing which the Lord swore to your fathers, to
Abraham, to Isaac and to Jacob. And you [must] acknowledge that the
Lord your God is not giving you this good land to possess because of your

7. Or "he allotted their land" (i.e., separated their land to their tribes by casting lots).

8. That is, the confessional history was recited in two ways: one to glorify God for his
mighty acts (cf. Psalm 105) and the other to confess Israel's faithless response to God at
each juncture (cf. Psalm 106, and Wright, "The Lawsuit of God . . . ," *Israel's Prophetic Heritage*
[ed. by Anderson and Harrelson], pp. 26–67). Stephen's defense is a particularly vigorous
recital in the second vein. Both are woven together, of course, in the epic.

9. Literally, "a people for his possession"—clearly an attempt to translate into Greek the
special word *sĕgullāh* in Exod 19:5.

righteousness. Indeed, you are a stiff-necked people. Remember and do not forget how you provoked the Lord your God in the wilderness. From the day when you came out of the land of Egypt until your coming into this place you have been rebellious against the Lord.

Israel thus is an agent in God's overall purposes as the Suzerain of history. And if one is an agent in conflict, that does not necessarily involve a moral superiority. Indeed, in Israel's conquest it definitely does not involve any connotation of a superior goodness. The evidence is quite to the contrary. Yet as a result of corruption the divine government has decreed the end of Canaanite civilization.[10] At the same time, a new and redemptive purpose for mankind is expressed in the promises to the Fathers (that is, in the Abrahamic covenant; cf. Gen 12:1–3; 15:12–21; 17:1–8).

In any case, the events in Joshua cannot be attributed to primitivism in Biblical theology. The Bible's most advanced interpretations in later ages saw there nothing but a most dramatic illustration of the power, grace, and justice of God.

. . . .

⟦129⟧ There is only one theological context in which the institution of holy war in early Israel can be dealt with meaningfully. Certain components are as follows:

1. Ultimate power or "the field of power" is actively experienced in history in both positive—i.e., creative and redemptive—and negative—i.e., destructive and judgmental—ways. Yet in the long run I put my faith in the creative and redemptive as the context of the whole, because of the manner in which I feel I must interpret the structure of existence.

2. The use of the Divine Monarch theme involves also that of the Divine Warrior because the Monarch's chief concern is universal order. We cannot assume, therefore, that blood and God are ⟦130⟧ contradictory terms, so that where the one is, the other simply cannot be.

3. Our human world stands in defiance of its pretensions. It is in dreadful disorder, a faithful copy of all the Apostle Paul says in Romans 1 that it becomes when men worship the creature rather than the Creator. All war is fought by sinners who are employing evil structures of power to their own ends.

4. God works in this world as it is by mediate means. He has his men, whether they know it or not, who serve as his agents, doing what is appro-

---

10. There is indeed evidence of the decline of Canaanite civilization during the thirteenth century B.C. On the other hand, the Israelite conquest in the thirteenth century and the Aramean and Philistine conquests of the twelfth century confined most remaining Canaanites to the coastal regions of Lebanon where in due course the remarkable Phoenician trading empire was developed.

priate for the immediate issue. Our problem is to know and do what we are called to do. But by failure of mind and will, we seldom get our duty straight or do what we know we should.

5. From this standpoint, Israel's holy war—something that looks to us today as a kind of fanaticism—can be conceived as an agency which God made use of at one time for his own purposes and without in any way sanctifying the participants. Similarly, the world powers of Assyria and Babylon were subsequently used to destroy Israel and Judah—and for just cause, so the literature maintains. Yet each moment is unique. A past pattern of response by an agent can be used as a guide only with great caution in the present. Israel's wars of conquest become no mandate for wars by God's people today.

6. God the Warrior is the theme that furnishes hope in time. What is, cannot be sanctified for the future because a vast tension exists between the will of the Suzerain and that of his vassals. Our world is under judgment. Wars and rumors of wars are a Biblical reality, a present reality, and we see no immediate surcease of them in the future. Yet the strong, active power given language in the Warrior-Lord means that there is a force in the universe set against the forces of evil and perversity. Life, then, is a battleground, but the Divine Warrior will not be defeated.

Now if one thinks this type of language is too strong, let him only remember that God the Warrior is simply the reverse side of God the Lover or God the Redeemer. The seeking love of God is only one side of the Suzerain's activity, because, to change the figure, [[131]] divine love is a two-edged sword. It is power in action in a sinful world, and redemption is disturbing, painful, resisted.

. . . .

[[145]] The purpose of this sampling of Biblical material is not to make a bibliolatrous point. That is, just because these things are Biblical, one should not automatically assume they must be central to our own theology. Indeed, with regard to the themes surveyed in this and in the preceding two chapters it would be simple to suggest that we forget that they exist. Yet when one reviews the attempts at theology in recent years which proceed on this very suggestion, I for one find much that is not satisfying. The conscious rejection of political language as appropriate to an interpretation of my existence leaves me without a firm anchor to what appears to be my central problem as a human being. That is, how I can see my life as possessing freedom for positive ends that encompass more than myself? Since as a social and historical being I was not a person as a fetus in the womb, but only became a person in interaction within my environment of other people and institutions within a context of relatedness to fellow men with our vocational choices, and within a social organism which has its history and traditions, what is the "ground" of my life? To disregard the political is to disregard this central and social aspect of myself as a self-in-relation. To reduce the language patterns to the family and love with the family, to say that my only need is to be "brother" to my neighbor, is simply to neglect the larger contexts of my relatedness, of institutions, of other people and nations whom I do not know. Does "love" here become a passion for justice[11] which soon goes far beyond what any model drawn from the family can provide?

Shall I disregard the real structure and history of the self and assume with current existentialisms that my only duty is to myself, to courage, and to "authentic" existence, whatever I may decide that to be? But self-preoccupation is the first and basic disease of the neurotic. It is only as I give my loyalty to concerns larger than [[146]] myself that I can find freedom from the tyranny of self-preoccupation.[12]

Perhaps we should say that the first and most important thing to admit about ourselves is that we are simply an integral part of nature and of nature's process. If so, then perhaps ancient polytheism has its point and the process and power of life in all its forms should provide the chief categories for self-understanding. There is great merit in some sort of process philosophy as a background for current theology. Yet the difficulty always encountered is that set forth as basic presupposition by Reinhold Niebuhr in the first chapter of his *Nature and Destiny of Man*. The first thing to be said about man is that he is a child of nature. Yet one cannot stop there without making the equally important observation that man is a child of God. By the latter one refers first of all to man's power of self-transcendence and to all that distinguishes him in and from nature. Man is the creator of cultural tradition. As phenomenon he creates and lives in a present which contains its past, but he also transcends the present by foresight, planning, even controlling to some degree his own evolution. That is, historical man

11. See Reinhold Niebuhr, *Nature and Destiny of Man*, Vol. II (New York: Charles Scribner's Sons, 1943), pp. 244ff.

12. See the final section of Chap. 1 for additional discussion, esp. for the query as to whether the popular form of existentialism being used currently in theology is not just as artificial a construction, as an attempt to describe my existence, as any of the past systems, Hegelianism, e.g., that it supersedes. The attempts of several modern "sons" of Bultmann to suggest that if existential categories are drawn from "the later Heidegger," the problems of the school with regard to history would be removed, have been wordy but not very impressive: see, e.g., James M. Robinson and John B. Cobb, eds., *The Later Heidegger and Theology* (*New Frontiers in Theology*, Vol. I; New York: Harper & Row, 1963); and the critique of Hans Jonas, "Tenth Essay. Heidegger and Theology," *The Phenomenon of Life* (New York: Harper & Row, 1966), pp. 235–261.

is equally significant with natural man, and both aspects of our being must provide the terms of basic reference. Nature's process is insufficient to expound human life and history.

Perhaps the easiest course to follow is the popular one today among Christians. That is simply to drop all talk of God and live as a Christian humanist, Christ forming a model of what the good for us can be. Yet here again the structures of historical existence are so complex that the very simple, idealized model thus created from the life of Jesus, one abstracted almost completely from its own environment, furnishes a very limited and limiting context in which I must attempt to face the human struggle with and for civilization.

⟦147⟧ It will be suggested in the next chapter that human beings live with their fellows in a cultural environment in which communication is by a language that has a variety of symbolic expressions to convey meaning. The images or symbols are abstractions of experienced realities by which and within which thinking and action take place. To demythologize is to destroy an organism of meaning because it generally turns out to be desymbolization instead of resymbolization. Without the latter, no thought or action is really possible. And one thing seems certain about my existence: I cannot express a sufficiently comprehensive or coherent set of meanings and values for myself, my fellow men, or my world without the use of social and political language models. Such language is simply basic to my life as a fellow man and as a member of a social organization, which includes but is ultimately much larger and more complex than the family alone or nature alone can possible provide.

Summary

The heuristic value of the Bible's version of the cosmic government has been suggested in this and in the preceding chapters. The particular conception and language pertaining to it are by no means simple, and they are so frequently misunderstood and misrepresented simplistically. However, they successfully hold together the relativity of so much of our human activities and valuations. At the same time they present a structural model which preserves the positive importance of values themselves and their relation to what can be conceived as stable and permanent in the cosmos. In this context all human activity exists in tension with ultimate goals, and thus ⟦148⟧ forbids all claims of absolution for our earthly existence. It sets forth a very realistic picture of the world and its history, holding the positive and the negative together in tension but setting forth grace, love, and justice—positive goals—as the primary context of all action. It presents a much more "secular" and realistic Christ than the simplistic improvisations to which we are prone.

One thing clear, however, is that one cannot adopt the cosmic government model for self-understanding and for communication without a creative attempt to deal with the fundamental and necessary engagement of all life in conflict for continuous adaptation to a changing environment. This conflict too often spills over into overt and often evil uses of force because of our sin and finitude. Hence, if God is Lord, he must also be Warrior. Unless he is, there is no ground for hope, for there is knowledge that human evil is not the last word, that the cards are stacked in behalf of the Kingdom of God, rather than the Kingdom of Satan.

In conclusion, I would like to summarize a conversation with a theologian about the substance of this chapter. This man is one to whom I have looked for guidance as a theological mentor since our thinking runs in parallel paths on most issues. Let me refer to him as "Mr. X." He was reared within a community of one of the historical "peace churches," a relationship which he still retains. I, on the other hand, was reared in a Presbyterian environment which has generally been more a part of the establishment in this country than its critic. Consequently, my basic question about the use of force immediately concerns its proper use, the restraints that must be employed, and some kind of casuistic analysis as to the relative weight of the positive and negative goals of the use of force in a given situation. Mr. X will indulge in much of the same kinds of consideration but in a context in which nonviolence is accepted as an absolute guide to action in conflict situations.

He also agrees with my basic thesis that God the Suzerain of cosmic government is the primary area in which the unifying threads are to be discovered in the vast variety of literature in both Testaments. He agrees that early Israel's institution of holy war was an agency which the Suzerain could be said to have used as a device for implanting Israel in Palestine, without conferring moral ⟦149⟧ value on the agent or the institution. He agrees that God as King, Judge, Warrior, Father, and Shepherd is accorded these roles, not as contradictory expressions, but as deriving from royal language which thus expresses the various activities of the Divine Monarch. He also agrees that the common attitude about that Monarch, as given expression in the quotation from Whitehead in Chapter 2, is a misunderstanding and inadequate presentation of what the Bible means.

Yet when we come to the New Testament, Mr. X says that Christ is the supreme and final revelation of the will of God for Christians. This means that nonviolence and love are always the ethical imperatives, and in situations of conflict they must always be employed in every situation. The reason we must retain the image of God the Lord and Suzerain is that only the ruling power of God actively at work in history can assure the ultimate success of the nonviolent imperative.

[handwritten: but why must judgment be violent?]

Yet since conflict itself must be viewed as both opportunity for change, growth, and broadening, on the one hand, and judgment for failure, on the other, why is it not true that the response of "love" is also two-edged? Love in situations of conflict obviously does not involve surrendering individual integrity, while concern for the needy and for justice to the oppressed may involve the active use of power in ways that cannot be described in every instance as nonviolent. Can it not be said that when the absolutes of the Kingdom-ethic are translated into absolutes for the present age, trouble always ensues? In the life we lead we are always involved in mental casuistry because two or more absolutes are in conflict in so many situations we have to face. Nonviolence can always be defended in a given instance as the best means to obtain a necessary and quite specific objective. Yet to absolutize it as the only form of action love can take in conflict would from my perspective and tradition be far too limiting for the flexibilities needed to reach necessary goals when we are faced with the principalities and powers of darkness.[13] In any event, such a position enables me to see far more [[150]] symbolic value in the New Testament's apocalyptic material than Mr. X has been able to appropriate. For him God the Warrior was necessary and proper in its time and setting, but it no longer can have positive use as an appropriate symbol in Christian ethics.

[handwritten: who is this, and why the dissembling?]

[handwritten: philosophically violence doesn't necessarily mean Force]

[handwritten: ⟶ see Millard Lind or Lois Barrett's The Way God Fights]

---

13. Needless to say, I am stating this in the most general of terms, and, if this means a position in general support of a given war, it would not lead me to a self-righteous support of a given "just war" theory as background for that war. Since all wars exemplify human evil in its most virulent expression, one can only set up guidelines as limits of coercive action, such as the Geneva conventions, etc.

GERHARD VON RAD

b. 1901   d. 1971

Eighth-Century Prophecy

Theological Synopsis

Gerhard von Rad was one of the twentieth-century giants of Old Testament scholarship. Along with Albrecht Alt and Martin Noth he was a pioneer in developing both form-critical and traditio-historical methodologies. Von Rad's influence has been felt by succeeding generations of Old Testament scholars on every continent.

He produced over two hundred publications; many of the major ones have been translated into several modern languages. His earliest publications, which began in 1929, dealt with the Hexateuch, especially Deuteronomy. The bulk of his scholarly publications (listed in Wolff 1971: 665–81) appeared in the post–World War II period, encompassing commentaries, books, essays, book reviews, dictionary articles, and the like, on historical, prophetic, and wisdom traditions of the Old Testament and the complexities related to historical-critical reconstructions.

Contrary to much present activity on Old Testament theology, von Rad published his monumental two-volume *Old Testament Theology* (German 1957, 1960) after about thirty years of teaching, research, and writing. Thus, in the tradition of the old masters his tomes are the result of mature reflection, summarizing as it were nearly a lifetime of traditio-historical research on the Old Testament.

The basis for understanding von Rad's Old Testament theology is the "recognition of its form-critical and traditio-historical presuppositions and foundations" (Knight 1973: 97–142, quotation at p. 124). In contrast to the traditional God–man–salvation scheme of writing an Old Testament theology, thoroughly opposed by Walther Eichrodt as early as the 1930s (who in turn developed the cross-section method based on a center or theme), von Rad creatively pioneered a traditio-historical Old Testament

120

theology that was diachronic in method and nature (Hasel 1982b: 69–75). He denied that the Old Testament had a "center" (*Mitte*). As to the philosophical perspective of von Rad, it has been shown that there is a close relationship between the philosophy of Hans Georg Gadamer and von Rad (Oeming 1985: 20–103).

Among the major issues raised by von Rad's Old Testament theology are the following: (1) the methodological starting point of an Old Testament theology; (2) the relationship between history and *Heilsgeschichte*; (3) the connection between faith and history; (4) the idea of *retelling* as "the most legitimate form of theological discourse on the Old Testament" (von Rad 1962: 121); (5) the nature of traditio-historical reconstruction; (6) the relationship between the Old Testament and New Testament; and (7) whether the Old Testament has a "center."

The stimulation provided by von Rad's reconstruction of Old Testament theology has led one prominent scholar to speak of Old Testament theology before and after von Rad (Schmidt 1972). While no one has yet followed his diachronic traditio-historical Old Testament theology in writing another such theology of the Old Testament, he has stimulated others (e.g., Hartmut Gese and Henri Clavier) to develop further the traditio-historical model. On the other hand, von Rad's Old Testament theology brought Theodorus C. Vriezen to rewrite completely his own Old Testament theology in a second English edition (1970), so as to counter von Rad on major points. More recently Brevard Childs used his "canonical approach" in full-fledged opposition to the traditio-historical approach for Old Testament theology (Childs 1986: 4–16). Certainly von Rad's Old Testament theology is unique; it has stimulated scores of scholars pro and con for decades.

Gerhard von Rad was born in 1901 into the home of Lutheran parents in Nuremberg, Germany. He was educated at the universities of Erlangen and Tübingen. His teaching career began in Leipzig in 1930, later transferring to the universities of Jena (1934–45) and, after the war, to Göttingen (1945–49). Finally, he was called to the University of Heidelberg where he taught from 1949 until his death in 1971. He wrote about himself, "My task as academic teacher was and is to learn to read and to teach how to read" (cited in Wolff 1971: 659).

G.F.H.

Writings by von Rad

1957   *Theologie des Alten Testaments.* Volume 1: *Die Theologie der geschichtlichen Überlieferungen Israels.* Munich: Kaiser.

1960   *Theologie des Alten Testaments.* Volume 2: *Die Theologie der prophetischen Überlieferungen Israels.* Munich: Kaiser.

1962   *Old Testament Theology.* Volume 1: *The Theology of Israel's Historical Traditions.* Translated by David M. G. Stalker. New York: Harper & Row/ Edinburgh: Oliver & Boyd.

1965   *Old Testament Theology.* Volume 2: *The Theology of Israel's Prophetic Traditions.* Translated by David M. G. Stalker. New York: Harper & Row/ Edinburgh: Oliver & Boyd.

1966   *The Problem of the Hexateuch and Other Essays.* Translated by E. W. T. Dickens. Edinburgh: Oliver & Boyd.

Writings about von Rad

Crenshaw, James L.

1978   *Gerhard von Rad.* Makers of the Modern Theological Mind. Waco: Word.

Davies, G. Henton

1970   Gerhard von Rad: *Old Testament Theology.* Pp. 63–89 in *Contemporary Old Testament Theologians.* Edited by Robert B. Laurin. Valley Forge, Pennsylvania: Judson.

Rendtorff, Rolf, and Klaus Koch (editors)

1961   *Studien zur Theologie der Alttestamentlichen Überlieferungen* (Gerhard von Rad Festschrift). Neukirchen: Neukirchener Verlag.

Spriggs, David G.

1974   *Two Old Testament Theologies: A Comparative Evaluation of the Contributions of Eichrodt and von Rad to Our Understanding of the Nature of Old Testament Theology.* Studies in Biblical Theology 2/30. London: SCM/ Naperville, Illinois: Allenson.

Wolff, Hans W. (editor)

1971   *Probleme biblischer Theologie: Gerhard von Rad zum 70. Geburtstag.* Munich: Kaiser.

Gerhard von Rad's
Approach to Old Testament Theology

Excerpted with permission from Gerhard von Rad, *Old Testament Theology* (New York: Harper & Row, 1962), vol. 1: pp. 105–12, 121–28.

Methodological Presuppositions

The Subject-Matter of a Theology of the Old Testament [[105]]

This belief in Jahweh, whose vitality we have described in brief outline, had very many ways of speaking about him. It never ceased speaking of his relationship to Israel, to the world, and to the nations, sometimes through the impersonal media of the great institutions (cult, law, court, etc.), sometimes however through the mouths of priests, prophets, kings, writers of narratives, historians, wise men, and Temple singers. Now, from this extremely abundant witness to Jahweh it would be perfectly possible, as has already been said, to draw a tolerably complete and, as far as comparative religion goes, a tolerably objective picture of the religion of the people of Israel, that is, of the special features in her conception of God, of the way in which Israel thought of God's relationship to the world, to the other nations and, not least, to herself; of the distinctiveness of what she said about sin and had to say about atonement and the salvation which comes from God. This has often been attempted, and needs no doubt to be attempted repeatedly. While Christian theologians may have played a decisive role in fostering this enterprise, the task in itself, however, falls within the province of the general study of religion; and it is therefore fitting that in recent times Orientalists, sociologists, ethnologists, ethnopsychologists, investigators of mythology, and others too have to a considerable extent co-operated in its accomplishment. The theological task proper to the Old Testament is not simply identical with this general religious one, and it is also much more restricted. The subject-matter which concerns the theologian is, of course, not the spiritual and religious world of Israel and the conditions of her soul in general, nor is it her world of faith, all of which can only be reconstructed by means of conclusions drawn from the documents: instead, it is simply Israel's own explicit assertions about Jahweh. The theologian must above all deal directly with the evidence, that is, with what Israel herself testified concerning Jahweh, and there is no doubt that in many cases he must go back to school again and learn to interrogate each [[106]] document, much more closely than has been done hitherto, as to its specific kerygmatic intention.[1] The tremendous differences evinced in the specific literary units will be dealt with later on in this volume. None the less we must anticipate, and mention briefly, what unites them all. They are far from comprehending equally all the wide range of statements about God, man, and the world which are conceivable and possible in the religious sphere. In this respect the theological radius of what Israel said about God is conspicuously restricted compared with the theologies of other nations—instead, the Old Testament writings confine themselves to representing Jahweh's relationship to Israel and the world in one aspect only, namely as a continuing divine activity in history. This implies that in principle Israel's faith is grounded in a theology of history. It regards itself as based upon historical acts, and as shaped and re-shaped by factors in which it saw the hand of Jahweh at work. The oracles of the prophets also speak of events, though there is the definite difference, than in general they stand in point of time not after, but prior to, the events to which they bear witness. Even where this reference to divine facts in history is not immediately apparent, as for example in some of the Psalms, it is, however, present by implication: and where it is actually absent, as for example in the Book of Job and Ecclesiastes, this very lack is closely connected with the grave affliction which is the theme of both these works.

Both at this point and in the sequel, we are of course thinking, when we speak of divine acts in history, of those which the faith of Israel regarded as such—that is, the call of the forefathers, the deliverance from Egypt, the bestowal of the land of Canaan, etc.—and not of the results of modern critical historical scholarship, to which Israel's faith was unrelated. This raises a difficult historical problem. In the last 150 years critical historical scholarship has constructed an impressively complete picture of the history of the people of Israel. As this process took shape, the old picture of Israel's history which the Church had derived and accepted from the Old Testament was bit by bit destroyed. Upon this process there is no going back, nor has it yet indeed come to an end. Critical historical scholarship regards it as impossible that the whole of Israel was present at Sinai, or that Israel crossed the Red Sea and achieved the Conquest *en bloc*—it holds the picture of Moses and his [[107]] leadership drawn in the traditions of the Book of Exodus to be as unhistorical as the function which the Deuteronomistic book of Judges ascribes to the "judges." On the other hand, it is just the most recent research into the Hexateuch that has pro-

---

1. It would be well to scrutinise from this point of view the chapter-headings in our translations or interpretations of the Bible, which often completely miss the intention that the specific narrators had in mind.

ceeded to deal with the extremely complicated origin of the Old Testament's picture of Jahweh's saving history with Israel. Scholars are even beginning to allow a scientific standing of its own to the picture of her history which Israel herself drew, and to take it as something existing *per se* which, in the way it has been sketched, has to be taken into account as a central subject in our theological evaluation. Research into the Hexateuch has established that this picture is based upon a few very old *motifs* around which subsequently have clustered in organic growth the immense number of freely circulating separate traditions.[2] The basic *motifs* were already pronouncedly confessional in character, and so were the separate traditions, in part very old, which made the canvas so very large. Thus the Hexateuch shows us a picture of the saving history that is drawn up by faith, and is accordingly confessional in character. The same holds true for the Deuteronomistic history's picture of the later history of Israel down to the exile. These two pictures of Israel's history lie before us—that of modern critical scholarship and that which the faith of Israel constructed—and for the present, we must reconcile ourselves to both of them. It would be stupid to dispute the right of the one or the other to exist. It would be superfluous to emphasise that each is the product of very different intellectual activities. The one is rational and "objective"; that is, with the aid of historical method and presupposing the similarity of all historical occurrence, it constructs a critical picture of the history as it really was in Israel.[3] It is clear that in the process this picture could not be restricted to a critical analysis of the external historical events: it was bound to proceed to a critical investigation of the picture of Israel's spiritual world, her religion, as well.

The other activity is confessional and personally involved in the events to the point of fervour. Did Israel ever speak of her history [[108]] other than with the emotion of glorification or regret? Historical investigation searches for a critically assured minimum—the kerygmatic picture tends towards a theological maximum.[4] The fact that these two views of Israel's history are so divergent is one of the most serious burdens imposed today upon Biblical scholarship. No doubt historical investigation has a great deal that is true to say about the growth of this picture of the history which

---

2. M. Noth, *Pentateuch*.

3. "The historical method, once it is applied to biblical science . . . is a leaven which transforms everything and finally explodes the whole form of theological methods." "The means by which criticism is at all possible is the application of analogy. . . . But the omnicompetence of analogy implies that all historical events are identical in principle." E. Tröltsch, *Über historische und dogmatische Methode*, Tübingen 1889 (*Gesammelte Schriften*, vol. II, pp. 729ff.).

4. N. A. Dahl, *Der historische Jesus als geschichtswissenschaftliches und theologisches Problem*, *Kerygma und Dogma*, Göttingen 1955, p. 119.

the faith of Israel painted: but the phenomenon of the faith itself, which speaks now of salvation, now of judgment, is beyond its power to explain.

It would not do, however, simply to explain the one picture as historical and the other as unhistorical. The kerygmatic picture too (and this even at the points where it diverges so widely from our historical picture) is founded in the actual history and has not been invented. The means by which this historical experience is made relevant for the time, the way in which it is mirrored forth in a variety of pictures, and in sagas in type form, are those adapted to the possibilities of expression of an ancient people. But it would be a very hasty conclusion if critical historical scholarship were minded to be itself taken as the only way into the history of Israel, and if it denied to what Israel reports in, say, her sagas a foundation in the "real" history. In some respects, this foundation is an even deeper one. Only, in these traditional materials the historic and factual can no longer be detached from the spiritualising interpretation which pervades them all.

We are not here concerned with the philosophical presuppositions of objective, rational, and critical scholarship, or the methods with which it works. On the other hand, the particular way in which Israel's faith presented history is still far from being adequately elucidated. Admittedly, we are acquainted with the various basic historical and theological ideas of the Jahwist, or of the Deuteronomist's history, or the Chronicler's. But we are much less clear about the mode of presentation of the smaller narrative units, although it is in fact the mass of these which now gives characteristic stamp to those great compilations. The way in which faith perceives things has its own peculiarities, and it is perhaps therefore possible to point to some constantly recurring features, certain "patterns," which are characteristic of a confessional presentation, particularly of early historical experiences. In this connexion a very common datum would have to [[109]] be taken into consideration by the theologian as well as by others—the fact that a great part of even the historical traditions of Israel has to be regarded as poetry, that is, as the product of explicit artistic intentions. But poetry—especially with peoples of antiquity—is much more than an aesthetic pastime: rather is there in it a penetrating desire for knowledge directed towards the data presented by the historical and natural environment.[5] Historical poetry was the form in which Israel, like other peoples, made sure of historical facts, that is, of their location and their significance. In those times poetry was, as a rule, the one possible form for expressing special basic insights. It was not just there along with prose as something one might elect to use—a more elevated form of discourse as it were then—but

5. The idea of poetry as an "organ for the understanding of life" goes back to Dilthey. Cf. P. Böckmann, *Formgeschichte der deutschen Dichtung*, Hamburg 1949, pp. 17ff.

poetry alone enabled a people to express experiences met with in the course of their history in such a way as to make the past become absolutely present. In the case of legend, we now know that we must reckon with this coefficient of interpretation. But in thinking of the literary stories, which extend from the Hexateuch to 2 Kings, and which we must also regard to begin with as poetry, we have to learn to grasp this coefficient more clearly in its special features in any given story.[6] As far as I can see, Israel only finally went over to the prosaic and scientific presentation of her history with the Deuteronomistic history. Thus, right down to the sixth century, she was unable to dispense with poetry in drafting history, for the Succession Document or the history of Jehu's revolution are poetic presentations, and are indeed the acme of poetic perfection. No wonder that in Israel, and in her alone, these historical narratives could develop so profusely and in such perfection—the faith needed them. On the other hand, there is no mistaking that the effort to interpret historical events in this poetic-theological guise imposes a limit upon the possibilities of our understanding such narratives. The understanding of lists and annals is independent of the presuppositions of faith. But these poetic stories appeal for assent; they address those who are prepared to ask questions and receive answers along like lines, that is, those who credit Jahweh with great acts in history.

If some stories, chiefly older ones bordering upon legend, represent ⟦110⟧ events which happened to a group as connected with an individual, this is doubtless mainly a poetic proceeding. They are removed from the realm of political history and projected into the wholly personal world of an individual. This usage which personalises and at the same time symbolises can be plainly seen in the stories about Ham and Canaan (Gen 9:25), and in those about Ishmael or Judah (Gen 16:12, 38:1). But exegesis probably must take still greater account of it in the patriarchal stories dealing with Abraham and Jacob. To symbolise things in a single person in this way is in itself not at all peculiar to Israel. But since it also crops up in stories which are markedly minted by faith, we must make ourselves familiar with it. In every case, through this transference into a personal picture these stories have been given an enormous degree of intensity, for events or experiences of very different times have been pulled together as a single episode in an individual's life. Thus, for our historical and critical understanding, stories such as these have from the very start only an indirect relationship with historical reality, while their relation to what was believed by Israel is much more direct. We have further to consider that in their presentation of religious material the peoples of antiquity were not

---

6. A few more specific references are to be found in G. von Rad, *Der Heilige Krieg im alten Israel*, pp. 43ff.

aware of the law of historical exclusiveness, according to which a certain event or a certain experience can be attached only to a single definite point in history. In particular, events bearing a saving character retained for all posterity, and in that posterity's eyes, a contemporaneousness which it is hard for us to appreciate.[7] The upshot is that, in what they present, the later story-tellers blatantly make capital of experiences which, although they are invariably brought in on the basis of the ancient event in question, still reach forward into the story-teller's own day. It is only from this standpoint that the story of Jacob's struggle (Gen 32:22f.), or the story of Balaam (Numbers 22–24), or the thrice-repeated story of the endangering of the ancestress of the race (Gen 12:10ff., 20:1ff., 26:5ff.) can be interpreted as they should. What is historical here? Certainly some definite but very elusive particular event which stands at the primal obscure origin of the tradition in question—but what is also historical is the [[111]] experience that Jahweh turns the enemy's curse into blessing, and that he safeguards the promise in spite of all failure on the part of its recipient, etc. Israel did not dream up this confidence, but came to it on the basis of rich and wide experience, of her history in fact; and, symbolising it in a person, she illustrated it in a story. This of course occasions another and rather severe clash with our critical way of thinking about history. Did the historical Balaam actually curse, or did his mouth really utter blessings? We may assume that it was only in the story that that which was given to Israel's faith became presented as a visible miracle. This process of glorification is quite clear in many of the stories about the Conquest—the events are depicted with a splendour and a strong element of the miraculous which are impossible to square with older strands in the report.[8] The later story-tellers are so zealous for Jahweh and his saving work that they overstep the limits of exact historiography and depict the event in a magnificence far transcending what it was in reality.[9] These are texts which contain an implicit eschatological element, since they anticipate a _Gloria_ of God's saving action not yet granted to men.

---

7. L. Köhler, _Hebrew Man_, trans. P. R. Ackroyd, London 1956, p. 39. This cannot of course be taken as meaning that "the conception of history itself hardly plays any noticeable part" for Israel. These words are incomprehensible in face of the fact that Israel's faith gave itself sanction in a series of ever vaster theological sketches of her history.

8. It is well known that an older and less miraculous picture of the events is given in Judg 1:1ff. than in the larger complex in Joshua 1–9.

9. "Poetry is not the imitation of a reality which already exists in the same quality prior to it . . . ; the aesthetic faculty is a creative power for the production of a concept which transcends reality and is not present in any abstract thinking, or indeed in any way of contemplating the world." W. Dilthey, _Gesammelte Schriften_, Leipzig 1914–18, vol. VI, p. 116. In this "production," the chief force in Israel in forming tradition was Jahwism.

In the Old Testament it is thus this world made up of testimonies that is above all the subject of a theology of the Old Testament. The subject cannot be a systematically ordered "world of the faith" of Israel or of the really overwhelming vitality and creative productivity of Jahwism, for the world of faith is not the subject of these testimonies which Israel raised to Jahweh's action in history. Never, in these testimonies about history, did Israel point to her own faith, but to Jahweh. Faith undoubtedly finds very clear expression in them; but as a subject it lies concealed, and can often only be grasped by means of a variety of inferences which are often psychological and on that account problematical. In a word, the faith is not the subject of Israel's confessional utterances, but only its vehicle, its mouthpiece. And even less can the "history" of this world of faith by the subject of the theology of the Old Testament. Admittedly, the presentation ⟦112⟧ of the "ideas, thought, and concepts of the Old Testament which are important for theology" will always form part of the task of Old Testament theology.[10] But is this all that there is to it? Would a history confined to this leave room for discussion for example of the saving acts of grace, on which the faith of Israel regarded itself as based, and with reference to which it lived its life? A world of religious concepts later systematically arranged is of course an abstraction, for such a thing never existed in Israel in so complete and universal a way. So too the idea of a "religion of Israel," that is, the idea of the faith as an entity, appears more problematical still as a result of the investigation of the history of tradition in our own time. There were up and down the land many traditions which little by little combined into ever larger complexes of tradition. Theologically, these accumulations were in a state of constant flux. Religious thought cannot be separated out from these traditions and represented thus in abstract. If we divorced Israel's confessional utterances from the divine acts in history which they so passionately embrace, what a bloodless ghost we would be left with! If, however, we put Israel's picture of her history in the forefront of our theological consideration, we encounter what appropriately is the most essential subject of a theology of the Old Testament, the living word of Jahweh coming on and on to Israel for ever, and this in the message uttered by his mighty acts. It was a message so living and actual for each moment that it accompanied her on her journey through time, interpreting itself afresh to every generation, and informing every generation what it had to do.

· ·

The Oldest Pictures of the Saving History ⟦121⟧

Even the earliest avowals to Jahweh were historically determined, that is, they connect the name of this God with some statement about an action in

10. Köhler, *Theology*, p. 1.

history. Jahweh, "who brought Israel out of Egypt," is probably the earliest and at the same time the most widely used of these confessional formulae.[11] Others are such as designate Jahweh as the one who called the patriarchs and promised them the land, etc. Alongside these brief formulae, which are content with a minimum of historical subject-matter—as a species they are generally cultic invocations—there were very certainly soon ranged confessional summaries of the saving history, covering by now a fairly extensive span of the divine action in history.[12] Among these the most important is [[122]] the Credo in Deut 26:5–9, which bears all the marks of great antiquity:

> A wandering Aramean was my father; he went down with a few people into Egypt and there he became a nation, great, mighty, and populous. But the Egyptians treated us harshly, they afflicted us, and laid hard toil upon us. Then we cried to Jahweh, the God of our fathers, and Jahweh heard us, and saw our affliction, our toil, and oppression. And Jahweh brought us out of Egypt with a mighty hand and an outstretched arm, with great terror, with signs and wonders, and brought us to this place and gave us this land, a land flowing with milk and honey.

These words are not, of course, a prayer—there is no invocation or petition—they are out and out a confession of faith. They recapitulate the main events in the saving history from the time of the patriarchs (by the Aramean, Jacob is meant) down to the conquest, and they do this with close concentration on the objective historical facts. As in the Apostles' Creed, there is no reference at all to promulgated revelations, promises, or teaching, and still less any consideration of the attitude which Israel on her side took towards this history with God. The exalted mood which lies behind this recitation is merely that of a disciplined celebration of the divine acts, and in the process a note was struck which henceforward was to remain the predominant one in Israel's religious life. Israel was always better at glorifying and extolling God than at theological reflexion.[13] In spite of

11. The content of the old confessional formulae and the problem of their connexion is dealt with by Noth, *Pentateuch*, pp. 48ff.

12. In no circumstances are these historical summaries to be judged as later than those short historical epicleses, as for example in the sense of an organic development as their subsequent combination, for both are very different in respect of species and each could have its life in its own place contemporaneously.

13. The question of the age of this Credo in ancient Israel's life is fairly unimportant for us here. Noth emphasises the original cultic independence of the various themes out of which it is composed (deliverance from Egypt, the promise to the patriarchs, guidance in the wilderness, etc.), *Pentateuch*, pp. 48ff. The literary material seems to justify him, for in the majority of cases the "themes" seem to be independent. Nevertheless these single themes themselves always presuppose an idea of the whole. Guidance in the wilderness cannot be thought of apart from the deliverance from Egypt and vice versa. Again, the promise to the patriarchs, after it

being cast in the form of words spoken by God, the retrospect of the history given in Josh 24:2ff. ⟦123⟧ is closely allied to Deut 26:5ff. Admittedly, it goes into considerably greater detail in the presentation of the saving history; but the two are alike in confining themselves to the objective facts. And, in particular, in Joshua too the starting-point is the period of the patriarchs while the end-point is Israel's entry into the promised land. Some of the psalms make it perfectly clear that, originally, this span of time, and this alone, was regarded as the time of the saving history proper. Psalm 136 is certainly a much later litany, but apart from the fact that it starts with the creation, it keeps to the same canonical pattern of the saving history. The same is true of Psalm 105, which also is certainly not old. Psalm 68 does indeed go beyond the conquest—down into the period of the monarchy. But just in so doing it serves as a proof of our thesis. While it is able to depict Israel's early period down to the conquest with a real wealth of concrete historical data (vss. 12–55), its presentation after vs. 50—that is, exactly at the point where the canonical pattern of the saving history leaves it in the lurch—is jejune and slight. (Still, it does mention the loss of Shiloh and the election of David and Zion.) Even stranger is the disproportion in the picture of the saving history in Judith 5:6ff. Its picture of the conquest takes up ten verses, but for the whole period from then down to 586 the narrator can only report trite generalities concerning constant apostasy. He jumps a span of more than 600 years in two verses! These historical summaries in hymn form are still thoroughly confessional in kind. They are not products of a national or even a secular view of history, but clearly take their stand on that old canonical picture of the saving history, the pattern of which was fixed long ago for all time.[14] They are of course no longer confessions in the strict sense of Deuteronomy 26. Concentration on the facts alone has been abandoned. A tendency towards epic elaboration, and also towards reflexion, is apparent: more than anything else, contrasting with the chain of the divine saving acts, the infidelity and disobedience of Israel now increasingly become objects of importance in the presentation. If we imagine a considerably greater advance still in this

---

passed over from the cultic communities of the people belonging to Abraham and Jacob to Israel, was immediately referred to the deliverance from Egypt, etc. At the same time, regarding the patriarchal tradition, there is much to be said for the assumption that the Credo itself presupposes the combination of an originally independent set of traditions with the central Exodus tradition. Even afterwards the two traditions, of the Exodus and of the patriarchs, are found side by side in marked independence, and clearly discriminated in references to them. K. Galling, *Die Erwählungstraditionen Israels,* Bei⟦hefte zur⟧ Z. A. W. No. 48, Giessen 1928.

14. On the reappearance of the saving history in the Psalms cf. A. Lauha, "Die Geschichtsmotive in den alttestamentlichen Psalmen," in *Annales Academiae Scientiarum Fennicae,* Helsinki 1945.

process of connecting a narrative to the old pattern and widening its theological range by means of all kinds of traditional material, then we find
ourselves face to face with the work of the Jahwist or the Elohist. Starting
as the latter does [[124]] only with the history of the patriarchs (Genesis
15), he comes closer to the old canonical pattern of salvation. But both
with the Jahwist and the Priestly Document too, their allegiance to, and indeed their rootedness in, the old confessional tradition is beyond doubt.
Once this process of giving a narrative connexion to the old plan and widening its scope was given free play, it is no wonder that the plan was also
supplemented by theological traditions originally alien to it. The most important of these additions, of which not even a hint is to be found in the
old transmitted pattern, is the prefixing to it of an account of the creation
and the primeval history, and the insertion of the Sinai pericope, which as
a block of tradition has a completely different derivation.[15] As far as form
goes, this expansion of the ancient Credo by the Jahwist and the Elohist
led to the creation of an extremely involved and highly detailed presentation of the history. Finally, the subsequent combination of the three great
works J, E, and P produced a literary structure of the history, whose dis-
proportions can only cause astonishment to anyone who looks for an artistic harmony and an inner balancing of these tremendous masses of
material. There is in fact much to be learned from a comparison of how
the story of Jacob or Moses is presented with that of the Homeric Odys-
seus, for in both cases the pictures are due to the coalescence of originally
independent traditions. The main difference lies in the fact that in the
rendering of her story Israel handled the old material much less freely
than the Greeks. A later age could not venture to recast the old legends in
respect of theme and thought and to combine them so as to give rise to
what was in fact a new history complete in itself. They were bound in a
much more conservative way to what had come down to them, and especially to the forms in which they had received it—that is, they handled it
much more as if it were a document. The result of this for the theological
elaboration of the old traditions upon which J, E, and P were indeed in-
tensively engaged, was a completely different form of theological handling
of the tradition. If the possibility of bringing the several traditions into inner unity with one another and of balancing them as they were amalgamated, was ruled out, it was nevertheless still possible to insert expressly
directive passages at important nodal points in the events. And this possi-

15. The free variations on the old Credo do not mention the events at Sinai either. The
first mention is in Neh 9:6ff. This was then the first place where the picture which J and E expanded made an impression.

bility was in fact used again and ⟦125⟧ again.[16] But the chief method employed in the theological unfolding of the tradition was a different one still: it was much more indirect, for it consisted in the way in which separate pieces of material were connected. The lay-out of the primeval history, the story of Abraham, the relationship of the period of the patriarchs to that of Joshua, etc., is arranged in such a way that quite definite theological tensions, which the great collector intended, arise out of the sequence of the material itself. This indirect theological way of speaking through the medium of the traditional material and its arrangement makes clear once more that remarkable preponderance of the matter-of-fact historical over the theological which is so characteristic of the witness of Israel. Even in its final form, the Hexateuch retained a confessional stamp, though not in that restrained form of celebrating the divine deeds and them alone which is found in the old Credo; for as well as dealing with them, this historical work also deals with the institution of offices and rites, and with men standing up to the test, and still more with failure and rebellion. If we say a confessional stamp, this means that the later Israel saw in the historical witness of the Hexateuch something that was typical for the people of God, and that what was there related remained of immediate concern for every subsequent generation, because of a latent contemporaneousness in it.

Meanwhile, however, something of decisive importance for the faith of Israel had come about. As early as the time when the theological elaboration of the old Credo was still at its beginnings, Jahweh had further dealings with Israel. The history with God did not come to a standstill. Jahweh had raised up charismatic military leaders to protect Israel, he had chosen Zion and established the throne of David for all time, Israel had become disobedient, and so he had sent prophets, and finally he repudiated Israel in the twofold judgments of 722 and 587. The realisation that with David something new began had certainly come to life fairly soon in Israel. This is without any doubt itself the background of the great narrative complex describing "David's rise to power" and in particular of the Succession Document, which are so ⟦126⟧ important theologically.[17] But Israel did not arrive at a clear consciousness of this new epoch in her history with Jahweh as a whole until it had, in such a fearful way, already come to its end in the exile. Then, with the help of a great mass of already

16. Gen 12:1–9, for instance, is such a unit in the story of Abraham lying outwith the saga material handed on. The prologue to the Flood in the primeval history of J (Gen 6:5–8) is to be judged in the same way. In the realm of the story of Jacob the prayer in Gen 32:10ff. [9ff.] would call for mention, and in that of the Deuteronomistic histories the freely composed discourses in Joshua 23; 1 Samuel 12; 1 Kings 8.

17. For the history of David's rise to power see Noth, *Überl. Studien*, p. 61. For the history of the succession to David see L. Rost, *Thronnachfolge*, pp. 82ff.

available historical material, the great theological history which we call the Deuteronomist's came into being. It carried the thread of the history with God down from the conquest to the catastrophe of the exile, and presented and interpreted this period up to Israel's final shipwreck from quite definite and very individual theological points of view. The second stage in Israel's history with Jahweh was clearly not simply conceived of as the unilinear prolongation of the first; from the theological point of view, it ran its course under essentially different presuppositions. As concerns the good gifts of salvation promised by Jahweh, it does not go beyond the old one—the good gift of the land was always the ultimate for Israel, which nothing could surpass and which could only be won or forfeited. But this era stands rather under the sign of the law of judgment, and accordingly the question as to how Israel stood up to the test thrusts itself more and more into the foreground: indeed it becomes decisive for Israel for life and death before Jahweh. And the sum-total of this Deuteronomistic historical work is that Israel, possessed as she already was of all the good gifts of salvation, chose death. It is to be noticed that the decision about this termination of her monarchical period was thus in the Deuteronomist put in the hands of Israel. In the "canonical" saving history, from the patriarchs down to the entry into Canaan, it was Jahweh who made the truth of the promise good in face of all the failure of Israel; and he did not let any part of his great plan in history, least of all the final part, be taken out of his own hands. But in the Deuteronomist's history Jahweh allowed Israel to make the decision.

The exile was a period devoid of saving history. The Deuteronomistic historical work gave an authoritative interpretation of the riddle of the standstill in the divine history with Israel: the catastrophes were the well-merited judgment upon the continued apostasy to the Canaanite cult of Baal. At the time, who could know whether this judgment was final or only temporary? In keeping with Israel's whole religious attitude, this question could in fact be answered only by Jahweh's beginning to act anew in history. As it happened, about 550, through ⟦127⟧ Cyrus, history began to move very mightily in the immediate surroundings of the exiles. But at this point Israel's witness parts company with itself. After Babylon had fallen, and the worship in the Temple had been reconstituted in Jerusalem, and later, when even a large section of the exiles had returned home, Israel could only see in these events a fresh act of grace; and, as the historical summaries in Neh 9:6ff. and Judith 5:5ff. show, she carried the thread of history with God which had been so abruptly snapped, down with praise and thanksgiving into the present time. This theological link with the pre-exilic history with God is established by means of elaborate argumentation, especially in the Chronicler's history, the main concern of which is to legitimate the cultic restoration in the post-exilic period on the basis of a legacy of David's which had not been brought into effect until his time. But the prophets Jeremiah, Ezekiel, Zechariah, and, more than anyone else, Deutero-Isaiah, placed a very different interpretation upon the breaking-off of the history with God up to then. The tenor of their message is this: the old is done away with; now Jahweh will bring about something completely new, a new Exodus, a new covenant, a new Moses. Israel's old confession of faith is present now only as something which is done away with, since Jahweh is about to act along the lines of his earlier saving acts in an even more splendid way.[18]

Now this sequence given by the great pictures of the history, with their very different conceptions of the progress of the saving history, prescribes the way in which we too have to unfold the witness of the Old Testament. What other starting-point can we take than the colossal theological structure which Israel raised on the foundation of her oldest confession of Jahweh? We have therefore first to attempt to sketch the basic traits of a theology of the Hexateuch. This must be followed by a description of the new experience which Israel gained on her journey from the conquest to the disasters at the end of the period of the monarchy; for a description of the outcome of this second phase of the history with God was, of course, the task which the Deuteronomistic writer imposed on himself. Following on that, we shall finally have to deal with the great interpretation which Israel later drew up in the Chronicler's history of the final phase of her history with God, the period from David to Nehemiah. Then, in a second part, we will have to speak about the situation in which Israel felt herself to be placed as a result of this revelation and of God's activity in ⟦128⟧ history, and about her praises, her justice, her trials, and her wisdom. What was distinctive in the response which Israel made to the revelation of Jahweh will therefore be dealt with there.

The most accurate test of the starting-point and arrangement of a theology of the Old Testament is, however, the phenomenon of prophecy. At what point has it to be dealt with, and in what connexion? If we are resolved on giving a systematic and connected presentation of the religious ideas, then we shall have occasion to speak about prophecy throughout— in dealing with the holiness of Jahweh, the beliefs about creation, the idea of the covenant, etc. But in so doing would we do justice to its message? We should also, however, do it an injustice if we reserved treatment of it for a special section dealing with Israel's thought about her own and the nations' future.[19] This is not the way to bring the message of the prophets

---

18. Especially Isa 43:16–20; Jer 21:31ff., and also Hos 2:16ff.

19. So for example E. Jacob in his *Theology of the Old Testament*, London 1958.

into organic connexion with the religious ideas of Israel. However over-
poweringly diverse it may be, it nevertheless has its starting-point in the
conviction that Israel's previous history with Jahweh has come to an end,
and that he will start something new with her. The prophets seek to convince their contemporaries that for them the hitherto existing saving ordinances have lost their worth, and that, if Israel is to be saved, she must
move in faith into a new saving activity of Jahweh, one which is only to
come in the future. But this conviction of theirs, that what has existed till
now is broken off, places them basically outside the saving history as it had
been understood up to then by Israel. The prophets' message had its
centre and its bewildering dynamic effect in the fact that it smashed in
pieces Israel's existence with God up to the present, and rang up the curtain of history for a new action on his part with her. So prophecy needs
separate treatment in a theology of the Old Testament.

Synopsis of von Rad's *Old Testament Theology* (1962, 1965)

Gerhard von Rad
On the New Element
in Eighth-Century Prophecy[1]

Excerpted with permission from Gerhard von Rad, *Old Testament Theology* (New York: Harper & Row, 1965), vol. 2: pp. 176–80, 183–87.

[[176]] Careful consideration of the distinctive features in the prophecies of Amos, Hosea, Isaiah, and Micah might well lead us to the conclusion that all comparisons are dangerous, because once we have discovered the radical differences between them it is difficult to avoid the temptation of going on and smoothing these out. What, in actual fact, do Hosea and Isaiah have in common? Hosea came from the farming world of the Northern Kingdom, he was opposed to everything that in his day was implied by the word "king"; of all the prophets he was the most deeply involved in patriarchal concepts deriving from the cult, and he paid particular attention to problems in the sacral sphere and to cultic irregularities. Isaiah was a townsman, brought up in a *polis* tradition, and a sharp-sighted observer of world politics; he explained all the changes in the political kaleidoscope as part of Jahweh's rational scheme, he placed his confidence in the divinely guaranteed protection of the city, and he looked for a king who would bring peace and righteousness. Much the same can be said of Amos and Micah. Amos was apparently quite unmoved by Hosea's main topic, the threat of Jahwism from the Canaanite worship of Baal; and he is also different from Isaiah, for he does not inveigh against mistaken policies, against armaments and alliances. Finally, there is absolutely no bridge between Micah and the hopes cherished concerning Zion by Isaiah, his fellow-countryman and contemporary; Micah in fact expected Zion to be blotted out of the pages of history. Even the kind of prophetic office surprisingly discovered in the state documents of Mari, which makes it clear that the prophet could threaten even the king in God's name, does not give us any standpoint from which to summarise and categorise the prophetic role. If their close connexion with the king and their interest in political and military affairs is a particular characteristic of the "prophets" of Mari, then Israel has comparable figures not only in Isaiah, but in a whole series of prophets beginning with Ahijah of Shiloh, including Micaiah ben Imlah and [[177]] Elijah, and going down to Jeremiah.[2] On the other

1. Eichrodt, *Theology*, pp. 345–53; Vriezen, *Outline*, pp. 62–6.

2. S. Herrmann, *Die Ursprünge der prophetischen Heilserwartung im Alten Testament*, Leipzig Dissertation 1957, pp. 65ff., 73ff.

137

hand, it is impossible to bring Amos into this category. Nevertheless, in spite of all these great differences, there is a great deal of common matter which links the eighth-century prophets to one another; for their religious ideas led them to an absolutely common conviction, one so novel and revolutionary when compared with all their inherited beliefs, that it makes the differences, considerable as these are, seem almost trivial and peripheral. We shall now make another attempt to find out which element in the prophets' teaching struck their contemporaries as being a departure from the religious standards of the time.

To begin with a very simple statement: these men were set apart from their contemporaries and they were very lonely. Their call gave them a unique knowledge of Jahweh and of his designs for Israel. We have already seen how, apparently to a much greater degree than any of their contemporaries, they are deeply rooted in the religious traditions of their nation; indeed, their whole preaching might almost be described as a unique dialogue with the tradition by means of which the latter was made to speak to their own day. Yet the very way in which they understood it and brought it to life again is the measure of their difference from all the contemporary religious heritage of their nation. When Amos said that Jahweh presided over the migration of the Philistines and the Syrians (Amos 9:7), he was departing pretty radically from the belief of his time. This novel and to some extent revolutionary way of taking the old traditions was not, however, the result of careful study or of slowly maturing conviction; rather, these prophets were all agreed that it was Jahweh who enlightened them and led them on from one insight to another. The reason for their isolation was therefore this—as they listened to and obeyed a word and commission of Jahweh which came to them alone and which could not be transferred to anyone else, these men became individuals, persons.[3] They could say "I" in a way never before heard in Israel. At the same time, it has become apparent that the "I" of which these men were allowed to become conscious was very different from our present-day concept of personality. For first of all, this process of becoming a person was marked by many strange experiences of compulsion, and one at least of its characteristics—we have only to think of the "be still" [[178]] in Isaiah's demand for faith—was passively to contemplate and make room for the divine action.[4] Yet, at the same time, this opened up freedom upon freedom for the prophet. He could even break out into an "exultation of the spirit" about this, as Micah once did when, as his *charisma* welled up

---

3. See [[von Rad 1965:]] pp. 76f. Eichrodt, *Theology,* p. 343.
4. Eichrodt, *Theology,* p. 357.

gloriously within him, he became conscious of his difference from other people:

> But as for me, I am filled with power,
> [with the spirit of Jahweh],
> with justice and might,
> to declare to Jacob his transgression,
> and to Israel his sin.   (Mic 3:8)

There is a very direct reflexion of the prophets' attainment of personal identity and of their religious uniqueness in their style, the way in which they speak of God and of the things of God. During centuries of reverent speech Israel had created a language of the cult, and had devised a conventional phraseology for speaking about God; yet there were times when he might also be spoken of in the way these prophets loved to do—in monstrous similes, with an apparent complete absence of any feeling for dignity or propriety.[5] These were *ad hoc* inspirations, the provocative inventions of a single person, whose radical quality and extreme boldness was only justified by the uniqueness of a particular situation and the frame of mind of the people who listened to them.

Even if we knew still less than we in fact do of the way in which the concepts of Jahwism were still a living force at the shrines and among the broad mass of the people at the time when these prophets were active, one thing could yet be said for certain—the new feature in their preaching, and the one which shocked their hearers, was the message that Jahweh was summoning Israel before his judgment seat, and that he had in fact already pronounced sentence upon her: "The end has come upon my people Israel" (Amos 8:2). The question has recently been asked whether the prophets did not base even these pronouncements of judgment on older tradition. Were there ceremonies [[179]] in the cult at which Jahweh appeared as his people's accuser?[6] So far nothing definite has materialised; and an answer to this question would not in any way be a complete answer to the other question: why did the prophets proclaim this message? Moreover, the devastating force and finality of the prophetic pronouncement of judgment can never have had a cultic antecedent, for it envisaged the end of all cult itself.   *why is this logical?*

---

5. Jahweh, the barber (Isa 7:20), the ulcer in Israel's body (Hos 5:12), the unsuccessful lover (Isa 5:1ff.); see also [[von Rad 1965:]] p. 375.

6. So E. Würthwein, "Der Ursprung der prophetischen Gerichtsrede," in *Z. Th. K.*, 49 (1952), pp. 1ff.; in a different way F. Hesse, "Wurzelt die prophetische Gerichtsrede im israeitischen Kult?" in *Z. A. W.*, 64 (1953), pp. 45ff.

For the proper understanding of what we have called this completely
new note in the prophetic preaching, we have not least to remember the
changing political situation, Assyria's increasingly obvious and steady advance towards Palestine. When in an almost stereotyped fashion Amos suggests that Jahweh's judgment will take the form of exile, this quite clearly
reflects how much the Assyrians occupied his thoughts. The prophets are,
however, obviously motivated not merely by one factor but by several. Let
us simply say that these men spoke of the divine wrath as a fact, and designated as its proper object their contemporaries' whole way of life, their social and economic attitudes, their political behaviour and, in particular,
their cultic practice. At all events, the favourite way of putting it, that this
is simply the emergence of new religious ideas, and as such only a new understanding of the relationship between God and Man, does not square
with the fact that in this matter the prophets most decidedly took as their
starting-point the old traditions of Jahwism. It was these that formed the
foundation of their attack, and time and again the prophets took them as
the basis of arguments with their audiences. Thus, as far as the old Jahwistic tradition was concerned, the prophets and their hearers were on
common ground: but they differed in their interpretation of these traditions, which the prophets believed were far from ensuring Israel's salvation. The classic expression of this aspect of prophecy are Amos's words—
her very election made the threat to Israel all the greater (Amos 3:1f.)!
This is therefore the first occasion in Israel when "law" in the proper sense
of the term was preached.[7] This is most apparent in the prophets' castiga-
tions of their fellow-countrymen for their anti-social behaviour, their com-
mercial sharp-practice. Here they do not in any sense regard themselves as
the revolutionary mouthpiece of one social group. Time and again we can
see them [[180]] applying provisions of the old divine law to the situation.[8]
Isaiah uses much the same procedure when he measures the behaviour of
the people of Jerusalem against the Zion tradition, and looks on armaments or security sought for in alliances as a rejection of the divine help. It
is also used by Hosea when he takes the saving gift of the land, which Israel still completely failed to understand, as his starting-point, and uses it
to show up the enormity of her faithlessness and ingratitude. Jahweh was
known to be the judge of sinners in early Israel also; and early Israel was
equally aware that a man's sin is more than the sum total of his several acts
(Genesis 3). Yet, the prophets' zeal in laying bare man's innate tendency
to oppose God, their endeavour to comprehend Israel's conduct in its

---

7. See [[von Rad 1962:]] pp. 195ff.; see [[von Rad 1965:]] pp. 395ff.

8. See [[von Rad 1965:]] pp. 135f. H.- J. Kraus, "Die prophetische Botschaft gegen das so-
ziale Unrechts Israels," in *Ev. Th.*, 15 (1955), pp. 295ff.

entirety, and to bring out what, all historical contingency apart, might be taken as typical of that conduct—this was something new, especially since its purpose was to give reasons for Jahweh's judgment. Thus, for example, Hosea included and discussed the whole story of the relationship between God and his people in his poem on Israel's failure to understand that the blessings of the soil of Canaan were gifts from Jahweh. This was a great intellectual achievement. The prophets' chief concern was not, of course, to summarise human conduct under the most general concepts possible by the method of abstraction, though this does sometimes happen;[9] they reached their goal in a different way. For while they seem to be describing only a particular failure of a particular group of men in a particular situation, they have really depicted, by their use of a few characteristic traits, something that was typical of Israel's general attitude to God.[10]

. . . .

[[183]] We may therefore describe the characteristic feature of the prophetic view of history as follows: not only does it recognise most clearly Jahweh's designs and intentions in history, it also sees the various historical forces involved in quite a different light from other people. The great powers which occupied the centre of the political stage did [[184]] not blind the prophets to God; these empires shrivel up almost into nothingness before Jahweh's all-pervasive power. It is the "I" spoken by Jahweh that pervades the historical field to its utmost limits. It is moving to see how Isaiah and his subjective certainty about his own view of history came into collision—a proof of its complete undogmatic flexibility and openness. As Assyria advanced, the interpretation he had put upon her as an instrument of punishment in the hands of Jahweh proved to be inadequate, or at least partial. The way in which she exterminated nations and the danger that she would treat Jerusalem and Judah in the same way gave rise to a question: did she not intend also to overrun Zion? Nevertheless, Isaiah was still able to interpret Jahweh's design; he explained the difficulty by saying that the Assyrians were exceeding the task assigned to them. The scope of their commission was merely to chastise, not to annihilate (Isa 10:5–7). This change in Isaiah's views is a further remarkable confirmation of the prophets' claim to be able to see history in its relation to God clearly and with perfect understanding. In Isaiah's view history can be analysed into the

9. Here one might think, for example, of Isaiah's characteristic reproach of pride (גבהות אדם Isa 2:11, 17) or of Hosea's equally characteristic term "spirit of harlotry" (זנונים רוח Hos 4:12, 5:4), or also of Amos's word about the "pride of Jacob" (גאון Amos 6:8). The comprehensive term "return" and the statement that Israel does not return, also belong here. H. W. Wolff, "Das Thema 'Umkehr' in der alttestamentlichen Prophetie," in *Z. Th. K.*, (1951), pp. 129ff.

10. The courtly monologues which the prophets put into the mouth of foreign kings also belong to this tendency to make types, Isa 10:8ff., 14:13ff., 37:24, Ezek 28:2, 29:3, 9, 27:3.

divine design and the co-efficient of arbitrary human power.[11] To come to this explanation—and we should make no mistake about this—Isaiah wrestled with the whole force of his intellect as well as of his faith. Written evidence of this expressly rational grappling with history is furnished by the generally accepted interpretation of the didactic poem in Isa 28:23–9, in which Isaiah makes the multifarious and carefully considered actions of the farmer's sowing and reaping into a transparent parable of the divine action in history. "Wonderful is his counsel and great his wisdom."[12]

So far, however, we have dealt almost too much with history in a general sense, with the result that misunderstanding could arise: it might be supposed that the prophets shared our concept of objective history. This is contradicted by the very fact that, as the prophets use the term, wherever history is spoken of, it is related in some sense to Israel. Even Isaiah's famous universalism still keeps to the idea that Jahweh directs history with reference to Israel. Yet, closer consideration of the prophecies of salvation shows that Jahweh's coming action in history upon Israel has still another peculiar characteristic. What comes in question here are not designs which Jahweh formed so to speak in perfect freedom, but only the fulfilment of promises he had already made to Israel in the old traditions. Whether we think of Hosea's [[185]] prophecy that Israel will once more be led into the wilderness and once more be brought through the valley of Achor into her own land (Hos 2:16ff. [14ff.]), or of the prophecy that Jahweh will once more gather nations together against Zion, though he is again to protect it, or of the prophecies about the anointed one who is yet to come in Amos, Isaiah, and Micah, we everywhere see to what an extent even the prophets' predictions of the future are bound to tradition; and this in the sense that on the prophets' lips the coming and, as we may safely call them, eschatological events of salvation are to correspond to the earlier events as antitype and type. Thus, even in what they say about the future, the prophets function largely as interpreters of older traditions of Jahwism.

At the same time they introduce a fundamentally new element, which is that only the acts which lie in the future are to be important for Israel's salvation. The old traditions said that Jahweh led Israel into her land, founded Zion, and established the throne of David, and this was sufficient. No prophet could any longer believe this; for between him and those founding acts hung a fiery curtain of dire judgments upon Israel, judgments which, in the prophets' opinion, had already begun; and this message of judgment had no basis in the old Jahwistic tradition. They believed, therefore, that salvation could only come if Jahweh arose to per-

---

11. See [[von Rad 1965:]] p. 163.
12. See [[von Rad 1965:]] p. 163, n. 21.

form new acts upon Israel, an event which they looked on as certain—and they entreated those who were still able to hear not to put their trust in illusory safeguards (Mic 3:11), but to "look to" what was to come, and to take refuge in Jahweh's saving act, which was near at hand.[13] The prophets were therefore the first men in Israel to proclaim over and over again and on an ever widening basis that salvation comes in the shadow of judgment. It is only this prediction of a near divine action, with its close relation to old election traditions and its bold new interpretation of them, which can properly be defined as eschatological.[14] Everywhere there were pious hopes and confident statements about the continuance of the divine faithfulness. What the prophets foretold was something completely different theologically. They take as their basis the "No" pronounced [[186]] by Jahweh on the Israel of their day, her relationship to Jahweh which had for long been hopelessly shattered. They were sure, however, that beyond the judgment, by means of fresh acts, Jahweh would establish salvation; and their paramount business was to declare these acts beforehand, and not simply to speak about hope and confidence.

Summing up, it may be said that in regard to both their "preaching of law" and their proclamation of salvation, the eighth-century prophets put Israel's life on completely new bases. The former can only be seen in its true light when it is considered in relation to the latter. We have already emphasised the fact that the prophets did not derive their conviction that Jahweh purposed judgment from any special revelation, independent of his saving acts, but from the old saving traditions themselves; thus, they interpreted the message in a way different not only from their contemporaries but also from all earlier generations. For them the traditions became law. Yet, they were not precursors of legalism; they did not reproach their fellows with not living their lives in obedience to law; their reproach was rather this, that as Jahweh's own people they had continually transgressed the commandments and not put their confidence in the offer of divine protection. How little the prophets' work was aimed at a life lived under the yoke of the law is made particularly clear in those places, which are, of course, few in number, where they go beyond negative accusations to positive demands. "Seek good, and not evil; hate evil, love good!" "Seek Jahweh, that you may live!" (Amos 5:14f., 6). This is not the language of a man who wants to regulate life by law. In Amos's view, what Jahweh desires

---

13. See [[von Rad 1965:]] pp. 160ff.

14. See [[von Rad 1965:]] pp. 118f. and 239. The term "prophetic," too, urgently requires a suitable restriction. There is no profit in expanding it, as for example Vriezen does, so as to see what is prophetic as something implanted into Jahwism by Moses (*Outline*, pp. 137, 257f.). In my opinion, what is specific to the prophet only appears with the determination of his characteristic attitude towards tradition (see [[von Rad 1965:]] p. 299).

from Israel is something very clear and simple; if not, how could he have described it by the perfectly general term "good" (cp. also Hos 8:3; Isa 5:20; Mic 3:2)? And listen to Micah. The prophet answers the excesses in the performance of legal and cultic rites to which Israel's anxiety was driving her: "he has showed you, O man, what is good and what Jahweh seeks from you: to do justly, to love kindness, and to walk humbly before Jahweh" (Mic 6:8).[15] This is [[187]] the quintessence of the commandments as the prophets understood them. There is no demand here for "ethics" instead of a cult, as if the prophet's desire was to lead men from one set of laws into another. No, something quite simple is contrasted with the arduous performance of works which can end only in destruction—a way along which men can walk before God. Exactly the same is true of the verse in Hosea which "reads like the programme of an opposition party," to the effect that what counts with Jahweh is not the offering of the proper sacrifices, but "loyalty to the covenant and knowledge of God" (Hos 6:6). The vow which this same prophet puts into the mouth of those who turn to Jahweh is given in negative terms, doubtless because it follows a literary category used in worship, but in principle it takes the same line. It does not expect the fulfilment of a legal demand:

> Assyria shall not save us, we will not ride upon horses;
> and we will say no more "Our God" to the work of our hands.
> (Hos 14:4 [3])[16]

Isaiah says practically nothing about the inner disposition of the purified remnant, with the result that it is not easy to imagine what this is. The remnant is composed of those from whom Jahweh has not hidden his face (Isa 8:17), those who have had faith. On one occasion he calls those who take refuge in Zion "the poor of his people" (Isa 14:32).

The eighth-century prophets were, of course, only the first to tread this new theological path. Their successors were to go further along it, and in particular were to have still more to say about the question of the new obedience. In general they were to take up the topics they inherited and to develop them in their own way; but they were also to enrich the prophetic preaching with new topics which for eighth-century prophecy had not as yet appeared on the horizon.

15. The meaning of הצנע is not perfectly certain. The term seems to belong to the language of Wisdom (Ecclesiasticus 16:25, 35:3), and tends in the direction of the idea of "measured." In his study, "Und demütig sein vor deinem Gott," in *Wort und Dienst, Jahrbuch der theologischen Schule Bethel,* 1959, pp. 180ff., H. J. Stoebe also finds the term principally in the language of Wisdom and translates it as "to be discerning, circumspect."

16. The negative formulation of the confession corresponds to model confessional formulations; von Rad, *Ges[[ammelte]] St[[udien zum Alten Testament,* Munich 1958]], p. 292.

EDMOND JACOB

b. 1909

The Spirit and the Word

Theological Synopsis

The decade of the 1950s has been described as the "golden age" of Old Testament theology. Edmond Jacob's volume, appearing at the decade's midpoint, joined at least eight others published in that decade.

The stage for this flurry of activity had been set in the preceding two decades during which German, French, Dutch, British, and American scholars had published theologies of the Old Testament. Walther Eichrodt's work, highlighting the theme of covenant, appeared between 1933 and 1939. Otto Procksch, Eichrodt's teacher, wrote a theology which was published posthumously in 1950. Other Germans to publish Old Testament theologies were Ludwig Köhler (1935) and Paul Heinisch (1940). Two publications out of Paris should be noted: Albert Gelin (1948) and Paul van Imschoot (1954–56). The work of the Dutch scholar Theodorus C. Vriezen appeared in 1949. British writers, while not writing books formally designated as theologies, were nevertheless writing in that field: H. Wheeler Robinson (1946), Harold H. Rowley (1956), and Norman H. Snaith (1944). And from the ranks of North Americans there had appeared three attempts: Millar Burrows (1946), Otto Baab (1949), and G. Ernest Wright (1952). James D. Smart therefore wrote quite appropriately about the rebirth of Old Testament theology (1943).

The wrangle about the relationship of history to theology, about which Eissfeldt and Eichrodt had written (see above, pp. 20–39), had not subsided, but the light was now green for biblical theology. Jacob, along with others, stressed that "in the Old Testament history is the most characteristic channel through which thought is expressed" (1958: 197). Still, ideas or themes were carried in the basket of language; therefore words and word

145

studies were critical. Jacob's book included numerous expositions that were essentially theological word studies, for example, holiness, righteousness, spirit, and heart. Jacob was clearly in touch with Ludwig Köhler's work: a lexicon, articles on the meanings of Hebrew words, and especially Köhler's Old Testament theology (1935). Like Köhler, Jacob emphasized the names of God, and like Köhler he concluded with a discussion of redemption. But Jacob did not share Köhler's view that the cult was "man's expedient for his own redemption" (1957: 181). Nor did Jacob follow Köhler in stressing revelation and covenant.

Jacob's *Theology of the Old Testament* (1958) had its own characteristics. He limited its scope primarily to a discourse about God. It was God's presence manifested in his sovereignty, and his activity as Savior which Jacob found most noteworthy. Among God's activities was his election of Israel. For Jacob this factor was more decisive than covenant, for it preceded covenant. Apparently influenced by Harold H. Rowley, who had written about both election and missions, Jacob elaborated on the missionary task of Israel, noting prophetic passages such as Zephaniah 3:9–10, Micah 4, Isaiah 2 and 54:1–3, Malachi 1:11, and Jonah. Not all Old Testament theologies take up the theme of Messiah, but for Jacob that theme belonged to "the consummation" and God's final triumphant work. In the preface to the second edition (1968) Jacob responded to criticism of his first edition, commented on von Rad's approach, and championed the role of a biblical theology.

Edmond Jacob was born at Beblenheim, France, in 1909. Son of a pastor's family, he received his education in Strasbourg, Paris, and Jerusalem, after which he served two pastorates. He became professor of Old Testament at Montpellier in 1941. In 1946 he assumed a similar position at the University of Strasbourg. He wrote books about Israel's history, Ugarit, and the Old Testament, and among his numerous articles were several that dealt with prophets.

E.A.M.

Writings by Jacob

1955   *Théologie de l'Ancien Testament: Revue et augmentée.* Paris/Neuchâtel: Delachaux & Niestlé.

1958   *Theology of the Old Testament.* Translated by Arthur W. Heathcote and Philip J. Allcock. London: Hodder & Stoughton/New York: Harper.

1968   *Théologie de l'Ancien Testament: Revue et augmentée.* 2d edition. Neuchâtel: Delachaux & Niestlé.

1970   *Grundfragen Alttestamentlicher Theologie.* Franz Delitzsch–Vorlesungen 1965. Stuttgart: Kohlhammer.

Writings about Jacob

Laurin, Robert B.
     1970b   Edmond Jacob: *Theology of the Old Testament.* Pp. 141–69 in *Contemporary Old Testament Theologians.* Edited by Robert B. Laurin. Valley Forge, Pennsylvania: Judson.

Edmond Jacob's
Approach to Old Testament Theology

Excerpted with permission from Edmond Jacob *Theology of the Old Testament* (New York: Harper & Row, 1958), pp. 11–13, 28–30, 32–33.

Historical and Methodological Considerations

Outline of the History of the Subject

⟦11⟧ The theology of the Old Testament may be defined as the systematic account of the specific religious ideas which can be found throughout the Old Testament and which form its profound unity. This subject is relatively new, since only from the eighteenth century onwards can we see it developing as an autonomous science and diverging from dogmatics, to which it was until then indissolubly bound. But the reality is older than the name. Within the Old Testament itself it is already possible to speak of theology. The Old Testament counts among its authors several real theologians, of whom the most ancient, the one called the Yahwist by the critics, portrays the history of humanity and of Israel's earliest days as a succession of events according to the principle of grace (God's initiative), of punishment (man's disobedience) and of faith (God's requirement and man's normal attitude towards him); an analogous plan is adopted by the writer of Deuteronomy, who insists more strictly on the divine punishment for man's rebellion. The so-called Priestly writer presents Israel's history in the form of four successive covenants and the writer of Chronicles sets out to show how all history must confirm the promise made to king David that his dynasty would be everlasting. ⟦12⟧ Similarly we could speak of the theology of each prophet. Among these Second Isaiah is the one whose book is a real theological treatise based on the three themes of creation, redemption and final salvation. We recall these early outlines because we hold that, even in the twentieth century, a theology of the Old Testament should be able to draw inspiration from them so as not to fit the Old Testament into a modern scheme or explain it according to a dialectic that is fundamentally foreign to it. The New Testament too is a theology of the Old Testament, for its essential purpose is to show that Jesus of Nazareth is the Christ, the Messiah promised to Israel to whom all Scripture bears witness. Certain of the New Testament writings assume more especially the appearance of theological treatises: the Gospel of Matthew is an historical treatise meant to prove that Jesus is a new Moses,

148

while the Epistle to the Romans and the Epistle to the Hebrews present the Old Testament from the point of view of the law and the promise in one case, and of priesthood in the other. The latter writing is particularly important for the exegetical methods of the early Church, it is not "the most finished specimen of allegory",[1] but a model of typological exegesis, for which the past is a preparation and an imperfect sketch of the future. According to this writing there is between the two Testaments the relationship of shadow to reality. In general, the Apostle Paul makes the same use of it, only giving up typology for allegory when he views the Old Testament apart from the general perspective of the fulfilment of Scripture in history.[2]

A theology of the Old Testament which is founded not on certain isolated verses, but on the Old Testament as a whole, can only be a Christology, for what was revealed under the old covenant, through a long and varied history, in events, persons and institutions, is, in Christ, gathered together and brought to perfection. Such a statement does not in any way mean that we should only consider the Old Testament in the light of its fulfilment, but a perfectly objective study makes us discern already in the Old Testament the same message of the God who is present, of the God who saves and of the God who comes, which characterizes the Gospel. Unless it is based upon the principle of the unity of the [[13]] two Testaments, and *a fortiori* on the internal unity of the Old Testament itself, it is not possible to speak of a theology of the Old Testament. The unity of the Old Testament is in no way incompatible with what critical and historical study has revealed about the very diverse elements that have gone to its composition, for the collections of books and traditions have not prevented the Old Testament from remaining as one book and the expression of one religion. That is an objective fact and consequently justifiable from scientific study.[3]

. . . .

The Place of Theology in Relation to Other Branches of Old Testament Study

[[28]] The third discipline [[in addition to introduction and archeology]] with which the theology of the Old Testament must of necessity collaborate is the history of the people of Israel. To know the way in which the nation was moulded, the political and social changes that it underwent, is

---

1. The expression is from P. Lestringant, *Essai sur l'Unité de la révélation biblique*, Paris 1943, p. 131.

2. Gal 4:21ff. is the clearest example of this.

3. The problem of the unity of the Bible has been most recently treated in a particularly profound manner by H. H. Rowley, *The Unity of the Bible*, 1953, which does full justice to the diversity of currents brought to light by historical and literary criticism.

as important as to know how the Old Testament itself was formed, knowledge that is all the more indispensable since theology does not work with ideas, but with historical facts. Questions of the spirituality, of the unity or of the foreknowledge of God are far less important for the faith of ancient Israel than questions of the Exodus from Egypt, of the Sinai covenant or of the conquest of Canaan. The "Credo"[4] of [[29]] the people was firmly based on the affirmation and remembrance of historical events. The Old Testament theologian therefore cannot have with regard to history that attitude of indifference or scepticism which is often shown towards historical questions by philosophers and dogmatists. It is then important to know—and it will only be known by virtue of the methods proper to historical study—whether the events which the Old Testament relates, and on which it bases its faith, really took place. This method cannot be applied, of course to the early chapters of Genesis, where we are in the presence of myths which give expression to supra-historical truths or to historical facts only in the eyes of a higher power, but we could not speak with the same authority of Abraham's faith if it were historically proved that the patriarch never existed. It is important, however, at the same time to state that it is not enough that an event should have taken place on a particular day in a particular place for it to be historical. In order to merit the title of "historical event", an event has to be conspicuous and that conspicuous quality is not necessarily a function of the event's primary importance in history: the death of Jesus passed unnoticed in Roman history and yet that historical event dominates world history and caused it to move in a new direction. Similarly, the Exodus of the Israelites must have been a quite trivial event, but that trivial event made its mark on the life of the Jewish people and, as a result, on universal history. We can grasp this significance of the historical event by considering the interpretation of history in the prophets and in the Psalms. We discover there that history is very freely used, that the sequence of events is sometimes reversed, as in Psalm 114 where the Jordan is mentioned before the Red Sea, and that the whole tendency is to set the principal themes in relief. Hence Old Testament theology, while remaining a descriptive subject, will not stop over details of history and will not be shackled by the chronological order of events, yet it will not launch into excesses of allegory.

So it is neither desirable nor possible to pose the dilemma: either the history of Israel's religion, or the theology of the Old Testament. Each has its proper function to fulfil while remaining in each case an historical and descriptive subject: the first will show the variety of the history and its evo-

---

4. Cf. G. von Rad, *Das formgeschichtliche Problem des Hexateuchs*, 1938, and Wright, *God who acts.*

lution, the second will emphasize its unity. But can one legitimately speak of "theology" and would it not be better, as has been recently suggested, to be content [[30]] to speak of the "phenomenology of the Old Testament"?[5] The objection would be valid if the history of Israel were not itself a part of the theology, that is to say a word and a revelation of God. And so we think it is better to use the word theology in a wide sense—one could speak of the theology of events and the theology of ideas—rather than to see in it only the expression of the piety and faith of the Church. In conclusion let it be said that there is no history without theology and no theology without history.

. . . .

The Place of Old Testament Theology in Relation to Other Theological Studies

[[32]] Old Testament theology will not be able to deal with all the questions that the Old Testament puts before us and it should not try to do so; drawing inspiration from all branches, it will not make the claim of being a possible substitute for them; faithful to its name, it will deal only with God and his relationship with man and the world. Piety, religious institutions and ethics are not part of Old Testament theology's specific domain.

This is the limitation which we have imposed in this present work, which makes no claim to be a "compendium" of the permanent or Christian values of the Old Testament. Two closely connected themes have come to our notice more forcibly than others, the themes of the *presence* and the *action* of God. The God of the Old Testament is a God who seeks to manifest his presence in order to be recognized as the sovereign Lord; that is why the fear of God is at the basis of all piety and all wisdom. But God also and especially seeks to manifest his presence in order to save man. A line not always straight, but none the less continuous, leads from the anthropomorphism of the earliest pages of the Bible, to the incarnation of God in Jesus Christ. God's action throws into relief the specifically Hebrew quality of that presence: the Old Testament does not bring us ideas about God, but acts of God, a God who leaves his transcendence to link his own destiny with the destiny of a people and through that people with the whole of humanity. A contemporary Jewish philosopher has given expression to this truth by saying that "the Bible is not the theology of [[33]] man, but the anthropology of God"[6] a profound statement which, in our view, found its fulfilment in Christ and which will be made fully real at the time when there comes to pass what is said in that book of the last days, each term of the statement being drawn directly from the Old Testament:

5. N. W. Porteous, "The Old Testament and some theological thought-forms" in *Scottish Journal of Theology*, 1954, pp. 153ff.

6. Abraham Heschel, *Man is not alone. A philosophy of religion.* New York 1951, p. 129.

'Ιδοὺ ἡ σκηνὴ τοῦ θεοῦ μετὰ τῶν ἀνθρώπων, καὶ σκηνώσει μετ' αὐτῶν, καὶ αὐτοὶ λαοὶ αὐτοῦ ἔσονται, καὶ αὐτὸς ὁ θεὸς μετ' αὐτῶν ἔσται ⟦'Now the dwelling of God is with men, and he will live with them. They will be his people, and God himself will be with them'⟧ (Rev 21:3).

Synopsis of Jacob's *Theology of the Old Testament* (1958)

Edmond Jacob on the Spirit and the Word

Excerpted with permission from Edmond Jacob *Theology of the Old Testament* (New York: Harper & Row, 1958), pp. 37–42, 121–34.

The Living God: Centre of Revelation and of Faith

[[37]] What gives the Old Testament its force and unity is the affirmation of the sovereignty of God. God is the basis of all things and all that exists only exists by his will. Moreover, the existence of God is never questioned; only fools can say, "There is no God" (Ps 14:1; 53:2; Job 2:10); and even when the prophet Jeremiah speaks of the unfaithful Israelites who denied Yahweh by saying, "It is not he" (*lo hu*) (5:12) he does not intend to speak of those who disbelieve in God but of rebels who question his sovereignty. The passages which can be invoked as proofs of the existence of God are meant to lay stress on certain aspects which can be discussed, but the reality of God imposed itself with an evidence which passed beyond all demonstration. The knowledge of God in the sense of the awareness of divine reality—and not in the profounder sense the prophets will give to it—is to be found everywhere. The entire world knows God; not only Israel but all the peoples praise him; even nature has only been created to proclaim his power (Ps 148:9–13). Even sin itself proclaims the existence of God by contrast, for it is either desertion from God or revolt against him; the sinner is a man who turns his back on God, but who does not dream of contesting his existence. The fact of God is so normal that we have no trace of speculation [[38]] in the Old Testament about the origin or the evolution of God: whilst neighbouring religions present a theogony as the first step in the organization of chaos, the God of the Old Testament is there from the beginning. He does not evolve, and the various names which are given him are those of originally independent gods and do not mark phases of his development. The Old Testament gives us no "history" of the person of Yahweh, who nevertheless existed in another form before becoming the national God of the Israelites, and the gods of the patriarchs only have a chronological and not a genealogical connection with Yahweh. From the time that Yahweh appears he is a major God whose eternity could be affirmed (Ps 90:2; 139:16), but the idea of eternity is secondary to that of life. God is not living because he is eternal, but he is eternal because he is living. The Israelite felt God as an active power before positing him as an eternal principle. God is never a problem, he is not the ultimate conclusion

153

of a series of reflections; on the contrary, it is he who questions and from whom the initiative always comes. Strongly typical in this respect is the sudden and unexpected appearance on the scene of history of the prophet Elijah, who justifies his intervention simply by the words, "Yahweh is living" (1 Kgs 17:1). Just as life is a mysterious reality which can only be recognized, so God is a power which imposes itself on man and comes to meet him without his being always prepared for it.

The expression "living God" (*ʾel chay, ʾelohim chayyim*) has a less deeply imprinted theological character than other formulae such as holy God or God the King, and so we do not agree with Baudissin[1] that it is of recent date and that it sprang into being from the polemic of Yahwism against the cult of dying and rising gods who claimed to have the monopoly of life, nor with L. Koehler[2] that it sprang up as an answer to the criticism that God had neither life nor power. To say of God that he was a living God was the elementary and primordial reaction of man in face of the experience of the power which, imposing itself on the entirety of his being, could only be envisaged as a person, that is, as a living being. It is to the power and succour of that person that the Israelites appeal [[39]] when they are menaced in their own personal life, *chay Yahweh* [['Yahweh's life']], and when Yahweh himself wishes to confirm by an oath the dependability of his threats or promises he introduces it by the affirmation of his life: "I am living, says the Lord Yahweh. . . . I will make the effects of my oath fall upon his head" (Ezek 17:19), but also: "I am living, oracle of the Lord Yahweh, I have no pleasure in the death of the wicked" (Ezek 33:11).

Life is what differentiates Yahweh from other gods; before it is expressed in a well formulated monotheism, the faith of Israel is confident of the feebleness of the gods of the nations and contrasts that weakness to the living God; the gods of the nations are stupid and foolish while Yahweh is the true God and the living God (Jer 10:9–10). Yahweh does not die: "Thou shalt not die" cries the prophet Habakkuk[3] (1:12). The idea of God as living also implies that Yahweh is the one who gives life: "As true as Yahweh lives, who has given us this *nephesh* [['soul']]" (Jer 38:16). It is because they see in the Living One essentially the source of life that believers regard as the supreme aspiration of piety the ability to approach the living

---

1. In *Adonis und Eshmun*, Leipzig 1911, pp. 450ff. The expression "living God" does not necessarily imply a relation to nature. Yahweh—to whom the title is given more often than to El or Elohim—is living because he is bound to a social group, which is a living reality *par excellence.*

2. L. Koehler, *Theologie des A. T.*, p. 35.

3. The actual form of the verse: "We shall not die" is due to a *tiqqun sopherim* designed to correct the disrespect which the mere thought of the death of God would involve.

God (Ps 42:3; 84:3); and finally it is belief in the living God which will lead to the affirmation of victory over death.

From a literary point of view, faith in a living God attained its best expression in anthropomorphic language; "the idea of a living God," writes F. Michaeli, "gives to the anthropomorphism of the Bible a significance quite other than that which applies to similar expressions about pagan idols . . . it is because God is living that one can speak of him as of a living man, but also in speaking of him as of a human being one recalls continually that he is living."[4] Anthropomorphism is found throughout the Old Testament; it is by no means a "primitive" way of speaking of God and it easily harmonizes with a highly spiritual theology, as, for example, in Second Isaiah: God speaks (Gen 1:3), hears (Exod 16:12), sees (Gen 6:12), smells (1 Sam 26:19), laughs (Ps 2:4; 59:9), whistles (Isa 7:18); he makes use of the organs suited to these functions: he has eyes (Amos 9:4), hands (Ps 139:5), arms (Isa 51:9; 52:10; Jer 27:5), ears (Isa 22:14), and feet (Nah 1:3; Isa 63:3) which he places on a footstool (Isa 66:1). His bearing is described with [[40]] the help of the most realistic anthropomorphisms: he treads the wine-press like a grape-gatherer (Isa 63:1–6), he rides on the clouds (Deut 33:26; Hab 3:8), he comes down from heaven to see the tower of Babel and to scatter its builders with his own hands (Gen 11:7), and he himself shuts the door of the ark behind Noah (Gen 7:16). Figures of speech borrowed from military language are particularly frequent. Yahweh is a *gibbor* [['mighty one']] and an *ʾish milchamah* [['warrior']] (Exod 15:3; Ps 24:8; Zech 9:13), because at the period which may coincide with the first age of settlement in Canaan war was the normal and even the only way for Yahweh to reveal himself.[5] Sometimes it is even the activity of animals which provides the term of comparison; when it is a matter of showing a terrifying aspect, the lion, the bear and the panther illustrate it in turn (Lam 3:10; Hos 5:14; 11:10; 13:7), and also the moth, which destroys more subtly but quite as surely (Hos 5:12); yet the sacred character of animals in the majority of pagan religions was bound to hinder Israel from making too large a use of theriomorphism. Anthropomorphisms are accompanied by anthropopathisms: God feels all the emotions of human beings—joy (Zeph 3:17), disgust (Lev 20:23), repentance (Gen 6:6) and above all jealousy (Exod 20:5; Deut 5:9).

There were mitigations of the anthropomorphism. Respect for divine transcendence led to the substituting for God of intermediaries for his communication with men, for example in the E editing of the J traditions, but it must be noted that these attenuations are attributable to ethical

4. F. Michaeli, *Dieu à l'image de l'homme*, p. 147.
5. G. von Rad, *Der Heilige Krieg im alten Israel*, 1951.

tendencies rather than to a spiritualizing for which the idea of a personal and present God was fundamentally unacceptable. Other limits to anthropomorphism are simply due to the fact that from the beginning Israel was aware that God was only partially the image of man. In the conception of God as a person Israel felt and expressed both the similarity and the separation, for such a person was felt not only as a different being but often indeed as a veritable obstacle; the "thou" who was God could say No! to the "I" of man, so that even while speaking of God in human terms account must be taken of the fact that one realized that between the two there was no common measure. God is not subject, like men, or at least not to the same extent as men, to changes of humour or feeling: "God [[41]] is not man, that he should lie, or a son of man, that he should repent. Has he said, and will he not do it? Or has he spoken, and will he not fulfil it?" (Num 23:19). "I am God and not man" (Hos 11:9); and then Isaiah summarizes the irreducible difference between God and man by the terms spirit and flesh (31:3), putting the opposition not between what is spiritual or corporeal, but between what is strong and what is feeble and ephemeral. Another limit to anthropomorphism is supplied by the very conception of man in Israel. According to the anthropology dominant in the Old Testament a man only exists as a member of a community, there is no isolated man, there are only *bene ʾadam* [['sons of man']], that is, participators in that great collective personality which is constituted by humanity and, more especially, Israel. But that idea of collective personality could not be applied to God: to exist and manifest his sovereignty, God has no need of the assistance of other beings; biblical anthropomorphism thus differentiates itself clearly from ancient anthropomorphism in general where the god is not only always associated with an attendant goddess, but where he is also surrounded by an entire court of equal or inferior personages like a human family. The Old Testament is unaware of any feminine partner to Yahweh and Hebrew does not even possess any term for goddess and uses the ambiguous word *ʾelohim* [['God']] (1 Kgs 11:5, 33, Astarté *ʾelohe Sidonim* [['god of Sidonia']]). Certainly it happened that, under the influence of the contemporary world and because of a very natural tendency of the human mind, the attempt was made to give a consort to Yahweh: Maacah, the mother of king Asa, made an idol which might serve as a feminine counterpart to Yahweh (1 Kgs 15:13), and the Jews of the military colony of Elephantiné did not hesitate to associate with Yahweh the great Canaanite goddess under the name of Anat Yahu; but these are deviations which were never admitted within the framework of the orthodox faith which only knew a single consort of Yahweh, namely the people of Israel, but the union with the people is the result of an act of pure grace and in no way corresponds to a necessity of the natural order. Transcendence of sex is also shown in the absence of a son of God: the *bene ha²elohim* [['sons of God']] of Gen 6:2 and of the prologue to Job are divine beings, but not sons in the proper sense. Finally, a last limit to anthropomorphism and one which clearly shows that anthropomorphism was unsuitable for expressing the divine personality in its fulness, is the prohibition of making [[42]] a visual representation of Yahweh;[6] consistent anthropomorphism necessarily ends in plastic representations. Even if in the course of history the people of Israel sometimes had difficulty in keeping to the Mosaic order (Exod 20:4, 22; Deut 4:12, 15–18), it must be recognized that the prohibition on the making of images of the deity and adoring them (for an image of the divine is made to be adored) represents the main trend of Israelite religion. To make a representation of God means to desire to imprison him within certain limits and God was too great for anyone to be able for an instant to dream of setting a limit to what clearly never ceased, namely his life.

. . . .

The Action of God According to the Old Testament

The Spirit

[[121]] The goal of divine action is to maintain and to create life; to achieve this aim Yahweh chiefly avails himself of two means which we encounter in varying intensities in all the realms of his manifestation: the Spirit and the Word. The striking resemblance between these two realities goes back to their common origin: the term *ruach* means originally and etymologically the air, which manifests itself in two forms—that of the wind in nature and of breath in living beings. Once it became the prerogative of God *ruach* threw off its material attachments though it never ceased to be an active power. Spirit and Word belong to anthropomorphic language; but since they continue to operate even apart from bodies they can be regarded as independent realities more easily than the hand or face of God.

Apart from some passages where it is the symbol of inconstancy and nothingness: Isa 26:18; 41:29; Mic 2:11; Job 16:3; Jer 5:13, wind as a physical

---

6. As a God of nomadic origin and bound to a human society, Yahweh had no need like other gods of fashioned representations in animal or human form, though one must beware of equating nomadism with spirituality. But contact with the religion of Canaan, where the power of the image was very great, might have led the Israelites to use the same procedures sometimes to represent Yahweh, without there being necessarily in origin an act of infidelity. The fashioned image of a bull was not always an adoration of Baal; and the ephod itself, a human or closely human representation of Yahweh (cf. 1 Sam. 19:10ff.), could appear perfectly legitimate and even necessary for affirming the power of Yahweh. But as these attempts ultimately struck at the uniqueness of Yahweh and especially at his jealousy, a radical condemnation of all images and an insistent reminder of the Mosaic requirements was brought into operation.

reality is always closely associated with God, it is one of his best servants (Ps 104:4) and is personified as the breath of his nostrils (Ps 18:16). The Exodus, that liberating event which became the type of salvation, was due to the intervention of Yahweh in the form of a strong wind which dried up the sea and gave the Israelites passage (Exod 14:21; 15:8). The wind ⟦122⟧ fulfils a double function exactly corresponding to that of God; it is the destructive power which dries up the springs (Hos 13:15), but at the same time and more importantly the force which by piling up the clouds brings fertilizing rain to the parched earth (cf. 1 Kgs 18:45). Another aspect of the wind, less spectacular but not less suggestive, connects it with God, namely its light and intangible nature; it knows no limits and is capable of bearing the deity on its wings to the extremities of the earth (Ps 68:4; 104:3) and no one can grasp its whence and whither. Power and mystery, such are the two characteristics of wind, and it is because the God of the Old Testament is both power and mystery that the wind is able to express so adequately the whole nature of the divine.

Although the wind accounts for life in nature and can be regarded without difficulty as the breath which gives life, the life of living beings should not be considered as an effect of the wind. The term *ruach* denotes the breath of life which is an effect of the breath of God. J. Hehn[1] has shown with numerous examples that this idea was to be found amongst the Egyptians, Babylonians, Assyrians, Canaanites, Phoenicians and Hebrews. It must have offered itself spontaneously to different peoples through the simple observation that life and breath ceased together, and because of the anthropomorphic picture of the deity the origin of this breath was attributed to his breath. Numerous texts in the Old Testament affirm that the breath of God is life-giving: Gen 6:17; 7:15; Num 16:22; Judg 15:19; Ps 104:29; Eccl 3:1; 9:21; 12:7; Isa 37:6, 8; Zech 12:1. Not only the origin of human life but its span is conditioned by the breath of Yahweh: "Thou hast granted me life and thy care has watched over my *ruach*" Job cries (10:12). This breath rarely, and only as a result of the systematization of language, becomes a merely anthropological reality; on the whole it always remains the property of God who is free at any instant to take it back to himself.

For the ancient Israelites the mystery which fills the world was not limited to certain natural happenings; even before the unique God Yahweh had assumed all aspects of power and mystery there was belief in the existence of powers more or less invisible, for the most part maleficent, and

---

1. "Zum Problem des Geistes im Alten Orient und im Alten Testament," *ZAW*, 1925, p. 210.

they were spoken of by the same term [[123]] *ruach*[2] in order to indicate their violent and mysterious character. In the present state of the texts, these evil spirits appear as subject to Yahweh, but their aspect as originally independent powers is shown by certain verbs which are used of their mode of action. Thus it is said of *ruach* that it clothes itself (*labash*), Judg 6:34; 1 Chr 12:18; that it falls upon an individual (*naphal*), Ezek 11:5; that it comes forth mightily (*tsalach*), Judg 14:6; 1 Sam 10:6, 10; 18:16; that it passes or traverses (*ᶜabar*), Num 5:14. If in these passages the term used had from the beginning referred to the spirit of Yahweh one cannot see why these early texts, which do not give ground before the most daring anthropomorphisms, did not simply say: Yahweh falls, Yahweh bursts in upon. Account must be taken of this sense of *ruach*. To get out of the difficulty by saying that the spirit is only the vivid personification of an evil power or passion,[3] is to by-pass the problem; in fact there is a notable difference between passages like Num 5:14, 30; Hos 4:12; 5:4; Zech 13:2, where we have a rhetorical style, and the very concrete description of spirits in 1 Kings 22[4] where they play the part of individuals subordinate to Yahweh but acting independently of him.[5]

Physical, biological and demonic reality, the spirit is yet primarily in the Old Testament the prerogative κατ' ἐξοχήν [['according to election']] of God and his instrument of revelation and action *par excellence*. It is probable that this identification of Yahweh with the *ruach* was not made at the outset.[6] The quite frequent combination of the term with *ᵓelohim* [['God']] might suggest that the divine spirit was thought of as a force able to act without Yahweh and even to escape his control; thus the transmission of Elijah's spirit to his successor seems to imply no participation by Yahweh (2 Kgs 2:9–15). However, from [[124]] the first traces of theological reflection about *ruach* as a divine power it was connected with Yahweh; a celebrated passage in the book of Isaiah shows that in the eighth century

2. P. Volz in his work *Der Geist Gottes im A. T. und im Spätjudentum* has insisted on this aspect of *ruach*. Cf. the same author: "Der Heilige Geist in den Gathas des Sarathuschtra", in *Eucharisterion* (Gunkel Festschrift), 1925, p. 323.

3. R. Koch, *Gottesgeist und Messias*; otherwise this work gives an excellent summary of the subject of the spirit in the O. T.

4. The spirit (*haruach*) which comes before Yahweh in 1 Kgs 22:21 plays a part comparable to that of Satan in the prologue of Job; Kittel, *Biblia hebraica* (3rd ed.) even proposes to alter *ruach* into *satan*, a purely gratuitous emendation.

5. In 1 Kgs 22:21 spirit is masculine, which indicates a more definite individualizing, though examination of all the texts does not allow any conclusions to be drawn from variations in gender of the word *ruach*.

6. According to Ed. Koenig, *Hebr.-aram. Wörterbuch zum A. T.*, the primitive sense may have been that of spirit, and the material sense of wind and breath derivative; that seems difficult to reconcile with Hebrew semantic principles about the priority of concrete meanings.

the spirit and Yahweh denote the same reality. The prophet reproaches the king and the people of Judah for the projected alliance with Egypt, for to seek salvation by military means is to reject Yahweh: "Egypt is man and not god (*'el*), his horses are flesh (*basar*) and not spirit (*ruach*). Yahweh will stretch out his hand and the protector will stumble and his protégé will fall and all will perish together" (Isa 31:3). The terms *'el* and *ruach* placed here in parallel signify that God alone has on his side power and immortality. The prophet does not go so far as the New Testament affirmation that God is spirit, but he implies—and everything suggests that he is not the first to do so—that spirit characterizes all that is contained in the word "god" and that Yahweh, once he has become the only God, is alone capable of giving it perfect fulfilment. It can therefore be said that the spirit is God himself in creative and saving activity; the spirit of God lies at the origin of creation (cf. Gen 1:2), it is ceaselessly present in the form of wind, but because of the uniqueness of Israelite religion it is chiefly history which is the place of his manifestation. The action of the spirit in history has not been experienced with equal intensity in the course of the ages, but it can be said without risk of hasty generalization that throughout history it is the spirit who directs events. In the early ages the spirit acts intermittently; he falls unexpectedly upon certain persons and makes them capable of extraordinary acts. Thus, it is through a momentary gift of the spirit that Samson is able to tear in pieces a lion and a kid (Judg 14:6); by this act Samson is able to ward off the Philistine danger and to restore the confidence of the people in Yahweh's power; through the gift of the spirit all these charismatic leaders are saviours (*moshi'im*) of the theocratic state and maintain the reality of the covenant. It has been very soundly written,

> These acts are not merely marvellous exploits, they are acts of liberation. Though isolated deeds of local heroes they belong to the one historical process, they mark the stages of the forward march which leads Israel to independence. It is this movement of liberation which gives them unity. The intervention of Yahweh's spirit at these different stages gives prominence to one of the directions of divine action in the Old Testament. The spirit of God is the source of the national community of [[125]] Israel.[7]

The prophets are animated by the spirit. The *nebi'im* [['prophets']] of the time of Samuel are possessed by the *ruach* and he who comes into contact with them is willy-nilly so infected as to become "another man" (1 Sam 6:10). The spirit could have effects upon men of God as violent as they were unexpected; it was commonly accepted that it could seize them and carry them to another place, even destroy them (1 Kgs 18:12; 2 Kgs 2:16).

7. J. Guillet, *Thèmes bibliques*, p. 233.

Nor is the spirit foreign to the activity of the great prophets; it is true that the pre-exilic prophets from Amos onwards never speak of the possession of the spirit in order to justify or authenticate their work. Opposition to the old nabiism and to its ecstatic manifestations produced by the *ruach* might explain this new attitude. According to Mowinckel[8] the prophets' reserve about the spirit may have been due to conflicts which some of them—Jeremiah in particular—had to suffer with the false prophets who boasted their possession of *ruach,* but which was really only "wind" (cf. Jer 5:13). It is clear that for all the prophets it is not the spirit but the word which qualifies them for their ministry, because only the word creates between the prophet and God a relationship of person with person. But the word presupposes the spirit, the creative breath of life, and for the prophets there was such evidence of this that they thought it unnecessary to state it explicitly. There are in addition a few passages which show that the true prophets were also conscious of being clothed with the spirit and of being thereby the heirs of the ancient *nebi³im* as an instrument of divine revelation in history. Hosea, after having announced punishment, elicits from his adversaries the sarcasm: "The prophet is a fool, the man of the spirit (*³ish haruach*) is mad" (9:7), a passage which clearly does not prove that the prophet attributes his inspiration to the spirit, but which shows that the prophets did not refuse to be called men of the spirit among the people. Micah puts the spirit into more direct relation with prophetic inspiration: "As for me, I am full of power, of the *ruach* of Yahweh" (3:8),[9] and Isaiah [[126]] says that to act without the spirit of Yahweh is to set oneself up against him and that to oppose the words of the prophet who is the mouthpiece of God is to reject God himself (Isa 30:1-2). Elsewhere the hand of Yahweh which seizes the prophet (Isa 8:11; 1 Kgs 18:12, 46; Ezek 1:3; 3:12; 37:1; 40:1) acts exactly like the spirit, so that in spite of the infrequent reference to the spirit the upheaval which takes place in the great prophets through their calling is placed on the same plane as the marvellous acts attributed to the spirit when it fell upon the judges and the first *nebi³im*. From the Exile the spirit becomes an essential element in the inspiration of the prophets. Ezekiel speaks and acts under the inspiration of the *ruach* (2:2; 3:24; 11:5, etc.), and it is to the spirit that he attributes both the reception of the divine word and the superhuman power which makes him capable of announcing it. Many of the post-exilic texts in which we

8. Mowinckel, "The spirit and the word", *JBL,* 1934, pp. 199ff.

9. This Micah passage, because of its unusual construction (*³et ruach Yahweh*), might be regarded as an addition to the text inspired by analogy with Isa 11:2; break in the rhythm has also been appealed to in support of its lack of authenticity; but instead of suppressing *ruach* we could just as well take *koach* as a gloss uselessly repeating *geburah* (cf. Giesebrecht, *Die Berufsbegabung der altt. Propheten,* 1897, pp. 123, 137).

have a kind of résumé of the history of salvation present that history as a result of the spirit manifesting itself through the prophets. Speaking of Israel's past, the great prayer of repentance of Nehemiah (chap. 9) recalls that activity: "Thou warnedst them by thy spirit through the medium of thy prophets, but they did not listen" (v. 30) and in an analogous context of thought the prophet Zechariach speaks in the same way: "They made their hearts adamant for fear of hearing the instruction and the words which Yahweh Tsebaoth had sent—by his spirit—through the medium of the prophets of the past" (7:12).

In a similar presentation of history, Moses becomes the man of the spirit, with which he is so richly endowed that he can without loss transmit some of it to others (Num 11:17, 25, 29). But it is not only past history which is a manifestation of the spirit; an even more splendid outpouring of the spirit is reserved for the future: the new age will be marked by abundance of vegetation, by prosperity and peace, all of which will be produced by the spirit of Yahweh "come from on high" (Isa 32:15ff.); the shoot of the stem of Jesse will be clothed with the spirit in a more complete and spiritual way than the leaders of the heroic age (11:2ff.); the spirit will also rest permanently on the servant of Yahweh (42:1ff.) but at the same time all the people will receive the benefit of this extraordinary gift: "I will pour forth my spirit upon thy race and my blessing upon thy posterity" (Isa 44:3) and since it will be shed in their hearts it will produce not a transient manifestation of power but a regeneration which will be the counterpart of the creative ⟦127⟧ function of the spirit in nature (Ezek 36:22–28). With stress laid upon its creative function, the spirit's sphere of action is enlarged. Each individual life is directed by the spirit in the moral realm (the request is made for the spirit to lead in the path of uprightness, Ps 143:10) as well as in that of intelligence (wisdom and artistic abilities are gifts of the spirit, Exod 28:3; 31:3ff.) and the Wisdom of Solomon will draw the consequences of that evolution by identifying the spirit with wisdom. The spirit being of the very essence of God was brought into relation with the holiness which constituted his principal attribute, but it is only in two passages that this relationship is explicitly stated. One post-exilic prophet represents the holy spirit as the means *par excellence* by which God asserts his presence in the midst of his people, a presence as personal as that of the angel or the fact against whom one can revolt and who can be grieved (Isa 63:10–11). The author of Psalm 51 has the very strong feeling that his faults deserve his removal far from God; so he begs that God, after having pardoned him, will not remove his holy spirit (v. 13), that is to say that he will not deprive him of his presence. Without the spirit—and on this point the testimony of the Old Testament in unanimous—it is not possible to have communion between God and man; but this theology of the spirit never took the form of an indefinite spiritism which would have undermined the personality of God.

The Word

That God reveals himself by his word is a trust confirmed by every one of the Old Testament books. It is by his word that he reveals himself as the living God and Second Isaiah, drawing the full consequences of anthropomorphism, will contrast Yahweh with pagan gods by the word of the one and the silence of the others. Of the false god made by human hands he says, "It is vain to cry unto him, he does not reply, he does not deliver from distress" (46:7; cf. also 41:21; 43:9; 45:20ff.). To understand the importance of the word of Yahweh it is necessary to remember the common belief throughout antiquity in the value and efficacy of a word. A spoken word is never an empty sound but an operative reality whose action cannot be hindered once it has been pronounced, and which attained its maximum effectiveness in formulae of blessing [[128]] and cursing. This dynamic quality of the word already appears in the names by which it is denoted. The most usual term and the one which has become classical for the word is *dabar* [['word']] which must probably be associated with a root which in Hebrew has the meaning of: to be behind and to push; *dabar* could then be defined as the projection forward of what lies behind, that is to say, the transition into the act of what is at first in the heart. The realistic character of *dabar* is always strongly stressed, so that the term will denote thing as well as word (Gen 20:10; 22:1, 20; 40:1; 48:1 etc.) and no term throws into clearer relief the fact that the Hebrew mind did not distinguish between thought and action. Realism and dynamism are features equally characteristic of the root *ʾamar* [['say']]; derived from a root having the sense to be raised up or to be clear, the word would be the visible manifestation of the thought and of the will. In distinction from *dabar*, the stress with *ʾamar* is chiefly upon the spoken word; the expression *lemor* [['to say']] which introduces speeches is generally preceded by *dabar* (*wayedabber lemor* [['and he spoke, saying']]) which alone possesses creative dynamism.

The power of the word of God is similarly met outside the Old Testament.[10] Sumerian hymns very often celebrate the greatness of the word; the believer in Enlil-Marduk addresses his god thus:

> thy word, a sublime net, stretches over heaven and earth, it falls on the sea,
> and the sea is rough, it falls on the cane plantation and the cane sprouts,
> it falls on the waves of the Euphrates, the word of Marduk stirs up vast waves.

10. The most abundant documentation is given in the work of L. Dürr [[*Die Wertung des göttlichen Wortes im A. T. und im antiken Orient*, Leipzig 1938]] and for the most recently discovered texts in that of Ringgren [[*Word and Wisdom*, Lund 1957]].

Belief in the creative power of the word appears in many proper names, with constructions such as "*Sin* gives the name" or "*Nabu* is lord of the name", showing that existence and life was attributed to the all-powerful word of the god. In Egypt we meet the same theme of the creative word with the stress laid more on the efficacious word of the king who, as the image and son of the god, shares his power.

The idea of the divine word is, therefore, by no means peculiar to Israel, but the God of Israel, being essentially different from the nature gods and the national gods of other nations, stamps his particular mark upon the theology of the word, so that under [[129]] analogous terms very different realities are expressed. It is impossible to study the theology of the word without relating it to the revelation of God in history. Whilst in Babylon and Egypt the divine word intervenes in isolated events which have no connection with one another, the word of God in the Old Testament directs and inspires a single history which begins with the word of God pronounced at the creation and which is completed by the word made flesh (John 1:14). Therefore it is in history that the word is revealed and its action in nature is only a pale reflection of its work in history. The laws and the oracles of the prophets are the two principal forms which that word assumes. Law belongs to the origins of Israelite history, not in its casuistical form but in that of brief apodictic declarations, to which just the name *debarim* [['words']] was given and of which the various decalogues give us the best known instances (Exod 24:3, 4, 8; 20:1; 34:1, 27, 28). These *debarim* constitute a revelation of God; in them Yahweh affirms that he is the Lord, but since God's affirmation is at the same time the manifestation of a power before which man can only bow, and therefore of an order which he can only obey, the word takes on the aspect of a law. The circumstances in which these *debarim* are uttered, their link with the establishment of the covenant, have conferred upon them an authority which in Judaism became merged with that of God himself.

The prophets never dream of questioning the authority of the ancient *debarim*; they were even to a large extent commentators upon the law, but with them the rôle of guardians of tradition is subordinate to the direct link which united them to God who places his words in their mouth, thereby affirming his presence not above but within the events of history.[11] The prophet is a man of the word; the wife of Jeroboam asks a *dabar* of

11. Two practices inspired the formulation of the prophetic oracles: on the one hand the proclamation of royal edicts and orders, and on the other the forms of communication oral or written (letters). Cf. the conclusive comments of L. Koehler, *Deuterojesaja, stilkritisch untersucht*, pp. 102f., and of W. Baumgartner in *Eucharisterion* (Gunkel Festschrift), pp. 145ff. This dual origin well illustrates the double rôle of the prophet as the representative of God and as the servant of his people.

Ahijah of Shiloh (1 Kgs 14:5); king Ahab asks a *dabar* of his prophets and of Micaiah ben Imlah (1 Kgs 22:15–13), and Jeremiah, in characterizing the various ministries, defines the prophet by the *dabar* (Jer 18:18). There is an important difference between the legal and the prophetic [[130]] word: *debarim* have a lasting value for all generations, whilst the word of the prophet, spoken in quite definite circumstances, has no bearing after its fulfilment. Thus the *dabar* which the prophet Elijah announced to king Ahaziah: "Thou shalt die" only exists for the king and loses its dynamic when it is fulfilled. The word of Micah about the ruin of Jerusalem and of the Temple (Mic 3:12) weighed like a heavy threat over the people until the time of Jeremiah (Jer 26:17ff.), but after the events of 587 B.C. it had no further significance. However, even in definite and individual cases, the prophets do not announce *a* word but *the* word of Yahweh. This means that each time the prophet speaks he reveals Yahweh in his totality under one of his essential aspects as judge or as saviour, and that revelation made to an individual has value as an example for all the people.

What is striking in a study of the word in the prophets is its objective and dynamic character. Jeremiah, who is the most explicit of all the prophets on the subject of prophetic experience, shows to what extent the prophet, in receiving the word, is seized by a mysterious power which sometimes crushes and tortures him (20:9), sometimes fills him with joy (15:16). The prophet is literally disturbed through and through by the *dabar* he receives, and which creates a new life within him. It is by this constraining power of the word which weighs upon him that Jeremiah authenticates his own ministry against that of the false prophets who also claimed to have received the words of Yahweh, but in whom no change in personal bearing was shown (23:11ff.) and Amos compares the situation of the prophet who has received the word to the terror which spontaneously seizes a man who hears the roaring of a lion (3:8).

The word is always far greater than the person of the prophet; he only receives it in order to transmit it, his function is that of a messenger. Even the form of prophetic discourses shows the nature of the prophets as men called and sent. The prophets in fact formulate their oracles in just the same way as a messenger transmits a message that has been entrusted to him; passages such as Num 22:16; Judg 11:12; 14:22; 1 Kgs 20:3; 22:27; 2 Kgs 18:28, which relate secular messages, have the same form as prophetic oracles. When the prophets introduce their discourses by the words: "Thus saith Yahweh", they imply the transmission of a message received without any addition of their own; and in other respects they [[131]] take care to distinguish the word of Yahweh from their own words; so in Amos 5:1–2 it is the prophet who speaks, in verse 3 Yahweh, in Isa 18:1–3 it is the word of the prophet, in verses 4–6 the word of Yahweh.

Once handed on, this word acts independently of the person of the prophet: "The Lord sends a word against Jacob and it falls on Israel" (Isa 9:7). It is like a projectile shot into the enemy camp whose explosion must sometimes be awaited but which is always inevitable, and these explosions are the events of history. It cannot be more explicitly stated that Yahweh is the sole author of history; human beings are the instruments of his word; even the Assyrian king Sennacherib represents his intervention as an order from Yahweh: "Yahweh told me: go up against this country and destroy it" (Isa 36:10; 2 Kgs 18:20). It is particularly in Deuteronomy, and in the great work of historical synthesis created under its inspiration, that the idea of the word in relation to history is systematized. The permanence of the word is assured by the prophetic succession;[12] according to the word put into Moses' mouth by Deuteronomy, Yahweh promises an uninterrupted succession of prophets (Deut 18:15–18). That prophetic succession was an historical reality, even though there were periods when the word of God was rare, that is to say practically non-existent and though the link connecting a prophet with his predecessors is less important than the direct and personal relationship which links him with God. After Deuteronomy the theology of the creative word in history found still greater expression in the work of Second Isaiah, whose book opens with the affirmation that in face of the succession of the generations the word of God abides eternally, and closes with the proclamation of that word's efficacy (40:8 and 55:11). This word is more to him than "the promises of the old prophets recorded in Scripture",[13] it is the entire action and revelation of God; with great power he shows its double aspect; noetic and dynamic. By his word God makes known the meaning of events; he makes them known in advance, for he who is the first and the last knows what will happen at the end of time (41:4; 43:10; 44:6; 48:12).[14] [[132]] Above all it is the dynamic aspect of the word which he is interested in stressing, though with him the dynamism which had ended in catastrophe, as the majority of his predecessors had announced, blossomed forth into salvation. This function of the word in producing salvation can be compared with that of the servant of Yahweh and it can be asked whether the intu-

---

12. Five stages of that succession can be distinguished, with R. B. Y. Scott, *The Relevance of the Prophets*, New York 1944: (*a*) Moses; (*b*) the prophets of the time of the Judges and of the first period of the kingdom: Samuel, Nathan, Gad, Shemaiah, Ahijah, Jehu ben Hanani; (*c*) Elijah and Elisha and their disciples; (*d*) the golden age of pre-exilic prophecy inaugurated by Amos; (*e*) the post-exilic prophets, often anonymous and hence difficult to date.

13. A. Robert, article "Logos" in *DBS*, col. 453.

14. There was no organic association between the prophet and the word. The word could fall upon the prophet at a moment when he was not expecting it, just as it could be refused him when he asked for it. Cf. the example of Jeremiah who had to wait ten days for the manifestation of a word (Jer 42:7ff.).

ition of the prophet did not already discern one and the same reality in the word which remains eternally and in the figure of the servant fulfilling his mission right to the end.

. . . .

⟦133⟧ The theology of the word resulted in two kinds of crystallizations; the first started with the fixation of the word in writing. While the *debarim* were from the start put into writing, which would ensure their permanence, the prophets had originally no other concern than that of transmitting the word orally to those for whom it was destined. Before Jeremiah only occasionally does the question arise of writing certain words down, as in Isaiah 8 with the purpose of reinforcing a symbolic action. The definite order which Jeremiah receives to write down his prophecies is probably not unrelated to the Deuteronomic reform. In the history of Israel Deuteronomy marks an attempt to reconcile and to identify the prophetic word with the legal word by presenting a book as the normative authority; in this book, which can always be consulted (Deut 30:11–14), life is truly found (Deut 32:47), so that any new revelation is superfluous. The *dabar* is, therefore, no more the hoped for reality whose manifestation was often awaited with anxiety, even by the prophets, it is given once for all and the Israelite will find there all that is necessary for his salvation. Only the backward glance matters, and every new revelation will have to assume an antique garb to avoid appearing new.[15] The part which this orientation towards the *dabar* has played in the destiny of Judaism cannot be disregarded. If we consider that because of it Judaism survived during the Exile, and if we measure the intensity of the piety aroused by the written word, then we appreciate all that was fruitful in that evolution. Nevertheless we are not prevented from regretting that, by opening the door to the idea of ⟦134⟧ complete and literal inspiration, it hampered an understanding of the dynamic of the word of God such as we find in the prophets.

The other attempt at crystallization appears in the tendencies towards making an hypostasis of the word. Although it is impossible to speak of an hypostasis of the word in the canonical books of the Old Testament,[16] it must be recognized that many of the affirmations point in that direction. To speak of the word as a reality which falls and which unlooses catastrophe (Isa 9:7), or as a devouring fire (Jer 5:14; 20:8; 23:29), or as a reality which is present with someone like one person with another (2 Kgs 3:12), is to look upon it less as an effect than as an active subject akin to the angel

---

15. This is why so many apocalypses are attributed to men of the past.

16. Instead of speaking about foreign influences it is better to see in the analogous expressions and speculations the mark of a fundamental structure of the primitive mind according to which the life of a person shows itself in the form of breath and word, dynamic realities *par excellence*.

or the face of Yahweh. The same hypostatic function of the word, which receives its full development in the pseudepigrapha, has its roots in the Old Testament without any need to admit foreign influences. The tendency to hypostatize was more obvious in the case of wisdom than of the word, but it is the latter which provided a foundation for the theology of wisdom.[17]

17. It is evident that in a text like Ecclus. 24:3 where Wisdom says, in speaking of itself: "I came forth from the mouth of the Most High" and in Wisd. 7:25 which represents wisdom as a "breath of the glory of the Almighty", the rôle attributed to wisdom is literally proper only to the word or to the spirit.

JOHN L. MCKENZIE

b. 1910   d. 1991

Cult

Theological Synopsis

Father John L. McKenzie was not known to follow tradition closely. Traditionally, Roman Catholics had addressed themselves to a philosophical or systematic theology, in nature like a student's handbook, which followed the topics of a dogmatic theology (e.g., Paul Heinisch, 1940). Paul van Imschoot, also a Roman Catholic, produced a theology of the Old Testament in 1954 and 1956 around the topics God, man, judgment, and salvation. McKenzie explained that the discipline of Old Testament theology was directed toward the totality of the biblical utterances; that which emerged from a study of this totality was something different from that which emerged from a study of the single utterances. Prior to writing a theology, McKenzie authored *The Two-Edged Sword* (1956), a "spiritual study of the Old Testament" (Flanagan 1975: 5), regarded by some as his finest book, and single-handedly produced *The Dictionary of the Bible* (1965), the work of six years.

Methodologically, McKenzie was not concerned to exhibit a structural system, like Eichrodt, for example, because the Old Testament has for its subject not a system, but a reality, namely Yahweh. Israel's experience of Yahweh is foundational. That experience was recorded in the Old Testament. It was the task of Old Testament theology, he felt, to present a synthesis of these records, utterances ultimately descriptive of Yahweh. In this approach McKenzie was quite unlike van Imschoot, whose self-declared aim was to "bring about a synthesis of the doctrines of the Old Testament" (1965: 3). Moreover, McKenzie deliberately did not address himself to the problem of how the Old Testament related to the New Testament because "the Old Testament is not a Christian book" (1974: 320). For him "the study of the theology of the Old Testament has never been advanced by the Christianization of the Old Testament" (1974: 268). He wrote, therefore as though the New Testament did not exist.

McKenzie's theology began with cult, because through cult came Israel's most frequent experience of Yahweh. In discussing cult, as well as other topics, McKenzie often compared Israel's belief with that of her ancient Near Eastern neighbors (e.g., 1974: 68, 76, 85, 132, 185). In this way he focused more sharply on the distinctive nature of Israel's experience with Yahweh. He claimed, for example, that the tradition of covenant law was "altogether without parallel in ancient religions" and that "the future orientation of much of the Old Testament and Judaism is a manifest and really unparalleled fact" (1974: 70, 268–69).

In elaborating on his chosen themes, McKenzie called attention to changing perceptions. Under the topic of revelation he treated matters such as God's saving acts, the gift of the land, and God's assessment of nations. This assessment was first made on the basis of the nations' relationship to Israel, but was later assessed, as in Amos, on the grounds of moral considerations (1974: 167–68). Similarly in the discussion of wisdom, McKenzie began with conventional wisdom, defined as folkloric in nature. Critical wisdom differed from conventional wisdom, for critical wisdom dealt, as in Job, with catastrophe. McKenzie's final chapter was on the future of Israel. The approach here, as throughout, was not the development of doctrine. Rather, McKenzie paid attention to the historical experiences which for Israel were an "encounter with God" (1974: 135–36), for he held that "historical events had everything to do with the development of different forms which the hope took" (1974: 270), and that changing perceptions came from Israel's new experiences with Yahweh.

John L. McKenzie was born and raised in the environs of Terre Haute, Indiana. He received his training in Jesuit schools in Kansas and Ohio and at Weston College, Massachusetts, where he received his doctorate in sacred theology. He was ordained a priest in 1939. He taught at West Baden, Indiana, for nineteen years and later at Loyola University, the University of Chicago, the University of Notre Dame, and at DePaul University in Chicago. A congenial and witty man, he challenged ecclesiastical authorities, often in trenchant fashion. About his *A Theology of the Old Testament* a colleague writes, "The vintage McKenzie is in these books: a thorough grasp of the materials presented with clarity and verve" (Munson 1975: 12).

E.A.M.

Writings by McKenzie

1956   *The Two-Edged Sword: An Interpretation of the Old Testament.* Milwaukee: Bruce.

1965   *Dictionary of the Bible.* New York: Bruce/London: Collier-Macmillan.

1974   *A Theology of the Old Testament.* Garden City, New York: Doubleday.

Writings about McKenzie

Flanagan, James W., and Anita W. Robinson (editors)
    1975   *No Famine in the Land: Studies in Honor of John L. McKenzie.* Missoula: Scholars Press/Institute for Antiquity and Christianity—Claremont.
Munson, Thomas N.
    1975   A Biographical Sketch of John L. McKenzie. Pp. 1–13 in *No Famine in the Land: Studies in Honor of John L. McKenzie.* Edited by James W. Flanagan and Anita W. Robinson. Missoula: Scholars Press/Claremont: Institute for Antiquity and Christianity—Claremont.

John L. McKenzie's
Approach to Old Testament Theology

Excerpted with permission from John L. McKenzie, *A Theology of the Old Testament* (Garden City: Doubleday, 1974), pp. 21, 23–25, 27, 29, 32–35.

Principles, Methods, and Structure

[[21]] The task of Old Testament theology may become easier and be more successfully accomplished if we remember that it is precisely the theology of the Old Testament, not the exegesis of the Old Testament, not the history of the religion of Israel, not the theology of the entire Bible, which is the object of the study. The religion of Israel included many factors which are not found in the Old Testament; some are unknown, others are poorly known. For the historian of Israelite religion, the temple and cult of Bethel are extremely important, and he is hampered in his task because so little is known of them. To the theologian of the Old Testament the temple and cult of Bethel are important only because of what Amos and Hosea said about them. To their contemporaries Amos and Hosea were not very important.

· ·

[[23]] I have asked, but not yet answered, whether we can use the word "systematic" of biblical theology in the same meaning in which it is used of systematic theology. The most ambitious venture in this area, the work of Eichrodt, has been successful in spite of the partial failing of the system as such. Von Rad's theology is not systematic in the sense I have already described, the sense in which certain basic principles are applied to each particular question so that the entire system is brought to bear on any particular problem. This type of system seems impossible in Old Testament theology, and we must anticipate a theological statement to explain why. Basic principles emerge in a rational system, which is a thing. What emerges in the Old Testament is not a rational system but a basic personal reality, Yahweh, who is consistent as a person is, not as a rational system. No particular problem is solved without reference to Yahweh, who is not a rational principle.

One seems, then, to be forced into the approach of particular topics; and in these treatments there is order and arrangement, but no system or structure. The topics are usually selected according to the personal studies and interest of the writers; this is not in itself deplorable, but it manifests

172

that biblical theology is an unstructured discipline. Yet there are other factors at work which deserve mention. Up to this time it has been difficult for a Catholic to write a theology of the Old Testament without an explicit section on messianism. A small essay of my own was criticized even in the editorial stage because this topic was not presented with sufficient emphasis. I have been convinced for years that messianism is a Christian interest and a Christian theme; that it is a Christian response to the Old Testament and should be treated as such; that in a theology of the Old Testament, as I have described it thus far, messianism would appear neither in the chapter headings nor in the index. It is not only not a dominant theme, but in the proper sense of the word it is doubtfully a theme of the Old Testament ⟦24⟧ at all. This theme is imposed upon the theologian by theological factors foreign to his area of study. He should be free to make his own selection and to make his own errors of judgment. Yet such a work deserves a title like "Essays in the Theology of the Old Testament," or "Towards a Theology of the Old Testament," or "Prolegomena to a Theology of the Old Testament."

We have already noticed the obvious fact that the principles, methods, and style of theology change, and usually change later than they ought. The change comes because the world and the Church are asking questions which theology is not answering or not even hearing. To illustrate: I have been a fairly convinced pacifist for twenty years. This conviction began with the teaching of the prophets. I do not remember any theology of the Old Testament which dealt with the problems of war and peace. They shall certainly be treated in this work; the purpose is not to promote pacifism, but simply to discern whether in that totality which we have mentioned there emerges some insight into this problem. Those who do not accept my insight are forced either to say that their insight is contradictory or that the Old Testament does not touch the problem at all. Such problems are not simply a question of relevance, but of meeting the development of theology. If this development is not to be met, there is no need for producing an additional theology, now or ever. Those we have are fully adequate. But since it is a biblical belief that whenever man encounters man, God is present as a witness and a party to the encounter, Old Testament theology must deal with such problems as war and peace, poverty, the urban problems, industrial and technological society, and such— not directly, of course, but by stating clearly what principles may emerge from the totality of the utterances. Theology keeps reforming its principles and its contents from the course of the human adventure. This is what gives the theologian the new questions. It is also one of the things, and perhaps the most important, which distinguishes theology from the history of religion.

If any structure emerges from the totality of the God-talk of the Old Testament, it ought to arise from the emphases of the Old Testament. These emphases, which have long been recognized, are simply those themes which occur most frequently and which [[25]] appear to be decisive in giving Old Testament belief its distinctive identity. The theologian can hardly divert much from his predecessors in his titles of chapters and sub-division. Nor can he avoid personal value judgments in the weight which he assigns to various topics and themes; if he were to present the themes with perfect objectivity, as if they were coins of the same denomination, he would not be faithful to his material. The order in which they are presented is not determined by the Old Testament, but by his own judgment of the most logical and coherent arrangement of material which was never arranged by those who wrote his sources. There is no reason in the Old Testament why biblical theology should begin with creation; in our own theology creation is the belief which is presupposed by all other beliefs. Biblical theology of the Old Testament, we have said, is written for modern readers who are probably religious believers, not for the scribes of Israel and Judaism who produced the source material of biblical theology. Their categories of thought must be of some importance for the arrangement of the material. But in whatever categories the material is arranged, the theologian is not going to escape a topical treatment; his problem is to rise above the merely topical treatment, the disconnected *quaestiones.*

. . . .

[[27]] The biblical theologian can scarcely avoid value judgments in his arrangement. Like the military historian, he should be able to distinguish the accessory and the inconclusive from the central and decisive. Not all parts of the Old Testament contribute equally to the total experience. Reviewers of Eichrodt noticed that he had difficulty including wisdom in his synthesis. Yet wisdom is more central in the Old Testament than one could judge from a covenant-centered theology. Wisdom simply has no reference to the covenant; it is older than the covenant, it is so basic to human experience that it has as many nonbiblical contacts as biblical. But it is an important part of Old Testament God-talk and includes themes which are scarcely touched in other books. Some of these themes are permanent in theological discussion and literature. The theologian ought to know that such value judgments are dangerous. But neither he nor his readers can escape their own history. It is difficult to imagine any theological question asked in this generation on which the book of Chronicles is likely to shed any light. But the theologian can write only in his generation.

. . . .

[[29]] The task of Old Testament theology can now be summarized as the analysis of an experience through the study of the written records of that experience. The experience is a collective experience which covers roughly a thousand years of history and literature. The experience is one because of the historical continuity of the group which had the experience and because of the identity of the divine being which the group retained as the object of its faith throughout the experience. The analysis must be done in certain categories and not merely by a chronological recital. We seek always the totality of the utterances and the insight which can be gained by assembling them. The theology of the Old Testament has to be a study of the reality of Yahweh. The Old Testament is the sole literary witness to that reality as the record of the experience of Israel, the sole historical witness.

. . . .

The Israelite Experience of Yahweh

[[32]] If we inquire in what ways Israel, according to its literary records, experienced Yahweh, certain categories suggest themselves; and these categories will furnish the structure of the theological analysis which we undertake here. With some brief remarks, we set them forth as a preliminary outline.

I place cult first as the normal and most frequent manner in which the Israelite experienced Yahweh. The importance of cult need not be measured exactly according to the space which is given it in the Old Testament, but the space given it is abundant. That the cult is a ritual encounter with the deity is a universal human belief; we do not have to validate it for Israel, but simply to see what the peculiarly Israelite understanding and practice of cult may have been. In the Old Testament we are almost always dealing with the religion and faith of a people described as such, very rarely with the phenomenon called "personal religion." Cult is by [[33]] definition the religious expression of a group and not a feature of personal religion. Cult is explicitly or implicitly a profession of faith.

Next I list revelation as the situation in which Israel experienced Yahweh. By this I mean revelation made through authentic spokesmen of Yahweh, and not revelation in an improper sense. One need know little about other religions to recognize that revelation as it was understood in Israel does not appear in other religions except those which claim some continuity with Israelite religion. Israelite revelation is distinguished both in form and content from the revelation known to us in other religions with which Israel had contact. No other religion of the ancient Near Eastern world claimed to be founded on a revelation of the deity which the community worshiped, and on a revelation of a code of conduct imposed by the deity. No other religion exhibits a type of religious spokesman which is more than remotely similar to the Israelite prophets.

In the third place I list history as the area in which Israel experienced Yahweh. The treatment of this area may overlap the treatment of revelation, for the "experience" of Yahweh in history often consisted of hearing the prophetic interpretation of history. Yet the Israelites exhibit a conviction, again without parallel, that their history was the work of the deity whom they worshiped. One sees in the Old Testament a firm belief that Yahweh acts with plan and purpose, that he is not subject to fate, that he is not hindered by other divine beings nor moved by irrational whim.

In the fourth place I list nature as an area where Israel experienced Yahweh. The religions of the ancient Near East can generally, if unsatisfactorily, be classified as "nature religions"; the perception of superhuman power in nature is another universal human phenomenon. Israel again had its own distinctive way of expressing this perception. The question of mythology arises under this heading, as well as the question of creation.

To speak of wisdom as an experience of Yahweh may seem to be stretching our principle more than we ought; yet it is a peculiarly Israelite belief that Yahweh alone is wise and that Yahweh alone gives wisdom. Most of the content of conventional Israelite wisdom can be paralleled in other ancient wisdom literature, but [[34]] not its religious quality. Similarly, the Israelite critical or "anti-wisdom" literature is not without parallel; but Job and Koheleth are recognized as two of the most original works of the Old Testament. In any scheme of Old Testament theology, wisdom is something of a deviant; it stands in its own category, and it has to be recognized as isolated from other parts of the theological structure.

With some hesitation we then take up a topic labeled the institutions of Israel. During its history the community of Israel appeared in several political forms and with variations in its social structure. The Old Testament writings present each of the developments in these fields as exhibiting theological aspects. The Old Testament is not acquainted with a purely secular politics or a purely secular sociology. One may say that it is acquainted neither with politics nor with sociology as theoretical disciplines; but the materials which we include in these disciplines present theological problems as these materials are presented in the Old Testament. Yet one hesitates to include these elements in a treatment of religious institutions.

Our final heading is a vague title: the future of Israel. This touches the topic of messianism. I have already indicated that I do not think that this topic, precisely defined, is a topic of Old Testament theology. But it is an unparalleled feature of Old Testament belief that it has a simple and impregnable faith in the survival of Israel. As long as Yahweh is, there will be an Israel. This faith is not found everywhere; Amos possibly did not have it. But the majority of the writings exhibit the conviction that there will be an

Israel, and the writers are compelled to visualize this future in some way. The variations in this vision of the future are numerous and remarkable, and this is not surprising. Each writer who thinks of the future which Yahweh will grant his people must think of those things in Israel which he believes are vital to its identity. Evidently not all Israelites thought of the same things. Still less did the Christians of the apostolic age think of all these things when they professed their belief that they were the fulfillment of the future which the Old Testament writers had seen.

At this point the theology of the Old Testament must end. The arrangement, it is hoped, will include all the God-talk which students of the Old Testament have found important. It is an ⟦35⟧ artificially unified analysis of a historical experience which has a different inner unity from the unity of logical discourse. A theology is also a theodicy. The experience of the totality, which we have insisted is the objective of Old Testament theology, shows the reality of Yahweh with a clarity which particular books and passages do not have. The Yahweh who was ready to kill Moses—on an impulse apparently—is not attractive, and obscure rather than mysterious (Exod 4:24–26); and it is certainly a pseudotheology which tries to identify this manifestation with the God whose loving kindness is above all his works. Not every biblical experience of Yahweh, not every fragment of God-talk, is of equal profundity; and it is only the totality of the experience that enables us to make these distinctions. Even though the theologian seeks the detached objectivity that modern scholarship demands, he is dealing with a collection of documents that present to those who believe in the documents a God who commands faith. Even if the theologian should not share this faith, he would be less than candid if he ignored the purpose of the literature that he analyzes. There was a time when an Israelite could give his faith to a God who could kill on impulse; many Old Testament writers wrote at length on the impossibility of faith in such a deity. Neither element should be omitted.

Synopsis of McKenzie's *Theology of the Old Testament* (1974)

John L. McKenzie on Cult

Excerpted with permission from John L. McKenzie, *A Theology of the Old Testament* (Garden City: Doubleday, 1974), pp. 48–54, 58–63.

Temple and Sanctuary

[[48]] The idea of the holy place is pervasive in religion, and it is remarkable that early Israelite religion deviates from the common pattern.[1] A holy object symbolizing the divine presence appears in the traditions earlier than the holy place and the holy building. The temples of Mesopotamia and Egypt had no counterpart in Israel before the monarchy.

The holy object was the ark, called the ark of the covenant, the ark of the testimony, the ark of Yahweh or of *elohim*, and some similar titles. This was a wooden box, described in the postexilic source P (Exod 25:10–22) as three feet nine inches by two feet three inches by two feet three inches. One tradition affirms that the ark contained the two tablets of the law inscribed by Yahweh for Moses. This was a portable shrine symbolizing the presence of Yahweh; and such a portable shrine would be at home in a nomadic tribe which lives in tents, not houses. The ark was housed in a tent until the reign of David and then was permanently installed in the temple of Solomon. Some scholars have suggested that the ark and the tent were two holy objects originally independent of each other. The tent was called "the tent of meeting," signifying the meeting of Yahweh with Israel; it was the place of revelation through oracular utterance. Like the ark, it was [[49]] a portable symbol; and it is curious that there was no permanent holy place during the period of the amphictyony, when Israel was settled on the land. No explanation of this somewhat foreign usage is available except the Israelite tradition that the worship of Yahweh came into the land with an immigrant tribe. The unreal tent of the priestly source (Exodus 26), constructed according to the dimensions of Solomon's temple, is a product of scribal imagination; but the tradition of the premonarchic tent is solid. It must be conceded that the symbolism of the ark and tent overlap somewhat. Both symbols exclude the idea of a sacred area (*temenos*); the deity is present where the portable symbol is set down, and he leaves the area when it is moved. He really dwells "in the midst of his people" and not on holy ground. The ark was carried at the

---

1. Van der Leeuw [[*Phänomenologie der Religion* (Tübingen, 1956)]].

head of the column when the tribe moved from place to place and at the head of the battle column (Num 10:33–35; 14:44; 2 Sam 11:11).

The precise quality of the symbolic presence is ambiguous and very probably shows considerable development. Yahweh is said to be enthroned upon the cherubim when the reference is to the ark (1 Sam 4:4; 2 Sam 6:2; Ps 80:2); and in the temple of Solomon the ark stood between the images of the cherubim, winged figures of guardian genii. But the configuration of the ark does not suggest a throne, and it is possible that the ark was not a chair but a footstool. Yahweh, who cannot be represented by image, stands invisible upon the footstool. A similar explanation of the calf of the temple of Samaria as an invisible footstool has been proposed.[2]

There is no parallel in ancient Near Eastern religions to the prohibition of images.[3] The prohibition touches images for worship, but in Israel and Judaism it has been understood as a general prohibition with a few exceptions like the cherubim in the temple of Solomon and the wall paintings in the synagogue of Dura-Europos. Palestinian archaeology has disclosed nothing which could be called an image of Yahweh; it has disclosed hundreds of images which are evidently presentations of non-Israelite gods [[50]] and goddesses, in particular female figurines of the fertility goddess.[4] These images illustrate biblical references to superstitious cults in Israel. The god Ashur was represented by an archer within a winged disk, and the Egyptian Aton as the solar disk with rays terminating in hands;[5] these are schematic, not representational, but they would fall under the Israelite prohibition.

The prohibition is comprehensive, covering anything that is susceptible of representation—that is, anything which is visible. Yet to say that the Israelites conceived of Yahweh as spiritual in the sense of immaterial says more than the texts will support. The anthropomorphisms of the Old Testament speak of Yahweh's eyes, ears, hands, arms, nostrils, mouth, and feet; yet while they may be spoken of, they may not be represented in art, and were not. Yahweh was not properly conceived as invisible; the sight of him was fatal to mortal eyes, which is not exactly the same thing as invisibility.

The implication of the prohibition is the statement that Yahweh is like nothing in the heavens above, the earth below, or the waters under the earth. These are the boundaries of the universe as the Israelites thought of them; Yahweh can be assimilated to nothing in the universe. He is "wholly other," to use the phrase of Rudolf Otto. One may find a theoretical

2. William Foxwell Albright, *From the Stone Age to Christianity* (2nd paperback ed., New York, 1957), 299–301; H. Th. Obbink, "Jahwebilder," ZATWiss 58 (1929), 264–74.

3. Exod 20:4–6; Deut 5:8–10; see also Lev 26:1; Deut 4:15–23.

4. William Foxwell Albright, *The Archeology of Palestine* (Harmondsworth, 1951), 107.

5. Pritchard, ANEP 536, 408, 409.

inconsistency between the prohibition of images and the anthropomorphisms of biblical language. One may even find a theoretical inconsistency
between the imageless Yahweh and the location of Yahweh symbolically
where the ark reposed; the Old Testament neither sought nor achieved
theoretical consistency. The prohibition of images went far towards preventing the assimilation of Yahweh to the deities of other ancient Near
Eastern religions. The books of the prophets attest that the danger of assimilation was real. The god who cannot even be symbolically represented
by anything in nature is above and outside nature.

Neither the throne nor the footstool suggests the covenant; and the
tradition of the tables of stone very probably reflected the historical reality
that the ark contained a document stating the [[51]] terms of the covenant.
We shall see in dealing with the covenant that the treaty documents on
which the covenant is most probably modeled were stored in the temples.
This association, however, must be a later reinterpretation of the ark,
which has in itself a satisfactory symbolism of presence with no reference
to covenant. As the ark of the covenant, the ark symbolizes not only the
presence of Yahweh among his people but also the union of the tribes with
Yahweh and with each other. It was as the symbol of Israelite unity that it
was brought to Jerusalem by David and finally installed in the temple of
Solomon.

The ark and the tent, which certainly came together in premonarchic
Israel, whether they originally belonged together or not, were authentically Israelite symbols of the presence of Yahweh. The temple of Solomon
was an imitation of non-Israelite symbols; and there is no reason to differentiate between the temple of Solomon and the temples erected at Bethel
and Dan in the kingdom of Israel. The temple was the symbolic palace of
the deity; like the tent, it was his residence. The ancient temple was not
built for the assembly of the worshipers, who assembled in the outer
courts; it was the palace of the god, and his privacy was protected by the
holiness of the place. The god lived in his temple as the king lived in his
palace. Both in Mesopotamia and in Egypt the temple was a symbol of ce-
lestial reality; in Egypt the temple symbolized the world in which the god
reigned, and in Mesopotamia the temple was the earthly counterpart of
the heavenly temple. It was a point of contact between heaven and earth;
the idea is echoed in the Old Testament story of the tower of Babel (Gen
11:4) and probably in the ladder of Jacob (Gen 28:12); Jacob recognized
that Bethel (the site of an Israelite temple) was the house of God and the
gate of heaven (Gen 28:17).[6]

6. Cf. "The Significance of the Temple in the Ancient Near East," *The Biblical Archeologist*
7 (1944), 41–63.

The temple of Solomon was such a deviation from traditional Israelite cult that it had to be authenticated by an oracle of Yahweh. This is found in 2 Samuel 7, pronounced by Nathan to David; the oracle had to be given to the founder of the dynasty and of Jerusalem, not to his son. The oracle clearly states that the temple was not built because Yahweh "needed" a house, and implies [[52]] that the temple is not only the house of Yahweh but also a symbol of the "house" (dynasty) which Yahweh will build for David. The selection of the site of the temple is also attributed to revelation (2 Samuel 24). There is no doubt that the site is the modern Haram esh Sharif, occupied since the ninth century A.D. by the Dome of the Rock. There is very little doubt that this was the site of a sanctuary in pre-Israelite Jerusalem, but the narrative of 2 Samuel 24 ignores this.

Few parallels have been found to the structure of the temple of Solomon; the narrative itself states that the temple was designed and built by Phoenicians, and almost no Phoenician temples from this period have survived. Compared to the great temples of Egypt and Mesopotamia, the temple of Solomon was quite small. The inner chamber, which elsewhere enclosed the image of the deity, housed the ark. In the earliest temple there is no doubt that the ark was visible through the main door as the image was visible in most other temples. Entrance, however, was prohibited to others than priests; this was normal. The altar stood in the outer court, and there the sacrificial ritual was performed.

The courts of the temple contained some symbols which are still not understood. These included the two free standing columns named Yakin and Boaz, and the enormous bronze vessel of water called the "sea." The character of these objects suggests that they were cosmic symbols—more precisely, symbols of Yahweh's cosmic dominion. It has been suggested that the names of the two columns were the first words of inscriptions. It has also been suggested that they were fire pillars, but the description seems to make them somewhat impractical for this purpose. As symbols of the pillars of the world they are perhaps more easily understood. The "sea" could hardly symbolize the monster of chaos, but rather the sea as subdued by Yahweh. This ornamentation can easily be related to the New Year festival in which Yahweh was celebrated as king and creator. Indeed, the act of creation may have been identified with the building of the temple-palace, as it was in both Mesopotamia and Canaan; the building of the temple was the climactic act of sovereignty asserted in creation.[7]

[[53]] Less explicit in the texts but implied in the architecture is a Davidic-messianic symbolism of the temple. The temple must have been notably smaller than the rest of the palace complex of which it was a part.

---

7. *Enuma Elish*, Pritchard ANET 68–69; Baal of Ugarit, Pritchard ANET 134.

Many find the term "royal chapel" improper for the temple of Solomon, but in spite of the uncertainties of the total design it is clear that the temple was incorporated into the buildings and courts of the palace. The description does not suggest that the temple courts had an entrance distinct from the gates of the palace courts. The covenant union of Yahweh with the house of David was effectively symbolized by the union of the temple with the palace. Furthermore, the covenant of Yahweh with Israel stood with the covenant with David. Zion, the temple mountain, was the residence of Yahweh. It will become the tallest of all mountains to which all peoples will stream (Isa 2:1–4; Mic 4:1–4). It becomes the mythological mountain of the north, the residence of the gods in Canaanite mythology (Ps 48:1–2). These are echoes of the ancient Near Eastern belief that the earthly temple is the counterpart of the heavenly temple; it is also the residence of the king of Judah.

The law of Deuteronomy 12 prescribes that the cult of Yahweh shall be carried on only at the sanctuary which he has chosen. Historians associate this law with the cultic reform of Josiah (2 Kings 22–23), instituted in 622–21 B.C. Before this reform, according to numerous allusions in the books of Kings, the people of Judah worshiped at the "high places." These high places were local shrines in towns and villages. If the name "high place" is correctly translated, they were located on hilltops and can be compared to the "high place" preserved at Petra, which is not only on an elevation but is difficult of access.[8] If cultic worship had been limited to the temple of Jerusalem, most Israelite males could not have been present, and this must have been the effect of the reform of Josiah. These allusions recommend the opinion that the temple of Solomon was a royal chapel and that it was a center of worship for the palace community, identical with the population of Jerusalem. The cultic experience of Israel and Judah was not [[54]] situated in the Jerusalem temple but in the local shrines of the towns and villages. Very little trace of this cult has been left in the Old Testament, in which the cult of the second Jerusalem temple has become the model of Israelite cult. There are numerous allusions to cultic abuses in the local shrines; not all of them were unfounded, it seems, but under the monarchy the standards of the Jerusalem cult were not established as normative. Indeed, it is quite clear that during the Assyrian period (735–640) the cultic abuses of the Jerusalem temple were as deplorable as any abuses elsewhere.[9]

. . . .

8. G. Lankester Harding, *The Antiquities of Jordan* (New York, 1959), 117–20.

9. Roland de Vaux, *Ancient Israel* (New York, 1961), 322.

Prophetic Criticism of the Cult

[handwritten note: what defines "cultic" worship? sacrifice?]

⟦58⟧ Cult is generally accepted in the Old Testament as the normal means by which the community encounters Yahweh. One needs little acquaintance with the history of religion or little experience with cultic worship to know that cult is open to many abuses which have often made people wonder whether cult is a legitimate approach to the deity. To many of our contemporaries cultic worship is superstition by essence. There are also some discordant voices in the Old Testament which show that the attitude of the Israelites towards cult was more complex than simple and naïve acceptance.

Criticism of the cult in varying severity is expressed in Ps 50:7–15, Amos 5:21–25, Isa 1:10–17, Jer 7:1–15 and 21–22, and Isa 66:1–4. Psalm 50 cannot be dated with any precision. Amos 5:21–25 is accepted as original by all critics. Isa 1:10–17 is not certainly from Isaiah, but it is very probably pre-exilic. Jeremiah 7 appears to be original with Jeremiah. Isa 66:1–4 belongs to the postexilic period. The criticisms come from different periods and they are not all of the same character.

Psalm 50 is the easiest to handle. The poet rather gently and ironically speaks in the person of Yahweh and tells the Israelites that he does not accept sacrifices to satisfy his hunger. It is very doubtful that any Israelite really believed that sacrifices satisfied Yahweh's hunger; they may very well have believed that Yahweh wanted sacrifices more than anything else or that they did something for Yahweh by offering sacrifice. The poet makes Yahweh prefer vows, prayers of thanksgiving, and sincere confessions of need. The Israelite liturgy did contain these elements; and the rebuke touched no more than a kind of naïve and pardonable superstition about sacrifice. The other passages are less kindly.

Both Amos and Jeremiah are thought by some scholars to express an acquaintance with a tradition of early Israel which had no institution of the sacrificial ritual as we now have it in the Pentateuch. In fact most of the liturgical passages of the Pentateuch come from the priestly source, which attributed the entire cultic system of the second temple to Moses. The older sources J and E ⟦59⟧ are much less explicit concerning the institution of the cultic system by Moses; and it is possible that both the prophets knew traditions which had no ritual institutions. The Israelite sacrificial system actually does not show any sharp differences from other sacrificial systems. There is, as is well known, considerable ambiguity concerning the knowledge of Moses and his work exhibited in the prophetic writings. The point is that nothing either in the criticisms of the Pentateuch or the prophetic writings imposes upon us the existence of a tradition in the eighth and seventh centuries concerning the institution of the sacrificial system by Moses.

To be more specific than this with the rhetoric of the two prophets is dangerous, but one can hardly evade the danger. Amos seems to deny not only the institution of the sacrificial system but even the offering of sacrifice during the desert sojourn. Jeremiah, on the other hand, rather speaks of the absence of any commandment of sacrifice. Amos adds a difficulty which Jeremiah does not have. Yet it seems scarcely possible that Amos could have had a tradition in which sacrifice was not mentioned, and one must suppose that he pushed it for all it was worth.

The common element in Amos, Jeremiah and Isaiah is that Yahweh speaks as rejecting sacrifices and not merely as criticizing abuses. The reasons for the rejection are the same in all the prophets: the offering of sacrifice is not joined with righteousness within the community. Both Amos and Jeremiah elsewhere announce the total destruction of all institutions, both religious and secular.[10] For Amos and Jeremiah there is no reason to take the rejection in any other sense than absolutely. Jeremiah predicts the destruction of the temple of Jerusalem in the same context. Isaiah is less precise in his predictions of a future destruction; but there is no reason to take his rejection as conditioned by something which he does not utter. None of the prophets speak of a reform of abuses as a way of solving the problem which they present. One need not suppose that they look to a noncultic religion of the future; they simply look to the abolition of the cultic system which they knew.

⟦60⟧ Whatever be the ambiguities of the pre-exilic prophets, there is no ambiguity in Third Isaiah. The prophet spoke in the cultic community of postexilic Jerusalem, the community which produced the priestly code and the elaborate ritual of P. He does not speak of a distinction between legitimate and superstitious cults, not even expressly of the moral corruption of the worshiping community as the pre-exilic prophets spoke of it. He simply enumerates several ritual actions and identifies them all as superstition. Heaven and earth are Yahweh's throne and temple, not the temple of Jerusalem. The prophet clearly repudiates the temple, the cult, and the priesthood.

These passages do not surprise us by their awareness that hypocritical worship is possible; they do create something of a problem by indicating that their authors seem ready to abandon cult without replacing it. In the same book of Jeremiah, a new covenant is presented with no intermediaries between Yahweh and the individual worshiper (Jer 31:31–34). Critics have often doubted that this passage came from Jeremiah, but it is in the same line of thought with the rejection of the cult; from both there

10. Amos 2:13–16, 3:12, 5:2–3, 6:1–3, 8:1–3, 9:8a; Jer 7:1–15 (the temple), 8:8–9 (the law), 22:29–30 (the monarchy), 23:33–40 (prophecy).

seems to follow a religion without social structure. Jeremiah and Amos both faced the possibility—indeed, the expectation—that the people of Yahweh as such would cease to exist; there would be no worshipping community of which the believer could be a member. Such a worshiping community did arise after the exile, but this was not within the vision of the prophets. In actual fact these prophets have very little to say to the Israelite who found himself uprooted from the community of his faith. These would have to find their hope and their encouragement elsewhere. For Amos and Jeremiah the judgment of Yahweh fell with the same totality upon the cult as upon the monarchy and the nation. No institution they knew would return in the form in which it disappeared. Third Isaiah expressed a rare disapproval of the restoration which was ultimately instituted. The future of Israel was not conceived as a mere revival of institutions which had failed to do their work. Yet to say that the cult had simply failed is again to say more than the texts permit. This will concern us in the sections to follow. The conclusion from the prophetic criticism is that cult did not have a 〚61〛 sacramental *ex opere operato* validity as a means of approaching Yahweh.

The Cultic Community

The postexilic community of Jerusalem was effectively and almost formally a cultic community. It was not founded as such, although one of the motives alleged for the restoration of Jerusalem was the restoration of temple and cult (Ezra 1:2–4, 6:2–12). But this restoration was not immediately accomplished, and indeed until the reforms of Ezra was not firmly established. Until these reforms the community struggled to survive as a small ethnic group in a sea of foreigners. After Ezra the community felt it had achieved the ancient ideal of Yahweh dwelling in the midst of his people. For this it needed no political institutions. As we shall see elsewhere, the postexilic community saw itself as a kind of messianic fulfillment, the saved remnant.

One cannot without reservations transfer this idea of the cultic community to Israel before the exile. At the same time, it is difficult to assess the importance of the cultic ritual in the formation and preservation of the Israelite faith and community. We have observed certain prophetic criticisms which reveal massive failures in the cult. These should be balanced against certain values, which have been well set forth by Sigmund Mowinckel.[11] In the ancient world we cannot assume that religious community was instituted and supported by doctrinal instruction. What the

11. *The Psalms in Israel's Worship*, 2 v. (New York, 1962), I, 97–105.

people believed and accepted as obligations was professed only in cultic ceremonial; as we have pointed out several times, this was the community's collective experience of the deity. The individual person could not think of a purely personal experience; ritual performances for private persons were still ritual and fulfilled through the cultic and sacerdotal system. The Israelite prophets deviate sharply from the universal patterns, but even the prophets should not be taken outside of the cultic system in which they lived and in which they formed their basic ideas and beliefs about Yahweh and in [[62]] terms of which they addressed the Israelites. The hymns, as Mowinckel points out, are the best summary of what the Israelites thought Yahweh was; the hymns have their limitations, but they show the cultic system at its best.

In modern times a comparison between the cultic systems of Israel and its contemporaries is possible.[12] The comparison is most revealing when one observes a number of highly developed rituals which had no place in Israelite cult. Such are the rituals of divination which have left such extensive remains in Mesopotamia. The Israelites had certain oracular practices; the references to these are few and disclose no extensive apparatus for discerning the future by occult means. The Mesopotamian lived in a world where demons constantly threatened his fortunes and his health. The priestly offices and functions by which demonic attacks were averted matched the divining priesthood in their numbers and complications. Mesopotamian religion cannot always be distinguished from magic, which is really anti-religion; Israelite religion was liberated from this type of superstition. What the Mesopotamians expected from the rituals of divination and incantation the Israelites expected from Yahweh or did not expect at all. The Old Testament cultic experience of Yahweh left no room for divination or demonology. Here, however, it is necessary to recall the distinction between the history of Israelite religion and the theology of the Old Testament. There is ample evidence that superstitious rites flourished in the Israelite community; the belief in Yahweh which is expressed in the Old Testament repudiates these superstitions.

Mowinckel has pointed out that the limitations of the religion of the hymns lies precisely in their exclusively Israelite character. In the cult Yahweh is experienced as the God of Israel rather than as the God of the world and mankind. His saving power was celebrated mostly in the recital of his saving acts in behalf of Israel, whether in the past of the exodus and the possession of the land or in more recent victories. One does not find expressed in the hymns the prophetic awareness of judgment. Having said [[63]] this, one perhaps has not gone beyond the prophetic criticisms of cult.

12. Cf. Saggs, [[*The Greatness That Was Babylon* (New York, 1962)]] 299–358.

One returns, then, to the essential nature of cult as the rites by which the believing community recognizes and professes its identity and proclaims what it believes about the deity it worships and the relations between the deity and the worshipers. The Israelite cultic system did not succeed in professing the totality of Israelite belief. It failed to maintain Israelite faith in crisis. The prophetic criticisms are not the whole truth concerning Israelite cult. Cult was also the factor which sustained the framework of Israelite belief. Many modern critics believe that the cult was the most important source of the literature of the Old Testament. One must avoid premature and sweeping judgments, but the results of recent work suggest that earlier interpreters seriously underestimated the importance of cultic worship in the formation of Israelite belief and Israelite literature.

WALTHER ZIMMERLI

b. 1907   d. 1983

Life before God

Theological Synopsis

Walther Zimmerli, of the University of Göttingen, figures—along with Albrecht Alt, Martin Noth, Gerhard von Rad, and Claus Westermann—as one of the major Old Testament scholars of the European continent. He was to make his mark in biblical scholarship as a master exegete, using particularly the tools of literary criticism, form criticism, and tradition criticism. His expertise in these areas is displayed in his magisterial two-volume commentary on Ezekiel (1979, 1983).

The capstone of Zimmerli's scholarly career came in 1972, three years before his retirement, with his *Old Testament Theology in Outline* (English translation in 1978). The German edition was revised in 1975 with an expansion on the theology of the Chronicler (pp. 159–61) and a total rewriting of the chapter on Old Testament apocalyptic. The fourth German edition (1982a) was enlarged with bibliographical literature and a few changes, and the fifth edition appeared without changes in 1985. In 1972 Zimmerli had hoped that he could follow this *Outline* with an extensive Old Testament theology. Unfortunately this did not come about due to his unexpected death.

In contrast to von Rad who denied a center to the Old Testament and to Eichrodt whose center is the covenant and to Vriezen who built his theology around the "communion" concept, Zimmerli, while agreeing with Eichrodt, Vriezen, and others that there is a center in the Old Testament, put forth "Yahweh, the God of Israel, the Living One, the Free One" (1985: 9) as the center of the Old Testament. Thus "'Old Testament theology' has the task of presenting what the Old Testament says about God as a coherent whole" (1978: 12). This center-oriented, descriptive Old Testament theology by Zimmerli is opposed to traditio-historical diachronic (von

Rad, Hartmut Gese) and other approaches. Zimmerli starts with the exodus as the beginning of Israel. The picture of God in the pre-Mosaic period is "the task of a history of Israel's religion" (1978: 28)! One could ask why this should not also have theological significance.

The structure of Zimmerli's *Outline* starts with the various descriptions of Yahweh (as God of Israel, creator and king, God of Sinai), who bestows gifts through war and victory. He gives the land; he offers his presence. He also provides charismata of leadership and instruction. Yahweh is known as the God who gives commandments. Israel, in turn, is to live before God in obedience. Divine inspiration calls for the indicative of human response.

Zimmerli shares with von Rad and others the problem of integrating Old Testament wisdom into a theology of the Old Testament (1978: 155–56). In the final part of Zimmerli's Old Testament theology, attention is given to "Crisis and Hope" in primeval history, the historical narratives, the prophets, and apocalypticism, which has its roots in prophecy (1985: 209; here Zimmerli sides with P. von der Osten-Sacken against von Rad).

Walther Zimmerli was born in 1907 in Schiers, Switzerland. He studied theology and Semitic languages in Zurich, Berlin, and Göttingen. He was pastor in the Reformed tradition in Aarburg for a number of years. In 1935 he accepted a call to teach Old Testament, history of religion, and oriental languages at the University of Zurich. In 1951 he moved to the University of Göttingen, succeeding Gerhard von Rad who went to Heidelberg. He retired in 1975 and passed away in Switzerland on December 4, 1983.

G.F.H.

Writings by Zimmerli

1968   *Der Mensch und seine Hoffnung im Alten Testament.* Göttingen: Vandenhoeck & Ruprecht.

1969   *Ezechiel.* 2 volumes. Biblischer Kommentar: Altes Testament 13. Neukirchen-Vluyn: Neukirchener Verlag.

1971a   *Man and His Hope in the Old Testament.* Translated by G. W. Bowden. Studies in Biblical Theology 2/20. London: SCM.

1971b   *Die Weltlichkeit des Alten Testaments.* Göttingen: Vandenhoeck & Ruprecht.

1972   *Grundriss der Alttestamentlichen Theologie.* Theologische Wissenschaft 3. Stuggart: Kohlhammer.

1975   *Grundriss der Alttestamentlichen Theologie.* 2d edition. Theologische Wissenschaft 3. Stuttgart: Kohlhammer.

1976   *The Old Testament and the World.* Translated by John J. Scullion. Atlanta: John Knox.

1978   *Old Testament Theology in Outline.* Translated by David E. Green. Atlanta: John Knox/Edinburgh: Clark.

1979–83 *Ezekiel: A Commentary on the Book of the Prophet Ezekiel.* 2 volumes. Translated by Ronald E. Clements and James D. Martin. Edited by Frank M. Cross, Klaus Baltzer, Leonard J. Greenspoon, and Paul D. Hanson. Hermeneia. Philadelphia: Fortress.

1982a   *Grundriss der Alttestamentlichen Theologie.* 4th edition. Theologische Wissenschaft 3. Stuttgart: Kohlhammer.

1982b   *I am Yahweh.* Translated by Douglas W. Stott. Edited by Walter Brueggemann. Atlanta: John Knox.

1985   *Grundriss der Alttestamentlichen Theologie.* 5th edition. Theologische Wissenschaft 3. Stuttgart: Kohlhammer.

Writings about Zimmerli

Donner, Herbert, Robert Hanhart, and Rudolf Smend (editors)

1977   *Beiträge zur Alttestamentlichen Theologie: Festschrift für Walther Zimmerli zum 70. Geburtstag.* Göttingen: Vandenhoeck & Ruprecht.

Walther Zimmerli's
Approach to Old Testament Theology

Excerpted with permission from Walther Zimmerli, *Old Testament Theology in Outline* (Atlanta: John Knox, 1978), pp. 13–15, 17–26. The footnotes have been reconstructed from the bibliographies on pp. 21 and 26–27.

[[13]] The Old Testament comprises a set of documents that came into being over a period of almost a thousand years. During this period Israel, from whose world the documents contained in the Old Testament derive, underwent many changes. Nomadic beginnings give way to settled life in Canaan. Herdsmen become farmers and also infiltrate earlier urban cultures. A loose association of the groups constituting Israel in the period before there was any state develops into a state, first as a single kingdom, then as two. The latter are destroyed by the blows of the great powers, first the Assyrians and then the Neo-Babylonians. The people lose their identity as a separate state; a major portion of the intellectual leadership lives in distant exile in Mesopotamia. Then a new entity, something like an ecclesiastical state, consolidates itself around Jerusalem, first under Persian, then under Macedonian-Greek hegemony.

The change in sociological structures produced changes in liturgical life, resulting finally in the elimination of a multiplicity of sanctuaries and focusing on Jerusalem. And of course, alongside of this, the exile forced the establishment of places of worship in distant lands. Modern scholarship has revealed how this historical movement has its inward aspect in the faith of Israel. Religious traditions in new situations find new interpretations. According to the law of challenge and response, a new historical challenge brings about a novel formulation of the response.

A presentation of Old Testament theology cannot close its eyes to all this movement and change, the more so in that it is characteristic of the faith of the Old Testament not to live with its back turned to the world and to history, turning inward to guard its arcanum, but rather to relate closely to the world and the course of events and engage in dialogue with whatever it encounters in history.

On the other hand, this raises the question of whether the "coherent whole" of what the Old Testament says about God, which it is the task of an Old Testament theology to present, consists merely in the continuity of history, that is, the ongoing stream of historical sequence.

The Old Testament itself makes a different claim: it firmly maintains its [[14]] faith in the sameness of the God it knows by the name of Yahweh. Throughout all changes, it maintains that this God Yahweh takes an active interest in his people Israel. In the face of all vexation and anguish, when "the right hand of the Most High" seems to have lost its power (Ps 77:11), the devout person takes refuge in this confession and "remembers" the former works of Yahweh (Ps 77:12). Here, in Yahweh himself, who has made himself known in his deeds of bygone days, this faith believes it can find the true and authentic continuity on which it can rely.

Thus it is advisable to turn our attention first to this central focus, where alone we find the inner continuity acknowledged by the faith of Israel itself. But a second point must be added at once. This faith knows that Yahweh was not the God of Israel from the beginning of the world. In the account of how the world began, Israel does not yet appear in the great table of nations displayed in Genesis 10. Not until Genesis 12, with the beginning of the story of Abraham, and in the "fathers" descended from him, do we begin to hear distant echoes of the promise of the history of Israel. According to Gen 32:29 (35:10), the name "Israel" is given first to the patriarch Jacob. With the beginning of the book of Exodus we encounter Israel as a people.

This striking phenomenon goes hand in hand with another. As early as Gen 2:4b, that is, in the context of the story of how the world began, the earliest source stratum, J, speaks quite artlessly of Yahweh as creator of the world. But the two other narrative strands, E and P, on the other hand, know that the name "Yahweh" was first revealed to Moses, when he was commissioned to lead Israel out of Egypt. This obviously preserves the correct recollection that there can be no talk of the Yahweh of the Old Testament until he reveals himself as the God of Israel and accomplishes the deliverance of Israel from Egypt.

From this perspective, too, it is advisable to take as our point of departure that focal point where the faith of the Old Testament specifically confesses the God of Israel under the name of Yahweh. It will be clearly evident that this "focal point" does not present an "image" of God to be understood statically. The God who is invoked by the name "Yahweh" repeatedly demonstrates his freedom by dashing to pieces all the "images" in which humanity would confine him. This takes place not only in Exod 3:14, in the account of how the divine name is revealed to Moses, but to an equal degree in the great prophets, or, in the realm of wisdom, in Ecclesiastes and Job.

Zimmerli, Walther. "Alttestamentliche Traditionsgeschichte und Theologie." In *Probleme biblischer Theologie* (Festschrift Gerhard von Rad), pp. 632–647. Edited by Hans Walter Wolff. Munich: Kaiser, 1971. Reprinted in his *Studien zur alttesta-mentlichen Theologie und Prophetie*, pp. 9–26. Theologische Bücherei, vol. 51. Munich: Kaiser, 1974.

Smend, Rudolf. *Die Mitte des Alten Testaments.* Theologische Studien, vol. 101. Zurich: EVZ, 1970.

Hasel, G. F. "The Problem of the Center in the Old Testament Theology Debate." *Zeitschrift für die Alttestamentliche Wissenschaft* 86 (1974): 65–82.

Zimmerli, Walther. "Zum Problem der 'Mitte des Alten Testaments.'" *Evangelische Theologie* 35 (1975): 97–118.

Fundamentals

[[17]] *"I am Yahweh, your God, who brought you out of the land of Egypt, the house of servitude. You shall have no other gods beside me." (Exod 20:2–3; Deut 5:6–7)*

At the beginning of the great revelation to Israel at Sinai, the mountain of God, stands the proclamation of the Decalogue, introduced with full solemnity by the words quoted above. The God who here appears in the storm makes himself known through his name, recalling at the same time his act of delivering Israel from servitude. On the basis of this act his people may and shall know him.

The recollection of this deliverance and the subsequent journey to Canaan under the guidance of God, which re-echoes in later summaries and creed-like statements, constituted the nucleus of what is today the monstrously expanded first portion of the canon, the Pentateuch. It is therefore advisable in the fundamental exposition of this introductory section to take as our point of departure Yahweh (§1), the God of Israel since Egypt (§2). We shall then turn our attention to the discussion of the God of the fathers (§3), which precedes this nucleus, and of the creator of the world (§4), proclaimed in the primal history. We shall conclude by treating the theologoumena of election (§5) and covenant (§6), which describe in more detail the relationship between Yahweh and Israel. [[Only sections 1 and 2 are reprinted here.]]

The Revealed Name

The faith of the Old Testament knows its God by the name of Yahweh. This pronunciation of the tetragrammaton (יהוה), which is no longer recorded in the masoretic vocalization, can be shown to be highly probable on the basis of evidence from the church fathers.

The passages that deliberately avoid speaking of Yahweh by name can as a rule be understood on the basis of specific considerations. E and P do not speak of

Yahweh before the time of Moses because of a specific view of the history of revelation, which will be discussed below. The elimination of the name of Yahweh from the so-called Elohistic psalter (Psalms 42–83) is the result of editorial revision probably based on a dread of pronouncing the holy name of [[18]] God. In Judaism, this tendency later resulted in a total avoidance of pronouncing the tetragrammaton. This tendency appears also to have been at work in the book of Esther. In the book of Job, the name of Yahweh is avoided in the discourses of chapters 3–37 because the discussion is between non-Israelites; it is replaced by the more general terms אלוה *ĕlôah* or שׁדי *šaddai*. The introductions to the speeches of God and the framework narrative in chapters 1–2 and 42 use the name of Yahweh without hesitation. Elsewhere, too, as in the Joseph story, the name of Yahweh is not placed in the mouth of non-Israelites. In Ecclesiastes, the name is probably avoided because the wise man in question prefers to distance himself from God (see [[Zimmerli 1978:]] pp. 161–163). In the book of Daniel, too, the final chapters show clearly that the Lord referred to as "God of Heaven" or "the Most High God" or simply as "God" is none other than he who is called by the name of Yahweh. The prayer in Daniel 9 uses the name "Yahweh" quite naturally.

For the audience of the Old Testament, a "name" is more than a randomly selected label. Those who are named are vulnerable; they can be invoked by means of their name. Two questions arise in this context:

1. How does the faith of the Old Testament come by its knowledge of the name of its God? The Old Testament can be heard to give various answers:

a) J uses the name "Yahweh" without hesitation even in the primal history and the patriarchal narratives.

In the context of J, the statement in Gen 4:26 stands out: in the days of Enosh, who represents the third human generation, people began to call on the name of Yahweh. Since the name "Enosh," like "Adam," can simply mean "man," it is possible there was an earlier version according to which Yahweh was called upon in the generation of the very first man. According to Horst, the present text can be understood on the basis of the distinction common in comparative religion between the high god present from the beginning (i.e., the creator) and the god that people call upon in the cult of the historical present.[1] The special contribution of the Old Testament would then be the statement that the creator and the god called upon in worship are the same Yahweh.

b) E and P take a different approach. Each in its own way represents a specific view of how the name of Yahweh was revealed. According to both, this takes place in the time of Moses, the initial period of Israel's history as already mentioned. According to E, it is at the mountain of God that Moses learns to invoke God by name; in the earlier narratives the general term

---

1. Friedrich Horst, "Die Notiz vom Anfang des Jahwekultes in Gen. 4:26," in *Libertas Christiana* (Friedrich Delekat Festschrift; ed. Walter Matthias; Munich: Kaiser, 1957) 68–74.

אלהים *ĕlōhîm*, "God," was used, which could also be applied to non-Israelite deities. When Moses is commanded to lead his enslaved people out of Egypt, he asks the name of the God under whom this is to happen; the name of Yahweh is communicated to him in a veiled way that will be considered in more detail below (Exod 3:1, 4b, 6, 9–15).

c) P, whose peculiar organization of God's history with Israel will be discussed in more detail later (see [[Zimmerli 1978:]], pp. 55–57), exhibits a process by which the name of God is revealed in three stages. Like E, P uses the general term אלהים *ĕlōhîm* at the outset when referring to the acts of God in the primordial era. According to Gen 17:1, however, God reveals himself to Abraham, the earliest of the patriarchs of Israel, under the name אל שדי *ēl* [[19]] *šaddai* (see [[Zimmerli 1978:]], p. 41). Then, according to Exod 6:2ff., he encounters Moses with equal spontaneity, introducing himself of his own accord under his name Yahweh, while referring explicitly to Genesis 17: "I am Yahweh. To Abraham, Isaac, and Jacob I appeared under the name אל שדי *ēl šaddai*, but in my name Yahweh I was not made known to them." This passage expresses most emphatically the spontaneity and novelty of the revelation of the name Yahweh. The name by which Israel may call upon its God does not simply lie ready to hand for people to use. Neither, as in E, is it given in response to a human question; it is the free gift of the God who sends his people their deliverer, thereby forging a bond between himself and them (Exod 6:7).

2. Does the name of Yahweh, which Israel calls upon, reveal something of the nature of this God?

To answer this question, we must distinguish two directions of inquiry. (a) Quite apart from the statements made by the Old Testament texts themselves, we can inquire whether philological investigation can give us any information about the original meaning of the name "Yahweh." But of course an answer in these terms need by no means have any relevance for the faith of the Old Testament. The name might have taken shape in a totally different context. This does not hold true in the same way, however, if (b) we ask whether the Old Testament context itself says anything about the meaning of the name. With such a statement, whatever its original philological accuracy may be, we are in any case dealing with an actual statement of the Old Testament that is significant for an Old Testament theology.

a) There is no lack of suggestions about what the name "Yahweh" originally meant.

Philological investigation must first deal with the question of whether we should take as our point of departure the long form "Yahweh," an abbreviated form "Yahu" as found in many names (ישעיהו *yᵉšaʿyāhû*; ירמיהו *yirmᵉyāhû*; יהויקים *yᵉhôyāqîm*, etc.), or the monosyllabic form "Yah," as found, for instance, in the acclamation "Hallelujah" (הללו יה *haĺlû yâ*). Driver claimed that he could interpret the form

"Yah" as a shout of ecstatic excitement, which then turned into a divine name and, in association with the deliverance from Egypt, became the long form with the meaning "he who is" or "he who calls into being." Eerdmans derives the name from a disyllabic form, in which he hears what was originally an onomatopoetic imitation of thunder. There are good reasons to consider the long form original; it probably represents an imperfect form of a verb הוה *hwh*. But is this root related to the Arabic verb meaning "blow," which would suggest the name of a storm god, or to the verb meaning "fall," which would suggest a god of lightning and hail? Or should we take הוה *hwh* as equivalent to היה *hyh* and interpret it as "he is" or "he shows himself efficacious" or "he calls into being"? And are we then to follow Cross in thinking of an abbreviated form of the more complete יהוה צבאות *yahweh ṣᵉbā'ôt*, "he who calls the (heavenly) hosts into being" (see [Zimmerli 1978:], p. 75)?[2] It is unlikely that we are dealing with a noun form having the meaning "being."

b) We come next to the actual statements of the Old Testament itself. When Moses asks the name of the God who sends him to Israel, he is given, [20] according to Exod 3:14, the answer: אהיה אשר אהיה *ehyeh ăšer ehyeh* ("I am who I am . . . and so you shall say to the Israelites, 'I am [אהיה *ehyeh*] has sent me to you'"). Here the name "Yahweh" is unequivocally interpreted on the basis of the verb היה *hyh* (= הוה *hwh*).

This passage, therefore, has provided the basis for most attempts to interpret the name in a way consonant with the faith of the Old Testament. The Septuagint led the way with its translation *egó eimi ho ón*, "I am the one who is," transforming the verbal expression into a nominal participle and, following Greek example, finding an ontological concept of being in Exod 3:14. It was probably sensed, however, how inappropriate this concept was within the framework of Old Testament thought. Scholars have therefore gone on to ask whether היה *hyh* might not be better taken to mean "be efficacious" (Ratschow), "be there, be present" (Vriezen), "be with someone" (Preuss).[3]

But the name "Yahweh" is here not meant to be understood on the basis of the isolated verb היה *hyh*, but rather on the basis of the figure of speech "I am who I am." This form may be compared to the lordly statement of Exod 33:19: "To whom I am gracious I am gracious, and to whom I show mercy I show mercy." In this figure of speech resounds the sovereign freedom of Yahweh, who, even at the moment he reveals himself in his name, refuses simply to put himself at the disposal of humanity or to allow humanity to comprehend him. We must also take into account

2. Frank M. Cross, "Yahweh and the God of the Patriarchs," *Harvard Theological Review* 55 (1962) 225–59. [Zimmerli does not give the bibliographic data for the references to Driver and Eerdmans in this paragraph.]

3. Carl H. Ratschow, *Werden und Wirken* (Beiheft zur Zeitschrift für Alttestamentliche Wissenschaft 70; Berlin: Töpelmann, 1941); Theodorus C. Vriezen, [*An Outline of Old Testament Theology* (trans. S. Neuijen; Oxford: Blackwell/Boston: Branford, 1958) 235–36]; Horst D. Preuss, ". . . ich will mit dir sein!" *ZAW* 80 (1968) 139–73.

God's refusal to impart his name to Jacob in Gen 32:30: "Why do you ask about my name?" According to the statement of Exod 3:14, at the very point where Yahweh reveals his true name so that people can call him by it, he remains free, and can be properly understood only in the freedom with which he introduces himself.

This knowledge, which also lies behind God's free revelation of his name in Exod 6:2 (P), coming not in response to any human question, was given further expression in certain characteristic Priestly turns of phrase. In the laws of the Holiness Code in Leviticus 18ff., the legislation is underlined by copious use of the appended phrase "I am Yahweh" or "I am Yahweh, your God." Here, in the context of proclamation of the law, this formulaic phrase of self-introduction maintains the majesty of him who issues the law, who encounters people as their Lord. It is possible to ask, even if a definitive answer cannot be given, whether there were occasions in the liturgical life of Israel when this free self-introduction of Yahweh in his name was publicly spoken (by the priests?). The preamble to the Decalogue with its אנכי יהוה אלהיך *ānōkî yahweh ēlōhêkā* [['I am Yahweh your God']] may also support this suggestion.

In a different way this element centered into the prophetic formulation of the so-called "proof-saying" (*Erweiswort*), found repeatedly in the book of Ezekiel but apparently originating in earlier pre-literary prophecy and its messages from God in the context of the Yahweh war (1 Kgs 20:13, 28). Here a statement of what Yahweh will do with or for his people (expanded [[21]] by the addition of a motivation or stated without any motivation at all) can be concluded with the formula: "And you [he, they] will know that I am Yahweh." This formula declares the announced action of Yahweh to be the place where people will know—and acknowledge—Yahweh as he introduces himself. Yahweh declares himself in what he does. This rhetorical form is also found in Joel and the late exilic Deutero-Isaiah (see Isa 49:22–26). See also [[Zimmerli 1978:]] pp. 207, 229.

This freedom of Yahweh means he is never simply an "object," even in his name which he graciously reveals—the third commandment of the Decalogue seeks to protect the freedom implicit in Yahweh's name in a very specific way against "religious" abuse. And this freedom of Yahweh must be taken account of in all other statements about the faith of the Old Testament. In the only passage where the Old Testament itself attempts to provide an explanation of the name "Yahweh," it refuses to "explain" the name in a way that would confine it within the cage of a definition. It seeks to express the fact that we can speak of Yahweh only in attentive acknowledgment of the way he demonstrates his nature (in his acts and his commandments).

. . . .

Yahweh, God of Israel since Egypt

In Hos 13:4, we hear the words: "I, Yahweh, am your God since the land of
Egypt. You do not know any god except for me, or any savior except ⟦22⟧
for me." This statement corresponds in content with the beginning of the
Decalogue (Exod 20:2–3); like the latter passage, it says two things. First,
where Yahweh presents himself to the faith of the Old Testament, he does
so as the God of Israel, who will not tolerate any other god. And even
more clearly than the beginning of the Decalogue it underlines the fact
that this "God of Israel" is a relationship that has existed from the beginning of time, in the sense, for instance, that the Babylonian god Shamash
was the sun god by definition. Yahweh is the God of Israel by reason of
certain historical events associated with the name of Egypt (to which the
preamble to the Decalogue adds: "the house of servitude").

This phrase points to the events recorded in the book of Exodus, in
which the people of Israel first makes its appearance. Their forebears, as
Exod 1:11 maintains with historical accuracy, were compelled to perform
forced labor for the building of the provision cities Pithom and Ramses
during the reign of Ramses II (1290–1224 B.C.). Moses, who bears an
Egyptian name, led them forth at the command of Yahweh. At the Sea of
Reeds they escaped miraculously from the pursuing Egyptians, whose king
had refused to let them go. This event is recorded in the earliest hymn
preserved in the Old Testament, the Song of Miriam. "Sing to Yahweh, for
highly exalted is he; horse and rider he cast into the sea" (Exod 15:21).
What Israel experienced was no piece of chance good fortune such as
might be recounted dispassionately. In this experience Israel recognized
and confessed Yahweh, who refuses to be worshiped alongside others. The
glorification of this initial experience of the exodus also appears in the
observation that there is no other event in the entire history of Israel so
surrounded by a plethora of miraculous interventions on the part of Yahweh as the event of the deliverance from Egypt. Again and again the description of the exodus makes mention of the "signs and wonders"
performed by Yahweh for his people, "with mighty hand and outstretched
arm." Then the road leads out into the desert, toward the land that is to
be given to Israel. The Old Testament returns again and again to creed-
like mentions (von Rad)[4] of this event, in detailed summaries of Yahweh's
history with Israel as well as in succinct formulas like the preamble to the

---

4. Gerhard von Rad, *Das formgeschichtliche Problem des Hexateuch* (Beiträge zur Wissenschaft vom Alten und Neuen Testament 4/26; Stuttgart: Kohlhammer, 1938); repr. in his *Gesammelte Studien zum Alten Testament* (Theologische Bücherei 8; Munich: Kaiser, 1958) 9–86;
English translation: "The Form-Critical Problem of the Hexateuch," in *The Problem of the
Hexateuch and Other Essays* (trans. E. W. T. Dicken; New York: McGraw-Hill, 1966) 1–78.

Decalogue. When the farmer brings his offering to the sanctuary, he speaks in his prescribed prayer of what Yahweh did for his fathers (Deut 26:5–10). When a father tries to make the commandments meaningful to his son, he tells of this event (Deut 6:20ff.). According to Joshua 24, it was spoken of when Israel assembled at Shechem. The poetry of the cult recounts the exodus immediately after speaking of Yahweh's acts at creation (Psalm 136). Commandments in the Holiness Code can be underlined by reference to it (Lev 22:32–33; 25:55). Even the prophet Ezekiel, narrating the story of Israel's sins, with the two kingdoms personified in two girls with bedouin [[23]] names, says in Ezekiel 23 that they come from Egypt, where they became Yahweh's own. Cf. also Ezekiel 20; Isa 51:9–10).

Alongside such passages, there are a few that state that Yahweh "found Israel in the desert" (Deut 32:10; Hos 9:10; cf. Bach).[5] This can hardly refer to a different story of Israel's origins; these passages must be interpreted in the same light. In Ezekiel 16, the motif of the foundling has been incorporated into the story of Jerusalem's beginnings, a story organized very differently.

. . . .

We must now consider the significance of this fundamental confessional statement for the faith attested by the Old Testament.

1. In the first place, it is quite clear that the Old Testament, however much it thinks of Yahweh as majestic and free, knows this God from the very outset as the God who wants to involve himself with Israel. In the Old Testament we never come across any attempt to inquire into the nature of Yahweh *per se*. This could be observed even in the only passage that reflected on the significance of the name "Yahweh." How the God of Israel acts with respect to his people, with respect to the individual Israelite, and later, as the horizon of religious thought expands in head-on encounter with other forms of religious belief, with respect to all of creation and the nations dominates the Old Testament statements. [[24]]

2. At the beginning of the exodus story, on which the faith of the Old Testament never ceases to reflect, stands the great deliverance from the house of servitude. It is not really accurate to turn this event into an "exodus principle," which in turn produces a "principle of hope" (Bloch).[6] What is really central is not the fact of the "exodus," which would lead to

5. Robert Bach, *Die Erwählung Israels in der Wüste* (Ph.D. diss., Bonn, 1951).

6. Ernst Bloch, *Das Prinzip Hoffnung* (Gesamatausgabe 5; Frankfurt: Suhrkamp, 1959). For a discussion of Bloch's views, see Walther Zimmerli, *Der Mensch und seine Hoffnung im Alten Testament* (Kleine Vandenhoeck–Reihe 272S; Göttingen: Vandenhoeck & Ruprecht, 1968) 163–78; English translation: *Man and His Hope in the Old Testament* (Studies in Biblical Theology 2/20; Naperville, Illinois: Allenson, 1971) 151–65. See also Hans-Joachim Kraus, "Das Thema 'Exodus,'" *Evangelische Theologie* 31 (1971) 608–23.

new forms of "going out" into the future, but the encounter with the God who has pity on those who are enslaved. We often hear the Old Testament speak of the God who hears the crying of the oppressed and sends them their deliverer; this image becomes a category by which subsequent experiences in the history of Israel can be understood (the judges, Saul, David). Therefore even Ezekiel and above all Deutero-Isaiah can paint deliverance from the terrible distress of the exile in the glowing colors of a new exodus, in which the events of the first exodus out of Egypt return antitypically. In Trito-Isaiah we can observe how the images of exodus and roads in the desert begin to form part of the stock language of religious discourse (see [[Zimmerli 1978:]] p. 226).

3. Having seen that in the "exodus" we are dealing with an act of mercy on the part of the God who has pity on his people and delivers them, we must go on at once to say that the help Israel experiences sets it on a course on which God continues to be with it. The theme of "guidance in the desert" (Noth)[7] is intimately associated with the theme of "exodus." From the very beginning, Yahweh was known to Israel as the "shepherd of Israel," who accompanies it. Victor Maag has justifiably placed great emphasis on this heritage of Israel from its nomadic past.[8] But a sociological reference to "the nomadic heritage" will not in itself suffice for a theological understanding. We must go on to state that when Israel proclaims "Yahweh, your God since Egypt," as an element of its faith, it is also keeping alive the knowledge of the God who remains with Israel on its journey. Neither is this knowledge abrogated by all the later theologoumena about the presence of Yahweh in specific places (see [[Zimmerli 1978:]] §9). This knowledge makes it possible for Israel not to lose its God in all its subsequent "departures," when it is snatched out of the "rest" to which God brings it in the land (Deut 12:9–10), and to survive with the guidance of the "shepherd of Israel." Israel remains preeminently a people of hope.

4. In the confession of "Yahweh, the God of Israel since Egypt," Israel's faith receives an intimate association with a historical event. An initial historical deliverance, experienced by those escaping from Egypt, resounds in the earliest extant hymn of Israel. It has recently been accurately pointed out (Albrektson)[9] that it is quite inappropriate to set up a

7. Martin Noth, *Überlieferungsgeschichte des Pentateuch* (Stuttgart: Kohlhammer, 1948); English translation: *History of Pentateuchal Traditions* (trans. B. W. Anderson; Englewood Cliffs, New Jersey: Prentice-Hall, 1971).

8. Victor Maag, "Der Hirt Israels," *Schweizer Theologische Umschau* 28 (1958) 2–28; idem, "Das Gottesverständnis des Alten Testaments," *Nederlands Theologisch Tijdschrift* 21 (1966/67) 161–207.

9. Bertil Albrektson, *History and the Gods* (Coniectanea Biblica, Old Testament series 1; Lund: Gleerup, 1967).

contrast between Israel, with its sense of history, and the nature religions of the surrounding world, without any historical ties. The world of Assyria and Babylonia is also familiar with the intervention of the gods in the course of history and dependence on divine aid in historical crises. But it remains undeniable that Israel's basing ⟦25⟧ of its faith on that early act of deliverance, in which it knew that a single Lord was at work, not a multiplicity of powers, established a particularly intimate relationship between its faith and its historical experiences.

Having said this, we must still avoid the mistaken assumption that for Israel history as such became the revelatory word of Yahweh. Such an understanding of history as a phenomenon in its own right, to be taken as an independent quantity in God's revelation, is alien to the Old Testament. By the same token, an isolated fact of history is not as such simply a proclamation of Yahweh. Vast stretches of Israel's historical experience that come to light in the Old Testament remain silent, having nothing new to say. But then it can happen that messengers speaking for Yahweh appear unexpectedly in the context of exciting events, proclaiming the historical events to be Yahweh's call to decision. Here we recognize very clearly that "history" by no means simply proclaims Yahweh in its course of events; in the very midst of the historical disaster that is accompanied by the message of the prophets, it is especially urgent that Yahweh's word be heard. See ⟦Zimmerli 1978:⟧ §20 and §21.

Thus we must also remember in retrospect that the "deliverance from Egypt" was also accompanied by Yahweh's word. The preponderance of evidence still supports the assumption that Moses, the man with the Egyptian name, did in fact lead Israel out of Egypt "in the name of Yahweh" and thus, however we may go on to define the "office" of Moses more precisely, determined the subsequent "representation" (Noth)[10] of the acts of Yahweh in Israel.

5. In this event Yahweh declared himself for the faith of Israel. In what took place he made himself known as the deliverer of that company, which then handed on its confession to all "Israel" living at a later date in Canaan as the twelve tribes. Starting with this confession, he is the "God of Israel." Not because Israel chose him voluntarily or because he has a "primary relationship" with Israel, but simply because by a free act he delivered those who dwelt in the house of servitude in Egypt—therefore he is their God. What the self-introduction formula sought to express in its own way is defined in terms of this historical self-statement of Yahweh and

10. Martin Noth, "Die Vergegenwärtigung des Alten Testaments in der Verkündigung," *Evangelische Theologie* 12 (1952/53) 6–17; repr. in his *Gesammelte Studien zum Alten Testament* (Theologische Bücherei 39; Munich: Kaiser, 1969), 2:86–98.

given concrete meaning. Whatever those who dwelt in Egypt may previously have known of Yahweh, under this new event his name was either forgotten or subsequently incorporated into this "initial knowledge": he who is invoked in the name "Yahweh" made himself known as the God of those brought up out of the house of servitude in Egypt and became the "God of Israel" through an expansion of the circle of those confessing him in the land of Canaan. Only when this self-statement of Yahweh is recognized is the phrase "Yahweh, God of Israel since Egypt" properly understood.

6. This makes a final point clear. The event that bears significance for the beginning of "Israel's" faith in Yahweh has from the outset a political [[26]] dimension. The beginning does not consist in the illumination of a single individual who then assembles other individuals around him, like Buddha, but in the deliverance experienced by a cohesive group. This political dimension, relating to a people defined in secular terms, will subsequently remain a hallmark of Yahwism. The individual is not forgotten and individual responsibility is increasingly stressed as time goes on, but it remains clear even in the late statements of the book of Daniel that individuals are not isolated from the people of Yahweh as a whole, nor can they take refuge in a special relationship with their God such as might remove them from the concrete events of the "secular" world. On the special problems posed by "wisdom," see [[Zimmerli 1978:]] §18.

Synopsis of Zimmerli's *Old Testament Theology in Outline* (1978)

Walther Zimmerli on Life before God

Excerpted with permission from Walther Zimmerli, *Old Testament Theology in Outline* (Atlanta: John Knox, 1978), pp. 141–47. The footnotes have been reconstructed from the bibliography on pp. 147–48.

[[141]] It is reasonable to ask whether a section on "life before God" belongs in an Old Testament theology. Especially in a theology that takes as its point of departure the principle that the Old Testament faith derives from Yahweh's "statement" about himself in history. But our discussion has shown how the faith of the Old Testament knows its God not in an absolute transcendence but rather in his approach to Israel and the world, and how the Old Testament, in what it has to say about God, thinks of itself as a book of God's words addressed to people. And it is also true that in the "response" God expects from those he addresses God himself can be recognized as in a mirror.

This "response" is found in people's obedience to the commandments of God as formulated in his law. But it is also found when Israel submits to the gracious governance of its God, even when no specific commandments are formulated (§16). Yahweh's nature is also recognizable in those situations when people turn to him in thanksgiving or petition (§17). Even in situations in which individuals, sensible of their relationship to the creator, order their daily course according to reasonable decisions, making thankful and obedient use of the gifts given them by Yahweh, their creator, it is possible to recognize the God who guides their lives (§18). [[Only section 16 is reprinted here.]]

The Response of Obedience

As Parts II and III have made clear, Yahweh's love for his people has two aspects, which are inseparable from each other. It expresses itself in Yahweh's gracious guidance, beginning with his deliverance of Israel out of the house of bondage in Egypt, and subsequently in all his gifts bestowed on Israel and the world. But the gift always implies a requirement. This imperative aspect takes concrete form in the words of Yahweh's commandments, which expect very specific actions in obedience to them.

The response of obedience itself has two aspects. In the first place, it consists of obedience to the concrete requirements of the law as elaborated in Part III.

203

⟦142⟧ In this context, an important role is played by "hearing" (שמע *šmᶜ*, which can also mean "obey"), "observing" (שמע *šmr* in the sense of "keep, follow"), and "doing" (עשה *ᶜśh*; cf. the stereotyped formulas of the Sinai episode [Exod 19:8; 24:3; and 24:7 in conjunction with שמע *šmᶜ*]). They refer to a clearly delineated act of obedience.

Likewise, the response of faith consists of the acceptance and proper stewardship of the gifts given by Yahweh, which Israel receives within the framework of having its history guided and governed by its God. It is not always clear in any particular case at what point precisely the gift to be received with pure hands turns into the commandment that requires active obedience. The discussion to follow will illustrate this point clearly with reference to certain specific passages.

1. Yahweh, who comes to his people, wishes to have his nature reflected in theirs. This point is made especially clear in the statement that introduces the core of the legal material in the Holiness Code: "You shall be holy, because I, Yahweh your God, am holy (קדוש *qādôs*)" (Lev 19:2). Here the closeness between Yahweh's gift and his commandment is unmistakable.

. . . .

2. The projection of Yahweh's divine nature upon the community living before God, and at the same time the unmistakable tension between gift and commandment, indicative and imperative, can be seen even more clearly in the term צדקה (צדק) *ṣᵉdāqâ (ṣedeq)*, translated very imperfectly as "righteoussness." This circumstance conceals the fundamental theological problem of "divine and human righteousness."

Recent studies have shown clearly the the "righteousness" predicated of Yahweh must not be confused with the blindfolded "justice" that strictly apportions to every person the reward or punishment he or she deserves according to an objective norm that stands above all parties. When the Old Testament speaks of "Yahweh's righteousness," it means rather the social bond existing between him and his people and Yahweh's actions based on this bond. The plural form צדקות יהוה *ṣidqôt yahweh*, found as early as the Song of Deborah (Judg 5:11; also 1 Sam 12:7 and Mic 6:5), is best rendered "saving acts." The singular forms צדקה *ṣᵉdāqâ* and צדק *ṣedeq* are often used in the Psalms and in Deutero- and Trito-Isaiah, which come from the milieu of the Psalms, to refer to Yahweh's beneficent order, which can be recognized even in the realm of ⟦143⟧ nature. According to Jepsen, the masculine form צדק *ṣedeq* means "rightness," "order," while the feminine form צדקה *ṣᵉdāqâ* means the "conduct that aims at right order."[1] Schmid prefers to understand the term in its various ramifications on the basis of its Canaanite background, where it expresses the harmony of the world in all its different realms.[2]

---

1. Alfred Jepsen, "צדק und צדקה im Alten Testament," in *Gottes Wort und Gottes Land* (Hans-Wilhelm Hertzberg Festschrift; ed. Henning Graf Reventlow; Göttingen: Vandenhoeck & Ruprecht, 1965) 78–89.

2. Hans H. Schmid, *Gerechtigkeit als Weltordnung* (Beiträge zur historischen Theologie 40; Tübingen: Mohr, 1968.

Now it turns out that the term "righteousness," which characterizes the sphere of divine justice, understood in Israel with specific reference to Yahweh, becomes likewise the central term for human justice. The extent to which Israel sees this human justice as a reflection of Yahweh's justice is illustrated especially well in the twin acrostic Psalms 111/112. The former extols the glorious acts of Yahweh; the latter, the actions of the person who fears God. In verse 3b, each of them uses precisely the same words to refer to both God and the person before God: "His 'righteousness' is forever."

If we go on to ask for a more detailed description of human righteousness, the fact cannot be overlooked that it is associated with keeping the commandments. Ezek 18:5ff., for example, describes righteous persons in terms of their conduct with respect to a series of commandments: "Consider the man who is righteous and does what is just and right. He never feasts at mountain-shrines, never lifts his eyes to the idols of Israel, never dishonors another man's wife. . . . " According to this passage, it is individuals' right actions, according to the norm of the law, that constitute their "righteousness."

But the list culminates surprisingly in the repeated formula: "Such a man is righteous; he shall live." The first half of this statement is composed formally in the style of a priestly "declaration," like those found above all in the legislation governing leprosy in Leviticus 13 (Rendtorff).[3] Here it pronounces a general verdict upon the man. Von Rad has pointed out that more is involved here than an analytic statement.[4] The declaration must be seen in the context of the priestly entrance liturgies, which pronounce the general divine verdict of "righteousness" upon the pilgrim, who has been examined on some of the marks of the righteous person. Thus we see in Ps 24:4–5 how the one "who has clean hands and a pure heart, who has not set his mind on falsehood, and has not committed perjury" is granted entrance to the Temple; it is further said of him: "He shall receive a blessing from Yahweh, and righteousness from God his savior." Here "righteousness" is clearly something received at the sanctuary, not simply achieved by the individual. Gen 15:6 states that Abraham believed in God and "it was counted as righteousness"; von Rad has shown elsewhere that this statement is connected with "righteousness" accorded by declaration.[5] We see especially clearly in Job 33:26 how God restores "righteousness" to the sinner who has been warned by his illnesses and then prays to God.

In sum, all talk of human "righteousness," like that heard at the sanctuary, is like the talk of Israel's "holiness": there is obvious tension between

---

3. Rolf Rendtorff, *Die Gesetze in der Priesterschrift* (Forschungen zur Religion und Literatur des Alten und Neuen Testaments 62; Göttingen: Vandenhoeck & Ruprecht, 1954).

4. Gerhard von Rad, "'Gerechtigkeit' und 'Leben' in der Kultsprache der Psalmen," in *Festschrift Alfred Bertholet zum 80. Geburtstag* (ed. Walter Baumgartner; Tübingen: Mohr, 1950) 418–37; repr. in his *Gesammelte Studien zum Alten Testament* (Theologische Bücherei 8; Munich: Kaiser, 1958) 225–47.

5. Gerhard von Rad, "Die Anrechnung des Glaubens zur Gerechtigkeit," *Theologische Literaturzeitung* 76 (1951) 129–32; repr. in his *Gesammelte Studien zum Alten Testament* (Theologische Bücherei 8; Munich: Kaiser, 1958) 130–35.

what the law given by Yahweh seriously requires on the one hand, and on the other the concomitant superabundance that is an unearned gift. Neither aspect can simply be eliminated in favor of the other. The law that in the great legal corpora of Deuteronomy and the Holiness Code culminates in the alternatives of salvation and perdition, that confronts people with a promise and a threat, is not to be abrogated. But Israel is also familiar with the will of Yahweh to exercise a beneficent "righteousness" over Israel, only rarely (as in Ps 7:12) associated with his wrath: "God is a 'righteous' judge, and a God who is daily angered." Israel, living before God, knows that it is called to the "righteousness" that is indispensable for real "life." Therefore the theme of "righteousness" also dominates the prayers of the Psalms. At the beginning of the psalter there is placed, like a call to decision, the two-fold image of the "righteous" person and the "wicked," who is blown away like chaff at the judgment (Psalm 1), so that the worshiper will always keep in mind [[144]] that the prayer of the devout can never evade the question of being in the right before Yahweh.

3. Deuteronomy grounds Yahweh's election of the patriarchs on a simple reference to Yahweh's love; see [[Zimmerli 1978:]] p. 45. The images of marriage and childhood, which involve the notion of divine love, are also used to describe the relationship of Yahweh to Israel. "When Israel was a boy, I loved him; I called my son out of Egypt" (Hos 11:1). Besides the verb אהב *ʾhb*, "love," used in this passage, the relevant terminology includes the noun חסד *ḥesed*, which refers to the "grace" appropriate in the context of a specific social bond, and רחמים *raḥămîm*, which means natural love like that of a mother for her child. One of Yahweh's solemn adjectival predicates is רחום וחנון *raḥûm wᵉḥannûn* (Exod 34:6 and elsewhere).

Once again it is appropriate to cite the conclusion of the twin Psalms 111/112, where verse 4b applies the same adjectival predicate to Yahweh and to the righteous person. Here the notion is probably of compassion toward one's neighbor; elsewhere, most clearly once again in the parenetic sections of Deuteronomy, the emphasis is on human love for God. The full exposition of this theme in Deut 6:5 admonishes listeners to love Yahweh with all their "heart and soul and strength." But when this loving is immediately associated with keeping the commandments, with serving Yahweh and going by his ways (Deut 10:12; 11:22; cf. also the Decalogues: Exod 20:6; Deut 5:10), we can see how human love for God cannot simply be equated with God's love for Israel. Israel's reply is a response to Yahweh's initiative. The love for Yahweh referred to here is never simply free intrusion into the presence of God, but an approach to God along the road he has cleared. We will speak later about the "fear of God" that is associated with love for him.

Besides Deuteronomy, it is primarily several of the Psalms that speak of people's love for God (18:2 רחם *rḥm*; 116:1 אהב *ʾhb*[?]; 31:24 אהב *ʾhb*). That it is also possible to speak of loving the commandments of Yahweh (119:47) shows once more how love follows the summons of Yahweh along the paths which he maps out. Deut 30:6 transcends everything else that is said, speaking of this love in terms reminiscent of the New Testament talk of the charisma of love in 1 Corinthians 13 and calling it a consequence of a circumcision of the heart performed by God himself. Thus the Old Testament already suggests, if not especially often, at least in crucial passages, that people must respond to Yahweh's love with their own love.

4. Amos 3:2 used the verb "know" to describe Yahweh's election of Israel. Jeremiah, too, according to 1:5 realizes that Yahweh "knew" him and thus made him his prophetic instrument. Now if knowledge of Yahweh also plays a significant role in the life of people before God, it must be stressed even more than in the case of "love" for God that the human response of [[145]] knowledge does not share in the creative power of the Lord who chooses his people, but can only return to Yahweh along the road that he himself has pioneered.

. . . .

5. In Deuteronomy the requirement to love Yahweh was linked with the requirement to fear him. Far beyond the limits of Deuteronomy, this fear of Yahweh plays an important role in E (Wolff),[6] in circles antedating the writing prophets, in a series of Psalms, and above all in wisdom literature, where it practically becomes the supreme requirement. It is strikingly absent in P and Ezekiel. The juxtaposition of these two concepts may at first seem surprising. If love appears to bring people into the presence of Yahweh, "fear" appears to remove them from this presence.

Now it is doubtless true that the "fear of Yahweh" repeatedly recalls the distance that separates creatures from their creator and Lord. In all periods of its history, Israel has had a sense of awe before the Lord, who transcends all Israel's power to love and understand, and whose encounter [[146]] from time to time produces uncontrollable terror (Volz).[7] Israel encountered the mysterious side of God in its worship, which never eliminated the element of "holiness." Even when licensed into the very

6. Hans Walter Wolff, "Erkenntnis Gottes im Alten Testament," *Evangelische Theologie* 15 (1955) 426–31; idem, "Zur Thematik der elohistischen Fragmente im Pentateuch," *Evangelische Theologie* 29 (1969) 59–72; English translation: "The Elohistic Fragments in the Pentateuch," *Interpretation* 26 (1972) 158–73; repr. in *The Vitality of Old Testament Traditions* (ed. Walter Brueggemann; Atlanta: John Knox, 1975) 67–82.

7. Paul Volz, *Das Dämonische in Jahwe* (Sammlung gemeinverständlicher Vorträge und Schriften 110; Tübingen: Mohr, 1924).

presence of Yahweh, people have felt something of terror (Gen 28:17; Isa 6:5; Amos 3:8). In its wisdom musings (Ecclesiastes) and its attempts to understand the mysteries of human destiny (Job), Israel never evaded the terror evoked by Yahweh's impenetrability.

But it is a striking fact that, in all its talk of the fear of Yahweh, the faith of the Old Testament never was diverted into mere trepidation before God. This is probably in part because in Yahweh Israel knew that it confronted a Lord in whom it encountered not only mystery and arbitrary caprice, but a Lord who had promised to be Israel's God and who, in his law, had shown Israel the way that made life before him possible. Therefore in the Old Testament "fear of God" often becomes synonymous with obedience to the commandments of Yahweh.

· ·

Yahweh's law summons people into his presence. Obedience to his will promises life. This explains how the talk of fear of God as the proper attitude for people before Yahweh can, quite surprisingly, take on a decided note of confidence. "Fear of God" becomes quite generally a term for the piety that brings people within the orbit of Yahweh's protection: "In the fear of Yahweh there is confidence and trust, even for children he [Yahweh] is a refuge. The fear of Yahweh is a fountain of life, so that one may escape the snares of death" (Prov 14:26–27). Thus one might almost say: whoever fears Yahweh need have no fear, but whoever does not fear Yahweh must have fear. "The wicked are wracked with anxiety all their days, the ruthless man for all the years in store for him," says Eliphaz the Temanite (Job 15:20). How wisdom speaks of the fear of Yahweh will have to await detailed discussion in §18 〚not reprinted here〛.

6. The term "belief" or "faith" is sometimes used to describe the proper response of people to what Yahweh does. It does not occur frequently, but it is found in a few momentous passages. As in the case of the "fear" of 〚147〛 Yahweh, we are no longer dealing with an attitude that reflects Yahweh's own attitude. The term refers instead to the way a person who is weak derives stability from someone else, who is strong.

The notion of mere "holding an opinion," which is one of the senses of the English word "believe," is totally absent from the Hebrew האמין *heʾĕmîn*. This word derives from the root אמן *ʾmn*, "be firm, stable, secure," familiar to everyone from another derivate, "amen," which can be used as a response to emphasize a curse (Deut 27:15–26; Num 5:22), a royal command (1 Kgs 1:36), a wish (Jer 28:6), or even a prayer (Ps 41:14 and elsewhere, concluding a subsidiary collection of Psalms). One theory holds that האמין *heʾĕmîn* should be understood as a declarative hiphil, so that belief represents a responsive "amen" to a promise made by Yahweh. Against this theory, it must be pointed out that the word is usually constructed not with the expected accusative but with the preposition ב *bᵉ*, "in," and sometimes with ל *lᵉ*, "to." According to Wildberger, it is to be understood intransitively; when used with ב *bᵉ* in theological contexts, it means "find security in," "place trust in."[8] Thus the statement in Gen 15:6 (quoted in Romans 4 and Galatians 3) about Abraham, to whom, though childless, God promised descendants like the stars of heaven in number, is to be understood as meaning: "Abraham found security in Yahweh, and Yahweh accounted this as righteousness." This "finding security" in Yahweh makes people "righteous" in the eyes of God. The absolute use of the term, in which Smend claims to find the origin of talk about "faith" in the Old Testament, occurs in Isaiah.[9] In an hour of great danger, Isaiah promises King Ahaz that the plans of the enemy will miscarry, using an elegant pun that employs the root אמן *ʾmn* twice: "If you do not believe, you will not endure"; or, literally, "If you do not find security [i.e., in Yahweh's promise], you will not be secured [= preserved]" (7:9). And Isa 28:16 refers to Yahweh's establishment of Zion (see ⟦Zimmerli 1978:⟧ pp. 76–77): "He who believes will not waver." Belief or faith means security, repose within God's promise. But because this promise is spoken through men sent by Yahweh, Exod 14:31 can say that the people believed Yahweh *and* his servant Moses. Exod 4:1, 5; 19:9 speak of Moses alone as the messenger to be believed. 2 Chr 20:20 calls upon the people to believe Yahweh and his prophets. Ps 119:66 speaks of God's commandments as the object of "belief."

In none of these passages is "belief" or "faith" to be understood as passive quietism. Jonah 3:5 says that the people of Nineveh, when they heard Jonah's message, "believed God and ordered a public fast and put on sackcloth, high and low alike." Belief effects repentance and conversion. In Exod 4:1, 5 it is signs that evoke belief among the people. Isaiah, too, offers the hesitant Ahaz such a sign (7:10ff.). In Exod 14:31 the great event of deliverance from the Egyptians is patent to the eyes of all. According to the Old Testament, then, Yahweh now and then gives belief the aid of a sign or even direct vision. But Gen 15:6 shows very clearly how people must venture to believe even contrary to what they can see with their own eyes—what kind of evidence is the view of the starry heavens that is given to Abraham? And yet it is possible to say that faith bears knowledge within it. Isa 43:10 states that Israel must be Yahweh's witness, "that they may gain insight and believe and know that I am He." But Ps 106:12 clearly states the purpose of belief: "Then they believed his [Yahweh's] promises and sang his praises." Belief sings God's praises.

---

8. Hans Wildberger, "'Glauben': Erwägungen zu האמין," in *Hebräische Wortforschung: Festschrift zum 80. Geburtstag von Walter Baumgartner* (Vetus Testamentum Supplement 16; Leiden: Brill, 1967) 372–86.

9. Rudolf Smend, "Zur Geschichte von האמין," in *Hebräische Wortforschung: Festschrift zum 80. Geburtstag von Walter Baumgartner* (Vetus Testamentum Supplement 16; Leiden: Brill, 1967) 284–90.

RONALD E. CLEMENTS

b. 1929

Law and Promise

Theological Synopsis

Brevard S. Childs of Yale identified the problems besetting the task of Old Testament theology in his book, *Biblical Theology in Crisis* (1970). The decade of the 1970s, however, rivaled that of the 1950s for the number of Old Testament theologies published as scholars tried to surmount the shortcomings of their predecessors.

Clements's *Old Testament Theology* (1978) was subtitled *A Fresh Approach.* The "fresh approach" was introduced by two questions: Who has most utilized the Old Testament and how? The answer to the first question was two groups, Jews and Christians, for both of whom the Old Testament is Scripture. The answer to the second was that Jews have understood the Old Testament primarily as *torah.* The Christians have seen it primarily as promise, but for both groups it has been a book of both law and promise. An Old Testament theology, then, might appropriately have for its centerpiece the dual notions of law and promise. Dialogue between Christians and Jews would then be facilitated.

That conclusion was buttressed by another "fresh approach," namely an examination of the Hebrew form of the canon with its two basic parts: Law (*torah*) and Prophets (promise), with the Writings as modulations on the two themes. Clements declared that one should "be critical of any presentation of an Old Testament theology which fails to show clearly the movements which led to the production of a canon of Old Testament scripture" (1976: 131). With attention to the canon, Clements, like Childs, introduced a fresh factor, a lead which continues to be explored.

Such an approach, while underscoring the unity of the Old Testament, cast that unity in a form quite unlike that of Eichrodt's unity built around the one theme of covenant. Clements was one among an increas-

210

ing number who synthesized the Old Testament around two poles in dialectical or elliptical fashion (cf. Georg Fohrer's "rule of God/communion," and Samuel Terrien's "ethics/esthetics").

For Clements the Book of Deuteronomy was a key in the canonization process. Moreover, Deuteronomy described itself as *torah* (Deut 4:44–45), a term later attached to the Pentateuch and understood as "the comprehensive list of instructions and stipulations by which Israel's covenant with God is controlled" (1978: 110). Highlighting Deuteronomy's theological message in *God's Chosen People* (1969), Clements explained how the people of God, and also God, became a context for law and promise.

Clements proposed that Judah's seventh century became the context for promise and hope to come to the fore. It was in the Deuteronomic movement and its ambition to reestablish a united Israel, rather than in the postexilic period, that we first see signs of hope and expectation, according to Clements. The promise factor was large in the prophets, even though, for reasons which Clements lists, critical scholars have not so interpreted them. But they well might, says Clements, if they recognized how the New Testament used the Old Testament as promise, as also did intertestamental literature, including Qumran. One should recognize, too, that the original prophets had an openness to further interpretation (cf. Shear-jashub in Isa 7:3; 10:20–23; 11:11, 16). Moreover, the prophets' writings may well have been brought together around a theme. From the standpoint of canon, once the prophets were interpreted as promise, so were the books brought alongside them, such as the Psalms and even the Pentateuch. In short, the promise theme, like the theme of law, is pervasive, and so both are central to the Old Testament.

Ronald E. Clements received bachelor's and master's degrees from Spurgeon College in London and Christ College in Cambridge, respectively. His Ph.D. degree is from the University of Sheffield in 1961. He has been a minister of Baptist churches in Sheffield and Stratford-on-Avon. His appointments included lecturer at New College, Edinburgh (1960–67), and at the University of Cambridge (1967–83). He is currently the Samuel Davidson Professor of Old Testament at King's College, University of London. He has written commentaries, among others, on Exodus, Isaiah 1–39, and Jeremiah.

E.A.M.

Writings by Clements

1969 *God's Chosen People: A Theological Interpretation of the Book of Deuteronomy.* Valley Forge, Pennsylvania: Judson/London: SCM.

1976   *One Hundred Years of Old Testament Interpretation.* Philadelphia: West-
        minster. [British edition: *A Century of Old Testament Study* (Guildford/
        London: Lutterworth).]
1978   *Old Testament Theology: A Fresh Approach.* New Foundations Theological
        Library. London: Marshall, Morgan & Scott/Atlanta: John Knox.
1980   *Isaiah and the Deliverance of Jerusalem: A Study of the Interpretation of
        Prophecy in the Old Testament.* Journal for the Study of the Old Testa-
        ment Supplement 13. Sheffield: JSOT Press.

Ronald E. Clements's
Approach to Old Testament Theology

Excerpted with permission from Ronald E. Clements, *Old Testament Theology: A Fresh Approach* (Atlanta: John Knox, 1978), pp. 15–19, 201.

The Problem of Old Testament Theology

⟦15⟧ All of these factors bring us back to a fundamental consideration about the aim and purpose of an Old Testament theology. It should be concerned to provide some degree of theological insight and significance in relation to the Old Testament literature which we have. This canonical form of the literature represents the 'norm', if only in the sense that it represents the way in which the Old Testament is read and interpreted in the Jewish and Christian communities. To probe behind this canonical form is important, and should provide a basis for obtaining a better understanding of it, as also is the way in which this canonical form has subsequently been understood and interpreted in Jewish and Christian tradition. The questions of tradition and canon are interrelated, since the canon of the Old Testament represents a kind of 'freezing' of the tradition that was central to Israelite-Jewish religion at a critical moment in its history.

The Old Testament as Canon

All of these considerations lead us to recognise the great importance that attaches to the form, function and concept of the Old Testament as canon. It has therefore been a welcome feature of recent approaches to the problem of biblical theology to have rediscovered the notion of canon as a central feature of the Old Testament, which must be allowed to play its part in the presentation of an Old Testament theology.[1] At a very basic level we can see that it is because the Old Testament forms a canon, and is not simply a collection of ancient Near Eastern documents, that we can expect to find in it a 'theology', and not just a report of ancient religious ideas. There is a real connection between the ideas of 'canon' and 'theology', for it is the status of these writings as a canon of sacred scripture that marks them out as containing a word of God that is still believed to

1. Cf. B. S. Childs, *Biblical Theology in Crisis* (1970); J. A. Sanders, *Torah and Canon* (1973); and D. A. Knight (ed.), *Tradition and Theology in the Old Testament* (1977), pp. 259–326.

be authoritative. There are good reasons, therefore, ⟦16⟧ why it matters a great deal that the historical and literary problems relating to the formation and acceptance of the canon should occupy a place in our discussion.

One point becomes immediately clear, and this is that the date of composition of a document, or writing, in the Old Testament does not, of itself, determine its place in the canon. Similarly where, as is supremely the case in the Pentateuch, there is evidence that a great multitude of sources have been used to create the extant whole, then we are in a real way committed to trying to understand this whole, rather than to elucidating the separate parts.

Perhaps most of all, however, the concern with canon forces us to realise that the Old Testament has a distinctive, and in many ways unexpected, shape. This becomes clearest as soon as we follow out the guideline provided by the Hebrew (Jewish) shape of the canon, which must be accorded full authority as the oldest, and most basic, form of it. The earliest Christian Church took over the Old Testament in its Greek (Alexandrine) form, whereas the separation between Judaism and Christianity led Judaism to revert exclusively to the Hebrew (Palestinian) form. In spite of many problems and historical obscurities concerning the way in which the formation of the canon developed in the first century B.C. and in the ensuing century, we may confidently recognise that this Palestinian form of the canon represents the oldest, and most basic, form of the Old Testament. In this it is made up of three separate parts: the Pentateuch, or *tôrâh*, the Prophets (later subdivided into the Former and Latter Prophets), and the Writings. These three parts correspond to three levels of authority, with the Pentateuch standing at the highest level, the Prophets below this and the Writings further down still. When therefore the New Testament characterises the entire Old Testament as a book of 'Law' (Greek *nomos* translating Hebrew *tôrâh*) this reflects the canonical priority accorded to the Pentateuch. In a similar fashion the characterising of the historical narratives from Joshua to 2 Kings as 'Prophets' is not without significance when it comes to understanding them as a whole.

From a literary perspective, enlightened by historical criticism, one feature becomes very marked in regard to the structure ⟦17⟧ of the canon. This is that each part contains material from very different ages, spread rather broadly over the period from 1000 B.C. to approximately 200 B.C., or a little later. Age is not of itself therefore a determinative factor in explaining why particular books are in the part of the canon where they are now found.

In addition to this we also discover as a result of source criticism that there are interesting areas of overlap between some of the circles to which we must ascribe authorship of parts of the Pentateuch and Prophets. This is most evident in regard to the book of Deuteronomy in the Pentateuch and the 'Deuteronomic' character of prominent editorial tendencies in the Former and Latter Prophets. Other literary affinities are also to be seen, as for example between some psalms and certain parts of the prophetic corpus.

Yet further literary puzzles reveal themselves, for historical-literary criticism shows us that the Pentateuch has in some respects acquired its canonical status in a curious reverse order. There is widespread agreement that the book of Deuteronomy, the last book of the Pentateuch, was the first to acquire canonical status, albeit in a somewhat different form from that which it now has. Furthermore it is now widely accepted that it once was joined on to form the first 'chapter' of a work which stretched from Deuteronomy to 2 Kings, and thus combined 'the Law and the Prophets'. The point need not be explored further here, although its consequences will be referred to again later. For our immediate concern it is sufficient to note that the canonical shape of the Old Testament cannot be assigned to the result of accident, nor to a simple process of aggregation of documentary material until it formed a massive whole. There is evidently some design and system about the shape that has been accorded to the material.

Our concern at this juncture is to draw attention to the way in which the structure of the canon affects its interpretation. As the canon is primarily made up of the Law and the Prophets, so its contents are broadly to be interpreted as either 'Law' or 'Prophecy'. In fact we quickly discover that 'Law' is a somewhat inadequate term by which to reproduce the Hebrew *tôrâh*, but a legal connotation is not altogether to be discounted. [[18]] So far as interpretation is concerned, we find that the categories of 'Law' and 'Prophecy' are not rigidly restricted to their separate parts of the canon, but each tends to spill over to affect other parts. Hence we find, for example, in Matt 11:13 that 'the Law and the Prophets' are both said to 'prophesy', so that parts of the Pentateuch can be treated as prophecy. Similarly we find in Mark 2:23–28, for example, that a narrative from the Former Prophets is made into an affirmation of a 'law', or *tôrâh*. Even more importantly from the point of view of understanding the New Testament use of the Old we find that numerous passages from the Psalms can be treated as prophecy (cf. Acts 2:25–28, etc.). The details of these categories of interpretation need not detain us at this point, since it is sufficient for our purpose to note the way in which the shape which is given to the canon has served to establish an elementary, but significant, basis for interpretation. The literary context inevitably serves to create a basis of ideological context, for the Old Testament was not meant to be read as a collection of independent 'proof texts', but as a series of three *[handwritten margin notes: protestant understanding of Canon / intertextual quality of Bible itself (whether it's self-interpreting or not, it's certainly self-referencing)]*

great literary wholes. This is in line with the contention we have already mentioned that scripture should be interpreted by scripture.

Another point also falls to be considered in relation to the canon. If Old Testament theology is intended to be an examination of the theological significance of the Old Testament as it now exists as a canon, then this supports our view that it should not be a purely historical discipline concerned only with the world of ancient Israel and Judaism in which this canon was in process of formation. Rather it must address itself to those religious communities who accept and use this canon as a central feature of their religious life. This points us to both Judaism and Christianity as the religious communities who can be expected to concern themselves with the Old Testament as theology.

In this light we cannot remain altogether indifferent to the liturgical use made of the Old Testament within these communities. This, too, provides part of the context in which the Old Testament is understood. It is inevitable that the situation in worship in which the Old Testament is read, as well as the [[19]] particular choice and ordering of it, play a part in its being heard as the word of God. The 'I and Thou' of scripture become readily identifiable with the 'I and Thou' of worship in which God addresses man and vice versa, and it is of the utmost importance that the theological justification for this identification should be considered. We cannot tolerate a divorce between theology and liturgy, and we cannot therefore be indifferent to the way in which the Old Testament is used liturgically. A very clear example of this need for a theological reflection upon liturgical use is provided by the Psalter and its extensive employment in Christian worship.

However, the issue does not end there, but affects the whole use of the Old Testament, as is most strikingly exemplified by the use of 'messianic' prophecies in Christian Advent services. A wide range of theological questions are raised, which relate to the canonical form and use of the Old Testament. We cannot in consequence leave the question of the canon out of reckoning in an Old Testament theology. On the contrary, it is precisely the concept of canon that raises questions about the authority of the Old Testament, and its ability to present us with a theology which can still be meaningful in the twentieth century. If we restrict ourselves solely to reading the Old Testament as an ancient text, and endeavour to hear in it nothing that the ancient author could not have intended, then we should be denying something of the tradition which asserts that God has continued to speak to his people through it. In reality we do not need to insist on such a rigidly historicising approach, if we believe that the Old Testament does present us with a revelation of the eternal God.

Synopsis of Clements's *Old Testament Theology: A Fresh Approach* (1978)

Ronald E. Clements on Law and Promise

Excerpted with permission from Ronald E. Clements, *Old Testament Theology: A Fresh Approach* (Atlanta: John Knox, 1978), pp. 104–10, 140–50, 153–54, 203, 205.

The Old Testament as Law

[[104]] We remarked in considering the problems of method associated with the writing of an Old Testament theology that it is of great importance to the subject that it should take fully into account the nature of the Old Testament as literature. This must necessarily include some attention to the literary form and structure of its constituent books, but also it should look at those broad categories by which the Old Testament as a whole has been understood. The importance of doing this is all the greater on account of the far-reaching consequences that develop from the way in which the unity of the canon is understood.

Two factors can assist us in finding this basis of unity. One is the structure of the canon itself with its division into three literary collections of Law, Prophets, and Writings, in a three-tier level of authority. The second factor is provided by the way in which the early Jewish and Christian interpreters of the Old Testament have set about their task, with the indications which they give of the particular assumptions and presuppositions which they bring to the literature. Here immediately we encounter the most widespread and basic category which has been employed to describe the nature of the material which the Old Testament contains. This is that of 'law', or more precisely *tôrâh* since the question of how far 'law' is a very satisfactory translation of the Hebrew *tôrâh* remains to be considered. Certainly it raises the question of what kind of law, and what legal authority and sanctions it may be thought to possess.[1]

In the New Testament a quotation from Ps 82:6 is said to be written 'in your law' (John 10:34). Thus even the third part of the Old Testament canon, the Writings, could, by a kind of extension, be regarded as falling within 'the Law'. Evidently the priority and importance of the first part of the canon was felt to be such that it carried over to affect other parts also. [[105]] Certainly we readily discover other indications that this was so for the Prophets. In Mark 2:25–26 we find the citation of an incident regard-

---

1. For the understanding of the Old Testament as law, see P. Grelot, *Le sens chrétien de l'Ancien Testament* (*Bibliotheque de Théologie* Vol. 3) (Tournai, 1962), pp. 167–208.

ing David and the eating of the Bread of the Presence which is recorded in 1 Sam 21:1–6. This incident from the Former Prophets is interpreted as an example of the fundamental principle, applied to Old Testament laws and regulations, that the humanitarian demand for preserving life is of greater importance than the more specifically cultic demand of respect for holiness. The background and assumptions of this interpretation need not detain us. It is simply a clear illustration of the way in which the record of narrative incidents, which were originally preserved for specific purposes of quite another kind, could later be interpreted out of the basic presupposition that they are *tôrâh*—law. Nor is this approach a uniquely Christian one, or we find very strikingly that it pervades almost completely the mainstream of Jewish interpretation of the Old Testament. The Mishnah, and later the Talmud, are full of citation and interpretative comment upon the Old Testament which regard it as *tôrâh*.

Certainly we cannot put aside this fundamental category by which post–Old Testament Jewish and Christian interpreters of this literature have set about understanding it as though it were imposed upon it entirely from outside. We have already noted that the literary structure of the Old Testament supports such a pattern of interpretation by its three-tier ordering of the canon. From a literary point of view the Old Testament is *tôrâh*, and the fact that it contains a great deal else in addition to this, has to be understood in some kind of relationship to this *tôrâh* structure.[2] What has evidently happened is that the concept of a *tôrâh* literature has been used to provide some element of co-ordination and unity to a very varied collection of writings. It offers a unifying guideline, or motif, which has served to impose some degree of order upon what would otherwise be a rather strange miscellany of writings.

As we move further away in time from the editorial and redactional activity which has shaped the Old Testament into its present form, so we tend to find that the assumption that it is all *tôrâh* has tended to become more and more dominating in its effect upon the way in which the material is understood. [[106]] More diverse elements tend to become submerged under the weight of conviction that all the literature is *tôrâh*. At least this is so in respect of Jewish interpretation, since we find that in the mainstream of Christian exegesis a rather different category came to predominate. This is that of 'promise', which we must discuss later. In considering the structure of the Old Testament, therefore, we find ourselves facing a number of questions about its role as *tôrâh*. How far is this category endemic to the literature itself, and how far is it simply a structural framework, lightly built around writings of a more diverse character? Secondly, if we find that the

2. Cf. J. A. Sanders, *Torah and Canon* (1973).

category of *tôrâh* does have a real and fundamental place in the formation of the Old Testament, what exactly is this *tôrâh*? What kind of 'law', or 'instruction' is it?

The Meaning of Tôrâh

The word *tôrâh* occurs very frequently in the Old Testament to denote 'instruction' of various kinds. Its etymology is contested, and two possibilities present themselves. Either it has been formed from the verb *hôrâh* (√*yārāh*) with the meaning 'to direct, aim, point out', or it is a Hebrew counterpart of the Babylonian word *tertu*, 'oracular decision, divine instruction'. Most probably the former is correct, in which case the word means 'guidance, instruction'.[3] As such it could be the kind of instruction which any person might give in a whole variety of situations. However, we find that the word is predominantly used for religious instruction, and especially for the kind of instruction which could be given by a priest. The clearest confirmation of this is to be found in Jer 18:18:

> Then they said, 'Come let us make plots against Jeremiah, for *tôrâh* shall not perish from the priest, nor counsel from the wise, nor the word from the prophet. Come, let us smite him with the tongue, and let us not heed any of his words.'

The assumption here is evidently that *tôrâh* would especially be given by a priest. Yet we find in the Old Testament that others besides priests give *tôrâh*. Hence the prophet does so (cf. Isa 8:16); so also does the wise man (cf. Prov 3:1; 4:2), and also apparently the king (cf. Isa 2:3). To what extent any clear [107] development or extension of meaning can be traced over a period is hard to determine with confidence. Evidently a word of *tôrâh* was particularly the kind of instruction that the ancient Israelite expected to learn from a priest, so that it was a religious direction, the ultimate source of which was to be found with God.

What kinds of rulings might be the subject of such priestly *tôrôth* can only be inferred from the particular duties and concerns which fell to the priest to take care of in ancient Israel. Obviously matters concerning the protection of the holiness of a sanctuary, the obligations of worshippers at the major festivals, and what perquisites belonged to the priests and their families would form a part of this. The fact, however, that a much wider range of concerns dealing with the health of the community, the avoidance of unclean foods, and even sexual and social manners, counsels us against drawing any very narrow conclusions about the nature and scope of *tôrâh*. Cultic, ethical and hygienic interests could all be made the sub-

---

3. The question of the meaning and use of *tôrâh* is discussed extensively by G. A. Ostborn, *Torah in the Old Testament. A Semantic Study* (Lund, 1945).

ject of priestly *tôrôth.* That the word could readily be extended to cover matters where the traditions of the past, most naturally thought to be in the custody of the priest as the guardian of the community's lore, could all be included is not difficult to see. What is noticeable is that it does not specifically apply to juridical traditions in the narrower sense of 'law', nor is it a broad word for general ethical admonition, although it could include this.

So far as the formation of the Old Testament is concerned a quite fundamental development is to be found in the book of Deuteronomy, where *tôrâh* becomes applied to the law-book itself:

> This is the *tôrâh* which Moses set before the children of Israel; these are the testimonies, statutes, and the ordinances, which Moses spoke to the Israelites when they came out of Egypt . . . (Deut 4:44–45).

This summarising introduction to the central part of the book of Deuteronomy is particularly helpful to us in showing the way in which the idea of *tôrâh* was developed and extended. It must once have formed an opening introduction to an edition [[108]] of the book, and so clearly was intended to apply to a written text. Hence it has carried over the idea of an orally given *tôrâh,* delivered as occasion demanded, to a more permanently recorded account of what constituted the *tôrâh* of Israel.

There is clearly also a very marked effort present to achieve comprehensiveness, as is shown by the definition which follows and the wide range of rulings and injunctions which the book contains. The definition in terms of testimonies (Hebrew *ʿēdôt*), statutes (*mišpāṭîm*) and ordinances (*ḥuqqîm*) is interesting for the way in which it brings together words denoting laws, decrees, and admonitions under one all-embracing category. From this time onwards *tôrâh* came to signify the most comprehensive type of instruction in which legal, cultic, and more loosely social obligations were brought together. To obey *tôrâh* was to satisfy the demands of religious, social and family life in the broadest possible compass. Even quite directly political obligations would appear to be included.

The definition that is given in Deut 4:44f., therefore, provides a valuable summarising note about the kind of duties that are brought under the hearing of *tôrâh* in the book of Deuteronomy. When we look at the contents of this book this anticipation is fully borne out. Very decidedly the book is addressed to each and every Israelite, who bears the responsibility for bringing its contents to the attention of his children (cf. Deut 6:7; 11:19), and of reflecting upon them carefully himself (cf. Deut 11:18). No exceptions are envisaged or allowed for. Included in the book are rulings of a markedly legal character concerning the processes of law and the way in which serious crimes are to be dealt with (cf. Deut 19:14–21).

Murder, theft, adultery, and the problems arising therefrom about the trial and punishment of offenders, are all included. But so also are matters of an exclusively religious kind such as the observance of cultic festivals (Deut 16:1–17), which even incorporates notes on how the festivals are to be interpreted. Perhaps more surprising in a document of this kind, which is concerned to spell out precisely the nature of the individual's responsibilities and obligations, is that moral attitudes are commanded, particularly those of love and respect (cf. Deut 15:7–11). Even more prominently is this carried over into the ⟦109⟧ religious realm, so that it becomes a prime duty to love God, and to feel and express gratitude to him (cf. Deut 6:5; 9:4–5). Beyond these broad ethical admonitions, we find that a wide area of life comes under the heading of *tôrâh*. Obligations for military service, the care of buildings, the conservation of the environment and the protection of slaves are all included (cf. Deut 20:1–20; 21:10–17; 22:6–7; 23:12–14).

So far as the threat of punishment for disobedience to particular *tôrôth* is concerned, two points call for comment. The first is that the entire machinery of the state, with all its sanctions, is involved in dealing with all offences against the injunctions laid down. Hence religious offences, especially apostasy, are to be dealt with by the most severe sanctions (Deut 13:5, 8–11). In some cases, as for instance in that of failing to show a right attitude, it would clearly have been impossible to adjudicate the fault. Yet this highlights the second feature concerning punishment, which is that, over and above the particular punishments and sanctions that society could impose, there stood a larger sanction. This is that Israel would have shown itself to be disobedient to the covenant with Yahweh, and would forfeit all its privileged status as his chosen people. We have already considered this earlier in relation to the Deuteronomic teaching concerning Israel and the covenant.

This brings us to note the wider theological context in which the book of Deuteronomy places the notion of *tôrâh*. This is not treated simply as 'good advice', which might, through social pressure and the good sense of the hearers, be accepted by men of good intention everywhere. It is directed specifically to Israel and is the *tôrâh* of the covenant by which Israel's relationship to God is governed. It is as a consequence of belonging to the elect people of Yahweh that the Israelite finds himself committed in advance to obedience to *tôrâh*. Hence he found that it was imperative for him to know *tôrâh*, to understand it correctly, and to be reminded of it regularly, if he were to remain as a member of his people. Furthermore, it was upon the sincerity and willingness of each individual Israelite that the well-being of the whole nation was made to depend.

When we come to ask the question 'What is *tôrâh?*', therefore, the clearest and fullest answer that we have is that which is ⟦110⟧ provided by the book of Deuteronomy. *Tôrâh* is the comprehensive list of instructions *def* and stipulations by which Israel's covenant with God is controlled. What we have now to do is to enquire further how far this understanding of *tôrâh* has affected the Old Testament as a whole.

. . . .

The Old Testament as Promise

Prophecy and Hope

⟦140⟧ The problem of the origin and meaning of the prophecies of hope and restoration for Israel must find answers to two main questions. The first concerns the circumstances in which it is possible for us to see that such a message would have been entirely appropriate. The second question concerns the reason why this message of hope has been added to each of the prophets, and why it takes very much the same form in each of them.

The first question has generally been answered by noting the real birth of the message of hope during the years of Babylonian exile, and regarding this as the first truly appropriate moment for it to have arisen. However, not all scholars have been convinced that no place for a message of hope existed in the eighth century B.C. We may consider the problem in relation to one particular text, that of Amos 9:11–12:

'In that day I will raise up the booth of David that is fallen,
    and repair its breaches and raise up its ruins, ⟦141⟧
    and rebuild it as in the days of old;
that they may possess the remnant of Edom
    and all the nations who are called by my name,'
says the LORD who does this.

The use of the metaphor of the 'booth', or 'shelter', of David to signify his kingdom raises a number of questions. The reference could be to the collapse of the united kingdom of David, which took place with the division into two kingdoms after Solomon's death. Or it could be to the downfall of the northern kingdom in 722, which had once been an important part of the territory ruled by David. It could, however, also refer to the fall of the Davidic dynasty from the throne of Judah, which did not take place until Zedekiah's deposition in 587 B.C. A large number of scholars have taken the reference in the latter sense, so that the promise in these two verses, as well as that which follows in Amos 9:13–15, have been ascribed to the post-exilic age. On the other hand, G. von Rad, in arguing that the reference is back to the disruption in the tenth century B.C., has defended the authenticity of the saying from Amos.[1]

In itself the saying scarcely allows a very clear-cut decision to be made. However, when we compare it with comparable sayings in Hosea (e.g. Hos 2:5), and Isaiah (e.g. Isa 9:2–7; 11:1–9; 32:1–8) regarding the restoration of the united Davidic kingdom, the picture gains a clearer perspective. The recent recognition that a very significant and substantial editing of a collection of Isaiah's prophecies occurred during the reign of Josiah (640–609 B.C.),[2] enables us to see that a very attractive case can be made out for recognising that the age of Josiah witnessed a very marked resurgence of hope for the restoration of Israel. The clearest indication of this is to be found in the Deuteronomic movement and its ambition of re-establishing a united Israel modelled after the old kingdom of David. Certainly by this time in the seventh century B.C., there were indications of the weakening of the Assyrian grip on Judah, and substantial signs of new hope and expectation abroad in the land. There is no reason, therefore, why all the hopeful prophecies to be found in Amos, Hosea and Isaiah should be later than this time. The assumption that all of them must be post-exilic is [[142]] unnecessarily rigid. In fact several scholars have concluded that, even if serious doubt remains about the presence of a clear word of hope in Amos, at least with Hosea and Isaiah these prophets looked for a restoration of Israel beyond the judgments which they foresaw.[3] There are strong reasons, therefore, why it should be fully recognised that a message of hope entered into the mainstream of Israelite-Judean prophecy no later than the seventh century B.C., and probably before this time.

It remains doubtful, however, whether this message of hope can be properly called eschatological, for the simple reason that Judah had survived to become a remnant of the old kingdom of Israel. Very possibly the beginning of the 'remnant'-theology in Isaiah is to be traced back to this time, although the original prophecy had looked in a very different direction. What was anticipated was a resurgence of Israelite power and independence after the disastrous years of Assyrian oppression and suzerainty. Such a hope could take up the themes and images which belonged to a far older stage of Israel's worship and religious life. Especially here we can see an influence from the older Jerusalem traditions associated with the Davidic monarchy and the great festivals celebrated in the temple there. All of these belong to the general theme of hope, rather than with an eschatology in the full sense.

---

1. G. von Rad, *Old Testament Theology*, Vol. II, p. 138.

2. H. Barth, *Israel und das Assyrerreich in den Nichtjesajanischen Texten des Protojesajabuches* (Diss. Hamburg, 1974).

3. Cf. J. Bright, *Covenant and Promise*, pp. 92ff.

What was lacking for an eschatology was a sense that a full and complete end had overtaken the survivors of Israel, so that an entirely new beginning needed to be made. This is the new element that came with the disaster which overtook Judah in 587, with the destruction of the temple and the removal of the Davidic king. The two institutions which seemed to have achieved most in providing a sense of continuity with the greatness of Israel's past were swept away. From this time onwards the whole direction of the prophetic faith turned to look for the return of that part of the community of Judah which had been carried into Babylonian exile in 598 and 587. We find this very fully demonstrated in the way in which the book of Jeremiah has been expanded and developed. The prophet's words of hope for a renewal of normal life in Judah (cf. esp. Jer 32:15) have been very fully and extensively elaborated by Deuteronomistic editors to show that this fulfilment could only come when the [[143]] return from exile took place (Jer 24:1–10; 29:10–14; 32:36–44). We find a similar hope of a return from the Babylonian exile at the centre of the message of Ezekiel (cf. Ezek 36:8–15; 37:15–23; 40–48), and then coming into full flower in the preaching of the prophet of Isaiah 40–55 (Isa 40:1–5; 43:1–7, 14–21; 45:20–23).

The prophets who followed after the time of Babylon's downfall, when the first company of returning Jews made their way back to their homeland, elaborate still further on this hope of a return. They do so, however, in language which becomes increasingly extravagant, and which displays a growing frustration with the political and social possibilities of the times. The prophetic hope of a return to the land and a restoration of Israel acquires a marked supernatural and apocalyptic character (cf. Isa 60:1–22; 61:1–7; 66:12–16). In this way the prophetic eschatology appears to have slipped further and further away from the realities of history, and to have moved into a strange world of apocalyptic images and themes. Yet these themes and images themselves derive from the older cult and prophecy of Israel.

When we look at the canonical collection of the Latter Prophets we find that there is a certain connectedness between the different prophets, and signs that their preaching has been treated as a part of a larger whole. It is the conviction that all the prophets were speaking about the death and rebirth of Israel that has brought together prophecies which stretch across more than two centuries. Beginning with Amos and the onset of the threat from Assyria in the middle of the eighth century, and continuing until the early returns of the fifth century, Israel and Judah had suffered traumatic disasters. The specific and individual circumstances of threat and danger have been swallowed up in a wider portrayal of doom and judgment which applies to all Israel. History has become subsumed in eschatology. Yet in a comparable fashion, the message of hope that began no later than the middle of the seventh century has become an all-embracing message of Israel's restoration and future greatness. No hesitation and compunction has been felt, therefore, by the editors of the separate prophetic books in applying this message of hope to each of the books. Such a hope belonged to the prophetic 'message', even though, from a [[144]] strictly literary viewpoint, it did not derive from each individual prophet. Individual prophetic hopes and promises have become part of a much greater theme of 'promise' which came to be seen as characteristic of prophecy as a whole.

The Forms of Prophetic Hope

The particular way in which the prophetic books have been put together, supplemented and expanded to form a large canonical collection, has clearly been the result of a very extended process. Nevertheless, within this process a number of basic concepts and themes have played a dominant role. Where the modern critical scholar is rightly desirous of listening to the differing sound of each of the prophetic voices, the editors of the collection have worked with a different aim, and have tended to obscure these different tones by the way in which they have edited the collection into a whole. The result now is that we frequently find difficulty in determining the authenticity or otherwise of particular sayings, as we have already noted especially in the case of the hope expressed by Amos and Hosea. Certainly it has not been the needs of liturgical use alone that have determined this, but rather the conviction that the prophetic message is a unity, the ultimate author of which is God himself. The theological student of the meaning of prophecy must consequently be content at times to accept some degree of uncertainty as to when a particular saying was added to a book, since to note this has not been in any way a concern of the original editors.

However, this way of treating the prophetic books, in which some consistency of pattern and ideas is evident, does enable us to see the importance of a number of recurrent themes which form the centre of their message of hope. We may now note briefly what these are. At the head of them we can undoubtedly place the expectation of a return from exile (cf. esp. Jer 24:1–10; 29:10–14; Ezek 36:8–15; Isa 40:1ff.). The plight of those deported to Babylon has become a kind of model or symbol of the plight of all the scattered and dispossessed Jews who formed the Diaspora. The very word 'exile' comes to take on a larger significance as a description of the scattered Jews of every land.

[[145]] Behind this we can also detect the importance of the consequences that arose from the Assyrian deportations from the northern kingdom in the late eighth and seventh centuries B.C. (cf. Jer 31:7–9; Ezek

36:8–15; Isa 49:6). The return of these people too, however completely they appeared to have become lost among the nations, became a part of this hope of a return. So the return to Jerusalem and to Mount Zion became the classic image of how Israel's restoration would take place (cf. Isa 60:1–22; Joel 3:9–17). With this is coupled a related theme that members of Gentile nations will join with them, to pay homage to them and to act as their servants (cf. Isa 33:1–24; 35:1–10). This theme of 'return' also implies the great importance that was attached to the promise of the land. Never is there the slightest suggestion that Israel's misfortune of being scattered among the nations should be a permanent condition, or that it might re-establish its national existence in some other territory than that promised to the patriarch Abraham. This land itself becomes central to the theme of promise.

There is, however, a very deep concern in the prophetic message of hope that Israel should recover its status as a nation. In particular, the division into two separate kingdoms of Israel and Judah is viewed as an act of sin, which must not be repeated. The Israel of the future is consequently foreseen as a single united Israel under a single ruler (cf. Ezek 37:15–23).

This brings us to the third of these basic prophetic themes of hope, which is that the new Israel is to come under a restored king of the Davidic line (Amos 9:11–12; Hos 2:5; Isa 9:2–7; 11:1–9; 32:1; 33:17; Jer 33:19–26; Ezek 37:24–28). This hope, which found a basic point of reference in the older Davidic promise tradition delivered by the prophet Nathan in 2 Sam 7:13, became the foundation of the later 'messianic' hope. Since the restored king was to be an 'anointed' ruler (Hebrew *māšiaḥ*) of the Davidic family, there is some basis for speaking of a 'messianic' hope. Yet this was certainly not the full expectation of a remarkable superhuman figure such as developed in later Judaism. Rather, it was a hope of the restoration of a Davidic ruler, based on the belief that this dynasty alone had been entrusted with this privilege by God.

Two factors in particular belonged to this hope. In the first [[146]] place it was important, since the renewal of the monarchy would signify for Israel the return to full political independence. In this particular form the hope was destined never to be realised, even though the possibility that it would be at one time seemed real and even imminent (Hag 2:23). In the second place the expectation of a return of the kingship, restricted to the Davidic line, was important for the concept of the unity of Israel. It is no surprise, therefore, to discover that eager eyes must have surveyed the fortunes of the Davidic family for a long time after Zerubbabel's death (cf. 1 Chr 3:16–24). Throughout the period when this hope was at its greatest, it is evident that the main weight of interest lay with the belief in the divine destiny of the descendants of David, rather than with any deep commitment to the monarchy as an institution on the part of Israel. In this form the hope appears gradually to have waned, only to re-appear later in a more radical form with the expectation of a messiah of more transcendant proportions, but once again descended, as prophecy foretold, from the house of David.

In relation to the messianic hope we find how the written form of prophecy lent new possibilities to the interpretations which could be placed upon it. The hope of a restoration of a Davidic kingship became transformed into a wider portrayal of the coming of a heavenly saviour figure. The prophecies on which the later hope was built, as in the Messianic Testimonia from Qumran,[4] were the earlier prophecies seen in a new context of expectation. It is in no way the special divine status of the king in ancient Israel which has aroused this pattern of interpretation, but rather the unique importance of the Davidic family in Israel's history.

A further basic theme, or model, of the prophetic hope is the belief in an ultimate glorification of Mount Zion as the centre of a great kingdom of peace. Jerusalem itself becomes a place of the greatest importance, with its rebuilt temple looked to as the place where God's 'glory' or 'presence' would appear (cf. Ezek 48:35; Mal 3:1). To this the nations would come as an act of pilgrimage and homage, rather in the way that their representatives had done long before in the short-lived kingdom of David (Isa 2:2–4 = Mic 4:1–5; cf. Isa 60:14; 61:5).

[[147]] It becomes evident on examination that all of these images of what the restoration of Israel would bring have been drawn in one way or another from the tradition of Israel's past history as a nation. The central role of Israel as the people of God is everywhere assumed and used as a basis for depicting the future. Yet this is not in any way out of a conviction that history is cyclic in its nature, and that an inevitable 'return to the past' would take place as future years unrolled. In general such a deterministic view of history appears to have been almost completely alien to the Israelite tradition of thought. It is instead the belief that Israel's election must mean something, both for Israel itself and for the nations which would be blessed through it, that lies at the heart of these convictions. In calling Abraham, God had begun a task which he had not completed. Indeed the intransigence of the old Israel and its resort to idolatry were regarded as having frustrated this purpose. Yet the purpose itself had not, and could not, be abandoned. God would bring to fruition that which he had begun. By an understandable human reaction, the very frustrations and disappointments of the post-exilic age appear to have intensified the

4. Cf. G. Vermes, *The Dead Sea Scrolls in English* (1962), p. 245.

strength and firmness of the conviction that the final goal of God's purpose—the eschatological age of salvation—would certainly come.

It is difficult, to the point of impossibility, to speak of this element of 'promise' and eschatological hope in the Old Testament in terms of a 'doctrine,' or of a rounded theology. Its literary form is primarily that of prophecy, and its ideas are expressed through images and thematic models, and not through firm doctrines or fixed schemes in which the sequence of events could be determined. The very flexibility of the literary and verbal expression of such hopes and images meant that there could be no single form of interpretation which could be heralded as self-evidently correct.

It is against this background that we must understand the rise of certain key-words and sometimes bizarre images in Jewish hope. In some circles this gradually developed into a new literary form, which we can call apocalyptic, of which the book of Daniel is the only full example in the Old Testament.[5] This new type of literature, however, which for a period flourished extravagantly in Judaism, arose out of earlier [[148]] prophecy, and carried its images and themes to strange extremes. For this to have happened one essential prerequisite was necessary, and this was that prophecy should already have become an accepted part of a canonical literature. The new 'prophecy' was essentially the ability to discover the further messages that were believed to lie hidden in the old (cf. Dan 9:2).

With the arrival of apocalyptic the concept of God's promise to Israel acquired a new medium of expression. Yet already we find an abundance of indications that it was a medium with genuine antecedents in the way in which earlier prophecy had been studied, interpreted and re-applied by the editors of the prophetic books themselves. There is no clear and broadly acceptable definition by which the passage from prophecy to apocalyptic can be readily traced. The strange images and symbols of the latter have their antecedents in the poetry and conventional descriptions of divine activity which we find in the former. With this new literary form there went a clear pattern of interpretation which could treat all prophecy as a kind of apocalyptic, with hidden meanings contained in every word, and names and numbers used as ciphers. Hence it is no surprise to discover from the way in which the prophetic books of Nahum and Habbakuk were interpreted at Qumran that they could be regarded as though they were a form of apocalyptic.[6] All prophecy had come to be seen as a

---

5. For the origin of apocalyptic and its relation to prophecy, see P. D. Hanson, *The Dawn of Apocalyptic. The Historical and Sociological Roots of Jewish Apocalyptic Eschatology* (1975).
6. Cf. G. Vermes, *The Dead Sea Scrolls in English*, pp. 230–40.

veiled form of revelation, the fundamental message of which was the judgment that still awaited the sinners of the earth and the salvation that was to come for Israel.

Already, therefore, we discover that the particular assumptions about Old Testament prophecy that we find in the New Testament are firmly anticipated in the Old. If we are to seek some defence of the early Christian claim that the prophetic message of the Old Testament had been fulfilled in the events concerning Jesus of Nazareth, then we must begin to trace critically and historically the way in which prophecy itself developed from the preached utterances of inspired individuals to become a written series of texts, collected together and edited to form great books. These were then subsequently interpreted as a vast repository of hidden truths and revelations which the [[149]] skilful interpreter and the discerning student of events could use to discover the will of God.

The Promise in the Law and the Writings

So far we have looked at the theme of promise in the Old Testament in relation to the books of the prophets. Attempts that have been made from time to time to trace the ultimate origin of this concept of promise further back than the prophets, to discover its roots either in an ancient mythology or a particular tradition of the cult, must be rejected. It is the way in which the prophets gave new hope to Israel and Judah, after the ruination of the old kingdoms had occurred in the eighth to the sixth centuries B.C., that has given rise to this fundamental theme of promise.

Yet when we turn to the New Testament for some guidance upon the way in which the promise was being interpreted in the first century A.D. we find that passages from the Pentateuch and the Writings could be interpreted as though they were prophecy. This is most notable in the way in which royal psalms are interpreted as foretellings of the coming of the messiah in early Christian preaching, so that the text of the psalm, which was certainly originally composed and intended for liturgical use, is treated exactly as though it were prophecy. The divine declaration of Ps 2:1–2 is interpreted in Acts 4:25–26, as a prophetic foretelling of the sufferings of Jesus, in precisely the same way as though it had been preserved in a book of prophecy:

> Why did the Gentiles rage,
>   and the peoples imagine vain things?
> The kings of the earth set themselves in array,
>   and the rulers were gathered together,
>   against the Lord and against his Anointed.

Even in the case of a psalm which carries in itself no special indication that it was a royal psalm (Psalm 118), we find that it could be treated as containing a prophecy of the rejection of the messiah by God's people in Acts 4:11. Evidently what has taken place is that the category of prophecy, and the assumptions and [[150]] methods of interpretation that were believed to belong to it, have been carried over to other parts of the Old Testament. This recognition is of great importance in the modern critical attempt to uncover the origins of the messianic hope in ancient Israel. It also matters greatly in connection with attempts to claim a far greater number of the psalms as being concerned with the kingship of Israel than any explicit statement in the text warrants. So attempts have been carried through in which the institution of kingship itself, and the distinctive high ideology associated with this, have been regarded as the real basis of Israel's 'messianic' hope.[7] Yet this can be true only by reaching a very extended understanding of what such a hope truly entails.

We have already seen that, so far as the main essential of the 'messianic' hope was concerned, this derived from the expectation of the restoration of the Davidic family to the kingship of a renewed Israel after the Babylonian exile. The distinctive elements of the old royal ideology as such, difficult as this is to define on account of its highly symbolic language, came to be caught up in this, but was not its main stimulus. The prophetic interpretation of specific psalms has not arisen because these psalms were originally thought to be prophetic in their nature, but rather as a consequence of the trends and developments which were taking place in the formation of a collection of canonical texts.

. . . .

[[153]] From this perspective we can see that the early Christian claim that the whole Old Testament is a book of prophetic promise cannot be regarded as something imposed on the literature from outside. Rather it reflects an understanding which exists within the Old Testament canon itself. We find, therefore, that the Old Testament is presented to us with two major themes governing its form and establishing a basis of understanding from which all its writings are to be interpreted. It is a book of *tôrâh*—of the 'law' of the covenant between God and Israel. Yet it is also a book of promise, for it recognises the tensions that have arisen within this covenant relationship and the fact that Israel stands poised between the election of God, with all the promises that this entails of land, national life, and the tasks of bringing blessing to the nations, and its fulfilment.

7. Cf. A. Bentzen, *King and Messiah* (ed. G. W. Anderson, [2]1970); and T. N. D. Mettinger, *King and Messiah. The Civil and Social Legitimation of the Israelite Kings* (*Coniectanea Biblica. Old Testament Series* 8, Lund, 1976).

The law itself is both a gift and a goal. While we can see that historically the theme of 'law' belongs primarily to the Pentateuch and that of 'promise' to the Prophets, in practice all parts of the literature could be interpreted from the perspective of both themes. However, their mutual interrelationships, and the questions of priority between them, do not appear with any ⟦154⟧ rigid fixity. In their own ways, both Judaism and Christianity saw the relationships differently as they built upon the Old Testament and established their own priorities in interpreting its demands upon the continuing 'Israel of God'.

WALTER C. KAISER JR.

b. 1932

Promise

Theological Synopsis

Kaiser's book, *Toward an Old Testament Theology* (1978), despite its title, advocated a specific approach and argued for a specific theme—promise—as the central theme of the Old Testament. In the 1970s the debate continued whether the Old Testament had a center. With the publication of Brevard S. Childs's *Biblical Theology in Crisis* (1970), the emphasis on the canonical shape of the text was gaining adherents. Moreover, in North America the evangelical movement was becoming more articulate and was gaining some momentum. An editorial in *Christian Century* referred to 1976 as "the year of the evangelical" (Wall 1976: 1165).

Earlier, Edward J. Young, an evangelical, wrote *The Study of Old Testament Theology Today* (1958), J. Barton Payne published *The Theology of the Older Testament* (1962), and Chester Lehman, *Biblical Theology: Old Testament* (1971). Kaiser himself was strongly influenced by Willis J. Beecher's 1905 book, *The Prophets and the Promise*.

Kaiser is indebted for his method to the impulses of *Heilsgeschichte*, or salvation history. This view of a "divinely guided history of redemption" was championed by Johann C. K. von Hofmann (1810–77) of the Erlangen school in a work dealing with prophecy and fulfillment in the Old and New Testaments (1841–44). Kaiser, like Gerhard von Rad, proceeds through the Old Testament diachronically—by eras or centuries. That is, in tracing the theme of promise, he follows the story, or rather history, which for him is the medium of revelation. Unlike von Rad, he eschews the historical-critical method, but adopts a syntactical-theological method (1981: 89). For Kaiser the accent falls on "a network of interlocking moments in history" (1978:34). He returns often to the concept of "antecedent Scripture." He maintains that at any given point listeners then

233

understood, as readers today must understand, a statement "against the backdrop of an accumulated theology" (e.g., Day of the Lord; 1978: 190).

Kaiser proposes the concept of *promise* as the center of an Old Testament theology. Since the point of departure for a *Heilsgeschichte* is Abraham, so also, understandably, the promise text of Gen 12:1ff. is pacesetting. Promise, never sharply defined, but predicated on a divine plan, incorporates a "constellation of terms" including *blessing* and *covenant.* While the promise issues eventually in the Messiah, the promise is not to be only narrowly construed. Thus, in the Mosaic era, Kaiser expounds on the "people of the promise." Here exposition consists of specific texts, frequently interspersed with word studies (e.g., my son, my firstborn, my possession, kingly priests, a holy nation, law of God, a tabernacling God).

Wisdom materials are handled in the chapter entitled "Life in the Promise" and are incorporated in "salvation history" largely through the term *fear of God,* found, significantly, in both Deuteronomy and Proverbs. The postexilic prophets, such as Haggai, Zechariah, Malachi, along with the materials in Chronicles, Ezra–Nehemiah, and Esther, dealt with the "Triumph of the Promise," and so prepared the way for the New Testament in which "promise" (*epangelia*) is a key term.

Walter C. Kaiser Jr. is a professor of Semitic languages and Old Testament and dean and vice-president of education at Trinity Evangelical Divinity School (Chicago). A graduate of Wheaton College (Illinois), he received his doctorate in Mediterranean studies from Brandeis University. He taught at Wheaton College for eight years and has been at Trinity since 1964. He has authored commentaries and has strong interest in biblical theology and interpretation. He is an ordained minister in the Evangelical Free Church of America.

                                                                    E.A.M.

Writings by Kaiser

1978	*Toward an Old Testament Theology.* Grand Rapids: Zondervan.
1981	*Toward an Exegetical Theology: Biblical Exegesis for Preaching and Teaching.* Grand Rapids: Baker.
1983	*Toward Old Testament Ethics.* Grand Rapids: Zondervan.
1987	*Toward Rediscovering the Old Testament.* Grand Rapids: Zondervan.

Walter C. Kaiser Jr.'s
Approach to Old Testament Theology

Reprinted with permission from Walter C. Kaiser Jr., *Toward an Old Testament Theology* (Grand Rapids: Zondervan, 1978), pp. 11–14, 32–35.

The Method of Old Testament Theology

[[11]] Is there, then, a distinctive methodology for this discipline? Or has all the toil of the last half century been for no real purpose? Is there an inner, persistent, distinctive, and characteristic theme or plan that would mark off the central concern for the OT? And would it aid the theological curriculum or even the general reader's appreciation of the text to have this plan laid out in its successive installments? Does all this amount to a system or a logic that builds within the Old Testament? And does this pattern give evidence that it expects additional events and meanings even beyond the range of its canonical writings? Even more critical, can it be shown from the claims of the original participants in the events and thoughts of these OT texts that they were conscious of a continuing stream of events, meanings, and ideas which preceded them and that they felt themselves obligated to acknowledge some type of permanent, normative demands laid on their beliefs and actions? These are the hard, methodological problems which the past generation and ours have found difficult to answer, especially since this discipline was viewed as the synthesis of all the "assured results" of OT study over the past two centuries. Unfortunately, some of these results represented as great bondage to grids, systems, and philosophies as those the discipline had originally attempted to evade in 1933.

Our proposal is to distinguish sharply biblical theology's method from that of systematics or the history-of-religion. There is an inner center or plan to which each writer consciously contributed. A principle of selectivity is already evident and divinely determined by the rudimentary disclosure of the divine blessing-promise theme to all men everywhere as the canon opens in Genesis 1–11 and continues in Genesis 12–50. Rather than selecting that theological data which strikes our fancy or meets some current need, the text will already have set up priorities and preferences of its own. These nodal points can be identified, not on the basis of ecclesiastical or theological camps, but by such criteria as: (1) the critical placement of interpretive statements in the textual sequence; (2) the frequency

235

of repetition of the ideas; (3) the recurrence of phrases or terms that begin to take on a technical status; (4) the resumption of themes where a forerunner had stopped often with a more extensive area of reference; (5) the use of categories of assertions previously used that easily lend themselves to a description of a new stage in the program of history; and (6) the organizing standard by which people, places, and ideas were marked for approval, [[12]] contrast, inclusion, and future and present significance.

Not only must the job of selectivity be initiated and guided by textual controls set by the authorial truth-intentions of the writers of the OT, but these same men must also be closely followed in the evaluation of all theological conclusions drawn from these "selected" theological data.

If the value judgments, interpretations, and estimates which they placed on these key events and persons in the text be deleted, dismissed, neglected, or replaced with those of our own, we will need to blame no one but ourselves if the authority of the Bible seems to also have evaporated beneath our own best scholarly efforts. The truth of the matter, for better or for worse, is that these writers claim they were the recipients of divine revelation in the selection *and* evaluation of what was recorded. Consequently, all serious theologies will need to reckon with both aspects of this claim, not to speak of the claim itself to have received revelation.

To repeat then, in our proposed methodology, biblical theology draws its very structure of approach from the historic progression of the text and its theological selection and conclusions from those found in the canonical focus. Thereby it agrees in part with the historical and sequential emphasis of the diachronic type of OT theology and the normative emphasis of the structural type.

Yet it does more than merely synthesize or eclectically accept a new combination of what has been heretofore a set of antithetical methods. It deliberately attempts to derive its theology from the exegetical insights of canonical sections, whether it be a summarizing paragraph or chapter, a key teaching passage, a strategic event as evaluated in the context where it first appeared and in subsequent references in the canon, or a whole book or group of books which are so closely connected in theme, approach, or message as to provide an explicit unity.

Amidst all the multiplexity and variety of materials, events, and issues, it is our contention that there does exist an eye to this storm of activity. Such a starting point is *textually* supplied and *textually* confirmed as the canon's central hope, ubiquitous concern, and measure of what was theologically significant or normative. While the NT eventually referred to this focal point of the OT teaching as the promise, the OT knew it under a constellation of such words as promise, oath, blessing, rest, and seed. It

any inductive work depends on a hermeneutical principle → where does that come from?

was also known under such formulas as the tripartite saying: "I will be your God, you shall be My people, and I will dwell in the midst of you" or the redemptive self-assertion formula scattered in part or in full form 125 times throughout the OT: "I am the Lord your God who brought you up ⟦13⟧ out of the land of Egypt." It could also be seen as a divine plan in history which promised to bring a universal blessing through the agency of an unmerited, divine choice of a human offspring: "In thee shall all families of the earth be blessed" (Gen 12:3).

So crucial is the passage rendering of Gen 12:3 (also 18:18; 28:14—all niphal form verbs) that Bertil Albrektson[1] acknowledges that if the niphal form is passive here and not reflexive as most modern translations claim, then a clear reference to a divine plan by which Abraham is chosen to be God's instrument to reach all the nations of the earth is explicitly taught in the text. But, alas, he feels constrained to reject it on the basis that this formula appears in the hithpael form (usually a reflexive form) in Gen 22:18 and 26:4: "Bless oneself."[2]

But a strong protest must be raised at this point for several exegetical reasons. First of all, in Gen 12:2 the divine blessing already is said to be attached to Abraham's person: "And thou [or "it," referring either to Abraham's name or nation] shalt be a blessing." Hence, neither he nor the nation are merely to be a formula of blessing; neither will he merely bless himself! Instead, even apart from the controversial niphal of verse 3, Abraham is to be the medium and source of divine blessing. Such was his destined mission in the first set of promises of verse 2 before moving on to another and higher statement of purpose on verse 3.

All five passages in Genesis (both the niphal and hithpael forms of the verb "to bless") are treated in the Samaritan, Babylonian (Onkelos), Jerusalem (Pseudo-Jonathan) Targums as passives. Indeed, the harmonistic interpretation which insists on rendering three niphals by two hithpaels is also misinformed when it insists on a uniform reflexive meaning of the hithpael, for that is not true.[3] Thus it cannot be assumed so facilely that the sense of the hithpael is clear and therefore it should be made the basis of rendering the sense of the "disputed niphal." The sense of both of

---

1. Bertil Albrektson, *History and the Gods* (Lund, Sweden: C. W. K. Gleerup Fund, 1967), p. 79.

2. For the hithpael form of this verb, see Ps 72:17 and its parallelism in context, but note the LXX and Vulgate *passive* rendering.

3. The most definitive discussion of this problem ever is O. T. Allis's "The Blessing of Abraham," *Princeton Theological Review* 25 (1927): 263–98. See especially p. 281 where he lists these possible examples of a passive meaning for the hithpael: Gen 37:35; Num 31:23; Deut 4:21; 23:9; 1 Sam 3:14; 30:6; 1 Kgs 2:26; Job 15:28; 30:16, 17; Ps 107:17, 27; 119:52; Isa 30:29; Lam 4:1; Ezek 19:12; Dan 12:10; Mic 6:16.

these stems changed under the pressure of polemical interest in Rashi, then Clericus, and now the greater majority of linguists and exegetes. [[14]] Meanwhile, O. T. Allis's linguistic challenge has stood unrefuted and even unacknowledged by contemporary scholars—the meaning is clearly passive and the implications for OT biblical theology are massive!

The focus of the record fell on the *content* of God's covenant which remained epigenetically constant, i.e., the accumulation of materials as time went on grew around a fixed core that contributed life to the whole emerging mass. This content was a given word of blessing and promise. It was a declaration guaranteed by a divine pledge that God would freely do or be something to a certain person(s) in Israel there and then and to later Jewish descendants in the future so that God might thereby do or be something for all men, nations, and nature, generally. The immediate effects of this word were divine blessings (happenings or arrival of persons) usually accompanied by a promissory declaration of a future work or completion of the series—a divine promise. Accordingly, men received the promise and waited for the promise all in one plan.

But in its composition, it contained such variegated interests as to include: (1) material blessings of all men and beasts; (2) a special seed to mankind; (3) a land for a chosen nation; (4) spiritual blessing for all the nations; (5) a national deliverance from bondage; (6) an enduring dynasty and kingdom that would one day embrace a universal dominion; (7) a forgiveness of sin, and on and on.

No principle foisted as an "abstract divining rod" over the text could be expected to yield so great a theological payload. Only a textually supplied claim could have pointed our attention to such a constellation of interconnected terms and contents as are found in this single plan of God—His promise. The progress of this doctrine can be historically measured and described. Further, it will include its own pattern for a permanent, normative standard by which to judge that day and all other days by a yardstick which claims to be divinely laid on the writer of Scripture and on all subsequent readers simultaneously.

. . . .

Canonical Precedence for a Center

[[32]] OT theologians have missed the only way for safe passage through these treacherous waters. That way must be an *inductively* derived theme, key, or organizing pattern which the successive writers of the OT overtly recognized and consciously supplemented in the progressive unfolding of events and interpretation in the OT. If amidst all the variety and multiplexity of the text there does, as we [[33]] contend, exist an eye to this storm of activity, it must be *textually* demonstrated that it is the canon's own "starting point" and *textually* reconfirmed in the canon's united witness that it is its own ubiquitous concern, central hope, and constant measure of what was theologically significant or normative!

Such a textually derived center, what the NT eventually was to call the "promise" (*epangelia*), was known in the OT under a constellation of terms. The earliest such expression was "blessing." It was God's first gift to the fish, fowl (Gen 1:22), and then to mankind (v. 28).

For men, it involved more than the divine gift of proliferation and "dominion-having." The same word also marked the immediacy whereby all the nations of the earth could prosper spiritually through the mediatorship of Abraham and his seed: this, too, was part of the "blessing." Obviously, pride of place must be given to this term as the first to signify the plan of God.

But there were other terms. McCurley[1] counted over thirty examples where the verb *dibber* (usually translated "to speak") meant "to promise." The promised items included (1) the land (Exod 12:25; Deut 9:28; 12:20; 19:8; 27:3; Josh 23:5, 10); (2) blessing (Deut 1:11; 15:6); (3) multiplication of God's possession, Israel (Deut 6:3; 26:18); (4) rest (Josh 22:4; 1 Kgs 8:56); (5) all good things (Josh 23:15); and (6) a Davidic dynasty and throne (2 Sam 7:28; 1 Kgs 2:24; 8:20, 24–25; 1 Chr 17:26; 2 Chr 6:15–16; Jer 33:14). Also note the noun *dābār* ("promise") in 1 Kgs 8:56 and Ps 105:42.

To these "promises" God added His "pledge" or "oath," thus making the immediate word of blessing and the future word of promise doubly secure. Men now had the divine word and a divine oath on top of that word (see Gen 22; 26:3; Deut 8:7; 1 Chr 16:15–18; Ps 105:9; Jer 11:5).[2]

The case for this inductively derived center is even more wide-ranging than the lexicographical or vocabulary approach traced so far. It also embraced several epitomizing formulae which summarized that central action of God in a succinct phrase or two. Such was what we have called the tripartite formula of the promise. This formula became the great hallmark of all biblical theology in both testaments. The first part of the formula was given in Gen 17:7–8 and 28:21, viz., "I will be a God to you and your descendants after [34] you." When Israel approached the eve of nationhood, again God repeated this word and added a second part, "I will take you for My people" (Exod 6:7). Thus Israel became God's "son," His "firstborn" (Exod 4:22), "a distinctive treasure" (Exod 19:5–6). Finally, the third part was added in Exod 29:45–46 in connection with the construction of

1. Foster R. McCurley, Jr., "The Christian and the Old Testament Promise," *Lutheran Quarterly* 22 (1970): 401–10, esp. p. 402, n. 2.

2. Gene M. Tucker, "Covenant Forms and Contract Forms," *Vetus Testamentum* 15 (1965): esp. pp. 487–503, for the use of "oath" with promise.

the tabernacle: "I will dwell in the midst of you." There it was: "I will be your God; you shall be My people, and I will dwell in the midst of you." It was to be repeated in part or in full in Lev 11:45; 22:33; 25:38; 26:12, 44–45; Num 15:41; Deut 4:20; 29:12–13; et. al. Later it appeared in Jer 7:23; 11:4; 24:7; 30:22; 31:1, 33; 32:38; Ezek 11:20; 14:11; 36:28; 37:27; Zech 8:8; 13:9; and in the NT in 2 Cor 6:16 and Rev 21:3–7.

Another formula, found in Gen 15:7, "I am Yahweh who brought you out of Ur of the Chaldeans," was matched by an even greater work of redemption: "I am the Lord your God who brought you out of the land of Egypt" (found almost 125 times in the OT). Still another formula of self-prediction was, "I am the God of Abraham, Isaac, and Jacob." All such formulae stress a continuity between the past, present, and future. They are parts of God's single ongoing plan.

As the record progressed, an accumulation of various metaphors and technical terms began to emerge. Many of these focused around the Davidic descendant. He was the "Seed," "Branch," "Servant," "Stone," "Root," "Lion," etc.[3] More often than not, the text had a backward glance to previous contexts which contained parts of the same metaphors and technical terms.

Nevertheless, neither the vocabulary nor the formulae and technical terms by themselves would make the case for a unified plan to the entirety of the OT progress of theology. The accent must ultimately fall where it fell for the writers themselves—on a network of interlocking moments in history made significant because of their content, free allusions to one another, and their organic unity. The focus of the record fell on the *content and recipients* of God's numerous covenants. The content remained epigenetically constant, i.e., there was a growth—even a sporadic growth from some points of view—as time went on around a fixed core that contributed vitality and meaning to the whole emerging mass. The content was a divine "blessing," a "given word," a "declaration," a "pledge," or "oath" [35] that God Himself would freely do or be something for all men, nations, and nature, generally.

Consequently, the revelatory event and/or declaration was frequently an immediate "blessing" as well as a promissory "word" or "pledge" that God would work in the future or had already worked in some given event or situation. God had done so in a way that significance had been given to man's present history and by this, simultaneously to future generations, also.

---

3. Dennis C. Duling, "The Promise to David and Their Entrance into Christianity—Nailing Down a Likely Hypothesis," *New Testament Studies* 20 (1974): 55–77.

Synopsis of Kaiser's *Toward an Old Testament Theology* (1978)

Walter C. Kaiser Jr.
on the Promise Theologian: Isaiah

Reprinted with permission from Walter C. Kaiser Jr., *Toward an Old Testament Theology* (Grand Rapids: Zondervan, 1978), pp. 204–5, 207–10, 212–19.

[[204]] Beyond all question, Isaiah was the greatest of all the OT prophets, for his thought and doctrine covered as wide a range of subjects as did the length of his ministry. While his writing can be divided into two parts, chapters 1–39 keyed mainly to judgment and chapters 40–66 primarily emphasizing comfort, the book stands as a unit with its own continuity features such as the unique and distinctive phrase "the Holy One of Israel," which occurs twelve times in the first part and fourteen times in the second part.[1]

[[205]] The second part of Isaiah's work is a veritable OT biblical theology in itself. It might well be called the "Old Testament book of Romans" or the "New Testament within the Old Testament." Its twenty-seven chapters cover the same scope as the twenty-seven books of the NT. Chapter 40 begins with the predicted voice of John the Baptist crying in the wilderness as do the Gospels: chapters 65–66 climax with the same picture as the Apocalypse of John in Revelation 21–22 of the new heavens and the new earth. Sandwiched between these two end points is the midpoint, Isa 52:13–53:12, which is the greatest theological statement on the meaning of the atonement in all Scripture.

No less significant, however, is the first part of Isaiah's writing. Its successive "books," to use Franz Delitzsch's term,[2] are the books of Hardening (chaps. 1–6), Immanuel (7–12), Nations (13–23), the Little Apocalypse (24–27; 34–35), the Chief Cornerstone and Woes (28–33), and Hezekiah (36–39).

In our view, Isaiah must be called the theologian's theologian. And when the continuing promise of God was being considered, Isaiah excelled both in his use of the antecedent theology of the Abrahamic-

---

1. Conservatives have pointed to some forty additional phrases or sentences that appear in both parts of Isaiah as evidence for its unity, cf. Gleason L. Archer, Jr., *A Survey of Old Testament Introduction*, rev. ed. (Chicago: Moody Press, 1974), pp. 345ff.

2. Franz Delitzsch, *The Prophecies of Isaiah*, 2 vols. in C. F. Keil and F. Delitzsch, *Biblical Commentary on the Old Testament*, 25 vols., trans. James Martin (Grand Rapids: Eerdmans, 1969), 1:v–vii; 2:v.

Mosaic-Davidic promise and in his new contributions and development of that doctrine.

. . . .

The Branch of Yahweh

⟦207⟧ Who is the "sprout" or "branch" (*ṣemaḥ*) of Isa 4:2–6? Very few doubt that the one who is afterward called "the Branch" is the Messiah. Nor do they doubt that later prophets directly depend on Isa 4:2 for that title. Those products who use this title for Messiah are:

"Branch of Yahweh" (Isa 4:2)
"Branch of David" (Jer 23:5–6)
"The Branch, My Servant" (Zech 3:8)
"Branch, a man" (Zech 6:12)

In Isa 4:2 the "Branch of Yahweh" is the Davidic dynasty in its human ("fruit of the land") nature as well as its divine ("of Yahweh"). In this case "Branch" would be an equivalent term for "Anointed" or "holy One."

But many object that "Branch" was not yet a fixed designation for Messiah; besides, its parallelism with "the fruit of the land" (4:2) favored a reference to the sprouting forth of the land under the beneficent influence of Yahweh. However, as the following chapters of Isaiah show, Messiah was the Mediator of these benefits and He Himself was the greatest of all the benefits.

Is it any wonder then that the later prophets applied this title to the living personal source of all these gifts in the last days? Some of those gifts found already in this passage are (1) the promise of the fruitfulness of the land; (2) the certainty of a remnant of "survivors"; (3) the holiness of the remnant; (4) the cleansing and purification of the moral filth of the people; and (5) the radiant glory of the personal presence of Yahweh dwelling in Zion with His people forever. The "holy nation" of Exod 19:6 would finally be completely realized as would the permanent "dwelling" of Yahweh in their midst. Even the "cloud by day" and "fire by night" (4:5) were to be renewed. For just as they were the visible proofs of God's presence in the wilderness (Exod 14:19ff.), so they would be a shade by day and illuminate the night to shield the city of God from all violence.

Immanuel

What the previous "Branch [or Sprout] of the Lord" passage left indefinite was now given personal shape and definition in the Immanuel ⟦208⟧ prophecies of Isaiah 7–11. This word came against the background of the Syro-Ephraimitic War in which Pekah, king of Israel, made an alliance

with Rezin, king of Syria, to advance against Ahaz, king of Judah, with a
view to installing the son of Tabeal as king on David's throne. This threat
to Jerusalem and Judah was countered by Isaiah's invitation to Ahaz to
"believe" God in order that Ahaz himself might "be believed," i.e., established (7:9). In fact, God would validate His good offer in so improbable a
situation by performing any sign (i.e., miracle) Ahaz might choose from
Sheol or heaven.

But Ahaz, true unbeliever that he was, piously rejected Yahweh's help
with an oblique reference to Deut 6:16 about not tempting the Lord his
God. The truth of the matter was that he expected little from Yahweh;
moreover, he had probably already secretly sought the support of Tiglath-
pileser, king of Assyria (2 Kgs 16:7ff.).

Nevertheless, the Lord proceeded to give a sign. It was: "Behold,
[you] the virgin are pregnant and bearing a son; you shall call his name
Immanuel" (7:14). Now it is important to note several things: (1) the word
ᶜalmâh denotes a "virgin" in every case where its meaning can be determined;[3] (2) it has the definite article, "*the* virgin"; (3) the verb "to call" is
second person feminine and not third person feminine; and (4) the
wording of this verse made use of older biblical phraseology: at the birth
of Ishmael (Gen 16:11); at the birth of Isaac (Gen 17:19); and at the birth
of Samson (Judg 13:5, 7). Thus, the sign given to Ahaz consisted in repeating to him the familiar phrases used in promising the birth of a son.

But this passage dealt with the birth of three children, all three being
signs in Israel (8:17–18). Each of the three was introduced and then was
later the subject of an expanded prophecy as follows:

1. Shear-Jashub—"remnant shall return"
   7:3 → 10:20, 21, 22; 11:11, 16
2. Immanuel—"God with us"
   7:14 → 8:8, 10
3. Mahershalalhashbaz—"haste spoil, hurry prey"
   8:1, 3, 4 → 10:2, 6

In each of these passages we have the mention of a child born in fulfillment of the promise that had been made to David, to the [[209]] effect
that his seed should be eternal . . . In the second half of his discourse on
the three children, Isaiah thus reiterates the promise that had been made
to David, and insists upon it. He makes it the foundation of his rebuke to
the people for their corruptions . . .

3. Besides this text, it appears in the account of Rebekah (Gen 24:43); the sister of
Moses (Exod 2:8); in the phrase "the way of a man with a maid" (Prov 30:19); and in the plural in Ps 68:25 [26]; Song 1:3; 6:8; and the titles to Psalm 46 and 1 Chr 15:20.

Those who heard him understood that when Ahaz refused to ask the offered sign, the prophet repeated to him, in a new form, Jehovah's promise concerning the seed of David, and made that to be a sign that Jehovah would both keep his present pledge and punish Ahaz for his faithlessness. It may be doubted whether any of them had in mind the idea of just such a person as Jesus, to be born of a virgin, in some future century; but they had in mind some birth in the unending line of David which would render the truth, "God with us," especially significant.[4]

Furthermore, before this son, the most recent birth in the line of David, was able to understand right from wrong (7:16–17), a political revolution of major proportions would remove both Pekah and Rezin from power. But several other facts must be borne in mind at once if one is rightly to identify this "son." According to 8:8, 10, he is addressed as the prince of the land ("thy land, O Immanuel") and as the expected anointed one of David's house in 9:6–7 [5–6] ("There will be no end of the increase of his government and peace [as he rules] on the throne of David over his kingdom . . . forevermore"). Also Isaiah, like his contemporary Micah, everywhere presupposes that a period of judgment must precede the glorious messianic age. Therefore, whatever this sign and birth is, it cannot be the completion of the "last days."

Who then was this child? His messianic dignity totally excludes the notion that he may have been Isaiah's son born to some maiden newly married to the prophet after Shear-Jashub's mother supposedly died. Still less likely is it a reference to any marriageable maiden or some particular ideal maiden present at the time of the proclamation of this prophecy since the prophet has definitely said "the virgin." It is preferable to understand him to be a son of Ahaz himself, whose mother Abi, daughter of Zechariah, is mentioned in 2 Kgs 18:2—namely, his son Hezekiah. It is well known that this was the older Jewish interpretation, but it is also supposed that Hezekiah could not be the predicted "sign" of 7:14 since on present chronologies he must have already been nine years old at that time (about 734 B.C.). That last point is to be thoroughly studied before it is adopted. The chronology of Israel and Judah has been well secured with only one minor exception—a ten year difficulty in the [[210]] rule of Hezekiah. Without arguing the point at this time, I would like to boldly suggest that only Hezekiah meets all the demands of the text of Isaiah and yet demonstrates how he could be part and parcel of that climactic messianic person who would complete all that is predicted in this Immanuel prophecy. Only in this, the most recent installment in the Abrahamic-Davidic

4. Willis J. Beecher, "The Prophecy of the Virgin Mother: Isa. vii:14," *Homiletical Review* 17 (1889): 357–58.

promise, could it be seen how God was still being "with" Israel in all His power and presence.

In Isa 9:6, a series of descriptive epithets are given to this newborn son who is to climax the line of David. He is "wonderful Counsellor," "mighty God," "Father of eternity,"[5] and "Prince of Peace." These four names represent, respectively, (1) the victory due to His wise plans and great skills in battle; (2) the irresistible Conqueror (cf. 10:21); (3) the fatherly rule of Messiah and His divine attribute of eternality; and (4) the everlasting peaceful reign of Messiah. His government and the peace during His regime would know no boundaries, for He would establish His kingdom in justice and righteousness forevermore (Isa 9:7). Unique among the descriptions of peace that will be observed during that era is the picture of all nature at rest and devoid of hostility (11:6–9). Again, there is a graphic prediction of the restoration of both the north and south to the land "in that day" (vv. 10–16). And from the stump of David's father, Jesse, would come that "shoot," even a "branch" (*nēzer*), upon whom the sevenfold gift of the Spirit of the Lord would rest as He ruled and reigned righteously and awesomely (vv. 1–5). The whole picture of the future person and work of the Messiah was cast in terms of the Davidic promise as a glowing encouragement for Israel.

. . . .

Short Theology of the Old Testament

[[212]] One of the most remarkable sections of all the OT is Isaiah 40–66. In its general plan, it is laid out in three enneads: chapters 40–48, 49–57, and 58–66. In each of these three sets of nine messages the focus is directed to the particular aspect of the person and work of God. It is as close to being a systematic statement of OT theology as is the book of Romans in the NT. Its majestic movement begins with the announcement of the person and work of John the Baptist and spins to the dizzy heights of the suffering and triumphant servant of the Lord by the time the middle of the second ennead is reached. But this climax is again superseded by the concluding message on the new heavens and the new earth.

In each of the three sections there is a central figure. In Isaiah 40–48 the key figure is a hero who would come from the East to redeem Israel from captivity, namely, "Cyrus." The revelation of this hero, coming as it did right in the middle of the addresses (44:28–45:10), served as a bold challenge to the idols or deities embraced in that day to do likewise for the people. However, their inability to speak anything about the future

---

5. It is not "Father of booty," which does not match the permanent attribute of "Prince of Peace"; rather, the Hebrew *ʾab ʿad* is "Father of Eternity" as *ʿad* means in Gen 49:26, Isa 57:15, and Hab 3:6.

could only lead to one conclusion: Yahweh was indeed the only God, and they were nothing at all.

In Isaiah 49–57 the central figure is the "servant of the Lord," who combined in his person all the people Israel, the prophet and [213] prophetic institution, and the Messiah in His role as Servant. Again the climactic description and his most important work was located at the middle point of this ennead: 52:13–53:12. The salvation effected by this servant had both objective and subjective aspects (54:1–56:9); indeed, its final and concluding work would involve the glorification of all nature.

The third ennead, 58–66, triumphantly announces the dawning of a new day of salvation for nature, nations, and individuals. At the center of this ennead was a new principle of life—the Spirit-filled Messiah (61:1–63:6) who bore the powers and dignities of the prophetic, priestly, and kingly officers.

Thus in each successive ennead another aspect of the Godhead and God's work was celebrated. In order, the emphases on the persons of the Godhead are Father, "Servant" [Son], and Holy Spirit. In work, they are Creator—Lord of history, Redeemer, and sovereign Ruler over all in the "eschaton." The five major forces in Isaiah's message are God, the people of Israel, the event of salvation, the prophet, and the word of God. Finally, this message even has several distinctive stylistic features. It has a plethora of divine self-asseverations such as "I am the first and the last," or "I am Yahweh"; a long series of participial phrases after the formula "Thus says the Lord" or "I am the Lord" which continue on to detail His special character; and a profuse number of appositional words appearing after the names of Yahweh or Israel as well as a great abundance of verbs to describe Yahweh's work of judgment or salvation. Such is the style of this most magnificent section of the OT. But let us treat each of these enneads in turn to examine that theology more closely.

The God of All (Isaiah 40–48)

The theme of Isaiah's call returns in this section as the holiness and righteousness of God are praised repeatedly. God is "the Holy One" (40:25; 41:14, 16, 20; 43:3, 14; 47:4; 48:17; and it continues in the later sections in 49:7 bis; 54:5; 55:5). He also is righteous (*ṣedeq*), i.e., straight, right, and faithful to a norm, His own nature and character. His righteousness could best be seen in His work of salvation, for the prophet often joined His righteousness and His performance of the covenant promise together (e.g., 41:2; 42:6–7; 46:12–13; note later 51:1, 5, 6, 8; 54:10; 55:3; 62:1–2). Only of God could it be said, "He is right" (41:26) or He is "a righteous God and Savior" (45:21), who declares "what is right" (v. 19) and who brings men near to His righteousness (46:13).

His nature is especially to be seen in His singleness and self-sufficiency. In Isaiah's famous set of six variations on the formula of self-predication, he set forth the incomparability[6] of Yahweh: Beside [[214]] Him there was no other God (44:6, 8; 45:5–6, 21). Thus the question remained: "To whom then will you liken Me?" (40:18, 25; 46:5). The forms of self-predication[7] are:

"I am Yahweh" or "I am Yahweh your God"	41:13; 42:6, 8; 43:3, 11; 45:5, 6, 18
"I am the first and I am the last"	41:4; 44:6; 48:12
"I am He"	41:4; 43:10, 25; 46:4; 48:12
"I am God"	43:13; 46:9
"I am your God"	41:10

But God's works were likewise enumerated in this first ennead. He was Creator, Kinsman-Redeemer, Lord of history, King of all, and Discloser of the future.

Repeatedly Isaiah stressed the fact that God had "created" (*bārā*ʾ); "made" (ʿ*āśâh* or *pāʾal*); "spread out" (*nāṭâh*), "stretched out" (*rāqaʿ*), "established" (*kûn*), and "founded" (*yāsad*) the heavens and the earth. In this vocabulary, so reminiscent of Genesis 1–2, he established God's ability to create as part of His credentials as rightful Lord of man's present history and final destiny (40:15, 17, 23–34; 42:5; 43:1–7; and later 54:15–16).

Yahweh was also a Kinsman-Redeemer (*gôʾel*) as Boaz was to Ruth. The verb to redeem (*gāʾal*) and its derivatives appear twenty-two times. Here Isaiah used the motif of the Exodus as his source (cf. Exod 6:6; 15:13; Isa 45:15, 21). Involved in this redemption were (1) physical redemption from bondage (43:5–7; 45:13; 48:20; and later 49:9, 11, 14; 52:2–3; 55:12–13); (2) inward, personal and spiritual redemption with the removal of personal sin for Israel (43:25; 44:22; 54:8) and Gentiles (45:20–23; 49:6; 51:4–5); and (3) the eschatological redemption when Jerusalem and the land were rebuilt (40:9–10; 43:20; 44:26; 45:13; 49:16–17; 51:3; 52:1, 9; 53:11–12). Yahweh was a Kinsman-Redeemer without equal.[8]

---

6. For an excellent study on this concept, see C. J. Labuschagne, *The Incomparability of Yahweh in the Old Testament* (Leiden: E. J. Brill, 1966), esp. pp. 111–12, 123f., 142–53.

7. See the discussion by Morgan L. Phillips, "Divine Self-Predication in Deutero-Isaiah," *Biblical Research* 16 (1971): 32–51.

8. See F. Holmgren, *The Concept of Yahweh as Gôʾel in Second Isaiah* (Diss., Union Theological Seminary, New York: University Microfilms, 1963). Also Carroll Stuhlmueller, *Creative Redemption in Deutero-Isaiah* (Rome: Biblical Institute Press, 1970).

[[215]] Currently, Yahweh was in charge of history itself, and the nations did not frighten Him at all (40:15, 17). In fact, foreign leaders were raised up to do His bidding in history (as is so aptly illustrated by Cyrus in 41:1–4); and they were ransomed or conquered on His authority (43:3–14; 44:24–45:8; 47:5–9). No wonder He was called "King" on four occasions. He was "King of Jacob" (41:21); "your King," O Israel (43:15); "King of Israel" (44:6); and as 52:7 summarized, "Your God is King." Isaiah also used the additional royal titles of "Shepherd" (40:9–11), "Witness," "Commandment-Giver," and "Leader" in Isa 55:3.[9]

One more word must be added before leaving the theology of this ennead: Yahweh was the discloser of the future. Before things happened, the prophet was told about them (41:22–23, 26; 42:9; 43:9–10; 44:7–8; 45:21; 46:10–11; 48:5). The challenge to the gods, who were poor rivals and actually nonentities at best, was to declare what was to come to pass in the future, be it good or bad. The most graphic of all the predictions was the naming of Cyrus and two of his greatest works for Israel almost two centuries before they took place (44:28). On such works as these Isaiah rested his case. Yahweh was God of gods, Lord of lords, King of kings and beyond all comparison. He was the God of all.

The Savior of All (Isaiah 49–57)

Two words would summarize the second plank in Isaiah's minitheology book: servant and salvation. But it was the figure of the servant of the Lord that captured the limelight in this section.

The advances in the portrayal of this corporate figure of "servant" are already observable in the use of the singular form twenty times in Isaiah 40–53 and in the plural form ten times in Isaiah 54–66.[10] To demonstrate that the servant is a collective term as well as an individual one representing the whole group can be done from two sets of data: (1) the servant is all Israel in twelve out of the twenty singular references (41:8–10; 43:8–13; 43:14–44:5; 44:6–8, 21–23; 44:24–45:13; 48:1, 7, 10–12, 17); (2) the four great servant songs of Isa 42:1–7; 49:1–6; 50:4–9; and 52:13–53:12 all present the servant as an individual who ministers to Israel. Therein lies one of the greatest puzzles for those scholars who reject the corporate solidarity of the servant.

[[216]] Israel, the servant, is the "seed of Abraham," the patriarchal "friend" of God (41:8). "Abraham . . . was called and blessed" when "he was but one" and was subsequently "made . . . many" (51:2; cf. 63:16). Now

9. Carroll Stuhlmueller, "Yahweh-King and Deutero-Isaiah," *Biblical Research* 11 (1970): 32–45.

10. Isa 54:17; 56:6; 63:17; 65:8–9, 13 ter, 14–15; 66:14.

God had already called Abraham His servant in Gen 26:24; and so had Moses referred to Abraham, Isaac, and Jacob as servants of the Lord (Exod 32:13; Deut 9:27). In fact, all Israel was regarded as His servants in Lev 25:42, 55. Thus the seed was still the center of God's blessings (43:5; 44:3; 45:19, 25; 48:19; 53:10; 54:3; 59:21; 61:9). "The seed shall be known among the nations . . . that they are a seed whom Yahweh has blessed" (65:9, 23; 66:22). That seed was God's "servant," or as it regularly appears in Isaiah 54–66, His "servants." As John Bright noted,

> The figure of the Servant oscillates between the individual and the group . . . He is the coming Redeemer of the true Israel who in his suffering makes the fulfillment of Israel's task possible; he is the central actor in the "new thing" that is about to take place.[11]

In the four servant songs, many of the individual's titles or descriptions are matched by identical ascriptions made of Israel in the Isaianic poems, for example:

An Individual		*All Israel*
42:1	"my chosen"	41:8–9
49:3	"my servant"	44:21
49:6	"a light to the nations"	42:6; 51:4
49:1	"called me from the womb"	44:2, 24; 43:1
49:1	"named my name"	43:1b

Yet, striking as this evidence might be, the servant of the songs has the task and mission "to bring Israel back" and "to gather" Israel to Himself, "to raise up the tribes of Jacob and restore the preserved of Israel" (49:5–6). Therefore, the servant of the Lord cannot be totally equated with Israel as the servant in all respects. The apparent ambivalence is the same type of oscillation found in all the collective terms previously observed in the promise doctrine. They were all-inclusive of all Israel, but they were simultaneously always focused on one representative who depicted the fortunes of the whole group for that present time and the climactic future. The connection was to be found not in some psychological theory of personality but in the "everlasting covenant," even the "sure loyal love for David" (Isa 55:3; 61:8; cf. 2 Samuel 7). The servant of the Lord was the messianic person in the Davidic line then and finally that [[217]] last new David who was to come and who was known as the Seed, the Holy One (*ḥāsîd*), the Branch, etc.

---

11. John Bright, *Kingdom of God* (Nashville: Abingdon, 1953), p. 150ff.

The second ennead also detailed the salvation won by the Servant. In a real turn of events, the prophet Isaiah had God take the cup of God's wrath from Israel's lips and put it to her oppressor's mouth instead (51:22–23; cf. the seventh century prophet Nahum [1:11–14]). Furthermore, a new exodus and redemption were envisaged for the future (52:1–6). This "good news" (*mᵉbaśśēr*) to Zion. Then all the ends of the earth would see God's salvation (52:9–10; cf. 40:9).

This servant who would personally rule, a fact that would startle all the kings of the earth (52:15), would also be the One who would suffer on behalf of all humanity so as to make God's atonement available. The first advent of this Servant would amaze many (vv. 13–14), but His second advent would catch the breath of even the kings of the earth (52:15)—therein lay the mystery of the Servant. His rejection followed: men would reject His message (53:1), His person (v. 2), and His mission (v. 3). But His vicarious suffering would effect an atonement between God and man (vv. 4–6); and though He would submit to suffering (v. 7), death (v. 8), and burial (v. 9), He would subsequently be exalted and richly rewarded (vv. 10–12). On the Servant of the Lord, then, was laid the iniquity of all humanity.

The result of the Servant's suffering was that the "seed" would "possess the nations"; for their tent would be enlarged, the ropes lengthened, and the pegs driven in deeper (54:2–3). Yahweh would then be "the God of the whole earth" (54:5; 49:6). Thus, as "it was in the days of Noah," so it would be when Yahweh returned to "gather Israel" and extended His "steadfast love" (*ḥeseḏ*) and "covenant of peace" (54:5, 9–10). Meanwhile, the free offer of salvation was extended to all nations through David's son (55:3–5; cf. 55:1–2, 6–9; 49:6; and the NT comment in Acts 13:45–49; 26:22–23).

The End of All History

The inauguration of the "eschaton" was sharply demarcated by the ending of the "former things"[12] (41:22; 42:9; 43:9, 18; 44:8; 46:9; 48:3) and the introduction of God's "new thing." There would be a "new" sincere repentance (58–59), a "new" Jerusalem (60), and a "new" heavens and "new" earth (65:17–25; 66:10–24; cf. 2 Pet 3:13; Rev 21:1–4).

[[218]] This would be the aeon of the Holy Spirit according to 63:7–14. A call would go forth for a new Moses to lead a new exodus (vv. 11–14) and give them that "rest" (*nûaḥ*) promised long ago to Joshua. As the servant

---

12. C. R. North, "The Former Things and the 'New Things' in Deutero-Isaiah," *Studies in Old Testament Prophecy*, ed. H. H. Rowley (Edinburgh: T. & T. Clark, 1950), pp. 111–26.

was empowered by God's Spirit (42:1), so was this "anointed" Person. Indeed, He was equated with the servant in Isa 61:1 — "The Spirit of the Lord God is on me because the Lord has anointed me." There He described the joy of His mission (vv. 1–3) and the content of His message (vv. 4–9) including:

1. "You shall be called priests of the Lord and ministers of our God" (v. 6; cf. Exod 19:6).
2. The "everlasting covenant" will be carried out (v. 8).
3. Their "seed" would be known among the nations as those whom God had truly blessed (v. 9).

Even the equipment and character of this Spirit-filled messianic Servant were noted in 61:10–11. He would be clothed with the "garments of salvation" and "cause righteousness and praise to spring forth before all nations."

The Redeemer would come in the last day "for the sake of Zion" (Isa 59:20). He would be dressed as a warrior (59:15b–19) and would wage war on all evil and sin, especially that type of hypocritical life style described in Isa 57:1–59:15a. He would be invested with God's words and His Spirit (59:21). Then Jerusalem would experience violence no longer, for the Lord of glory would be her greatest asset (60). The wealth of the nations would pour into Jerusalem as all humanity arrived to praise the Lord (60:4–16) Then the exalted city of Jerusalem would be at peace forever, and the presence of the Lord of everlasting light would make the need for the sun or moon obsolete (vv. 17–22).

While the "day of vengeance" (63:4–6) and "year of redemption" brought judgment on the nations when God trampled down the nations in His winepress, even as Obadiah and Joel had proclaimed, God's irrevocable purpose for a rebuilt city of Jerusalem which would be inhabited by the "holy people" of God would be realized (62). Even though the clothes of the Hero were sprinkled with the blood of the winepress (63:1–6; cf. Isaiah 34; Joel 3:9–16; and later Zechariah 14; Ezekiel 38–39), He would be vindicated as this aeon drew to a close and the new aeon began.

Part of that renewed—for so the word "new" should be understood—world to come, where righteousness dwelt, included new heavens and new earth. Once again, Isaiah's paradisiacal pictures of peace in nature came to the fore (cf. Isaiah 11 and 65:17–25; 66:10–23). [[219]] Death would be abolished (cf. Isa 25:8), and the everlasting world-wide rule and reign of the new and final Davidic King would begin. Only the judgment of eternal torment on the wicked and finally unrepentant interrupted this picture, for they were perpetually in agony and forever apart from God.

So Isaiah ended his magnificent shorter theology. His dependence on antecedent theology was evident at almost every turn. While relating the "servant" to the earlier teaching about the "seed" (Isa 41:8; 43:5; 44:3; 45:19, 25; 48:19; 53:10; 54:3; 59:21; 61:9; 65:9, 23; 66:22) and to the "covenant" already given (Isa 42:6, 49:8; 54:10; 55:3; 56:4, 6; 59:21; 61:8), not to mention "Abraham" (41:8; 51:2; 63:16) or "Jacob" (41:21; 44:5; 49:26; 60:16) or "David" and the "everlasting covenant" (55:3; 61:8), Isaiah carefully systematized to a large degree the total plan, person, and work of God in the short scope of twenty-seven chapters. No wonder his theology has so profoundly affected men over the centuries.

If you broaden the term of covenant (or anything else) sufficiently, it's possible to demonstrate OT unity. But is it possible to broaden a term so much that it becomes virtually meaningless? Is this only a matter of personal judgment, or is there still more to it?

SAMUEL LUCIEN TERRIEN

b. 1911

Presence in Absence

Theological Synopsis

The magisterial theologies of Walther Eichrodt and Gerhard von Rad came to dominate the discussion about Old Testament theology in North America. Each in its own distinctive way, these theologies managed to embrace the entire Old Testament within a governing principle (Eichrodt) or method (von Rad). Yet the very disagreements between them showed that many problems remained unresolved. The absence of covenant language from much of the Old Testament cast doubt on Eichrodt's theology from the beginning. It seemed to some an unwarranted imposition of a single theme on diverse Old Testament materials. On the other hand, von Rad's claim to find no overarching (or undergirding) theological unity in the Old Testament seemed equally unsatisfactory. In addition, the problematic answers of Eichrodt and von Rad to the question of the Old Testament's relation to the New raised fresh issues, including the existence of Judaism. Samuel Terrien found in these various difficulties the opportunity for a fresh approach to Old Testament theology.

In fact, Terrien's book, *The Elusive Presence*, incorporates both Testaments in a *biblical* theology, a "biblical theology of presence" (1978: 43). Terrien draws on both the tradition-history research of Scandinavian scholars, with its emphasis on myth and ritual, and the form-critical research of German scholars, with its emphasis on salvation history and covenant. Along with the former, Terrien links Israel's religion to its ancient Near Eastern environment; with the latter, he emphasizes Israel's uniquely historical theology. Underlying the diverse expressions of that theology in the Old Testament is what Terrien calls "the Hebraic theology of presence," which the New Testament interprets with reference to Jesus (1978: 411). With this emphasis on presence—God's always *elusive* pres-

254

ence—Terrien is able to integrate, more adequately than either Eichrodt or von Rad had done, Israel's wisdom literature. Indeed, Terrien argues that it is wisdom that holds together the theologies in the Old Testament that otherwise stand in an unresolved tension: "The figure of personified Wisdom brings together the theologoumenon of the name, with its response of the ear, and the theologoumenon of the glory, with its response of the eye" (1978: 473). That statement indicates Terrien's dialectical approach to Old Testament theology, as well as his attention to esthetic dimensions of faith and worship that the strongly historical and ethical approaches of Eichrodt and von Rad omitted. Terrien finds the "play" of wisdom most adequate to the self-hidden God who is always present (*Deus absconditus atque praesens*; 1978: 470). That Judaism and Christianity interpret this self-hidden presence differently does not deny the legitimacy of either.

Terrien suggests that the motif of the presence of God may account best for both "the homogeneity of the Old Testament literature in its totality, . . . [and] the historical and thematic continuity which unites Hebraism and large aspects of Judaism with nascent Christianity" (1978: 475–76). The question is whether such a broad and flexible motif accounts for too much, and thus obscures the particularity of the biblical texts and their individual witness to the identity of God.

Samuel L. Terrien studied in Paris between 1927 and 1933, and in 1933–34 at the École Biblique in Jerusalem. In Paris he studied under Éduard Dhorme, with whom he shared a life-long interest in the Book of Job. From 1935 to 1941, he studied Old Testament at Union Theological Seminary in New York, where he earned his Th.D. He taught at Wooster College in Ohio from 1936 until 1940, and after that until his retirement in 1976 at Union Theological Seminary, New York. He stands within the French and Swiss streams of the Reformed tradition. His work has centered around the theme of wisdom in the Bible and in the ancient and modern worlds, and especially on the Book of Job. Terrien has published monographs and commentaries on Psalms and Job, as well as many books and articles on biblical, theological, and cultural themes.

B.C.O.

Writings by Terrien

1978   *The Elusive Presence: Toward a New Biblical Theology*. Religious Perspectives 26. San Francisco: Harper & Row.

1981   The Play of Wisdom: Turning Point in Biblical Theology. *Horizons in Biblical Theology* 3:125–53.

Writings about Terrien

Gammie, John G., Walter A. Brueggemann, W. Lee Humphreys, and James M.
Ward (editors)
   1978   *Israelite Wisdom: Theological and Literary Essays in Honor of Samuel Terrien.*
             New York: Union Theological Seminary/Scholars Press.
Sanders, James A.
   1978   Comparative Wisdom: L'Oeuvre Terrien. Pp. 3–14 in *Israelite Wisdom:*
             Theological and Literary Essays in Honor of Samuel Terrien. Edited by John
             G. Gammie, Walter A. Brueggemann, W. Lee Humphreys, and James
             W. Ward. New York: Union Theological Seminary/Scholars Press.

Samuel L. Terrien's
Approach to Old Testament Theology

Excerpted with permission from Samuel L. Terrien, *The Elusive Presence: Toward a New Biblical Theology* (San Francisco: Harper & Row, 1978), pp. 31–43, 57–62. Some footnotes have been omitted.

The Quest for a Biblical Theology

[[31]] In the face of the multiplicity of rituals and beliefs represented in the Bible, many scholars have restricted their endeavors to describing the religious phenomena which have received literary formulation. Recent interpreters have therefore tended to present only the history of the religion of Israel and the history of primitive Christianity. Even writers of an Old Testament theology, like Gerhard von Rad,[1] or of a theology of the New Testament, like Rudolf Bultmann,[2] have stressed the plurality of theological responses within Scripture rather than run the risk of distorting historical complexity through oversimplification.

At the same time, it is not possible to ignore the place the Bible has occupied for centuries—and still occupies today—at the heart of both Judaism and Christianity. The books of the Hebrew Bible for Judaism and of both the Old Testament and the New for Christianity exerted an inward stimulus and a power of restraint on faith long before these writings received [[32]] recognition of authority by synagogue or church. It was neither the synagogue nor the church which initially decreed that Scripture was to be the rule of faith and order or "the Word of God."[3] Rather, the books of the Hebrew Bible and of the New Testament imposed themselves upon Jews and Christians as the regulating standard of their religious commitment and ethical behavior. *Canon* was originally not a dogmatic structure imposed from without by institutionalized collectivities but an unspoken force which grew from within the nature of Hebrew-Christian religion.[4] The obligations of the Sinai covenant were remembered as the

huh?

---

1. G. von Rad, *Old Testament Theology*, I–II, tr. by D. M. G. Stalker (New York, 1960–65).

2. R. Bultmann, *Theology of the New Testament*, I–II, tr. by K. Grobel (New York, 1951–55).

3. The rabbinical college at Jamnia (ca. A.D. 97) did not promulgate the canon of the Hebrew Bible. It decided on the canonicity of marginal or doubtful books. Likewise, it is piquant to observe that the Western church lived for centuries without an official canon of scripture, which was formulated by the Protestant Confessions of the sixteenth century and the decrees of the Council of Trent in response to the Protestant challenge.

4. See G. E. Wright, "The Canon as Theological Problem," *The Old Testament and Theology* (New York, 1969), pp. 166ff.

"torah" of Yahweh, a growing collection of instructions which were inserted within the context of the narratives of the Sinai theophany. Thus, the cultic *anamnesis* of the event during which the divine presence disclosed itself to the people through the mediation of Moses prepared and promoted the development of the canon.[5] The idea of the canonicity of a "scripture" was a *fait accompli* when a written document was found in the temple of Jerusalem in 622 B.C. and led to the reform of Josiah and the renewal of the Sinai covenant (2 Kgs 22:1ff.). The "book of the law" (approximately Deut 12:1–26:19) became the nucleus of "the Bible" (*ta biblia*, "the books") because Huldah the prophetess found it conformed to the living word of the Deity (2 Kgs 22:13ff.). Canonicity went back to the cultic memories of the Sinai-Horeb theophany. It is significant that the final edition of the Deuteronomic law opened with a cultic rehearsal of those memories (Deut 1:1ff.) in which the motif of covenant is subordinated to the story of theophanic presence (Deut 5:2–4).

Likewise, it appears that the letters of Paul, which constituted the original nucleus of the New Testament, were circulated throughout the churches of the Mediterranean world and they were read ceremonially at the paracultic celebrations of nascent Christendom, side by side with the portions of the Law and the Prophets traditionally appointed for the sabbath service and the [[33]] festivals. Canonicity imposed itself from within, little by little, in the context of the Christian community at worship.

The inwardness of scriptural canonicity and of its growth in the course of several centuries suggests that a certain homogeneity of theological depth binds the biblical books together beneath the heterogeneity of their respective dates, provenances, styles, rhetorical forms, purposes, and contents. The search for the principle of this homogeneity which spanned a considerable period of time points to the dynamic aspect of a continuity of religious aim rather than to a static unity of doctrinal conformity.[6]

As soon as the historian of the Hebrew-Christian religion seeks to determine the nature of this continuity, he goes beyond a merely phenomenological description of rites and beliefs. He does not disregard on that account the historical fluidity of their origin and growth, but he asks the question of the possibility, the legitimacy, and perhaps even the inevitability of biblical theology.

The disrepute in which this discipline is held in some quarters depends on several factors, one of which is the hostile attitude which many biblical theologians of the past century displayed against modern methods of literary and historical criticism. Another of these factors is related to the de-

5. See [[Terrien 1978: 51]] note 100.

6. See J. Barr, *The Bible in the Modern World* (New York, 1973), p. 181; J. A. Sanders, "Reopening Old Questions About Scripture," *In.*, 28 (1974): 322f.

nominationalism which has colored not a few treatises of biblical theology in which one or another of the scriptural themes was enlisted as the ancillary justification of a dogma peculiar to individual church, sect, or tradition.

Ironically, the idea of a "biblical theology" originated as a reaction of the Pietists against the scholastic Lutheranism of the eighteenth century.[7] In 1787, in an academic discourse now well-known [[English translation on pp. 489–502 below]], Johann-Philip Gabler assigned the "new" discipline with the task of describing in historical sequence the thoughts and feelings of the sacred authors "concerning divine things." Gabler's intention was chiefly to obtain for biblical [[34]] interpreters a freedom of inquiry from the dogmatic theology of his time. The new discipline, however, fell almost immediately under the spell of the age of the enlightenment. Most treatises published in the nineteenth century under such titles as *Biblical Theology*, *Old Testament Theology*, and *New Testament Theology* were systematic presentations of the ideas of the Bible on God, man, sin, and salvation.[8]

It is now recognized that such attempts, inherited in part from Platonic conceptual thinking and Aristotelian logic, were bound to translate the *sui generis* thrust of biblical faith into the alien idiom of didactic exposition. Many interpreters have therefore questioned the legitimacy of the discipline of biblical theology.

At the dawn of the twentieth century, the vast majority of scholars restricted themselves to composing essays on the history of the Hebrew religion, the "life" of Jesus, and the "religious experience" of the early church, especially that of Paul. The discipline of biblical theology entered into an eclipse. The concern for *historicism*, on the one hand, and the revival of the Marcionite prejudice against the Hebrew Bible, on the other, introduced the fashion of an atomistic approach to the study of Scripture. Harnack even proposed the "removal" of the Old Testament from the Christian canon.[9]

A new era began during the First World War. In 1920, Rudolf Kittel spoke of the "future of Old Testament science"[10] and urged the rediscovery

7. The distinction between "biblical theology" and "scholastic theology" appeared in the *Pia Desideria* of Philip Spener in 1675, although the expression *theologia biblica* was first used by Wolfgang Jacob Christmann in 1624 and Henricus a Diest in 1643. A *Biblische Theologie* was published by Carl Haymann in 1708. A. F. Büsching wrote in 1758 on the "advantages of a biblical theology over a scholastic or dogmatic theology."

8. See the works, among others, of C. F. Ammon (1792), G. L. Bauer (1796), W. M. L. de Wette (1813–16), E. W. Hengstenberg (1829–35); B. Bauer (1838–39); F. C. Baur (1847), J. C. Hoffmann (1840–44), G. F. Oehler (1873), H. Schultz (1869), A. B. Davidson (1904).

9. See A. von Harnack, *Marcion: das Evangelium vom fremden Gott, eine Monographie zur Geschichte der Grundlegung der kathohlischen Kirche. Neue Studien zu Marcion* (Leipzig, 1924).

10. R. Kittel, *ZAW*, 39 (1921): 84; cf. C. Steuernagel, "Alttestamentliche Religionsgeschichte," *ZAW*, 43 (1925): 266–73; J. D. Smart, "The Death and Rebirth of Biblical Theology," in *The Interpretation of Scripture* [[Philadelphia, 1961]], pp. 270ff.

of the significance of the entire Bible for the religious thinking of modern
man. Quite independently of Karl Barth's thunderous proclamation of the
Bible as the "Word of God,"[11] a few exegetes who had been trained in the
rigors of the critical method slowly assumed a new stance. While they refused to serve the interests of a particular church tradition, and retained intact their respect for the scientific approach, they moved away from a
position of analytical compartmentalism and antiquarian remoteness, and
they sought to restate in [[35]] modern terms the meaning of the Bible for
contemporary theologians.

In 1926, Johannes Hempel published *God and Man in the Old Testament*, in which he attempted to stress those features of the faith "which
came from God and led to God, and which also lead us to God."[12] The
same year, Otto Eissfeldt sensed the need to build a new bridge between
the religious history of Israel and the theological significance of the Old
Testament.[13] In 1929, Walther Eichrodt put squarely the question, "Does
the Old Testament theology still have an independent significance within
Old Testament studies?"[14] During the following decade, Eichrodt brought
out his monumental three-volume *Old Testament Theology*,[15] for which he
used the tools of modern research and at the same time sought to discover in the covenant the principle of coherence for the understanding of
the Old Testament in its entirety.

Eichrodt's treatment was thorough, incisive, and in many places original. It is still indispensable after a whole generation of further study.
Nevertheless, a "pan-covenant" approach to Old Testament theology over-

---

11. Barth was aware of the sterility of *Historismus*, but he tended to telescope the entire
history of Israel into a Christology. Paradoxically, his reaction against the neo-marcionism of
Harnack led him to neglect the historical concreteness and complexity of "the people of
God," either in the Hebraic period or at the birth of the church. His influence has generally
been felt by systematic theologians rather than by biblical exegetes. One notable exception is
that of W. Vischer, who, like Barth and indeed E. W. Hengstenberg (*Christologie des Alten Testaments*, 1829–33), interpreted the Old Testament as "a witness to Christ." Among the many
books and articles dealing with Barthian hermeneutics, cf. O. Cullmann, "Les problèmes
posés par le méthode exégétique de Karl Barth," *RHPR*, 8 (1928): 70–83; German tr. in *Vorträge und Aufsätze* (Tübingen und Zürich, 1966), pp. 90–101.

12. J. Hempel, *Gott und Mensch im Alten Testament. Studie zur Geschichte der Frömmigkeit*
(Stuttgart, 1926; etc.).

13. O. Eissfeldt, "Israelitisch-jüdische Religionsgeschichte und alttestamentliche Theologie," *ZAW*, 44 (1926): 1–12 [[English translation on pp. 20–29 above]].

14. W. Eichrodt, "Hat die alttestamentliche Theologie noch selbständige Bedeutung
innerhalb der alttestamentlichen Wissenschaft?" *ZAW*, 47 (1929): 83–91 [[English translation
on pp. 30–39 above]].

15. *Theology of the Old Testament* (1933–39), tr. by J. A. Baker from the 6th German ed.
(1959), 2 vols. (Philadelphia, 1961–64; etc.).

looks the multi-faceted complexity of Hebrew religion.[16] In the ten centuries covered by biblical literature, the importance of the covenant motif was only sporadic. In addition, the wisdom books[17] by and large ignore covenant ideology. This omission is the more remarkable when it is remembered that sapiential circles in Jerusalem during the monarchy were closely related to the royal court and might have been expected to pay strict attention to the theological significance of the Davidic covenant.[18] A covenant-centered interpretation of Old Testament thinking on God and man necessarily underplays the significance of Hebrew wisdom.[19]

In spite of its limitations, Eichrodt's work proved to be the chief incentive for numerous reappraisals of the issues involved in the elaboration of an Old Testament theology.[20] In 1946, H. Wheeler Robinson laid down the principles for a new Old Testament [[36]] theology which would adequately discover in the historical traditions of Israel the locus of revelation.[21] E. Jacob, Th. C. Vriezen and G. E. Wright—each in his own style and with his own emphasis—have persuasively presented the dynamic aspect of the self-disclosure of Yahweh in the context of the Hebrew epic traditions.[22]

In 1957, G. von Rad called for an abrupt change of approach. In his two-volume *Old Testament Theology*,[23] he undertook to discern the theological significance of the Hebrew Bible not so much in the sequential continuity of a theological theme in the history of Israel's religion as in

16. See [[Terrien 1978:]] pp. 22–27.

17. See R. E. Murphy, "The Kerygma of the Book of Proverbs," *In.*, 20 (1966); 9ff.; "The Interpretation of the Old Testament Wisdom Literature," *In.*, 22 (1968); 290ff.; B. L. Mack, "Wisdom Myth and Mythology," *In.*, 24 (1970): 3ff.; R. B. Y. Scott, "The Study of the Wisdom Literature," *In.*, 24 (1970): 20ff.

18. F. C. Prussner, "The Covenant of David and the Problem of Unity in Old Testament Theology," in J. C. Rylaarsdam, ed., *Transitions in Biblical Scholarship* (Chicago, 1968), pp. 17–41.

19. W. Zimmerli; "The Place and Limits of the Wisdom in the Framework of the Old Testament Theology," *SJT*, 17 (1964): 146–58; W. Brueggemann, "Scripture and an ecumenical Life-Style," *In.*, 24 (1970): 3–19.

20. Cf. W. G. Most, "A Biblical Theology of Redemption in a Covenant Framework," *CBQ* 29 (1967): 1–19; J. Jocz, *The Covenant: A Theology of Human Destiny* (Grand Rapids, Mich., 1968); G. W. Buchanan, *The Consequences of the Covenant* (Leiden, 1970); see also [[Terrien 1978: 51]] note 96. Although many essays on biblical theology are still written in the traditional framework of doctrinal ideas, they usually assign a prominent place to the soteriological complex of cultic obedience and faith, even if they present a didactic pattern. See, among others, the works of L. Köhler (1936), P. Heinisch (1940), A. Gelin (1949), P. van Imschoot (1945), and O. Procksch (posthumously published in 1956).

21. H. Wheeler Robinson, *Inspiration and Revelation* (Oxford, 1950).

22. E. Jacob, *Theology of the Old Testament*, tr. by A. W. Heathcote and Ph. J. Allcock (New York, 1958); Th. C. Vriezen, *An Outline of Old Testament Theology*, 2nd ed. (Oxford, 1970).

23. See note 151 above [[note 1 in this reprint]].

the constant revising and reformulating of the creedal confessions in the light of historical change. Although von Rad's achievement remains to his day epoch-making, it cannot justify the title *Old Testament Theology*, for the dichotomy between the theologies of the confessional reinterpretations, on the one hand, and the theologies of the responses of the psalmists, the prophets, and the wisemen, on the other, has not been successfully overcome, nor has a principle of theological homogeneity capable of accounting for the growth of the Hebrew Bible been convincingly elucidated. Neither Eichrodt nor von Rad has discovered within Old Testament religion that organic and specific element which not only points to the gospel of Jesus and the early church but also leads inevitably to the New Testament.[24]

While Eichrodt and von Rad were carrying out this work, intensive research was being undertaken among interpreters on the interrelation between faith and history. G. E. Wright looked for the principle of biblical continuity in the activity of Yahweh as creator, Lord, and warrior;[25] B. S. Childs tended to stress the importance of the community pattern as a vehicle of divine intervention within history.[26] Others have discussed the purposes and methods of Old Testament theology in the light of contemporary trends;[27] G. Fohrer, especially, has proposed that at the center of Old

24. Not more successful has been von Rad's effort to justify mutual complementariness of Old Testament and New Testament. To maintain that the first Christians reinterpreted the creedal confessions of Judaism in a way not unlike that of the Deuteronomists and the Chronicler with regard to the cultic traditions of ancient Israel (cf. von Rad, "The Actualization of the Old Testament in the New" and "The Old Testament's Understanding of the World and Man, and Christianity," in *Old Testament Theology*, vol. II, pp. 319–56) is possible only through the application of a form of typological exegesis which raises serious problems of hermeneutical methodology. Cf. W. Eichrodt, "Typologische Auslegung des Alten Testaments," *Ev. Th.*, 12 (1952): 17ff.; H. Conzelmann, "Fragen an G. von Rad," *Ev. Th.*, 24 (1964): 113ff., and von Rad's subsequent disquisition *Ev. Th.*, 24 (1954), pp. 388ff. See also Eichrodt's comments on von Rad's methods and purpose in the revised edition of his *Theology of the Old Testament*, tr. by J. A. Baker (London, 1967) I, p. 34; and those of Vriezen, in "Basis, Task and Method in Old Testament Theology," *An Outline of Old Testament Theology*, pp. 118ff.

25. G. E. Wright, *The Old Testament and Theology* (New York, 1969), pp. 70ff.

26. B. S. Childs, "The God of Israel and the Church," in *Biblical Theology in Crisis* (Philadelphia, 1970), pp. 201ff.

27. J. Barr, "The Problem of Old Testament Theology and the History of Religion," *CJT*, 3 (1957): 141–49; R. de Vaux, "Peut-on écrire une théologie de l'Ancien Testament?" *Bible et Orient* (Paris, 1967), pp. 59–71; E. Jacob, "La théologie de l'Ancien Testament: Etat présent et perspectives d'avenir," *De Mari à Qumran. Festschrift J. Coppens* (Gembloux et Paris, 1969), pp. 259–71; H.-J. Kraus, "Geschichte als Erziehung. Biblisch-theologische Perspektiven," in *Probleme biblischer Theologie: Festschrift G. von Rad*, ed. H. W. Wolff (München, 1971), pp. 258–74; N. W. Porteous, "Magnalia Dei," *ibid.*, pp. 417–27; G. F. Hasel, *Old Testament Theology: Basic Issues in the Current Debate* (Grand Rapids, Mich., 1972); W. Zimmerli, *Grundriss der alttestamentliche Theologie* (Stuttgart, 1972).

Testament faith lies neither the covenant ⟦37⟧ ideology nor the concept of community but the motif of divine presence, now and on the last day.[28]

The quest for an authentically "biblical" theology is being renewed more actively than ever before,[29] and there are signs that the present generation of New Testament scholarship no longer works in isolation from Old Testament science. Like their Old Testament colleagues, New Testament critics have been interested for many years in history rather than in the theological significance of Scripture. In 1897, W. Wrede reduced the task of "the so-called New Testament Theology" to the historical description of early Christianity.[30] While treatments of a New Testament theology conceived as a system of doctrinal ideas continued to appear, the discipline was no longer the concern of modern exegetes, although a few of them refused to reduce the New Testament either to a series of historical sketches or to a merely didactic exposition.

As early as 1885, A. Schlatter clearly discerned that the thought of Jesus and the apostles was inseparable from their faith and ethics.[31] A generation later, when the impact of the comparative history of religions convinced the students of primitive Christianity that the New Testament documents could not be interpreted in isolation from the sects and the cults of the Mediterranean world, W. Bousset assigned to the ceremonial worship of the Christian communities a major part in the formulation and the transmission of the gospel.[32] In the light of the subsequent discoveries made on the Hellenistic mystery cults, Gnostic groups, and especially the Jewish sectarians of Qumran, many historians of the early church have stressed the need to revise long-standing attitudes concerning the neglected discipline of New Testament theology.

In the meantime, Rudolf Bultmann drew out the theological consequences of his form-critical analysis of the gospel tradition. His *New*

28. G. Fohrer, *Theologische Grundstrukturen des Alten Testaments* (Berlin & New York, 1972), pp. 95ff. A useful survey of various suggestions for the "central" concept of the Old Testament will be found in G. Hasel, *Old Testament Theology: Basic Issues in the Current Debate* (Grand Rapids, Mich., 1972), pp. 49ff.

29. See H.-J. Kraus, *Die biblische Theologie: Ihre Geschichte und Problematik* (Neukirchen-Vluyn, 1970), pp. 279ff.; E. Ladd, "The Search for Perspective," *In.*, 25 (1971): 41–62.

30. W. Wrede, *Über Aufgabe und Methode der sogenanntlichen neutestamentlichen Theologie* (Göttingen, 1897).

31. A. Schlatter, *Der Glaube im Neuen Testament* (1885); *id.*, *Theologie des Neuen Testaments* (1909–18); *id.*, *Die Geschichte des Christus* (1921); cf. Kraus, *Die biblische Theologie* (1970); pp. 175ff. See also the influential book of M. Kähler, *The So-Called Historical Jesus* (2nd. German ed., 1896), tr. by C. E. Braaten (Philadelphia, 1964).

32. W. Bousset, *Kyrios Christos. A History of the Belief in Christ from the Beginnings of Christianity to Irenaeus*, tr. by J. E. Steely (Nashville and New York, 1970; original German edition, 1913).

Testament Theology,[33] the culmination of many years of exegetical research, is comparable in its field to the [[38]] masterpieces of Eichrodt and von Rad in the field of Old Testament theology. The considerable achievements of Bultmann are marred by his inability to see the organic affinities which link the faith of Jesus and the early Christians to the theological thrust of Hebraism rather than the speculations of popular Judaism.

With respect to the Old Testament, Bultmann proved to be a neo-Harnackian.[34] In addition, he failed to appreciate the historical foundations of the Christian *muthos*. He did not ask seriously whether the faith in the resurrection of Jesus and later in his virgin birth might not be indissolubly related to, and organically dependent upon, the historical reality of his personality as well as his teaching.[35] He relegated the sayings and the ministry of Jesus to the Jewish background of New Testament theology, as if the faith of the early church had suddenly emerged of itself as a new and particular *gnosis*. While his presentations of Paulinism and Johannism possess qualities of exceptional incisiveness, his theological understanding of the New Testament is largely reduced to anthropological and psychological concerns. Through an exegetical and philosophical *tour de force*, Bultmann has succeeded in eradicating the transcendental dimension of justification by faith.

In a laudable effort to be relevant to the cultural chaos that followed Nazism and the Second World War, Bultmann excessively reacted against the very excesses of historicism, but he undermined and almost negated the historical foundation of New Testament faith. By demythologizing the Christian kerygma, he paradoxically de-historicized the humanity of Jesus and the concreteness of the faith of the early church. Ironically, transforming New Testament theology into an anthropology of existential self-understanding, he failed to grasp the existential involvement of the church in the political, moral, and cultural realities of history.

A powerful corrective to Bultmann's Marcionic and docetic [[39]] tendencies was provided by Oscar Cullmann's insistence on the biblical reality

---

33. See note 152 above [[note 2 in this reprint]].

34. R. Bultmann, "The Significance of the Old Testament for Christian Faith," in *The Old Testament and Christian Faith*, ed. by B. W. Anderson (New York, 1963), pp. 8–35. Among the various contributions to this critical appraisal of Bultmann's position, see especially C. Michalson, "Bultmann Against Marcion," pp. 49–63, and E. Voegelin, "History and Gnosis," pp. 64–89. Cf. Bultmann's typical treatment of the Old Testament in his article on "Knowledge" in *TWNT*. The literature on Bultmann is considerable. Among others, see P. Barthel, "Bultmann et l'interprétation du Nouveau Testament," *RHPR*, 37 (1957): 257–64; N. J. Young, *History and Existential Theology: The Role of History in the Thought of Rudolf Bultmann* (Philadelphia, 1969).

35. See [[Terrien 1978: 56]] note 136.

of time.[36] For him Christian faith is centered less on an existential discovery of self-awareness than on a cultic participation in salvation history. He does not deny that faith requires an existential decision, but he maintains that such a decision is always founded upon the certainty that "a divine history" unfolds in the universe and across the generations of men.[37] Christian existence takes place between the "already" and the "not yet" of an eschatological hope which is at once past and future.[38] Cullmann's stress on the interpenetration of *Heilsgeschichte* and eschatological expectation has inspired intensive research concerning faith and history.

In the meantime, biblical theologians have been led to work more closely with the systematic theologians and the philosophers of language in raising the issue of hermeneutics.[39] The distinction between biblical theology, a historical discipline which seeks to elucidate the meaning of the Bible itself, and systematic theology, which attempts to translate biblical dynamics of faith and cultus into the contemporary idiom, needs to be carefully preserved.[40] Biblical theologians are increasingly aware of the relativity of historical research and of the dangers of *historicism*. They recognize the need of becoming critically explicit regarding their epistemological presuppositions, and they constantly remind themselves of their own limitations in attempting to penetrate scriptural meaning and to remain faithful to that meaning while seeking to translate it into the language of the cultural world view of the twentieth century. In addition,

---

36. O. Cullmann, *Christ and Time: The Primitive Christian Conception of Time and History*, rev. ed., tr. by F. V. Filson (London, 1957); *Christology of the New Testament*, tr. by Sh. C. Guthrie and Ch. A. M. Hope (Philadelphia, 1959); *id.*, *Salvation in History*, tr. by S. G. Sowers (New York, 1967): this is in effect a modern treatment of the theology of the New Testament which presupposes the theological significance of the Old Testament for Christians.

37. Cullmann, *Salvation in History*, pp. 313ff.

38. *Ibid.*, pp. 283ff., 289ff.

39. The problem of the interrelation of exegesis and epistemology has been revived in the past twenty-five years through the development of linguistic analysis and philosophical inquiry concerning the question of objectivity and subjectivity. See F. Bovon, et al., *Analyse structurale et exégèse biblique* (Neuchâtel, 1971); J. A. Sanders, "Hermeneutics," *IDB, Suppl. Vol.* (1976), pp. 402ff.; *id.*, "Adaptable for Life: The Nature and Function of the Canon," *Magnalia Dei: The Mighty Acts of God* [*In Memoriam G. E. Wright*] (Garden City, N. Y., 1976), pp. 531ff.

40. In his book, *Biblical Theology in Crisis* (New York, 1969), B. S. Childs referred not to "Biblical Theology" in the historical sense of the word (p. 18, *et passim*), but to various forms of a neoorthodox theology which appeared on the North American continent in the middle of the twentieth century and was sometimes known as "the Biblical Theology Movement." This misleading expression designates a loose group of heterogeneous trends that have been influenced by Kierkegaard, Dostoievski, Barth, Brunner, Bultmann, Tillich, R. Niebuhr, Sartre, Heidegger, and even Camus. Although several of the representatives of this theological movement have taken seriously the theological significance of the Bible, their work should not in any way be confused with "biblical theology" in the proper sense.

they know that to assume their proper responsibility toward the work of systematic theologian, they must perform the "descriptive task" of biblical theology, as it has been called,[41] in a way which goes beyond the mere cataloguing of the mythopoetic formulations of the biblical documents, from the Yahwist epic in the tenth century B.C. to the Johannine Apocalypse at the end of the first century A.D.

[[40]] By their parallel insistence on *Heilsgeschichte*, biblical theologians like Eichrodt, Vriezen, Jacob, von Rad, Cullmann, and Wright have offered a platform for further research.[42] The warnings of Ebeling on the problematic character of theological coherence within each Testament deserve scrupulous attention,[43] but the arguments that he directed against the unity of the Bible have now lost their sharpness, for contemporary discussion no longer attempts to expound biblical "ideas." It centers on the dynamic continuity of biblical fields of force.[44] Furthermore, general agreement has been reached on Ebeling's plea to understand Scripture in the context of the ancient Near Eastern and Mediterranean cultures, with special emphasis on the extracanonical literature of Judaism in Hellenistic, Hasmonean, and Roman times.[45]

Above all, the very use of the word "theology" in connection with the Bible requires critical scrutiny. Going beyond Ebeling's challenge,[46] the biblical theologian will refuse to apply the word *theo-logia* to the content of the Bible as if it were still overloaded with connotations that are either patristic, medieval, scholastic, or Tridentine on the one hand, or Protestant, modernist, and postexistential on the other. Instead he will seek to discover the biblical meaning of the notion which the Greek term *theo-logia* fails to convey. Plato and Aristotle employed it in the sense of "science of

41. See K. Stendahl, "Biblical Theology, Contemporary," *IDB*, 1 (1962): 429ff.; cf. "Method in the Study of Biblical Theology," in *The Bible in Modern Scholarship*, ed. by J. Ph. Hyatt (Nashville, 1965), p. 199.

42. See B. Albrektson, *History and the Gods: An Essay on the Idea of Historical Events as Divine Manifestations in the Ancient Near East and in Israel* (Lund, 1967); S. Amsler, "Les deux sources de la théologie de l'histoire dans l'Ancien Testament," *RTP*, 19 (1969): 235–46.

43. G. Ebeling, "The Meaning of Biblical Theology," *JTS*, 6 (1955): 210–25; revised and rep. in *Word and Faith* (Philadelphia, 1963), pp. 79–97; see esp. pp. 91f.

44. See P. R. Ackroyd, *Continuity: A Contribution to the Study of the Old Testament Religious Tradition* (Oxford, 1962). New Testament scholars generally tend to continue presenting theological themes separately, although several of them are trying to bring these themes into a single focus. See H. Thyen, *Studien zur Sündenvergebung im Neuen Testament und seinen alttestamentlichen und jüdischen Voraussetzungen* (Göttingen, 1970).

45. See J. Barr, "Le judaïsme postbiblique et la théologie de l'Ancien Testament," *RTP*, 18 (1968): 209–17.

46. "What the Bible testifies to and strives after is not theology, but something that happens to man in God's dealings with the world" (Ebeling, *Word and Faith*, p. 93).

divine things."[47] Quite differently, the Hebraic expression *daᶜat Elohim*, "knowledge of God," points to a reality which at once includes and transcends intellectual disquisition. It designates the involvement of man's total personality in the presence of Yahweh through the prophetic word, the cultic celebration, and the psychological mode of communion in faith. In the Hebraic sense of "knowledge of God," theology does not mean an objective science of divine things. Although it uses the critical faculties of the mind, it proceeds both from an inner commitment to a faith and from ⟦41⟧ a participation in the destiny of a people which transcends the national and racial particularities of the times.

Theology in this sense implies the dedication of the self, its orientation toward the demands of a specific vocation, and its acceptance of a corresponding mode of living. At its highest level, it aims at promoting a stability of faith independent of the normal fluctuations of the human character, and at facilitating a transmission of that faith to the next generation. It is based on the cultic commemoration of presence and the cultic expectancy of its renewal. It is nurtured by the celebration of presence in the midst of the community of faith which extends from the theophanic past to the epiphanic end of history.[48]

Not on account of an editorial accident of juxtaposition but through a conscious intent which reveals a theological grasp have the Deuteronomists made the *Shemaᶜ* ("Hear, O Israel, Yahweh thy God, Yahweh is one") inseparable from the invitation to love God. In the words of Israel's creed (Deut 6:6ff.), faith in Yahweh means love of Yahweh, first with the whole of one's mind (*lebh*), second with the whole of one's living being, its instinctual drives and its persistence in selfhood (*nephesh*), and third with the whole of one's potentiality, the abundance or "muchness" (*meʾôd*) of eros, which leads to the extension of the individual into the family, the continuation of the self into the self of one's children and the future generations of man.[49]

It is therefore not on account of a second editorial accident of juxtaposition that Israel's creed was used as a preface for the first textbook on religious education in the history of western culture: "And those words,

47. Plato, *Rep.*, 379*a*; Aristotle, *Meteor.*, 2, 1–2, *id.*, *Metaph.*, 2, 4, 12; 10, 7, 7; 11, 6, 6; etc. See F. Kattenbusch, "Die Entstehung einer christlichen Theologie. Zur Geschichte der Ausdrücke *theologia, theologos, theologikos.*" *ZTK*, 11 (1930): 161–205; W. W. Jaeger, *Theology of the Early Greek Philosophers* (Oxford, 1947), pp. 4–5.

48. It is significant that in the revised edition of *An Outline of Old Testament Theology* (Oxford, 1970), Th. C. Vriezen emphasizes the reality of communion between Yahweh and his people above all other factors (see esp. pp. 150, 175).

49. See J. W. McKay, "Man's Love for God in Deuteronomy and the Father/Teacher—Son/Pupil Relationship," *VT*, 22 (1972): 426–35; S. D. McBride, Jr., "The Yoke of the Kingdom: An Exposition of Deuteronomy 6:4–5," *In.*, 27 (1973): 273–306.

which I command thee this day, shall remain in thy intellectual consciousness, and thou shalt teach them to thy sons by sing-song rote (*we-shin-
nànetâ lebhanèkâ*)" (Deut 6:6ff. [Heb. 7ff.]). The pericope concludes with
the kerygmatic summary of the *Heilsgeschichte*: "Then, thou shalt say to thy
son, "We were Pharaoh's slaves in Egypt . . . " (Deut 6:21 [Heb. 20]). [[42]]
Theology is the knowledge of God, but this knowledge is love with the
whole of one's mind in the context of a corporate obligation toward the
past and the future. Biblical theology as the biblical knowledge of God is
indeed the object of science, provided that the biblical theologian is also
subject to a personal involvement in the "knowledge" of that God. Biblical
theology is thus indissolubly married to biblical spirituality, which in turn
remains inseparable from the continuity of the cultic celebration of presence. It is the knowledge of God which provides the clue to the mystery of
the people of God, whether Israel or the Church. Such a knowledge
points to what has been felicitously called "the sacramental prophetism"
of the Bible in its entirety.[50]

Covenant ideology and covenant ceremonial may have played significant roles at critical moments in the history of Israel, and especially in its
eschatological form at the birth of the Christian church. Nevertheless, this
ideology and ceremonial proved to be chiefly the means of reform in
times of corruption or cultural chaos. Covenant making constituted a rite
which depended on the prior affirmation of a faith in the intervention of
God in a peculiar segment of history. By contrast, the reality of divine
presence proved to be the constant element of distinctiveness throughout
the centuries of biblical times. It is this reality which produced the power
of a "canonical" Scripture, and it is this reality which may renew this
power in contemporary Christianity.

Israel maintained her historical existence as a people only in so far as
she remembered and expected the manifestation of divine presence. It
was the presence which created peoplehood. An individual member of
that people partook of the life of the community only in so far as he
shared in the presence, either through cultic celebration or by associating
himself with the mediators of presence who had experienced its immediacy. When the structure of the covenant exploded, as it did during [[43]]
the exile in Babylon, the people remained conscious of their peoplehood
only when they improvised paracultic celebrations of the presence and
thereby ritually anticipated the final epiphany.

50. J.-J. von Allmen, *Prophétisme sacramentel; neuf études pour le renouveau et l'unité de
l'Eglise* (Neuchâtel, 1964), p. 19; cf. S. Amsler, "Le thème du procès chez les prophètes d'Is-
raël," *RTP*, 24 (1974): 116–31, esp. p. 130.

Because it brings together the divine asseverations, "I am Yahweh," of the Hebraic theophany, and "I am the Lord," of the Christian faith in the resurrection of Jesus, the motif of presence induces a magnetic field of forces which maintains a dynamic tension, in the whole of Scripture, between divine self-disclosure and divine self-concealment.[51] The proximity of God creates a memory and an anticipation of certitude, but it always defies human appropriation. The presence remains elusive.

It is symptomatic of our age that the crisis of contemporary theology is related to the problem of authority in all domains, and that the search for the perennial authority of Scripture requires new tools of semantic interpretation. The problem of responding to the biblical record of the revelation of God from Abraham to Paul moves again to the forefront of the theological enterprise. The Hebraic theology of presence leads to the Christian theology of the eucharistic presence. Because it refuses to accept a separation between cultus and faith and carries at the same time the seed of corporate continuity in history, the biblical theology of presence may provide a prolegomenon to a new biblical theology that in its turn may play a central part in the birth of an authentically ecumenical theology.

Synopsis of Terrien's *Elusive Presence* (1978)

51. K. H. Miskotte, *When the Gods are Silent,* tr. J. W. Doberstein (New York, 1967), pp. 257ff.

Samuel L. Terrien
On the Psalmody of Presence

Excerpted with permission from Samuel L. Terrien, *The Elusive Presence: Toward a New Biblical Theology* (San Francisco: Harper & Row, 1978), pp. 320–26, 347–48.

Presence in Absence

⟦320⟧ As the kingdom of David crumbled from within and eventually fell to Babylonian imperialism, the temple psalmodists continued to praise Yahweh as the lord of Zion, the sovereign of nature, and the judge of history. With candor, they also confessed their own agonies. Although they sometimes borrowed ⟦321⟧ hackneyed formulas which went back to Sumerian laments, they also gave poetic shape to their original insights into the crucible of religious discovery. As lyrical poets of sickness, harassment, doubt, and guilt, a few became channels of divine revelation. Some of the psalmodic theologians labored under the plight of their spiritual isolation. They sang the hidden God. Others were tortured by an obsession for God. They sang the hauntingness of presence. A few reached a plateau of confident serenity. They sang the sufficient grace.

The Hidden God

When the prophet Isaiah of Jerusalem observed that "Yahweh concealed his face" (Isa 8:17) or the Second Isaiah in Exile mourned the absence of Yahweh from the fate of his own people, saying,

> Verily, verily, thou art a God that hidest thyself   (Isa 45:15)

their complaint amounted in effect to a confession of faith. To be aware of divine hiddenness is to remember a presence and to yearn for its return. The presence of an absence denies its negativity.

The poet who composed Psalm 22 was a theologian of dereliction.[1] His cry, "My God, my God, why hast thou forsaken me?", has been echoed by legions who have been tormented by cosmic solitude. In a sense, the psalmist showed that he had been a poet of cultic presence, but he

---

1. See R. Martin-Achard, "Notes bibliques: Remarques sur le Psaume 22," *Verbum Caro,* 17 (1963): 119ff.; N. H. Ridderbos, "The Psalms: Style, Figures, and Structures . . . ," *OTS,* 12 (Leiden, 1963): 43ff.; L. R. Fisher, "Betrayed by Friends. An Expository Study of Psalm 22," *In.,* 18 (1964): 20ff.; R. Kilian, "Ps 22 und das priesterliche Heilsorakel," *BZ,* 12 (1968): 172ff.; H. Schmid, "Mein Gott, mein Gott, warum hast du mich verlassen?" *Wort und Dienst,* NF, 11 (1971): 119ff.

ignored the myth of holy space. He substituted for the category of the sanctuary the living reality of the act of praise offered by the whole community—past, present, and future—of the people of God:

> . . . Thou art holy,
> enthroned upon the praises of Israel   (vs. 3 [Heb. 4])

[[322]] It is only through exegetical legerdemain that commentators discern in this phrase an allusion to the ark upon which Yahweh of Hosts was believed by some to have been ceremonially seated. The psalmist used a spatial verb with an auditive object that belonged to the realm of humanity. The ear triumphed over the eye. The mystery of divine nearness depended less on the *hagios topos* than upon the social reality of adoration.

Now, the lamenter has been cut off from the source of his life. Not only has he been deprived of the protection he expected from the Lord of history, but he has also been dispossessed of his divine filiality.

> . . . Thou art he who took me from my mother's womb,
> Thou caused me to feel safe on my mother's breasts,
> Upon thee was I cast from my mother's womb,
> And from my mother's belly thou hast been my God!
> (vss. 9–10 [Heb. 10–11])

These ritual gestures of paternal adoption may indicate that the lament was intended to be intoned by the king at the ceremonial of the New Year, if indeed such a drama of royal humiliation, torture, and execution did take place at any time in the temple of Jerusalem (vss. 19–21 [Heb. 20–22]).[2] Unfortunately, the Hebrew text of the critical lines is obscure and probably corrupt. In any case, in mid-course the lament becomes a hymn of praise, as if the hero has been raised from symbolic death to a new life (vss. 22–30 [Heb. 23–31]).

From dereliction, the perspective of the psalmist broadened its scope to include "all the families of the nations." In a reminiscence of the Abrahamic promise (Gen 12:1–3), the reborn hero hailed Yahweh's kingdom "to the extremities of the earth." His horizon has now transcended the categories of time. Both the dead and the generations yet to be born are invited either to eat at the heavenly banquet or to hear the good news of the *Opus Dei*.[3]

---

2. See discussion in G. Fohrer, *History of Israelite Religion*, tr. by D. E. Green (Nashville and New York, 1972), pp. 142ff.

3. See C. Krahmalkov, "Psalm 22, 28–32," *Biblica*, 50 (1969): 389ff.; E. Lipiński, "L'hymne à Yahwé Roi au Psaume 22, 28–32," *Biblica*, 50 (1969): 153ff.; O. Keel-Leu, "Nochmals Psalm 22, 28–32," *Biblica*, 51 (1970): 405ff.

[[323]] Inasmuch as the motif of divine hiddenness in Psalm 22 was unrelated to any sense of sin—a most unusual omission in Near Eastern and Hebraic laments—and on account of the universalism of its eschatology, the early Christians appropriated this extraordinary poem of presence lost and regained to describe the passion of Jesus, his death in forsakenness, and his triumph over mortality and time in the life of his followers.[4]

Psalm 22 constitutes an exception in the psalmody of presence. Other laments which complained of the veiling of the Deity were confessions of sin. In Hebraic theology, Yahweh concealed his face from human criminality. If the hero of the poem was not a king but a single member of the community, his plight must have been the more intolerable, for he had no answer to the question "why" and he found neither justification nor meaning in his spiritual, as well as physical, agony. After his ordeal, however, he was ushered into the future. Looking back, he understood that absence was presence deferred. His dereliction had been the prelude to what Kierkegaard many centuries later called "the moment before God." The cruelty of his trial proved to be as disproportionate as the magnitude of his eventual mission.[5]

The appeal from dereliction to communion is heard in the psalter especially when laments are confessions of sins. When a guilty man asks for forgiveness and rehabilitation, he begs at the same time for the renewal of presence. The penitential psalm *par excellence*, known as the *Miserere* or Psalm 51, exhibits the intricacy of the theological transition which links the request for mercy with the request for presence.[6]

In an unexpected way, the psalmist at first used the motif of hiddenness in a reversed form. He begged the Deity to hide from his sins:

4. See A. Rose, "L'influence des Psaumes sur les annonces et les récits de la Passion et de la Résurrection dans les Evangiles," in R. de Langhe, ed., *Le Psautier* (1962), pp. 297ff.; H. Gese, "Psalm 22 und das Neue Testament," *ZTK*, 65 (1968): 1ff.; H. D. Lange, "The Relation Between Psalm 22 and the Passion Narrative," *Concordia Theological Monthly*, 43 (1972): 610ff.; J. A. Soggin, "Notes for Christian Exegesis of the First Part of Psalm 22," in *Old Testament and Oriental Studies* (Rome, 1975), pp. 152ff.; J. H. P. Reumann, "Psalm 22 at the Cross: Lament and Thanksgiving for Jesus Christ," *In.*, 28 (1974): 39ff.

5. The MT merely reads, "that Yahweh did" (vs. 30b). Modern translators err when they supply the pronoun "it" as a direct object. The verb is used intransitively in an absolute sense. The psalm ends on the evocation of the act of God in the history of the world.

6. Among the many monographs on Ps. 51, see especially those which deal with vss. 10–12 (Heb 12–14): R. Press, "Die eschatologische Ausrichtung des 51.Psalms," *TZ*, 11 (1955): 241ff.; P. Bonnard, "Le psaume de pénitence d'un disciple de Jérémie," *Bible et vie chrétienne*, 17 (1957): 59ff.; id., "Le vocabulaire du Miserere," *Festschrift A. Gelin* (Paris, 1961): 145ff.; E. R. Dalglish, *Psalm Fifty-One in the Light of Ancient Near Eastern Patternism* (Leiden, 1962); L. Neve, "Realized Eschatology in Ps 51," *ET*, 80 (1968–69): 264ff.; P. Auffret, "Note sur la structure littéraire de Ps LI 1–19," *VT*, 26 (1976): 142.

> Hide thy face from my sins
> and blot out my guilt! (vs. 9 [Heb. 11])

⟦324⟧ The exact nature of the petitioner's lawlessness is unknown. Since the worshippers of the Second Temple during the Persian centuries ascribed some thirteen psalms to specific events in the life of David, it is quite understandable that this poignant confession of criminality would have been related to the king's notorious murder of Uriah, Bathsheba's husband (Ps 51:1; cf. 2 Sam 12:14ff.). The horror of the deed and the total incapacity of its perpetrator to make amends led the poet to ask in effect for the death of his inward self and for his rebirth under the mythical trope of a cosmic creation:

> Create in me a pure heart, O God,
>   and make new within me a steadfast spirit,
> Cast me not away from thy presence.
>   and take not the spirit of thy holiness away from me.
> Restore unto me the mirth of thy rescue
>   and let the spirit of nobility uphold me
> (vss. 10–11 [Heb. 12–14])

God comes only to those who are pure of heart, but how can the heart of man be pure? God alone is able to cleanse an enormous guilt (ᶜ*awônôth*, a superlative). No ritual will suffice,[7] for man is utterly depraved.[8] More than ceremonial ablutions or characteral amelioration are needed. Nothing less than a radical innovation is required. The psalmist borrowed the verb *baraʾ*, "to create," from the cosmogonies of the sapiential circles,[9] and he dared to apply it to his own, minuscule, situation. As God creates a world, so also can he create a man.

The idea of the new being was articulated within the theology of presence. The poet reflected on his estrangement, no longer in terms of God's hiddenness, but according to the image of his own expulsion: "Cast me not away from thy presence!" He also developed his hope of communion

---

7. Cf. A. Caquot, "Ablution et sacrifice selon le Ps 51," *Proceedings of the XIth International Congress of History of Religion*, II (Leiden, 1968), pp. 75ff.

8. Cf. Job 14:1 with Ps 51:7 [Heb. 9]. See J. K. Zink, "Uncleanness and Sin. A Study of Job XIV and Psalm LI 7," *VT*, 17 (1967): 354ff. The statement of Ps 51:7 (Heb. 9) does not refer to the sinfulness of sexuality but implies the universality of sin and the solidarity of the human race from generation to generation.

9. The story of creation in Gen 1:1–2:4a represents ancient traditions which have affinities with wisdom poetry. See G. M. Landes, "Creation Tradition in Proverbs 8:22–31 and Genesis 1," *Festschrift J. M. Myers* (Philadelphia, 1974), pp. 279ff.

through the triple use of the word "spirit." First, the newly created being needs the power ⟦325⟧ of survival, or the gift of self-maintenance. He therefore must be able to resist temptation and to overcome self-doubt: "Make new within me a steady, firmly attached, coherent spring of moral behavior!" Second, estrangement must be enduringly bridged. The power which will permanently heal the poet's alienation from God will be so penetrating that holiness itself will flow from God to him. "Do not take away from me the spirit of thy holiness!"[10]

Since the ancient notion of holiness connoted the dread of "the wholly other," the psalmist's prayer was unprecedented. He viewed the holy no longer as the *mysterium fascinans atque tremendum*, forever exterior to man as the numinous force which attracts and repels him at the same time, but as the source of vitality which sharpens conscience, activates the will to shun evil, and stirs the imagination to do the good. A world is aborning also within man. Creation may be microcosmic as well as macrocosmic. Presence and spirit coalesce to animate the new being.

Third, the slave of egocentricity discovers freedom from the self. "Let the spirit of nobility uphold me!" A noble man is one who assumes his obligation of social responsibility. A knight is not a knave. He helps and respects others with the ease, elegance, and style of a prince. The new being is a moral aristocrat, not of birth but of service. Freedom to be oneself implies the power to serve willingly. A fresh innocence will obliterate the murderous past. The poet has joined those

> who were so dark of heart they might not speak,
> a little innocence will make them sin.[11]

The psalmists exhibited theological maturity because they were forced to a recognition of their true selves vis-à-vis their God, even when that God was hiding from their plight. By evading ⟦326⟧ their pleas, that God became more and more manifest to them, even when he seemed to

> . . . adjourn, adjourn . . .
> To that farther side of the skies.[12]

---

10. The traditional rendering, "thy holy spirit," risks anachronistic connotations with the Jewish and Christian hypostasis. Moreover, the context shows that the word *ruaḥ* is used three times in the sense of "virtue" as energy. Although it is unlikely, the psalmist may have referred to "the angel of the presence," an expression which appeared after the Babylonian exile in parallel with the spirit of God's holiness (Isa 63:9; cf. vss. 10–11).

11. e. e. cummings, *XAIPE*, no. 51, in *Poems 1923–1954* (New York, 1954), p. 456.

12. Peter Viereck, "Incantation at Assisi," *The First Morning: New Poems* (New York, 1952), p. 39.

It was that very hiding which disclosed to them not only the meaning of their existence but also the intrinsic quality of divinity. The God of the psalmists made them live in this world, and they lived without using him. It is when man tries to grasp him that God veils himself. The *Deus revelatus* is the *Deus absconditus.*

CLAUS WESTERMANN

b. 1910

God's Judgment and God's Mercy

Theological Synopsis

In the post–World War II period the scene in Old Testament scholarship in Germany was dominated by figures such as Martin Noth, Albrecht Alt, Gerhard von Rad, and Walther Zimmerli. This period was marked by hermeneutical discussions and other advances in critical biblical scholarship. Claus Westermann made major contributions with studies on the Book of Genesis, the Israelite prophets, the Psalms, and Job. His massive three-volume Genesis commentary (1984–86) is a masterpiece of form-critical analysis. His form-critical study on the prophets (1967), his commentary on Isaiah 40–66 (1969), his books on Old Testament salvation oracles (1987), his three volumes of collected essays (1964, 1974, 1984), and many other monographs and publications reveal the depth and breadth of study typical of this giant of Old Testament scholarship.

He produced two books on Old Testament theology in the post–von Rad period. He delivered the Sprunt Lectures at Union Theological Seminary, Virginia, which were published under the title, *What Does the Old Testament Say about God?* (1979). His work on Old Testament theology appeared in German in 1978.

Westermann objects to Gerhard von Rad's notion of "retelling." The task of Old Testament theology is to describe and view together what all parts of the Old Testament have to say about God (1979: 11; 1982: 9). In contrast to reducing to concepts what the Old Testament says about God, such as salvation, election, covenant, faith, revelation, and redemption, as was typical of previous Old Testament theologies, "the structure of an Old Testament theology must be based on events rather than concepts" (1979:

276

12; 1982: 9). Westermann insists that "instead of looking at the Word of God for its thought-content, we shall have to approach it as an *action* between God and people and determine its functions" (1979: 13, italics his). The systematic aspect of the structure of Old Testament theology is not a center (*Mitte*) or a central theme (*pace* Eichrodt, Vriezen, and others) but a dialectical interaction between God and humankind (1979: 13; 1982: 12). Westermann maintains that the debate between von Rad's retelling of the confessional salvation history in Old Testament theology and Franz Hesse's attempt to ground faith in historical science (followed recently by James Barr among others) starts from false presuppositions on both parts, "since both presuppose the distinction between reality and the reality of faith" (1982: 13). The fundamental difference between the modern historical (-critical) science and the Old Testament story is that "what the Old Testament says about reality, it says about God; what it says about God, it says about reality" (1979: 14; 1982: 13).

On the whole Westermann is close to von Rad in various ways, but moves beyond von Rad and other form-critics and tradition-critics by emphasizing a systematic aspect in Old Testament theology. The Old Testament is speaking about God *and* there is a human response. Westermann proposes a biblical theology which is verb-dominated, and follows a historical structure of what the Old and New Testaments have to say about God and what happens between God and humanity (1979: 96; cf. 1982: 231).

During World War II Claus Westermann served in the German army. While interned as a prisoner of war, he started to work on the esthetic in the Old Testament and turned to the theme of praise in the Psalms. Subsequently he studied at the universities of Tübingen, Marburg, and Berlin. His doctoral degree was earned at the University of Zurich. After serving as a Lutheran pastor, Westermann began a teaching career at the Kirchliche Hochschule in Berlin. In 1958 he transferred to the University of Heidelberg, serving as Professor of Old Testament. He is now professor emeritus at Heidelberg.

G.F.H.

Writings by Westermann

1960   *Grundformen prophetischer Rede.* Beiträge zur evangelischen Theologie 31. Munich: Kaiser.

1964   *Forschung am Alten Testament: Gesammelte Studien.* Theologische Bücherei 24. Munich: Kaiser.

1966   *Das Buch Jesaia Kapitel 40–66.* Das Alte Testament Deutsch 19. Göttingen: Vandenhoeck & Ruprecht.

1967   *Basic Forms of Prophetic Speech.* Translated by Hugh C. White. Philadelphia: Westminster.

1968   *Der Segen in der Bibel und im Handeln der Kirche.* Munich: Kaiser.

1969   *Isaiah 40–66: A Commentary.* Translated by David M. G. Stalker. Old Testament Library. Philadelphia: Westminster/London: SCM.

1974   *Forschung am Alten Testament: Gesammelte Studien II.* Edited by Rainer Albertz and Eberhard Ruprecht. Theologische Bücherei 55. Munich: Kaiser.

1974–82 *Genesis.* 3 volumes. Biblischer Kommentar: Altes Testament 1. Neukirchen-Vluyn: Neukirchener Verlag.

1976   *Die Verheissungen an die Väter: Studien zur Vätergeschichte.* Forschungen zur Religion und Literatur des Alten und Neuen Testaments 116. Göttingen: Vandenhoeck & Ruprecht.

1977   *Der Aufbau des Buches Hiob.* 2d edition. Stuttgart: Calwer.

1978a *Blessing: In the Bible and the Life of the Church.* Overtures to Biblical Theology. Translated by Keith Crim. Philadelphia: Fortress.

1978b *Theologie des Alten Testaments in Grundzügen.* Göttingen: Vandenhoeck & Ruprecht.

1979   *What Does the Old Testament Say about God?* Edited by Friedemann W. Golka. Atlanta: John Knox/London: SCM.

1980a *The Promises to the Fathers: Studies on the Patriarchal Narratives.* Translated by David E. Green. Philadelphia: Fortress.

1980b *The Psalms: Structure, Content and Message.* Translated by Ralph D. Gehrke. Minneapolis: Augsburg.

1981   *The Structure of the Book of Job: A Form-Critical Analysis.* Translated by Charles A. Muenchow. Philadelphia: Fortress.

1982   *Elements of Old Testament Theology.* Translated by Douglas W. Stott. Atlanta: John Knox.

1984   *Erträge der Forschung am Alten Testament: Gesammelte Studien III.* Edited by Rainer Albertz. Theologische Bücherei 73. Munich: Kaiser.

1984–86 *Genesis: A Commentary.* 3 volumes. Translated by John J. Scullion. London: SPCK/Minneapolis: Augsburg.

1987   *Prophetische Heilsworte im Alten Testament.* Forschungen zur Religion und Literatur des Alten und Neuen Testaments 145. Göttingen: Vandenhoeck & Ruprecht.

Writings about Westermann

Albertz, Rainer, Hans-Peter Müller, Hans W. Wolff, and Walther Zimmerli (editors)

1980   *Werden und Wirken des Alten Testaments: Festschrift für Claus Westermann zum 70. Geburtstag.* Göttingen: Vandenhoeck & Ruprecht/Neukirchen-Vluyn: Neukirchener Verlag.

Claus Westermann's
Approach to Old Testament Theology

Excerpted with permission from Claus Westermann, *Elements of Old Testament Theology* (Atlanta: John Knox, 1982), pp. 9–12, 230–32, 235.

What Does the Old Testament Say about God?

Preliminary Methodological Considerations

[[9]] The answer to this question must be given by the entire Old Testament. A theology of the Old Testament has the task of summarizing and viewing together what the Old Testament as a whole, in all its sections, says about God. This task is not correctly understood if one declares one part of the Old Testament to be the most important and gives it prominence over the others; or if one regards the whole as determined by one concept such as covenant, election, or salvation; or if one asks beforehand what the center of the Old Testament is. The New Testament clearly has its center in the suffering, death, and resurrection of Christ, to which the Gospels are directed and which the Epistles take as their starting point. The Old Testament, however, bears no similarity at all to this structure, and it is thus not possible to transfer the question of a theological center from the New to the Old Testament.[1]

If we wish to describe what the Old Testament as a whole says about God, we must start by looking at the way the Old Testament presents itself, something everyone can recognize: "The Old Testament tells a story" (G. von Rad). With that statement we have reached our first decision about the form of an Old Testament theology: If the Old Testament narrates what it has to say about God in the form of a story (understood here in the broader sense of event), then the structure of an Old Testament theology must be based on events rather than concepts.

But how can we define this structure of events more exactly? There seems to be an obvious answer to this question. The task of a theology of the Old Testament could simply consist of re-narrating the story of the Old [[10]] Testament in an abbreviated and summarized form. This was certainly how Gerhard von Rad understood it: "Re-telling the story is therefore still the most legitimate way for theology to speak about the Old Testament." This would be possible if the whole of the Old Testament

1. G. von Rad, *Old Testament Theology*, p. 127f.; R. Smend, ThSt 101; G. F. Hasel, ZAW 86; W. Zimmerli, EvTh 35.

consisted of a continuous story from the first to the last chapter. However, this is not the case.

The Old Testament has come down to us in a threefold structure in which it also originated: the Torah, the Prophets, and the Writings; or the historical, prophetic, and didactic books, the nucleus of which is the Psalms. According to the traditionists' conception here, the Bible of the Old Testament includes the story narrated, but also the word of God inhering in the story and humanity's response in calling to God. The narrative of the historical books from Genesis to Chronicles does contain texts in which the word of God enters the action, and texts which contain the response of praise or lament; but the structure of the Old Testament in its three parts indicates that the narrative in the Old Testament is determined by the word of God occurring in it and by the response of those for whom and with whom this story unfolds.

It is therefore the canon of the Old Testament itself which shows us the structure of what happens in the Old Testament in its decisive elements. We have thus found an objective starting point for an Old Testament theology which is independent of any preconceptions about what the most important thing in the Old Testament is and independent of any other prior theological decisions. If one asks what the Old Testament says about God, this threefold structure shows us the way.[2]

But how can what the Old Testament says about God be viewed and described together in its many and diverse forms? How can it be expressed along broad and simple lines? In previous Old Testament theologies, this has been attempted predominantly by reducing what the Old Testament says about God to comprehensive terms such as *salvation, election, covenant, faith, kerygma, revelation, redemption, soteriology, eschatology*, etc. By using these noun concepts scholars moved away from the language of the Old Testament, which is overwhelmingly dominated by verbs. In addition, this meant a loss of the diversity in which the Old Testament speaks of God.[3]

If we wish to inquire concerning these broad lines determining the whole way in which the Old Testament speaks about God and yet not overlook the many forms in which it occurs, we shall therefore have to start from *verb structures.* This demands a complete change of our way of thinking. The story [[11]] told in the Old Testament is then not a salvation history in the sense of a series of God's salvation events, but rather a history of God and man whose nucleus is the experience of saving. It does

2. B. S. Childs points to the significance of the canon for OT theology; see also G. W. Coats—B. O. Long.

3. The history of OT theology can show how difficult it is to present the variety of Old Testament talk about God as a whole. E. Würthwein gives an overview, ThR NF 36, 3.

not, however, remain only a story of deliverance. In the middle of the Pentateuch stands the confession of praise of those who experienced this saving, and in the middle of the Deuteronomistic historical section (Joshua to 2 Kings) the confession of sin of those on whom judgment was passed. The Pentateuch is further subdivided into primeval history, patriarchal history, and history of the people. Within this subdivision, the beginning of the history of the people (Exodus through Deuteronomy) receives a forestructure which encompasses God's activity in the world and human life and thus God's blessing.

In the prophetic books, the framework of the presentation does not emerge from what the individual prophets said, but rather from the structure of the judgment oracle common to all judgment prophets (to which corresponds the confession of sin in the middle of the Deuteronomistic historical work) and its correspondence within the salvation oracle. The varying individual prophetic pronouncements are then to be understood from the perspective of these constants.

In the Psalms, this constant factor is given by the structure of the Psalms of lament and praise, and two major types, from which then both the varying individual expressions and any subordinate forms are to be understood.

Wisdom has no place within this basic framework of an Old Testament theology, since it originally and in reality does not have as its object an occurrence between God and man; in its earlier stages wisdom is overwhelmingly secular. A theological wisdom develops at a later stage, and is then to be understood according to its theological statement (e.g., from the perspective of the contrast between the pious and godless). The theological home of wisdom can be found within the context of human creation; the creator gives humanity the ability to understand its world and to be oriented within it.[4]

So far we have only hinted at a few main features. They should show that from such a starting point of an Old Testament theology, the whole of what the Old Testament says about God continually stays in view. The theology of the Old Testament thus remains determined in every aspect by the outline of a story entrusted to us which includes the occurrence of God speaking and the response of those who experience these events.

With that the structure of Old Testament theology acquires a systematic [[12]] as well as historical aspect. The systematic aspect emerges from the talk about God which remains constant throughout the entire Old

---

4. See [[Westermann 1982:]] pp. 85f.; cf. C. Westermann, BK I/1, pp. 436–467 concerning Gen 4:17–26, and ThB 55, pp. 149–161; similarly: W. Zimmerli, *Old Testament Theology in Outline*, p. 141f.

Testament. This constant is found primarily in an interaction between God and man (more precisely; between God and his creation, his people, humanity), and includes speaking and acting on both sides. In addition to this we find a series of other constants throughout the entire Old Testament, e.g., the fact that both saving and blessing belong to God's acts from beginning to end, or that human response finds its center in lament and praise, or that from beginning to end God is *one.*

The historical aspect emerges from the fact that this God of whom the Old Testament speaks has bound himself to the history of his people. Since this is a people like any other, it, too, is subject to historical change and historical contingency. This accounts for the fact that the elements of this interaction between God and humanity change in the course of history. So, for example, the facticity of response in service remains constant, while the worship service itself is subjected to changes during the course of this history. Or it manifests itself in the fact that the saving God is simultaneously always the judging God, although both God's saving and judging occurs in a history in which each, in and for itself, as well as their relationship to each other, changes. This simultaneity of constants and variables inhering in this talk about God also accounts for the fact that the history of God with his people as a whole—in this structure of constants and variables—is characterized by absolute singularity and uniqueness. The elements, however, out of which this whole is put together are able to represent a connection between the religion of Israel and other religions (see [Westermann 1982:] pp. 58–61).

. . . .

The Question of Biblical Theology

[230] What we have found in investigating the relationship of the Old Testament to Christ are not conceptual relations and contrasts but rather correspondences or contrasts which relate to a sequence of events, a history between God and humanity. This history, with which both the Old and New Testaments deal, occurs in two circles: the wider, which stretches from the creation to the end of the world, and the more limited one, which is the history of God with a specific section of humanity, the people of God. The Old and New Testaments deal with the history of the wider circle. Both speak about the God who created heaven and earth and who ultimately leads the world and humanity to a final goal. And both deal with the narrower circle which has two sections, the first treated in the Old Testament, the second treated in the New. The history of God's people in the Old Testament leads away from power and toward salvation on the basis of forgiveness. The new people of God can no longer preserve its existence by means of victories over other peoples, but rather only through its exis-

tence *for* the rest of humanity, as was already suggested by the servant songs in Deutero-Isaiah. The same transformation occurs in the case of the saving of the individual through God. Because Christ died on the cross even for his enemies, the ⟦231⟧ charge of the pious against their enemies is dismissed. The saving of the faithful no longer implies death for nonbelievers. This also removes the curse from the suffering of believers. The book of Job already allows the new insight emerge that human suffering does not have to be God's curse or punishment. It acquires a positive meaning through the suffering of Christ.

In the history recounted by the Old Testament we can thus see a movement toward a goal which points to what the New Testament says about Christ. In the light of Christ a Yes and Amen are spoken to the Old Testament as the way which leads to this goal. At the same time, with Christ a No is spoken to that which, through the work of Christ, is overcome and now ended: the association of God's salvation with power which is also the power of destruction, and the association of the salvation of the individual with the request against the unrighteous which aims at his destruction.

This Yes to the Old Testament from the perspective of Christ, and this No to the Old Testament from the perspective of Christ, however, are not dogmatic and not theoretical, but are rather historical. One cannot say that what the New Testament says about God is correct, and what the Old Testament says false. That part of what the Old Testament says about God which has come to an end is done away with by the historical event of the coming of Christ as God's final word and final act.

Then the history of the church or the history of the Christian churches becomes a section of the whole history of God with his people between the coming of Christ and his return, which must be seen in the light of the *entire* Bible. From the perspective of the whole Bible, we then need to ask whether the period in church history in which the church once again became associated with power is not a regression behind the extraction of the people of God from political power, as already shown in Deutero-Isaiah. The question should then be directed to New Testament theologians whether it is not possible to return from an intellectual and conceptual structure of New Testament theology to a verb-dominated or historical structure to present what happens in the New Testament between God and humanity. The first step toward this would be the recognition that what happened is more important than what was thought about it. What the New Testament says about Christ also has essentially the form of a report or story: first in the Gospels, which lead up to the death and resurrection of Christ, and then in the Book of Acts, which starts from the death and resurrection of Christ and is directed toward Christ's return, with which Revelation also deals. Here, [[232]] too, there is a correspondence to the Old Testament which should not be overlooked. While the Old Testament points from creation beyond the history of God's people to the "center of time," the New points from the center of time to the end of time. Thus Old and New Testaments belong together so that, side by side, they can report the history of God with his people and can place this history into the broader horizon of the history of God with humanity and with the world.

If this basic historical structure of what the Old and New Testament say about God were recognized in Old as well as in New Testament studies, we could return to a biblical theology which included the Old as well as the New Testament and which was based upon both. A biblical theology is necessary for the incipient ecumenical era of the Christian churches.

Synopsis of Westermann's *Elements of Old Testament Theology* (1982)

Claus Westermann
On Judgment and Mercy

Excerpted with permission from Claus Westermann, *What Does the Old Testament Say about God?* (Atlanta: John Knox, 1979), pp. 53–61, 74–80, 103–5.

God's Judgment and God's Mercy

Sin and Judgment: The Prophets of Doom

[[53]] When the Bible mentions the fact that God punishes or acts as a judge, this seems to contradict what the Bible says about God otherwise: God created men—so why didn't he just create them in such a way that he would never need to punish them? God blesses people; he saves those threatened by death—so why does he destroy his saving and blessing again and again by punishments?

Sin as a Human Phenomenon. This latter question points to an insurmountable limitation of man in deed as well as in thought. It is simply a human limitation that people transgress, that they sin. Thus they can only speak of God by including judgment and punishment. This contradiction cannot be solved; it is part of human existence. Therefore sin, human transgression and God's intervention against it, is already part of the primeval history; this indicates that this human transgression which we call sin is characteristic of human beings: no religion and no structure of society can change the fact that people of all times, all races, and all [[54]] ideologies transgress by nature. When, then, in the primeval history human sin is each time followed by God's intervention, this is motivated by the hindering, disturbing, and destruction effect of sin. An Egyptian text once called human sin "the great disturbance." By sin something or somebody is always endangered, whether this becomes immediately apparent or remains hidden for a long time.

It is the intention of the Yahwist in his narratives of guilt and punishment in Genesis 1–11 to depict human transgression in its many varied possibilities in order to make clear the impending danger to man in these possibilities: the transgression of the individual against the creator in an act of disobedience which threatens the relationship of trust between God and man (Genesis 3), fratricide (Genesis 4), and the despising of a father (Gen 9:20–27).[1]

---

1. Claus Westermann, *Genesis*, 1:374–380; idem, "Der Mensch im Urgeschehen," *Kerygma und Dogma* 13 (1967): 231–246.

285

To this has to be added the possibility of collective sin in the crossing of the border into the superhuman (Gen 6:1–4; 11:1–9) and the corruption of a whole generation (Genesis 6–9). In all these stories the narrator of the primeval history describes sin as a universal phenomenon. At the same time the writer points out an important distinction in the reaction of God the creator to human transgressions. On the one hand God intervenes as judge, especially in Genesis 3 and 4, where this judicial intervention corresponds precisely to the profane trial, which can be found universally in the institution of courts (discovery of the crime—hearing—defense—sentence). It is God the creator who in the worldwide institution of the independent court opposes the transgressor and restricts evil. On the other hand the flood story shows a different reaction of God to human transgression: the flood is an act of God's judgment for the hybris of a whole generation which has grown beyond all limits (Gen 6:5a, 7a, J). But at the end of the flood the creator declares solemnly that such a destruction shall never occur again: "'I will never again curse the ground because of man, for the imagination of man's heart is evil from his youth'" (Gen 8:21). In this decision at the end of the flood the creator promises the preservation of the world in spite of all human inclination to evil. God wishes to preserve and keep humanity as it is. His reaction to the human inclination to evil is patient suffering; it is not the reaction of the judge. Jesus says likewise: "'for he makes his sun rise on the evil and on the good, and sends rain on the just and on the unjust'" (Matt 5:45). [[55]]

Sin in the History of God's People. From sin as a human phenomenon, human transgression which is part of human existence, we have to distinguish the sin of the people of God and its individual members in the mutual relationship of Israel to her God. This sin only becomes possible through the encounter of Israel with Yahweh; it is a process in the history of Israel with her God. Every possible transgression, every possible sin has already been preceded by something, namely Israel's experiences with God, the experience of the acts of saving and the receipt of his gifts.[2] It is sufficient to point out one word which makes this connection clear: the word "forget." It is often used by Jeremiah in his accusation. The transgressions of the people of Israel which lead to his accusation are rooted in this act of forgetting: only because the present generation has forgotten God's deeds and gifts for Israel could such transgressions arise.

These transgressions of Israel can only be understood in close connection with her history; they are themselves a historical phenomenon and as such subject to change (in contrast to the concept of sin in the

2. Very often the prophets point to this, above all in the contrast-motif; cf. my *Basic Forms of Prophetic Speech*, pp. 181–188.

Western Christian tradition—in which sin has become an unhistorical timeless phenomenon). The unique characteristic of the history of Israel, as described in the Old Testament, consists of the very fact that the sin of Israel towards her God has been taken so very seriously that it decisively determined the history. Israel's sin begins when Israel itself begins: the exodus from Egypt contains the event of the golden calf (Exodus 32–34). Israel's history with God is like an incline: the guilt of Israel before God grows to such an extent that it leads to his intervention against his own people in judgment. This is the very nucleus of the message of the prophets of judgment: the announcement that God will punish or even destroy his own people, based on an accusation.[3]

Remember that Israel's sin is not something which exists of necessity; Israel is *not* by its very nature a sinful people. On the contrary, at the beginning a good and intact relationship between God and his people is presupposed. This is the meaning of the frequently used image of marriage. In Deuteronomy, remaining in the promised land and the continuation of the blessing are made dependent on the obedience of the people; it is presupposed that this condition can be fulfilled [[56]] and that therefore the relationship between God and his people can remain intact. Similarly in the review of the Deuteronomistic History the idolatry of the kings of Israel and Judah, which causes God's judgment, is not general: David and a few other kings are exempt.

It is not only in prophecy that the guilt of Israel in the context of its history is seen. The Deuteronomistic History also shows this incline which led to the catastrophe.[4] The clearest sign of this incline is the fact that the prophets of judgment before Amos have voiced *no* accusation against Israel as a whole nation. Therefore the accusation against the whole nation has an added stress. It is voiced from the time of Amos up till Jeremiah and Ezekiel, and it gives the reason for the announcement of catastrophe.

The Prophecy of Judgment. There has been a phenomenon like prophecy—take in a very broad sense—in many religions. There has even been a form of prophecy that shows similarity in its very wording to the prophecy of Israel: the prophecy of Mari by the Euphrates. But only in Israel has there been this succession of prophets from Amos to Jeremiah and Ezekiel, who through this long period of time have stedfastly announced the intervention of a god against his own people in judgment. The prophecy of judgment has to be seen in close connection with the beginnings of

---

3. *Basic Forms of Prophetic Speech*, pp. 169–175.

4. Hans Walter Wolff, "Das Kerygma des deuteronomistischen Geschichtswerkes," *Zeitschrift für die alttestamentliche Wissenschaft* 73 (1961): 171–186; also in *The Vitality of Old Testament Traditions*, ed. Brueggemann, pp. 83–100.

Israel: with the saving from Egypt and the guidance through the wilderness, which only then made Israel a people. Israel obtained its very existence as a nation by God's acts of saving; if Israel forgot God, if it turned against this God and away from him, then it would thereby lose the basis of its existence.[5] This is the reason for the appearance of the prophets. Their accusations and announcements of judgment were concerned with Israel's existence. Thus the saving God is now the judging God; the judgment announced by the prophets is the necessary continuation of the saving working of God. This judgment is aimed, paradoxically, at the saving of Israel—through and after the judgment. God's acts in saving and judging his people belong closely together.

We can illustrate this point even more clearly. The prophetic accusation is not concerned with individual sins nor with the fact that [[57]] Israel is a sinner in a general and abstract way; it is concerned rather in each case with transgressions which put the existence of Israel as the people of God in danger. The Old Testament knows no abstract and timeless concept of sin, which would be similar to a concept of being. Sins and transgressions are only mentioned when they threaten human existence, the human community, or the community between God and man. This threat is never the same; it is derived from the historic, economic, cultural, and religious circumstances; consequently it changes.[6]

This historic character of sin is clearly manifest in the prophetic accusation. It is not always the same, it changes from one prophet to another and also within the same prophet from one period of his ministry to another. The accusations of the prophets before Amos were mostly directed towards a king; they have to be understood against the background of the historical situation, just as the prophetic tradition afterwards is still a part of the historical tradition. Nathan's accusation against David and Elijah's against Ahab have their respective meanings only in the situation in which a threat to Israel arises from the behavior of the king; and it is against this that the accusation is directed. Thus the emphasis of the accusation changes from one prophet to another and we obtain from them a surprisingly accurate reflection of the cultural, social, economic, political, and religious events of their respective times. Sometimes the emphasis is on social accusation (especially Amos and Micah), sometimes an idolatry (Hosea and Ezekiel), on political accusation combined with an attack on hybris (Isaiah), on the deserting and forgetting of Yahweh (Jeremiah), or on worship which has become insincere (Amos, Jeremiah). These are only examples; they show the surprising liveliness of the prophet accusa-

---

5. Cf. chapter II: "The Saving God and History."
6. See the article "*nabi*" in *Theologisches Handwörterbuch zum Alten Testament*.

tion. The prophets are never interested in compiling catalogues of vices to demonstrate to their contemporaries what kind of bad people they are; on the contrary, they point to the respective crises, i.e., where the threat lies in the present hour.

But this is only possible when the prophets pit their whole existence on their commission: to announce God's judgment on the basis of these accusations of Israel. The prophets' total identification of themselves with their office is a characteristic of prophecy in Israel. [58] This has two sides: one of them is manifest in the language of the prophets. Each speaks his own language and introduces into this language the tradition in which he has grown up, so that we can recognize more or less clearly his "geistige *Heimat*" (intellectual and spiritual home, Hans Walter Wolff). It is in most cases a profane language, differing strongly from the language of a priestly-sacral school; it is the language of a living man, whose personal fate, whose thoughts and emotions, whose involvement in the message which he has to pass on, all form part of this language. The prophets as mediators of the word of God are men of their time; while in the very midst of experiencing the present, they are under commission to accuse and to announce judgment on it. They themselves are sitting in the boat whose capsizing they have to announce. The other side has thus already been hinted at: the commission brings them no reward or honor, but it can certainly bring them suffering. From the history of Israel's apostasy springs the history of the suffering of those individuals who in their message oppose this apostasy: the suffering of the mediator. How the suffering of the mediator forms part of the new context of God's mercy beyond judgment, we shall discuss in the following.

God's Compassion and the Prophecy of Salvation

The "Inconsequence of God" and the Prophets. In its talk about God, the Old Testament contains a very peculiar feature which makes God's actions at a certain point appear very human. As opposed to other contexts, which emphasize the holiness of God in contrast to man, here a human emotion is attributed to God: the emotion of compassion. The Hebrew word of this, *rḥm* (or its plural), actually means "mother's womb"; or the compassion of the father for his child (Psalm 103) can become the image of this divine compassion.[7] It is very often connected with an "inconsequence of God"; i.e., this divine compassion frequently occurs where a totally different reaction of God would be appropriate. This is why this

---

7. Here the whole group of words pertaining to God's mercy or goodness has to be considered, e.g., *ḥesed*, in *Theologisches Handwörterbuch zum Alten Testament*, 1:600–621. The most important references are in the descriptive praise (hymns); cf. chapter V: "The Response." The praise of God's mercy, however, is a response to the merciful intervention of God.

divine compassion appears so human. In the narratives of guilt and punishment in Genesis 1–11, God's reaction to the human guilt never ends
⟦59⟧ simply with the punishment. Somehow he always moderates the
punishment; e.g., at the expulsion from the garden, God makes skirts
from skins for the man and his wife, so they need not be ashamed. This
divine compassion acquires the most decisive significance after the occurrence of the divine judgment by the destruction of the state, the kingship,
and the temple. The "inconsequence" of God which is connected with his
compassion is most apparent at this point in the entire history of Israel:
the destruction has been announced by the long sequence of prophets of
judgment—but in spite of this a turning occurs for the remnant.

As the prophets had been the messengers of God's judgment, so once
again the prophets were the messengers of this turning. The prophets
were never messengers of doom alone. At certain times the prophets of
judgment have spoken oracles of salvation too, especially Isaiah, e.g., in
chapter 7. These messages of compassion are special, however, and are always connected with the prophet's message of judgment. This can be particularly recognized in Hosea and Jeremiah. The language of compassion
is connected immediately with the announcement of judgment in Hos
11:8–9: "How can I give you up, O Ephraim! How can I hand you over, O
Israel! . . . My heart recoils within me, my compassion grows warm and
tender." Here too the same inconsequence: compassion breaks through in
spite of the announcement of judgment. In Jeremiah, we find something
similar in the peculiar motif of God's lament which is connected with the
announcement of judgment, e.g., Jer 9:10–12, 17–22. God suffers under
the judgment that he has to bring upon his people.

We have to point to a further connection: in the visions of Amos (7:1–
9; 8:1–3; 9:1–6) the prophet as intercessor begs for the compassion of
God upon the people's need, and in the first two visions (7:1–3, 4–6) this
is granted. In the three subsequent visions, however, this compassion is
denied: "'I will never again pass by them!'" (7:8; 8:2; 9:4). The announcement of judgment takes the place of God's turning towards Israel in compassion. God can now no longer show compassion, he can no longer
forgive his people. Still, God's compassion is not extirpated, it is only with-
held, until it breaks through again after the judgment. This is the very
message of Ezekiel and Deutero-Isaiah: after judgment, there can be a
message of comfort (Isa 40:1–11). As ⟦60⟧ in the visions of Amos, the lament of the people in need is presupposed; it is the many-sided lament after the catastrophe (e.g., Isa 40:27), to which the message of the prophet
in the form of the oracle of salvation comes as the divine answer. And it is,
once again (as in the first two visions of Amos), the answer of divine compassion (Isa 40:28–31; 41:8–16; 43:1–7).

God's Mercy and Forgiveness.   But in this new compassionate turning of God towards his people, which brings the time of judgment to an end, a difference has to be noted in comparison with former demonstrations of God's compassion. Compassion is only possible in connection with God's forgiveness. The forgiveness of the guilt which had accumulated during the time of the announcement of judgment has to be explicitly stated and has to be pronounced immediately to the people of God. Compassion without forgiveness would have no meaning in this situation—it could not bring about a real change. There can only be a change when the relationship between God and his people becomes intact again, and this is only possible through forgiveness. Therefore Deutero-Isaiah's message of comfort has as its very first words an announcement of forgiveness: "cry to her that her time of service is ended, that her iniquity is pardoned!" (Isa 40:2). The complete agreement of the two exilic prophets in this is important. Ezekiel also assumes that the restoration of the people (Ezekiel 37) will be combined with a cleansing of the people from their sins (Ezek 36:16–38).

With this we have to compare what has been said about God's compassion to his people at the beginning of the history of Israel, at the beginning of the book of Exodus: "'I have seen the affliction of my people who are in Egypt, and have heard their cry because of their taskmasters; I know their sufferings'" (Exod 3:7). In this case it is God's pure compassion with these sufferers: "I know their sufferings"; this turning is brought about simply by the saving out of need, need caused by suffering. In this case no history has yet taken place and no guilt has accumulated; God's compassion is simply the compassion towards the suffering creature, in the same way as his compassion turns towards the child dying of thirst in Gen 21:17.

⟦61⟧ It is on the basis of this compassion for the sufferer that the promise on its way through the Old Testament must be understood, beginning with the promises to the patriarchs, taken up by the prophets of salvation, and ending with the promises in the context of apocalyptic. The way of the promise through the Old Testament is the strongest expression of continuity in the history of the people of God; it holds together large epochs—for example, the promises to the patriarchs bind that period with the period of the people in Canaan.[8]

Both therefore have their place, their meaning and their necessity: God's compassion which turns towards the suffering creature and God's compassion on the basis of forgiveness which heals a broken community. It is of great significance for the Old Testament's talking about God that

---

8. Claus Westermann, *Die Verheissungen an die Väter* (Göttingen: Vandenhoeck & Ruprecht, 1976).

both are mentioned. Both are part of God's mercy: the compassion towards the sufferer and the compassion towards the sinner.

. . . .

The Response in Action

[[74]] Just as God's word and deed are both relevant in every relationship of God to man, the human response is not only in words but in deeds also; in both cases the whole being of God and the whole being of man are included.

The Commandments and Laws

The commandments and laws belong together in the context of the word of God. Moreover, they are also a part of the human response, especially that of Israel, because in the context of them Israel is shown how she can answer God through her own action.

The Connection with the Sinai Theophany. The commandments together with the laws are associated with the Sinai experience.[1] They can only become an integral part of the Pentateuch, of the Torah, through this association with the theophany at Sinai. We know that the laws in Israel had a long history; we also know that the series of commandments arose gradually. The decalogue of Exodus 20 and Deuteronomy 5 carries within itself the signs of its gradual origin. The same holds true for the history of the legal corpus.[2] Thus the association of the commandments and laws with the theophany at Sinai gives them a greater significance. Why did this happen? Israel's worship, and especially its worship of the transition to settled life, is based on this Sinai theophany. Significant for the worship of Israel after it is settled is the new divine relationship of Lord and servant, which is distinct from that of the period of wandering and which corresponds to that of the enthroned king and his attendant servants. As described by the Priestly writing with the concept of *kabod* (Exod 24:15–18), the majesty of the Lord belongs to the God revealed at Sinai.[3] While the guiding God is the God who directs the way, or who commands departure or indicates a direction, [[75]] the lord enthroned in majesty becomes the God who reveals his will through the series of com-

---

1. W. Malcolm Clark, "Law," *Old Testament Form Criticism*, ed. John H. Hayes, pp. 99–139.

2. Martin Noth, *Die Gesetze im Pentateuch* (Halle [Saale]: Max Niemeyer Verlag, 1940), also in his *Gesammelte Studien zum Alten Testament* (Munich: Chr. Kaiser, 1957), pp. 9–141. English translation: *The Laws in the Pentateuch and Other Studies* (Edinburgh and London: Oliver & Boyd, 1966), pp. 1–107.

3. Claus Westermann, "Die Herrlichkeit Gottes in der Priesterschrift," *Forschung am Alten Testament, Gesammelte Studien*, II:115–137.

mandments, and then through the laws and the collections of laws.[4] The people declare themselves ready to serve this lord, as the representatives of the people attest at Shechem (Joshua 24).[5] The commandments and laws explain how the people of Israel can serve their God. And then, a great arch spans from the first commandment, which bases the exclusive acknowledgment of one Lord upon the liberation from Egypt, across and beyond the series of commandments (the two tablets) which is linked to this basic command, to the gradually growing corpus of law which determines the epochs of the history of the Israelites. It spans all the way to the Priestly law, in which the law became an extensive cultic law, corresponding to the way in which the worship of Israel was established by the theophany, as the Priestly law expressly states in Exodus 24ff.[6]

The Difference Between Law and Commandment. When we consider this large complex of commandments and laws, we are confronted with a difficult question for the theology of the Old Testament. Throughout the entire Jewish and Christian tradition, this large complex is understood, interpreted, and judged theologically by *one* concept, that of the Law. The question is, can we continue to maintain that in the Old Testament commandment and law have the same theological meaning and can thus be brought together under the concept of Law?[7]

The texts of the Old Testament reveal a completely clear and unequivocal distinction between commandments and laws. The commandment—or prohibition—is a single statement in which God speaks directly to people: "Thou shalt not. . . . " The law consists of two statements, an assumed situation and a determination of the consequences: whoever does this and that—such and such a thing will happen to that person. The commandment is a direct proceeding between God and people, and in this regard corresponds to a commandment to depart or a direction to follow, in the pre-settlement period. In contrast, the law is not a direct word of God; in every case it is tied to human institutions, since punishment requires some agency to execute the punishment. Laws about slavery presuppose a specific social order. This is also the reason why the laws within the ⟦76⟧ legal corpus of the Old Testament are much more

4. Walter Zimmerli, *Grundriss der alttestamentlichen Theologie*, pp. 39–48. English translation: *Old Testament Theology in Outline*, pp. 48–58.

5. See the articles on ʾabad and šērēt in *Theologisches Handwörterbuch zum Alten Testament*.

6. Claus Westermann, "Die Herrlichkeit Gottes in der Priesterschrift," *Forschung am Alten Testament, Gesammelte Studien*, II:115–137.

7. This is the main problem with the fundamental work of Albrecht Alt, *Die Ursprünge des israelitischen Rechts* (Leipzig: Hirzel, 1934). English translation: "The Origins of Israelite Law," *Essays in Old Testament History and Religion* (Garden City, N.Y.: Doubleday, 1967), pp. 101–171. By using the same term, "Recht," for the two forms—apodictic and casuistic—he merely exchanges the governing concept of "Gesetz" for the governing concept of "Recht."

subject to change than the commandments. The laws for sacrifices, for example, were bound to become inoperative when the temple was destroyed; the laws about slavery, when slavery was done away with. The commandments of the Decalogue, however, are not subject to such changes; commands such as "thou shalt not steal," "thou shalt not commit adultery" still stand today. This is also the reason why the Ten Commandments could be taken over by the Christian church and have retained their significance far beyond it.[8]

However, all this simply corresponds to the situation in the Old Testament itself: only in the Sinai account of the Decalogue does the word of God issue directly from the mountain of God to Israel; and the Decalogue in Deuteronomy 5 is definitely placed before the laws which follow in chapters 12–26. It was only in the late postexilic period that a comprehensive concept of the law arose which made the commandment subordinate to the law. One can only conclude from this fact that commandments and laws do not have the same theological significance in the Old Testament. Only the commandment is the direct and immediate word of God; it was only subsequently that the laws were explained as God's word. In the Old Testament as well as in the New, the *commandment*, as God's instruction for human behavior, is necessary and indispensable for the relationship of God to man. This does not apply to the *laws* in the Old Testament in the same way. They are only necessary where they develop God's commandments and apply them to the various sectors of settled life; in the process they can change, and can even become inoperative.

In view of this situation, what Paul says in his letters about the Law must be reconsidered. He uses Law in the tradition of the linguistic usage of the late postexilic period, as a general concept for commandments and laws. The negative judgment of Paul concerning the Law can no more apply to the commandments of God in the Old Testament than it does to the commands and instructions of Jesus in the New. Speaking and acting are both the response of the person who has heard God's word and experienced God's action. It is on the basis of the instructions and commandments of God that a person can act. ⟦77⟧ If the commandments which God gave to the people of Israel extend their validity and their significance into our present age, far beyond the Jewish people and the Christian church, then we may regard this as a sign of the power and quality of God's instructions which have survived the changes of history.

Worship

Further, serving God has in the Old Testament—as in many other religions—the specific sense of worshiping God. Individuals can serve God

---

8. The specific meaning of the commandments finds a convincing representation in Gerhard von Rad's *Old Testament Theology*, 1:190–203.

insofar as they acknowledge God as their Lord in daily life, and do God's will; they can also serve God by bringing him an offering in the act of worship, at the holy place, at the sacred time. The institution of worship, however, is not solely concerned with the fact that people serve God with their offerings; it is rather that in the worship the relationship to God as a whole finds an institutionalized expression. All important parts of Old Testament theology come together in worship, which, therefore, really ought to form a special part of it.

In the Old Testament, worship is a reciprocal event between God and people. In it God acts and speaks, and people also act and speak.[9] This reciprocal event between God and people takes place at a special place at a special time, at the sanctuary on festival days. Since it happens at a special time and place, it is sacred; that is, an event removed from everyday life. As such, it requires a mediator of the holy, the priest. The worship of Israel in this form was established through the theophany at Sinai. Here, the group liberated from Egypt, on its way through the wilderness, experienced for the first time the holy place, the sacred time, and the word of God addressed to them in the theophany. Moses became the mediator of the holy in this event. What was established at Sinai was the worship of the later, settled form of life, as the Priestly writing shows: the tabernacle which God commanded to be built in the revelation at Sinai is the model for the temple. [[78]]

Viewpoints for Understanding Worship in the Old Testament

Two Types of Cult. Worship in the Old Testament has a history. The most important caesura is the transition to the settled life. Only with this transition does the *Grosskult* first arise, in which a large festive congregation comes together in the sanctuary, the "House of God," on festival days. This is preceded by the early cult which we know from the patriarchal accounts, in which the congregation consisted of only a small family group, into whose life the cult was still fully integrated. In this early cult the holy place was not yet made by hands; it was the mountain, the rock, the tree, the spring. There were no priests as yet; the father received God's word and dispensed the blessing.[10] The second caesura is the establishment of kingship, which acquires major significance for the worship of Israel. The king himself becomes the mediator of blessing (Psalm 72), he dispenses the blessing (1 Kings 8); the priests in Jerusalem become officers of the king. The third caesura is the exile, introduced by

---

9. In the well-known definition of Martin Luther, worship is represented as a reciprocal event between men and God. But this is limited to the spoken word.

10. Claus Westermann, *Genesis*, pt. 2, "Die Religion der Väter—der Gottesdienst"; Roland de Vaux, *Histoire ancienne d'Israel*, 2 vols. (Paris: Gabalda, 1971), 1:255–273; idem, *Ancient Israel: Its Life and Institutions*, pp. 289–294.

the destruction of the temple. The offering of sacrifices ceases; at first, worship consists of nothing more than gatherings for lamentation, then a new type of worship by word arises alongside the restoration of worship by offering. In it, many features of the early cult come to life again, and the family regains a significant role in worship.

Blessing and Saving in Worship. The action of God in worship is, first and foremost, a blessing rather than a saving action.[11] The liturgical blessing, dispensed by the priest, is an essential part of worship; the blessing flows out from the sanctuary across the land. The constant character of worship, with its regular annual cycle of returning festivals, corresponds to the blessing. The blessing is vitally important to the everyday life of the congregation gathered together in worship. The saving action of God cannot take place in worship itself. But it is present in the service, on the one hand in the announcement of saving in response to the laments of the people and of the individual (the so-called oracle of salvation); and on the other hand in the word, in the remembrance of the saving acts of God in various forms, and above all in the association of the annual festivals with the working of God in the history of Israel.[12]

[[79]] In addition to this the word of God has a decisive significance for the worship of Israel in the proclamation of the commandments, and in the representation of history in various forms and words which introduce and accompany the liturgical actions, as e.g., the words spoken for the dispensing of the blessing. How far the exhortation, as encountered in Deuteronomy, had a liturgical function is not yet certain. God's word in worship ought to be distinguished from the word of God to people outside the service—from, for instance, a messenger of God. Its particular character stems from the fact that, at a holy place and at a sacred time, it occurs against the background of quietness which hints at the presence of God, as the theophany in Exod 24:15–18 shows. The willingness of the congregation gathered in worship to hear God's word is associated with this quietness. The possibility of the transmission of God's word is based on this particular character.

The human action in worship is the offering. Rather than go into the whole history of sacrifice,[13] I should like to make only two remarks about it: Although sacrifices were originally offered by the head of the family, the priest gradually takes his place. Although originally the offering had many different functions, in the later period the sin offering takes prece-

11. See Gerhard Wehmeier, *Der Segen im Alten Testament;* Claus Westermann, *Der Segen in der Bibel und im Handeln der Kirche.*

12. Robert Martin-Achard, *Essai biblique sur les fêtes d'Israel.*

13. Hans-Joachim Kraus, *Worship in Israel,* pp. 112–124; Roland de Vaux, *Ancient Israel: Its Life and Institutions,* pp. 415–456.

dence; hand-in-hand with this goes a quantitative increase in sacrifices. The prophetic criticism of sacrifices is to a large extent caused by this trend.[14] What the worshipers say in worship is, on the one hand, the words which accompany the actions, which, like the sacrificial saying at the presentation of the first fruits, can be expanded into a creed (Deuteronomy 26). On the other hand, there is the singing of Psalms by the congregation and by the individual, the meaning of which has already been discussed.

Worship as the Focal Point in the Life of the People. The relevance of worship in Israel lies in its function as the focal point of the life of the people. What is decisive is not what happens in the isolated service, but rather what happens in worship for the whole people and the whole land. Therefore, the walk from the house to the service, and from the service back to the house, is an important factor of the service itself. What is brought into the service on these walks from the outside life, and also what is taken back into everyday [[80]] life from the service, are necessarily a part of the act of worship as well. Only in this way can worship be the center of the entire life of the people. Only in this way is criticism of worship also possible, as in the prophetic criticism of a worship which has become false. The reciprocal event of worship from God to people and from people to God receives meaning solely from the fact that it becomes the center of events outside the service.

The Universal Aspect of Worship. The Psalms show that in them the collective life of the community, and of the individual outside the service, extends into the service itself. Moreover, they show that worship in Israel had a strongly universal character. The praise of God has a tendency to expand. Even the kings and the nations are called to praise, and moreover all creatures, as is particularly evident in Psalm 148. Since the God of Israel is also the creator of heaven and earth, worship must encompass the entire span of creation. Looking back on the response of man in words and in action, we can see now how this response encompasses all of human life in speaking and in acting. There is a center of all the thousands of words each person speaks during life. This center is one's speaking to God, voicing the suffering, voicing the joy of life.

There is a center of all human actions throughout life, year after year, day after day. This center is one's doing the will of God, the obedience which seeks God's will, and the knowledge that worship can be the quiet center of all human activity.

14. H. H. Rowley, *Worship in Ancient Israel* (Philadelphia: Fortress Press, 1967), chapter 5: "The Prophets and the Cult," pp. 144–175.

ELMER A. MARTENS

b. 1930

Land and Lifestyle

Theological Synopsis

Elmer A. Martens belongs to a rich evangelical tradition of scholars of the last five decades who have engaged in biblical or Old Testament theology. Examples of such scholars would be Geerhardus Vos (1948), J. Barton Payne (1962), Chester K. Lehman (1971), William A. Dyrness (1979), and Walter C. Kaiser Jr. (1978)—all of whom work with evangelical presuppositions.

Martens believes that organizing principles such as revelation (Vos, Lehman), covenant/testament (Payne, and earlier Gustaf F. Oehler, Walther Eichrodt, etc.), promise/fulfillment (Kaiser), and others are wanting for doing Old Testament theology. He is concerned for a proper move from historical exegesis to theology. In his book he views biblical theology as a descriptive enterprise standing between exegesis and systematic theology. Martens aims at a "correlation of texts, themes and thrusts" (1977: 129) in the move from exegesis to biblical theology. His own proposed "unifying factor" (1977: 132) or "overarching theme" of the Old Testament as a whole is "God's design, a design that incorporates four components: deliverance, community, knowledge of God, and the abundant life" (1981: 3). This "unifying and organizing principle of the Old Testament material arises from an exegesis of several comparable biblical texts, the first of which is Exodus 5:22–6:8" (1981: 12).

This center-oriented approach seeks to overcome the limitations of other center-oriented approaches in that the choice of the center of the Old Testament is chosen or grounded in a biblical text (Exod 5:22–6:8). Its four themes set the tone for Yahweh's design or plan for the future of his people in the Old Testament (and beyond).

298

Martens wishes to be "descriptive" and divides his presentation into three major sections on God's design in the pre-monarchy, monarchy, and post-monarchy eras. A feature of his Old Testament theology is that it is descriptive in only one sense. Martens has at the end of various major parts of his discussions what he calls "theological reflections" (1981: 59–64, 154–56, 187–89, 234–36, 247–48). These serve as models for relating biblical messages and practices to the believer in today's world. This makes Martens's approach both descriptive and constructive and more than a prolegomenon to Old Testament theology (*pace* Reventlow 1987: 252).

Martens shares with many other Old Testament theologians the interest to move beyond the Old Testament to the New Testament. He does this by tracing the four components of the divine design in Matthew and Romans. He notes that these themes receive their particular fulfillment in Christ in history, but beyond history, in eternity, "that design will be not only fully plain, then, but fully realized" (1981: 260).

Elmer A. Martens, a Canadian by birth, received his education at the universities of Saskatchewan and Manitoba. His B.D. was earned at the Mennonite Brethren Biblical Seminary in Fresno, California, where he has taught as professor of Old Testament since 1970 and where for nine years he was president. He completed his Ph.D. degree at the Claremont Graduate School in 1972 in Biblical Studies–Old Testament. Professional activities have taken him to Europe, Asia, and Africa. He served on and as contributor to translations teams for the New American Standard Bible and the New King James Version, as well as theological wordbooks. His commentary on Jeremiah was the first in the Believers Church Bible Commentary series (Herald Press) of which he is the Old Testament editor.

G.F.H.

Writings by Martens

1977   Tackling Old Testament Theology. *Journal of the Evangelical Theological Society* 20:123–32.

1981   *God's Design: A Focus on Old Testament Theology.* Grand Rapids: Baker. [British edition: *Plot and Purpose in the Old Testament* (Leicester: Inter-Varsity).]

1986   *Jeremiah.* Believers Church Bible Commentary. Scottdale, Pennsylvania: Herald.

Elmer A. Martens's
Approach to Old Testament Theology

Reprinted with permission from Elmer A. Martens, *God's Design: A Focus on Old Testament Theology* (Grand Rapids: Baker, 1981), pp. 11–23. Some footnotes have been omitted.

A Pivotal Text about Yahweh and His Purpose

[[11]] The task of adequately stating the central message of the Old Testament is a challenging one, and that for several reasons. The diversity of the Old Testament material, quite apart from its size, offers a challenge to anyone who intends to provide a summary statement of its contents. The Old Testament includes stories, poems, laments, judgment speeches, proverbs, songs, and laws. Can one from such diversity of material written over a period of several centuries arrive at a single central theme? Is there even a single theme? Scholars have not been unanimous in their answer.

The challenge of describing the heart of the Old Testament is compounded by the variety of proposals already given by scholars, even in the last fifty years.[1] For some, God's covenant with Israel seems all-important.[2] Others organize their theological statements around the concept of God's sovereignty, or the communion of God with men, or God's promise, or God's presence.[3] Asked to summarize the Old Testament message in one sentence, a group of college graduates gave these answers: 'God acts in history'; 'God is active in reconciling fallen men to himself'; 'The central message of the Old Testament is the preparation for the first coming of

1. A good survey, though somewhat technical, is offered in Gerhard F. Hasel, *Old Testament Theology: Basic Issues in the Current Debate* (Grand Rapids: Eerdmans, 1972, ²1975). A readable summary of scholarly positions is given in Robert Laurin, *Contemporary Old Testament Theologians* (Valley Forge: Judson Press, 1970). A helpful discussion of the issues facing the biblical theologian is given in Walter C. Kaiser Jr, *Toward an Old Testament Theology* (Grand Rapids: Zondervan, 1978), pp. 1–40. Cf. John Goldingay, The Study of Old Testament Theology: its Aims and Purpose, *Tyndale Bulletin* 20 (1975), pp. 34–52.

2. E.g. Walther Eichrodt, *Theology of the Old Testament*, 2 vols. (Philadelphia: Westminster Press; London: SCM Press, 1961, 1967); J. Barton Payne, *The Theology of the Older Testament* (Grand Rapids: Zondervan, 1962). An author who eschews a single concept as the centre is Gerhard von Rad, *Old Testament Theology*, 2 vols. (New York: Harper & Row; London: Oliver & Boyd, 1962, 1967).

3. E.g. on sovereignty, E. Jacob, *Theology of the Old Testament* (New York: Harper & Row; London: Hodder & Stoughton, 1958); on communion, Th. C. Vriezen, *An Outline of Old Testament Theology* (Newton, Mass.: Charles T. Branford; Oxford, Blackwell, 1956, ²1970); on promise, Walter C. Kaiser Jr, *Toward an Old Testament Theology*; on presence, S. Terrien, *The Elusive Presence: Toward a New Biblical Theology* (San Francisco: Harper & Row, 1978).

the Messiah.' Some answers get closer to the heart of the Old Testament than [[12]] others. The answers are not mutually exclusive, of course, though some are more capable of embracing the bulk of the Old Testament material than others. One scholar has aptly said: 'When there is one landscape, many different pictures may nevertheless be painted.'[4] The challenge remains, however, to paint the best possible picture.

The attempt to describe the core message of the Old Testament is challenging, for clarity about the Christian faith will depend on a grasp of the Old Testament. The Old Testament supplies the fibre for the Christian faith. But unless the message of the Old Testament is clearly articulated, its relevance to the New Testament and to Christians today will remain fuzzy.

The proposal of this book is that God's design is the key to the content of the Old Testament. This proposal assumes that it is legitimate to examine the Old Testament in search of a single central message. The following chapters attempt to offer compelling reasons for such an assumption. The emphasis on a design of God as a unifying and organizing principle of the Old Testament material arises from an exegesis of several comparable biblical texts, the first of which is Exodus 5:22–6:8.

The approach advocated in this book is distinctive in that the answer to the question about the central message is derived from a specific set of texts. It is in the language of the Bible itself that God's fourfold purpose is described, so that what we have here is a biblical theology rather than a systematic theology. It is with exegesis that we begin in order to get an outline for our picture.[5]

Someone might respond that selections of other texts would yield other outlines of a message. Why choose a certain text in Exodus from which to develop the central Old Testament message? The answer to this question will be clearer once the Exodus text has been understood.

A Significant Answer to a Crucial Question: Exodus 5:22–6:8

> Then Moses turned again to the LORD and said, 'O LORD, why hast thou done evil to this people? Why didst thou ever send me? [23]For since I came to Pharaoh to speak in thy name, he has done evil to this people, and thou has not delivered thy people at all.'

4. James Barr, 'Trends and Prospect in Biblical Theology', *Journal of Theological Studies* 25:2 (1974), p. 272.

5. See E. A. Martens, 'Tackling Old Testament Theology: Ex. 5:22–6:8', *Journal of the Evangelical Theological Society* 20 (June 1977), pp. 123–132.

¹But the L ORD said to Moses, 'Now you shall see what I will do to Pharaoh; for with a strong hand he will send them out, yea, with a strong hand he will drive them out of his land.' ⟦13⟧

²And God said to Moses, 'I am the L ORD. ³I appeared to Abraham, to Isaac, and to Jacob, as God Almighty, but by my name the L ORD I did not make myself known to them. ⁴I also established my covenant with them, to give them the land of Canaan, the land in which they dwelt as sojourners. ⁵Moreover I have heard the groaning of the people of Israel whom the Egyptians hold in bondage and I have remembered my covenant. ⁶Say therefore to the people of Israel, "I am the L ORD, and I will bring you out from under the burdens of the Egyptians, and I will deliver you from their bondage, and I will redeem you with an outstretched arm and with great acts of judgment, ⁷and I will take you for my people, and I will be your God; and you shall know that I am the L ORD your God, who has brought you out from under the burdens of the Egyptians. ⁸And I will bring you into the land which I swore to give to Abraham, to Isaac, and to Jacob; I will give it to you for a possession. I am the L ORD."'

This text presents a dialogue between Moses and God, an observation which the usual chapter division obscures. The conversation occurs after an initial attempt by Moses to seek the Egyptian Pharaoh's permission for the slave people of Israel to leave the country. Moses addresses God, primarily with questions. The larger part of the text is given to God's reply. We may already note a somewhat curious fact, namely that there are two introductions to God's speech. 'But the L ORD said to Moses . . . ' (verse 1) is followed, though there is no reply by Moses, by 'And God said to Moses . . . ' (verse 2). The structure of this text, which consists of a twofold reply to a speech by Moses, which is also in two parts, is an important clue to the message of this text unit.

Moses' Crucial Question: Exodus 5:22–23

The situation which gives rise to the questions posed by Moses before God involves a public confrontation with the Pharaoh in the land of Egypt. Moses' initial appeal to Pharaoh to let the Israelites, for years slaves in Egypt, go to freedom to the land of promise, has been met with rebuff. Pharaoh has taunted, 'Who is the L ORD, that I should heed his voice and let Israel go?' In defiance Pharaoh has responded: 'I do not know the L ORD, and moreover I will not let Israel go' (5:2). Aggressive action has followed assertive word. The production quota imposed by Pharaoh on the Israelites ⟦14⟧ has remained the same, but straw for bricks is no longer provided by the Egyptians: the Israelites must secure the straw themselves. The Israelite foremen, not able to meet the new demands satisfactorily, are beaten by their Egyptian task-masters and complain to Pharaoh. The Pharaoh grants no reprieve. The foremen turn on Moses, claiming that he is to blame.

Moses takes his frustration before God, from whom he hast received the assignment to lead a people out of bondage. His speech to God consists of two parts. He asks two questions and files a complaint.

The questions are already of an accusatory nature. 'Why hast thou done evil to this people?' Just as the foremen blame Moses, their superior, so the leader Moses now blames God, whose call he has reluctantly followed. As often happens in accusations of this kind, Moses overstates the case, for God has not actively brought evil upon his people. True, the events which have led to harsh treatment by the Pharaoh have been set in motion by Yahweh, but only indirectly. The second question registers impatience, if not accusation: 'Why didst thou ever send me?' This is hardly a question asking for information. After all, the directives had been clear when Moses received his commission at the burning bush: he was to bring a slave population into freedom. Is there in Moses' question a request for some further clarity, however? Is he calling for a rationale, for purpose, for objective? A hesitation, an uncertainty, underlies his question. In colloquial language one might phrase that question, 'God, what are you up to?' The whole enterprise of the anticipated deliverance is called into question. Moses has just entered into his assignment. He thought he knew what was involved, but now that opposition has set in more vehemently, he steps back and in measured cadence asks the elementary but entirely basic question about his mission: 'Why didst thou ever send me?' (5:22).

The questions, posed in a reproachful tone, are followed by a forthright complaint: 'For since I came to Pharaoh to speak in thy name, he has done evil to this people, and thou hast not delivered thy people at all' (5:23). Moses confronts God with a breach of promise. The attempts to gain a favourable response from Pharaoh have met with obstinacy on Pharaoh's part. The glorious promise of God seems at this point to be a hollow promise. With the forthrightness, if not bluntness, characteristic of some of God's servants through the ages, Moses files his complaint. Clearly Moses is in a difficult position. He has been rebuffed by Pharaoh, he has been accused by leaders of the people he is to deliver. Therefore he has turned to God for help.

God's Deliberate Reply

God's reply, like the statement of Moses, is in two parts. The first word from God is reassuring: 'Now you shall see what I will do to Pharaoh; for with a [[15]] strong hand he will send them out, yea, with a strong hand he will drive them out of his land' (6:1). A divine rebuke might be expected in response to the accusations, but Moses receives a promise instead. He is being asked to rely on the naked word of God. This initial reply addresses the last part of Moses' speech, the complaint. The procedure is reminiscent of the lecturer who says, 'I will take the last question first.' Moses charges, 'Thou has not delivered thy people at all.' God's answer is that deliverance is future but sure. The immediate agent for that deliverance will be Pharaoh himself; he will in due time virtually expel the people from his land. Thus the objection of Moses is answered by a straightforward statement, without elaboration.

God's further reply in 6:2–8 is much more extensive. It addresses the weightier part of Moses' speech, for it takes up the question of rationale and objective, a question basic for Moses. The longer reply is clearly structured. The first part revolves around the self-identification of God (6:2b–5); the second part is a series of instructions to Moses. Together the two parts speak to Moses' concern: 'God, what are you up to anyway?'

God's Self-identification as Yahweh. God's reply to Moses begins with a simple but highly significant assertion: 'I am the LORD' (6:2). In the English translation the force of this statement is not at once apparent. It is essentially the name of the deity that is at issue. In this reply the self-identification formula 'I am the LORD' appears three times (verses 2, 6, 8).

The name for God is given in most English Bibles as 'the LORD'. The Hebrew consonants are YHWH, and with certain vowels customarily written with these consonants, the pronunciation for the name suggested by earlier scholars was Yehovah (Jehovah). Modern scholars hold that the name of God was pronounced Yahweh. This conclusion is based on an understanding of the way in which in oral reading Jewish people came to substitute a title for the written name of God because of their deep reverence for the name of God. Yahweh, then, is the proper name for God. Some modern translations of the Bible employ the name Yahweh rather than the accustomed 'the LORD', and perhaps for good reason. In the English language 'Lord' is a title and properly translates ʾaḏōnāy, master. LORD, all in capital letters, as a translation of Yahweh,[6] does not convey the force of a personal name. In this passage it is not a title but a specific name that is revealed. Since great importance was attached to names in ancient Israel, and among Semites generally, it is of considerable importance, especially for a theology of the Old Testament, to gain clarity on the meaning of the name Yahweh.

[16] To answer the question about the meaning of the name Yahweh, we must reach back a little in the narrative. The name had been

---

6. For an extended discussion of the name see G. H. Parke-Taylor, *Yahweh: The Divine Name in the Bible* (Waterloo, Ont.: Wilfred Laurier University Press, 1975). His conclusions differ, however, from those presented here.

given to Moses earlier in connection with his call (3:1–4:17). There Moses had heard God identify himself as 'I AM WHO I AM' (3:14), a phrase that plays on the Hebrew verb 'to be'. Building on the derivation of the word Yahweh from the verb 'to be', some scholars hold that the expressions 'I AM WHO I AM' and 'Yahweh' refer to the actuality of God's existence. The name, then, marks the certainty of Yahweh's existence. Given a western mindset, such an explanation seems plausible; yet scholars have challenged that interpretation on the basis that such abstractions as 'existence' were not characteristic of the Hebrew way of thinking.

Since linguistically the phrase could be translated, 'I cause to be that which I cause to be', others have argued that the words refer to the creative activity of God. This view has been contested, however, on the grounds that the specific verb form involved (causative) is not found in the Hebrew for the verb 'to be'. Still others have suggested that 'I will be who I will be' indicated that God was sufficient for every circumstance. Paraphrased, this would mean, 'I will be for you the kind of God you have need of.' A Jewish scholar holds that the name El Shaddai, which also occurs in the text and is rendered 'God Almighty', was a name that was associated with fertility. The patriarchs, this scholar says, knew God as 'God Almighty', but did not know God as the one who fulfilled promises; now, at the time of the exodus, the name Yahweh was to be associated with the keeping of promises. That is, Yahweh represents 'He who is with his creatures, and He who is constantly the same, that is, he is true to his word and fulfills his promise'.[7]

Or, to turn to an approach that sidesteps the attempt to translate the word, some have suggested that the name Yahweh was deliberately enigmatic. To know someone by name is to have a measure of control. One can summon him, for instance. Did God give to Israel so strange a name, a name that was no name, so that Israel would not manipulate God?[8] It is a distinct possibility. Man's inclination is to use God to his own advantage. But Yahweh is not a dispensing machine from whom can be secured at will his gifts of bounty, health, wisdom, etc. No, Yahweh remains free to act. His acts are carried out in freedom. He is who he is, and is not determined, except by himself.

Attractive as some of these suggestions may be, it is best, if one wishes to know the meaning of the name Yahweh, to give close attention to the context of Exodus 3. As Eichrodt has noted, the significance of the name lies in part in the promise of his presence. Moses has already been given

7. U. Cassuto, *A Commentary on the Book of Exodus* (Jerusalem: Magnes Press, ET 1967), p. 77.

8. See G. von Rad, *Old Testament Theology*, 1, p. 182.

the assurance of God's presence earlier when God declares, in response to
[[17]] Moses' objection, 'But I will be with you' (3:12).[9] The context is also
one in which God promises deliverance. God says: 'I promise that I will
bring you up out of the affliction of Egypt' (3:17). This promise gives support to the meaning of the name Yahweh as being the saving name. Yahweh is the name by which God represents himself as present, here and
now, to act, especially to deliver. It is in this way, essentially in a new way,
that Israel will experience Yahweh. Yahweh is a salvation name. This
name, the most frequent name for God (YHWH occurs more than 6,800
times in the Old Testament) becomes a frequent reminder that God is the
saving God.

The identity of Yahweh, as our text emphasizes, is not to be divorced
from the story of the patriarchs. 'I appeared to Abraham, to Isaac, and to
Jacob, as God Almighty, but by my name the LORD (Yahweh) I did not
make myself known to them' (6:3). The same God who now speaks to
Moses, though under a new name, Yahweh, had earlier committed himself
to the patriarchs through a covenant to them, which, among other things,
included the gift of the land of Canaan. With this statement the relationship of God to the patriarchs, described already in Genesis 12, is reviewed,
or affirmed, or better yet, made the platform from which the further
promises are now launched. The promise of land to Abraham is made in
Gen 12:7. The covenant with Abraham is described in greater detail in
Genesis 15 and 17 and is related to the initial blessing of a multitude of
descendants promised to Abraham (Gen 12:2). Along with the promise of
descendants, God promised Abraham territory. 'On that day the Lord
made a covenant with Abram saying, "To your descendants I give this
land, from the river of Egypt to the great river, the river Euphrates . . . "'
(Gen 15:18). The triple promise of descendants, territory, and blessing is
embraced in a covenant given to Abraham in his ninety-ninth year (Gen
17:1–8). Reiterated to Isaac (Gen 26:3) and to Jacob (Gen 28:19; 35:9–
12), the promise continued to have a threefold gift of descendants, territory, and blessing. God's word to Moses is that he has remembered that
covenant, not in the sense of merely recalling it, but in the sense of
honouring it. One phase of the promise, that of offspring, is realized, in
part, for the families of Israel have been exceptionally fruitful (Exod 1:7).
Fulfillment of the remaining part of the promise, that of land, will now be
brought under way.

The statement of God in Exod 6:3–5 then ties in with the patriarchs
historically, by reviewing the past, and theologically by providing continu-

---

9. W. Eichrodt, *Theology of the Old Testament*, 1, p. 191.

ity of the name Yahweh with the name God Almighty. What follows in the Yahweh speech is directed to the future.

Yahweh's purpose. The name Yahweh, judged by the context in which it is first given (3:14) and the special attention devoted to it in the present ⟦18⟧ passage (5:22–6:8), signals a divine presence to save. The name Yahweh, one is led to expect, will introduce a new chapter in God's work in the world. In his reply to Moses, God as Yahweh describes his intention.

Yahweh's initial design for his people is deliverance: 'I will bring you out from under the burdens of the Egyptians, and I will deliver you from their bondage, and I will redeem you with an outstretched arm and with great acts of judgment' (6:6). These three statements resemble, by reason of parallelism, lines of Hebrew poetry. Three synonyms are used to elucidate Yahweh's action. 'I will bring out' is in the causative form of 'go' (*yāṣā᾿*) and might be rendered: 'I will cause you to go out.' The causative is also employed in the following verb: deliver (*nāṣal*). It is the common verb used to refer to God's actions of rescue. The verbal form (*nāṣal*) is repeated with considerable frequency (135 times). The word rendered 'redeem' (*gā᾿al*) has its linguistic home in regulations governing tribal peoples and property. A redeemer (*gô᾿ēl*) was one whose responsibility it was to buy out the property of a kinsman who had forfeited it, or who was on the verge of forfeiting it, perhaps because of debt. The prophet Jeremiah purchased a piece of land from his cousin Hanamel and so acted as a redeemer (Jer 32:6ff.). A more familiar example is Boaz, who as a near relative buys the property of Naomi (Ruth 2:20; 4:4–6, 9). Or the redeemer might buy out a kinsman who had become the slave of a foreigner (Lev 25:47–54), or avenge the blood of a relative who had been murdered. The sense of restoration to a former state or the healing of tribal brokenness is an underlying component of the term. In Exodus 6 the redeemer is Yahweh, and the deliverance is specified to be of large proportion: 'from the burdens of the Egyptians' and from 'their bondage'.

Secondly, Yahweh's design is to form a godly community. 'And I will take you for my people, and I will be your God' (Exod 6:7a). God's purpose is that the people now to be formed are to be distinctly his people. But, characteristically, God's demand is not apart from his promise: he himself will be their God. This second statement makes it clear that deliverance, though it is Yahweh's initial intention, is only preparatory to larger concerns. The redeemed lot are to stand together as a community marked as God's special possession. The vocabulary is covenant vocabulary. The formula, slightly altered, occurs in the major sections of the Old

Testament (e.g. Lev 26:12; Deut 26:17ff.; Jer 7:23; Ezek 11:20). The implications of this statement will receive attention later.

Thirdly, Yahweh's intention is that there be an on-going relationship ⟦with⟧ his people. 'And you shall know that I am Yahweh your God who has brought you out from under the burdens of the Egyptians' (Exod 6:7b). They are to know (that is, experience) him as Yahweh their God. This means, among other things, that he offers himself to be known. He invites his ⟦19⟧ people into the adventure of knowing him. The means by which this knowledge occurs and the nature of the resultant experience can be deduced from the exodus event, but further descriptions of Yahweh's encounter with his people will be in evidence later.

Finally, Yahweh's intention for his people is that they enjoy the good life. The words of the text are: 'and I will bring you into the land which I swore to give to Abraham, to Isaac, and to Jacob; I will give it to you for a possession' (Exod 6:8). The land was already earlier the object of promise, where it was the concrete part of God's blessing for his people. Elsewhere the land is described as the land flowing with milk and honey (Exod 3:17), which is to say that it is a land in which life is pleasant and in which living is marked by abundance. The land comes before long to symbolize the life with Yahweh in ideal conditions, a quality of life which might be characterized as the abundant life.

The divine reply to Moses' question, 'Why did you ever send me?' embraces a discussion of the name Yahweh, and a disclosure of his purpose. Three times, as we have noted, the self-identification formula surfaces: 'I am Yahweh.' In the first instance it introduces the historical review in which emphasis is placed on the name itself since it had not been known in earlier times (Exod 6:3). In the second part of the speech, the self-identification formula occurs at the outset of the four statements of divine purpose (6:6). Curiously, and in a sense of finality, the 'I am Yahweh' phrase also terminates the speech (6:8). Unless we think of the reply as composed carelessly, we must ask, what is the force of this thrice-repeated assertion? If in the name Yahweh there is disclosed a new feature of Yahweh, and if the covenant with the patriarchs was already made earlier, apart from the name, then we must look for a new feature other than covenant as linked in a particular way with the name Yahweh. Is that new feature not to be found in the statement of the fourfold design? Salvation, a new people, a new relationship, and the gift of the land—these are the components of the purpose. Yahweh is the name that is associated at this crucial juncture with purpose, that which God intends or is about.

One may fully affirm the remark by Brevard Childs in conjunction with this passage: 'The content of the message which is bracketed by this self-identification formula is actually an explication of the name itself and contains the essence of God's purpose with Israel.'[10] Similarly, the Jewish scholar Cassuto states in commenting on this Exodus text: 'In our passage the king of the universe announces His purpose and the amazing plan of action that He proposes to carry out in the near future.'[11] We should wish to [[20]] amend this statement only by noting that the plan is not just for the near future, but embraces a large block of time, in fact the entire history of Israel.

. . . .

A Grid for the Old Testament Message

There is general agreement that the Old Testament has Yahweh for its central subject, but we may ask, what does one say after having said that? We may posit that the text in Exod 5:22–6:8 clarifies the way in which the central subject of the Old Testament, Yahweh, is to be elaborated. Yahweh has a plan. This plan is one to bring deliverance, to summon a people who will be peculiarly his own, to offer himself for them to know and to give to them land in fulfillment of his promise. This Scripture passage asks the question posed at the outset, namely, how to understand what the Old Testament is getting at. Formulated by Moses in the context of a frustrating and perplexing experience, the question, 'Why did you ever send me?' is helpful in supplying a handle, a definite clue to our investigation about the [[21]] central message of the Old Testament. As a preliminary check we might test our suggestion that the fourfold purpose of God is a satisfactory grid by casting our eye over one block of the Old Testament, namely the Pentateuch.

The concept of purpose, quite apart from detail, already underlies the book of Genesis. The family stories of Abraham, Isaac and Jacob presage a distinct destiny, especially since they are launched with the statement of design to Abraham: 'Go from your country and your kindred and your father's house to the land that I will show you' (Gen 12:1). The Joseph narrative at the conclusion of Genesis also hints at design. Joseph says to his brothers: 'As for you, you meant evil against me; but God meant it for good, to bring it about that many people should be kept alive, as they are today' (Gen 50:20).

Deliverance, the first phase of Yahweh's intention, is particularly the subject of the first half of the book of Exodus; the covenant community, now given detailed instructions, is the subject of Exodus 19–40. Through the sacrifice and other cultic institutions in Leviticus God makes himself

---

10. Brevard S. Childs, *The Book of Exodus* (Philadelphia: Westminster Press, 1974), p. 115 (= *Exodus*, SCM Press, 1974).

11. U. Cassuto, *Exodus*, p. 76.

known and the people experience him as Yahweh. Land, and the regulations pertaining to occupancy, are the frequent subject of Deuteronomy. Thus the fourfold design serves almost as a table of contents to the Pentateuch. Might this outline be pertinent, even adequate, for the remainder of the Old Testament?

It is the thesis of this book that the fourfold design described in Exod 5:22–6:8 is an appropriate and also adequate grid according to which to present the whole of the Old Testament material. This is a substantial claim, proof of which must be the pages which follow. Even should it be disputed that the proposed grid is adequate as a set of categories for the presentation of the Old Testament message, the insights gained from this approach promise to be considerable.

Two points could still be raised as requiring clarification. First, it might be asked why this particular passage in Exodus rather than some other in Exodus or elsewhere was chosen. Could some other passage serve equally well? Perhaps, but not too likely. The paragraph of Exod 5:22–6:8 commends itself for various reasons. It is the text in which the revelation of the name Yahweh is differentiated from other names of God. Even though a form of it is given to Moses earlier, attention is distinctly called here to Yahweh, the form of the name by which God will be primarily known in the remainder of the Old Testament canon. Secondly, this passage speaks of the beginnings of the people of Israel, with whom much of the Old Testament [22] deals. It could be expected that a programmatic statement would be found here. Moreover, this text is concerned with an interpretation of the exodus event, which according to some scholars is the fulcrum event in the Old Testament.[12] Most important, however, in commending this scripture as the Old Testament message in a nutshell is the consideration that the text addresses the question of God's ultimate purpose. Moses' question is our question too: 'God, what are you up to?' More than a clue is given here. The explicit statements supply specific, even if not fully detailed, indications of Yahweh's purpose. Those indications, it may be argued, are the controlling purposes of God within the Old Testament. But someone may still object by saying, 'Is not the notion of purpose and design an import from a western civilization which, especially in our time, is fascinated by ideas such as purpose?' The notion of design is basic, for instance, to such western concepts as 'management by objective'. Since it is our intention to let the Old Testament speak in its

---

12. James H. Cone: 'The Exodus was the decisive event in Israel's history, because through it Yahweh revealed himself as the Savior of the oppressed people.' 'Biblical Revelation and Social Existence', *Interpretation* 28 (1974), p. 423; cf. David Daube, *The Exodus Pattern in the Bible* (London: Faber and Faber, 1963).

own terms, the question is most appropriate. The remainder of the book is an attempt at an answer.

. . . .

⟦23⟧ Yahweh is a God with a purpose. In this respect Yahweh is different from other gods represented in ancient Near Eastern literature. Already the Genesis verdict, 'God saw that it was good', presupposes a purpose. To this fact of purpose the law gives evidence (Exod 5:22–6:8), as do the prophets (Isa 46:10; 14:26; Jer 32:18–19) an so also do the writings (Ps 33:11; Prov 19:21).

With these assertions about purpose generally, and the exegetical treatment of Exod 5:22–6:8 specifically, the shape of our task emerges with greater clarity. To comprehend Yahweh's design we shall have to talk about deliverance; about covenant and community; about the knowledge of God; and about land.

Synopsis of Martens's *God's Design: A Focus on Old Testament Theology* (1981)

Elmer A. Martens On Land and Lifestyle

Reprinted with permission from Elmer A. Martens, *God's Design: A Focus on Old Testament Theology* (Grand Rapids: Baker, 1981), pp. 108–15.

Land as Demanding a Specific Life-Style

[[108]] Human conduct and behaviour are understood to have a bearing on land, and conversely, land occupancy demands a particular quality of life-style. This association between life-style and land is found in scattered references through the books of Leviticus, Numbers, and Deuteronomy; but these references occur in sufficient number to command notice and have shown a point of view that is unique to the Bible. For a glimpse of this association between land and life-style we look in turn at moral and cultic responsibilities, specific rules relating to land use, and the cultic festivals which had an agricultural orientation. A discussion of these moral, economic and cultic regulations will clarify the theological aspects surrounding land.

As to moral, civil and cultic instructions, their association with the land needs first to be established biblically and then assessed. Various statutes are announced for observance at the time of entry into the land, often introduced by a general statement of which Deut 12:1 is typical: 'These are the statutes and ordinances which you shall be careful to do in the land which the LORD, the God of your fathers, has given you to possess' (cf. 11:31–32; 4:5, 14; 5:31; 6:1). From these statements it is obvious that a prescribed form of conduct is appropriate for life in the land. Thus the land is not only a promise or a gift; fulfilled responsibility is integral to land tenure.

These regulations range broadly. They deal with governance, for they speak to the possibility of the people's desire for a king and give direction for the establishment of a monarch (Deut 17:14). Cities of refuge are to be established for murderers in the land as a part of the civil-law complex regulating blood revenge (Deut 19:7). Religious and moral instruction in the Torah is to be undertaken in a family setting, and Moses, visualizing a permanent residence, commands that 'these words' are to be written on the doorposts of the house and on the gates (Deut 6:9). Dietary instructions are also given (Deut 12:20ff.). To occupy the land, as in modern occupancy of rental property, a willingness to submit to regulations of the owner is required. Israel is not at liberty to set its own behavior guidelines. Residence in the land means paying attention to what is fitting in the land.

312

But the case for law and land association is stronger than the words 'fitting' or 'propriety' indicate. Wrong behaviour, for instance, is not only unbecoming but it defiles the land. Harlotry is forbidden, for example, lest [[109]] 'the land fall into harlotry and the land become full of wickedness' (Lev 19:29). Shedding of blood pollutes the land and no expiation for it is possible, except the death of the murderer (Num 35:29–34). A man who is hanged for an offence is not to remain on the tree into the night—he must be buried, for a 'hanged man is accursed by God; you shall not defile your land which the LORD your God gives you for an inheritance' (Deut 21:23). Divorce is permitted, but not the remarriage of the husband to his divorced wife who has already married another. Not only is such a practice an abomination before the LORD, but it will 'bring guilt upon the land' (Deut 24:4). Marriage and family ethics are not in themselves associated directly with land—yet violations of these family-related moral and civil regulations are said to defile the land. In what sense? In the sense that Yahweh dwells in the midst of the land (Num 35:34). And in another sense also. Land is the 'middle term' between Israel and Yahweh. Land is a tangible symbol of Yahweh. It would not be conceivable that Yahweh could be defiled, therefore the negative consequence could best be stated by saying that the land will be defiled. So close is the association between Yahweh and land that an infraction against Yahweh has the effect of polluting or defiling the land. The land therefore symbolizes in a forceful way Israel's relationship with Yahweh.

Yet it is not only Israel, to whom the Torah belongs, who defiles the land: the Canaanites who are strangers to the Torah have by their abominations defiled the land. Israel is cautioned not to defile herself with such things as child sacrifice, for 'by all these the nations . . . have defiled themselves; and the land became defiled' (Lev 18:24–25). Pollution of self and pollution of land result from unlawful behaviour. Even apart from revelation the non-Israelite should know to abstain from such sexual perversion as bestiality and homosexual activity and from human sacrifice. These evils defile the land. Though they did not possess the Torah, peoples outside Israel are held responsible for their conduct in the land. It is not therefore that the land is rendered impure because of its relation to Israel. Again, it is defiled almost in its own right, or, perhaps more accurately, because of the close relationship of the land to Yahweh.

The case for the interdependence between moral behaviour and land is even stronger than the preceding discussion has suggested. There is more to be said than that obedience to Yahweh is fitting in the land and that disregard of Yahweh's instruction defiles the land. Continued occupancy of the land is itself conditioned by observance of the law. This means on the one hand that by faithful adherence to the admonitions,

Israel can continue in the land. Motivation for such observance of law includes the promise of continued residence: 'All the commandment which
I command you this day you shall be careful to do, that you may live and
multiply, and go in and possess the land' (Deut 8:1). Moses says: 'Justice
and only justice you shall [[110]] follow, that you may live and inherit the
land which the LORD your God gives you.' Obedience to the law brings
blessings, which, as the catalogue of blessing indicates, are primarily prosperity and fruitfulness in the land (Deut 28:1–14).

But if blessing follows obedience, curse within the land and even de-
portation from it will result from disobedience (Deut 28:15–68). Lack of
rain, defeat by enemies, internal confusion and disease are only a few of
the disasters which may be expected, and the ultimate disaster, apart from
ruin, is that 'you shall be plucked off the land . . . And the LORD will scatter you among all peoples' (Deut 28:63–64). Again, such drastic treatment as removal from land is not reserved only for a people like Israel
with a revealed Torah. It was because of the sinfulness of the Canaanites
that they were expelled from the land (Lev 18:24). Indeed, so much are
these infractions directly against the land that the land personified is described as vomiting out Canaanites (Lev 18:24). The threat for Israel too is
that unless she keeps the statutes and the ordinances, the land may vomit
up the people in it (Lev 20:22–26). By this one is to understand that violation of norms is so reprehensible that, quite apart from Yahweh's dis-
pleasure, the land itself cannot tolerate them: the land will spew out the
population.

It may seem at first glance that the stipulations accompanying the gift
of the land make the land not altogether a gift. A few passages indeed give
the impression that obedience to God's ordinance was a condition of entry
into the land (e.g. Deut 8:1). But these are not to be understood as quali-
fying people in a fundamental sense for the gift; rather they are to be
taken, as are the many statements cautioning Israel lest through disobedience they forfeit the right to continue on the land, as accompanying the
gift. To a gift, even a gift totally the result of grace, there is not inconsis-
tently attached stipulation for its use. A British company director who at
his death left £33,000, specified that £5,000 be given to each of his two
grandchildren—provided they did not spend the money on motorcycles.
This twentieth-century example, while not the norm for interpreting ancient Israelite practice, may still illustrate the basic principle that a gift may
have conditions. The land gift was unique in that Yahweh remained the
owner. He disposed of it, but not in a final sense by giving it over to Israel.
As the proprietor of the land, his right to make stipulations, along with his
claim to Israel, is everywhere assumed. Life in the land can continue provided a certain life-style, one marked by obedience, is maintained.

The subject of life-style is far too large to survey with any depth, but the regulations about land use can move us from generalities to specifics and can illustrate the tenor of conduct pleasing to Yahweh. [[111]]

Sabbath and Jubilee

Two regulations dealt with land use: the sabbath and the jubilee. From Mount Sinai Moses issued this instruction: 'When you come into the land which I give you, the land shall keep a sabbath to the LORD' (Lev 25:2; cf. 23:10f.). By this, as the explanation which follows shows, is meant that whereas for six years the land is to be sown and vineyards cultivated, in the seventh it is to be fallow. There is to be no seeding of the land, and vineyards are not to be pruned, nor is there to be reaping of that which grows by itself. The practice of leaving the land fallow for the purpose of rejuvenation was not uncommon among Israel's neighbours. The reason for such a practice in Israel, however, takes a decidedly different shape. The sabbatical year is for the benefit of the poor and for the benefit of wild life, 'that the poor of your people may eat, and what they leave the beasts may eat'. This purpose could be achieve if for individual farmers the seventh year came at different times. In Leviticus there is assumed a universal and uniform observance of the fallow year. But the purpose, while humanitarian, is not exclusively so. A religious motivation is announced in the terminology, 'a sabbath to Yahweh'. The land, by being left fallow, bears witness to Yahweh's ownership. The direct link between Yahweh and land is left intact; the land's rest is not disturbed by human intervention of tilling.

It is argued by some scholars that Deut 15:1–3 couples a regulation about the release of all debts every seven years to the command to fallow the land. While complicated in details, Deut 15:1–3 is best considered not as a cancellation of debts generally but as a case where land was mortgaged to a creditor. In the seventh year the creditor was not to demand annual payment of the land's harvest. This provision, also humanitarian, allowed the debtor some hope of meeting his obligations. If a loan were taken in the sixth year and not fully paid, it would not be payable till after the harvest of the eighth year, thus giving the impoverished Israelite an extended period of credit. The sabbath for the land was for Yahweh (Lev 25:2) and the practice of charity to the debtor was also performed 'before Yahweh' (Deut 15:2). The sabbath regulation, while clearly given as an obligation unto Yahweh, pointed two ways: to the land, and to the debtor whose land had been encumbered. Failure to observe these statutes is given as reason for drastic action of God's removal of people from the land (Lev 26:32–33, 43; 2 Chr 36:21).

A second ordinance that dealt especially with land use is the jubilee. The instructions about jubilee also require that the land be left fallow, not only every seven years but during the fiftieth year, namely after seven sevens of years (Lev 25:8ff.). It was unlike the seventh fallow year in that in the jubilee year the land was to revert to the family that originally claimed ownership. An impoverished Israelite, once he had mortgaged his land and his crops, [[112]] might find it necessary to 'sell' the land to his creditor, and even if a relative redeemed it, the unfortunate Israelite would still in all likelihood be working it for the benefit of his kinsman (Lev 26:36ff.). The purpose of the kinsman provision was to retain the land within the particular family of the clan; otherwise descendants of the unfortunate Israelite would be condemned to be property-less. The jubilee year, coming every few generations, was to remedy this eventuality, for in the jubilee year, even had the land remained in the clan through redemption, it was now to be returned to the particular family within the clan. The jubilee year also had provisions for the release of slaves. It is therefore clear that the regulations of the jubilee affected the economic life of a people by demanding magnanimous action by the well-to-do for the benefit of the less capable or unfortunate man. Without such a provision as a jubilee, territories of a clan could come into the hands of a few families, and the remaining clans people would be serfs. The jubilee aimed at the preservation of household units, ensuring their economic viability. The land belonged inalienably to the householder. This right of the household landowner to regain his property was not due to some belief about the right of property *per se*, but a belief in land as a gift from Yahweh, whose regulation stabilized the people's relationship with each other and with their God. It is not hard to see that in the Old Testament, [[113]] land, Israel and Yahweh belonged together, and that in this triad the rights of the family were particularly safeguarded.[1]

Festivals

With such agricultural practices as the sabbath year and the jubilee year, a life-style characterized by non-exploitation of land and of people was inculcated. A considerate and caring attitude was encouraged.

In addition a set of festivals, primarily agricultural, established yet another orientation and life-style attitude: thanksgiving and joy. Instructions about these festivals appears in each of the four law books (Exodus 23; 34; Leviticus 23; Numbers 28; Deuteronomy 16).

All of the three major annual festivals, each a week long, were held in connection with the harvest from the field. The festival of unleavened

---

1. I am indebted for material in this chapter and for the diagram to C. J. H. Wright's careful analysis of regulations governing land, 'Family, Land and Property in Ancient Israel—Some Aspects of Old Testament Social Ethics' (unpublished dissertation, University of Cambridge, 1976).

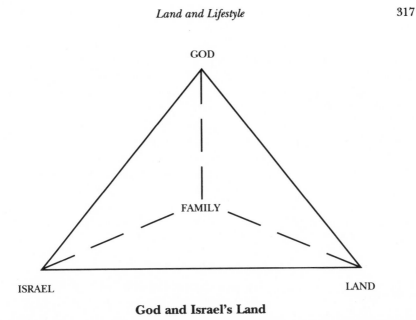

God and Israel's Land

bread was held in the spring of the year immediately following the pass-over observance. Scheduled for the beginning of the barley harvest in late April/early May, its important feature was the baking and eating of un-leavened bread. The bread of the harvest was deliberately not prepared with yeast, so that the firstfruits would be eaten untouched by a foreign element. The second festival, called a feast of harvest in the book of Exo-dus but more commonly a feast of weeks (Deut 16:10), came fifty days af-ter the sickle was first put to the spring grain. It was observed at the end of the wheat harvest, corresponding to our month of June. At this time the firstfruits of the farmer's labour were presented before Yahweh. Either the whole crop, the first of several in the agricultural year, or the first fruits of the barley grain harvest preserved from their first cutting to the end of the season, were brought to the sanctuary. The third agricultural festival was the feast of ingathering, known also as the feast of booths or tabernacles, because of a provision that during the week people should live in tents. This festival followed the day of atonement in the month of October, and centred on the harvest of fruits, especially olives and grapes.

Though agrarian-based, these festivals were not pagan orgies. They were religious occasions. In all three, males of the country were to present themselves at the sanctuary. Although social in character, with feasting and celebration, these were more than social events. The festivals were festivals 'to Yahweh'. The religious orientation emerged in the presenta-tion of animal offerings to Yahweh and also in the gift of first fruits of the grain and fruit to Yahweh. The detailed instruction for such a presentation of agricultural produce is given in Deut 26:1, and, while given for the particular occasion of the very first harvest, the instruction may also have been ritually ⟦114⟧ applied, especially at the feast of weeks and the feast of ingathering.

At these festivals the Israelite was not to appear before Yahweh empty-handed (Exod 34:20; 23:15). The worshipper with his produce in his basket would appear before the priest and begin his statement by saying: 'I declare this day to the LORD your God that I have come into the land which the LORD swore to our fathers to give us' (Deut 26:3). After rehearsing the history of his people, with emphasis on Yahweh's grace to them, he concluded with the words: 'And behold, now I bring the first of the fruit of the ground, which thou, O LORD, hast given me.' The priest either set the basket before the altar (Deut 26:4) or waved the sheaf before Yahweh (Lev 23:10–11, 20). The character of the festival as a festival to Yahweh was safeguarded through this ritual at the sanctuary in which through word and act Yahweh was acknowledged. The worshipper expressed his thankfulness and gratitude to Yahweh.

Now it is highly significant that the speech the worshipper made at the presentation of his offering is a rehearsal of the deeds of Yahweh in history. The dedication of the produce was motivated by recognition of Yahweh not so much as creator, but as deliverer. It was not as a creature who enjoys the yield of creation that the worshipper came before Yahweh, but as one who had experienced deliverance from oppression. His history was a history of salvation, and here the land is remarkably in focus. His ailing forefather Jacob migrated to Egypt with but a small family and without land. The population in Egypt had no land they could call their own. But now, the worshipper concluded, Yahweh had brought them into the land. The pagan worshipper by contrast addressed a god related to nature, from whom he expected the benefits of fertility in field, flock and family. But in Israel these ideas of God so closely and so exclusively associated with nature are absent. While Yahweh is a God of nature, and is so celebrated in the Psalms, he is a God of history; and his connection with the land is not only or even primarily as a God who makes it fertile, but as one who in response to his promise has brought his people to enjoy the abundance that the land offers. To this God of history, the worshipper offered his thanksgiving.

Judged by the instruction in Deuteronomy, the festivals, while foremost festivals for Yahweh, were also festivals for the people. The males appeared at the sanctuary but the festivals involved all—sons and daughters, servants and Levites. The fatherless and widow are singled out for special mention, but, more arresting from a sociological point of view, the sojourner was also to participate in the celebrations (Deut 26:11, 14). These celebrations were not to become exclusivist—the non-Israelite was to be included. The festivals, related so closely to the land, display, as did the land use regulations, a humanitarian concern. Israel was to recall that she had been a slave in Egypt (Deut 26:12). Love to God and love to neighbour came to expression in the ⟦115⟧ festivals.

Finally, the mood of the three-week-long annual festivals deserves mention. 'You shall rejoice before the LORD your God' (Deut 16:11). 'You shall rejoice in your feast' (Deut 16:14). 'You shall rejoice before the LORD your God seven days' (Lev 23:40). The imperative to rejoice, like the imperative to love, while strange, nevertheless indicates the basic posture for the Israelite. Philo, the Jewish philosopher-exegete of the first century A.D., described even the day of atonement as the 'feast of feasts'. Israelite worship was a worship of joy and praise. In the light of the ancient Near Eastern record and practice, no doubt, one scholar has gone as far as to say, 'There is hardly a word so characteristic of the Old Testament as the word joy.'[2] Festivals, as ordered by Yahweh, were an expression of this joyful mood.

Land, then, is more than acreage or territory. It is a theological symbol, through which a series of messages are conveyed. It is the tangible fulfilment of the promise. Land is a gift from Yahweh, and Israel, through preoccupation with it, has her attention continually called to Yahweh. Land requires a specific and appropriate life-style. Responsibilities concerning social behaviour are enjoined upon the people for the time when they will occupy the land, and they are warned that disobedience defiles the land and may result in loss of their privilege of tenancy. The specific regulations about land use, such as the sabbatical year and jubilee, take ecological and humanitarian concerns into account. Finally the festivals, associated with the production from the land, once again link land and Yahweh, point to social responsibilities, and portray the joyful spirit in which this people lives its life on the land, always before Yahweh.

But if land is more than acreage or territory and symbolic of promise, gift, blessing and life-style, it is nevertheless still soil and territory. It has theological aspects, but it is not thereby an ethereal thing, nor should it be spiritualized. Land is real. Earth is spatially definable. Life with Yahweh takes place here and now. The quality of that life is all-embracing—it relates to Yahweh, to neighbour, to environment. Life with Yahweh cannot be compartmentalized, as though his interest lies only within a small area. No, his interest extends to the total man and to the total society and to the

2. Ludwig Koehler, *Old Testament Theology* (Philadelphia: Westminster; London: Lutterworth, 1957), p. 151.

total environment. He is misrepresented, and his people's life misshaped, if the wholeness of life is not emphasized. The promise of land and all that it signifies keeps the entire design rooted in history and is thoroughly reality-related. We shall find the this-worldly and earth-affirming aspect strong and marked once again in the wisdom literature, especially in Proverbs. In the New Testament, the concept of discipleship is equally all-embracing.

BREVARD S. CHILDS

b. 1923

Canon

Theological Synopsis

The name of Brevard Childs is closely linked with biblical theology. In the earlier phase of his career, he was identified with the Biblical Theology movement. That is the name Childs himself gave to a collective effort, during the middle years of this century, to harness historical-critical study *def of Biblical Theology moved* of the Bible to Christian theological and churchly concerns. His first three books, *Myth and Reality in the Old Testament* (1960), *Memory and Tradition in Israel* (1962), and *Isaiah and the Assyrian Crisis* (1967), could all be seen to fall within the scope of the movement; all were published in the series "Studies in Biblical Theology." But already in the last of these books, there is indication of Childs's growing dissatisfaction with the way historical and theological questions were commonly treated. More specifically, Childs had come to believe that literary-historical investigations could not, of themselves, settle theological questions.

One of those questions concerned the diversity of Old Testament materials, which Gerhard von Rad had highlighted and which Childs uncovered in his own study of Isaiah. It was appropriate, Childs concluded, that literary-historical inquiry seek to discover the way in which the Old Testament handles *its own* theological diversity—the way in which later traditions take up and modify earlier ones, for example. But, he went on to *what's reasoning here?* conclude, it is also theologically appropriate "to bring to bear other norms than those found within the tradition" (1967: 126). Jewish and Christian communities have their own such "other norms," and Childs refused to discount these. In that refusal, and in his emphasis on the "Christian canon" as the appropriate "theological context" for interpretation (1967: 127), Childs began to chart a unique, even an iconoclastic, course in biblical studies.

He laid a more systematic foundation for that unique course in his *Biblical Theology in Crisis*, which pointed out the failures of the Biblical Theology movement, and went on "to defend the thesis that the canon of the Christian church is the most appropriate context from which to do Biblical Theology" (1970: 99). He then pitted this canonical approach against the dominant tradition of Old Testament scholarship in his *Introduction to the Old Testament as Scripture* (1979). Here he argued not just that the canon is the proper *context* of interpretation, but that the canonical (or final) form of each Old Testament book is the proper *object* of interpretation. Childs insists that this does not mean that traditional historical-critical approaches have no role to play; rather, they have their role in illuminating the form of the texts in which we have them, and in laying bare their "depth dimension" (1986: 11) by showing how they came to have the form in which we have them. Nonetheless, Childs assigns to his "concern with canon" a "negative role . . . in relativizing the claims to priority of the historical critical method" (1979: 83). Childs understands the forces that shaped the Old Testament texts to be primarily religious, rather than strictly historical, sociological, or political; they are texts of a *faith* community, the interpretive context, now, of another faith community.

In his subsequent introduction to the New Testament (1984) and in his Old Testament theology (1986) Childs carried forward his canonical approach. Whether it is ultimately more persuasive than was the Biblical Theology movement, whose "crisis" he once diagnosed, remains to be seen. In the meanwhile, it can be said that no Old Testament theologian has been more concerned than has Brevard Childs to take seriously the "theological" nature of Old Testament and biblical theology.

Brevard S. Childs graduated from the University of Michigan and Princeton Theological Seminary before studying for his doctorate in Old Testament at the University of Basel (1953), where his teachers were Walter Baumgartner and Walther Eichrodt. He taught at Mission House Seminary from 1954 to 1958; since then he has been at Yale University, where he is Holmes Professor of Old Testament Criticism and Interpretation at Yale Divinity School. Childs has been a leader in Old Testament and biblical theology in North America; all nine of his books have a clearly theological dimension. He has published introductions to both Testaments, an Old Testament theology, a commentary on the Book of Exodus, as well as numerous studies of individual biblical texts and themes, and issues in theology and interpretation. Childs is an active Presbyterian churchman.

B.C.O.

Writings by Childs

1960   *Myth and Reality in the Old Testament.* Studies in Biblical Theology 27. London: SCM/Naperville, Illinois: Allenson.

1962   *Memory and Tradition in Israel.* Studies in Biblical Theology 37. London: SCM/Naperville, Illinois: Allenson.

1967   *Isaiah and the Assyrian Crisis.* Studies in Biblical Theology 2/3. London: SCM/Naperville, Illinois: Allenson.

1970   *Biblical Theology in Crisis.* Philadelphia: Westminster.

1974   *The Book of Exodus: A Critical, Theological Commentary.* Old Testament Library. Philadelphia: Westminster/London: SCM.

1979   *Introduction to the Old Testament as Scripture.* Philadelphia: Fortress.

1984   *The New Testament as Canon: An Introduction.* Philadelphia: Fortress.

1986   *Old Testament Theology in a Canonical Context.* Philadelphia: Fortress.

Writings about Childs

Tucker, Gene M., David L. Petersen, and Robert R. Wilson (editors)

1988   *Canon, Theology, and Old Testament Interpretation: Essays in Honor of Brevard S. Childs.* Philadelphia: Fortress.

Brevard S. Childs's
Approach to Old Testament Theology

Excerpted with permission from Brevard S. Childs, *Old Testament Theology in a Canonical Context* (Philadelphia: Fortress, 1986), pp. 10–19.

A Canonical Approach to Old Testament Theology

⟦10⟧ The profile of the discipline of Old Testament theology which I am suggesting can perhaps be made more precise by briefly sketching its relationship both to Judaism and to biblical theology. I have emphasized that Old Testament theology is a Christian discipline which reflects on the scriptures held in common with the synagogue. One of the main reasons for the Christian use of the Hebrew text of the Old Testament rather than its Greek form lies in the theological concern to preserve this common textual bond between Jews and Christians. Historically, Christianity confronted first-century Judaism through the Greek form of the Jewish scriptures, and thus the New Testament is stamped indelibly by the Septuagint. Yet the theological issue of how Christians relate to the Jewish scriptures cannot be decided biblicistically by an appeal to New Testament practice, but must be addressed theologically. The debate transcends the historical moment of the first-century encounter, and turns on the church's ongoing relation to the authoritative scriptures which Israel treasured and continues to treasure in the Hebrew. A canonical approach takes the Hebrew scriptures seriously because of its confession that Israel remains the prime tradent of this witness. It remains an essential part of the church's theological reflection on the Old Testament to continue in dialogue with the synagogue which lives from the common biblical text, but often construes it in a very different manner. The goal of the dialogue is that both religious renderings be continually forced to react to the coercion of the common text which serves both to enrich and to challenge all interpretations.

The discipline of Old Testament theology also differs from biblical theology in several important ways. Biblical theology provides a disciplined reflection on the scriptures of both Old and New Testaments. Its emphasis differs because of the overriding problem of relating the witnesses of the two different Testaments. Moreover, because of its concern to interpret the entire Christian Bible theologically, it tends to be in dialogue more with the traditions of dogmatic theology than with the discrete problems which arise from the separate Testaments. However, the

324

theological approaches to the text of both Old Testament theology and biblical theology do not differ hermeneutically. Both are disciplines arising from within [[11]] Christian theology and both involve the application of descriptive and constructive tools in order to execute the task.

It is a basic tenet of the canonical approach that one reflects theologically on the text as it has been received and shaped. Yet the emphasis on the normative status of the canonical text is not a denial of the significance of the canonical process which formed the text. The frequently expressed contrast between a static canonical text and a 'dynamic' traditio-historical process badly misconstrues the issue. Similarly, to claim that attention to canon elevates one specific historical response to a dogmatic principle utterly fails to grasp the function of canon. Rather, the basic problem turns on the relationship between text and process. The final canonical literature reflects a long history of development in which the received tradition was selected, transmitted and shaped by hundreds of decisions. This process of construing its religious tradition involved a continual critical evaluation of historical options which were available to Israel and a transformation of its received tradition toward certain theological goals. That the final form of the biblical text has preserved much from the earlier stages of Israel's theological reflection is fully evident. However, the various elements have been so fused as to resist easy diachronic reconstructions which fracture the witness of the whole.

The controversy with the traditio-historical critics is not over the theological significance of a depth dimension of the tradition. Rather, the issue turns on whether or not features within the tradition which have been subordinated, modified or placed in the distant background of the text can be interpreted apart from the role assigned to them in the final form when attempting to write a theology of the Old Testament. For example, to seek to give theological autonomy to a reconstructed Yahwist source apart from its present canonical context is to disregard the crucial theological intention of the tradents of the tradition, and to isolate a text's meaning from its reception.

Even more controversial is the usual method of reconstructing an alleged traditio-historical trajectory which does not reflect actual layers within Israel's tradition, but is a critical construct lying outside Israel's faith. To draw an analogy, it is one thing to trace the different levels within the growth of the New Testament parables. It is quite another to reconstruct putative earlier levels apart from their reception and transmission within the community [[12]] of faith. The canonical approach to Old Testament theology is insistent that the critical process of theological reflection takes place from a stance within the circle of received tradition prescribed by the affirmation of the canon.

The canonical approach to Old Testament theology rejects a method which is unaware of its own time-conditioned quality and which is confident in its ability to stand outside, above and over against the received tradition in adjudicating the truth or lack of truth of the biblical material according to its own criteria. Of course, lying at the heart of the canonical proposal is the conviction that the divine revelation of the Old Testament cannot be abstracted or removed from the form of the witness which the historical community of Israel gave it. In the same way, there is no avenue open to the Jesus Christ who is worshipped by the Christian church apart from the testimony of his fully human apostles. To suggest that the task of theological reflection takes place from within a canonical context assumes not only a received tradition, but a faithful disposition by hearers who await the illumination of God's Spirit. This latter point has been developed so thoroughly by Calvin as to make further elaboration unnecessary (*Institutes*, I, ch. VII).

Then again, a canonical approach envisions the discipline of Old Testament theology as combining both descriptive and constructive features. It recognizes the descriptive task of correctly interpreting an ancient text which bears testimony to historic Israel's faith. Yet it also understands that the theological enterprise involves a construal by the modern interpreter, whose stance to the text affects its meaning. For this reason, Old Testament theology cannot be identified with describing an historical process in the past (*contra* Gese), but involves wrestling with the subject-matter to which scripture continues to bear testimony. In sum, Old Testament theology is a continuing enterprise in which each new generation must engage. An important implication of the approach is that the interpreter does not conceive of Old Testament theology as a closed, phenomenological deposit—Eichrodt spoke of a 'self-contained entity' (*Theology* I, 11)—whose understanding depends on the discovery of a single lost key. Much of the recent discussion of the so-called 'centre of the Old Testament' seems to have arisen from a concept of the discipline which views it simply as an historical enterprise (cf. Reventlow).

One of the important aspects within the shaping process of the [[13]] Old Testament is the manner by which different parts of the canon were increasingly interchanged to produce a new angle of vision on the tradition. The canonical process involved the shaping of the tradition not only into independent books, but also into larger canonical units, such as the Torah, Prophets and Writings. For example, law was seen from the perspective of wisdom; psalmody and prophecy were interrelated; and Israel's narrative traditions were sapientialized (cf. Sheppard). The canonical process thus built in a dimension of flexibility which encourages constantly fresh ways of actualizing the material.

There are some important implications to be drawn from this canonical process for the structuring of a modern Old Testament theology. This canonical structuring provides a warrant for applying a similar element of flexibility in its modern actualization which is consonant with its shape. In other words, a new dynamic issues from the collection which maintains a potential for a variety of new theological combinations. Even though historically Old Testament law was often of a different age and was transmitted by other tradents from much of the narrative tradition, a theology of the Old Testament according to the proposed canonical model seeks to exploit a theological interaction. Therefore, regardless of the original literary and historical relationship between the Decalogue and the narrative sections of the Pentateuch, a theological interchange is possible within its new canonical context which affords a mutual aid for interpretation. Of course, there are rules which control and govern the interaction which derive from the literature's structure, content, and intertextuality, but these can be best illustrated in practice. The recognition of this dimension of a canonical approach further sets it apart from the usual descriptive method which is bound to original historical sequence.

One of the hallmarks of the modern study of the Bible, which is one of the important legacies of the Enlightenment, is the recognition of the time-conditioned quality of both the form and the content of scripture. A pre-critical method which could feel free simply to translate every statement of the Bible into a principle of right doctrine is no longer possible. Of course, it is a caricature of the history of Christian theology to suggest that such a use of the Bible was universal in the pre-Enlightenment period. Augustine, Luther and Calvin—to name but a few—all worked with a far more sophisticated understanding of the Bible than the term 'pre-critical' [14] suggests. Nevertheless, it is still true that the issue of the Bible's time-conditioned quality became a major hermeneutical problem in the wake of the Enlightenment and the rise of the historical-critical method.

Modern Old Testament theologians have applied various hermeneutical approaches to the text in order to accommodate the problem. One sought critically to abstract the 'abiding truth' or 'elements of lasting value' from the literature. Or a history of moral progress was discerned which slowly sloughed off its primitive inheritance in order to reach its ethical goal, often found in the Sermon on the Mount. Finally, some mode of consciousness, egalitarian ideology, or elements of liberation were discovered and assigned a normative theological function. However, in spite of the tendentious nature of many of these proposals, it is significant to observe that a concern was always expressed to retain at least some understanding of biblical authority for the modern church, and to resist its complete relativity.

Summary of the way OT theology has tried to deal w/ the Bible's "time-conditioned quality."

hebrew text foundational to other versions which are interpretations of it → but problematic because there isn't a hebrew text

328

Brevard S. Childs

Child's proposal

The hermeneutic implied in a canonical understanding of the Old Testament moves in a strikingly different direction in seeking its resolution to the problem. The emphasis on scripture as canon focuses its attention on the process by which divine truth acquired its authoritative form as it was received and transmitted by a community of faith. Accordingly, there is no biblical revelation apart from that which bears Israel's imprint. All of scripture is time-conditioned because the whole Old Testament has been conditioned by an historical people. There is no pure doctrine or uncontaminated piety. Any attempt to abstract elements from its present form by which, as it were, to distinguish the kernel from its husk, or inauthentic existence from authentic expression, runs directly in the face of the canon's function.

but isn't the canon itself conditioned?

Moreover, to take seriously a canonical approach is also to recognize the time-conditioned quality of the modern, post-Enlightenment Christian whose context is just as historically moored as any of his predecessors. One of the disastrous legacies of the Enlightenment was the new confidence of standing outside the stream of time and with clear rationality being able to distinguish truth from error, light from darkness.

In conscious opposition to this legacy of the Enlightenment, the canonical approach seeks to approach the problem with a different understanding of how the Bible functions as a vehicle of God's ⟦15⟧ truth. By accepting the scriptures as normative for the obedient life of the church, the Old Testament theologian takes his stance within the circle of tradition, and thus identifies himself with Israel as the community of faith. Moreover, he shares in that hermeneutical process of which the canon is a testimony, as the people of God struggled to discern the will of God in all its historical particularity. Its shaping of the biblical tradition indicated how it sought to appropriate the tradition as a faithful response to God's word. In an analogous context of a received witness, the modern biblical theologian takes his stance within the testimony of Israel and struggles to discern the will of God. Fully aware of his own frailty, he awaits in anticipation a fresh illumination through God's Spirit, for whom the Bible's frailty is no barrier. Although such understanding derives ultimately from the illumination of the Spirit, this divine activity functions through the scriptures of the church; that is to say, completely within the time-conditioned form of the tradition. There is no one hermeneutical key for unlocking the biblical message, but the canon provides the arena in which the struggle for understanding takes place.

Canonical Approach and the Modern Debate

Space is too limited for a lengthy discussion with many of the classic issues which currently agitate the field. However, I would like briefly to suggest ways in which a canonical approach seeks to overcome some of the major problems at present under debate (cf. Reventlow).

(*a*) In respect to the disagreement between Eichrodt and von Rad, among others, as to whether an Old Testament theology should be organized 'systematically' or 'traditio-historically', I suggest that both of these alternatives arise from a view of a closed body of material which is to be analysed descriptively. Both writers have worked hard to discover inner-biblical categories, which is an effort not to be disparaged. Nevertheless, when Old Testament theology is viewed in its canonical context as a continuing interpretative activity by that community of faith which treasures its scriptures as authoritative, the issue of organization is sharply relativized. At times the shaping process introduced systematic features; at times it structured the material historically. However, even more significant, there are innumerable other options within the ⟦16⟧ theological activity of interpreting scripture which are available for grappling with the material. The real issue lies in the quality of the construal and the illumination it brings to the text.

(*b*) A canonical approach once again attempts to overcome the sharp polarity in the debate whether the object of an Old Testament theology is a faith-construal of history (*Geschichte*), according to von Rad, or based on a reconstructed scientific history (*Historie*), according to Hesse and others. It reckons with the fact that Israel bore witness to its encounter with God in actual time and space, and yet registered its testimony in a text through a complex multilayered manner which far transcends the categories of ordinary historical discourse. The canonical approach views history from the perspective of Israel's faith-construal, and in this respect sides with von Rad. However, it differs in not being concerned to assign theological value to a traditio-historical trajectory which has been detached from the canonical form of the text. To put the issue in another way, the canonical approach seeks to follow the biblical text in its theological use of historical referentiality rather than to construct a contrast between *Geschichte* and *Historie* at the outset. At times, the nature of an Old Testament passage has been so construed as to register little which is accessible to objective historical scrutiny. At other times, an event which is grounded in common historical perception, such as the destruction of Jerusalem in 587 B.C., is of central importance for the theological task. In sum, although different dimensions of history are freely recognized, by focusing on Israel's historical role as the bearer of the traditions of faith, these two aspects of Israel's experience are held together in a subtle balance within the shape of the canon, and should not be threatened by some overarching theory of history.

(*c*) Finally, in respect to the position of Pannenberg which has sought to identify history with revelation, the canonical approach looks with suspicion on any view of history as a bearer of theological value which is divorced from the concrete reality of historical Israel. Far more is at stake here than simply making an academic point. Rather, scripture serves as a continuing medium through which the saving events of Israel's history are appropriated by each new generation of faith. Thus God's activity of self-disclosure is continually being extended into human time and space, which lies at the heart of the debate over the nature of revelation through scripture. ⟦17⟧

The Importance of Old Testament Theology

Lastly, a word is in order to justify the importance of the discipline of Old Testament theology even when it is conceived of as a modest and restricted enterprise within the larger field of biblical theology.

(*a*) First, in terms of strategy, to focus solely on the Old Testament in theological reflection allows one to deal with the subject in much more detail and depth than if one sought to treat the entire Christian canon at once. It seems wise at some point to focus primary attention on the Old Testament before coming to grips with the sheer mass of material and the overwhelming complexity of issues which arise when the New Testament is also included.

(*b*) Attention to the Old Testament within a theological discipline provides a major check against the widespread modern practice of treating it solely from a philological, historical or literary perspective. The inability of most systematic theologians to make much sense of the Old Testament stems in part from the failure of the biblical specialists to render it in such a way which is not theologically mute.

(*c*) It is a major function of Old Testament theology to treat the Old Testament in such a manner as to guard it from being used simply as a foil for the New Testament. Rather, it is theologically important to understand the Old Testament's witness in its own right in regard to its coherence, variety and unresolved tensions.

(*d*) Finally, theological reflection on the Old Testament makes possible a more correct hearing of the New Testament by clarifying the effect of the Hebrew scriptures on the Jewish people from whom Jesus stemmed, to whom he preached, and from whom the early church was formed. As the history of exegesis eloquently demonstrates, a Christian church without the Old Testament is in constant danger of turning the faith into various forms of gnostic, mystic, or romantic speculation.

Bibliography

Eichrodt, W. *Theology of the Old Testament* (2 vols.; ET: London/Philadelphia 1961–1967).
Hesse, F. *Das Alte Testament als Buch der Kirche* (Gütersloh 1966).
Pannenberg, W. *Revelation as History* (ET: New York 1968/London 1969).
von Rad, G. *Old Testament Theology* (2 vols.; ET: Edinburgh/New York 1962–1965).
Reventlow, H. Graf. *Problems of Old Testament Theology in the Twentieth Century* (ET: London/Philadelphia 1985).
Sheppard, G. T. "Hearing the Voice of the Same God through Historically Dissimilar Traditions," *Interp* 36 (1982) 21–33.

Synopsis of Childs's *Old Testament Theology in a Canonical Context* (1986)

Brevard S. Childs
On a Theological Understanding
of Law and Priesthood

Excerpted with permission from Brevard S. Childs, *Old Testament Theology in a Canonical Context* (Philadelphia: Fortress, 1986), pp. 51–57, 145–54.

The Law of God

The Knowledge and Will of God

[[51]] To know God is to know his will. In the Old Testament to know God is not a mystical experience or merely an inter-personal relationship. Nor is it a feeling of spirituality. Rather, the knowledge of God is defined throughout as obedience to his will which has a content. When God reveals himself in his name, 'I am Yahweh', he also reveals his will (Exod 20:2ff.). Just as the knowledge of God is based on his disclosure, so also his will is made known simultaneously. Israel does not first know God, and then later discover what God wants. Knowledge of his person and will are identical, and both are grounded in his self-revelation. To lack knowledge of God is described as disobeying his will and therefore it evokes his anger.

Isaiah speaks of a disobedient people dying for lack of knowledge (5:13), and Hosea describes the consequences of the failure of knowledge as lawlessness (4:1). The latter condemns a people who have broken the covenant, transgressed the Law, and yet cry, 'My God, we, Israel, know thee' (8:2). Conversely, God is present and known where the oppressed are freed, and the naked are covered (Isa 58:6ff.).

The Divine Imperative

God has expressed his will from the beginning: 'The Lord God commanded the man saying. "You may freely eat of every tree of the garden; but of the tree of the knowledge of good and evil, you shall not eat . . . "' (Gen 2:16). For the writer of Genesis 2, to be human consists in living in freedom, within a community, and under the divine imperative. Again, God commanded Abraham, [[52]] saying, 'Go from your country and your kindred . . . to the land that I will show you' (Gen 12:1). Or to Jacob, 'Return to your country, and to your kindred and I will do you good' (Gen 32:9). God also charged Moses, 'Come, I send you to Pharaoh that you may bring forth my people . . . out of Egypt' (Exod 3:10). When Moses then resisted the command, God was willing even to negotiate for his plan until the real grounds for Moses' resistance emerged as unbelief. In sum, God appears throughout the Old Testament as a person with a will which he freely communicates.

Conversely, it is a divine judgment of the severest sort when the word of God becomes 'rare' in the land (1 Sam 3:1). Amos pictures the judgment of God:

> not a famine of bread, nor a thirst for water,
> but of hearing the words of the Lord.
> They shall wander from sea to sea,
>   and from north to east;
> They shall run to and fro to seek the word of the Lord
>   but they shall not find it (8:11–12).

Saul despairs of his life because 'God has turned away from me and answers me no more' (1 Sam 28:15). It is a deep biblical conviction that when God withdraws his presence, man does not know what to do!

God's Will and Its Realization

The creation account of Genesis 1 bears clearest witness that there is no hiatus between the will of God and his action. When God said 'let it be', it was. It therefore belongs to the divine attribute of grace when there is a temporal distinction between prophecy and fulfilment. God delays his decision of judgment in order to give his people every chance for repentance.

One of the truly remarkable chapters on this topic consists of a dialogue between God and Abraham before the destruction of Sodom (Gen 18:22ff.). God takes Abraham into his confidence and reveals to him his decision to destroy Sodom because of its great evil. Then God allows Abraham to persuade him to refrain from his judgment for the sake of ten righteous inhabitants. In the course of the dialogue, Abraham implies a distinction between God's will and his action: 'Shall not the judge of all the earth do right?' [53] However, the tension is only an apparent one— it serves as a literary device in the chapter—and is resolved by God's matching his will for justice with his acts of mercy by accepting Abraham's compromise.

In a similar vein, the Hebrew idiom of God's 'repenting of his resolve' retains the integrity of the divine will, but allows for decision and flexibility in relation to a genuine human history (cf. Jeremias).

The Canonical Shape of the Sinai Witness

The fullest and most direct expression of the will of God in the Old Testament is found in the revelation of the Law at Sinai. In a real sense the book of Genesis is its prologue and the book of Deuteronomy its epilogue, but the heart of the Pentateuch lies in the tradition of Sinai contained in the middle books of Exodus, Leviticus and Numbers.

The usual procedure of critical commentaries and Old Testament theologies is to begin any discussion of the theology of the Law by rehearsing the many literary problems within this complex of tradition which stretches from Exodus 19 to Numbers 10. The various discrete units, such as the Decalogue, Covenant Code, Holiness Code, and Priestly legislation, are distinguished and separately evaluated. However, in spite of much evidence that these chapters have indeed undergone a complex history of development, in my opinion it is methodologically a mistake to make the writing of an Old Testament theology directly dependent on its historical reconstruction. Rather, the approach being proposed is to describe the theology of the Old Testament according to the intertextuality of its canonical shaping and to seek to understand how this corpus of material was ordered and rendered within the context of scripture. To the extent that a depth dimension illuminates the canonical text, and is not viewed as a rival construal, its use can be often a great help.

Certain broad interpretative lines become immediately apparent. The revelation of Sinai (Exodus 19) is integrally connected with the deliverance from Egypt. The giving of the Law (Exodus 20ff.) and the sealing of the covenant (Exodus 24) form the climax of the formation of the people of God (19:4–6). Moreover, the Decalogue has been assigned a special place within the Old Testament tradition, which is apparent by its form, terminology and position within the narrative. [[54]] The commandments of the Decalogue are tied closely to the divine revelation at Sinai, and bear witness to a direct, unmediated communication from Yahweh himself: 'God spoke all these words, saying. . . . '

The Decalogue is distinguished from most other legal corpora by having little or no reference to a specific historical period of Israel's history, or to a particular institution such as a central sanctuary. In its canonical role the Decalogue forms a theological summary of the entire Sinai tradition. All the detailed legislation which follows is therefore subordinated to and interpreted by the heart of the Law found in the Ten Commandments. The Book of the Covenant which follows in Exod 20:21ff. has been assigned a role as additional commandments delivered through the mediation of Moses when the people fled in terror from the divine theophany (20:18ff.). That all this legislation was seen in the context of establishing a covenant is made clear from ch. 24.

The laws of the book of Leviticus, regardless of their prehistory, have been firmly tied to the Sinai events. This connection is made explicit in Leviticus 8–9, which forms the literary continuation of Exodus 29, namely, the inauguration of Aaron and his sons. Moreover, the ceremony unfolds according to the exact execution of the will of God, 'as Yahweh commanded Moses' (8:9, 13, 17, 21, 29, etc.). The same intention to bind the laws of Leviticus to Sinai is again made explicit in the concluding subscription to the laws of sacrifice (7:37–38). The editor of Leviticus has structured the material in order to show that the sacrificial system which commenced with the inauguration of Aaron in chs. 8–9 stemmed from a divine revelation at Sinai through Moses (7:38). The sacrifices which Aaron initiated did not derive from mere custom, but in direct compliance with the divine will. Aaron's inauguration became an instantiation of obedience and response in proper worship whereas Nadab and Abihu illustrated judgment on unholy malpractice (Lev 10:1ff.).

The canonical effect of structuring the book of Leviticus in such a way as to connect all the material directly to the revelation at Sinai is of crucial importance in understanding its role as authoritative scripture for Israel. The laws of Leviticus which stemmed originally from very different periods, and which reflected remarkably different sociological contexts, are subordinated to the one overarching theological construct, namely, the divine will made known to Moses at Sinai for every successive generation. This hermeneutical move is [[55]] not to be characterized as simply a dehistoricizing of the tradition. Rather, in the book of Leviticus one historical moment in Israel's life has become the norm by means of which all subsequent history of the nation is measured. If a law functions authoritatively for Israel, it must be from Sinai. Conversely, if it is from Sinai, it must be authoritative. Clearly a theological understanding of Sinai is at work in the canonical process which is different in kind from a modern reconstruction of the historical origins of Israel's laws.

Finally, crucial to any understanding of the theological significance of the Sinai material is a correct analysis of the canonical role assigned to the book of Deuteronomy. Once again the canonical approach does not deny that forces from Deuteronomy's long growth have left an imprint on the material; however, the decisive exegetical issue lies in determining how these earlier levels function within the context of a canonical corpus.

The first chapter of Deuteronomy makes it immediately clear that the purpose of Moses' addressing the people is to 'explain the Torah' (v. 5). To the new generation who was about to cross into the land, Moses interprets the Sinai covenant. He does not offer a new law, but by means of a rehearsal of the history of Israel since Sinai, seeks to inculcate obedience to the divine law which had once and for all constituted the nation (5:22). Moses applies the divine law to the new situation in which the people would shortly enter. It is, therefore, built into the canonical function of Deuteronomy that a new application of old tradition is being offered. The

[handwritten marginal note at top: So the canon as a whole demonstrates hermeneutical principles: it shows as well as a product, it also normative. Interpretive principles as well as the process is ... & the ...]

new interpretation seeks to actualize the traditions of the past for the new generation in such a way as to evoke a response to the divine will in a fresh commitment to the covenant.

The setting forth of the Law is now placed within the context of the new, hitherto unexperienced situation of Israel occasioned by the entrance into the land (18:9; 19:1ff.). Israel is not to continue as before (12:8), but is given a new charter by Moses. This implies that the very different character of the laws of Deuteronomy has been recognized within the canonical process and the change has been accommodated within the framework of the new historical condition of the conquest (cf. 14:24ff.). The effect of the ordering of the laws within chs. 12–26 is to legitimate the principle of change within the Law, and at the same time to subordinate all the various forces at work within the historical development to one theological category. This is to say that the process of canonical ordering [[56]] worked into the final form of the book a great variety of different laws, but virtually disregarded the specific socio-political forces which produced the new forms of the Law.

The theological implications of the canonical role of Deuteronomy for understanding the Sinai traditions are fundamental. Moses is portrayed as explaining the divine will to a new generation which had not itself experienced the formative events of its religious history. Deuteronomy, therefore, serves as an authoritative commentary on how future generations are to approach the Law and how it functions as a guide for its interpretation. Thus, God's covenant is not tied to past history, but is still offered to all Israel of every generation. Again, the promise of God still lies in the future and Israel can only anticipate in faith the possession of the heritage. Again, Deuteronomy teaches that the Law demands a response of single-hearted commitment. The Deuteronomic writer strives to inculcate the Law into the will of the people. The Law of God remains a dynamic imperative which evokes an active choice to share in the living traditions of God's people. Finally, the ability of Deuteronomy to summarize the Law in terms of loving God with heart, soul and mind is a major check against all forms of legalism. According to Deuteronomy, the whole Mosaic law testifies to the living will of God whose eternal purpose for the life of his people provides the only grounds for life and salvation.

Theological Implications of the Law

(*a*) In spite of the variety and diversity of the various Old Testament laws, there is a theological coherence to the material as expressing the one will of God to his covenant people. Within the context of the historical covenant, the commandments served different functions in transforming historical Israel into the people of God. One can, therefore, rightly speak of the Law of God, comprising the first part of the Hebrew canon and constituting the covenant relationship.

(*b*) The Law contains both promise and threat. It calls forth decisions which result in either life or death. Commandments which serve the faithful as guides to life similarly work death to the disobedient. The dual side of the Law is highlighted throughout the Pentateuch, both in the ceremony which sealed the covenant (Exodus 24) and in the ritual of blessing and cursing. The execution of [[57]] judgment announced by the prophets was contained within the Law itself from the beginning.

(*c*) The Law of God was a gift of God which was instituted for the joy and edification of the covenant people. It was not given as a burden, but as a highest treasure and a clear sign of divine favour. The profoundest testimony to the original intent of the Law is found in Psalm 119:

> How love I thy law,
> It is my meditation all the day . . .
> I will never forget thy precepts,
> for by them thou hast given me life (vv. 97, 93).

(*d*) The clearest sign of the brokenness of the covenant and of the alienation of Israel from God emerged when his Law became a burden and a means of destroying the nation. This terrifying point was reached in Ezekiel, when the prophet testified that, 'God gave them statutes that were not good and ordinances by which they could not have life . . . I (Yahweh) defiled them through their very gift in making them offer by fire their firstborn that I might destroy them' (20.25f.). However, for the full implications of this understanding of the Law, one has to await the testimony of the apostle Paul.

Bibliography

Childs, B. S. *Exodus* (London/Philadelphia 1974) 385–496.

Clements, R. E. "The Old Testament as Law," in *Old Testament Theology: A Fresh Approach* (London 1978) 104–30.

Eichrodt, W. *Theology of the Old Testament* (ET: London/Philadelphia 1961), 1:70–97.

Ellul, J. *The Theological Foundation of Law* (ET: New York 1960).

Gese, H. "The Law," in *Essays on Biblical Theology* (ET: Minneapolis 1981) 60–92.

Jeremias, Jörg. *Die Reue Gottes* (BSt 65; Neukirchen-Vluyn 1975).

Mendenhall, G. E. *Law and Covenant in Israel and the Ancient Near East* (Pittsburgh 1955).

Noth, M. *The Laws in the Pentateuch and Other Studies* (ET: Edinburgh/Toronto 1966; reissued London 1984).

von Rad, G. "The Law," in *Old Testament Theology* (ET: Edinburgh/New York 1965), 2:388–409.

Schechter, S. *Some Aspects of Rabbinic Theology* (New York 1923) 116–60.

Urbach, E. E. *The Sages: Their Concepts and Beliefs* (ET: Jerusalem 1975), 1:286–314.

Zimmerli, W. "The Theological Relevance of the Law," in *The Law and the Prophets* (ET: Oxford 1965/London 1967) 46–60.

· ·

The Theological Role of Priesthood

[[145]] Few Old Testament problems are as complex as that of the priesthood. There is much continuing scholarly debate, but few lines of broad consensus have been established. I shall try to avoid excessive detail, and seek rather to illustrate the problem of reflecting theologically on the subject.

The Nature of the Critical Problem

There is no more powerful way of focusing on the problem than to confront Wellhausen's brilliant chapter on 'Priests and Levites' (*Prolegomena*, 121ff.), which poses the critical issues with extraordinary sharpness. According to Wellhausen, the Old Testament portrayal of the priests and Levites in its canonical—that is, its traditional—form is completely incomprehensible. In order to make any sense of the biblical text, it is necessary to reconstruct the record according to its genuine historical development, which has been badly misconstrued.

What, then, is the difficulty of understanding the office of priesthood in the Old Testament? According to the present biblical order the cult was established by Moses at Sinai. Exodus 28 describes the selection of Aaron and his sons, and their consecration to an eternal priesthood (Leviticus 8–10). Essential to the Mosaic cult is the sharp distinction between priests and Levites. The priest in the line of Aaron performed the essential cultic rites, whereas the Levites were viewed as minor cultic personnel in charge of the external maintenance of the tabernacle. The book of Numbers continues the same distinctions for Israel on the march.

The first major friction arises in the book of Deuteronomy because no distinction appears between priests and Levites; rather, the term [[146]] 'Levitical priest' is now used. Moreover, every Levite can function as a priest, although various priestly duties are recognized. According to Wellhausen, the problems grow even more intense when one reaches the early historical books. In Judges and Samuel all signs of a professional clergy of Aaronites disappear. Eli, the chief priest, is from the tribe of Ephraim, and there is only a loose description of the role of Levites (Judges 19).

Then again, there are enormous tensions surrounding David's cultic role. The portrayal of Israel's cult in Samuel/Kings diverges greatly from that of Chronicles, which again carefully separates priests and Levites. Although the reader gets the impression that something very important happened with Josiah's reform (2 Kings 23), only hints are given of the significance of the removal of the non-Jerusalemite priests from the high places. Finally, Ezekiel 44 offers a legitimation for Zadok's predominant role, but the effect is to defend a distinction which Ezekiel regards as new, though it has already been assumed as normative in the books of Leviticus and Numbers.

Wellhausen next offers his brilliant theory by which to explain the confusion. The basic problem of interpretation arises from a false analysis of the biblical literature. The Priestly material of Exodus 25–40, Leviticus and Numbers is not Mosaic in age, but rather post-exilic. Similarly, the book of Deuteronomy is not Mosaic, but stems from the period of the late monarchy. Moreover, in addition to this erroneous dating, the traditional interpretation failed to see that the key to the historical development of the priesthood was to be found in the centralization under Josiah in 621 B.C., which effected a fundamental change in the character of the priesthood.

However, lest anyone is tempted to dismiss Wellhausen's position as extreme and no longer to be taken seriously, its similarity to von Rad's formulation is to be noted:

> . . . the rigid demarcation of the priests from the Levites which we find everywhere in P, and without which its whole theological sacral picture is incomprehensible, was set in motion by an event which only took place in the late monarchical period, namely Josiah's centralization of the cult (I, 249).

Wellhausen next sets out to reconstruct the true history of the development of Israel's priesthood in his three classic stages. Early Israel had no professional classes, which explains why judges and [[147]] kings sacrificed freely. The second stage occurred with the reform of Josiah, who centralized Israel's worship by disenfranchizing the non-Jerusalemite priesthood. The policy, which was politically motivated by the Aaronite priesthood of Jerusalem, succeeded in subordinating the rival priestly clans, namely, the Levites, to the line of Zadok. Both Ezekiel 44 and the conflict stories in the Pentateuch, such as Numbers 16, reflect this struggle for hegemony. The final stage, which is found in the post-exilic Priestly code and in Chronicles, occurred when the one line of the priestly line of Zadok established its complete control of the priesthood and the Levites were demoted to hierodules.

How should one react to Wellhausen's massive challenge to the traditional position? Soon after the first shock from his critical assessment of the priesthood, a flood of articles and books appeared which sought to buttress the traditional view (cf. e.g. Curtiss). Significantly, these conservative responses shared the same historically referential reading of the Old Testament as the critical, but they differed in trying to identify the canonical presentation with the actual historical development of the Israelite priesthood. By and large, the conservative rejoinders were deemed unsuccessful by the scholarly guild. However, more significant was the hermeneutical effect of the ensuing debate. The conservatives wanted to reconstruct a less radical picture than Wellhausen's, but in the end they based their exegesis on a reconstruction of Israelite history which also differed from the biblical presentation.

During the last hundred years since Wellhausen posited his brilliant reconstruction there have been many efforts to modify and correct it. Certainly one of the most impressive of the recent attempts has been that of Frank M. Cross. He has argued in detail that all the various tensions which were pointed out by Wellhausen can be resolved by positing an ancient and prolonged struggle between two priestly houses. On the one hand, there was the Mushite (Mosaic) priesthood which flourished at the sanctuaries of Dan and Shiloh along with local shrines in the Negeb. On the other hand, there was the opposing Aaronite priesthood centred in Bethel and in Jerusalem. Cross opposes Wellhausen's reconstruction at several crucial places, but especially he is successful in showing the ancient roots of the priesthood extending far back into the pre-monarchial period. However, the major point to be made is that hermeneutically Cross's historical reconstruction is equally as radical as Wellhausen's [[148]] in rejecting the traditional view and in hypothesizing a true historical development which only a modern critical historian could recover. Cross fully agrees with Wellhausen that the present form of the canon is hopelessly confused and must be thoroughly reworked in order to be properly interpreted.

In the light of the great discrepancies between the traditional view of the priesthood and the various critical reconstructions, one is at first tempted to argue that there is no theological relationship between the actual, historical development of the priesthood and the biblical portrayal. These are two separate realms which function fully independently of each other. One can accept either Wellhausen's or Cross's historical reconstruction and then proceed to describe a theological interpretation based on the Old Testament canon as a separate enterprise without any historical referent.

However, in my opinion, there are major theological and hermeneutical difficulties with such an approach. If Wellhausen or Cross were right that the present form of the Old Testament priesthood reflects a completely artificial construct, and that the real forces determining the priestly institution were internal political struggles for power, then one could no longer meaningfully speak of a canonical shape. It would be virtually meaningless to focus on the religious use of authoritative traditions in order to form a theological witness if the forces at work were really of a radically different sort. I do not wish to oversimplify the canonical process. No human action is without ambiguity and no religious force is entirely isolated from so-called secular influences. However, it runs directly in the face of a canonical understanding to assume that the present form of the text is merely a cover for the real political forces which lie behind it, or to posit that the later theological use transformed the tradition into something different in kind from the original secular function. To use a crude analogy: one cannot take Richard Nixon's Whitehouse tapes and transform them into literature akin to Augustine's Confessions!

To summarize up to this point, although I have been highly critical of a historical referential reading of the Old Testament in the preceding chapters, the reverse construal is just as unsatisfactory, namely to lay claim to a completely non-historical reading of the Bible. To identify the canonical approach with structuralism, as J. Barton suggests (cf. ch. 1), is very far from the truth. The main hermeneutical point to stress is that the canon makes its theological [[149]] witness in numerous ways in relation to historical referentiality. At times it forms a very loose connection, whereas at other times a genuinely historical component belongs to the heart of the witness. It is fully inadequate to restrict the nature of the Old Testament's theological witness either by demanding absolute historical coherence or by positing in principle no relationship whatever. The attention to the text's canonical shape arises precisely from the concern to discern how the biblical material was construed in faith within the world of common human experience.

Fortunately, some recent research on Old Testament priesthood by modern scholars has opened up other options, so that one does not simply have to choose between Wellhausen and a pre-critical traditional reading. A good illustration is the monograph of Gunneweg, *Leviten und Priester*. Space is too limited to offer a detailed review of his criticisms of Wellhausen's reconstruction. However, he makes the rather convincing case that the distinction between priests and Levites is not just a post-exilic construct to legitimate an ideology, but reflects ancient, pre-exilic tradition which was subsequently refined and schematized. Or again, he argues that Deuteronomy's apparent identification of priest and Levite is placed in a very different light when seen as a programmatic claim of the writer for the purity of worship in which the Levitican zeal for the law subsumed the entire institution under a religious ideal. Finally, Gunneweg does much to relativize the close linkage of Josiah's reform with the downgrading of the Levites, and he outlines a very different historical process from that of Wellhausen.

I do not wish to be misunderstood. I am not saying that one can now accept Gunneweg's reconstruction instead of Wellhausen's or Cross's and build an Old Testament theology on top of it. I am still opposed to any direct historical referential reading as a substitute for the canonical witness. Nevertheless, I am concerned to show that a reconstruction which is totally alien to the canonical construal can have a negative effect in preventing a theological understanding by robbing the text of its freedom.

Towards a Canonical Construal of the Priesthood

The theological task is to try to sketch a theological understanding of the office of priesthood which does justice to the peculiar shape of the literature. According to the clear witness of the Pentateuch, the [[150]] worship of Israel was established by God at Sinai and formed an integral part of the divine will along with the giving of the Law. The goal of the exodus from Egypt was to establish a holy nation, a kingdom of priests (Exod 19:6). Moses is viewed as the founder of the priestly order who was faithful when tested (Exod 33:7–11; Lev 8:1ff.; Deut 33:8). The role of the priest was not merely to sacrifice, but to instruct the people in the ways of God. In Exodus 24 Moses ascended Mt. Sinai to receive directions regarding the building of the tabernacle and the institution of the priesthood. Exodus 28 speaks of the preparation of Aaron's consecration which was then executed in Leviticus 8–10. Leviticus summarizes the great task of the priesthood: 'You are to distinguish between the holy and the common, and between the unclean and the clean, and you are to teach the people of Israel all the statutes which Yahweh has spoken to them by Moses' (Lev 10:10–11; cf. Ezek 44:23). Moreover, a clear distinction was made between priests and Levites, the latter being appointed to minister over the tabernacle and the furnishings (Num 1:47ff.).

However, the Levites are integrally connected with another basic witness in the Pentateuch. In Exodus 32 Aaron the priest led the people astray into idolatry. The threat of false worship was present even at Sinai. Both Exodus 32 and Deuteronomy 10 derive the special role of the Levites from their zeal for Yahweh. Deuteronomy 10 elaborates on their distinction of being separated with a special inheritance: 'The Lord set apart the tribe of Levi to carry the ark of the covenant . . . to stand before the Lord to minister to him and to bless his name . . . ' (v. 8). Similarly, Deut 33:8f. stresses their role as guardians and keepers of the covenant. Throughout the rest of Deuteronomy they are always mentioned along with the poor and the landless of Israel, who must be invited to Israel's festivals in order rightly to share in the joy of God's blessing (12:19ff.; 18:6ff.).

→ leads to a typological, almost allegorical
reading of scripture → or is it just "application"?
see also Van Rad

Canon   343

Other prime examples of the threat to Israel's proper worship are represented in the Pentateuch by the narrative of Nadab and Abihu, the sons of Aaron, who offered 'unholy fire' (Lev 10:1–3), and by the revolt of Korah, who was a Levite (Num 16:1ff.), but who rebelled against Moses in an effort to gain priestly privilege for himself. It is very likely that both Exodus 32 and Numbers 16 reflect some earlier stages within the tradition, and show evident signs of struggles within the priesthood between competing clans. However, the canonical process had largely blurred these original contours in ⟦151⟧ order to make the stories now function as representatives of false claims of priesthood. Conversely, the special role of the Levites as zealous adherents of the faith has been anchored literally to one particular historical moment in the Mosaic period according to which the office was defined.

Then again, the period of the judges has been interpreted canonically as one of decline and disobedience. The results of lawlessness are illustrated by reference to the abuses of the cult, particularly in the story of Micah's idols and the role of the wandering Levite (Judg 17:1ff.). The loss of the ark to the Philistines (1 Sam 4:1ff.) is also construed to the same effect. This period which Wellhausen interpreted as reflecting historically the early stages within Israel without an organized priesthood is used canonically to illustrate a retrogression from the ideal of Moses. Similarly, the priesthood of Eli and his wicked sons (1 Sam 2:2ff.) receive the divine judgment. Significantly, this theological use of the material has left enough tensions within the various stories to demonstrate that one cannot simply identify the canonical construal with the historical development of the cult within Israel, as traditionalists have often attempted.

Again, the historical development of the priesthood under David and Solomon remains quite obscure. That there was a political struggle is clear from the story of Abiathar's involvement in the succession story and his replacement by Zadok (1 Kgs 2:26). The canonical construal interprets the establishment of Zadok typologically as a representative of a righteous priesthood and Abiathar's rejection as the fulfilment of the prophetic word against Eli. Nowhere is there a hint that Zadok stemmed from a Canaanite priestly clan of pre-Davidic Jerusalem, as has occasionally been suggested.

The picture in Chronicles of the Levites is again idealized to represent the struggle for a purified, zealous priesthood against various forms of corruption. Recent critical research on the book of Chronicles has rightly rejected the extreme theories of de Wette and Wellhausen which spoke largely in terms of fabrication. Rather, the Chronicler has systematized and expanded the role of the Levites to represent a programme which conforms theologically to the laws of Leviticus and Numbers.

Within the canonical context of 2 Kings the Josianic reform has been assigned a much more modest role than that afforded it by ⟦152⟧ critical scholarship. In both Kings and Chronicles it has been set in continuity with the earlier reform of Hezekiah as a restoration of the legitimate and purified worship of God found in Deuteronomy. It is not construed as a political innovation. However, 2 Kgs 23:9 does record that the priests of the high places did not come to Jerusalem to minister, but remained in their villages. Significantly, the canonical construal which did not tie this demoting of the local priests with the Levites, as suggested by Wellhausen and many others, has been vigorously defended as historically accurate by Gunneweg. It is also clear that the biblical account has passed over the many serious social and political effects of the purification of worship through centralization which critical historians have often been able to discern.

Ezekiel 44 is another highly significant passage in evaluating the role of the priesthood, but again it is difficult to recover the exact historical circumstances surrounding the controversy. The singling out of Zadok is set against the vague historical background of the pre-exilic Levites who went after idols, led Israel astray, and therefore must bear their punishment. The canonical interpretation is consistent in seeing the history as a corruption of the revealed will of God for the priesthood and not as an innovation. The close parallels between Ezekiel and the priestly writings of Leviticus serve canonically to support the interpretation that God's purpose was one of the restoration of pure worship.

In general, the same pattern of a return to the original Mosaic ideal is continued in the books of Ezra and Nehemiah. Of course, there is recognition of the changing historical situation which the exile produced. Thus Ezra discovers that not enough Levites had returned from Babylon to support the needed ecclesiastical staff (Ezra 8:20). However, basically the new arrangements of the priests and Levites for the service of God in Jerusalem were made to conform to what 'is written in the book of Moses' (Ezra 6:18). The same contrast between the faithful and disobedient priest is voiced throughout the books of Ezra and Nehemiah (Ezra 10:5; Neh 11:10).

Summary of the Theology of Priesthood

Let me attempt briefly to summarize the theological implications of the canonical construal of the priesthood within the Old Testament. [153]

(*a*) The Old Testament offers a theological interpretation of the priesthood which derives from its own particular use of the tradition within the canonical process. The actual historical development of the priesthood is not afforded canonical status, but left in the background of the text as prehistory. Rather, the post-exilic form of the Israelite priesthood has been made normative. The canonical shape reflects a variety of moves by which to render its witness, such as schematizing, idealizing and typologizing the tradition. For this reason an interpretation which is directly dependent on a historically referential reading is theologically inadequate. It reorders the text diachronically and in so doing misses the Old Testament's unique message. Conversely, an interpretation which cuts all connections with Israel's peculiar history is unable to do justice to the canon's interpretation, which has incorporated crucial elements of the history into its testimony.

(*b*) The role of the priest is viewed primarily as the guardian of the will of God to separate the clean and the unclean, the pure and the sacred. A faithful priesthood was constitutive of an obedient, worshipping people of God from the beginning and was grounded in the theophany at Sinai. Especially the role of the Levites emphasized the unity of the will of God for the proper forms of worship, the distortion of which remains a constant threat.

(*c*) The canonical construal saw fit to blur and omit many of the historical features of the priestly institutions. Its main stress lay on contrasting the ideal, obedient forms of the priesthood with the recurring inroads of corruption (golden calf, Korah, Baal-Peor, Bethel). In my judgment, the challenge of Old Testament exegesis is not to rest content with refocusing the biblical text in order to reconstruct its prehistory. Rather, its theological responsibility lies in following with precision the direction which is given by the shaping of the biblical text itself, and to relate one's modern theological reflection to the unique dynamic which arises from the Bible's intertextuality.

Bibliography

Cody, A. *A History of Old Testament Priesthood* (AnBib 35; Rome 1969).
Cross, F. M. *Canaanite Myth and Hebrew Epic* (Cambridge, Mass./London 1973) 195–215.
Curtiss, S. I. *The Levitical Priests* (Edinburgh 1877).
Greenberg, M. "A New Approach to the History of the Israelite Priesthood," *JAOS* 70 (1950) 41–47.
Gunneweg, A. H. J. *Leviten und Priester* (FRLANT 89; Göttingen 1965).
Haran, M. *Temple and Temple-Service in Ancient Israel* (Oxford 1978).
Kraus, H.-J. *Worship in Israel: A Cultic History of the Old Testament* (ET: Oxford 1966).
Möhlenbrink, K. "Die levitischen Überlieferungen des Alten Testaments," *ZAW* 52 (1934) 184–231.
Polk, T. "The Levites in the Davidic-Solomonic Empire," *StBib* 9 (1979) 3–22.
von Rad, G. *Old Testament Theology* (ET: Edinburgh/New York 1962), 1:232–79.
Robinson, R. B. "The Levites in the Pre-Monarchic Period," *StBib* 7 (1978) 3–24.
Wellhausen, J. *Prolegomena to the History of Israel* (ET: Edinburgh 1885) 121–51.
Zimmerli, W. *Old Testament Theology in Outline* (ET: London/Atlanta 1978) 93–99.

Theological Synopsis

The political and cultural upheavals of the 1960s, including perhaps especially the Vietnam War, presented new challenges to the churches and to biblical scholars who wanted to serve them. It was, in some respects, an apocalyptic era, and it may not be accidental that Paul Hanson's early research on apocalyptic eschatology was done in that era. In his research Hanson discovered in the postexilic prophets of Judah a set of polarities around the question of God's purposes (1975). On the one hand were those who believed that God's purposes were fulfilled in the establishment of cultic worship. On the other hand were those who believed God's purposes lay in a transformed future. Drawing on Karl Mannheim, Hanson called the first set of beliefs ideological, the other he called utopian. Hanson also discovered that these respective beliefs were located in two different social groups, two communities—a priestly majority and a prophetic or apocalyptic minority. Each community drew on earlier biblical tradition to oppose the other; they were competing heirs to a diverse confessional history. These discoveries were significant. They led Hanson to lay stress on *both* the diversity of the Bible *and* the responsibility of communities of faith to interpret that diverse tradition as witness to the ongoing, dynamic activity of God—and as a guide to their own action in the present. In that respect, Hanson was faithful to his teacher, G. Ernest Wright (see pp. 100–119 above).

In two shorter works, Hanson explicitly took up the conceptual problems surrounding the notion of "act of God" (1978) and the theological problem of the diversity of scripture (1982). Hanson resolves both problems, ultimately, by appealing to the community of faith—both ancient and contemporary. It is in the faith community's interpretation and ap-

346

propriation of its confessional heritage that "act of God" is understood, and that God's action can be perceived; and it is by attending to the diversity of that heritage, as it developed through history, that the community of faith develops its own dynamic vision of God's ongoing action. He goes so far as to say that this can be understood *only* in the community of faith (1986: 525). On Hanson's view, the authority of the Bible lies not so much *contra Childs* in its declaration of the truth, but in its value as a record of those events by which the confessional heritage came to be formed—and continues to be formed. For that reason, historical-critical study of the Bible is of crucial importance to Hanson, because it is the only means we have of reconstructing those events that underlie the dynamic tension of its witness to God's activity.

In many respects, Hanson's theology is reminiscent of nineteenth-century attempts to harness historical-critical study to the unfolding revelation of God. So thorough is his historicism that Hanson can trace God's action, confessionally understood, right through the Old Testament and into the New; and it does not stop even there! Hanson's emphasis on the process rather than the content of faith puts him in sharp conflict with another of his former teachers, Brevard Childs. It remains to be seen whether this is a "dynamic tension" within Old Testament theology, or whether it forces an either/or choice.

Paul D. Hanson has taught at Harvard Divinity School his entire career, where he is now Bussey Professor of Divinity and Old Testament. He earned his Ph.D. at Harvard under Frank M. Cross Jr., and he also studied at Gustavus Adolphus College and Yale Divinity School. Hanson has written extensively on the topic of Old Testament and Jewish apocalyptic literature, and on Israel's postexilic prophets. A Lutheran, his work reflects a commitment to the church and to the vitality of the Bible and the biblical vision of God within it. Theological issues were incipient in his first book (1975), a revision of his dissertation, and he has continued to elaborate those issues in much of his later work (1986).

B.C.O.

Writings by Hanson

1975   *The Dawn of Apocalyptic: The Historical and Sociological Roots of Jewish Apocalyptic Eschatology.* Philadelphia: Fortress.

1978   *Dynamic Transcendence: The Correlation of Confessional Heritage and Contemporary Experience in a Biblical Model of Divine Activity.* Philadelphia: Fortress.

1980   The Responsibility of Biblical Theology to Communities of Faith. *Theology Today* 37:39–50.

1982   *The Diversity of Scripture: A Theological Interpretation.* Overtures to Biblical Theology. Philadelphia: Fortress.

1984   The Future of Biblical Theology. *Horizons in Biblical Theology* 6/1:13–24.

1985   Theology, Old Testament. Pp. 1057–62 in *Harper's Bible Dictionary.* Edited by Paul J. Achtemeier. San Francisco: Harper & Row.

1986   *The People Called: The Growth of Community in the Bible.* San Francisco: Harper & Row.

Paul D. Hanson's
Approach to Old Testament Theology

Excerpted with permission from Paul D. Hanson, *The People Called: The Growth of Community in the Bible* (San Francisco: Harper & Row, 1986), pp. 531–37, 540–44, 546.

Underlying Presuppositions and Method

Levels of Discernment: Vision of Divine Purpose

[[531]] For its part, the field of biblical theology can contribute another type of formulation of this vision, namely a description of the purposeful movement that it discerns unfolding through the writings of Scripture and that it regards as an essential source of our knowledge of God's will and of the perspective from which we can understand the events of this world and the role of the community of faith in relation to those events. The fresh new metaphors of liberation movements and the more conceptual descriptions arising from biblical scholarship should be allowed to enrich one another as complementary aspects of one united effort. In this ongoing process, it is the responsibility of biblical theology to resist all attempts to reduce the vision to narrow, self-serving formulations. This is one reason among many why the interdenominational character of biblical scholarship should be fostered. Unfortunately, in pursuit of the central meaning of Scripture, and no doubt in response to the partial perspectives of the specific theological traditions of which they are a part, biblical theologians have often contributed to parochialism and oversimplification. For example, Gerhard von Rad [[532]] selected as normative for his biblical theology the history of salvation tradition, to the virtual neglect of other important streams within the Hebrew Bible. Such oversimplification threatens the biblical principle that God's presence cannot be captured in the univalent formulation or the immutable image. Believers can hope to communicate to posterity a faithful vision of that presence only by preserving its rich confessional diversity as a witness to its encounter with God in the whole range of life settings and experiences.

As one struggles with the question of how to foster a vision of God's ongoing universal purpose without losing a sense of the rich diversity that resists verbal idolatry, it seems necessary to visualize the transcendent dynamic of Scripture as one that unfolds precisely within the tensions and polarities represented by divergent biblical traditions. One must be able to appreciate how the lofty visions of seers and the pragmatic policies of

priests both contribute to our vision of divine purpose. One must be able
to recognize the contribution that kingship made to social form and stability, and at the same time see that life under kings was quickly debased
when left unscrutinized by prophets with their vision of a heavenly order
of reality and their dedication to the reform of every structure that grants
privilege to some and excludes others. One must even be able to visualize
the importance of the tension between the cosmic dimension of reality
portrayed by mythical, sapiental, and hymnic traditions in the Bible and
the theological dimension described by the history of salvation tradition.[1]

Obviously the picture of the community of faith emerging from this
dynamic and often tension-filled vision of divine purpose is dynamic and
often tension-filled as well. What comes into view in this study therefore is
something very different from a timeless blueprint for contemporary faith
communities. It is rather a verbal portrait of an emerging community, one
constantly growing in response to divine initiative. What will be held before the contemporary community of faith therefore is the model of a
community with a vision of God's presence in the events of its world, and
with the courage to allow itself to be drawn toward that presence as a servant of the broken, the oppressed, and the despised.

But why locate the significance of the Bible for the contemporary community of faith in this model and the vision of divine purpose to which it
is related rather than in a simpler structural model; for example, the polity
of the pastoral epistles? The answer is rooted in the presuppositions underlying this study that were described earlier, and can be stated thus: the
transcendent dynamic discernible in Scripture in response to which a community becomes a people of God does not stop abruptly at the end of the
biblical era. If the biblical vision of a God [[533]] acting true to a plan of
universal peace and justice is trustworthy, that activity does not end with
the last event recorded in the Bible, for up to the final stages of the formation of Scripture the fulfillment of God's plan is still awaited in the future.
According to this model, a contemporary community of faith is thus not
primarily an archive where members can study records about ancient happenings, or an institution committed to perpetuating structures of a bygone age, but rather a community called by God to participate in an
ongoing drama. This necessitates the same interpretive process that was an
essential characteristic of most communities of biblical times, namely, one
drawing from the paradigms of its confessional heritage and from its vision
of divine purpose a perspective from which to understand the religious
and moral issues raised by contemporary realities, and then responding in

1. See further, P. D. Hanson, *The Diversity of Scripture* (Philadelphia: Fortress Press,
1982), pp. 14–82.

keeping with this understanding in confession and action. The magnitude of this challenge must not be minimized; identifying where God is present (for example, on what side of a conflict) is perhaps the most risky of all human enterprises, and description of contemporary events in terms of their relation to a universal plan of justice is not something a community dares to engage in lightly, especially when one calls to mind the mixed record of communities that have been guided by transcendent visions in the past. If a contemporary faith community is to make sense out of a complex world by bearing witness to a unifying vision and at the same time is to avoid the snares of triumphalism and self-aggrandizement, it must take seriously the biblical motif of the servant people, a people responding with fear and trembling to God's initiatives and mindful of its solidarity with the entire human family. From this perspective, the diversity that characterizes biblical traditions is interpreted not merely as an indication of divisiveness within the religious communities of biblical times. On a deeper level, it can be seen to reflect deference vis-à-vis the mystery of divine presence, a tentativeness that did not deem inappropriate the coexistence of responses that on the surface appear self-contradictory—for example, the fulfillment was now (realized eschatology) and not yet (futuristic eschatology); God's reign would come down from heaven (spatial metaphor), or it would come at the end of time (temporal metaphor). On the model of the biblical community, contemporary faith communities can hear openly the often diverse testimonies of their own seers and prophets, whose differing angles of vision contribute to the modesty befitting those living in the presence of God, and to the self-criticism that is an essential component of any genuinely humane community. Here the existentialist perspective can enrich the eschatological; the black liberation position can contribute to the feminist; the Marxist critique can be taken seriously by more traditional religious groups. Although this model guarantees debate and tension, it is totally in keeping with the spirit of a community that derives its sense of direction from a very long confessional history [[534]] and its sense of vocation from the desire to participate in the unfolding of an order of peace and justice intended by God for *all* people, and subject to the parochial claims of *none*.

The description of its vision of divine purpose is therefore an aspect of the hermeneutical task that demands a high degree of graciousness and judiciousness. The record of divine activity in Scripture is not reducible to a simple formula. And as overall patterns of meaning emerge from the paradigms, we must not be tempted into making a community's task of relating the overall trajectory of its heritage to contemporary events easier by eliminating fundamental polarities. On the other hand, it would only invite despair if biblical theology were to commend to the communities it served an unordered set of dichotomies that seemed to imply blatant contradictions. On this level, the challenge is to describe the vision of divine purpose running through our confessional heritage in a manner true to the mystery of divine presence and the complexity of mundane reality, and at the same time to delineate the dynamic Reality active through all time and space in the creation and preservation of a righteous habitation—that is, an order wedding justice and peace. Only by fostering such a nuanced description of its transcendent vision combined with vivid descriptions of the fundamental paradigms can biblical theology discharge its responsibility of offering the community of faith a reliable point of reference for defining its proper relation to the overarching reality within which every mundane reality finds its rightful place.

Although useful in the theological task of grasping the contemporary meaning of Scripture, technical terms such as "paradigm" and "vision of divine purpose" must not obscure the inextricable relationship of biblical research to the worship of life of actual communities of faith and their life of engagement in the everyday world. Nor can they be allowed to obscure the communal nature of the mission of the church in both aspects of its engagement—that is, in relating Word and world. There is no denying that Scripture embraces a richness and diversity of testimony to God's activity that challenges the most discerning and well trained of minds. But it is equally clear that the schoolchild or the illiterate adult is able to grasp and be grasped by the central paradigms of faith in Scripture. This complexity and simplicity corresponds to the world we live in. The questions of how a community living forth into the world from its confessional heritage is to respond to the peaceful use of nuclear energy, to various forms of abortion legislation, and to different monetary theories are difficult to the extreme. Yet, because of their impact on human well-being, they represent a direct challenge to believers possessing specialized training and wisdom in the fields in question. Yet who can deny the simplicity and purity of love's mandate in the vast majority of our experiences as human beings?

This polarity of the simple and the complex is another aspect of the [[535]] rich diversity that characterizes the life of faith, and here too unity is found as the polarity itself is drawn into the unity of the divine mystery in worship and devotion. This means that a religious community that locates its unity in communion with God will not be tempted into premature dissolution of the polarities of Scripture or the polarities of this world. How often have not a religious group's "simple" answers been the by-product of its own insecurity, its need to display to the world a superficial (and dishonest) unity because of its failure to ground true unity in worship of and devotion to the one living God! A community grounded in the God of mystery whose presence faithfully guides all worlds to their final goal is a community capable of treating every opinion honestly and fairly with a freedom rooted in communion with the ultimate Reality, in whom all polarities find their final rest.

Once believers accept their role within such a hermeneutic of engagement, and witness their diversity gathered up in the unity of worship, both competitiveness and envy will give way to a partnership in which God alone is exalted. When understanding is obscured by the scholar's stammering attempts to describe God's presence through technical formulations, the fresh metaphor born of the struggles of the poor against the oppressor will refocus the community's vision. When the preacher's exposition fails to correlate the ancient Word with a suffering world, the tender courage of the peacemakers in the congregation may keep alive the testimony of Scripture. It is within the vast choir of witnesses to God's presence in our world that the message is proclaimed that a people is God's people not when it copies a past polity or perpetuates its own image, but when, guided by its scriptural and confessional heritage, it glimpses God's presence in the world, and responds faithfully to that presence in confession, worship, and action. For that glimpse and that response have constituted the true community of faith through all ages. They form the heart of its transcendent vision.

A Hermeneutic of Engagement and the Problem of Biblical Authority

For some people, the suggestion of openness to God's new initiative in contemporary social and political events threatens the authority of Scripture. Undoubtedly a static view of authority, a view of the Bible as a collection of immutable laws and infallible truths, poses less problems for leaders of some religious groups. But such a static view and the alliances between religious bodies and repressive political powers that it commonly engenders pose too blatant a contradiction of the biblical view of reality to enjoy the support of biblical theology. From a biblical perspective, world events are viewed as the arena of an ongoing salvation drama, and communities adopting this perspective must be open to the God who is engaged in their world to "raise up the poor from the dust." This openness to the presence of the living God implies for a community of faith the need for constant renewal and reform.

〖536〗 The authoritative guide to the communal life dedicated to renewal and reform of self and world is not a static organizational structure, but the living example of a merciful God that moves the responsive community to adopt the role of servant within a suffering world. Although the process of working out an authentic communal form and style is inextricably tied to engagement with the concrete realities of this world, it does not exclude but draws on disciplined study as well. Indeed, it is through careful study of the paradigms of the confessional heritage that a community of faith is able to recapture and even sacramentally relive the events in which its spiritual ancestors patterned their lives after the example of the Deliverer God. And through the efforts to capture the central meaning of its scriptural heritage with the aid of the master image, the root metaphor, or the imaginative description of its vision of divine purpose moving through space and time, it begins to glimpse the creative, redemptive stream that flows steadily through the heart of all reality, unifying all life as it draws all reality toward its final fulfillment.

A community of faith submits to its proper authority to the extent that it allows itself to be drawn into that redemptive stream, giving up all penultimate values for the one eternal value, the universal order being created by the Redeemer God. Submission to such an authority is not a simple matter, but one replete with struggle, testing, and difficult decisions. But while resisting eternal tests of verification, it is an authority that proves itself to be self—authenticating within the servant community that takes the side of the weak and the oppressed as its divine calling. The dynamic manner in which this inner authority functions is exemplified in the history covered in this book, for its nature is most readily learned from the individuals and groups of the past that lived intimately with the divine presence.

We turn to our scriptural heritage, therefore, as an essential dimension of our response to God in an ongoing, living relationship. We draw on the patterns of transcendent meaning that emerge in Scripture as a guide to our own effort to make sense of an often baffling world. It is not with a merely antiquarian interest that we look to the people of God in the Bible. They are our spiritual ancestors, and their encounters with God were instrumental in the formation of a concept of life that has been bequeathed to us as the foundation on which we can construct an authentic life of faith and humaneness. As people responding to the creative, redemptive God today, we represent an extension of the biblical community of faith. Their ontology, as responding agents in God's purposeful activity, is our ontology. Their notion of community is the source of our own efforts to renew life as God intends it within a human family embodying righteousness and compassion. Without a clear understanding of the biblical community's role as participant in the unfolding of God's order of universal peace and justice out of chaos and sin, we shall fail to define adequately our own identity to ourselves or to our world.

[537] It is therefore salutory that we look to the Bible for orientation, for it is in effect our spiritual autobiography as people drawn to the living God. By tracing the life of the biblical community of faith—its birth, its growth amid crisis and struggle, its fragmentation and near de-

mise, its rebirth and further pilgrimage—in this way we clarify who we are, where we have come from, where we are going, and above all, to whom we belong. In recognizing the disparity between our ancestral community's vision of divine purpose and its partial response, a disparity that led to fragmentation and confusion of identity, we are led to a posture that repudiates the temptation to idealize and defend our past. It leads instead to repentance of the unresponsiveness of our spiritual forebears and of ourselves. It creates a deep desire to be reconciled with those from whom we are cut off due to misunderstandings and conflicts growing out of our confusing our own "tribalism" with God's universal reign. Where communities of faith allow themselves to be guided by such a biblical realism, there is hope for the overcoming of the temptation to employ Scripture to justify perversities such as the arrogant presumption of some to have earned special privileges within the human family and to have escaped from the harsh realities of this world into blissful otherworldly delights. The result can be a sense of discernment distinguishing clearly between God's steadfast love that is in the central theme of Scripture and the persistent hardness of a human family preferring its idols to life in the presence of the true God. This sense of discernment will establish for biblical theology the unco-optable function of subjecting all structures and beliefs to critique in submission to the sole authority of the living God, and in full acknowledgment that every human response, even those found in the Bible, participate in and perpetuate elements of a partial and often idolatrous vision. Within Scripture, faith encounters the basis for a thorough-going critique that alone can purge religious communities of their idols, and reestablish communities of faith as servant communities dedicated to the earthly vocation of mercy and justice as a part of the perennial stream that has borne faithful servants of all ages, upholding them in their struggles for God's reign, and enabling them to repudiate all who seek to substitute human desires for God's will, even when such include some of the most powerful political and religious leaders of the world.

. . . .

The Historical Relationship between the Communities of the Two Testaments

[[540]] Paul treats the relationship between the people of the first covenant and the new "Israel of God" most extensively in Romans 9–11. There he anguishes over the unwillingness of the "kinsmen by race" to accept the gospel, and goes on to describe their special history: "They are Israelites, and to them belong the sonship, the glory, the covenants, the giving of the law, the worship and the promises; to them belong the patriarchs, and of their race, according to the flesh, is the Christ." This splendid heritage evokes a doxology: "God who is over all be blessed for ever. Amen" (9:4–5). Against this background, Paul puzzles through the phenomenon of the rejection of the Christ by the majority of his kinsfolk, and the election of the Gentiles: "But it is not as though the word of God had failed. For all who are descended from Israel belong to Israel, and not all are children of Abraham because they are his descendants" (9:6–7a). This Paul illustrates by pointing to Jacob and Esau, and the fact that the promise was not handed down by natural inheritance or by human merit ("though they were not yet born and had done nothing either good or bad"), but "in order that God's purpose of election might continue" (9:11). He then draws on an ancient liturgical formula (Exod 33:19) to identify the source of God's election: "I will have mercy on whom I have mercy, and I will have compassion on whom I have compassion" (9:15). And thus it is that Paul explains the new Israel of God, "even us whom he has called, not from the Jews only but also from the Gentiles" (9:24). In this new chapter of God's relationship with the human family, in which righteousness is based on faith, the people of God is a people in which "there is no distinction between Jew and Greek" (10:10). As indicated by Paul's frequent quotation of prophetic texts to support his argument, this conception of the people of God breaking with a strict ethnic definition is rooted deeply in Hebrew prophecy, a conception mediated in the postexilic period within apocalyptic circles.

At the same time as Paul makes his case for this spiritual understanding of the Israel of God, he also hastens to observe that the new people of God is threatened by the same temptation on which the first Israel stumbled, pride of election. Therefore he goes on to teach a lesson that speaks urgently to every Christian individual and congregation, not only in Paul's day, but in every age down to our own, a lesson in what I earlier called "biblical realism": God, in an act that was at once judgment and mercy, broke off some of the branches of the original Israel, in which place the Gentiles ("a wild olive shoot") were grafted on. The warning to the newly grafted people is clear: "Do not boast over the branches" (11:18a). Rather, the Gentiles were to acknowledge the direction [[541]] of dependency, that is, the true nature of the indebtedness (recalling the heritage enumerated in 9:4–5):

> If you boast, remember it is not you that support the root, but the root that supports you. You will say, "Branches were broken off so that I might be grafted in." That is true. They were broken off because of their unbelief, but you stand fast only through faith. So do not become proud, but stand in awe. For if God did not spare the natural branches, neither will he spare you. Note then the kindness and the severity of God: severity to-

ward those who have fallen, but God's kindness to you, provided you continue in his kindness; otherwise you too will be cut off. (Rom 11:18–22)

Boasting is excluded, ultimately (as Paul insists) because justification comes by faith alone, and "it is the root that supports you," and excluded historically because of the distinction between the "natural branches" (Israel), and those "cut off from what is by nature a wild olive tree and grafted, contrary to nature, into a cultivated and live tree" (the Gentiles).

The overall witness of Scripture, therefore, as well as this specific elucidation of salvation history by Paul, gives us the order that must be followed if we are to understand the community of faith within the only context that reveals its essential being, the context of God's creative and redemptive activity from creation to the coming of God's reign. The order is sketched by Paul in Rom 9:4–5, and traces the history of the Israelites, to whom "belong the sonship, the glory, the covenants, the giving of the law, the worship . . . the promises, and the patriarchs." Only by reliving the history of God's intimate relationship with God's first people can communities of faith today avoid the trap of blind arrogance and instead grow into a realistic and mature understanding of what it means to be "God's people," "the children of the promise." And only by reliving this rich history are Christians prepared to enter the next chapter mentioned by Paul, "and of their race, according to the flesh, is the Christ."

The reason why this *praeparatio* in the history of God's first people is essential to understanding the Christ and the community of Christ's followers is clear. In the birth of a people of God in Christ, God's anointing Jesus as the Messiah was not a solitary happening, but one within a long history of salvation. Jesus is not a gnostic savior, a disembodied spirit emanating from the *pleroma* to draw forth divine sparks entrapped in this aeon within prisons of flesh. Jesus, who was anointed God's Messiah to go to the lost of the tribes of Israel, is the carpenter's son from Nazareth; that is, of a particular people according to the flesh. That people is the Jewish people. The Christian kerygma goes on to profess that to that people, and then to all the nations of the earth for which the Jews were called to be a blessing, Jesus came as the Messiah; that is, the anointed King long awaited out of the House of David who would deliver the people from their dark prison. Christians today [542] are as indebted as were those in Paul's Roman audience to their ancestors in the faith, God's first people the Jews, for the perspective that alone can protect us from the arrogance that evokes God's wrath. That perspective alone can safeguard us in our calling to be a servant people of God, the perspective of God's universal purpose revealed first to Israel and then spreading from this servant people to the ends of the earth.

one of the significant biblical witnesses is that God's redemptive work is universal & not, ultimately, tribal

Paul, moreover, goes on in Romans 11 to explain that we are indebted to God's first people for our essential orientation not only by virtue of our origins in Israel's past, but also in view of Israel's future role in God's purpose: "Now if their trespass means riches for the world, and if their failure means riches for the Gentiles, how much more will their full inclusion mean!" (11:12). God's history with God's first people has by no means come to an end. For the present, those who do not persist in their unbelief, will be grafted in, for God has the power to graft them in again. For if we have been cut from what is by nature a wild olive tree, and grafted, contrary to nature, into a cultivated olive tree, how much more will these natural branches be grated back into their own olive tree" (11:24). But Paul goes even further in penetrating the mystery of God's relation to the Jewish people: "Lest you be wise in your own conceits, I want you to understand this mystery, brethren: a hardening has come upon part of Israel, until the full number of the Gentiles come in and so all Israel will be saved" (11:25). On what basis can Paul make this confession? The trustworthiness of God's promises: "For the gifts and the call of God are irrevocable" (11:29).

In relation to the past in which the nature of our calling as God's people was born and developed, and in relation to the future toward which our participation in the unfolding of God's purpose impels us, we are dependent for our sense of orientation on God's relationship with the people through whom the nations of the world will bless themselves, the Jews. I personally do not derive from the overall trajectory of Scripture or from Paul's penetrating interpretation of that trajectory a millennialistic historiography such as that expressed by Jürgen Moltmann in *The Church in the Power of the Spirit.* It seems rather that Paul uses a teleological framework to portray the unique role of the Jews in God's purpose of God's creation, and while that purpose certainly has an historical dimension, this is accompanied by an existential dimension as well. In this respect, Paul's vision of God's relation to the Jews is analogous to the view of God's reign that grows out of the Gospels: Christians celebrate the advent of God's reign in Jesus' life and preaching and its victory in his resurrection, awaiting its culmination in the return of the Son of Man, and at the same time engage in its present inbreaking as their vocation in the world. In a similarly multivalenced manner, Christians should celebrate the peoplehood of God's 〚543〛 first Israel in the foundational events recorded in the Hebrew Bible, and look forward to God's new "covenant with them when I take away their sins" (11:27). But at the same time, we live with the present ramifications of God's purposes with God's first people: "For the gifts and the call of God are irrevocable."

Our relation to the Jews thus implies both present communion and future hope. This is a view sympathetic to that of Moltmann, with the exception that it is critical of a millennialism that lacks solid support either in Romans 9–11 or more broadly in Scripture as a whole.

We must acknowledge with deep sadness that, taken as a whole, the history of Christendom's relation to God's first (and God's future!) people was summarized accurately by Paul, "wise in your own conceits." All too frequently Christians have laid claim to being God's people with an arrogance reminiscent of that which called forth God's wrath on ancient Israel in the time of the prophets. Too often Christians have sought to insulate themselves against God's judgment on sectarian pride by narrowing the vision of the peoplehood of God so as to identify it exclusively as a Christian possession. What more vivid proof of this could be given than the long history of wrongs committed by Christians against Jews, beginning in the early centuries of the church, continuing through medieval and reformation times, and culminating in the greatest human atrocity of modern history, the Nazi holocaust. Within the church, this shameful record calls for a repentance leading to a more accurate understanding of the Jewish-Christian relationship: "natural branches" related to branches "cut off from what is by nature a wild olive tree, and grafted, contrary to nature, into a cultivated olive tree." For clarity on this historical relationship will keep Christians mindful of the dependency implicit in this relationship: "Remember, it is not you that support the root, but the root that supports you." Acknowledgment of their historical dependence on God's first people in turn prepares Christians to acknowledge their ultimate dependence on God.

Much is to be gained by finally healing this important relationship and placing it firmly upon a true historical foundation. If Christians learn to reaffirm their covenant with God by reaffirming the eternal validity of God's covenant and promise with Israel, they will recapture a clear vision of their place as a covenant people in God's universal plan for Israel and the whole human family.

From the perspective of this vision alone can Christians hope to develop an authentic relationship with Judaism, a relationship opened up by repentance of past sin and by devotion to God's reign of righteousness first revealed to the Jews. Without claiming to know the mind of God by specifying timetables for God's future with the Jews or precise formats for contemporary rapprochement between Jewish and Christian communities, Jews and Christians together can take an important ⟦544⟧ step forward by living with faith and quiet trust based on the testimony of their common biblical heritage to God's fidelity to God's plan for the human family. That is to say, because that plan is one, and is inclusive of all God's people, Jews and Christians can work together, pray together, and celebrate together in the confidence that all those doing justice and loving-kindness, and walking humbly with their God are on a pilgrimage leading toward the reign of peace that one day will unite all the faithful under God's righteous sovereignty.

. . . .

⟦546⟧ In tracing the development of the notion of the community of faith in the Bible, we use all available tools and sources of data so as to reconstruct the unfolding of this phenomenon as accurately and as comprehensibly as possible. What comes into view is an ongoing chain of the community of faith's responses to historical events interpreted as episodes in one divine drama. The situation varies among these responses regarding the degree of accuracy with which construction can be accomplished. And it is clear that the overall reconstruction of the emergency of the community of faith in the Bible that we sketch will be subject to constant revision. Nevertheless, we believe that one of the lessons gained from this study will be this: if we open our eyes to the community of faith that took shape in biblical times, the way in which we look on the communities of faith of which we are a part will be radically transformed.

Synopsis of Hanson's *The People Called* (1986)

Paul D. Hanson
On Deuteronomy: A New Formulation
of the Community of Faith

Excerpted with permission from Paul D. Hanson, *The People Called: The Growth of Community in the Bible* (San Francisco: Harper & Row, 1986), pp. 167–76.

[[167]] Early Yahwism formulated its vision of what it meant to be the people covenanted with God in the Book of the Covenant and the Decalogue. This formulation served as a light guiding the faithful through many troubled times, times in which the covenant notion was challenged by rival Baal cults and even by a rival conception of covenant coming from within the nation itself in the form of the royal ideology of Jerusalem. In the prophets, we have come to recognize the chief defenders of the early Yahwistic notion of community against both of these threats. Especially in northern prophecy, the qualities of community embodied in the Book of the Covenant and the Decalogue, as well as in the narrative traditions reporting the saving deeds of Yahweh, were interpreted and refined in the light of God's new activity in the prophetic word. During this entire span of time down to the mid-seventh century, however, no new formulation of the community of faith was attempted.

Amos and Hosea, however, prepared the way for such an attempt by maintaining the independence of the Yahwistic notion of God's people from entanglements with Baal worship or the native forms of royal ideology. According to them Yahweh was neither the patron of a royal temple nor the instrument of a nationalistic policy. Yahweh was the righteous and compassionate God who desired "steadfast love and not sacrifice, the knowledge of God, rather than burnt offerings" (Hos 6:6). By thus resisting co-option by political or religious institutions, prophetic Yahwism survived the collapse of both Northern Kingdom and cult during the Assyrian invasion of 724–722. In fact, the resulting destruction itself called attention to the truthfulness of the severe mercy proclaimed by these prophets. If there was to be a future for God's people, surely it was to be found among a people confessing, "Assyria shall not save us, we will not ride upon horses; and we will say no more, 'Our God,' to the work of our hands" (Hos 14:3). The deep darkness of the times allowed the light the prophets had refused to extinguish through compromise or assimilation to shine forth as Israel's only [[168]] hope: "Hate evil, and love good, and establish justice in the gate; it may be that the Lord, the God of hosts, will be gracious to the remnant of Joseph" (Amos 5:15).

The task formally undertaken by the authors of Deuteronomy was thus already anticipated in the activity of Amos and Hosea. They acknowledged one norm alone for the life of the community, the one true God, whose will was revealed in the Mosaic covenant and its law. And in anticipation of the Book of Deuteronomy, they sought to apply that norm to the new situations facing the people. Although their engagement with concrete situations as they arose did not give rise to as comprehensive and systematic a reformulation of the covenant understanding of community as that found in Deuteronomy, their address was not haphazard, but was always consistent with a clear vision of what it meant to be God's people, that being the vision of early Yahwism. One God, one covenant, one *tôrâ* interpreting that covenant to the community united under the sovereignty of God—this was the background of their prophecy. If they had sat down to formulate it in comprehensive terms, it would have resembled the Book of Deuteronomy, with one exception: the emphasis on the centrality of worship in one sanctuary would have been lacking. That likely entered this northern tradition after its migration to the south.

Often the positive vision of the righteous covenant community is not noticed by readers of the eighth-century prophets, since the unrighteousness of the people forced them repeatedly to carry on God's controversy and to intone the corresponding indictments and sentences. But it was precisely their vision of God's intended order that led them fearlessly to take up the cause of the poor and the oppressed, and to oppose any person or group that by commission or neglect contributed to the impoverishment of the land and the people. For them the greed and abuse of power by kings, priests, nobles, and false prophets were not a mere matter of personal misconduct, but an attack on the righteous community intended by God, and thus a repudiation of God's sovereignty. These prophets were thus the unflinching defenders of the early Yahwistic notion of community formulated in the Book of the Covenant and the Decalogue. In a spiritual succession reaching them from Gilgal, Shechem, and Shiloh, they stood in unbroken continuity with the redeemed slaves who first were gathered by Yahweh into the covenant community. Thus even to the rampant apostasy of that time, for example, Hosea responded with a unique formulation of Yahweh's judgment: It would be a return to the wilderness, where God could speak to them undistracted by the Baals and other seductions of the fertile land. The wilderness, as a return to the beginning, as a place for a new start, as an opportunity for covenant renewal, was the most promising place for the reformulation of the Yahwistic notion of the covenant community.

⟦169⟧ "These are the words that Moses spoke to all Israel beyond the Jordan in the wilderness" (Deut 1:1a). Deuteronomy picks up on Hosea's suggestion that the wilderness was the location where the covenant could be *re*-presented to the people of Israel. In the austerity of the desert could be found the intimacy of undistracted communion with their Deliverer.

But where might the carriers of this northern prophetic tradition re-create this wilderness setting? Their original home in the Northern Kingdom was no longer the place of new beginnings. There God had spoken a definitive word of judgment on the nation, its king, and its cult. Amos's vision of a remnant was accurate. Only a small circle of witnesses survived the dispersion of a nation. But beyond judgment Amos and Hosea had glimpsed a new beginning. Where could the remnant proclaim their message of repentance and covenant renewal?

Since the time of Ahijah of Shiloh, the prophet, while conceding a political division of Israel, never recognized a religious division. Their hope remained fixed on the restoration of Yahweh's whole people. It was quite natural, therefore, that when Samaria fell in 722 B.C.E., the heirs to the prophetic tradition moved to Judah to carry on their work. And specifically, the traditions preserved by northern prophecy seemed to be borne by a circle of levitical teacher-priests, no doubt in company with followers of such prophets as Hosea. Their teaching and exhortation is recorded in the Book of Deuteronomy.

These Levites asked a life-and-death question: What could prevent the catastrophe of the north from repeating itself in Judah? Only a return to the true covenant of God, was their reply, that is, to the covenant that early Yahwistic tradition traced to Sinai (Horeb), in which the one true God elected Israel to be a holy people living in obedience to the will of God expressed in the *tôrâ*. Deuteronomy is nothing less than a new formulation of this notion of the community of faith, embodying the traditions of early Yahwism as they had been handed down especially in the north, now applied to the new setting in seventh-century Judah. Here the testimony of freed slaves to a new notion of community would live on in that portion of Israel that had escaped the destruction of the Assyrians. Here was the wilderness where God could again speak to the hearts of his people:

> Hear, O Israel, the statutes and the ordinances which I speak in your hearing this day, and you shall learn them and be careful to do them. The Lord our God made a covenant with us in Horeb. Not with our fathers did the Lord make this covenant, but with us, who are all of us here alive this day. (Deut 5:1–3)

Deuteronomy was thus an invitation to Israel to renew the covenant with Yahweh "that you may live" (5:33). It also reformulated the *tôrâ* in which Yahweh described for the people the conditions and the qualities [[170]] of the covenant of life. It is thus no accident that close connections exist between the Book of the Covenant and this "second *tôrâ.*"[1] Nor is it a coincidence that the major themes of the northern prophetic traditions that succeeded early Yahwism find their systematic formulation here: "Their concern for the observance of covenant law, their adherence to the ideology of Holy War, their strong attachment to the principles of charismatic leadership and their critical attitudes toward the monarchy."[2] For Hosea, prophetic Yahwism (as the authentic carrier of early Yahwism) began with Moses and the exodus (Hos 12:13). And in Deuteronomy, Moses again takes up the discourse in formulating God's word for the people. In the words of the introduction to the original edition of the book: "This is the law which Moses set before the children of Israel; there are the testimonies, the statutes, and the ordinances, which Moses spoke to the children of Israel when they came out of Egypt" (4:44–45).

The reformulation of what it meant to be God's covenanted community found in Deuteronomy is an impressive witness to the vitality of this tradition. It moved from the ashes of the Northern Kingdom into the south as a daring effort to return what remained of Israel to the God of the exodus and Horeb. As is necessary in any viable hermeneutical effort, it made necessary adjustments to the new environment. It acknowledged implicitly (without mentioning Jerusalem, which in the mouth of Moses may have been deemed unacceptable anachronism) the central sanctuary of the Southern Kingdom as the place where "the Lord your God will choose out of all your tribes to put his name and make his habitation there" (12:5). It likewise acknowledged the office of kingship (17:14–20). But remarkably, it made these adjustments without compromising the principal themes of prophetic Yahwism. Thus at no point is the legitimacy of the Davidic Covenant (with its unconditional commitments to the House of David and to Zion) granted, which could have been accomplished without disrupting the literary fiction of the wilderness address by making reference to it in the law of the king in chapter 17. Rather, the sole authority of the conditional covenant permeates the entire book. Even the king is to follow carefully "the words of this law and these statutes, . . . doing them, that his heart may not be lifted up above his brethren, and that he may not turn aside from the commandment . . . , so that he may continue long in his kingdom, he and his children in Israel" (17:19b–20).

---

1. O. Eissfeldt, *The Old Testament: An Introduction* (New York: Harper & Row, 1965), pp. 220–221.

2. E. W. Nicholson, *Deuteronomy and Tradition* (Oxford, England: Blackwell, 1967), p. 69. Cf. A. Alt, "Die Heimat des Deuteronomiums," *Kleine Schriften zur Geschichte des Volkes Israel,* vol. 2 (München: C. H. Beck, 1953), pp. 271–272.

The boldness of this effort is also seen in its consistent reference to the nation as a whole. The message of Deuteronomy was not limited to a remnant, but appealed to all Israel. As R. E. Clements has written, "Deuteronomy therefore stands out as a last great attempt to call Israel [171] to national reform, including everyone in its appeal to repentance and renewal."[3] In it the attempt was made to show how every aspect of life, personal and public, could be conformed to the righteous standards of the holy God. Deuteronomy reformulated Israel's covenant as a total program for the whole people. The liturgical format used to structure the book would have awakened in its audience memory of the covenant renewal ceremony celebrated by Joshua at the beginning of Israel's history as God's people.[4] What were the essential features of the Deuteronomistic program for renewal?

As is the case of the unbroken continuity that can be recognized running through the Book of the Covenant, the Decalogue and the early prophets, in Deuteronomy the people of Judah were not presented with a new theology, but rather with a fresh formulation of God's original revelation. Thus they found the Decalogue at the head of the Torah section (5:6–21). And its definitive nature was emphasized: "These words the Lord spoke to all your assembly at the mountain . . . and he added no more" (5:22). What follows, therefore, would have been understood as an elaboration, one that—we can add on the basis of modern study—beautifully dignified the original "charter document" of the Yahwistic community.

Fully in the spirit of the Decalogue, the *tôrâ* of Deuteronomy focused first on the heart of Yahwism; that is, on worship of the one true God:

> Hear, O Israel: The Lord our God is one Lord; and you shall love the Lord your God with all your heart, and with all your soul, and with all your might. And these words which I command you this day shall be upon your heart: and you shall teach them diligently to your children, and shall talk of them when you sit in your house, and when you walk by the way, and when you lie down, and when you rise. And you shall bind them as a sign upon your hand, and they shall be as frontlets between your eyes. And you shall write them on the doorposts of your house and on your gates. (Deut 6:4–9)

As subsequent generations of Jews have realized down to our own day, acknowledgment of the sole sovereignty of God, and a response to this Sovereign in a love that is undivided and total, constitutes the center of faith.

3. R. E. Clements, *God's Chosen People: A Theological Interpretation of the Book of Deuteronomy* (London: SCM, 1968), p. 37.

4. Cf. Joshua 24, and commentaries that draw attention to the covenantal structure of the Book of Deuteronomy, such as G. von Rad, *Deuteronomy*, trans. D. Barton (Philadelphia: Westminster Press, 1956).

It was from this center that the entire Book of Deuteronomy emanated. From this center arose the covenant and the *tôrâ* that described it (Deuteronomy 7–26). Through the worship of this one Sovereign and through obedience to God's holy will, God's *šālôm* was allowed to permeate the entire community and its habitation in the world of nature (Deuteronomy 27–28).

Not only was Yahweh acknowledged as the center of faith. Yahweh was also confessed to be the source of the specific qualities that entered the life of the community so as to establish it in peace and righteousness [172]:

> When your son asks you in time to come, "What is the meaning of the testimonies and the statutes and the ordinances which the Lord our God has commanded you?" then you shall say to your son, "We were Pharaoh's slaves in Egypt; and the Lord brought us out of Egypt with a mighty hand; . . . and he brought us out from there, that he might bring us in and give us the land which he swore to give to our fathers. And the Lord commanded us to do all these statutes, to fear the Lord our God, for our good always, that he might preserve us alive, as at that day. And it will be righteousness for us, if we are careful to do all this commandment before the Lord our God, as he has commanded us." (Deut 6:20–21, 23–25)

The qualities Israel was to embody in its community were justice and love. Israel was to be a holy people because God was holy. Israel was to be a righteous and compassionate people, because God was righteous and compassionate. For this reason, the remembering of the exodus tradition was so important to the Deuteronomists, "that you may live" (8:1–10), even as forgetting Yahweh's gracious saving acts elicited the most dreadful of threats, "you shall surely perish" (8:11–20). Therefore, occasions for remembering were instituted as a regular part of Israel's life as a community, such as the Passover, with its pageant of the exodus (Deuteronomy 16), and the festival of first fruits with its recitation of the *magnalia dei* (26:1–11). God's grace had thus been manifested in God's delivering Israel from its bondage, and drawing it into a covenant of love, even as God's grace continued to be shown in the gift of the *tôrâ*. For in remembering and in obedience Israel was to find the abundant life. But not only in forgetting could Israel go astray. The very consciousness of the covenant relationship, of being "a people holy to the Lord you God," of being chosen "to be a people for his own possession, out of all the peoples that are on the face of the earth" (7:6) could become the occasion for a terrible sin, hubris. We have seen how Amos and Hosea struggled with this distortion of God's election, and with its repercussions in a perverted cult. In their moving homiletic style, the Deuteronomists also struggled to guard the hearts of the people from sinful pride:

It was not because you were more in number than any other people that the Lord set his love upon you and chose you, for you were the fewest of all peoples; but it is because the Lord loves you, and in keeping the oath which he swore to your fathers, that the Lord had brought you out with a mighty hand, and redeemed you from the house of bondage, from the hand of Pharaoh king of Egypt. (Deut 7:7–8).

Life in community for Israel was life in an intimate and life-sustaining relationship. Israel was called into existence solely by the gracious initiating act of God. To this Israel contributed nothing, neither unique beauty nor numerical advantage that could draw Yahweh's attention, nor special power to assist in its deliverance—nor, as 9:4–5 adds, was it [[173]] "your righteousness or the uprightness of your hearts." To the contrary, these people were present in the world as the fewest of all peoples. One source of motivation alone explained Israel's deliverance from bondage to freedom: God's love and God's faithfulness to the promises made to Israel's ancestors.

For the community of faith, the divine gifts of deliverance and freedom had created the context for the authentic life; that is, life of service and joyful obedience to God's will. But the God who was true to promises made centuries earlier to Israel's patriarchs could scarcely tolerate on the part of the people a response of unfaithfulness and contempt of the covenant relationship. They were called to a holy purpose, they were drawn into a distinct mission, and if they cast aside the life of righteousness for a life of greed and shamefulness, they became a hindrance to God's will rather than a blessing on the earth. The Deuteronomic theology made perfectly clear, therefore, that the response demanded by God's gracious acts of deliverance and creation of a people was unequivocal.

Know therefore that the Lord your God is God, the faithful God who keeps covenant and steadfast love with those who love him and keep his commandments, to a thousand generations, and requites to their face those who hate him, by destroying them; he will not be slack with him who hates him, he will requite him to his face. You shall therefore be careful to do the commandment, and the statutes, and the ordinances, which I command you this day. (Deut 7:9–11)

When tempted to take their freedom for granted and to insult God's grace, the people of Israel had the commandments of the covenant to remind them that even as deliverance of the enslaved was a matter of great urgency for God, obedience and zeal for justice were to be matters of urgency and greatest seriousness for them as well. They were God's possession not for a life of sinful self-indulgence, but righteous service. For it was in sharing God's love with others that they remained open to God's life-sustaining love.

Deuteronomy thus reformulated the notion of the community of faith of early Yahwism. And in so doing, its authors remained true to the original vision of a people called into being solely by the antecedent grace of God, and called to "be to me a kingdom of priests and a holy nation" (Exod 19:6a). It also demonstrated that the Yahwistic notion of community was a dynamic one, based on faith in a God active in every new generation. Thus Deuteronomy placed a new generation, faced with serious threats to faith and nationhood, before the God whose will had been revealed at Horeb. The result was a deepening of the essential qualities of the Yahwistic notion of community.

In this formulation, the Yahwistic understanding of righteousness was broadened to demonstrate how God's holiness applied to every aspect of life, cultic, social and political. With a remarkable comprehensiveness, [174] *tôrâ* was explicated so as to leave no area uncovered, no social class unaddressed. At the same time, comprehensiveness did not lead to an abstract legalism, for Deuteronomy was infused with an urgent and passionate appeal to the heart of every Israelite. Here was not a vocation reserved exclusively for kings and priests. Every individual was responsible for upholding the covenant in everyday life.

In a depth hitherto not reached, righteousness was clothed in compassion, creating a dynamic interaction between these two qualities that had a profound effect on the Yahwistic notion of community. Using an idiom earlier favored by Hosea, the Deuteronomists traced the quality of compassion to Yahweh's *love* for Israel; there was no explanation for Israel's election aside from the fact "that the Lord set his love upon you and chose you." Moreover, "the Lord your God is God, the faithful God who keeps covenant and steadfast love with those who love him and keep his commandments" (7:7b and 9a). Love between God and humans was thus characterized by a reciprocity that tied cult and morality together in an indivisible relationship.

Here we can note only a few examples of the effects of this deepening of understanding of righteousness and compassion and of their interrelationship. In the section regarding the release of slaves, the discrimination against female slaves found in the Book of the Covenant was eliminated:[5]

> If your brother, a Hebrew man, or a Hebrew woman, is sold to you, he
> shall serve you six years, and in the seventh year you shall let him go free

5. Cf. P. D. Hanson, "The Theological Significance of Contradiction Within the Book of the Covenant," in G. Coats and B. Long, eds., *Canon and Authority* (Philadelphia: Fortress Press, 1977), p. 116.

from you. And when you let him go free from you, you shall not let him go empty-handed; you shall furnish him liberally out of your flock, out of your threshing floor, and out of your wine press; as the Lord your God has blessed you, you shall give to him. (Deut 15:12–14)

Moreover, the motivational basis for this new sense of equality was located explicitly in the antecedent gracious acts of God: "You shall remember that you were a slave in the land of Egypt, and the Lord your God redeemed you, therefore I command you this day" (15:15). Similarly, in the cultic festivals, the discrimination found in the Book of the Covenant was eliminated: All were to attend, "you and your son and your daughter, your manservant and your maidservant, the Levite who is within your towns, the sojourner, the fatherless, and the widow who are among you" (7:11), and again motivation was grounded in Yahweh's initiating act of grace: "You shall remember that you were a slave in Egypt; and you shall be careful to observe these statutes" (17:12).

Other vivid examples of the wedding of righteousness and compassion in laws derived from the gracious acts of Yahweh related to "the justice due to the sojourner" and "the fatherless" and "the widow" [[175]] (Deut 24:17–18), and to the provision of gleanings for these same vulnerable classes (24:19–22). A deepened sensitivity is also found in the Book of Deuteronomy to the ramifications of the Yahwistic belief that the land was a gift from Yahweh, a gift for all the people to enjoy. Since some could find this right denied them due to misfortune, the specific provision of the third-year tithe was made for the Levite (who had no possession), the sojourner, the fatherless, and the widow (14:28–29). Such observance of the *tôrâ* was not merely a legal observance, but was an integral part of the order of *šālôm* established by Yahweh: That these vulnerable classes may "come and eat and be filled" was inextricably related to the blessing "of all of the work of your hands that you do" (14:29b).

The organic relation between God's antecedent grace toward Israel and their response in compassionate righteousness is beautifully expressed in the transition from the description of Yahweh to the commandment to Israel in Deut 10:17–19: "For the Lord your God is God of gods and Lord of lords, the great, the mighty and the terrible God, who is not partial and takes no bribe. He executes justice for the fatherless and the widow, and loves the sojourner, giving him food and clothing. Love the sojourner therefore; for you were sojourners in the land of Egypt." This passage leads us to the third quality of the Yahwistic notion of community, for in it we can discern how righteousness and compassion could be maintained in the heart of God. When Israel responded to the love of God in worship, it found the motivation from which righteousness and compassion alone could enter the life of community and individual. In

Deuteronomy, the center of life—the one true God, celebrated in worship—was described more vividly than in any previous Yahwistic document, from its most sublime formulation in the *šĕmāᶜ* (Deut 6:4–9) to the
persistent application of this belief to every area of life in its specific expositions of *tôrâ*. The effects of this central confession can be seen throughout the book. As one example we note that, although the Deuteronomists
accepted the existence of kingship, at no point was the privileged status of
the king normally associated with the Davidic covenant allowed to en-
croach on Yahweh's sole sovereignty. The king, like every Israelite, stood
under the sole authority of the Horeb covenant, with its unconditional
stipulations and absolute commandments. Similarly, while the centrality
of the cult was accepted, the royal traditions according Zion unconditional promises are nowhere to be found. Even the implication that the
ark might represent a special material link between God and people was
removed. No longer was it described as the throne on which the invisible
deity was seated, but rather as the container for the tablets of the law. As
for Yahweh's presence, it was expressed through a carefully formulated
theologumenon; that is, by [[176]] reference to the divine name, which
Yahweh would put in the place of his choosing (e.g., 12:5), a concept
again congruous with early Yahwism (cf. Exod 20:24) and resistant to the
royal theology's concept of the election of David and Zion. Against the
background of this strict observance of the central theme of early Yahwism, one can understand why the Deuteronomic law itself included both
a very careful formulation of "limited kingship" (17:14–20) and provision
for the charismatic presence of the prophet such as Moses (18:15–22);
both were intended as guardians of the central confession of Yahwism.

   We thus see how the Deuteronomistic notion of community was essentially faithful to the early Yahwistic notion, and dynamic in the way it
broadened and deepened the concept. With beauty and power, it pictured a people whose holiness derived solely from its center in worship of
the one true God. From this center there emanated outward into the
community a powerful divine example of acts of righteous compassion, interpreted by *tôrâ* and inviting embodiment in the life of the people. The
obedient response of the people in turn facilitated the flow of Yahweh's
šālôm into all nature, restoring a covenant of universal blessing. Passionately, therefore, the book appealed to the people to remember and to
live. For in remembering what Yahweh had done, Israel would respond in
grateful obedience to the *tôrâ*, which is to say, in a life of worship, righteousness, and compassion. And in that dynamic triad alone was the life of
blessing and peace to be found.

Part 3

The Way Forward:
Old Testament Theology
in the Twenty-first Century

The Future of Old Testament Theology: Prospects and Trends

GERHARD F. HASEL

This reader in Old Testament theology indicates that there is a multivarious and nonuniform picture regarding the sources, methodologies, nature, purpose, function, and design. Most issues are and remain debated. However, it is commonly agreed that there is such a discipline as Old Testament theology which is separate from both biblical theology on the one hand and systematic (dogmatic) theology on the other (Gaffin 1976; Hasel 1984). Judging from the many publications on Old Testament theology (Hasel 1991), representatives of which are excerpted in this reader, Old Testament theology as a subject is more alive today than at any other time in its history, despite the pessimistic view of some scholars. While this seems undeniable, for example, it has been stated flatly, "Biblical theology is a subject in decline" (Collins 1990: 1); or, "Most assessments [of the future of biblical theology] these days are marked by deep pessimism" (Hanson 1984: 13). These are opinions of Old Testament scholars who each in their own way attempt to change or expand present models of Old

---

GERHARD FRANZ HASEL was born in Vienna, Austria, and grew up in Frankfurt, Germany. He received a licentiate in theology from the Marienhoehe Seminary in West Germany in 1958. His subsequent education was taken at Andrews University in Berrien Springs, Michigan (M.A. in systematic theology, 1960; B.D. in New Testament, 1962). His doctoral thesis (1970) at Vanderbilt University in biblical studies was on the subject of "remnant." Following a brief pastoral experience, he was ordained to the ministry in the Southern Union of the Seventh Day Adventist Church in 1964. Since 1967 he has been professor of Old Testament and biblical theology at the Andrews University Theological Seminary at Berrien Springs, Michigan. For seven of those years he was academic dean, and since 1981 he has directed the school's Ph.D. and Th.D. programs. Since 1973 he has been associate editor of *Andrews University Seminary Studies*. For some of his published works, see pp. 508–9.

Testament theology based on modern paradigms of biblical study. Most scholars, however, see some future for Old Testament theology, though that future is perceived in vastly differing ways.

The Possibility of "Critical Old Testament Theology"

A recent dissenter about the program of Old Testament theology is R. N. Whybray, who considers Old Testament Theology "a non-existent beast" (1987). He does not believe that it is possible to unite the divergent pictures in the Old Testament into a unified theological construct.

James Barr has become more and more skeptical about a bright future for Old Testament theology. He suggests that we are moving away from and not toward Old Testament theology (1989), because (*a*) Old Testament theology is too complex a project, (*b*) the historical model upon which it was traditionally based is replaced by scholars with literary and structural models of study for the Old Testament, (*c*) the issues raised by a discussion of a Jewish theology of the Hebrew Bible seem unlikely to be settled, and (*d*) his interests in natural theology move in directions other than the witness of revelational theology (1988). Barr allows for Old Testament theology to stay alive but believes that its role is likely to change. For Barr, "biblical theology [and Old Testament theology] is descriptive" and clearly not normative or prescriptive (1988: 11). It is integrally linked with historical criticism and is best seen in sharp distinction from dogmatic (systematic) theology (1988: 13–17). Without explicitly using the Stendahl distinction of "what it meant" and "what it means," Barr's approach to Old Testament and biblical theology remains deeply indebted to this dichotomy.

John J. Collins makes a case for a "critical biblical theology" which includes Old Testament theology and New Testament theology. The term *critical* is particularly significant in his proposal. He says that G. Ernest Wright and Gerhard von Rad, for example, each in his own way, allowed "dogmatic convictions to undercut its avowedly historical method" (Collins 1990: 4). He strongly disallows the canonical approach to biblical theology as advocated by Brevard S. Childs (1986). In contrast to Childs's approach, which Collins sees as confessional in nature and built on a "dogmatic conception of the canon," his own proposal for a critical biblical theology is grounded in full-fledged historical criticism (Collins 1990: 7). He acknowledges that neither does the historical-critical method give us objective facts as argued in an earlier period (for example, by William Wrede [1859–1906] 1973; cf. Hasel 1978: 43–53), because "reasoned calculation" cannot and will not produce more than probability (Collins 1990: 8), nor can the historical-critical method be expanded with the "principle of consent" which is "open to the language of transcendence" (Stuhlmacher 1977: 88–89; Stuhlmacher 1979: 206–8). Collins goes to great length to defend the "principle of criticism" within the historical-critical method. This principle implies that historical research so conceived "produces only probabilities, a conclusion which raises questions about the certainty of faith and its object in theology" (Krentz 1975: 57). This state of affairs does not seem to be of much concern to Collins. He sees the shift from the historical paradigm to that of "story" in some segments of recent scholarship as a useful tool to address the issue of the nature of history. He approvingly cites literary critics such as Robert Alter, who argues that the "sacred history" of the Bible should be read as "prose fiction," and Meir Sternberg, who suggests that "history-writing is not a record of fact . . . but a discourse that claims to be a record of fact" (Collins 1990: 10). Sternberg changes the historical attachment of factual truth in history-writing by holding that fiction-writing is opposed to factual truth (Sternberg 1985: 25). In Collins's view the shift from history to story is useful for a critical biblical theology, because "biblical narratives are imaginative constructs and not necessarily factual. . . . Their value for theology lies in their function as myth or story rather than in their historical accuracy" (Collins 1990: 11).

In Collins's critical biblical theology what counts is not factual truth but functional usage, for biblical narratives function as both fiction and theology. Accordingly, "historical criticism lends itself most readily to a view of biblical religion as a functional system where myth and cult are supporting devices to regulate the conduct that is the heart of religion" (Collins 1990: 13). This conception of biblical religion as a functional system in which God-language functions as an underpinning for regulating human and communal conduct is a view of religion that remains open to debate. It remains to be seen whether it will be readily accepted by all or a large segment of biblical scholars. There is a tacit admission that there is no way to know whether biblical beliefs were well founded. The shape of the historical-critical method advocated by Collins is, in his words, a "hermeneutic of suspicion" (a designation borrowed by Collins from Stuhlmacher). This leads him to the conclusion that "assertions about God or the supernatural [in Scripture] are most easily explained as rhetorical devices to motivate behavior" (Collins 1990: 14).

In short, Collins's model of a critical biblical theology has several basic elements: (1) it is based upon an acceptance of the presuppositions of the historical-critical method and its three principles of criticism, analogy, and correlation (1990: 2–3); (2) it is incompatible with a confessional biblical theology (*pace* Childs); (3) it is a subdiscipline of historical theology that contributes to the broader subject of theology (Collins 1990: 9, 13), indeed overlapping with the history-of-religion approach; (4) in another sense it is a part of narrative theology and "more broadly it is an experiential, symbolic theology" (1990: 12); (5) it is to go beyond the simple description of what was thought or believed (*pace* Wrede [and Stendahl with followers]; Collins 1990: 14); (6) it is to clarify "what claims are being made, the basis on which they are made, and the various functions they serve" (Collins 1990: 13); and (7) it is "based on some canon of scripture" without any "qualitative difference over against other ancient literature but only a recognition of the historical importance of these texts within the tradition" (Collins 1990: 8). All in all a critical biblical theology as perceived in this proposal is a full-fledged "functional biblical theology." Its strengths and weaknesses will be assessed in relationship to its methodological foundations (cf. Maier 1977; Wink 1973: 1–18; Gottwald 1985: 10–26), its functional purposes (cf. Kelsey 1975), and its faithfulness to the nature of Scripture.

Old Testament Theology, Theology of the Hebrew Bible, and/or Tanakh Theology

In some areas of recent scholarship there has been a shift from the designation of "Old Testament theology" to the "theology of the Hebrew Bible," a designation that seeks to void any account of the relationships between the Old Testament and the New Testament.

In the latter part of the 1980s some members of the Jewish scholarly community, which is itself very broad and diverse, have opened up the debate as to whether Jews can participate in the enterprise of the "theology of the Hebrew Bible." Moshe H. Goshen-Gottstein (1987) of the Hebrew University in Jerusalem argues forcefully for what he calls a "Jewish biblical theology" or "Tanakh theology." The latter designation uses the term *Tanakh* as an equivalent for what is also designated Hebrew Scriptures, Jewish Bible, or simply among Christians the Old Testament. In Goshen-Gottstein's view Tanakh theology (i.e., Jewish biblical theology) is a complementary approach to that of the discipline of the history of ancient Israel: "Tanakh theology must be created as a parallel field of study" to that of Old Testament theology in which Christians engage (1987: 626). He suggests that the purely historical enterprise of Old Testament theology would be "nontheology," arguing against the Stendahl position in which Old Testament theology or biblical theology is seen as a purely "descriptive" enterprise. Goshen-Gottstein is of the conviction that scholars, regardless of whether Jews or Christians, invariably stand within their own religious traditions that in some fashion or other shape their theologizing.

Another highly respected Jewish scholar, Jon D. Levenson, now teaching at his alma mater, Harvard University (see pp. 427–44 below), argues with vigor that Jews are not interested in "biblical theology," because it assumes an "existential commitment" that "will necessarily include other sources of truth (the Talmud, the New Testament, and so on)" (Levenson 1987: 286). Because of this inevitable bias one can pursue either "Jewish biblical theology" or "Christian biblical theology," but *biblical* is not a neutral term in these instances. It has differing meanings for either group of scholars. In the view of Levenson the last one hundred years or so of "Old Testament theology" was distinctly colored by anti-Semitism; until recently it was non-Catholic; and it is still non-Jewish (1987: 287–93). He maintains that "the effort to construct a systematic, harmonious theological statement out of the unsystematic and polydox materials in the Hebrew Bible fits Christianity better than Judaism because systematic theology in general is more prominent and more at home in the church than in the yeshivah and the synagogue" (1987: 296). He insists that biblical theology of the Hebrew Bible is an enterprise not interesting to the Jews, and that there is an implicit admission that a biblical theology is a theological enterprise determined by the community of faith (Christian or Jewish) in which one stands. If this is the case, one could ask whether a Jewish biblical theology might not still be possible, for it need not be unilinear, unithematic, or interconfessional. Indeed, Levenson now believes that there can be a "contextualized" Jewish or Christian biblical theology which will be able to serve the respective religious communities (Levenson 1988b: 224–25).

In contrast to these two affirming voices on the side of scholars with Jewish background, there is the non-affirming voice of Matitiahu Tsevat of Hebrew Union College/Jewish Institute of Religion. He argues vigorously against the notion of a Jewish biblical (Old Testament) theology (Tsevat 1986: 50). He suggests that theology should be redefined as philology. He means that the Old Testament, or the Hebrew Bible, is literature and not theology. Literature is a category of philological study, but theology is influenced for the Jew by the Jewish tradition and for the Christian by the Christian perspective. In one case the theological enterprise will Judaize the Old Testament and in the other it will Christianize it. But the "theology of the Old Testament" should be practiced from an objective point of view as "that branch of the study of literature which has the Old Testament for its subject; it is philology of the Old Testament" (1986: 48). Tsevat's notion that the Old Testament is literature seems to be directly or indirectly influenced by the "new criticism" in which the study of the Old Testament (Hebrew Bible) has a literary base before it has a theological consequence. On the other hand, Tsevat does not seem to recognize that the kind of objectivity that he is calling for cannot be had even if one considers the study of the Old Testament to be a branch of the study of literature. To reduce the study of the biblical text to the level of philology as he proposes seems to move to concepts of literature that in themselves are highly debated and the subject of much criticism (cf. Kort 1988; Goldberg 1982).

These points of view of Jewish biblical scholars raise the inevitable issues whether Old Testament theology is indeed a Christian enterprise. Some will argue that Old Testament theology is not a Christian enterprise per se. These have seen, since the beginning of the discipline in the eighteenth century, the enterprise of biblical theology in terms of a "descriptive/historical" enterprise (Gabler 1980) or they hold to the distinction of "what it meant/descriptive" and "what it means/normative" (Stendahl 1984, and followers), and they maintain that biblical theology is descriptive, but not prescriptive for the church or communities of faith. Believer or nonbeliever alike should be able to engage in the same undertaking, because the undertaking is nonconfessional. On the other hand, there is an admission that has grown in recent years that this traditional distinction of "meant/means" or "descriptive/prescriptive" can hardly be maintained (Hasel 1988: 149–55; Ollenburger 1986). Even Collins, who remains deeply rooted in the historical-critical method, is dissatisfied with the descriptive/normative distinction. It is, therefore, not surprising in the least that scholars raise the inevitable issue, whether or to what degree Old Testament theology is a Christian and not a Jewish enterprise. Historically it was the Christian scholars who engaged in the enterprise of a biblical theology. In recent times that stance has been affirmed with distinction by Brevard S. Childs. He asserts that "the discipline of Old Testament theology is essentially a Christian discipline, not simply because of the Christian custom of referring to the Hebrew Scriptures as the Old Testament, but on a far deeper level" (Childs 1986: 7).

From a variety of perspectives, as we have seen, there is a recognition that Old Testament theology is indeed not uniquely or purely a descriptive/historical enterprise and likewise not a branch of pure historical study but belongs to the realm of theology. In saying that it is an enterprise of theology we do not mean that it belongs to systematic theology. It is an enterprise of biblical theology, which is to be distinguished from the historical enterprise (*pace* Gabler, Wrede, Stendahl, and followers) and from the enterprise of systematic theology which functions with philosophical categories. This definition can be expected to receive further discussion as we move on into the twenty-first century.

Old Testament Theology as Theology

A major trend in recent reflection on Old Testament theology is to overcome the sharp criticisms leveled against the practitioners of the historical-critical approaches for imprisoning the Bible in the past. In the words of Walter Wink, historical criticism has become "a stifling orthodoxy in its own right, swept along by the momentum of its own technical apparatus and indifferent to the life questions which gave birth to the texts themselves and to the scholars' original interest in studying them" (1980: 103). As long ago as 1973 Wink startled his colleagues by opening his book on a paradigm shift in Scripture study with the unexpected affirmation, "Historical biblical criticism is bankrupt" (Wink 1973: 1). Historical biblical criticism "has increasingly been divorced from vital communities. . . . The questions they [historical biblical critics] ask are not those on which human survival and development hinge, but those for which their technology can provide answers" (Wink 1980: 103). It is acknowledged today that the historical-critical method has run its course and is in need of serious self-correction (Krentz 1975: 67–72), expansion into a "hermeneutics of consent" open to transcendence (Stuhlmacher 1977: 83–90; Stuhlmacher 1979: 205–25), reduction into a "moderate biblical criticism" (Brown 1989: 34), or replacement by a "historical-theological" hermeneutic (Maier 1977), a "community-building hermeneutic" (Lindbeck 1989), or some other synthesis (Ratzinger 1989).

Whatever hermeneutic is developed, we need to be reminded that "the relationship between historical criticism and its results on the one side [and] the meaning of the Bible for Christian faith on the other side constitute the unsolved basic problem of historical-critical biblical exegesis of today" (Reventlow 1985a: 48). The result has been a "double vision" approach (what it meant/means; descriptive/prescriptive; nonnormative/normative) in biblical study, the result of which tends to place biblical interpretation in the university in opposition to biblical interpretation in the church (Dreyfus 1975). Interpretation of the Bible as text, history, literature, source, etc. is set in contradistinction to the interpretation of the Bible as Scripture, theology, canon, and norm.

In view of the hermeneutical crisis surrounding the historical-critical method, as hinted at above, "at least two major paradigms, or related sets of methods, have emerged in an attempt to get around the present impasse in the study of the Hebrew Bible" (Gottwald 1985: 22). One paradigm that has had some influence in Old Testament study is built on social science methods. It seeks to understand the Old Testament in terms of "changing social structures, functions, and roles in ancient Israel over a thousand years or so" (Gottwald 1985: 22).

The other paradigm shift that has taken place considers the Old Testament as a "literary production that creates its own fictive world of meaning and is to be understood first and foremost, if not exclusively, as a literary medium, that is, as words that conjure up their own imaginative reality" (Gottwald 1985: 22). The consideration of the Old Testament (and the New Testament) as literature means, among many other things, "a new concept of scripture," which "has a literary base before it has a theological consequence" (Kort 1988: 1, 3). Collins attempts to link the literary-narrative approach to his historical-critical biblical theology proposal since both seem to share nonfactual imaginative construals of reality.

It was none other than the renowned New Testament scholar Rudolf Bultmann who was concerned that "the act of thinking" be not torn apart from "the act of living" (Bultmann 1955: 250–51). In other words, Bultmann fully realized that the reconstruction of the biblical text according to the historical-critical method produced a reconstructed "what it meant" (which is not necessarily what actually happened), which should not be separated from "what it means," or as he terms it "the act of living" in the present. Bultmann bridged this gap between the past of the text and the present of moderns by translating the reconstructed biblical message of the past with the help of the philosophical system of existentialism into a meaningful message for modern humanity. Is it the task of the biblical (or Old Testament) theologian to use a philosophical system for bridging the gap?

Paul Hanson of Harvard University (see pp. 346–70 above), while having little to do with Bultmann, is very interested in the meaningfulness of Old Testament (biblical) theology for the communities of faith (Hanson 1980). Hanson insists that the Old Testament or biblical theology cannot be reduced to "a strictly descriptive discipline or to an attempt to proceed in a positivistic manner" (Hanson 1985: 1062). He sees the task of the Old Testament theologian as "open to the contributions of contemporary philosophy and the social sciences, for they offer concepts and tools that both aid in interpreting the ancient events and in drawing out the contemporary significance of those events in a manner understandable to modern individuals and communities" (1985: 1062). This process as envisioned by Hanson involves a dialectical move "between descriptive and normative aspects of interpretation. It does not seem advisable to leave that latter strictly to the systematic theologians" (1985: 1062). He explains further that it is the biblical (Old Testament) theologian's task to span bridges over vast centuries to make the message of the biblical text relevant for modern communities.

Thus the Old Testament theologian and Old Testament theology is not and must not be limited to the descriptive task; it has to be a theological undertaking. Hanson betrays the influence of the philosophies of Whitehead, Hartshorne, and Gadamer. Old Testament theology is clearly conceived to be a theological enterprise. Old Testament theologians are not historians but actual theologians. The question to be raised is whether systems of philosophy with their categories are necessarily the key to translating or applying the biblical message to modern human beings.

Brevard S. Childs, who pioneered the canonical approach to Old Testament theology (see above pp. 321–45; Hasel 1988: 151–55), which is still another point in the wide spectrum of conceptions mentioned above, argues for a "combining [[of]] both descriptive and constructive features" (Childs 1986: 12). Here too, description alone is not adequate. The constructive task, however, is not to be executed with systems of philosophy. When the latter is used there is a blending, if not a fusion, of the task of the biblical (Old Testament) theologian with that of the systematic theologian who builds his/her theological system on a chosen philosophical system. While it is "unrealistic to maintain that [[Old Testament]] theology should be a purely descriptive discipline" (Goldingay 1987: 185), it is equally unrealistic that Old Testament theology should be constructed on implicit or explicit philosophical foundations. The explication of the Old Testament material by a Christian can never be executed as if the New Testament does not exist (*pace* McKenzie 1974: 319), yet the Old Testament (biblical) theologian must not Christianize the Old Testament. The explication of the Old Testament materials should be shaped by the internal Old Testament notions of actualization and not by the chronological actualization (viz., von Rad, Gese, etc.). The latter procedure is not to be dubbed a success (Groves 1987).

Continuing Issues in Old Testament Theology

In addition to the vital issues as outlined above there are other issues of continuing debate and dialogue that are expected to draw the attention of students of the Old Testament and Old Testament theology in the years to come.

The matter of the *Mitte* or "center" of the Old Testament remains an unresolved problem for Old Testament study. As the fragmentation of the Old Testament traditions continues in certain segments of Old Testament scholarship, the matter of the center is pushed further into the background (Hasel 1974; Hasel 1985: 37–40; Hayes and Prussner 1985: 257–60; Reventlow 1985b: 125–33; Høgenhaven 1988: 38–44). A distinction is made between the center as a structuring approach for the systematizing of Old Testament theology and as a theological concept. There are various scholars who argue that the Old Testament has a *theological* center but that there in no *historical* center for the structuring of an Old Testament theology. Then there are those who deny any center to the Old Testament on any level (viz., Barr). Is there an undergirding theological center in Israelite religion? Is there a unifying element in the Old Testament, or are there unifying elements?

The issues of history, tradition, salvation history, and story/narrative are more intense today than at any other time. Some have said goodbye to salvation history (Franz Hesse, and followers) and others have built their understanding on the program of tradition history (von Rad, Gese) with chronological actualization. The whole paradigm shift from history to literature (with its emphasis on narrative and story and its nonhistorical, imaginative concept of reality) has the potential to profoundly influence aspects of the future of Old Testament theology. Will Old Testament theology give way to narrative theology? Will it remain independent or will both merge?

The undertaking of canonical criticism as developed by James A. Sanders (1987) with its levels of canonical authority that extend from the initial sacred story via various stages to the sacred text of the canon of Scripture and on to the modern communities of faith must be reckoned with. In what ways and to what extent this approach, which is not to be confused with the canonical approach of Childs, will exert an influence on the direction of Old Testament theology is to be awaited.

A further matter of major proportions is the relationship of the Old Testament to the New Testament. Is the Old Testament part of "one" Bible (Baker 1976)? Is the Old Testament the Bible (Jewish tradition)? Is the Old Testament the Bible and the New Testament an appendix (Kornelis H. Miskotte)? Is the Old Testament the Bible of a non-Christian religion (F. Baumgärtel)? Is the Old Testament a lower form of religious expression than the New Testament along the line of progressive revelation? Are both Old Testament and New Testament equally Scripture? These and other matters (Mayo 1982; Reventlow 1986: 10–144; Hasel 1991) will remain burning issues for Old Testament theology in years to come.

In addition to proposals found in the excerpts that follow, I offer several suggestions for Old Testament theology as an undertaking of a theological-historical nature. In contrast to various types of proposals based on diachronic-historical paradigms and linguistic-literary paradigms, all of which have significant contributions to make, and in partial overlap with several of them, I suggest an Old Testament theology approach based on a "canonical paradigm," which could be designated a "multiplex canonical Old Testament theology," with the following essentials:

1. The task of Old Testament theology is to provide summary explanations and interpretations of the final form (i.e., canonical form) of the individual books or blocks of writings of the Old Testament. The aim of this undertaking is to let the various themes, motifs, concepts, and

ideas contained in each book or block of material emerge in their full richness and relatedness.

2. The content of Old Testament theology is indicated beforehand by the entire Old Testament canon. This does not exclude an appreciation of the Old Testament in its historical setting nor an appreciation of the content of the Old Testament in relationship to the thoughts of ancient Near Eastern surroundings, but sees the latter in comparison and contrast to the Old Testament canonical norm.

3. The structure of such an Old Testament theology follows along the lines of a procedure in harmony with the multiplex approach. This implies that there is no single, dual, or multiple center which will dominate the entire structure. The full richness of the Old Testament will be allowed to emerge in all its aspects and variety. The theologies of the various books or blocks of writings will be expected to stand next to each other in their complete variety and richness, while exhibiting a unity of mutual complementarity.

4. A second part of the multiplex approach will treat the richness of themes, motifs, concepts, and the like along longitudinal lines in the historical sequence of appearance and development. The book-by-book presentation has the advantage of highlighting historical sequence of the material.

5. Bringing together the longitudinal themes and motifs and concepts will allow for the presentation of their growth, progression, and expansion throughout the flow of Old Testament times.

6. For the Christian Old Testament theologian, the Old Testament is part of a larger whole. The Scripture includes both testaments. The New Testament will not be allowed to superimpose itself on the Old Testament, but there is a forward flow in the Old Testament that reaches its climax in the New Testament. The Old Testament will be allowed to speak on its own terms, but it seems inevitable that there will also be some reciprocal relationship with the New Testament which cannot be brushed aside.

Based on these minimal aspects, the purpose of Old Testament theology remains both descriptive and also constructive on its own terms and germane to its own subject (see Hasel 1991 for a detailed presentation).

HARTMUT GESE

b. 1929

Tradition History

Theological Synopsis

Hartmut Gese's programmatic essays on biblical theology build on his mentor Gerhard von Rad and the traditio-historical method of research (1974: 11–30; 1977a; 1977b: 9–30). Gese goes beyond von Rad, however, in his development of a traditio-historical method of biblical theology that includes both Old Testament and New Testament. His approach is related to aspects of Peter Stuhlmacher, his former New Testament colleague at the University of Tübingen (Hasel 1982b: 75–77).

Following von Rad, Gese does not find unity in the Old Testament or between the Testaments in a "center" which may function as an organizing principle for a systematic presentation of biblical theology. Gese's traditio-historical model aims at the supposed tradition-building process that began in the Old Testament and is continued in the New Testament where it is brought to its end (Gese 1977b: 11). This tradition process provides continuity within the Old Testament and between the Testaments, thus giving them unity (1974: 13–15): "The New Testament forms the conclusion of the tradition process which is essentially a unit, a continuation" (1974: 14). While Gese insists on the canon as the context for his model of biblical theology, he rejects the Hebrew Masoretic canon as sufficient and maintains that the apocrypha needs to be included in the traditioning process. He argues against those who insist that the "final" form of the canon is to be seen as normative (cf. Brevard Childs and others), because no single stage in the traditioning process can be absolutized (1977a: 325). According to Gese, Old Testament theology, or biblical theology, is a phenomenology of tradition building. Biblical theology has the task of teaching revelation as history, that is, not a history of stages where the latter one(s) annul the former, but revelation history manifested through the various

384

stages of human existence which are evidenced in the traditioning processes uncovered by traditio-historical research.

It has been pointed out that Gese's model of tradition history is influenced both by the philosophies of the later Heidegger and particularly by Hans-Georg Gadamer's concept of tradition (Oeming 1985: 107–9). Among scholarly objections to Gese's proposals is the charge that he transforms biblical theology into "a phenomenology of tradition history" built upon a new ontology (Kraus 1977: 67–73), or that he engages in a "methodological narrowing," since the traditioning process is hardly as unilinear as is suggested (Schmid 1977: 81). Furthermore, Gese's identification of revelation and the tradition process and the identification, consequently, of theology with the description of this process is said to result in "methodological confusion" where "there would seem to be little hope for either sound historical research or responsible theological analyses if this path is followed" (Høgenhaven 1988: 50). Since the 1970s Gese has provided programmatic statements on Old Testament theology or, better, biblical theology. Despite various strong reactions (H.-J. Kraus, H. H. Schmid, S. Wagner, W. Zimmerli, G. Strecker, B. S. Childs, M. Oeming; see Hasel 1988: 147–48), he has not responded to them directly. Gese's formation of the tradition model of biblical theology has many ramifications that will keep the discussion about this approach alive.

Hartmut Gese took his theological training in West Germany. He wrote his dissertation on a traditio-historical investigation of Ezekiel 40–48 in the mid-1950s and followed this with a study on Old Testament wisdom in 1958. His teaching career commenced with a call in 1958 to teach at the Lutheran Theological Faculty of the Eberhard-Karls-Universität, Tübingen, Germany, where he remains to the present.

G.F.H.

Writings by Gese

1957   *Der Verfassungsentwurf des Ezechiel (Kap. 40–48): Traditionsgeschichtliche Untersuchung.* Beiträge zur historischen Theologie 25. Tübingen: Mohr.

1958   *Lehre und Wirklichkeit in der alten Weisheit: Studien zu den Sprüchen Salomos und zu dem Buche Hiob.* Tübingen: Mohr.

1974   *Von Sinai zum Zion: Alttestamentliche Beiträge zur biblischen Theologie.* Munich: Kaiser.

1977a   Tradition and Biblical Theology. Pp. 301–26 in *Tradition and Theology in the Old Testament.* Edited by Douglas A. Knight. Philadelphia: Fortress.

1977b   *Zur biblischen Theologie: Alttestamentliche Vorträge.* Munich: Kaiser.

1981a   *Essays on Biblical Theology.* Translated by Keith Crim. Minneapolis: Augsburg.

1981b   Wisdom, Son of Man, and the Origins of Christology: The Consistent Development of Biblical Theology. *Horizons in Biblical Theology* 3:23–57.

1983   *Zur biblischen Theologie: Alttestamentliche Vorträge.* 2d edition. Munich: Kaiser.

Writings about Gese

Schmid, H. H.

1977   Unterwegs zu einer neuen biblischen Theologie? Anfragen an die von H. Gese und P. Stuhlmacher vorgetragenen Entwürfe Biblischer Theologie. Pp. 75–95 in *Biblische Theologie heute.* Edited by K. Haacker. Neukirchen-Vluyn: Neukirchener Verlag.

Harmut Gese
Tradition and Biblical Theology

Excerpted with permission from Harmut Gese, "Tradition and Biblical Theology," in *Tradition and Theology in the Old Testament*, edited by Douglas A. Knight (Philadelphia: Fortress, 1977), pp. 301–26. Translated by R. Philip O'Hara and Douglas A. Knight.

[[301]] The appropriate form for presenting biblical theology or even Old Testament theology alone is a controversial subject. In fact, it is even problematic to determine exactly how its subject matter should be distinguished from a systematic-theological (dogmatic) presentation of biblical *doctrine*. Nevertheless, we can proceed from the justification given biblical theology in Johann Philipp Gabler's Altdorfer inaugural address in 1787, "*De iusto discrimine theologiae biblicae et dogmaticae regundisque recte utriusque finibus*" ("On the correct distinction between biblical and dogmatic theology and the proper determination of the goals of each" [[English translation on pp. 489–502 below]]). According to Gabler, biblical theology has a basically historical orientation and should clarify the different theological positions of the writings and (as we would say today) of the traditions combined in the biblical corpus: "*Est theologia biblica e genere historico, tradens quid scriptores sacri de rebus divinis senserint*" ("Biblical theology is of an historical nature, transmitting what the holy writers thought about divine matters"). Systematic theology can present dogmatics supported by biblical texts, but in contrast to this, biblical theology emerges from historical analysis of individual texts and should therefore present the historical differences. With the impressive discovery and expansion of historical knowledge in the nineteenth century, this biblical theology progressively took on the form of a history of religion. Not only an historical but increasingly also a dogmatic distinction [[302]] fundamentally between the Old and New Testaments accompanied these discoveries. As a result, the comprehensive biblical-theological perspective gave way to separate Old and New Testament theologies. The New Testament discipline maintained a conscious tie to the canon, thus setting limits to the disintegration of New Testament theology into a history of primitive Christian religion. In part this was due to the proximity of the discipline to dogmatics, but also because the New Testament materials had gone through a much shorter historical expansion than had those of the Old Testament. In comparison, the Old Testament field often lost sight of its connection with the canon. As a "collection of the national literature of Israel," the

Old Testament became the main source for reconstructing a history of Israelite religion, and this took the place of a biblical theology.

Since the 1920s this development, which had been particularly evident within Protestant circles, has been replaced by a general effort to
reflect upon the distinctive tasks involved if one is to make a description
that is both historical and also theological. The various contributions and
suggested solutions cannot be reviewed here, but it would be well to mention the essential viewpoints and their consequences:

(1) In contrast to a history of Israelite religion, Old Testament theology must relate to Old Testament literature as *canon*. However, it is not
enough for this theology to adopt—simply for practical reasons—the
canon and its historical affirmation. Instead, this canon must be theologically grounded in the heart of the Old Testament itself.

(2) Only the *testimony* of the Old Testament—and not Israel's piety—
can constitute material for Old Testament theology. Depending on one's
proximity to Kerygmatic Theology, this basic premise was underscored
and the testimonial character determined. However, such a premise derives from the very relation of Old Testament theology to the canon—regardless of one's own theological position. This is true to the extent that
〚303〛 the canon as such is characterized as a binding witness and consequently a religious "foundation"—and thus is more than a document of
religious piety or religious "praxis."

(3) In contrast to a dogmatic presentation of theological doctrine, a
theology of the Old Testament must be *historically* derived from the Old
Testament itself. However, that cannot mean merely describing the historical character of a *theologoumenon* but must also involve determining its
historical conditionedness, indeed its very essence which resides in its origins and in its historical crystallization and development. This historical
character must be preserved regardless of whether Old Testament theology takes the form of a more or less systematically structured design, or
describes the content in the form transmitted in the Old Testament, or
presents its historical development, or is conceived as some combination
of these approaches.

(4) It is not simply that in an Old Testament theology the relation of
the materials to *history* must not become lost; indeed, this relation must
determine its very structure. The historical path ("*Heilsgeschichte*") witnessed to in the Old Testament is not merely one among several features
of the Old Testament, but is of fundamental significance for every element of Old Testament theology. However, with respect to its content it
does not suffice simply to understand Old Testament theology as a theology of "*Heilsgeschichte*," especially since some important Old Testament
materials cannot be subsumed under the rubric of history. Rather, the-

ology must be understood essentially as an historical process of development. Only in this way does such a theology achieve unit, and only then can the question of its relationship to the New Testament be raised. Thus when individual *theologoumena* can be located in history, they acquire thereby a significance extending beyond historical precision and delimitation; they become classified functionally in this developmental process.

Contributions to Old Testament theology since the 1950s [304] illustrate progress in two directions. On the one hand, G. von Rad, drawing on the previous work of several predecessors, utilized the results of form criticism for the method of Old Testament theology. Since the Old Testament as a literary work develops from kerygmatic intentions, form criticism can to a considerable extent expose this kerygmatic structure, and a presentation of the traditions recovered by modern form criticism leads automatically to a presentation of the Old Testament kerygma. Thus, "retelling" (*"Nacherzählung"*) can be the "most legitimate form of speaking theologically about the Old Testament." The lively discussion following von Rad's work questioned whether form criticism was not being taxed too greatly in its significance for theology since the content behind the form should be more important than the form itself. Furthermore, the question was raised whether simply accepting the Old Testament view of history, instead of assessing the Old Testament traditions critically, would do justice to the task of Old Testament theology. Nevertheless, this whole discussion was not able to eliminate the impression that theological relevance resides not only in the "content" of Old Testament materials but also in its form-critical assessment and formation—and indeed that distinguishing between these two aspects is itself no mean problem.

On the other hand, the question of the unity or center of the Old Testament became acute as a result of the awareness, emerging from form criticism and tradition history, that the Old Testament displays a variety of elements and lines of tradition. Careful attention had been paid the Old Testament witness in its individual parts, and this raised the question about some overriding content. It was thought that a systematic presentation transcending historical description would become possible if one could somehow determine the center of the Old Testament. Yet there is still a problem of how this complies with the basic character of the Old Testament as a witness to a specific history and not simply to human historicality [305] (*"Geschichtlichkeit"*). Moreover—and this question is felt to be especially urgent—how can both Testaments be related to each other if New Testament theology is presented in an analogous manner?

This aspect of biblical theology has been expressed increasingly clearly in recent years, although the means for accomplishing it are more contested now than ever before. As much as it is emphasized that the Old

Testament is open to the New Testament, viewing the Old Testament as an entity *sui generis*, fundamentally different from the New Testament in many ways, nonetheless has just as great a countereffect. It is often felt that the Testaments are separated by a sizable historical gulf, occupied by the so-called apocryphal literature. This gulf is made even wider by the usual habit of devaluating the post-exilic Old Testament texts. With all of this, little is to be gained by referring to the subsequent history of Old Testament texts in the New Testament or by pointing out the complementary function of the New Testament with respect to the Old Testament. For if the New Testament is not simply to become an appendage to the Old Testament, then the Old Testament, if fundamentally different, must remain behind at the threshold of the New Testament. The demand for an historically, not dogmatically, oriented biblical theology, however, arises from the feeling that our present historical and theological knowledge and methods could disclose the internal and external coherence between the Old and New Testaments. This would transcend the fundamental distinction between Old and New Testament theology, which is affected essentially by systematic points of view, and it would transcend also the nonbinding character of a mere history of Israelite religion.

If we are to do justice to the above-mentioned demands on an Old Testament theological method, then out of necessity we must look to tradition history, which has gained special importance in modern research of the Old Testament. For, if (1) Old Testament theology needs to proceed from the canon and [[306]] yet also to understand this canon as something which is theologically grounded and not just historically given, then it must appeal to the theological development which led to the formation of the canon, and this is the history of tradition. (2) This makes it evident that not only the individual text but also the whole Old Testament has a testimonial character. Tradition does not grow as a document of piety but in its function for the life of faith—namely, as a witness to revelation and to its history. Tradition with no compelling character is unthinkable. (3) Tradition history resulted from a refinement of historical work on the tradition corpus in the Old Testament. And (4) precisely this structure of the Old Testament articulates the relation of the Old Testament to the history of Israel: what is handed down does not deal only with its experience of history; rather, stretching throughout history, tradition reflects Israel's experience of God in its history, and this historical character of revelation assumes tangible form as a process of tradition formation. The most recent development in the discipline of Old Testament theology confirms this significance of tradition history. Von Rad is particularly concerned not to bring foreign criteria to bear on an Old Testament theology but to let the Old Testament, in light of its formal structure, speak for itself in a "retelling" manner. This approach is essentially founded on traditio-historical research of the Old Testament. And with a possible traditio-historical connection between the two Testaments, the question about the relation of the Old Testament to the New could finally be liberated from the fruitless conflict over references and antitheses between their respective contents. As a result, one could instead turn to the question of how the Old Testament may provide a traditio-historical foundation for the New Testament.

Consequently, it is absolutely necessary for the method of biblical theology to become aware of the significance, indeed the essential function that tradition history can have for it. We can attempt to determine the importance of tradition history [[307]] for biblical theology in three directions: (1) with respect to the text as a whole; (2) with respect to the total subject matter of biblical theology, the canon, and the relationship between the Old and New Testaments; and (3) with respect to the theological consequences of laying a traditio-historical foundation for biblical theology—revelation history.

The Text as a Whole

The basic task of biblical theology consists in facing the multiform complex of texts, which differ sharply in their history and subject matter, and attempting to describe the theology of this complex. Simply setting out what all the texts might have in common would mean losing essentials which appear in the individuality of a text. But even for practical reasons such a process of reduction is quite impossible since a text's theological whole is more than the sum of its individual theological parts. On the other hand, we also cannot get at this plurality of theologies through merely juxtaposing them all in a biblical theology, for example, in historical order. For there is undoubtedly an internal connection among the texts (or their theologies) which gives this plurality a character extending far beyond their simple compilation.

This fundamental problem of biblical theology, that of comprehending unity in plurality, does not exist only with respect to the extensive complex of texts, but as a rule is present even in a single original text. For a biblical text is not the product of an author in the literary sense, even if we ignore all redactional arranging and reworking. For instance, a psalm is affected by a certain range of form, language, and ideas—existing antecedent to the psalm and having its own theological import— even though the author expresses his own, occasionally even his very personal "position" in this psalm. These antecedent theological elements are by no means mere externalities, as if they were only the media used for the author's real message. Rather, in his selection of precisely this form and formulation [[308]] we can perceive how the author classifies his own message. There is such a variety of formal and linguistic structures that the author is not compelled to follow a simple schema, but appropriates selectively and affirmatively. In fact, the structures of form and language are so much alive that with their inherent power they can actively convey the author's message. The author stands within a particular tradition both unconsciously and consciously.

We are advocating that biblical theology has the task of determining the theology of the whole tradition and that it can accomplish this neither by isolating a dogmatic doctrine as the unifying factor of the whole, nor by descriptively rendering historical diversity as the assemblage of the whole, but only by attempting to grasp the totality as a cohesion. Consequently, this task confronts (a) the individual text with its preliterary antecedents, (b) the development of the text as literature with its own literary classification, and (c) the growth of the text tradition into a corpus embracing the whole.

The Individual Text

The genesis of Old Testament texts usually includes an early stage of oral tradition. And even when the text appears in writing from the very outset, it is possible to speak of a prior stage, viz., its basis in the antecedent traditions. Tradition history in the narrower sense describes the preliterary, oral transmission of the text or its contents; in its broader sense, tradition history describes a text's formal and substantial presuppositions, taken from tradition. So ascertained, this formation of the text is of decisive theological importance—by no means simply a *quantité négligeable* or just a factor of very limited or circumscribed significance. The reason for this great importance is that the biblical texts grow out of *life processes* and exist in *life contexts*.

In the first place, this is true in the immediate sense in which form criticism and genre criticism speak of the "*Sitz im Leben.*" [[309]] Certain life processes in Israel lead to certain texts. The fact that the older historical traditions are totally under the influence of the legend-form ("*Sage*") can be traced back to the life situation in which historical events were narrated (and heard). The background for the collections of priestly instructions, the *tôrôt*, is the process of educating and instructing; for the laws it is that of adjudication. The prophetic reproaches and warnings derive from the process of prophetic proclamation of judgment. Cultic songs, whether lament, hymn, or song of thanksgiving, grow out of the vital process of cultic celebration. Even artistic wisdom sayings are unimaginable without the didactic discourse of the sages or without the ancient schools. This list of examples can be expanded as desired. In this regard, even late, purely literary appropriation of a genre should not be automatically excluded on principle from such basis in life processes. For even if at this point there is no longer an actual life process behind the text, this artificial connection to a suitable form shows that the writer is endeavoring to associate consciously, in a sublimated manner, with this life process. It is therefore not surprising when such texts, cut off from their direct processes in life, later find their way back to these life processes (e.g., when songs expressing individual piety become cultic songs again).

Thus we see that biblical texts relate to life processes in that these texts in their early stages grow out of such processes, or at least can be understood form-critically in terms of such processes. This is true in a deeper sense as well: what takes place in these life processes is what makes Israel into the biblical Israel. In these situations Israel's faith takes on form; revelation becomes apparent as lived life (*"gelebtes Leben"*) and can be articulated and proclaimed. As the great historical events are narrated and heard, Israel's memory is formed, and it becomes conscious of divine guidance in its history. Objective reporting of history can never manage to express history as it is lived or experienced, yet this is possible for the legend, which [[310]] grows out of the living process of narrating and listening. The life process of prophetic preaching is an immediate effluence of divine inspiration. Israel's piety survives in the processes of cultic life, giving birth to the cultic song. And the regulations of Israel represent its life lived, or at least perceived, under the aspect of revelation.

The Bible does not teach us revealed truth in doctrinal form. Revelation comes in the form of truth experienced in Israel's life processes—and even at that, this lived life is almost immeasurably diverse and even seemingly contradictory. This fact, of course, is connected with the very nature of this revelation. It is not revelation of the deity as such. It is the revelation of God as Self, in a self-disclosure to his personal counterpart, Israel. It is the revelation of the divine "I" in association with the "Thou." It is revelation in an exclusive relation, in an ultimate union between God and humanity: "I am YHWH, your God." Revelation in this exclusive personal relationship therefore enters into the very life of this Israel and is rooted in Israel's life processes. And the secret of Israel and of its historical path all the way to the point of identifying with all humanity—this is the essence of biblical revelation as truly human revelation, of divine self-disclosure projected into human life.

The biblical text thus begins in the life process of Israel. And only the traditio-historical approach can constitute the method for tracing this dimension of a text back into the lived life of Israel. Only tradition history opens up, as it were, the basis of the text in Israel's life processes. Yet this is not limited to the point of origin. Just as the individual legend develops

into a literary form, into the form of a text, and just as the corpora of Torah and law are crystallized from the life context, and just as the process
of prophetic preaching assumes a form amenable for transmission, and
just as the various possible and actually spoken proverbs converge into the
form of a text which stands the test of practical instruction, and just as apostolic parenesis [[311]] leads to the church epistle, and just as apostolic
tradition yields the peculiar form of gospel—so also it is essential to describe the traditio-historical path all the way until the text is formed, and
not only to penetrate back to some original situation. For the life context
of the text unfolds fully on this very path to the textual whole. This is true
first of all because only those life processes which the future also finds important can leave transmitted texts; only that which has proved itself can
become stable tradition. Secondly, it is true because certain bodies of material develop which alone present the form appropriate for the subject.

This can be clarified with the help of an example. We can certainly assume that there were very many prophetic incidents in Israel about which
no text reports because these incidents did not lead to the formation of
some text. As decisive as these events may have been in the particular
situation, their importance was too ephemeral for a long-lasting tradition
or for transmission in the form of a text. On the other hand, inclusion of
incidents in the continuing tradition must be differentiated from the determination of their form. Quite similar life processes can lead to completely different forms of tradition. The prophetic proclamation of Elijah
and Elisha unfolded in historical processes, were "fulfilled" in them, in
such a way that the legitimate form for tradition was the prophetic legend,
presenting the living experience of these processes. However, prophetic
proclamation in the eighth century was not "fulfilled" solely in the events
of Assyrian domination. These historical processes constitute only the beginning, and the fullness of what was proclaimed would not be actualized
until the future. Accordingly, in this case tradition usually had to retain
the prophetic word in its direct form. It is especially interesting how the
forms of tradition overlap in Isaiah. We can see clearly that the legend-
form in Isaiah can single out only one element of the Isaianic proclamation, the positive reference to the Zion tradition. Thus while tradition is
being formed [[312]] into a text, significant processes of selection and interpretation are occurring, and the life of Israel is as much behind these
processes as it is behind the initial formation of tradition.

The Literature

With literary fixation of a text, tradition relates to it differently in several
respects. In contrast to the rather fluid preliterary form, it is possible to
change the fixed form only through a conscious act of intervention. The

transmitted text carries its own authority, and a traditionist who engages this text must reckon with this, especially since he will in most cases be related to the circle preserving the tradition of this text. However, this does not mean that the tradition is confined to only editorial corrections and compositions and that otherwise the formation of tradition is terminated. On the contrary: since only those items are transmitted which meet the demands of life, literature does not exist for itself but has vital functions in life; therefore by being true to these functions it assumes a new form in the context of life. Deuteronomy does not attain significance only for the Deuteronomic reform; it represents a theological movement which affects and forms life in Israel long after the time of Josiah. Complexes of historical texts cannot be characterized simply as biblical archives; they give an account of Israel's past in order to provide a point of orientation for present self-understanding. Prophetic traditions describe future expectations as events which already begin to be fulfilled now in the real present.

The continued authenticity of a text is reflected in its redaction, composition, reinterpretation, and above all its selection and incorporation into new text complexes that are being formed. Only tradition history, which includes this viewpoint and thus embraces also redactional and compositional history, is in a position to describe and assess properly the theological developments occurring here. This continuing history of tradition [[313]] can show how, for example, additions to a text—beyond simply replenishing it as may be necessary—can result in an actualization of the text which opens it up to a totally new theological perception. Through apocalyptic additions a complex of prophetic texts can acquire an altogether new character, representing old truth on a new ontological level. This is more than merely requisite modernizations or adjustments to modern ways of thinking; preservation of the truth of the old text is at stake. Thus if apocalyptic thought significantly broadens the perspective in which revelation is perceived, then prophetic tradition, which of course had led to this expansion, can be viewed in this new light. If in a new ontology the Davidic king becomes the messiah, then the ancient Davidic traditions can be understood anew—indeed have to be understood in a new way if one wants to comprehend the truth retained in them. Psalm 110 does not maintain old truths out of necessity, but directs them toward a new plateau. We find ourselves today in the wake of an historical research which is interested primarily in the origin of an historical phenomenon and which exists in order to reconstruct "historically" this origin, in contrast to the later tradition; in this approach we are governed by our own modern perception of reality. Consequently, we are accustomed to evaluating this continuing history of tradition as something which is of secondary importance in comparison with the actual origin of the text. Yet as valuable as this historical viewpoint is, it will not do justice to the character of biblical literature as tradition. The import of additions and supplements, of redaction and composition, is not that "genuine" and "nongenuine" materials are mixed together or that a "counterfeit" impression according to the interests and taste of the successors is created— as if we should be grateful that all of this can be annulled by critical analysis. Rather, the texts incorporated into the tradition were living phenomena, and the point is for us to preserve them in their life context and not allow them to be reduced to [[314]] merely historical documents. This conservative character in tradition formation becomes understandable when we consider how tradition grows toward a whole.

The Totality

Tradition does not represent a series of individual stages in the material and formal evolution of truth. In such a case each stage would have to eliminate antiquated, no longer adequate elements, or at least "modernize" them rigorously. On the other hand, tradition is also not a compilation of materials perceived as truth at some point in time. In such a case it would have to confine itself to a rigid, non-innovative preservation of ancient texts. In contrast, tradition is like a living process of growth in which the old is preserved while being understood as the new. For example, a new understanding of the creation event is recorded in the Priestly text of Gen 1:1–2:4a, but this does not require that an older notion, such as that in Gen 2:4bff., be regarded as untenable and be eliminated. The edition retains the older tradition because it is still truth; indeed the story of the so-called Fall could not be understood at all without it. Yet through a definite form of complementary coordination the older tradition is not without relation to the younger. In this way tradition becomes a polyphonic choir of voices without relativistically surpressing any part. Intelligible co-ordination and subordination yield a totality and not merely coexistence. Tradition does not attempt simply to compile but also to mold a whole.

This formation of a totality is a necessary consequence of the fact that tradition grows along a continuum of meaning. New truth exists in revelatory identity with old truth: the same Israel experiences the same God, even when this experience becomes more advanced. This later experience, also immersed and amplified in being, does not suppress and replace the earlier experience, and this is in accord with the growing structure of history in which the past affects the present and the future is [[315]] embryonically existent in the present. Just as revelation is tied to Israel's history and is fulfilled in it, so also Israel's formation of tradition is connected with its history, and the path is retraceable only through traditio-historical means. As little as history is a mere succession of incidents, so little is tradition a mere juxtaposition of materials. A totality must necessarily emerge.

This growth toward a whole comes into view most clearly in the material ties between tradition strata. At this point we can perceive a developmental continuum of notions, motifs, elements, and structures, and this can describe content-related tradition history in its wider sense, embracing the history of a concept, the history of a motif, and similar entities. A line leads from the Davidic king to the messianic ideal-king of Isaiah 9 and of Isaiah 11, to the messiah of peace in Zechariah 9, to the heroic messiah of Zechariah 13; this is not a development in which one stage replaces another, but in which the former is retained so that a whole is formed. The notion of Moses as the *ᶜebed YHWH* ("servant of YHWH"), which in turn corresponds to the prophetic conception of Elijah, constitutes a representation of revelation in man; this becomes understood as the personification of Israel and thus leads to the Deutero-Isaianic *ᶜebed*-notion and, on the other hand, paves the way for the conception of the Son of Man. Wisdom theology can conceive of wisdom as a preexistent, personal, mediating figure, as the "co-enthroner of God," which is transformed into *logos*-Christology. These developments are often described today along merely religio-historical lines, whereby one considers the diverse possibilities of foreign, external influences as a basic impetus for development. But this manner of viewing the situation does little justice to the essence of tradition formation. Only that which promotes the growth process, that which is already implicit in the present, that which accords with the entirety of tradition can be appropriated or can have influence. And referring to external, political-historical conditions as the decisive basis for [[316]] the theological "superstructure" ("*Überbau*") of tradition fails to recognize that precisely the theological tradition determines how external history will be experienced; only this subjective experience and not an objective historical event itself could be relevant for the "superstructure." For example, the Assyrian domination can be "processed" according to the view of an Isaiah or that of an Ahaz. Only traditio-historical description related to the contents can understand tradition formation as such. It does not get lost in the quest for individual historical factors, for these cannot be properly evaluated by themselves but only in the total structure.

Against this viewpoint of the growing whole it cannot be objected that formation of tradition, like any historical occurrence, is subject to an untold number of contingencies which prohibit us from viewing the result as a developed whole. For by regarding the persistence of traditions as a result of chance one overlooks the life process which is active in the formation of tradition and which creates a totality. To be sure, the history of tradition is replete with contingencies; how much has been destroyed through external influence, how significantly have expansions and developments been hindered from without! Yet we do not disturb the contingent character of history if we pay attention instead to the lively thrust of tradition, replacing omitted elements, compensating for discontinued developments, eliminating meaningless and disruptive elements and wrong directions. If tradition formation is the living answer to the challenges of history in this external sense as well, then we have no grounds for speaking of accidental results. On the contrary, historical catastrophes appear to have benefited the formation of tradition considerably.

One could ask whether irreplaceable elements did not become lost in the course of history, as filled with misfortune as it is. What would it mean if, through an improbable occurrence, archaeology would supply us with an original testimony from a familiar Old Testament prophet? Should this document [[317]] properly belong to the prophet's canonical traditions? As important as such a discovery would be for historical research, it cannot correct the formation of tradition. For this prophetic utterance—not "heard," not esteemed, not transmitted—did not enter the life process of tradition formation. Only preaching which was heard, understood, and received constitutes the truth which sustained the life of Israel. This utterance found subsequently may be as "correct" as it can be, yet it is not truth in the sense of revelation to the Israel that lived. Revelation obtains its *organon* only in the formation of tradition.

This example makes it evident how different the historical viewpoint can be from the traditio-historical perspective, and we must recognize that only tradition history (to be sure, in its double sense) can describe biblical theology. It is only by these means that the historical as well as the kerygmatic character of revelation becomes manifest; it is only by these means that revelation can be understood as something which entered Israel's history and yet which forms a totality. Tradition history can become the method of biblical theology because it goes beyond historical facts and religious phenomena and describes the living process forming tradition.

The Canon and the Relationship between Old and New Testament

Canonization is the final result in the formation of tradition. The path from the text's origin in life situations, via complexes of tradition in the form of literature, and on to a comprehensive corpus of tradition leads to the final collection and compilation, the canon. Of course, this progressive consolidation of tradition is not possible without a substantive process behind it which directs the development of tradition toward a goal. But at this point we need to restrict our attention to the more formal side of the phenomenon.

Just as a long process is needed in order to accomplish the precanonical consolidation of tradition, so also canonization itself is ⟦318⟧ to be understood as a process. At the outset, the canonized text is neither a plumb-line of orthodoxy nor a sacred, inviolable text. Rather, the textual corpus in the pre-canonical period passes almost imperceptibly over into the canonical period. There is less change in the character of the text than there is in the Jewish community which is maintaining it. What is the nature of this process?

In the context of a comprehensive theocratic reorganization of the post-exilic Jewish political structure, Nehemiah's administration achieved relative independence through direct subordination to the Persian province of Transeuphrates, but under Bagoas internal difficulties resulted from conflicts between civil and religious powers (fratricide by the high priest within the temple, defilement of the temple, sacrificial tax, and more). Against this background, Ezra in 398 B.C. leads the Jewish community into a binding relationship to the codified Jewish "law," and this obligation is given external and legal form. This new obligatory character of the corpus of tradition represents the transition to the stage of canonization. At first little change occurs in the manner of relating to the more or less fixed textual tradition of the Pentateuch; even after Ezra the Pentateuchal text can be submitted to limited additions and redactions. We can observe the new relation to the text most clearly in the liturgical phenomenon of word-oriented worship ("*Wortgottesdienst*"), introduced by Ezra. The community, that is, "all who were able to hear with understanding," gathers not in the temple but in the square before the Water Gate. Following specific liturgical forms of giving reverence to God, the reading and interpreting of the text begin; indeed the present text in Nehemiah 8 speaks of Levitical instruction on the text, that is, preaching. This marks the beginning of sermons in synagogal and Christian worship, and this new liturgical relation to the text is the actual sign of canonization. The binding character of the text is expressed, and so is its authoritative and closed totality. In the face of this, any actualizing now is ⟦319⟧ understood as interpretive preaching. Alongside worship in the temple, a new form of obligatory and conscious appropriation of the revelation retained in tradition comes to the fore. The process of tradition formation had prepared the way for this long in advance, especially in the Deuteronomic demand for consciously internalizing tradition, but now it finally became possible by the virtual end of the development of the Torah.

One might think that the canonization effected at this point is tied to the preceptive character of the Torah, that is, that the form of the binding text derives from the character of the precepts themselves. However, we are dealing here with more than just commandments, which are of course a priori compulsory and which had for a long time been practiced as such in the form of the Decalogue and other legal collections. In addition to the law in its strict sense there is a plentitude of other materials in the Pentateuch which can by no means be regarded as accessories. Through the establishment of the Priestly document as the foundation and through the addition of older materials in the Tetrateuch, the *heilsgeschichtliche* structure acquired essential significance from the outset. And on the other hand, the legal material, even in Deuteronomy, often has a didactic character (for teaching "order") and thus extends beyond the normal practice of law. The understanding of Torah current in Ezra's age could have affected Pentateuchal canonization, but it is so complex (consider the influences from sapiential theology) that more was at stake in this canonization than simply elevating a certain legal tradition to the position of binding law. Instead, we must consider that the essence of revelation, the bestowal of being in community before God and with God, includes law at a decisive point, and we must comprehend the obligation being expressed in canonization in terms of this essence of revelation.

For this reason we can also understand that the canonization of the Pentateuch was only the beginning of a canonization process [[320]] and that this process did not apply to the Torah tradition alone but to the entirety of tradition: the historical tradition about the prophets succeeding Moses in the period following the Mosaic *Urzeit*, the prophetic tradition itself, the sapiential tradition, the "cult-lyrical" tradition, and the rest. With the conclusion of the prophetic age—the first signs of the end of this tradition formation can be sensed in Zechariah—the second part of the canon takes its place beside the Torah, before the close of the third century B.C.: the completed prophetic tradition, including both the historical tradition of the post-Mosaic age (which is understood as a prophetic period) as well as the tradition of the prophetic utterances. But it was never doubted that canonization did not end here. The Psalter was practically closed already, yet it could not be fitted into this prophetic section. The formation of apocalyptic tradition, which had previously occurred in direct contact to the prophetic traditions for the purpose of adding to and editing them, was continued in independent form. Sapiential tradition, as old as it might have been, now came to full bloom for the first time. These were joined by the historical tradition of the post-exilic period and many other elements. The extent and form of a third part of the canon remained open for a long time, even though the fact of such an additional section was recognized and recorded, for example, in the prologue to Sirach where mention is made of "the other books coming down from the fathers," "the remaining books" besides the law and the prophets.

When was this third part completed, and what was its extent? This question is controversial primarily for dogmatic reasons. According to the late Jewish (after 70 A.D.) theory of the canon, the third part is also delimited by the traditio-historical boundary-line of Ezra, or the time of Artaxerxes; in fact, determination of all three canonical sections is attributed to Ezra (4 Ezra 14:45). Here the third part o the canon has the small scope of the Masoretic tradition, and this is attested to by Josephus (*Against Apion* I,40) who in all probability stands ⟦321⟧ chiefly in Pharisaic tradition. We are informed that in Jamnia ca. 100 A.D. an affirmative decision was made that these controversial writings belong to this third canonical section. This indicates that this delimitation of the canon per se is not early, but at most the principle may be early insofar as only those writings were accepted which appeared old and enjoyed a certain respect. Synagogal worship does not usually have the third part of the canon in its scriptural readings, and this fact shows that for this stage of liturgical development the third section cannot in its entirety be presupposed as canonical.

The New Testament is familiar only with the law and the prophets (e.g., Matt 5:17; 7:12) as completed parts of the canon, and possibly also the psalms (Luke 24:44) as the beginning of a third section. However, the number of writings that are cited or that are implicitly presupposed extends far beyond the later Masoretic limit, and it can indeed even surpass the normal Septuagint circle, which is more comprehensive than the Masoretic (cf., e.g., the citation from 1 Enoch 1:9 in Jude 14–15). This corresponds entirely to the archaeologically ascertainable evidence of tradition formation prior to the upheavals of 70 A.D.: a flowering formation of tradition with a plentitude of writings, especially apocalyptic and sapiential but also historical and other types, with a variety of mixed forms. Disregarding perhaps the psalms, one cannot draw a line between writings which have acquired definitive canonical status and those which have not or have not yet achieved canonical maturity. At the most, inferences can be made about common recognition on the basis of circulation.

These circumstances can permit only one judgment—that a third part of the canon was in the process of being formed in the period prior to the New Testament. Certain individual writings had already attained greater or quasi-canonical recognition; others were only beginning to win recognition and distribution or were even still in the developing stage, and still others clearly in a traditio-historical marginal position were ⟦322⟧ not able to move beyond a narrowly limited circle of tradition and therefore had to withdraw from the common formation of tradition. In this traditio-historical stage of the development of the Old Testament, the events of the New Testament take place and are then followed by the formation of the New Testament tradition. In other words, there existed no closed Old Testament prior to the New Testament, and—provided that we do not reject the formation of the New Testament tradition in principle—we can speak really of only one single tradition process at the end and goal of which the New Testament appears.

A unity of the Bible is not to be established artificially through exegetical cross-references between the Old and New Testaments. A unity exists already because of tradition history. The gulf supposedly between the Old and New Testaments does not exist traditio-historically at all, and no dubious bridges are needed to span it. There is a difference between the Old and New Testaments insofar as the New Testament represents the goal and end, the *telos* of the path of biblical tradition. With the death and resurrection of Jesus, that event takes place toward which the earthly *Heilsgeschichte* of biblical revelation is moving. The apostolic principle, tied to those who witnessed Jesus' resurrection (for Paul, the Damascus incident), defines the end of forming the New Testament and thus the biblical tradition. In the process, of course, the apostolic tradition can be shaped by the circle forming around the apostle, as is only to be expected when considered traditio-historically; as a rule it is only in this way that the total amplitude of apostolic testimony can assume the form of tradition. There is no opposition in content or in tradition history between the Old Testament and the New Testament. The Old Testament prepares for the New in every respect: the doctrine of the new covenant, the structure of Christology, etc.

Objections to this view could be raised on formal and fundamental grounds. Formally, the New Testament seems to separate itself from the Old Testament through the Greek [[323]] language and through new literary forms. In answer to this, we can point out that even during the forming of Old Testament tradition a transition could be made to "ecumenical" languages, Official Aramaic and then Greek. Certainly, deeper reasons, not just superficial ones, lead to this transition, which we find, for example, in Daniel 7 and in Wisdom of Solomon. Yet we must note that the intellectual world of Hebrew does not simply disappear with this but helps to determine thinking in these trans-cultural languages. Regarding the other point, the new literary forms of gospel and apostolic epistle result traditio-historically of necessity from the subject matter itself; they are developed for the first time in the formation of New Testament tradition. But aside from these, the individual parts of the New Testament are to be understood form-critically entirely in terms of the Old Testament.

On fundamental grounds, the post-Christian Jewish viewpoint must result in rejecting the unity of biblical tradition because the legitimacy of the New Testament tradition is repudiated. Remarkably, though, Judaism does not continue developing Old Testament tradition parallel to the Christian forming of tradition (the latter would then appear to be a digressive, premature conclusion to the biblical tradition; cf. the Samaritan tradition). On the contrary, it leads to as extensive a reduction as possible and to a canonization of the third part of the canon, thereby terminating the whole tradition process. Through this reduction to the indispensable texts, which moreover as *kĕtûbîm* ("Writings") were not even made cultically equal to the first two parts of the canon, they rejected developments which appeared to be faulty from their perspective after 70 A.D. They appealed entirely to Ezra as the starting-point of the canon. Thus the Old Testament was closed through a reform in the spirit of Pharisaism, which rejected the Hellenistic Old Testament. Alongside the Old Testament, halakhic and aggadic explication of the Torah emerged as a new formation of tradition.

〖324〗 This later Jewish view of the Old Testament has, strangely enough, also become a widespread Christian view in modern times. To a certain extent, one has carried out the same canonical reduction, has ceased regarding the later Old Testament traditions as genuinely biblical, and has thereby made it impossible to preserve the continuity from the Old to the New Testament. In turn, even the pre-Hellenistic Old Testament was thought to be more strongly affected by "Jewish legality," which one was unable to understand at all. Actually, the preaching of the literary prophets was the only point where one dared to draw close connections to the New Testament. Consequently, the New Testament's whole understanding of the Old Testament was brought under suspicion, even though the method with which the New Testament interprets the Old Testament is in principle no different from that of later strata of the Old Testament, and is fully consistent traditio-historically. A biblical theology had become impossible through this view; two entities were set in juxtaposition: the Old Testament leading to Jewish religion and the New Testament leading to Christian religion. Access to a biblical theology can be opened only by revising, through the traditio-historical perspective, this fundamental evaluation of the relationship between the Old and New Testaments. This would also affect the way we perceive the relationship between Judaism and Christianity. We would have to recognize that the relation is not a juxtaposition ("*Nebeneinander*") but an interpenetration ("*Ineinander*"). Christianity would have to perceive itself as old-new Israel and would have to identify with the Old Testament history of experience. Judaism would have to recognize that it has not moved past Christianity, but that it has consciously taken a holding position prior to the messianic encounter.

Revelation History

Biblical theology can be described traditio-historically; it can be comprehended as a continuous, holistic process. In this totality, [[325]] no single level or element can be torn out of its context and absolutized. For example, as useful and important as it is to determine the theology of the historical Isaiah, biblical theology cannot be content with this historical viewpoint nor with translating this historical view into a systematically developed theology. It must perceive Isaiah's traditio-historical roots not simply as an historical condition but as an essential classification and connection: without the truth of the theology of Zion we cannot understand the truth of Isaiah, who transcends the old theology of Zion. Biblical theology must also see that the biblical Isaiah is not the historical Isaiah but the dynamic force, the Isaiah tradition, which stems from Isaiah and achieves its effect traditio-historically, stretching from the first redaction all the way to the New Testament view of "fulfillment."

Just as we cannot, in view of the holistic character of biblical theology, absolutize preliterary tradition, or the formation of the text, or certain redactional stages, or the canonical composition—so also we cannot understand the *telos* of the New Testament as the "final" form which has surpassed and thus done away with all prior forms. The New Testament has absolute character with regard to the *telos* which appears in it—but not absolute over against the Old Testament traditions leading up to it. Precisely because the Old Testament is "contained" in the New, we cannot divorce it from the latter. Practically speaking, the New Testament is not understandable without the Old because the New Testament lays its foundation in the Old. We often fail to realize this because we are no longer conscious of the Hellenistic Old Testament and because we regard "Hellenistic" and "Old Testament/Jewish" actually as strict alternatives. Without Sirach 24 *logos*-Christology is cut off from older wisdom theology, and theological evaluation of such development within revelation history has become impossible. Also, setting different theologies within the New Testament in sharp and mutually exclusive contrast to each other, which then leads to a desperate search for a "canon within the canon," [[326]] stems from this disengagement of the New Testament way of thinking from that of the Old Testament. On the one hand, one does not see the multiplicity of traditio-historical starting-points or the linguistic and interpretational fields which must be appropriated from the late Old Testament. And on the other hand, one often presupposes a much too simple and exaggerated theology within late Old Testament texts; this could be shown especially for the concept of the law. A New Testament theology is not feasible until it becomes a part of biblical theology.

Tradition history renders a biblical theology possible because it can describe revelation as history—not as a history of stages which relieve each other and are annulled in succession, but as a total process in which being is made known in the self-disclosure of God. As revelation is truly human-oriented disclosure of God, it does not appeal to a specific human situation but seizes the human entirely, that is, in one's historical dimension. This full revelation can only be revelation *history*. God's self-disclosure in union with the "Thou" can unfold only as a *process*, as a proceeding toward the goal—that God himself appears in the deepest depth of the human, in his uttermost distance from God.

Biblical theology is the comprehending presentation of this revelation history, which leads through all stages of human existence in the historical process. It is the secret of Israel to have been shown this path all the way to the inclusion of the whole world, to have perceived it, and to have handed down this truth. Biblical theology has the task of teaching us to comprehend this tradition, this path.

Theological Synopsis

The 1970s represented a third wave in the production of Old Testament
theologies, after the first wave in the 1930s and the second wave in the
1950s. But resolution to a variety of methodological problems had not
necessarily come. The time was ripe in the 1980s to take stock or to offer
new proposals. Walter Brueggemann did both.

Brueggemann's interest in Old Testament theology was apparent in
publications such as *The Message of the Psalms: A Theological Commentary*
(1984), and the monograph on *The Land* (1977). In fact, the latter
launched the series "Overtures to Biblical Theology" of which Brueggemann is the Old Testament editor. The series, intended to make fresh
probings and explore new hints, has expanded in a dozen years to more
than a dozen monographs covering theological subjects in Old and New
Testaments.

Brueggemann was intrigued, like Claus Westermann, with the polarities within the Old Testament, as well as with trajectories associated with
such polarities. For example, he identified the trajectories that move out
from the Mosaic and the Davidic covenants. The Mosaic trajectory stressed
freedom, tended to be socially revolutionary, and valued transformation.
Occupied with the concrete and focused on the justice and righteousness
of God's will, it was lodged, sociologically, in a marginal group. The royal
trajectory, anchored in David and lodged with people of power, was
different. It moved not so much in the arena of history, as in myth. It was
concerned with stability, even control, and, oriented more universally, it
focused on God's glory and holiness (1979).

Further stocktaking followed (1980). Three theological proposals, each dialectic in form, were reviewed. The first was Westermann's proposal of deliverance/blessing. The second was Samuel Terrien's magnetic opposites, such as God's presence/absence, God's name/God's glory, and summarized as ethical/esthetic. The third was Paul Hanson's cosmic vector/teleological vector. Brueggemann brought the three together in two halves: the deliverance/ethical/teleological half, and the blessing/esthetic/cosmic half. Did such a schema, Brueggemann asked, signal a new direction, one that would not be caught with the totalitarianism of Walther Eichrodt's "center" or the historicism of Gerhard von Rad?

Brueggemann went beyond stocktaking. Leaning on his earlier notion, he offered a newly minted proposal: "The *bi-polar* construct I suggest is that OT faith serves both *to legitimate structure* and *to embrace pain*" (1985: 30, italics his). The first participated in the "common theology" of the ancient Near East, stressed stability, allowed for no slippage, and presented a God tuned to reward and punishment. It could be characterized as "a contractual theology." The second, more of a minority strand, was in irresolvable tension with the first. It focused on grief and compassion, both in God and in Israel. It had elements of protest, as in Israel's laments. It pictured God within the fray of human experience and not detached, outside it.

Walter Brueggemann has been professor of Old Testament at Columbia Theological Seminary in Decatur, Georgia, since 1986, when he completed twenty-five years of teaching at Eden Theological Seminary in Webster Groves, Missouri, his alma mater. His doctorate in theology is from Union Theological Seminary (New York); he also holds a doctorate in education from St. Louis University.

Brueggemann, a scholar with a fertile and imaginative mind, is a prolific writer. He has produced monographs on wisdom, prophecy, and aspects of Old Testament theology, and has written commentaries—often with a decided theological component—on Genesis, Psalms, and Jeremiah. An ordained minister in the United Church of Christ, his churchly interests surface as associated editor of *Journal for Preachers* and as contributing editor of *Sojourners*.

E.A.M.

Writings by Brueggemann

1972   *In Man We Trust: The Neglected Side of Biblical Faith.* Richmond: John Knox.

1977   *The Land: Place as Gift, Promise, and Challenge in Biblical Faith.* Overtures to Biblical Theology. Philadelphia: Fortress.

1979   Trajectories in Old Testament Literature and the Sociology of Ancient Israel. *Journal of Biblical Literature* 98:161–85.

1980   A Convergence in Recent Old Testament Theologies. *Journal for the Study of the Old Testament* 18:2–18.

1984a   Futures in Old Testament Theology. *Horizons in Biblical Theology* 6/1:1–11.

1984b   *The Message of the Psalms: A Theological Commentary.* Augsburg Old Testament Studies. Minneapolis: Augsburg.

1985   A Shape for Old Testament Theology, I: Structure Legitimation; II: Embrace of Pain. *Catholic Biblical Quarterly* 47:28–46, 395–415.

Walter Brueggemann
A Shape for Old Testament Theology

Excerpted with permission from Walter Brueggemann, "A Shape for Old Testament Theology, I: Structure Legitimation; II: Embrace of Pain," *Catholic Biblical Quarterly* 47 (1985) 31, 395–402, 407–15.

Structure Legitimation

⟦31⟧ So the thesis I propose is this: OT theology fully partakes in "the common theology" of its world and yet struggles to be free of that same theology.

(a) Insofar as it partakes of that "common theology," it is *structure-legitimating*. It offers a normative view of God who is above the fray and not impinged upon by social processes.

(b) Insofar as it struggles to be free of that "common theology," it is open to *the embrace of pain* which is experienced from "underneath"[1] in the processes of social interaction and conflict.

(c) Insofar as this faith enters the fray of Israel's experience, it reflects the *ambiguity of our experiences* about structure and pain caused by structure. I understand this to be at the heart of Gottwald's argument that Israel's sense about God has arisen precisely in connection with ambiguity and pain of historical experience.

(d) Insofar as this faith makes claims beyond the fray of experience, it offers to the faithful community *a normative standing place* which may not be derived from the "common theology," but which articulates a normative truth about God not subject to the processes of the articulation. I understand this point to be implied in the canonical position of Childs.

(e) A careful understanding of the literature shows that we are not free to resolve the tension. The OT both partakes of the "common theology" and struggles to be free from it. The OT both enters the fray of ambiguity and seeks distance from the fray to find something certain and sure. The God of Israel is thus presented variously as the God above the fray who appears like other ancient Near Eastern gods and as a God who

---

1. K. Popper, in a discerning and quite unexpected judgment, has observed that whereas the "winners," those "above," regularly write history (and I should argue create theology), it is the story of Jesus and Jesus' people who remember history from below. I should make the same argument about decisive elements of the OT. I cannot now find the exact reference in Popper; but see more broadly *The Open Society and Its Enemies II* (Princeton: Princeton University, 1966), chap. 25.

is exposed in the fray, who appears unlike the gods of "common theology," a God peculiarly available in Israel's historical experiences.[2]

. . . .

Embrace of Pain

⟦395⟧ My first argument, put forth in Part One of this essay, is that OT faith fully partakes in the "common theology" of the ancient Near East, as outlined by Morton Smith.[3] In its basic articulation and view of reality, the OT agrees with the "common theology" of sanctions:

(1) This theology provides an ordered sense of life that is lodged in the sovereignty of God, beyond the reach of historical circumstance. It is a way of speaking about God's non-negotiable governance.

(2) This theology appeals to God as creator in relation to creation. It satisfies a religious yearning by an affirmation of providence. Not only does God govern, but there is an order that works through the processes of history, even if that purpose is not always visible. ⟦396⟧

(3) Such a theology tends to serve the ruling class, which regularly identifies the order of creation with the current social arrangement, so that the "system is the solution." What purports to be an ontological statement always comes out of a process of social interaction.[4] The end result

---

2. P. D. Miller, Jr. ("God and the Gods," *Affirmation* 1/3 [1973] 37–62) has most helpfully explored this issue.

3. See "A Shape for Old Testament Theology, I: Structure Legitimation." *CBQ* 47 (1985) 28–46. The phrase "common theology" is appropriated from Morton Smith, "The Common Theology of the Ancient Near East," *JBL* 71 (1952) 135–47. By the term, Smith refers to a set of standard assumptions and claims of religion that are pervasive in the ancient Near East and are shared in the literature of ancient Israel. Among those pervasive elements Smith includes: (1) Worshipers believe in a high god who is praised extravagantly. (2) This god is claimed to be effective in all realms of history, nature, and morality. (3) This god is acknowledged as just and merciful, to be loved and feared. (4) This god rewards and punishes according to a rigorous pattern of retribution. (5) Prophets in such religion are to be taken seriously, because they can announce the behavior that will lead to reward and avoid punishment. Norman Gottwald (*The Tribes of Yahweh* [Maryknoll, NY: Orbis, 1979] 670–91) has taken up Smith's categories and utilized them most helpfully with a more rigorous sociological method.

4. See the suggestive statement of Carl A. Keller, "Zum sogenannten Vergeltungsglauben in Proverbienbuch," *Beiträge zur alttestamentlichen Theologie* (ed. Herbert Donner, Robert Hanhart, Rudolf Smend; Göttingen: Vandenhoeck & Ruprecht, 1977) 223–38. Keller's thesis is: The "deed-consequence" construct is not primarily linked to a cosmic principle as "world-order" or self-actualizing "sphere of destiny," but is a formulation derived from specific social processes (p. 225). In the language of our first argument, it is that these views are evoked "in the fray." Keller is clear (perhaps against my view) that these are not theological constructions, but are observations out of actual experience. The point is that the claims that seem to be beyond historical experience are in fact fashioned within the experience.

serves to legitimate the precarious earthly settlement held at a particular time in a particular circumstance.

(4) While this theology always speaks of God's rule as settled and "above the fray," the fact is that this theology is always worked out and concerned with being "in the fray." That is, this "contractual theology" is never disinterested, detached, objectively clear or perfectly obvious. It is wrought by power agents who have a socio-political point to score and who mean to defeat alternative views and legitimate their own. Methodologically, it is important to recognize that the theological functioning of structure-legitimation in heaven always carries with it a hint of the legitimation of certain structures on earth.

Clearly the OT is not simply one more statement of "common theology." There is something else going on here to which we must pay careful attention. As the OT is a statement of "common theology," it also states the crisis in "common theology." The crisis comes about because that theology does not square with Israel's experience of life or Israel's experience of faith, i.e., Israel's discernment of God.[5]

Biblical faith, of course, is not static. It is not a set of statements which are always and everywhere true. Therefore, contemporary biblical theology must not be reductionist in order to make it all fit together. Rather, the OT is a collage of documents which bring to speech what seems to be going on in Israel's strange linkage with Yahweh. These two, Yahweh and Israel, are [[397]] lodged in a "common theology" on their way together. But it is important that they are on the way together, and not in a resting place together.[6]

In Israel's practice of "common theology," one may suggest that two moves are underway at the same time, and in opposite directions. On the one hand, there is an *intensification of Yahweh's anger and impatience.* Israel grows more wayward and less inclined to obedience. And, as "common theology" anticipates, Yahweh grows more taut and harsh. The building of intense anger is evident in the prophets of the eighth and seventh centuries, in the theological constructs of the Deuteronomists, in the events of 587, and in the telling response of Lamentations. The prophets move through all kinds of warnings and indictments to the extreme conclusion of Jeremiah that Yahweh wills the end of the city, of the people, and even

---

5. On the crisis of "common theology" see Herbert N. Schneidau, *Sacred Discontent: The Bible and Western Tradition* (Baton Rouge, LA: Louisiana State University, 1977). He understands that the OT is foundationally committed against common myths. Therefore, the community shaped by this book is destined for cultural alienation.

6. For the metaphor of "conversation on the way" as a means of thinking about the theological process, see Paul van Buren, *Discerning the Way* (New York: Seabury, 1980).

of the temple. In the south of Jeremiah, there is a second actualization of Amos' announcement of the end of the north (Amos 8:2). Jerusalem is driven to say that the south has no safe conduct (Jer 7:1–15). Jerusalem will be a dead crater like Shiloh in the north. This intensification of anger is not chagrin that the end has brutally come. It is rather amazement that the end is so long in coming. In retrospect it is clear that the destruction is inevitable and inexorable. The "common theology" has its say. The outcome of judgment for Jerusalem is tightly tied to disobedience.

But in the telling of its faith, Israel discerned a second move. In the heart of God there is an enormous patience, a holding to promises, even in the face of disobedience, a resistance to the theological categories which conventionally give God self-definition. It is clear that this God has reluctance about the singular role of structure-legitimation. The God of Israel wills to be other than "the enforcer." And so there emerges an unbearable incongruity. The incongruity concerns a God committed to a structure of sanctions, and yet with a yearning for a relationship with this disobedient partner.

It is this incongruity in the person of God which forces the issue that scholars are pleased to call the issue of theodicy.[7] But such a labeling, as [398] usually handled, is much too speculative and cerebral. Rather, the problem is that the God of Israel must decide again how much he is committed to the "common theology," how much he must implement its claims, and how much he can resist. That question, of course, is brought to eloquence in the poem of Job, which belongs in the dramatic presentation of this issue. Job makes the argument that the response of God in judgment is disproportionate to any identifiable guilt. The anger of this God seems to go beyond any recognizable warrant, as Job understands it. Perhaps the question raised by this seeming mismatch of disobedience

7. The theological problem of theodicy is regularly handled in OT scholarship. See James L. Crenshaw, "Theodicy," *IDBSup* (New York: Abingdon, 1976) 895–96, for a brief presentation of the issues and the several settlements offered in the text. See also the collection of papers edited by Crenshaw, *Theodicy in the Old Testament* (Issues in Religion and Theology 4; Philadelphia: Fortress, 1983). However, the issue of theodicy cannot be contained in a purely literary, reflective treatment. Peter Berger (*The Sacred Canopy* [Garden City, NY: Doubleday, 1967], chap. 3) has seen that theodicy becomes a problem when the world of plausibility is overwhelmed by facts and social reality that it cannot explain or contain. Jon Gunnemann (*The Moral Meaning of Revolution* [New Haven: Yale University, 1979], chap. 2) has gone further with a sociological understanding of theodicy. That is, it is an argument not that the rules have been wrongly administered, but that the rules are wrong. Thus, revolution means to nullify the settlements made about conduct and payoffs, about who has access and who is denied access. One can make the argument that the exodus event itself was a rejection of the theodicy that was sponsored and legitimated by the Egyptian empire (no doubt with the support of Egyptian religion). The crisis of theodicy is the rejection of the "contract" and of "contractual theology."

and punishment is not, "Does Job serve God for nought?," but "Does Yahweh judge Israel for nought?" The intensification of anger drives Israel's poets to unthinkable thoughts. And so the OT undertakes dangerous intellectual and theological probes against the "common theology."

There is more here than the intensification of anger. If that were all there was, Israel would not break from the "common theology." Israel's theology would be unambiguously structure-legitimating, and it would not be very interesting. OT theology must be bipolar. It is not only about structure-legitimacy, but also about the embrace of pain which changes the calculus. And so my argument in this second statement is that OT theology must attend to *the embrace of pain* as a posture of both Yahweh and Israel. By *embrace of pain* is meant the full acknowledgment of and experience of pain, and the capacity and willingness to make that pain a substantive part of Israel's faith-conversation with its God. Such an act of *embrace* means to articulate the pain fully, to insist on God's reception of the speech and the pain, and to wait hopefully for God's resolution. The term "pain" here refers to any dysfunction in the relationship with God, and any derivative dysfunction in the disorder of creation or society. The pain may be experienced in quite public or quite private ways. But it is all of a piece, because such acknowledgment and articulation are an assertion that the modes of common theology are not adequate or functional to this experience, which is no longer denied. This is the move made against common theology.

Before proceeding to an exposition of this theme, I wish to make three preliminary comments: [[399]]

(1) The practice of pain-embrace *must always be in tension* with the legitimation of structure, never in place of it. It is this tension that is the stuff of biblical faith and it is the stuff of human experience. However, simply to choose the embrace of pain instead of legitimation of structure as a rubric for theology is romanticism. Israel will have none of that. The tension must be kept alive and visible.

(2) The embrace of pain is *a crucial minority voice* in the OT that peculiarly characterizes both the God of Israel and the people of Israel. It is surely a minority voice, always fragile against the dominance of structure-legitimation, which I have already traced. It can only be and must always be a minority voice. But it is a crucial voice. It is this embrace of pain which opens the OT to the future. It is this radical probe of a new way of relationship which runs toward the theology of the cross in the NT and which runs in our time toward and beyond the Holocaust, as Wiesel and Fackenheim have seen so well.[8] It is precisely this fragile minority voice

---

8. See most recently Emil Fackenheim, *To Mend the World* (New York: Schocken, 1982), esp. pp. 278–94.

that gives a future. For without this voice, the unchallenged tendency of structure-legitimation will absolutize the present, so that there can be no future which stands apart from and over against the present.[9]

(3) It is the *disregard* (*or censoring*) *of pain-embrace* in our time and in every time which permits persons and institutions to be unconditionally committed to structure-legitimation. Where pain is not embraced, critical uneasiness about every crushing orthodoxy is banished. It is certain that, where there is the legitimation of structure without the voice of pain embraced, there will be oppression without compassion. There will be competence without mercy. There will be no need for or possibility of good news. Where there is only the legitimacy of structure without pain-embrace, there is only the good news that "the system is the solution," whether the solution is in heaven or on the earth. Good biblical theology, indeed good pastoral theology, keeps alive the tension which dares not to be resolved.

I will consider the embrace of pain as a theological datum in Israel in two parts. Gottwald has considered the issue in sociological categories. But it remains for us to consider the *theological aspects of pain-embrace* in Israel. When it is handled only as sociology and not as theological activity, it likely has no serious future.

[[400]] There is a restlessness in Israel which seeks to move through and beyond or against the "common theology." And that restlessness is articulated in *Israel's practice of lament.*[10] Israel's lament is a way of protesting against the "common theology." The lament in Israel is a way of asserting that the structure cannot always be legitimated, but that the pain needs also to be embraced. This pain, when brought to public speech, impinges upon every structure and serves to question the legitimacy of the structure. The laments of Israel, as Westermann has seen, are not marginal, but decisive for the faith of Israel.

The moment when Israel found the nerve and the faith to risk an assault on the throne of God with complaint was a decisive moment against

9. On the critical relation of past, present, and future, see Gary A. Herion, "The Role of Historical Narrative in Biblical Thought," *JSOT* 21 (1981) 25–57.

10. The practice of lament in the faith of Israel has been most carefully studied by Claus Westermann, *Praise and Lament in the Psalms* (Atlanta: John Knox, 1981). See also W. Brueggemann, "From Hurt to Joy, from Death to Life," *Int* 28 (1974) 3–19; and Patrick D. Miller, "Trouble and Woe," *Int* 37 (1983) 32–45. Following the lead of Westermann, a number of scholars have now seen that the structure of the lament psalm characteristically moves to resolution of the trouble, to praise, and to a restored, though changed, relationship. This, however, does not argue against embrace of pain, nor does it mute the power of such speech. Rather, it is to notice that embrace of pain is the only way in which pain can be submitted to God and thus resolved. See my extended discussion of this matter in *The Message of Psalms* (Minneapolis, MN: Augsburg, 1984) 81–88.

legitimation. The lament is a dramatic, rhetorical, liturgical act of speech which is irreversible. When spoken, it is done and cannot be recalled. It makes clear that Israel will no longer be a submissive, subservient recipient of decrees from the throne. There is a bold movement and voice from Israel's side which does not blindly and docilely accept, but means to have its dangerous say, even in the face of God. In risking this form of speech, the conventional distribution of power is called into question. It is no longer placidly assumed that God has all the power and the covenant partner must simply submit. Pain speaks against legitimacy, which now for the first time is questioned as perhaps illegitimate.

Legitimated structure can never again be utterly indifferent to the embrace of pain. It is like Rosa Parks's refusing to move to the back of the bus in Montgomery. Such a refusal means there can be no more "business as usual." Such an act of the public embrace of pain makes the questioned structure less "above the fray" than it has ever appeared to be before. That irreversible risk was so the first time it was uttered. It is so every time this action is undertaken again.

(1) Consider what an enormous risk it takes to speak such a lament. Lament-speech takes courage because it pushes the relationship to the boundaries of unacceptability. It takes risk because one does not know how the great God would receive it. It might have been an act of disobedience which [[401]] would be crushed according to the normal rules of authority and propriety. It requires deep faith, but not only deep—it requires faith of a new kind. It takes not only nerve but a fresh hunch about this God. The hunch is that this God does not want to be an unchallenged structure, but one who can be frontally addressed. Such is the hope and yearning of lamenting Israel. The outcome of such challenge is not known in advance, until the risk is run to test the hunch. Such dangerous, restless speech could have been received and reckoned as irreverent, disrespectful disobedience. But because the restlessness is not only Israel's but also Yahweh's, this bold speech of assault is in fact received at the throne not as disobedience, but as a new kind of obedience. The gain of Israel's faith is the discernment that this ultimately legitimated structure is indeed open to the embrace of pain, open both for Israel and for God. That can never be known theoretically. It can only be known concretely. The wonder of Israel's faith is that it is concretely risked.

In the risk there emerges a new mode of faith between Yahweh and Israel. In the public utterance of such pain, both parties emerge with freshness. Obedience turns out to be not blind, docile *submissiveness* required by "common theology." It is rather a bold *protest* against a legitimacy that has grown illegitimate because it does not seriously take into account the suffering reality of the partner. Where the reality of suffering is not dealt with, legitimate structure is made illegitimate when the voice of pain assumes enough authority to be heard.

(2) Before moving on, we may ponder the ways in which conventional theological tendency and conventional church practice have nullified the laments. The laments are not widely used among us, not printed in most hymnals, not legitimated in our theology. For many Christians, they are thought to be superseded by some christological claim. In fact, we have in practice reneged on the bold break made in Israel's protest against the "common theology." And unwittingly, by silencing the break of embraced pain, we have embraced the uncritical faith of structure-legitimation. Much biblical faith, as commonly held, has in fact become a support for the status quo, by using a theological mode that understands God primarily in the categories of structure-legitimation. Such a move is reflected both in liturgical use, where the laments have largely fallen out of the repertoire, and in popular theology as reflected in the catechisms, to say nothing of popular proclamation.

(3) The laments are Israel's primary and distinctive departure from the "common theology." Gerstenberger[11] has argued that these speech-forms are not in fact "laments" but "complaints," not *Klagen* but *Anklagen*. That is, [[402]] they are not acts of resignation, but acts of protest. They are not self-pitying meditations on trouble; rather, they are addressed to God. They are speeches which force a new connection between the Lord of Life and the troublesome reality of life, where Israel must live. In this dramatic exchange, Yahweh is recharacterized as the one who must take account of the trouble. God is no longer a trouble-free God. And the trouble is recharacterized as something that now is the proper agenda of Yahweh. Indeed, in these speeches trouble is presented in such a way that it impinges upon Yahweh. Yahweh is no longer free to be a trouble-free God who presides over untroubled legitimated structures. That is, Israel's enormous chutzpah forces a newness upon Yahweh and in Yahweh. Israel's laments force God to recharacterization. To be sure, this act of forcing God to recharacterization is not an unproblematic venture, theologically. It is in deep tension with the reality of God's sovereign freedom to be who God chooses to be. Nonetheless, in this liturgical, rhetorical, passionate moment of extremity, such an action is taken. And the remarkable experience of Israel is that God is impinged upon in decisive ways by such an act. While this rhetorical pattern is a matter of literary interest, it is also a matter of theological marvel, which lives in tension with more static theological categories.

(4) As Gerstenberger has shown, the laments are refusals to settle for the way things are. They are acts of relentless hope which believes no situa-

11. Erhard Gerstenberger, "Jeremiah's Complaints," *JBL* 82 (1963) 393–408, esp. n. 50.

tion falls outside Yahweh's capacity for transformation. No situation falls outside Yahweh's responsibility. Israel is the community which refuses to settle for the way things are, refuses to accept the legitimated structures, refuses to accept a God who is positioned "above the fray," refuses to accept guilt and blame for every dysfunction. Indeed, such a theological hunch does not believe that the doctor knows best, does not believe all authority is ordained by God, does not believe city hall (in heaven or on earth) cannot be fought.

This is a rhetorical form of civil (sometimes uncivil) disobedience that turns out to be a way of obedience.[12]

. . . .

[[407]] It is clear that this restlessness against the intensity of anger impinges upon Israel. But note that the same restlessness with "common theology" is at work with God. Here are hints (only hints) that God begins to feel increasingly uneasy about conventional forms, about standard characterizations of what makes a god a god.

Now in saying this, I am making some delicate assumptions about the nature of the biblical text. I am not arguing that this is simply a clever literary fiction, in which the biblical writers present whatever god they needed to keep the play going. Nor am I arguing that this is flat, descriptive reporting on the mind of God. Rather, I am assuming that the biblical text is an imaginative literary enterprise, in which the writers are like dramatists who create new scenes about God, but who are readily surprised by the moves made by the lead character, almost against the intent and beyond the imagination of the author.[13] The hints we shall consider portray the surprising efforts of Yahweh to break beyond convention and articulate a new identity.

Yahweh is indeed getting free of the pigeonhole due to "common theology." Throughout the OT, it is likely correct that Yahweh never fully breaks through. But there is a restlessness, a probing, a daring alternative that is proposed and lingered with, only then to be withdrawn.[14] And these restless probes may be the primary material for OT theology.

---

12. It is clear that much of "proper faith" is in fact an act of civility to keep the issues of injustice from having visibility. See the insightful analysis of John M. Cuddihy, *The Ordeal of Civility* (New York: Basic Books, 1974), and Norbert Elias, *Power and Civility* (New York: Pantheon, 1982).

13. See in this connection Dale Patrick, *The Rendering of God in the Old Testament* (Philadelphia: Fortress, 1981). Note particularly his references to Hans Frei and David Kelsey.

14. Such bold probing of God has been eloquently characterized by Samuel Terrien, *Job: Poet of Existence* (Indianapolis: Bobbs-Merrill, 1957) 113–17. Terrien quotes T. S. Eliot to good effect:

(1) The first such narrative text is the flood of Gen 6:5–8:22.[15] Bernhard Anderson has studied the structure of the flood narrative in its wholeness, and that need not be repeated here.[16] The main issue is that the flood narrative is not about destructiveness or about a lot of water, but about the troubled heart of God. Or said another way, the narrative is not about the anger of God but about the grief of God.

⟦408⟧ At the beginning of the narrative, two motifs are in tension. The text is carefully wrought to hold the tension in place. On the one hand, we have conventional lawsuit theology:

> The indictment: There is wickedness of imagination, evil continually.
> The sentence: I will blot out. (Gen 6:5, 7)

This is "contractual theology." Such wicked acts warrant such responses of punishment. If that were all we had, it would be a simple, uninteresting story. But on the other hand, intertwined with that structure is a disclosure of the heart of God:

> The Lord was sorry,
> It grieved him to the heart,
> I am sorry I have made them. (vv 6–7)

These lines take us into the interiority of God, where things are troubled and far from clear.[17] The former system gives the public facts of the case. The disobedient deserve to die. The other inclination reveals the internal sense of God that does not easily move into a public form. This combination of public system and internal inclination is a radical theo-

---

> There are only hints and guesses,
> Hints followed by guesses; and the rest
> Is prayer, observance, discipline, thought and action.
> The hint half-guessed, the gift half-understood, is
> Incarnation.

That is how it is with the probes we mention here.

15. See my exploration of this text, *Genesis* (Atlanta: John Knox, 1982) 73–88.

16. Bernhard W. Anderson, "From Analysis to Synthesis: The Interpretation of Genesis 1–11," *JBL* 97 (1978) 23–29.

17. This aspect of God's character is affirmed from an unexpected source. Bertil Albrektson (*History and the Gods* [Lund: Gleerup, 1967]) is best known for his insistence that the biblical God is not unique for action in history. But on p. 122 he writes, "We learn about Yahweh's purposes and intentions, his true nature and the innermost thoughts of his heart, his gifts and his claims, which make him different from all the other gods of the ancient Near East." It is that distinctiveness that is narrated in this text. See N. Gottwald, *The Tribes of Yahweh*, 674–75, for his comment on Albrektson.

logical disclosure. God has an internal life which does not conform to contractual norms. Things are at play and are yet to be decided. There is anguish, uncertainty, ambiguity, mixed feelings, and presumably some option. This is not how the high gods work who punish evil and reward good. So we are put on notice of a theological risk here on the part of Yahweh.

The narrative proceeds just as it should have, if there were only "common theology." There is water, destruction, and death. The story could and should have ended in Gen 7:24. There is more to the story only because there is more to God. "God remembers."[18] God is self-reflective and has a past to which appeal is made. God makes commitments and subsequently honors [[409]] them. God is not an automatic principle. At the center of the story is a person who cares. Caring is what legitimated structure cannot do.[19]

The conclusion of this narrative in Gen 8:20–22 is, of course, well-known. In the end, the waters are driven away. There is a promise that it will not happen again. Yahweh makes a new resolve and a new promise. In the end only one thing remains the same: "Man's imagination of his heart is still evil." That has not changed. Humankind is seen to be resiliently and relentlessly evil.

Yet a new relation is possible. The heart of "man" in 8:21 is as it was in 6:5. The change which makes a new future possible is wrought not in the human heart, but in Yahweh's heart, which is filled with sorrow, grief, regret. The flood is about the inundation of God's person. The narrative tells about a new resolve on God's part, which takes God outside the framework of "evil imagination" and "blotting out," i.e., outside the lawsuit of contractual theology. There is here a disclosure that Yahweh has heart trouble, knows something of pain, and does not act finally to legitimate order. To be sure, in 8:22 there is again a guaranteed order, but it is on the other side of God's turned heart. Pain for Yahweh has caused a turn in the flood and a turn in the narrative, and—we dare to think— a turn in the theological enterprise.

---

18. On "God Remembers," see Ralph W. Klein, "The Message of P," *Die Botschaft und die Boten* (ed. Jörg Jeremias and Lothar Perlitt; Neukirchen-Vluyn: Neukirchener V., 1981) 57–66. Klein argues that, in the P tradition, "signs" such as the rainbow and circumcision are established to help God remember. In the flood narrative, such special reminders are not necessary. The importance of Klein's argument for our discussion is that it also points to the interiority and life of freedom which Yahweh has.

19. I do not want to push the theme of "caring" too far, but reference might be made to Carol Gulligan, *In A Different Voice* (Cambridge: Harvard University, 1982). The theme has theological, as well as psychological, developmental dimensions.

(2) In Gen 18:16–19:22,[20] there is a complex narrative concerning Sodom and Gomorrah. I suggest this narrative presents the same tensions we have been considering elsewhere. In 19:1–29, there is the old, patterned story. Except for the mitigation concerning Lot's family in vv 12–23, the story is flat and predictable, according to "contractual theology":

> vv 1–11 the presentation of wickedness and outcry—indictment
> vv 24–28 fire and brimstone—sentence

The structure is a simple judgment story, befitting conventional, traditional theology.

But what interests us more is the counternarrative in 18:16–33, which lives in tension with the older narrative of 19:1–29. In 18:16–19, there is an extravagant credentialing of Abraham, perhaps the most extravagant of all of scripture. The simple story of guilt in chap. 19 could be operative without Abraham. But the introduction of Abraham in this alternative version allows for slippage and surprise. In 18:30 there is the verdict. But there is no flat, automatic rush to judgment. Abraham is present and his presence means there are promises to be kept and impossibilities to ponder (see v 14).

[[410]] Verses 22–23 contain some of the most remarkable material in the OT.

(a) Verse 22 contains a most important textual issue. The corrected text, as we have it, has Abraham standing before the Lord in a posture of proper deference. But we are told that the "uncorrected" form of the text reversed postures and placed Yahweh deferentially before Abraham for questioning and instruction. And indeed, that is the tone of the narrative.

(b) In vv 13–24, Abraham poses the question to Yahweh about the judge judging equitably. Admittedly the issue is not very much developed. It is not argued here that the presence of the innocent should save the guilty. It is only proposed that the innocent should not be destroyed with the guilty. But the question introduces for Yahweh a new theological sensitivity. It is as though Abraham has posed for Yahweh a new question about what kind of god to be, whether to notice people in their concreteness or to operate like the usual gods in rather summary fashion.

(c) The double question is answered by Abraham in v 25: "Far be it from thee!" The term is *ḥll*, which may mean unworthy, profane, unacceptable, i.e., incongruous with the holiness of God's character, upon

---

20. See my exploration of this text, *Genesis*, 162–76. Joseph Blenkinsopp ("Abraham and the Righteous of Sodom (Gen. 18:23–32)," *JJS* 35 [1982] 119–32) has provided a most discerning history of interpretation of this passage.

which God had not yet reflected. Abraham identifies such harsh judgment as inappropriate to and incompatible with the character of God, though God has not yet arrived at this insight about self-characterization.

The acknowledgment by Yahweh of the rightness of Abraham's argument is given in v 26. There then follows in vv 27–33 the wonderful and amusing negotiation between God and Abraham about the minimum number which might save the city. In its outcome, the narrative is thoroughly Jewish because the bottom line is the minimum of ten, a minyan. The story ends rather abruptly with the mutual departure. Abraham and Yahweh had gone as far as they could with this bold and dangerous exploration of a new characterization of God and a new practice of righteousness.

It is clear that the narratives of Gen 18:16–33 and 19:1–29 reflect very different theological efforts, the second being written out of exactly the purview presented by Smith. The present form of the text links them together, but they do not flow easily. Chap. 19 is an automatic playing out of the story of guilt and punishment. But chap. 18 lingers over the decisions that Yahweh has yet to make. In this narrative God is open to and instructed by Abraham about the reality of hurt and need in the human arena.

In the present form of the text, one can, of course, conclude that after such a radical probing, the narrative pushes along with business as usual to its terrible, predictable ending. Abraham's dangerous proposal to God is in vain. The *probe* of chap. 18 did not change the *convention* of chap. 19. The standard act of structure-legitimacy is not penetrated by the embrace of this more nuanced human reality. But perhaps that is to miss the point of literary finesse. The unthinkable has now been thought. The unutterable has now [[411]] been uttered. The question has now been asked of the judge of all the earth: "Shall not the judge of all the earth do right?" Will not the *šōpēṭ* do *mišpāṭ*? The question cannot be unasked. It lingers in the mind of God and God must decide afresh what that means. The effect of such a probe is to give God some distance, so that there are options, so that God is not taken for granted. The voice of real human hurt is embraced here in the context of the question of righteousness and justice. And though the old theology is implemented in chap. 19, it has been questioned and placed in jeopardy by the probe of chap. 18. The old, presumed systems of settlement are now placed in question. As we shall see, the question persists.

(3) Our third text, Hos 11:1–9, is well-known and perhaps the most important for the point being made. This poem is a rather conventional lawsuit form. Much of the tradition of Hosea adheres to lawsuit conventions and is even more rigorous and harsh than is much of Amos. Indeed,

stereotypes which treat Hosea as a "prophet of love" without further reflection miss the main point. In this text, vv 1–3 are a recital of God's graciousness, intertwined with an indictment:

> They went from me . . .
> they kept sacrificing to Baals,
>   and burning incense to idols.
> They did not know I healed them.

They forgot who was God (cf. 8:14). And the sentence in vv 4–7 is flat and predictable: exile, even death. That much is "common theology." And that should be the end of that. There the poem might have ended. That is where we conventionally stop with "contractual theology." The wonder is that the poet stays with the poem beyond this point. The greater wonder is that the God rendered in this poem focuses attention on the continuing question of Gen 18:25, when one might have thought vv 4–7 to be God's last thought on the question.

But it is precisely where the end is expected and justified that the poem takes on a new vitality. In v 8a there are four rhetorical questions which God asks "himself."[21] They are introspective questions, to which the answer is not known ahead of time, even to God. That is, this is not mere rhetoric, but a genuine probe. Yahweh probes for a new way of relating that moves beyond the end to which v 7 had brought things. It is important that the poem, in moving to this newness wrought in pain, makes explicit reference to the dilemma of Genesis 18–19. The reference to Admah and Zeboiim is to be taken as a reference to Sodom and Gomorrah. It is as though God now recalls that narrative. God now remembers what was done there against the [[412]] urging of Abraham, how painful it was, and whether it would be done again, this time against the proper, beloved covenant-partner. The question is a dangerous one for God to ask. All the old notions about what it means to be God come into play. The question is asked four times. Then there is a reflection on what this question does to God.

The reference back to Genesis 18–19 may be intensified by the use of the verb *hāpak*, which RSV renders "recoil." It is the verb used in Gen 19:25, 29 to characterize the earthquake. In that narrative God is not touched by the destruction which is externally executed against the wicked cities. Now, in this remarkable turn by the poem, God does not cause the earthquake against Israel, which is as deserving of it as Sodom and Gomorrah.

21. J. Gerald Janzen, "Metaphor and Reality in Hosea 11," *Semeia* 24 (1982) 7–44.

Now God takes to God's own heart the pain and the upheaval that one expects to be actualized. God's heart is impinged upon (not unlike in the flood story). God is unable to do the warranted act, precisely because God is no longer able to be a one-dimensional legitimator of structure. Now God is transformed by the embrace of pain in God's own person, which changes the calculus with reference to Israel. What had been done to Sodom and Gomorrah is now done to God's own person.[22] The next phrase in v 8 is difficult. It the term *nḥm* is retained, it holds for us the same term used to characterize God's regret in the flood narrative. If the conventional emendation is taken and the term is rendered as *rḥm*, then the impact upon God's own body is intensified.

So the probing questions of v 8 are answered in v 9. There will be no destruction. "The Holy One" is the one who makes the new decisions. This Holy One knows that there are promises to keep. What happens in this moment of the poem is that God's holiness is recharacterized as compassion. The move made here is not unlike the one proposed in Gen 18:23–25 by Abraham, though the words are different. Finally in v 9, God resolves not to act like *ʾiš*. God will not act in destructive, retaliatory ways, because God has broken with the usual human notions of retribution.[23] It is as though the whole enterprise of "contractual theology" is here treated as an unworthy human construct. God has until now been laboring under this reading of reality. But in this moment of acute pain, when the hurt of Israel is taken into [[413]] God's own heart, that conventional reading of earth and heaven is nullified and God assumes a new posture toward the covenant partner.

This is bold poetry on the part of Hosea, for the poet hazards the mind of God. What is discerned is that God has broken all the conventions. "Common theology" is rejected as a human construct and a human expectation, a mode to which God need not conform.

God's break with the "common theology" is not an easy step. It is a break wrought only in moving grief, only in solidarity with the grief of Israel. It is when God can grieve that there is a possibility of breaking out of such conventional categories.

---

22. I would not want to press the poetry into excessively rigid categories, but I take warrant from Eliot's "hint-guess of Incarnation." This formulation of the matter, when read in light of Genesis 18–19, affirms that God takes into God's person what rightly belongs to Israel. It is a step in the direction of saying, "He died that we might live."

23. Psalm 82 is also a discussion over what constitutes the godness of God. It is argued that care for the marginal is what makes God God. The other gods are condemned to die as "men," no doubt because they lack the compassion of God and only serve themselves according to human standards. The term "men" there is *ʾādām* (not the same term as in Hos 11:9), but the point seems parallel.

(4) The poem of Jer 30:12–17 presents yet another articulation of the same issue in Israel's discernment of God. The key literary problem in this poem is how to relate vv 12–15 to vv 16–17. The first element announces that the pain in incurable and the last two verses promise healing. The theological issue is how God makes the move from harsh rejection to positive intervention. Conventional critical treatment assumes that vv 16–17 are a later redactional addition to soften the previous verses. The problem with such an approach, of course, is that it violates the poem and dissolves all of the possible poetic playfulness.

If we are to take the poem as it stands,[24] then we must seek within the poem ground for the move to v 15. In v 14 Yahweh asserts that "no one cares." The odd turn is justified, if the final *kî* in v 17 is read as causative. that is, I will be healing *because* "they have called you an outcast." In v 17, the nations are said to repeat the very formula that was in the mouth of Yahweh in v 14.

That is intolerable. As long as the issue is between the two covenant partners, Yahweh can be harsh and final. But when the nations (as outsiders to the relationship) make the same judgment, Yahweh is evoked (or provoked) to new action which turns out to be saving. I submit that the break with contractual, structure-legitimating theology articulated in vv 16–17 is made because Yahweh is brought much closer to the hurt that Israel experiences. Contact with that hurt causes Yahweh to assume a new posture and to recharacterize the future of Israel.

Now to be sure, we have touched only a few texts and even these could be probed in greater depth. Other texts could be cited; but even with the other texts, the OT offers no more than a probe, a hint, or an urging. This is ⟦414⟧ not the main presentation of faith, which is still dominated (as indicated) by the power of structure-legitimation. But the presence of such texts is important for discerning the dynamic of OT theology.

The following conclusions may be suggested on the basis of these considerations.

(1) The dominant mode of the OT is contractual, a *quid pro quo*—a mode which serves to legitimate structure in heaven and on earth.

(2) Where the countertheme of pain-embracing is present, it does not supersede or nullify structure-legitimation, but only lives in tension with it. And that tension must be kept alive in all faithful biblical theology. I do not believe one can say there is a development from one to the other, but there is an ongoing tension, unresolved and unresolvable.

---

24. See my discussion of this passage, "The 'Uncared For' Now Cared For (Jer 30:12–17): A Methodological Consideration," forthcoming in *JBL* ⟦104 (1982) 419–28⟧.

(3) In the OT, the voice of pain is a minority wonderment, never a central proposal. But it is this which gives vitality and openness to the entire enterprise. Thus, these texts of probing perform a function in OT theology disproportionate to their number and strength.

(4) Insofar as OT theology is related to the life of the church, this way of organizing our understanding of the text may be peculiarly poignant in our cultural context. There is a great tendency now, both religiously and politically, to want the text to serve purposes of structure-legitimation. This is no doubt powered by the enormous fear and sense of chaos that are close at hand. But such a way of treating the text, for whatever reason, requires pushing the text unambiguously back into a pattern of "contractual theology" which ignores the hints and probes that are offered. The probes of pain-embrace affirm that the text asserts more than mere contract. The text understands that God's good news consists in more than structure-legitimation. Human personhood in the image of this God always entails pain-embrace, which causes transformation and breaks beyond contractual relationships.

Israel, from its earliest time, had understood this. In the early and programmatic formulation of Exod 34:6–7, the tension is already spelled out.[25] On the one hand, God takes violators seriously, well into the future. On the other hand, this same God is merciful and gracious. No doubt the text contains a deep incongruity. But the God of the Bible does not flinch from this incongruity. It is this incongruity that makes human life possible and makes biblical theology endlessly problematic and promising. It is my suggestion that this double focus can be carried through in a biblical theology that [[415]] probes what structure-legitimation and pain-embrace mean for our understanding of God, of Israel, of human personhood, of church, of creation.

The God portrayed here is an ambiguous one, always in the process[26] of deciding. For Israel the issue is whether to be "like the nations" or to be a "holy people." Israel dared to say that its God, Yahweh, lived in the same

25. On this crucial passage, see N. Gottwald, *The Tribes of Yahweh*, 686–91. The continuing power of this tension and the continuing vitality of the articulation of Exod 34:6–7 is evident in Walter Harrelson, "Ezra Among the Wicked in 2 Esdras 3–10," *The Divine Helmsman* (ed. James L. Crenshaw and Samuel Sandmel; New York: Ktav, 1980) 21–39. On pp. 35–39, Harrelson comments on the remarkable exegesis of Exod 34:6–7 offered in 2 Esdras.

26. In the terms offered here, there is no doubt that God is "in process." It may be that such an articulation opens to an interface with so-called process theology. Perhaps so. But I am unconvinced about the enormous metaphysical superstructure of process philosophy as being useful for interpreting the Bible. It appears to me much simpler and more effective to deal with social/covenantal/personal metaphors on the Bible's own terms. In another context I have suggested that process theology is inherently more conservative than is recognized in some quarters.

ambiguity: whether to be "like the other gods" or to be a holy God, "the Holy One in our midst," who had learned from Abraham fresh subversive notions of *ṣĕdāqâ* and *mišpāṭ*.[27] The God-question is intimately linked to the character of Israel in the OT. And the sociological tracings of Gottwald are intimately linked to theological questions proper. Israel as a social experiment could have little positive prospect unless it sojourned with a God who noted, responded to, and embodied the pain that Israel was also to embody. Yahweh's probe of godness away from the gods of the Egyptian empire is at least as important as Israel's probe of a sociology alternative to that of the empire.

27. Robert Polzin (*Moses and the Deuteronomist* [New York: Seabury, 1980] 36–43) has seen that, at least in Deuteronomy, the issues of Yahweh's uniqueness and Israel's distinctiveness are intimately linked together.

JON D. LEVENSON

b. 1949

Creation and Covenant

Theological Synopsis

It may seem that Old Testament theology would be an inquiry in which Jews and Christians could cooperate. According to Jon Levenson, "the sad fact, however, is that the endeavor known as 'Old Testament theology' has been, as its name suggests, an almost exclusively Gentile affair" (1985: 1). This is a "sad fact," says Levenson, not because Jews have neglected to join Christians in Old Testament theology—"Old Testament" is itself a Christian term—but because Christian biblical theologians have refused to consider whether Jewish tradition is an aid in understanding the religion of ancient Israel. Instead, even those scholars who take a historical-critical approach to the Bible tend to share a distinctly Christian prejudice against Israel's central institutions, the Torah and the Temple. Jews are not eager to join a discipline whose anti-Semitism has been apparent (1987: 287–91). Furthermore, Levenson argues that biblical theology has reflected a distinctly Protestant commitment to "repristinization" (1987: 292), trying to move behind tradition to the original purity of the Bible. Such a commitment is incompatible with Judaism, for which the Bible cannot simply be isolated from the history of commentary on it. Finally, Jews do not share the interest of Christian biblical theologians in finding a systematic unity within the Bible; the diversity of the Bible, or of the Old Testament, is a problem for Christians, not for Jews (1987: 296–300).

These considerations lead Levenson to conclude that "the message of the Hebrew Bible is a function of the tradition in which it is contextualized" (1987: 300). If Old Testament theology, or a theology of the Hebrew Bible, does aim to determine the message of the Bible, then on Levenson's accounting the Bible will have to be "contextualized" within either Judaism or Christianity. That rules out the possibility that biblical theology can

427

simply be an ecumenical venture between Jews and Christians. While not ruling out all cooperation between Jews and Christians, Levenson limits and defines its possibilities: "Only within the limited area of the smaller literary and historical contexts is an ecumenical biblical theology possible, and only as awareness grows of the difference that context makes shall we understand where agreement is possible and where it is not, and why" (1988b: 225).

Levenson pursues his theological study within the literary context of the Hebrew Bible, and within the historical context of ancient Israel. He does so, though, with an eye for the continuities between the Hebrew Bible and the literature of rabbinic Judaism. Two biblical themes of central importance to Judaism are covenant and creation. Levenson shows the kind of importance they have, and he shows how critical study of the Hebrew Bible can illumine them—for both Jews and Christians. In that way, he opens a conversation within and about Old Testament theology. In addition, Levenson shows from a distinctively Jewish perspective how critical biblical scholarship can continue to be theologically interested and related constructively to the religious communities it sometimes serves.

Jon D. Levenson is a graduate of the Near Eastern studies program at Harvard University, where he took his Ph.D. in 1975. He taught Hebrew Bible at Wellesley College (1975–82) and in the University of Chicago's Divinity School (1982–88). In 1988, he returned to Harvard as the Albert A. List Professor of Jewish Studies. Levenson's published scholarship ranges widely; it includes studies of the Hebrew Bible, methods in biblical scholarship, Jewish interpretation of the Bible, and theology. Levenson's theological contributions are especially important, since he confronts the predominantly Christian interpretation of the Bible directly and knowledgeably.

B.C.O.

Writings by Levenson

1985   *Sinai and Zion: An Entry into the Jewish Bible.* Minneapolis: Winston.

1987   Why Jews Are Not Interested in Biblical Theology. Pp. 281–307 in *Judaic Perspectives on Ancient Israel.* Edited by Jacob Neusner, Baruch A. Levine, and Ernest S. Frerichs. Philadelphia: Fortress.

1988a   *Creation and the Persistence of Evil: The Jewish Drama of Divine Omnipotence.* San Francisco: Harper & Row.

1988b   The Eighth Principle of Judaism and the Literary Simultaneity of Scripture. *Journal of Religion* 68:205–25.

Jon D. Levenson
Idioms of Creation and Covenant

Excerpted with permission from Jon D. Levenson, *Creation and the Persistence of Evil: The Jewish Drama of Divine Omnipotence* (San Francisco: Harper & Row, 1986), pp. 131–39, 174–75; and Jon D. Levenson, *Sinai and Zion: An Entry into the Jewish Bible* (Minneapolis: Winston, 1985), pp. 38–41, 80–86.

The Two Idioms of Biblical Monotheism
[from *Creation and the Persistence of Evil*]

[131] In the subordination of the other gods to Marduk in the *Enuma elish*, we see the emergence of a pattern that can, with appropriate qualification, be termed monotheism. Marduk, it will be recalled, demanded as the terms for his taking on Tiamat that his father Ea "convene the assembly and proclaim my lot supreme" so that he, instead of them, might "determine the destinies" and whatever he creates "shall remain unaltered."[1] Anxious to avert the lethal threat, the gods hold court and, in an atmosphere of bibulous festivity, carefree and exalted at last, they proclaim him their lord and erect him a royal dais.[2] The keynote of the homage that they then pay him is his incomparability: "You are [the most] important among the great gods" and "none among the gods shall infringe upon your prerogative." "To you," they announce, "we have given kingship over the totality of the whole universe."[3] This preliminary exaltation of Marduk at the expense of the other gods is ratified and established in perpetuity when he wins his victory and receives his temple and temple-city. In building these, the gods demonstrate their gratitude to Marduk for having beaten back the threat of chaos and for having liberated them from drudgery through the creation of humanity.[4] His acts of prowess, together with the gods' formal acknowledgment of the legal implications of them, thus become the basis of both cosmic and political order. They are the foundation of Babylon's very existence and the ground of her claim to world dominance.

---

1. *Enuma elish* 2:122–129 (Alexander Heidel, *The Babylonian Genesis*, 2nd ed. [Chicago: University of Chicago, 1963], 29–30).
2. *Enuma elish* 3:138; 4:1 (Heidel, *Babylonian Genesis*, 36).
3. *Enuma elish* 4:5, 10, 14 (Heidel, *Babylonian Genesis*, 36, except that I have modernized Heidel's archaic second person forms).
4. *Enuma elish* 6:49–54 (Heidel, *Babylonian Genesis*, 48).

As it appears in the *Enuma elish,* the creation of the world involves a movement from plurality to unity, from the fragile and cumbersome system of "primitive democracy" among the gods to the tougher and more efficient monarchy of the divine military [[132]] hero, Marduk.[5] Consensus is not, however, abolished. Rather, the endless and tiresome process of deliberation is reduced to the formulation of only one resolution— whether to accept Marduk's offer, whether to make him king. On this alone is consensus necessary and, it must be noted, easy to reach in light of the certain defeat that lies ahead without his leadership. In short, their choice for him is not much of a choice at all, the alternative being death. This is underscored by the imprisonment of those who confederated with Tiamat and the obvious absence of neutrality as an option. It is, nonetheless, remarkable that even the emergence of monarchy is here presented as having required a vote, as it were, and the supremacy of Marduk is not seen as primordial, self-evident, and self-sufficient, but as dependent upon the consent of the other gods.[6] In practice his elevation ends their autonomy, but in theory it does not nullify it. In full autonomy, they choose to subordinate themselves forever in order to live and be free. The paradox of world order is, to adapt Paul Ricoeur's characterization of Pharisaism, that it rests on "voluntary heteromony."[7] It is the gods' glad willingness to *choose heteronomy* that allows order, safety, and even liberty to appear.

The periodic public recitation of the *Enuma elish,* especially during the New Year's festival, indicates that this choice of heteronomy, the willing acceptance of Marduk's lordship, was never so final as a superficial reading of the great creation poem might suggest. Tzvi Abusch has recently opposed the conventional view that the *Enuma elish* is simply a reflection of the ascent of Babylon to hegemony, preferring instead to date it to "some time during the early first millennium in a period of political *weakness* of the city Babylon."[8] This fits nicely with my argument that in Israel the combat myth of creation increasingly tended to appear in moments in which YHWH and his promises to the nation seemed discredited.[9] In both cases the myth and its ritual reiteration would have had a compensa-

---

5. See Thorkild Jacobsen, "Primitive Democracy in Ancient Mesopotamia," in *Toward the Image of Tammuz and Other Essays on Mesopotamian History and Culture,* ed. William L. Moran, HSS 21 (Cambridge: Harvard University, 1970), 157–70, esp. pp. 163–169.

6. On the theory and practice of acclamation in both Mesopotamia and Israel, see Baruch Halpern, *The Constitution of the Monarchy in Israel,* HSM 25 (Chico: Scholars, 1981), esp. pp. 51–148.

7. Paul Ricoeur, *The Symbolism of Evil* (Boston: Beacon, 1969), 127.

8. I. Tzvi Abusch, "Merodach," in *Harper's Bible Dictionary,* ed. Paul J. Achtemeier (San Francisco: Harper & Row, 1985), 627 (my italics).

9. See [[Levenson 1988a:]] pp. 17–25.

tory or restorative role, serving to counter the persistence of the dark forces identified with the chaos monster. By reciting the *Enuma elish*, the cultic community overtly casts its lot with the gods acclaiming Marduk and differentiates [[133]] themselves from the army of Tiamat, destined for perdition. Covertly, they acknowledge the incompleteness of Marduk's supremacy and the persistence and resilience of the evil whose destruction *in illo tempore* they celebrate. The recitation of the *Enuma elish* is, in part, a reestablishment of social consensus, which readily dissolves when the community evades their task of self-subordination. Only the inextinguishable urge to do so accounts for the continuing pertinence of the poem.

In spite of the commonplace that Israel was monotheistic and thus radically distinct from the rest of the ancient world, clear echoes of this subordination of the pantheon to its king are to be heard in the Hebrew Bible as well:

> [1]Ascribe to the LORD, O divine beings,
> ascribe to the LORD glory and strength.
> [2]Ascribe to the LORD the glory of His name,
> bow down to the LORD when He appears in holiness.
>
> [10]The LORD sat enthroned at the Flood;
> the LORD sits enthroned, king forever.   (Ps 29:1–2, 10)[10]

That Psalm 29 is a YHWHistic adaptation of Baal hymns has long been recognized.[11] This, together with the context, makes it all the more certain that the "Flood" in v. 10 is not the great deluge of Noah's time, but rather the assault of chaos upon order in the form of the sea monster's bellicose challenge to the pantheon. It is possible that this allusion hints at a time when YHWH had not yet attained to supremacy, becoming, like Marduk, king only upon his victory. Even if this be so, the emphasis in the hymn is not upon the old and presumably failed arrangement of "democracy" in the pantheon, but upon the awesomeness of YHWH's mastery and the corollary obligation of the lesser gods to render him homage. Were those gods nonexistent or that homage never in doubt, Psalm 29 would have no point.

In Exodus 15, the Song of the Sea, we again read the hymnic affirmation of YHWH's incomparability: [[134]]

---

10. The translation departs from the NJV at the end of v. 2 for reasons laid out by Frank Moore Cross, "Notes on a Canaanite Psalm in the Old Testament," *BASOR* 117 (1950): 21.

11. See especially Theodore H. Gaster, "Psalm 29," *JQR* 37 (1946): 55–65. The earliest observation of the Canaanite roots of the psalm was that of H. L. Ginsberg, *Kitve Ugarit* (Jerusalem: Bialik, 1936), 129ff.

> Who is like You, O LORD, among the gods;
> Who is like You, majestic among the holy ones,
> Awesome in splendor, working wonders?   (Exod 15:11)[12]

The difference is that here YHWH's band of loyal confederates is not divine, but human, the people he acquired through manumission and settled on his mountain, the site of the sanctuary in which his everlasting kingship is proclaimed. Similarly, the confederates of the vanquished enemy are also human—Philistia, Edom, Moab, and Canaan, all of them panicked and aghast at the sight of YHWH's deliverance of Israel at the sea.[13] Israel's indomitability follows from her identification with the cause of YHWH, just as the defeat of her neighbors follows from their failure to submit to him and their choice of other gods. This too becomes explicit in the Psalter:

> ⁷All who worship images,
>   who vaunt their idols,
>   are dismayed;
>   all gods bow down to Him.
> ⁸Zion, hearing it, rejoices,
>   The towns of Judah exult,
>   because of Your judgments, O LORD,
> ⁹For You, LORD, are supreme over all the earth;
>   You are exalted high above all gods.   (Ps 97:7–9)[14]

The other gods and their worshipers are forced into submission, even as Judah and its Temple Mount, Zion, rejoice at the decrees (*mišpāṭîm*) of YHWH, great king and greatest God.

If we bear in mind this partial replacement of the other gods with the people Israel, then we shall see that in its broadest outlines, the Exodus–Sinai narrative conforms to the same pattern as that of the *Enuma elish*. An enslaved people calls out to YHWH to rescue them, and he responds in a wondrous way, saving them at the sea and drowning the picked troops of the god incarnate of Egypt. Israel acclaims YHWH as incomparable, their king forever, and he, having brought them to Sinai, offers them a covenant, by which they may become his "treasured possession among all the [135] peoples . . . a kingdom of priests and a holy nation." Unanimously

---

12. Again, the translation departs from the NJV in order to bring out the full implications of *ʾēlîm* and *qōdeš*. See Frank Moore Cross, *Canaanite Myth and Hebrew Epic* (Cambridge, Mass.: Harvard University, 1973), 129, n. 61.

13. Exod 15:13–18.

14. "Gods" in vv. 7 and 9 is a departure from NJV's pale and misleading "divine beings."

they accept: "All that the Lord has spoken we will do."[15] The entire revelation at Sinai is a specification of what that commitment entails. First and
foremost is the demand that no other god infringe upon the claim of him
who redeemed Israel from the house of bondage.

In spite of some demurrals, there is today wide agreement among
scholars that the theology of the Pentateuch is deeply imbued with the
idiom of the Near Eastern suzerainty treaty: YHWH, acting in the role
of an emperor, cites the record of his benefactions to his needy vassal Israel and elicits from her a sworn commitment to observe the stipulations
he imposes, to the benefit of both so long as she keeps faith.[16] As persuasive as the treaty analogy is, it should be noted that much the same
pattern can be detected in mythic literature, such as the *Enuma elish* and
its Canaanite and Israelite parallels: the gods willingly and gladly accept
the kingship of their heroic savior, grant him the right to determine the
destinies, and redefine themselves as his servitors. It is this act of voluntary heteronomy that, by establishing his kingship and ensuring their
survival, works to the benefit of both lord and liege. There is, of course,
a vast formal difference between the covenant and the combat myth.
The first originates in the world of diplomacy, the second in cult. But
when the language of diplomacy is transposed into theology, YHWH replacing the emperor, and the language of cult is substantially histori-
cized, people (largely) replacing gods, the convergence is remarkable.
In the Hebrew Bible, covenant and combat myth are two variant idioms
for one ideal—the exclusive enthronement of YHWH and the radical
and uncompromising commitment of the House of Israel to carrying out
his commands. If "monotheism" refers to anything in the conceptual
universe of biblical Israel, it refers to that ideal.

The great threat to monotheism, so understood, is defection. In the
mythic idiom defection takes the form of a challenge to YHWH's supremacy among the gods. The allusions to YHWH's composure in the face of
the angry, roiling sea reflect such a challenge, although in a rather demythologized way.[17] More pertinent [[136]] are the instances in which
YHWH pronounces a verdict upon other gods, as in Psalm 82, in which
the failure of the others to practice justice (in the classic form of special
protection for the poor and the orphan) results in a death sentence. In a
few other passages, mostly in the prophets, we find allusions to a lost myth

15. Exod 19:5, 8.

16. The most exhaustive discussion is Dennis J. McCarthy, *Treaty and Covenant*, AnBib
21A (Rome: Biblical Institute Press, 1978). See also Jon D. Levenson, *Sinai and Zion* (San
Francisco: Harper & Row, 1987), esp. pp. 23–80. The most recent survey from a revisionist
perspective is Ernest W. Nicholson, *God and His People* (Oxford: Oxford University, 1986).

17. E.g., Ps 93:3–4.

in which, having failed to make good on his claim of sovereignty, a god is ejected from the pantheon.[18] Later this story of the excommunicated deity will fuse with the biblical figure Satan, the heavenly attorney general, to produce the myth of Lucifer, the fallen angel who rules hell in Christian demonology. But in the Hebrew Bible, the fusion has not taken place, and the myth of the primordial theomachy or the revolt in heaven (*which* of them is unclear and must be determined in each case) is barely recoverable. That snippets of it are indeed to be found evidences profound insecurity about YHWH's kingship even within the world of Israelite myth. The absence of the full-blown myth has been taken by Kaufmann and others as proof of the radical demythologized character of Israelite religion.[19] To me it seems more consistent and more reasonable to conclude the opposite: it is precisely what is most dangerous and most alluring that must be repressed. That the myth of theomachy or rebellion has been repressed rather than destroyed accounts for the fact that we now have snippets, and only snippets.

In the other idiom of monotheism, the idiom of covenant, defection takes the form of Israel's worship of other gods, either in place of YHWH or alongside him. This aspect of biblical monotheism derives from the demand of ancient Near Eastern covenant lords (suzerains) that the vassal forswear allegiance to rival suzerains, taking special precautions to avoid the appearance of obeisance to any but his own lord in covenant. "Do not turn your eyes to anyone else," Mursilis, Hittite emperor of the fourteenth century B.C.E., warned his vassal, Duppi-Tessub of Amurru.[20] One of the great breakthroughs in the study of covenant occurred when William L. Moran identified "love" as one of the central items in the vocabulary of this idea of exclusive allegiance.[21] In an Assyrian treaty of the seventh century B.C.E., King Esarhaddon, anxious that [[137]] his vassals may break faith with his designated successor, Assurbanipal, stipulates that "You will love Assurbanipal as yourselves." Elsewhere, the vassals swear that "the king of Assyria, our lord, we will love."[22] It is this covenantal use of "love" that makes the transition between the first two verses of the great Jewish affirmation, the *Shema^c*, smooth and natural:

---

18. E.g., Isa 14:9–14.

19. See Yehezkel Kaufmann, *The Religion of Israel* (New York: Schocken, 1972), 60 and 142–147; and Jon D. Levenson, "Yehezkel Kaufmann and Mythology," *CJ* 36 (1982): 36–43.

20. *ANET*, 204.

21. William L. Moran, "The Ancient Near Eastern Background of the Love of God in Deuteronomy," *CBQ* 25 (1963): 77–87.

22. Ibid., 80.

⁴Hear, O Israel! The LORD is our God, the LORD alone. ⁵You shall love the LORD your God with all your heart and with all your soul and with all your might. (Deut 6:4–5)

The threat to covenant love is the allure of the other gods. By and large, the texts in the Hebrew Bible that show the most affinities with the suzerainty treaties also regard the other gods as extant, real, and potent:

²If there appears among you a prophet or a dream-diviner and he gives you a sign or a portent, ³saying, "Let us follow and worship another god"—whom you have not experienced—even if the sign or portent that he named to you comes true, ⁴do not heed the words of that prophet or that dream-diviner. For the LORD your God is testing you to see whether you really love the LORD your God with all your heart and soul. ⁵Follow none but the LORD your God, and revere none but Him; observe His commandments alone, and heed only His orders; worship none but Him; and hold fast to Him. ⁶As for that prophet or dream-diviner, he shall be put to death; for he urged disloyalty to the LORD your God—who freed you from the house of bondage. (Deut 13:2–6)

In this text, a false prophet is defined by his allegiance, to a god other than YHWH, and that allegiance, in turn, is defined by disregard for YHWH's directives or obedience to the other deity. Had that god been only a lifeless, storyless fetish in the Israelite mind, as Kaufmann thinks, then the temptation to abandon YHWH for him would have been slim, and the centuries of hard-fought competition between YHWH and his rivals for the heart, soul, and mind of Israel would never have been. In fact, however, texts such as this one are struggling to neutralize the *power* in Israel of deities other than YHWH by providing a YHWHistic explanation of their appeal. The supernatural gifts of their prophets and ⟦138⟧ diviners testify not to the power of those gods (unlike the supernatural gifts of exclusively YHWHistic prophets and diviners), but to the desire of YHWH to test Israel's exclusive allegiance to him: will Israel abandon him and his *mitsvot* for the other gods and their cults, or will they cleave devotedly to him even in the face of the dramatic and persistent inducements to do otherwise?

The fact that the urge to serve the other gods continues and is, to all appearances, validated by compelling empirical evidence, is itself proof that Israel's consent to serve YHWH alone was never so final and unshakable as a reading of the passages about revelation at Sinai would suggest. Instead, YHWH's kingship in Israel, like his kingship in the pantheon and his mastery over creation, remained vulnerable and in continual need of reaffirmation, reratification, reacclamation. The re-presentation of the Sinaitic moment on the plains of Moab, which is the burden of Deuteronomy, is born of a profound awareness of the waywardness of Israel, on the one hand, her indispensability to the suzerainty of YHWH, on the other. The covenant of Sinai has not the fixity and irrevocability of a royal decree; demanding human participation, it is fully realized only with the glad consent of the cultic community of Israel, a consent that is often denied—such is the risk that the consensual basis of the covenant entails—yet never destroyed. Texts like the one in Deuteronomy 13, previously cited, are attempting to make the consent to obey YHWH alone the prime and irreducible element in Israel's collective and individual life. Obedience is not to be predicated upon YHWH's ability to work miracles and predict the future; the prophets of the other deities can do these as well, and when they do, this empirical evidence on behalf of those deities is to be disregarded in the name of an increasingly nonempirical faithfulness, a faithfulness founded upon YHWH's acquisition of Israel through the nonrepeating foundational event of the exodus. The failure of the present to match the glories of the past, in which YHWH did his work in a pyrotechnic spectacular, is no grounds for defection or faithlessness. The very existence of the non-YHWHistic Israelites is to be seen as treasonous;[23] they and their gods are classified in Deuteronomy [139] as intolerable and unassimilable foreigners. Only the fragility of YHWH's covenantal lordship can account for this nervousness and defensiveness with the presence of an alternative to him and his cult. The theology of the fragile lordship of YHWH is, in turn, partly a reflection of the fragility of religious consensus within Israelite society in biblical times.

A long process of development lies between this theology and the mature Rabbinic thought of the Talmud. One difference is that the later is more rigorously monotheistic, treating the other gods as unreal and nonexistent. This, however, makes it all the more remarkable that the ideas of the fragility of God's reign in Israel and the continual necessity of Israel's active consent to it remain central to Rabbinic Judaism. The recitation of the *Shema^c*, already the watchword of the faith, became early on in Rabbinic law an obligation incumbent upon the Jew every morning and every evening. Its covenantal acclamation of the uniqueness of YHWH and his exclusive claim upon Israel, a claim honored by observance of his *mitsvot*, became known as the "acceptance of the yoke of the kingdom of heaven." The Jew begins and ends his day with a miniature covenant renewal ceremony.[24]

---

23. See Moshe Weinfeld, *Deuteronomy and the Deuteronomic School* (Oxford: Oxford University, 1972), 91–100, esp. pp. 92–93.

24. See Levenson, *Sinai and Zion*, 80–86.

More striking still this late midrash:

"So you are My witnesses
—declares the Lord—
And I am God." That is, if you are My witnesses, I am
God, and if you are not My witnesses, I am, as it were, not God.[25]

Here the consensual basis of the divinity of the God of Israel and the fragility of his reality in the world appear with shocking clarity. God depends, "as it were," upon the witness of Israel: without it, his divinity is not realized. The actualization of the full potential of God requires the testimony of his special people. Like Marduk in the *Enuma elish* or YHWH himself at Sinai, the elevation of the God of Israel is partly a function of those who elevate him. In the covenantal idiom of monotheism, Israel is the functional equivalent of the pantheon,[26] wisely and joyfully acclaiming their lord and deliverer.

Sinai, the Mountain of the Covenant
[[from *Sinai and Zion*]]

The Theology of the Historical Prologue

[[38]] It is significant for our understanding of the nature of the religion of Israel among the religions of the world that meaning for her is derived not from introspection, but from a consideration of the public testimony to God. The present generation makes history their story, but it is first history. They do not determine who they are by looking within, by plumbing the depths of the [[39]] individual soul, by seeking a mystical light in the innermost reaches of the self. Rather, the direction is the opposite. What is public is made private. History is not only rendered contemporary; it is internalized. One's people's history becomes one's personal history. One looks out from the self to find out who one is meant to be. One does not *discover* one's identity, and one certainly does not forge it oneself. He *appropriates* an identity that is a matter of public knowledge. Israel affirms the given.

The given that is affirmed in the covenant ceremony is not a principle; it is not an idea or an aphorism or an ideal. Instead, it is the consequence

---

25. *Sifre Deuteronomy* 346 (Finkelstein ed.). The biblical quote is Isa 43:12.
26. This is probably to be associated with the democratization of kingship and even divinity in Israel, as attested, for example, in Psalm 8 and Gen 1:26–27. See [[Levenson 1988a:]] pp. 114–16.

of what are presented as the acts of God. Israel accepts her place in the suzerain-vassal relationship. "YHWH our God we will serve; him alone we will obey" (⟦Josh 24:⟧24). In other words, those who come to the Hebrew Bible in hopes of finding a philosophical system flowing smoothly from a theorem will be disappointed. The religion of Israel was not a philosophical system; it had no such theorem. To be sure, every religion is the heritage of a particular community with a history of its own, and this element of history introduces a factor that frustrates the philosophical impulse in every religion. But in the religion of the Hebrew Bible, the philosophical impulse, if it exists at all, is stunted. We see no profound observation at the base of it, like the observation in Buddhism that desire is the source of suffering. Even the oneness of God, we shall soon see, is a consequence of other factors and not a proposition from which the essential religion of Israel can be derived.

Israel began to infer and to affirm her identity by telling a story. To be sure, the story has implications that can be stated as propositions. For example, the intended implications of the historical prologue is that YHWH is faithful, that Israel can rely on God as a vassal must rely upon his suzerain. But Israel does not begin with the statement that YHWH is faithful; she infers it from a *story*. And unlike the statement, the story is not universal. It is Israel's story, with all the particularities of time, place, and *dramatis personae* one associates with a story and avoids in a ⟦40⟧ statement that aims at universal applicability. In other words, if there is a universal truth of the sort philosophers and even some religions aim to state, Israel seems to have thought that such truth will come *through* the medium of history, through the structures of public knowledge, through time, and not in spite of these. History, the arena of public events (as opposed to private, mystical revelation and to philosophical speculation), and time are not illusions or distractions from essential reality. They are means to the knowledge of God. The historical prologue is a miniature theology of history.

When did the history summarized in the prologue commence? If one wishes to read the entire Torah as a covenant text, history begins at the beginning, the creation of the world and the story of primordial humanity (Genesis 1–11). But this is not where the historical prologues in the proper sense start their story. In Exod 19:3b–8, the story begins and ends with the Exodus from Egypt, when YHWH brought Israel, as on eagles' wings, to himself. In Joshua 24, the horizon is larger: history begins with the backdrop to Abraham's migration, the generation of his father, the Mesopotamian Terah. Most of the recapitulations of the sacred history begin, like Joshua 24, some time in the Patriarchal period. "An Aramean about to perish was my father," begins one little summary

(Deut 26:5) in an allusion to Jacob/Israel, from whom the nation took its name, and it is the descent into Egypt by the eponymous ancestor which tends to function there as the trigger for the action of the whole history of redemption, what German scholars call *Heilsgeschichte*.[1] Theologically this means that Israel's identity is not rooted in cosmic symbols, such as those that appear in the first account of creation in the [[41]] Torah (Gen 1:1–2:4a). Her identity is not cosmic and primordial, but historical in a sense not so distant from that in which modern people use the term. Israel was not created on day one or at any other moment in the seven days of creation. Instead, she was called into existence at a moment in ordinary time and at a specifiable place, Haran (11:31). Israel is to carry a metahistorical identity through her journeys in history.

. . . .

The Ever-Renewed Covenant

[[80]] The renewal of covenant was a central aspect of Israel's worship in biblical times. Psalm 81, chanted today on Thursday mornings, seems to have related the Sinaitic experience in some kind of regular liturgical celebration, also in its original setting. Although much of this psalm is obscure, v 4 would seem to locate its context in the celebration of the first day of the lunar month, on analogy with the celebration of New Year's Day (*Rosh Ha-Shanah*) so well known from later tradition, and comparable festivities for the day of the full moon, two weeks later.[2] What is most pertinent to us is that the liturgy for these holy days seems to have stressed the Decalogue. Vv 10–11 are a transparent restatement of the Second and First Commandments, according to the Jewish enumeration.[3] Vv 6b–8, in which YHWH becomes the speaker, perhaps through the mouth of a priest or prophet, and v 17 restate the the historical prologue, with its emphasis upon all that the suzerain, in his graciousness, has done for his vassal. The curses of covenant can be heard in vv 12–13, in which YHWH disowns a disobedient people, but in vv 14–16, the blessings balance this with their promise of victory if only Israel walks YHWH's path.[4] In short, Psalm 81 evidences a regular liturgical occasion in which the Sinaitic

1. On these summaries of *Heilsgeschichte*, see the title essay in G. von Rad, *The Problem of the Hexateuch and Other Essays* (New York: McGraw-Hill, 1966) 1–78. I do not endorse von Rad's belief that the *Heilsgeschichte* narratives grew out of short historical credos, but I do believe that he rendered a service in drawing attention to them. They are abstracts of the *Heilsgeschichte* stories presented in order to evoke an affirmation of covenant.

2. See [[Roland]] de Vaux, *Ancient Israel* [[New York and Toronto: McGraw-Hill, 1965]], 2:469–70, 476.

3. Exod 20:2–3 and Deut 5:6–7. See also Exod 20:5 and Deut 5:9.

4. Cf. Lev 26:7–8 and Deut 28:7.

covenant and the great choice it entails were re-presented to the Israelite congregation.[5]

[[81]] In the case of the book of Deuteronomy, the book of covenant *par excellence*, this insistence upon the relevance of the covenant of Sinai ("Horeb" in Deuteronomy) to the present generation reaches a pitch of intensity:

> [1]Moses called together all Israel and said to them: Hear, Israel, the laws and ordinances which I am proclaiming to you personally today. Study them, observe them, put them into practice. [2] YHWH our God made a covenant with us on Horeb. [3]It was not with our fathers that YHWH made this covenant, but with us—us!—those who are there today, all of us, the living. [4]Face to face YHWH spoke with you on the mountain, from the midst of the fire. (Deut 5:1–4)

The concern in this passage is that Israel may come to think of themselves as obliged in a distant way by the covenant of Sinai/Horeb, but not as direct partners in it. Lest the freshness of the experience be lost, v 3 hammers home the theme of contemporaneity in *staccato* fashion, with no fewer than six separate expressions: "with us"—"us!"—"those who are here"—"today"—"all of us"—"the living." The goal of this speech, as of the covenant renewal ceremony in which it probably originated,[6] is to induce Israel to step into the position of the generation of Sinai, in other words, to actualize the past so that this new generation will become the Israel of the classic covenant relationship (cf. Deut 30:19–20). Thus, life in covenant is not something merely granted, but something won anew, rekindled and reconsecrated in the heart of each Israelite in every generation. Covenant is not only imposed, but also accepted. It calls with both the stern voice of duty and the tender accents of the lover, with both stick (curse, death) and carrot (blessing, life) in hand. But it biases the choice in favor of life (Deut 30:19).

It is conventional to trace the influence of the covenant renewal ceremony and the formulary until the time of the disappearance [[82]] of the Dead Sea community (first century c.e.) and no further.[7] The tacit assumption is that these institutions did not survive into the next phase of Jewish history, the rabbinic era. In this, there is a certain truth. The idea of covenant does not seem to have had in rabbinic religion the centrality it had held since at least the promulgation of Deuteronomy in the sev-

---

5. On the psalms and covenant renewal, see S. Mowinckel, *The Psalms in Israel's Worship* (New York and Nashville: Abingdon 1967) 1:155–61. On covenant renewal in general, see Mowinckel, *Le Décalogue* (Paris: Félix Alcan, 1927) 114–62; H.-J. Kraus, *Worship in Israel* (Oxford: Blackwell, 1966) 141–45.

6. See von Rad, *Studies in Deuteronomy*, SBT 9 (London: SCM, 1953).

7. See [[Klaus]] Baltzer, *Covenant Formulary* [[Oxford: Blackwell, 1971]].

enth century B.C.E., although its importance for the rabbis must not be minimized.[8] There is no rabbinic ceremony in which the Jews are said explicitly to be renewing their partnership in the Sinaitic covenant, as the eight day old boy is said, for example, to be entering the covenant of Abraham (Gen 17:1–14) during his circumcision. There is, however, a text which is central to the rabbinic liturgy, in fact arguably *the* central text of the rabbinic liturgy, which is composed of three Pentateuchal passages (Deut 6:4–9; 11:13–21; Num 15:37–41)[9] expressive of the classical covenant theology. The prayer is known as the *Shma*, after its first word. The first verse of the *Shma* is correctly rendered, "Listen, Israel: YHWH is our God, YHWH alone" (Deut 6:4).[10] It is manifestly an echo of [[83]] the requirement of the old suzerainty treaties to recognize one lord alone. Since in the biblical case the lord is divine, the verse is a classic statement of covenantal monotheism, i.e., the prohibition upon the service of other suzerains.

In fact, we sense apprehension about the possibility of just such defection in each of the three paragraphs. In the second one, we hear of the danger of seduction, in language that recalls the career of Hosea (Deut 11:16–17), and in the last paragraph, such defection is termed "whoring" (Num 15:39). It is this passage from Numbers which establishes the ground of obedience to YHWH precisely where we expect it, in the redemption from Egypt (v 41). This verse, like the First Commandment of the Decalogue (Exod 20:2), is a condensation of the historical prologue. The central stipulation of the *Shma* is one familiar to any student of Near Eastern covenants, the obligation to love YHWH, which is inextricable from the requirements to carry out all his commandments. As we shall see, the rabbis, like the more ancient architects of covenant, saw in the acclamation of divine lordship and the love commandment of the first paragraph the basis for the acceptance of all other commandments. The second paragraph, which stresses performance of

8. See E. E. Urbach, *The Sages* ([Hebrew] Jerusalem: Magnes, 1975), 466–77.

9. The verse, "Blessed be the name of his glorious kingship forever and ever," is whispered between Deut 6:4 and 5.

10. The verse is conventionally rendered into English as, "Hear, O Israel, the Lord our God, the Lord is one," an interpretation that reflects the philosophical monotheism of a later tradition more than the covenantal monotheism of the Torah in its original setting. My translation essentially follows that of the Jewish Publication Society new Torah translation (1962), which draws attention to the commentaries of Ibn Ezra and Rashbam in support of the rendering. The remarks of Rashbam (ca. 1080–1174, northern France) are especially apt: "HaShem alone is our God, and we have no other god with him. Thus the Book of Chronicles: 'We will serve HaShem our God, and we have not abandoned him,' That is to say, HaShem is our God and not the calves to whom you bow down. 'HaShem alone': Him alone we will serve, and we will not add any other god to serve with him. . . . "

the stipulations, derives mostly from the blessings and curses of the covenant formulary. Fidelity to YHWH and the exclusive service of him will bring abundance; defection will result in drought, famine, and death. Finally, we should note that the insistence that the "words" be constantly recited, bound to one's body, written upon one's house, and the commandments symbolized in one's clothes, is also a reflex of part of the covenant formulary, the deposition of the text and the requirement for its periodic reading. In short, the idiom and the theology of covenant permeate the *Shma*.

What is interesting in light of the putative disappearance of the covenant renewal ceremony is that the rabbis selected these three texts to make up one prayer, for the three are not contiguous in the Torah, and the first of them there, Num 15:37–41, appears last here. What links the three paragraphs is that they constitute ⟦84⟧ the basic affirmation of covenant. They confront us with the underpinnings of the entire Sinaitic dimension of the religion of Israel. The link between them is theological, and it is that theology that the rabbis considered basic to their own appropriation and adaptation of the biblical heritage. For they made the *Shma* a staple in the liturgy they wove for Jewry. In the requirement to "recite them . . . when you lie down and when you get up," they saw a *mitsvah* to recite the *Shma* twice daily, in the morning and evening every day of the year.[11] The *Shma* thus became one of the pillars around which those two services developed.

What, precisely, did the rabbis think happened when one recites the *Shma?* We find an answer in the reply of the Tannaitic master Rabbi Joshua ben Korhah to the question of why Deut 6:4–9 is positioned before 11:13–21:

> so that one might accept upon himself the yoke of the kingdom of heaven first; afterwards, he accepts upon himself the yoke of the commandments.[12]

"Heaven" in Talmudic language is usually a more delicate way of saying "God." Rabbi Joshua sees the *Shma*, therefore, as the acclamation of God's kingship. Only in light of such an acclamation do the *mitsvot* make sense. In light of the biblical ideas, we can say that one must first accept the suzerainty of the great king, the fact of covenant; only then can he embrace the particulars which the new lord enjoins upon him, the stipulations. If God is suzerain, his orders stand. But his suzerainty is not something irrational and threatening. It follows from his gracious character:

11. *m. Ber.* 1:3.
12. *m. Ber.* 2:2.

I am the Lord Thy God. Why were the Ten Commandments not said at the beginning of the Torah? They give a parable. To what may this be compared? To the following: A king who entered a province said to the people: May I be your king? But the people said to him: Have you done anything good for us that you should rule over us? What did he do then? ⟦85⟧ He built the city wall for them, he brought in the water supply for them, and he fought their battles. Then when he said to them: May I be your king? They said to him: Yes, Yes. Likewise, God . . .¹³

His past grace grounds his present demand. To respond wholeheartedly to that demand, to accept the yoke of the kingdom of heaven, is to make a radical change, a change at the roots of one's being. To undertake to live according to *Halakhah* is not a question of merely raising one's moral aspirations or of affirming "Jewish values," whatever that means. To recite the *Shma* and mean it is to enter a supramundane sovereignty, to become a citizen of the kingdom of God, not simply in the messianic future to which that term also refers (e.g., Dan 2:44), but also in the historical present. Thus, one can understand the horror a rabbinic Jew would have of failing to say the *Shma*, as exemplified in this story: There was a law that a bridegroom was exempt from the commandment to recite the *Shma*, probably because he was in no mental condition to give the prayer the concentration it required. But concerning one early rabbi, we read this exchange in the Mishnah:

> It happened that Rabban Gamaliel got married and recited the *Shma* on the first night. His students said to him, "Our master, have you not taught us that a bridegroom is exempt from the recitation of the *Shma* on the first night?" He said to them, "I am not going to listen to you and annul the kingdom of Heaven from myself for even a moment!"¹⁴

In other words, one who neglects the *Shma* when its recitation is due is rebelling against the sovereignty/suzerainty of God. Or, to put it positively, the *Shma* is the rabbinic way of actualizing the moment at Sinai when Israel answered the divine offer of covenant with the words "All that YHWH has spoken we will do" ⟦86⟧ (Exod 19:8). In short, the recitation of the *Shma* is the rabbinic covenantal renewal ceremony. It is the portal to continuing life in covenant.

There is, therefore, no voice more central to Judaism than the voice heard on Mount Sinai. Sinai confronts anyone who would live as a Jew with an awesome choice, which, once encountered, cannot be evaded—the choice of whether to obey God or to stray from him, of whether to observe

---

13. *Mek., Baḥôdeš*, 5. The translation is from *Mekilta de-Rabbi Ishmael*, ed. J. Z. Lauterbach (Philadelphia: Jewish Publication Society, 1933) 2:229–30.

14. *m. Ber.* 2:5. On the significance of the *Shma*, see Urbach, *Sages*, 348–70.

the commandments or to let them lapse. Ultimately, the issue is whether God is or is not king, for there is no king without subjects, no suzerain without vassals. In short, Sinai demands that the Torah be taken with radical seriousness. But alongside the burden of choice lies a balm that soothes the pain of decision. The balm is the history of redemption, which grounds the commandments and insures that this would-be king is a gracious and loving lord and that to choose to obey him is not a leap into the absurd. The balm is the surprising love of YHWH for Israel, of a passionate groom for his bride, a love ever fresh and never dulled by the frustrations of a storm courtship. Mount Sinai is the intersection of love and law, of gift and demand, the link between a past together and a future together.

Phyllis Trible

b. 1932

Overture for a Feminist Biblical Theology

Theological Synopsis

Issues of objectivity have dogged the trail of Old Testament theology since 1930 and even earlier. It seemed then that objectivity was possible when dealing with the phenomenon of a religion but questionable when sketching a belief system. Later, when the category of history was emphasized, scholars, using the historical-critical method, claimed objectivity. If from that history one now wished to adduce something about faith, could such a theology be "objective?" In the last half of the century, the issue of objectivity took a new turn. With the rise of feminism, women argued that even prior to the development of any theology, the basic exegesis of Scripture was hardly objective since it was done by men and was therefore biased. By the end of the 1980s, women had neither written a theology of the Old Testament nor laid out comprehensive proposals for the enterprise, but "feminist hermeneutics" was sure to affect biblical studies significantly, more significantly than, say, the production earlier by nineteenth-century feminists of *The Woman's Bible* (Stanton 1895–98).

At the centennial of the Society of Biblical Literature in 1980 several women participated in a panel discussion on "The Effect of Women's Studies on Biblical Studies" (Trible 1982). Katharine Doob Sakenfeld identified four effects: (1) a systematic inquiry into the status and role of women in ancient Israelite culture; (2) a rediscovery of long-overlooked traditions (e.g., the story of the daughters of Zelophehad); (3) a reassessment of famous texts (e.g., Genesis 2–3) in the light of the author's purpose; and (4) an alertness to new images for God (Sakenfeld 1982). To these could be added investigations about "the interpretative implications of androcentric language" and other concerns.

Phyllis Trible was something of a pioneer in studies by women in the field of biblical theology. The editors of the series "Overtures to Biblical Theology," in introducing her monograph *God and the Rhetoric of Sexuality*, the second in that series, wrote: "Trible's book is indeed an 'overture,' a hint of a quite fresh way of doing exegesis. . . . It is an offering of serious substantive theology that requires a rethinking of some most central aspects of biblical faith" (1978: xii).

Trible herself saw her work as a "theological vision for new occasions" (1978: xvi). She did not, however, propose "to offer a comprehensive program for doing biblical theology" (1978: xvi). She represented a mood, and in some ways also a distinct mode of procedure. Both in that volume and also in her second, *Texts of Terror* (1984), Trible followed a literary analysis which stressed rhetorical criticism, metaphor, and "close reading." Literary design, narrative flow, and patterns of word use took precedence over date, authorship, and social context. If the method was literary criticism, the perspective was feminist. For her, feminist interpretation was a critique of culture. God, for example, was sexually beyond male and female. In her first book she spoke of the Deity, but never in pronouns— masculine, feminine, or neuter. The feminist perspective, she argued, served to redress earlier imbalances, even distortions in exegesis, and would affect the construction of an Old Testament theology.

Phyllis Trible completed doctoral studies at Union Theological Seminary (New York) under James Muilenburg, her mentor, whose methods of rhetorical criticism she followed, and to whose memory she dedicated her 1978 book. Since 1979 she has taught at Union Biblical Seminary where she is now Baldwin Professor of Sacred Literature. Previously she taught at Andover Newton Theological School (1971–79) and Wake Forest University (1963–71). Invitations to lecture have taken her to Australia, Canada, England, New Zealand, and Japan, and to dozens of seminaries in the United States. Since 1985 she has been on the editorial board of *Journal of Feminist Studies in Religion*. Her 1984 book, or parts of it, has been translated into Dutch, German, Spanish, and Japanese.

                                                                    E.A.M.

Writings by Trible

1978   *God and the Rhetoric of Sexuality*. Overtures to Biblical Theology. Philadelphia: Fortress.

1982   (guest editor) The Effects of Women's Studies on Biblical Studies. *Journal for the Study of the Old Testament* 22:3–71.

1984   *Texts of Terror: Literary-Feminist Readings of Biblical Narratives.* Overtures
              to Biblical Theology. Philadelphia: Fortress.

1989   Five Loaves and Two Fishes: Feminist Hermeneutics and Biblical The-
              ology. *Theological Studies* 50:279–95.

Phyllis Trible
Feminist Hermeneutics and Biblical Theology

Excerpted with permission from Phyllis Trible, "Five Loaves and Two Fishes: Feminist Hermeneutics and Biblical Theology," *Theological Studies* 50 (1989) 279–95.

[[279]] When this journal began its life a half century ago, feminist hermeneutics was an unrecognized subject. In the U.S. the first wave of feminism had passed: the voices of women were restrained. Emerging from the great Depression, the nation hovered between two wars, without inclination to explore matters of gender. The theological enterprise reflected the culture.

Such reflection continues in our time, when a second wave of feminism influences the North American scene.[1] Over recent years *Theological Studies* has published articles and an entire issue on the topic.[2] This anniversary volume pursues the interest as the present article explores feminist interpretation and the Bible, specifically the Hebrew Scriptures.[3] The study begins with an overview of feminism, proceeds with a sketch of biblical theology, and concludes by joining the subjects to consider offerings and make overtures.

An Overview of Feminism

For the second wave of feminism, the date 1963 was pivotal. Betty Friedan voiced the voices of countless women with the publication of *The Feminine*

1. Note that the image of waves implies continuity between the periods. For background see A. S. Rossi, ed., *The Feminist Papers* (New York: Columbia University, 1973); J. Hole and E. Levine, *Rebirth of Feminism* (New York: Quadrangle Books, 1971); S. M. Rothman, *Woman's Proper Place* (New York: Basic Books, 1978).

2. See the issue subtitled "Woman: New Dimensions," *TS* 36 (1975) 575–765. See also, e.g., A. E. Carr, "Is a Christian Feminist Theology Possible?" *TS* 43 (1982) 279–97; J. H. Martin, "The Injustice of Not Ordaining Women: A Problem for Medieval Theologians," *TS* 48 (1987) 303–16; E. A. Johnson, "The Incomprehensibility of God and the Image of God Male and Female," *TS* 45 (1984) 441–65.

3. Nomenclature for the canon shared by Judaism and Christianity is currently a much-discussed issue weighted with theological import. This article recognizes, though does not solve, the problem. It intentionally refrains from using the designation "Old Testament" except where the description is proper to report views of others. For discussion see J. A. Sanders, "First Testament and Second," *Biblical Theology Bulletin* 17 (1987) 47–49; E. S. Frerichs, "The Torah Canon of Judaism and the Interpretation of Hebrew Scripture," *Horizons in Biblical Theology* 9 (1987) 13–25.

Mystique.[4] Symbolically and substantively this book reopened [[280]] the question of female and male. Its contribution belonged to a tumultuous year. The assassination of John F. Kennedy marked a time since which "nothing has been the same."[5] The bombing of a black church in Birmingham, Alabama, killing four little girls, underscored the evils of a racist society. Upheaval characterized the nation. Within that context feminism was hardly an isolated phenomenon.

From 1963 on, many women and some men began to examine the *status quo*, pronounce judgment, and call for repentance. They espoused a prophetic message. *The Church and the Second Sex* by Mary Daly (1968) brought a distinctly religious voice to the movement.[6] Like its secular counterpart, this speech multiplied abundantly.[7] While feminism may have first appeared no more than a cloud the size of a woman's hand, in time it burst forth as a storm of controversy and as spring rain reviving life. A brief analysis of emphases, especially as they relate to theology, stages our discussion.

As a hermeneutic, feminism interprets existence. Though not monolithic in point of view, it focuses on gender and sex.[8] The word "gender" pertains to masculine and feminine roles as culturally perceived (rather than grammatical categories). More narrow in scope, the word "sex" denotes the biological distinction between male and female. While sex is given and for the most part unalterable, gender is constructed within particular societies and, theoretically at least, can be deconstructed. Historically, societies have used gender and sex to advocate male domination and female subordination. The term "sexism" denotes this ideology that fosters a system called patriarchy. Acquiring a definition beyond classical law, the word "patriarchy" describes the institutionalization of male dominance over women in home and society at large. Male authority does not necessarily imply that women have no power or that all women are

---

4. B. Friedan, *The Feminine Mystique* (New York: W. W. Norton, 1963).

5. This sentiment has been uttered repeatedly by countless Americans, most recently during commemorations of the 25th anniversary of the assassination, Nov. 22, 1988.

6. New York: Harper & Row, 1986. In an autobiographical preface to the reprinting of this book (1975), Daly disowns it, charting her "change of consciousness from 'radical Catholic' to post-christian feminist."

7. For a sampling, a decade after Daly's work, see *Womanspirit Rising: A Feminist Reader in Religion*, ed. C. P. Christ and J. Plaskow (San Francisco: Harper & Row, 1979).

8. See M. Gould and R. Kern-Daniels, "Towards a Sociological Theory of Gender and Sex," *American Sociologist* 12 (1977) 182–89. For a helpful exposition of these and other terms, see G. Lerner, *The Creation of Patriarchy* (New York: Oxford University, 1986) 231–43. Cf. R. Radford Ruether, "Sexism as Ideology and Social System: Can Christianity Be Liberated from Patriarchy?" in *With Both Eyes Open: Seeing beyond Gender*, ed. P. Altenbornd Johnson and J. Kalven (New York: Pilgrim, 1988) 148–64.

victims. Patriarchy has assumed diverse forms. To name the many manifestations constitutes one task of feminism.

⟦281⟧ In talking about sexism and patriarchy, feminism not only describes but convicts. It opposes the paradigm of domination and subordination in all forms, most particularly male over female, but also master
over slave and humankind over the earth.[9] Sex, race, class, and ecology
intertwine as issues. Theologically, the rule of male over female constitutes sin. This hierarchy violates the integrity of creation "in the image of
God male and female" by denying full humanity to women and distorting
the humanity of men. Consequently, both sexes suffer. Sexism as ideology
and patriarchy as system must be exposed and rejected. In assuming this
stance, feminism shows its prophetic base.

Prophecy calls for repentance. Beginning with a change of consciousness in individuals, it becomes a changing of society. Some feminists seek
reform and others transformation.[10] However the issue develops, repentance bespeaks a future vision of wholeness and well-being for female and
male. But feminists do not facilely claim this future. They know sexism is
insidious and obstacles are numerous.

The designation "prophetic" engenders other observations. First, by
definition prophetic movements advocate. This activity neither distinguishes nor demeans feminism but rather characterizes all theologies and
methods.[11] For centuries church, synagogue, and academy have advocated
patriarchy: the way things are and ought to be. In exposing their bias, feminism evokes a different hermeneutic. Second, as the generic term "prophecy" covers multiple perspectives, so the singular "feminism" embraces
plurality and diversity. Time, place, culture, class, race, experience—these
and other variables yield particular expressions of a shared cause. Though
particularities induce conflict and contradiction, they serve a salutary purpose. It pertains to a third observation. Prophetic movements are not exempt from sin. Feminism struggles with this awareness. Jewish feminist
theology, e.g., detects anti-Jewish sentiments in some Christian formula-

9. For a substantive statement of feminist theology, see R. Radford Ruether, *Sexism and
God-Talk: Toward a Feminist Theology* (Boston: Beacon, 1983); also A. E. Carr, *Transforming
Grace: Christian Tradition and Women's Experience* (San Francisco: Harper & Row, 1988).

10. This distinction resonates with the sociological categories of central and peripheral
prophets. Cf. R. R. Wilson, *Prophecy and Society in Ancient Israel* (Philadelphia: Fortress, 1980)
21–88.

11. At places in the current discussion this point seems to be missed, with the word "advocacy" assigned to feminism, as though it were, for better or worse, distinctive. Cf., e.g., the
unsigned editorial in *Interpretation* 42 (1988) 3–4; in these two pages some form of the word
"advocacy" appears no fewer than seven times to describe feminism and its proponents, but
not once to characterize its critics. Yet they too advocate.

tions.[12] Third World feminists criticize the [282] privileged positions of class and race that afflict First World feminism.[13] African-American women, claiming the identity "womanist," challenge white feminists.[14] On individual levels experiences of women differ, yielding diverse witnesses. Eternal vigilance is necessary. In announcing judgment on patriarchy and calling for repentance, feminism needs ever to be aware of its own sins.

This prophetic note concludes the overview of feminism; a sketch of biblical theology begins. The shift is jarring, as far as the east is from the west. Later, connections are forged.

A Sketch of Biblical Theology

Biblical theologians, though coming from a circumscribed community, have never agreed on the definition, method, organization, subject matter, point of view, or purpose of their enterprise. Drawing upon earlier studies, Johann Philipp Gabler (1787) formulated the discipline for the European world, particularly the German scene.[15] He deemed it a historical and descriptive undertaking distinguished from the didactic and interpretive pursuit of dogmatic theology. At the same time, he related the two fields by making biblical theology the foundation of dogmatics. For about a century afterwards the discipline flourished in disputation. Even the label "biblical theology" became suspect. Some scholars advocated the unity of Scripture; others separated the Testaments. The designation "Old Testament theology" emerged to specify a Christian bias that not infrequently disparaged the Hebrew Scriptures. Interpretive approaches began to contend with descriptive. Searches for unifying themes brought disunity. The concepts "universal" and "unique" vied for supremacy. Organizational differences furthered debate as chronologies of biblical content clashed

12. Cf. J. Plaskow, "Christian Feminism and Anti-Judaism," *Cross Currents* 28 (1978) 306–9. For a sampling of the diversity within Jewish feminism, see "Feminist Consciousness Today, Roundtable: The Women's Movement," *Tikkun* 2 (1987) 40–46; also J. Plaskow, "Standing Again at Sinai: Jewish Memory from a Feminist Perspective," *Tikkun* 1 (1986) 28–34.

13. See L. M. Russell et al., eds., *Inheriting Our Mothers' Gardens: Feminist Theology in Third World Perspective* (Philadelphia: Westminster, 1978).

14. The term "womanist" derives from A. Walker, *In Search of Our Mothers' Gardens: Womanist Prose* (San Diego: Harcourt Brace Jovanovich, 1983) esp. xi–xii. Cf. P. Giddings, *When and Where I Enter: The Impact of Black Women on Race and Sex in America* (New York: William Morrow, 1984).

15. See J. Sandys-Wunsch and L. Eldredge, "J. P. Gabler and the Distinction between Biblical and Dogmatic Theology: Translation, Commentary, and Discussion of His Originality," *Scottish Journal of Theology* 33 (1980) 133–58 [translation reprinted on pp. 489–502 below]. For a history of the discipline, with ample bibliography, see J. H. Hayes and F. C. Prussner, *Old Testament Theology: Its History and Development* (Atlanta: John Knox, 1985).

with categories of systematic theology. Before the end of the 19th century, then, biblical theology had developed in myriad ways compatible and incompatible.

[283] Thereupon followed 40 years of wilderness wanderings (1880–1920). Emphasis on history of religions threatened the discipline by promoting environmental rather than theological perspectives. But over time changes in the European climate, especially the impact of war and the rise of Barthian theology, revived interest. Two articles from the 1920s represented the discussion. Otto Eissfeldt argued for the legitimacy, yet discontinuity, of historical and theological approaches to the OT.[16] By contrast, Walther Eichrodt maintained that an irreconcilable separation was neither possible nor desirable.[17] He rejected Eissfeldt's description of OT theology as solely normative and interpretive. Like Gabler, he defined it as predominately descriptive and historical, even while acknowledging a role for faith.

The year Germany came under National Socialist control (1933), Eichrodt produced in Basel the first volume of his theology, with the second and third in 1935 and 1939.[18] He himself made no explicit hermeneutical connections with the political scene. He described the discipline as giving "a complete picture of the Old Testament realm of belief." This picture formed the center panel of a triptych. On one side, religions of the ancient Near East showed comparatively the uniqueness of the OT. On the other, the NT produced a theological union through the concept "the kingdom of God." Judaism Eichrodt denigrated. A "systematic synthesis" defined his method. Of the organizing categories—God and the People, God and the World, God and Humankind (*Mensch*)—the first was basic. Covenant constituted its symbol. Though largely a product of 19th-century thought, this formulation dominated biblical theology into the latter half of the 20th century.

Quite a different paradigm emerged in the work of Gerhard von Rad.[19] Volume 1 of his theology appeared just a little over a decade (1957) after the defeat of Germany in World War II; Volume 2 followed three years later (1960). Like Eichrodt, von Rad made no explicit

---

16. O. Eissfeldt, "Israelitisch-jüdische Religionsgeschichte und alttestamentliche Theologie," *Zeitschrift für die alttestamentliche Wissenschaft* 44 (1926) 1–12 [English translation on pp. 20–29 above].

17. W. Eichrodt, "Hat die alttestamentliche Theologie noch selbständige Bedeutung innerhalb der alttestamentlichen Wissenschaft?" *Zeitschrift für die alttestamentliche Wissenschaft* 47 (1929) 83–91 [English translation on pp. 30–39 above].

18. In English translation the three volumes became two; see W. Eichrodt, *Theology of the Old Testament* (Philadelphia: Westminster, 1961, 1967).

19. For the English translations, see G. von Rad, *Old Testament Theology* (2 vols.; New York: Harper & Row, 1962, 1965).

hermeneutical connections with the political scene. Form criticism and tradition history inspired his approach. Rather than positing a center (*Mitte*) for the theology or using systematic categories, he appealed to Israel's own testimonies about Yahweh's action in history. The first volume interpreted [[284]] the Hexateuch, the Deuteronomistic History, and the Chronicler's History, to conclude with Israel's response in the Psalter and the Wisdom literature. The second volume investigated prophecy as God's "new thing" in the land. A brief look at apocalypticism led to the final section, tracing the OT into the NT. Von Rad declared this movement the *sine qua non* of the enterprise. Without it, one had instead the "history of the religion of the Old Testament."

If Eichrodt be the *ʾaleph*, von Rad symbolized the *taw* of a prolific era in the history of biblical theology. During this time male German Protestant scholarship controlled the agenda. Its demise came through factors intrinsic and extrinsic to the discipline. Brevard S. Childs has chronicled these matters as they pertain to the North American scene.[20] Suffice it to note Childs's date for the end of this extraordinary period: 1963. From the perspective of this article, the timing is uncanny. That same year Betty Friedan wrote *The Feminine Mystique.*

In the last 25 years (1963–88) no major OT theologies have dominated the field.[21] Yet the subject has grown through experimentation. It includes conversation between sociology and theology,[22] discussion of canon,[23] and development of bipolar categories for encompassing scriptural diversity.[24] More broadly, biblical theology has begun to converse with the world.[25] To pursue this expansion in reference to feminism requires a few summary observations about the discipline throughout its 200-year history.

20. B. S. Childs, *Biblical Theology in Crisis* (Philadelphia: Westminster, 1970).

21. But see, e.g., R. E. Clements, *Old Testament Theology: A Fresh approach* (Atlanta: John Knox, 1978); for a theology spanning both Testaments, see S. Terrien, *The Elusive Presence: Toward a New Biblical Theology* (New York: Harper & Row, 1978).

22. See N. K. Gottwald, *The Tribes of Yahweh* (Maryknoll, N. Y.: Orbis, 1979) 667–709.

23. Cf. B. S. Childs, *Old Testament Theology in a Canonical Context* (Philadelphia: Fortress, 1985), and J. A. Sanders, *From Sacred Story to Sacred Text* (Philadelphia: Fortress, 1987).

24. See W. Brueggemann, "A Shape for Old Testament Theology, I: Structural Legitimation," *Catholic Biblical Quarterly* 47 (1985) 28–46; idem, "A Shape for Old Testament Theology, II: Embrace of Pain," ibid. 395–415.

25. Numerous volumes in the series entitled Overtures to Biblical Theology, published by Fortress (Philadelphia) from 1977 to the present and on, demonstrate the conversation. Overall, this series rejects the limitation of historical description to explore normative meanings. Distinctions between biblical theology and hermeneutics often collapse. Two recent titles illustrate the point: S. H. Ringe, *Jesus, Liberation, and the Biblical Jubilee: Images for Ethics and Christology* (1985), and J. G. Harris, *Biblical Perspectives on Aging: God and the Elderly* (1987).

First, biblical theology (more often OT theology) has sought identity, but with no resolution. Over time the discussion has acquired the status of *déjà dit*; proposals and counterproposals only repeat themselves.[26] [[285]] Second, guardians of the discipline have fit a standard profile. They have been white Christian males of European or North American extraction, educated in seminaries, divinity schools, or theological faculties. Third, overall, their interpretations have skewed or neglected matters not congenial to a patriarchal point of view. Fourth, they have fashioned the discipline in a past separated from the present. Biblical theology has been kept apart from biblical hermeneutics.[27]

Challenges to this stance now come from many directions. Liberation theologies foster redefinition and application.[28] Issues such as ecology, medical ethics, creationism, and spirituality press for dialogue. Racial, religious, and sexual perspectives also enter the discussion. African-Americans, Asians, and Jews, e.g., shape the discipline differently from traditional proponents.[29] In short, biblical theology, by whatever definition, method, or point of view, must grapple with contemporary hermeneutics. This recognition leads to connections between feminism and biblical studies.

26. See H. Graf Reventlow, "Basic Problems in Old Testament Theology," *Journal for the Study of the Old Testament* 11 (1979) 2–22; cf. J. Barr, "The Theological Case against Biblical Theology," in *Canon, Theology, and Old Testament Interpretation*, ed. G. M. Tucker et al. (Philadelphia: Fortress, 1988) 3–19.

27. For attention to the period since 1945, see George W. Coats, "Theology of the Hebrew Bible," in *The Hebrew Bible and Its Modern Interpreters*, ed. Douglas A. Knight and Gene M. Tucker (Philadelphia: Fortress, 1985) 239–62.

28. See, e.g., José Porfirio Miranda, *Marx and the Bible* (Maryknoll, N. Y.: Orbis, 1974); J. Severino Croatto, *Exodus: A Hermeneutics of Freedom* (Maryknoll, N. Y.: Orbis, 1981); Elsa Tamez, *Bible of the Oppressed* (Maryknoll, N. Y.: Orbis, 1982); Willy Schottroff and Wolfgang Stegemann, eds., *God of the Lowly: Socio-Historical Interpretations of the Bible* (Maryknoll, N. Y.: Orbis, 1984).

29. For the developing conversation between Judaism and biblical ("Old Testament") theology, see esp. J. Levenson, "The Hebrew Bible, the Old Testament, and Historical Criticism," in *The Future of Biblical Studies*, ed. R. E. Friedman and H. G. M. Williamson (Atlanta: Scholars, 1987) 19–59; idem, "Why Jews Are Not Interested in Biblical Theology," in *Judaic Perspectives on Ancient Israel*, ed. J. Neusner (Philadelphia: Fortress, 1989) 281–307. Cf. M. H. Goshen-Gottstein, "Tanakh Theology: The Religion of the Old Testament and the Place of Jewish Biblical Theology," in *Ancient Israelite Religion*, ed. P. D. Miller, Jr., et al. (Philadelphia: Fortress, 1987); also R. Rendtorff, "Must 'Biblical Theology' Be Christian Theology?" *Bible Review* 4 (1988) 40–43.

Feminist Hermeneutics and Biblical Studies

Perspectives and Methods

Joining biblical studies in the early 1970s, feminism has brought gender to the foreground of discussion.[30] It has exposed the androcentric bias of ⟦286⟧ Scripture and scholarship. Different conclusions result.[31] Some feminists denounce Scripture as hopelessly misogynous, a woman-hating document beyond redemption. Some reprehensibly use patriarchal data to support anti-Jewish sentiments. They maintain that ascendancy of the male god Yahweh demolished an era of good-goddess worship. A Christian version holds that whereas the "Old" Testament falters badly, the "New" brings improved revelation. Some individuals consider the Bible to be a historical document devoid of continuing authority and hence worthy of dismissal. In contrast, other feminists despair about the ever-present male power that the Bible and commentators promote. Still others, unwilling to let the case against women be the determining word, insist that text and interpreters provide more excellent ways. Thereby they seek to redeem the past (an ancient document) and the present (its continuing use) from the confines of patriarchy.

Whatever their conclusions, feminist biblical scholars utilize conventional methods in studying the text. Historical criticism, form criticism, tradition history, literary criticism, sociology, anthropology, archeology, history of religions, and linguistics—all these and others illuminate the document, contributing variously to theological formulations. Though traditionally tied to patriarchal interpretation, the methods produce different results when feminist hermeneutics appropriates them. A sampling indicates the terrain.

Working as a historical critic, Phyllis Bird has called for "a new reconstruction of the history of Israelite religion, not a new chapter on women."[32] A first step seeks to recover "the hidden history of women." She has contributed to this immense task in two articles examining women in

---

30. For a historical investigation, see D. C. Bass, "Women's Studies and Biblical Studies: An Historical Perspective," *Journal for the Study of the Old Testament* 22 (1982) 6–12; cf. E. W. Saunders, *Searching the Scriptures: A History of the Society of Biblical Literature 1880–1980* (Chico, Cal.: Scholars, 1982). For an overview of some recent developments, see K. Doob Sakenfeld, "Feminist Perspectives on Bible and Theology," *Interpretation* 42 (1988) 5–18.

31. Recent collections exemplifying or discussing many of these conclusions include *The Bible and Feminist Hermeneutics*, ed. M. A. Tolbert (Chico, Cal.: Scholars, 1983); *Feminist Perspectives on Biblical Scholarship*, ed. A. Yarbro Collins (Chico, Cal.: Scholars, 1985); *Feminist Interpretation of the Bible*, ed. L. M. Russell (Philadelphia: Westminster, 1985); *Reasoning with the Foxes: Female Wit in a World of Male Power*, ed. J. C. Exum and J. W. H. Bos (Atlanta: Scholars, 1988).

32. P. Bird, "The Place of Women in the Israelite Cultus," in *Ancient Israelite Religion* (n. 29 above) 397–419.

ancient Israel and in the Israelite cult.[33] Similarly, Jo Ann Hackett locates her research in "the new women's history."[34] It attempts [[287]] to recover the stories of females in their own right rather than measuring them by the norms of male history. In an examination of Judges 3–16, e.g., Hackett explores the leadership roles of women during a period of decentralized power. Paucity of evidence, difficulty of analysis, and resistance from established scholarship lead her to a pessimistic assessment about the impact of such work on so-called mainline scholarship.

More sanguine about the possibilities, Carol Meyers has recently prepared the first book-length study of Israelite women.[35] Using the tools of social-scientific analysis combined with the new archeology, she seeks "to discover the place of women in the biblical world apart from the place of women in the biblical text."[36] She argues that "the decentralized and difficult village life of premonarchic Israel provided a context for gender mutuality and interdependence, and of concomitant female power."[37] She sharply questions the validity of the description "patriarchal" for ancient Israelite society. Yet to be tested, this revisionist thesis enlarges options within feminist biblical scholarship.

Literary analyses also show the diversity. In considering the mother figure, Esther Fuchs avers that the Bible is riddled with "patriarchal determinants."[38] It "uses literary strategies in order to foster and perpetuate its patriarchal ideology."[39] By contrast, in a close reading of the Exodus traditions, J. Cheryl Exum detects "positive portrayals of women."[40] Examining mothers of Israel, she finds "strong countercurrents of affirmations of women" within the "admittedly patriarchal context of the biblical literature."[41] Thus she calls for "reassessment of our traditional

---

33. The above note identifies one article; for the other see "Images of Women in the Old Testament," in *Religion and Sexism*, ed. R. Radford Ruether (New York: Simon and Schuster, 1974) 41–88.

34. J. A. Hackett, "Women's Studies and the Hebrew Bible," in *The Future of Biblical Studies* (n. 29 above) 141–64.

35. C. Meyers, *Discovering Eve: Ancient Israelite Women in Context* (New York: Oxford University, 1988).

36. Ibid. 23.

37. Ibid. 187.

38. E. Fuchs, "The Literary Characterization of Mothers and Sexual Politics in the Hebrew Bible," in *Feminist Perspectives on Biblical Scholarship* (n. 31 above) 117–36.

39. Idem, "Who Is Hiding the Truth? Deceptive Women and Biblical Androcentrism," in *Feminist Perspectives on Biblical Scholarship* (n. 31 above) 137–44.

40. J. C. Exum, "'You Shall Let Every Daughter Live': A Study of Exodus 1:8–2:10," in *The Bible and Feminist Hermeneutics* (n. 31 above) 63–82.

41. Idem, "'Mother in Israel': A Familiar Figure Reconsidered," in *Feminist Interpretation of the Bible* (n. 31 above) 73–85.

assumptions about women's roles in the biblical story."[42] A similar view governs the work of Toni Craven.[43] She compares Ruth, Esther, and Judith, recognizing the social dominance of the male in these [[288]] stories but nevertheless asserting that "within this patriarchal milieu, the three women emerge as independent, making their own decisions and initiating actions in unconventional ways." Of whatever persuasions, these and other literary readings provide an exegetical base for theological reflection.

Feminist scholars who specialize in Wisdom literature also provide data for the theologian. With a multidisciplinary approach, Claudia V. Camp has explored female wisdom in Proverbs.[44] Viewing "woman Wisdom" as metaphor, she has isolated roles and activities within Israelite culture that influenced this personification. They include the figures of wife, lover, harlot, foreigner, prophet, and wise woman. The research joins the efforts of historians, sociologists, and literary critics.

This sampling, focused on the Hebrew Scriptures, concludes with three books that differ widely in interest, approach, and purpose but share a common grounding. Particular experiences motivated their authors. Unlike traditional male scholars, feminists often spell out hermeneutical connections between life and work. Citing an episode within her Jewish heritage as pertinent to her study, Athalya Brenner probes the familiar thesis that, as a class, women in Scripture are a second sex, always subordinate and sometimes maligned.[45] Her approach covers social roles and literary paradigms. Writing as a womanist, Renita J. Weems "attempts to combine the best of the fruits of feminist biblical criticism with its passion for reclaiming and reconstructing the stories of biblical women, along with the best of the Afro-American oral tradition, with its gift for story-telling and its love of drama."[46] Recounting unpleasant experiences within Roman Catholicism, Alice L. Laffey has prepared a "complement" to standard introductions of the OT.[47] She approaches texts, for weal or woe, with the principle "that women are equal to men." However scholarly judgments measure these works, the experiences that prompted their

---

42. Idem, "'You Shall Let Every Daughter Live'" 82.

43. T. Craven, "Tradition and Convention in the Book of Judith," in *The Bible and Feminist Hermeneutics* (n. 31 above) 49–61. See also idem, "Women Who Lied for the Faith," in *Justice and the Holy*, ed. Douglas A. Knight and Peter J. Paris (Atlanta: Scholars, in press 1989).

44. C. V. Camp, *Wisdom and the Feminine in the Book of Proverbs* (Sheffield: Almond, JSOT, 1985).

45. A. Brenner, *The Israelite Women* (Sheffield: JSOT, 1985).

46. R. J. Weems, *Just a Sister Away* (San Diego: LuraMedia, 1988). The combination proposed gives more weight to storytelling than to biblical criticism.

47. A. L. Laffey, *An Introduction to the Old Testament: A Feminist Perspective* (Philadelphia: Fortress, 1988). Regrettably, factual errors mar this book.

authors and the methods they employ show yet again the diverse terrain of feminist biblical studies.

All these samplings but hint at perspective and methods. Studying Scripture from the viewpoint of gender, feminism explores ideas and advances these shunned in traditional interpretations. Conventional methods produce unconventional results. Not all of them will endure. [[289]] Yet the ferment can be salutary, for the storehouse of faith has treasures new as well as old. They necessiate the perennial rethinking of biblical theology.

Overtures for a Feminist Biblical Theology

As a student of Scripture, I read biblical theology from duty and sometimes delight. As a student of feminism, I read feminist biblical scholarship from duty and sometimes delight. And then I ask: Can feminism and biblical theology meet? The question seems to echo Tertullian, "What has Athens to do with Jerusalem?" After all, feminists do not move in the world of Gabler, Eichrodt, von Rad, and their heirs. Yet feminists who love the Bible insist that the text and its interpreters provide more excellent ways. And so I ponder ingredients of a feminist biblical theology. Though not yet the season to write one, the time has come to make overtures.

At the beginning, feminist biblical theology might locate itself in reference to the classical discipline. Assertion without argumentation suffices here. First, the undertaking is not just descriptive and historical but primarily constructive and hermeneutical. It views the Bible as pilgrim, wandering through history, engaging in new settings, and ever refusing to be locked in the past. Distance and difference engage proximity and familiarity.[48] Second, the discipline belongs to diverse communities, including academy, synagogue, church, and world. It is neither essentially nor necessarily Christian. Third, formulations vary. No single method, organization, or exposition harnesses the subject: an articulation of faith as disclosed in Scripture. From these points of reference feminism takes its first step.

1) *Exegesis.* Mindful of the androcentricity in Scripture and traditional biblical theology, feminist interpretation begins with exegesis. It concentrates on highlighting neglected texts and reinterpreting familiar ones. The approach does not guarantee the outcome. Exegesis may show how much more patriarchal or how much less is a text. I start with passages that exhibit the latter.

---

48. See E. Schüssler Fiorenza, "The Ethics of Biblical Interpretation: Decentering Biblical Scholarship," *Journal of Biblical Literature* 107 (1988) 3–17.

Prominent among neglected passages are female depictions of deity.[49] Hebrew poetry describes God as midwife and mother (Ps 22:9f.; Deut 32:18; Isa 66:13). The Hebrew root *rḥm*, meaning womb in the singular and compassion in the plural, provides an exclusively female metaphor for the divine that runs throughout the canon. Supporting contexts [[290]] strengthen this meaning. Thus, Jer 31:15–22 constitutes a poem replete with female imagery. It moves from the mother Rachel weeping for her lost children to the mother Yahweh promising to show mercy (*rḥm*) upon the virgin daughter Israel.

Among familiar passages, depictions of deity may require reinterpretation. Hosea 11 illustrates the point. Verses 3–4 describe God the parent teaching Ephraim the child to walk, picking him up, and feeding him. Patriarchal hermeneutics has long designated this imagery paternal, even though in ancient Israel mothers performed these tasks.[50] Reclaiming the maternal imagery affects yet another verse (11:9). After announcing judgment upon wayward Ephraim, the Deity returns in compassion. A poignant outburst begins, "How can I give you up, O Ephraim!" It concludes, "I will not execute my fierce anger . . . for I am *ʾēl* and not *ʾîš*, the Holy One in your midst." Traditionally, translators have understood the words *ʾēl* and *ʾîš* to contrast the divine and the human. Though correct, the interpretation misses the nuance. Rather than using the generic *ʾādām* for humanity, the poet employs the gender-specific *ʾîš*, male. Thus the line avows: "I am God and not a male."

This translation makes explicit a basic affirmation needed in ancient Israel and the contemporary world. By repeatedly using male language for God, Israel risked theological misunderstanding. God is not male, and the male is not God. That a patriarchal culture employed such images for God is hardly surprising. That it also countenanced female images *is* surprising. If they be deemed remnants of polytheism, the fact remains that nowhere does Scripture prohibit them.

Shifting from depictions of deity to the human scene, feminist hermeneutics highlights neglected texts about women. The Exodus narratives provide several instances. So eager have traditional interpreters been to get Moses born that they pass quickly over the stories leading to his advent (Exod 1:8–2:10). Two midwives, a Hebrew mother, a sister, the daughter of Pharaoh, and her maidens fill these passages. The midwives,

49. See P. Trible, *God and the Rhetoric of Sexuality* (Philadelphia: Fortress, 1978). Throughout the discussion I draw upon this book.

50. Cf., e.g., "The Divine Father," in J. L. Mays, *Hosea* (Philadelphia: Westminster, 1969) 150–59; also H. W. Wolff, *Hosea* (Phialdelphia: Fortress, 1974) 197–203. For a recent attempt to hold fast to the paternal image, even while acknowledging the maternal, see S. Terrien, *Till the Heart Sings* (Philadelphia: Fortress, 1985) 56f.

given the names Shiphrah and Puah, defy the mighty Pharaoh, who has no name. The mother and sister work together to save their baby son and brother. The daughter of Pharaoh identifies with them rather than with her father. This portrait breaks filial allegiance, crosses class lines, and transcends racial and political differences. A collage of women unites for salvation; with them the Exodus originates. But existing biblical theologies fail to tell the tale.

[[291]] Likewise, these theologies neglect the distaff conclusion of the Exodus story (14:1–21). The figure Miriam provides continuity between beginning and end. First appearing discreetly at the Nile River, later she reappears boldly at the Reed Sea. With other women she leads Israel in a triumphal song. Though biblical redactors would rob Miriam of her full voice by attributing the Song of the Sea to Moses (Exod 14:1–18) and only a stanza to her (15:20–21), historical criticism has recovered the entire song for Miriam.[51] Feminist hermeneutics utilizes this work to show a conflict of gender embedded in the text. Miriam counters Moses. In time she questions his right to be the exclusive speaker for God (Numbers 11). Though the establishment censures her, fragments in Scripture yield another view. Unlike their leaders, the people support Miriam (Num 12:15). At her death nature mourns; the wells in the desert dry up (20:1–2). Centuries later Micah proclaims her a leader equal to Moses and Aaron (Mic 6:4). Jeremiah alludes to her prominence in his eschatological vision of restoration (Jer 31:4). Ramifications for biblical theology run deep when neglected Miriamic traditions emerge to challenge the dominant Mosaic bias.[52] Small things undermine patriarchal faith.

Even as it recovers neglected texts about women, feminist interpretation re-examines familiar ones. Genesis 2–3 is a prime example. Contrary to conventional understanding, this narrative does not proclaim male domination and female subordination as the will of God. Attention to vocabulary, syntax, and literary structure demonstrates no ordering of the sexes in creation. At the beginning "Yahweh God formed the human from the humus" (Gen 2:4b). Sexual identification does not obtain. At the end this creature becomes female and male in the sexually explicit vocabulary *ʾiššâ* and *ʾîš* (Gen 2:21–24). They are bone of bones and flesh of flesh, the language of mutuality and equality.[53] No concept of complementarity sets roles for them. The troublesome word *ʾēzer*, usually translated "helper" and applied to the woman as subordinate, actually connotes superiority.

51. See esp. F. M. Cross, Jr., and D. N. Freedman, "The Song of Miriam," *Journal of Near Eastern Studies* 14 (1955) 237–50.

52. See P. Trible, "Bringing Miriam Out of the Shadows," *Bible Review* 5 (1989) 14–25, 34.

53. See W. Brueggemann, "Of the Same Flesh and Bone (Gen. 2, 23a)," *Catholic Biblical Quarterly* 32 (1970) 532–42.

The phrase "corresponding to" or "fit for" tempers this connotation to signal equality.

But with disobedience the mutuality of the sexes shatters. In answering the serpent, the woman-shows theological and hermeneutical astuteness. She interprets the divine command faithfully and ponders the benefits of the fruit. By contrast, the man is mindless and mute. Opposing ⟦292⟧ portraits yield, however, the same decision. Each disobeys. The judgments that follow disobedience describe, not prescribe, the consequences. Of particular interest is the description, "Your desire is for your man, but he rules over you" (Gen 3:15). This condition violates mutuality. Thus it judges patriarchy as sin, a judgment that Scripture and interpreters have failed to heed.

Despite the passages cited thus far, feminist exegesis does not hold that all neglected and reinterpreted texts turn out to be less patriarchal than usually perceived. (Indeed, some feminists would disavow altogether the hermeneutics pursued here, to argue that patriarchy controls all biblical literature.) Exegesis also shows how much more patriarchal are many texts. The sacrifice of the daughter of Jephthah, the dismemberment of an unnamed woman, the rape of Princess Tamar, and the abuse of the slave Hagar constitute but a few narrative illustrations.[54] In prophetic literature the use of "objectified female sexuality as a symbol of evil" forms another set of passages.[55] Hosea employed female harlotry to denounce wayward Israel in contrast to the male fidelity of Yahweh (Hosea 1–3). Ezekiel exploited the female with demeaning sexual images (Ezek 23; 36:17). Zechariah continued the process by identifying woman with wickedness and envisioning her removal from the restored land (Zech 5:7–11). Legal stipulations also evince an overwhelming patriarchal bias.[56] Addressed only to men, the law viewed woman as property with concomitant results (Exod 20:17; Deut 5:21). While not excluded altogether from cultic functions, females were deemed inferior participants, obeying rules formulated by males. Not a few feminist exegetes find it sufficient to expose and denounce all such texts, asserting that they determine the biblical view of woman. Others recount them on behalf of their victims, thus establishing memorials in the midst of misery. However they are treated, such passages pose the question of authority—a central issue for all biblical theologies.

2) *Contours and Content.* Beyond exegesis, the next step envisions the contours and content of a feminist biblical theology. Following neither

54. See P. Trible, *Texts of Terror* (Philadelphia: Fortress, 1984).

55. See T. D. Setel, "Prophets and Pornography: Female Sexual Imagery in Hosea," in *Feminist Interpretation of the Bible* (n. 31 above) 86–95.

56. See Bird, "Images of Women in the Old Testament," 48–57.

the systematic-covenant model of Eichrodt nor the tradition-historical model of von Rad, it would focus upon the phenomenon of gender and sex in the articulation of faith. Without thoroughness and with tentativeness, the following proposals come to mind.

a. A feminist theology would begin, as does the Bible, with Genesis 1–3. Recognizing the multivalency of language, interpretation exploits the [[293]] phrase "image of God male and female," relating it positively to Genesis 2 and negatively to Genesis 3.[57] Allusions to these creation texts, such as Hos 2:16–20, would also come into play. This passage envisions a future covenant between God and Israel that disavows the hierarchical ordering of husband and wife. To base understandings of gender in mythical rather than historical beginnings contrasts what female and male are and are meant to be with what they have become. Creation theology undercuts patriarchy.

b. From a grounding in creation, feminist interpretation would explore the presence and absence of the female in Scripture, also taking into account relevant literature of the ancient Near East. Organization of this material remains unsettled. Narratives, poetry, and legal formulations need to be compared; minor voices, hidden stories, and forgotten perspectives unearthed; categories of relationships investigated. They include kinship ties of daughter, sister, wife, aunt, niece, and grandmother; social and political roles of slave, mistress, princess, queen mother, prostitute, judge, prophet, musician, adulterer, foreigner, and wise woman; and religious functions in cult, theophany, and psalmody.

c. Though it awaits sustained research, Israelite folk religion would become a subject for theological reflection. Denied full participation in the cult, some women and men probably forged an alternative Yahwism. What, e.g., is the meaning of worship of the Queen of Heaven (Jer 7:16–20; 44:15–28), of inscriptions that link Yahweh and Asherah,[58] and of female figurines at Israelite and Judean sites? What effect does folk religion have upon the character of faith, particularly debate about the unique versus the typical? Probing differences between the orthodoxy of the es-

---

57. Contra P. Bird, "'Male and Female He Created Them': Gen 1:27b in the Context of the Priestly Account of Creation," *Harvard Theological Review* 74 (1981) 129–59, a study that assigns the text but a single meaning and that a narrow one (procreation). Such restriction the text imposes neither upon itself nor upon the reader.

58. See Z. Meshel and C. Meyers, "The Name of God in the Wilderness of Zin," *Biblical Archaeology* 39 (1976) 11–17; W. G. Dever, "Consort of Yahweh? New Evidence from Kuntillet ʿAjrud," *Bulletin of the American School of Oriental Research* 255 (1984) 21–37; J. M. Hadley, "Some Drawings and Inscriptions on Two Pithoi from Kuntillet ʿAjrud," *Vetus Testamentum* 37 (1987) 180–213.

tablishment and the religion of the people might bring the female story into sharper focus.[59]

d. Feminist theology would be truly biblical in exposing idolatry. Under this rubric it investigates language for God. Juxtaposing verbal images, animate and inanimate, shows that Scripture guards against a single definition. Further, passages like the sacrifice of Isaac (Genesis 22), Elijah [[294]] on Mt. Horeb (1 Kings 19), and selected prophetic oracles (e.g., Isa 43:18f.; Jer 31:22) demonstrate that no particular statement of faith is final. Without rewriting the text to remove offensive language, feminism opposes, from within Scripture, efforts to absolutize imagery. The enterprise uses the witness of the Bible to subvert androcentric idolatry.

e. Similarly, the pursuit would recognize that although the text cannot mean everything, it can mean more and other than tradition has allowed.[60] Warrant for altering words and meanings runs throughout the history of interpretation and translation. No small example lies at the heart of Scripture and faith: the name of the Holy One. When Judaism substituted *Adonai* for the Tetragrammaton YHWH, it altered the text, "Thus is written; but you read." Christianity accepted the change. The authority of believing communities superseded the authority of the written word.[61] *Mutatis mutandis,* feminist theology heeds the precedent in wrestling with patriarchal language. The verb "wrestle" is key. In the name of biblical integrity, interpretation must reject facile formulations; in the name of biblical diversity, it must reject dogmatic positions. And like Jacob (Gen 32:22–32), feminism does not let go without a blessing.

f. Biblical theology would also wrestle with models and meanings for authority.[62] It recognizes that, despite the word, *authority* centers in readers. They accord the document power even as they promote the intentionality of authors. To explicate the authority of the Bible, a feminist stance might well appropriate a sermon from Deuteronomy (30:15–20). The Bible sets before the reader life and good, death and evil, blessing and curse. Providing a panorama of life, the text holds the power of a mirror

59. Cf. P. D. Miller, "Israelite Religion," in *The Hebrew Bible and Its Modern Interpreters* (n. 27 above) 201–37.

60. Cf. A. Cooper, "On Reading the Bible Critically and Otherwise," in *The Future of Biblical Studies* (n. 29 above) 61–79.

61. An appeal to canon as the prohibition to alteration is questionable, because canonization is a fluid as well as stabilizing concept, subject to the continuing authority of believing communities, including the power of translators; *pace* P. A. Bird, "Translating Sexist Language as a Theological and Cultural Problem," *Union Seminary Quarterly Review* 42 (1988) 89–95.

62. See L. M. Russell, *Household of Freedom: Authority in Feminist Theology* (Philadelphia: Westminster, 1987); C. V. Camp, "Female Voice, Written Word: Women and Authority in Hebrew Scripture," in *Embodied Love,* ed. P. M. Cooey et al., (San Francisco: Harper & Row, 1987) 97–113.

to reflect what is and thereby make choice possible. Like the ancient Israelites, modern believers are commanded to choose life over death. Within this dialectic movement, feminism might claim the entire Bible as authoritative, though not necessarily prescriptive. Such a definition differs from the traditional. In the interaction of text and reader, the changing of the second component alters the meaning and power of the first.

[295] These tentative proposals only initiate a discussion that seeks to join feminist hermeneutics and biblical theology. The descriptive and historical task would explore the entire picture of gender and sex in all its diversity. Beyond that effort, the constructive and hermeneutical task would wrestle from the text a theology that subverts patriarchy. Looking at the enormity of the enterprise, critics of all persuasions might well ask, "Why bother?" After all, east is far from west; Athens has nothing to do with Jerusalem. At best, constructive interpretations offer no more than five loaves and two fishes. What are they among so many passages of patriarchy? The answer is scriptural (cf. Matt 14:13–21). When found, rightly blessed, and fed upon, these remnant traditions provide more than enough sustenance for life.

Theological Synopsis

As Gerhard von Rad's student and assistant at the University of Heidelberg, Rolf Knierim was in a unique position to carry forward von Rad's project of Old Testament theology along traditio-historical lines. In fact, Knierim tells us that "for almost thirty years" he was among those who, following von Rad, were "certain that 'traditio-historical investigation shows the way' for an integrated view of the two testaments" (1981: 106). But it would be wrong to assume that Knierim is in any way hostile to the traditio-historical investigation he learned at the feet of its master and his teacher. The question he raised, after almost thirty years, was not about the legitimacy of traditio-historical investigation but about its adequacy for Old Testament theology.

In von Rad's theology of the Old Testament, there is a close fit between the history of Old Testament traditions and the decisively historical character of Israel's theology. While he in no way denies the importance of history, Knierim's study of revelation in the Old Testament led him to conclude that "the one-sided emphasis on history can only come at the cost of a considerable portion of the Old Testament material" (1971: 228). He reached that conclusion in an essay dedicated to Gerhard von Rad; it also marked the beginning of a departure from von Rad. Knierim's later work builds on his observation that the Old Testament speaks not only of history, and not only on the basis of history; it also speaks of the world and of creation, of world order. The task of Old Testament theology, then, is not just to investigate these traditions about history and creation, about Israel's deliverance and God's governance of the world, in their diversity and according to their own histories. Old Testament theology must also ask how these traditions are to be correlated, "and what the theological foundation is on which they all belong together" (1981: 107). Traditio-historical investigation alone is unable to answer those questions. Thus, for Knierim, von Rad's unity between the history of Israel's traditions and Old Testament theology as the investigation of that history is broken.

In its place, Knierim proposes that the task of Old Testament (or biblical) theology is a systematic one. To anyone familiar with biblical theology's history, that proposal is striking! It is so, because biblical theology struggled for a century to present the Bible in its own terms, rather than in terms and concepts borrowed from systematic theology or Christian doctrine. However, Knierim insists that the Old Testament's "plurality of theologies" requires a systematic analysis, "or we will not know how to read the Old Testament theologically" (1984: 29). The criteria for this analysis must come from the Old Testament itself, not from systematic theology. The supreme criterion for a theology of the Old Testament is "Yahweh's universal dominion in justice and righteousness" (1984: 49), the aspect of God's relation to reality that encompasses all others. This is, according to Knierim, more than just a central theme of the Old Testament; it is the criterion by which all themes and theologies are measured and evaluated.

Rolf Knierim was born and educated in Germany. He earned his doctorate at Heidelberg in 1962 and his Habilitation in 1965. He has taught for the past two decades at Claremont School of Theology and the Claremont Graduate School in California. Knierim has published several definitive studies on the methods of biblical interpretation, and these studies have clearly influenced his work on Old Testament theology. It reflects his own suggestion that Old Testament theology is the "relay-station between exegesis and systematic theology" (1984: 47).

B.C.O.

Writings by Knierim

1971   Offenbarung im Alten Testament. Pp. 206–35 in *Probleme biblischer Theologie: Gerhard von Rad zum 70. Geburtstag.* Edited by Hans W. Wolff. Munich: Kaiser.

1981   Cosmos and History in Israel's Theology. *Horizons in Biblical Theology* 3:59–123.

1984   The Task of Old Testament Theology. *Horizons in Biblical Theology* 6/1:25–57.

Rolf Knierim
The Task of Old Testament Theology

Excerpted with permission from Rolf Knierim, "The Task of Old
Testament Theology," *Horizons in Biblical Theology* 6 (1984) 25–31,
33–57. Some footnotes have been omitted.

The Problem

⟦25⟧ The Old Testament contains a plurality of theologies. This fact is
well established exegetically. It represents the theological problem of the
Old Testament. And the discipline of Old Testament theology is constituted by the task of addressing this problem.[1] The theological problem of
the Old Testament does not arise from the separate existence of its
particular theologies. It arises from their co-existence. The co-existence of
these theologies in the Old Testament demands the interpretation of

1. Our focus on the Old Testament in its own right is, while not exclusive, legitimate. Its
legitimacy does not depend on whether the Old Testament should be read together with the
New Testament, or whether it should be read by itself before being read with the New Testament. This question should not be determined by an either/or. As long as both testaments
are read together eventually, the question of where to start the process of reading is of secondary importance.

However, the claim that the Old Testament is theologically significant only when it is
read in light of the New Testament, or of Christ, has imperialistic implications and is theologically counterproductive: it is imperialistic because it censures the Old Testament's theological validity by external criteria; and it is counterproductive because the theological
significance of Christ or the New Testament, in as much as the Old Testament has something
to do with them, cannot be substantiated with reference to the Old Testament's theological
insignificance.

The legitimate focus on the Old Testament in its own right depends on some mutually
supportive reasons. *First*, this corpus is claimed by the Jewish as well as by the Christian tradition. The two claims conflict, and an arbitrating third party is not around. It should be clear,
at least for the Christians, that an interpretation of their Old Testament must be mindful of
that dissensus and therefore rest on the Old Testament itself, and not on their New Testament or an *a priori* combination of both. Such a combination of both testaments on the well
meant assumption by some Christians that Christianity is essentially Jewish because Jesus was
a Jew does not stand the test. Jews will recognize no Jewishness of Christianity on the ground
of Jesus' Jewishness, rightly so. And for Christians, the condition and ground for the election
of all humans into God's kingdom and salvation are not based on the Jewishness of Jesus.
Salvation may have come from or through a Jew, but it is not Jewish in nature. Christians owe
Jews a great debt indeed, for more than one reason. But Christianity is not essentially Jewish.

The recognition that Jews are no Christians, and by far most of the Christians are no
Jews, has nothing to do with racism. It amounts to a mutual recognition of difference. However, the denotation by Christians of the Jewish Bible as their Old Testament must not mean

their relationship or correspondence, a task that is more than and different from the interpretation of each of them in its own right which is done in historical exegesis—if exegesis does its work. And while generating this central theological problem and demand the Old Testament itself offers no direct approach and answer to it.

In the history of the discipline of Old Testament or Biblical theology, the ever increasing awareness of the plurality of theologies, as well as the danger of the Old Testament's theological disintegration and atomization implied in that plurality, has been met with attempts to identify holistic dimensions or perspectives which pervade all the Old Testament scriptures, messages, or theologies, or which embrace or undergird them. In fact, one of the primary postulates for the task of Old Testament theology has been that the Old Testament must be understood as a whole. And the ⟦26⟧ implication seems universal that as soon as a holistic dimension can be discerned the plurality of theologies in the Old Testament can be regarded as an enriching phenomenon rather than as a critical problem because the whole by definition represents nothing other than the semantic homogeneity of the plurality.

"passed away, inferior, invalidated, abolished." It can only mean antecedent to the New Testament historically even as this antecedence is not the basis for determining the relationship of the two testaments.

Secondly, the Christian tradition has distinguished, in essence, between two testaments in its Bible. Their relationship has been subject to varying and often controversial interpretation. However, each interpretation has always claimed to be legitimate, and not a usurpation or imperialization of one testament by the other. This claim must be taken seriously. The proper way for the Christian tradition to submit to its standards is to recognize the Old Testament in its own right before its relationship with the New Testament is determined.

Thirdly, there are, in a substantive sense, not only continuity and congruency connecting both testaments but also discontinuity and incongruency separating them. The question is open and indeed undecided as to which of the testaments interprets which, and what the role of continuity or discontinuity is in such interpretation, or whether any of the two testaments should be at all the basis for the interpretation of the other. This open situation suggests that the case not be prejudged in advance, and that each testament be understood as a whole in its distinctiveness before both are compared.

It is true that the title "Old Testament" presupposes the "New Testament" and, hence, the Christian Bible. This fact does not mean, however, that the Old Testament cannot be interpreted in its own right. It only means that the relationship of the two testaments must also be determined. Under discussion is whether this relationship is to be determined prior to and as the basis for, or after and on the basis of their independent interpretation.

Likewise, nothing is said against the need for a biblical theology. Emphasized is only that the approach to it must be based on a genuine comparison of the theologies of the two testaments for which the independent interpretation of each is at least as viable a starting point as their correlated interpretation from the outset.

This implication is indefensible.[2] The fact, e.g., that a plurality of theologies is held together or even generated by a holistic reality says *eo ipso* nothing about the kinds of their relationship, i.e., whether they agree or disagree, and even less about the degrees in which certain kinds are related. What is under discussion can be exemplified by the two types of holistic reality that have played the dominant role in the recent discussion: tradition-history and the canon.

Ancient Israel's theological tradition-history, certainly a type of holistic reality, generated the plurality of Yahweh-theologies. Yet the same holistic process did not clarify whether and how the theologies generated by it correspond among one another. It did not clarify the nature of the theological plurality itself even as it created the pluralistic fact. It is one thing to affirm all the Old Testament's theologies as the outgrowth of the tradition-history of Israel's Yahweh-faith. It is quite a different thing to ask how they are related among themselves. The question raised in the second aspect is not all resolved by what is affirmed in the first; nor is the answer to this question of the relatedness of the plural theologies a negligible issue. As long as the nature of the plurality, i.e., the relationship of the many theologies among one another, did not become self-evident through the historical process, the unavoidable result was that the dynamic process of tradition-history generated the problem of the relationship of these theologies even as it generated their plurality. It generated the plurality of [[27]] theologies as a central theological problem, and that ever more so as new generations kept extending the process.

2. The study of the understanding of the holistic dimension or perspective in the history of our discipline is fascinating. The book by H.-J. Kraus, *Die Biblische Theologie* (Neukirchen: Neukirchener, 1970) offers a convenient entry, among others. There are the attempts to define the whole in terms of a thematic-theological unity pervading the texts themselves. They have basically turned out to be unsuccessful. Again, the whole is seen as something in addition to or in difference from the texts, yet something that embraces or undergirds the texts and of which the texts, the messages or theologies are part: a common ontology such as a dynamic Yahweh-word-reality, an evolutionary or universal-historical process, or a process of some other sort, Israel's common theological, credo-oriented tradition-history, the history of Israel's living faith-community, Israel's common affirmation of the oneness and exclusivity of Yahweh, the canon of scriptures, and so on. Occasionally, the whole as a postulate for Old Testament theology is said to have to consist of the sum total of exegesis. Such an understanding of the whole is obviously deficient. The sum total of exegesis demonstrates the plurality of theologies and, hence, the theological problem. This problem cannot be answered by an exegetical summary, not even a total one.

The review of the history of this issue and of current literature shows that we urgently need a critical scrutiny of assumptions and definitions of the notion of the whole which are in operation, and a valid theory of it. The same is true for the widespread uncritical operation with the notion of plurality and pluralism, and finally for the relationship between holistic and pluralistic reality.

Thus, the whole itself of this process of tradition-history is essentially pluralistic. The whole process is not the answer to the problem arising from the plurality of ancient Israel's theologies. It partakes in that problem. It is itself in need of theological clarification from a different type of theological vantage point.

The canon has finalized the problem. In the process of canonization, authoritative theological traditions from many generations and diverse settings were condensed into close juxtaposition on the same synchronic level. In the canon, they have come together face to face, in conference so to say, and their canonic situation, if it means anything, authoritatively demands the clarification of their relationship. The question whether the various theological positions in the Old Testament are substantively or semantically in agreement or not and, if they are, how they appear to be related or can become related, becomes the key problem precisely because of their right and simultaneous canonic co-existence. In generating this problem without resolving it, the canon itself calls for the discernment of a theological criterion for the purpose of its own proper theological understanding.

The holistic dimensions that pervade or encompass the plurality of the Old Testament's theologies do not resolve the problem of the relationship of these theologies, or of the nature of the Old Testament's theological pluralism for that matter. The discussion must focus on the Old Testament's pluralism itself. This pluralism represents a fundamental problem precisely because it reveals *eo ipso* nothing about [[28]] the kinds and degrees in which the many theologies correspond among each other, and because it may represent a chaotic reality just as much as a harmonious one. The Old Testament's pluralism may mean that the various theologies are mutually inclusive, compatible, and homogeneous, or that they are mutually exclusive, incompatible, and heterogeneous. They may be subservient or dominant one to another, compete against each other, or coexist in mutual isolation. The theological pluralism of the Old Testament is in principle an ambiguous phenomenon which may be meaningful and justifiable or unjustifiable and meaningless.[3] Its theological identity and validity are not constituted by the fact of its existence. The fact of its existence is itself subject to theological scrutiny, identification and validation. Such scrutiny, identification and validation can only take place through the examination of the relationship or correspondence of its individual theologies. This examination must apparently concentrate

3. The classic example in the Bible is Paul's discussion with the Corinthians. This discussion involves two mutually exclusive kinds of pluralism: the pluralism of the Corinthians, a Christian congregation, was chaotic and self-destructive. Paul's own understanding of plurality reflects the orderly relationship of the members in the body under its head. And on the basis of his understanding of proper plurality, Paul rejected the pluralism of the Corinthians.

on the semantic aspect in their relationship which involves above all the comparison of their contents. It must focus on the substantive issues addressed in the theologies contained in Israel's tradition-history and the canon, rather than on that tradition-history or the canon as the substantive issue. And it must ask what the issue (die Sache) is all about in the comparison of the many issues (im Vergleich der Sachen).

I wonder what would have happened in Jerusalem around 612 had an encounter taken place between the deuteronomic theologians, the Jehovist, the priestly temple-theologians, some sages, and Jeremiah, Zephaniah, Nahum, and Habakkuk; or a hundred years later, around 515, how a theological encounter would have looked with all of those just mentioned present, but now also with the addition of Hezekiah and his school, the deuteronomistic school, Deutero- and Trito-Isaiah and their disciples, and Haggai [[29]] and Zechariah as well. Unfortunately, we are only left with their juxtaposition in the canon but not with any discussion about their relationship, neither their own discussion nor a discussion by those who juxtaposed them canonically. At this point appears the theological problem of their plurality. If we accept their coexistence at face value without asking how they relate to one another, we neglect the possibility of essential theological ambiguity or heteronomy in their pluralism. In effect, they would then be theologically valid because they exist as part of the tradition, and not because of what they say. The fact of their tradition would guarantee their right to exist regardless of their theological identity, and their right to exist would prove that they are right. Differences in substance, in kind and degree, would be irrelevant and negligible. Such a pragmatic and traditionalistic understanding of pluralism allows as much for the relativization and devaluation of what is important as for the upgrading or even monopolization of what is less or not important. Ultimately, it is capable of neutralizing substantive theological distinctions, and of establishing indifference or arbitrariness as the highest value. Then, the preponderance of the interpreter's subjectivity replaces her/his submission to priorities that can be discerned in the Old Testament itself. It is time for us to demythologize pluralism.

As soon as we recognize that the Old Testament's theological pluralism is itself under theological scrutiny, we will be forced to ask whether these theologies are semantically compatible or not, and what the criteria are under which they can be legitimately related to one another. The Old Testament has not solved this task for us. It is not its own theology. But it has posed the problem for us, and we must clarify it or we will not know how to read the Old Testament theologically.

[[30]] The theological problem of the Old Testament's pluralism comes even more into focus when we look at it from the point of theological substance. All theologies in the Old Testament are united in affirming Yahweh as the one and only God. Yet at the same time, their explications of this affirmation vary or differ. These varying or differing explications of the oneness and exclusivity of Yahweh reach to the heart of the theological problem of the Old Testament, especially as they coexist in the canon.

It is true that Yahweh has acted and spoken in many ways, and that the humans, especially his people, can approach and witness to Yahweh in many ways. However, this affirmation fails to address the real problem, namely, whether the various and diverse explications of Yahweh self-evidently reflect the oneness of Yahweh in the richness of his manifestations, or whether they reflect many and different Yahwehs and in effect the witnesses in the Old Testament to different gods. Let there be many ways to God! But how do we know that they all lead to the same God, and not to many gods? We have no problem with the pluralism of the Old Testament's mono-Yahwehism or monotheism; but we have a fundamental problem with the evidence for monotheism in the Old Testament's theological pluralism. Because of this pluralism, the affirmed monotheism is no longer self-evident. It can only become evident if we can show that the pluralism itself has a monotheistic structure. As long as this problem is not clarified we do not know whether the structure of the Old Testament's theological pluralism is monotheistic and in accord with the affirmation of the oneness of Yahweh, or whether it is polytheistic. Ultimately, we cannot know what the Old Testament means when affirming Yahweh.[4]

For the examination of the monotheistic structure of the Old Testament's theological pluralism the question of how the individual theologies relate or correspond to one [[31]] another becomes all the more important. In fact, it appears to be the only way by which to substantiate theologically the Old Testament's claim to monotheism. Once again, and now for the theological reason proper: The task before us is the examination of the correspondence or relationship of the Old Testament's theologies themselves. Under discussion is the substantive or semantic structure of the Old Testament's pluralism, and its theological identity and validity. This is the task of Old Testament theology because it reflects the Old Tes-

---

4. To those for whom this analysis appears unnecessarily abstract and pessimistic I should like to point out that it keeps just as much an eye on the controversial understanding of the God of the Old Testament throughout the entire history of the Church (from Marcion via the Reformers up to Harnack, Bultmann, *et al.*) as it is mindful of theoretical arguments and above all of the problems posed by the actual comparison of many of the Old Testament's own theologies. By analogy, we have to ask whether the understanding of Christ as expressed in diverse theological interpretations triggered by the New Testament is at times so controversial among Christians, today as throughout history, that they reflect a polytheistic more than a monotheistic christology or christianity.

tament's central problem. For such an examination, we need the proper criteria. These criteria have to be drawn from within the Old Testament itself. Their discernment and definition is the task of the methodology of or the prolegomena to Old Testament theology.

The Criteria

Our discussion so far points out that we need to determine a basis from which to conceptualize the Old Testament's theology. This basis must apparently be found in the comparison of the Old Testament's theologies themselves. For such a process, we need guidelines.

. . . .

⟦33⟧ In order to determine the relationship among the Old Testament's theologies we must be able to discern theologically legitimate priorities. We must ask which theology or theological aspect or notion governs others, and which is ⟦34⟧ relative to, or dependent on, or governed by others. Ultimately, we must ask whether there is one aspect that dominates all others, is therefore fundamental and must be understood as the criterion for the validity of all others.

Such relating of theological aspects under priorities is often done in the Old Testament itself. In fact, it is deeply rooted in Israel's understanding of reality, her ontology, sociology, and historiology. The same is especially true for the composition of text-units. Anyone who has ever studied the relationship of parts in the semantic structure of a text-unit has been confronted with this basic phenomenon. Also, the search for priorities in such relationship should come as no surprise to anyone. Wherever and whenever the Bible was and is read, priorities have been at work, whether accounted for or not. The problem is on what grounds they are chosen, not that they are at work. The grounds, or criteria upon which we define priorities is therefore the question that demands attention.[5]

---

5. These questions and problems clearly set the task of Old Testament theology apart from the task of Old Testament exegesis. They are not germane to the methodological repertoire of historical exegesis. They establish Old Testament theology as a necessary discipline in its own right. It presupposes exegesis. But its task is, strictly speaking, not to provide a sum total of exegesis, something like an appendix to an exegetical commentary. Nor do works in which theological notions are merely juxtaposed, like in a theological dictionary, deserve the name "Theology." Nor does Old Testament theology have to recount the history of the Old Testament's theologies which is done in a History of Israelite Religion and even in a History of the Israelite Literature. Old Testament theology has to systematize the theological traditions of the Old Testament. A good eye-opener in this respect, at least for theological students, is the assignment to ask how the chapters in one or several available Old Testament theologies are related among one another as parts of a systematic whole.

The criteria for discerning the theologically legitimate priorities must obviously be found in primarily substantive aspects. They depend on what is said, and not equally as much on how, where, when or how often something is said. It is irrelevant in the canonic convention of the Old Testament's theological tradition-history and form-sociology whether a decisive theological argument was made more or less often than others, whether it was made by a historian drawing from the past, by a prophet looking towards the future, a priest, a sage, or a layperson, a man or a woman. It is equally irrelevant whether an argument was made early or late in the history of Israel's faith, or at its "axis-time." Why should any of these different types of Yahweh's servants, or their time, have per se a greater validity than any other? Also, why should any generic form of language—narrative, [[35]] instructing, legal, prophetic, proverbial, hymnic, complaining, poetry, prose—have an a priori theological prevalence over the other? Why should the "telling of the story" (which covers only part of the Old Testament language anyway) be theologically more or less prevalent than language speaking in systematic concepts? Every exegete knows that the Old Testament also speaks conceptually in terms of doctrine. More, the exegesis of every text shows that semantically, form of expression and conceptual understanding are intrinsically interrelated, and that one form of its expression can be transformed into others. We have to look for criteria that reflect the heart of the theological substance.[6]

We must focus on those criteria by which priorities among the theological arguments themselves can be distinguished.

The Old Testament's theologies are expressions of Israel's Yahweh-spirituality. In their center stands Israel's experience of her encounter with Yahweh, and her affirmation of his oneness and exclusivity. This spirituality pervades the entire Old Testament and its tradition-history. It finds its particular expressions in Israel's knowledge of Yahweh's initial and ongoing revelations, in her remembrance and worship of Yahweh, and in her exclusive commitment to Yahweh. This spirituality reflects an anthropology in which a community experiences itself as structured theocentrically and monotheistically, and not anthropocentrically or polydynamistically. Invariably, Old Testament theology must from the outset and all the way focus on this central aspect if it wants to avoid missing its subject.

However, this aspect only represents the presupposition for the problem which Old Testament theology has to address. In fact, it sharply creates

6. This statement does not mean that the socio-historical data are theologically irrelevant. They indeed express in an endless variety of ways that theology is concrete witness always related to actual reality. However, neither a witness nor its concreteness are sufficient criteria for true knowledge of Yahweh. They are themselves subject to scrutiny with respect to whether their actualizations reflect what must be said in the context of Yahweh's total dominion.

the theological problem. For when affirming Yahweh's oneness and exclusivity, the Old Testament speaks neither about a lone Yahweh in [[36]] splendid isolation nor solely about the encounter between Yahweh and Israel. Yahweh relates to many realms of reality, and in many ways, and vice versa. Actually, the manifoldness of these relationships between Yahweh and reality, and of the types of these relationships, constitutes the particular question by which the interpretation of the plurality of the Old Testament's theologies, i.e., their relationship among one another, is guided. As long as these questions are not clarified, the nature of Israel's entire Yahweh-spirituality remains ambivalent. These questions also reveal that the criteria for the understanding of Yahweh are not found in Israel's Yahweh-centrism, mono-Yahwism, or mono-theism, but that the theological integrity and validity of Israel's mono-Yahwism, mono-theism, or Yahweh-centrism is to be found in those aspects that show the extent and the modes of Yahweh's relationship to reality.

The Old Testament, strictly speaking, does not speak about Yahweh. It speaks about the relationship between Yahweh or God and reality. The interpretation of this aspect represents the basic substantive task of Old Testament theology. More specifically: Old Testament theology must interpret the relationship between Yahweh/God and reality with respect to the Old Testament's affirmation of Yahweh's oneness and exclusivity.

In view of this task, two questions are constitutive: First, *how* are Yahweh and reality seen as related, and *how* are the various modes of this relationship related one to another? And secondly, *with whom* and *with what* is Yahweh related, and especially, how are the various realms with whom Yahweh is related, related among one another? The first question refers to the qualitative notions in relationship while the second question refers to its quantitative notion or to its extent.

[[37]] The qualitative modalities of Yahweh's relationship to reality are reflected in words or word-fields and concepts such as creation, sustenance, election, liberation, covenant, law, justice, righteousness, peace, atonement, forgiveness, judgment, mercy, etc. We find these aspects everywhere in the respective Hebrew word-fields, and in smaller and larger text units.

With regard to the plurality of these aspects, Old Testament theology must explain how Yahweh relates through them to reality, and how reality responds through them to Yahweh. It must explain, so to say, Yahweh's ethos towards reality and reality's ethos towards Yahweh—obviously in this order.

But Old Testament theology must especially explain how these modes are related among one another. Once these questions are asked it becomes clear that Old Testament theology has more to do than juxtapose essays on biblical words or concepts or on biblical books in nice isolation from one another, as in biblical dictionaries or commentaries or Old Testament Introductions or Histories of Israelite Religion, or as in our libraries where Barth and Bultmann and Calvin and Cobb stand peacefully side by side.

It is known, e.g., that in many parts of the Old Testament, the relationship between liberation and commandment is seen in a distinct and irreversible order. What seems to be less known but quite clear in the Old Testament is the kind of relationship between liberation and justice. Both notions are different and must not be used interchangeably. But they are related to one another in a distinct way in which liberation is neither the beginning nor the end of a process. It is always release from injustice, and it points towards the restoration or establishment of justice. It is [[38]] itself an act of, and part of a process of justice. The theology of liberation is no independent theology in the Old Testament. It is a sub-chapter of a dominant theology in the service of which it stands: the theology of justice and righteousness.

This is not the place for examining the qualitative kinds and degrees of relationship between Yahweh and reality, and their relationship among one another. But it is the place for emphasizing that herein lies the task of the Old Testament theologian, and that this task can be undertaken. In its pursuit we will discover semantic relationships and a semantic hierarchy in which priorities exist, in which theologies identify and validate each other in their respective place and function in relation to others, and in which lastly those aspects appear that show what the relationship between Yahweh and reality is first and last and always all about.[7] It is true that God spoke of old to the ancestors of the early Christians "in many and various ways" (Heb 1:1). In fact, he not only spoke "by the prophets," he also acted. But much more is at stake. The "many and various ways" do not mean that every way has the same place and function in the order of things, and that every theologian or preacher can afford to pick and choose or prioritize at will, at the neglect of the true biblical priorities. He/she may not turn the weights upside down and justify a pseudo-religion with reference to the pluralism attested to in the Bible. Heb 1:1 cannot be the basis for conceptualizing an Old Testament, or a New Testament, or a biblical theology, or for simply understanding any part of the Bible on equal footage with all others.

The quantitative aspect involves the extent or the realms of reality to which Yahweh is related, and the modes of their relationship among one

---

7. In the New Testament, Paul knows of a "better" way and of the ultimate criterion, in 1 Corinthians 13.

another. In the Old Testament, the essential realms are three: the cosmic and natural world, the corporate human existence including [[39]] Israel's, and individual human existence. In our terminology: Cosmos and Nature; History and Society; and Existentiality. Again, Old Testament theology must interpret how Yahweh is related to each of these realms, and *vice versa*. Especially, it must interpret how these realms are related among one another as they are related to Yahweh.

It is clear, e.g., that in the Old Testament, cosmic and natural world and human history are not unrelated, just as there exists a relationship between Yahweh and history on the other. The question we have to ask is which of the two relationships is more fundamental and the basis for the other, or which depends on which. For this type of question, the 200 year long history of our discipline finds us ill-prepared because that history has been preoccupied with the primary ontological and epistemological category of History, while cosmology and nature have fallen by the wayside. Ironically, the history of philosophy throughout the millennia was amazingly in touch with the problem of cosmology and nature, and with what we have come to call natural science. By contrast, the history of biblical theology has lost contact with natural science virtually totally, an unjustifiable situation with respect to both the evidence in the Old Testament and our current situation. The question involves not only the aspect of the cosmos proper but also of our earth and its natural life which are bound into and dependent on the cosmic order, including the provision of water, fertility, and food for the sustenance of the living. When has anybody bothered to include in an Old Testament theology a—massive!—chapter on a subject as trivial as a theology of food? Why should any serious theologian take G. Dalman's monumental work *Arbeit und Sitte in Palaestina* theologically seriously? Is the provision by Yahweh of food for all the product of historical existence on which cosmos and nature depend, or is it the product first of all of the [[40]] earth's cosmic-natural vitality without which human history including salvation-history and the believer's existence would cease to exist within less than a year? Which of these realms is the basis for which? Which depends on which, and which is independent of which even as each is related to Yahweh in its own way? Certainly, history is seen as the peak, the goal, the purpose of the creation of the world. But this does not mean that human history or existence are ever perceived as having nothing to do with the order of creation, or that the order of creation is not perceived as the criterion for the truth of history, even for the truth of the history of God's people.

And Yahweh is not the God of creation because he is the God of the humans or of human history. He is the God of the humans and of human

history because He is the God of creation.[8] For the Old Testament, just as
for the New Testament, the most universal aspect of Yahweh's dominion is
not human history. It is the creation and sustenance of the world. This aspect is at the same time the most fundamental because creation does not
depend on history or existence, but history and existence depend on and
are measured against creation.

Similar questions will have to be raised with regard to the relationship
of humanity's and Israel's corporate existence, and that not only under the
perspective of history, as is usually the case, but also under the perspective
of their relatedness in the order of creation. Which of Yahweh's relationships to any of these realms is more fundamental and has therefore priority
over which? The answers to these questions will also shed light on the problem of a particularistic or universalistic understanding of Yahweh as God.

⟦41⟧ As far as human existence, is it, according to the Old Testament, isolated from the order of creation and from history, or is it dependent on and constituted by them? In the Old Testament's understanding
of Yahweh's relationship to various realms of reality, where is the place
and function of human existence in the totality of Yahweh's dominion?

I have argued that the interpretation of the relationship between Yahweh and reality involves two basic aspects: the qualitative and the quantitative aspect. If we now ask which of these two aspects lastly controls the
other, we will realize that the one quantitative aspect of the relationship
between Yahweh and the totality of reality governs all the qualitative aspects just as it governs the rest of the quantitative aspects concerning the
less inclusive realms of Yahweh's dominion. The reason for this conclusion should be fairly obvious. Every exegete knows that the qualitative notions of justice, righteousness, liberation, peace, etc., are found in the
relationship between Yahweh and every known realm of reality. Justice,
peace, liberation can involve the cosmic order, Israel's or the individual's
life. They could be perceived universalistically, particularistically, or indi-
vidualistically. On what ground, however, are we to decide in any qualitative relationship between Yahweh and various realms of reality as to how
these realms are related to one another and which realm has priority over
which; Are, e.g., justice and righteousness in Israel revealed and required
because they reflect Yahweh's relationship to the totality of his creation
and of humanity, or because they stand for nothing but Yahweh's relationship to his elected regardless of his relationship to the rest of the world?

---

8. Psalm 8 sees it well: the humans stand on top of the pyramid of the order of creation.
And just as they pray to Yahweh, they understand themselves as part of and in the context of
the order of creation. It is in this context and on this basis, and not without them, that their
historical existence can unfold and hopefully remain at the top of the pyramid onto which
they have been placed.

Which realm of Yahweh's relationship to reality in justice and righteousness constitutes the ground and norm for which? It must be clear: Justice is indispensable. But the criterion for its ⟦42⟧ theological validity and for its protection from perversion and manipulation is the relationship in justice between Yahweh and the total dimension of his dominion. To this realm, justice among the elected is accountable, otherwise it is not accountable to Yahweh in the totality of his dominion; towards this realm, it must be transparent; and by this realm it is always transcended even as the actualization among the elected is socio-historically contingent.

The heuristic comparison of the modes and of the realms in which Yahweh and reality appear to be related shows that the aspect of the most universal extent of Yahweh's dominion represents the most fundamental theological criterion and, hence, the most fundamental theological priority. If Yahweh is not in principle and before everything else the God of all reality, he cannot be the one and only God because he is not God universal. Yahweh may be Israel's God in oneness and exclusivity, but if he is not Israel's God because he is first of all God of all reality and of all humanity, he is a nationalistic deity or an individualistic idol, one among others, actually a no-god. Without the critical notion of universality, the affirmation of Yahweh's oneness and exclusivity does not substantiate the affirmation of his true deity. This affirmation is substantiated only when Yahweh is perceived as the God of universal reality. The notion of universal reality which is basically reflected in the notions of Yahweh's creation of and dominion over heaven and earth is therefore the criterion for the Old Testament's affirmation of Yahweh the universal God, and for his true deity. It is the only persuasive argument for the significance of monotheism.

The notions of Yahweh's universality and of universal reality complement each other. Universality is their common denominator. This horizon represents the most fundamental of all theological aspects in the Old ⟦43⟧ Testament. It is most fundamental because it constitutes at once the ultimate criterion for Yahweh's deity and for the dimension of his dominion. No other theological notion can compete with it. In fact, all others are relative to it. They receive their validity from it. Moreover, Yahweh's relationship to universal reality as expressed in the theology of creation can be discerned in the final analysis as what is at issue in the Old Testament. In this horizon, human history, Israel's election, and individual existence as well receive their meaning because they all are part of and have their place and function in Yahweh's dominion of his world.[9] This horizon is not the only one in the Old Testament, but it is foundational to and the criterion for all others.

9. Jonah said it: "I am a Hebrew; and I fear Yahweh, the God of heaven, who made the sea and the dry land" (1:9).

Finally, when the universal horizon of the relationship between Yahweh and reality is coordinated with the semantic hierarchy of the modes of relationship in these realms, the basic vantage point for the concept of Old Testament theology emerges. I have already suggested that the notions of justice and righteousness seem to be governing the other qualitative notions, and that they represent the most fundamental of the modes in which the universality of Yahweh's relationship with reality is perceived.[10] It also seems that the other modes are either gradually relative to or elaborations of it. However that may be in detail, the ultimate concern discernible in the Old Testament and, hence, the ultimate vantage point from which to coordinate its theologies gravitates around *the universal dominion of Yahweh in justice and righteousness.* This dominion is expressed time and again directly in the categories of cosmic nature, of human history and existence, and most fundamentally in the theology of creation. Its interpretation represents the elementary task of Old Testament theology. To this dominion, all other kinds and degrees of relationship [[44]] between Yahweh and reality, quantitatively and qualitatively, and their own correlations as well, are subservient. They are not insignificant and must not be ignored. But their place in the whole and, hence, the degree of their theological validity can be understood only to the extent to which they reflect implementations or manifestations of Yahweh's universal dominion in justice and righteousness. For such an understanding, it is not necessary that all of the Old Testament's theologies speak about nothing but universality and justice and righteousness. But it is necessary to interpret how a qualitative notion relates to others, what the horizon of its extent is in a given text, and whether or not it can be understood as a case or paradigm for Yahweh's universal dominion and its fundamental nature.[11]

10. Cp. H. H. Schmid, *Gerechtigkeit als Weltordnung* (Tübingen: Mohr, 1968). This systematic conclusion is quite independent of the controversy over the historical origins of the concept of justice: from the Ancient Near Eastern cosmogonies or from the tradition of the ethos of clan-solidarity. For the importance of the motion of justice and/or righteousness in connection with the universal dominion of God also in the New Testament, cp., a.o., Matt 6:33; Rom 1:17; 2 Pet 3:13. Cp. Lloyd Gaston, "Abraham and the Righteousness of God" (*Horizons in Biblical Theology*, Vol. 2, 1980, pp. 39–68).

11. E.g., the theology of Israel's relationship to the nations in the promised land in Deuteronomy raises the question how this theology corresponds with other theologies concerning the same issue, how it corresponds with the Old Testament's theologies of peace, and whether or not it can be considered as a paradigm for Yahweh's universal justice and righteousness attested to in other theological strata in the Old Testament. The interpretation of this issue involves a complex set of aspects. Its task is very different from the exegesis of the deuteronomic theology. Cp. my paper: "Israel and the Nations in the Land of Palestine in the Old Testament" (*The Bulletin, Lutheran Theological Seminary*, Gettysburg, PA. Vol. 58, 4/1978, 11–21).

I must attempt to formulate summarily the task of Old Testament theology. This task is twofold.

Old Testament theology must first of all examine the semantic structure of the relationship between Yahweh and his world. In this pursuit, it must distinguish between Yahweh's relationship to the world, and between the world's relationship to Yahweh. It must furthermore distinguish between the quantitative extension and the qualitative nature of that relationship. Specifically, it must clarify the order in which the quantitative components on the one hand are related among each other, and in which the qualitative components are related among each other, on the other hand. Above all, it must identify those components that are fundamental and to which all others are accountable. They are assumed in this paper to be the theology of creation and dominion of the world, the most universal quantitative aspect, and the theology of justice and righteousness, the qualitative aspect governing all others.

This first task is systematic in nature. It is guided by systematic questions which arise from the theological [[45]] pluralism of the Old Testament. It draws its approach and its conclusions from substantive aspects, and avails itself of all the Old Testament scriptures regardless of their tradition-historical, generic, or canonic order. Its execution would have to fill the first, and programmatic, volume of an Old Testament theology. It is concerned not with one topic, a uniting theme, but with the criteria by which to relate all themes or *theologoumena* under theologically valid priorities.

Based on the understanding of the systematic relatedness of the Old Testament's theologies, Old Testament theology will, secondly, have to assess the individually exegeted messages, kerygmata, and or theologies in the Old Testament in light of the semantic structure of the relationship between Yahweh and reality.[12]

The approach to this task can follow the tradition-historical development as far as we know it, or the canonic order of the books, or a systematic order as found in many publications. The choice between these approaches is relative. As long as, in any chosen order, the individual

---

12. This assessment involves a theological critique of the individual theologies in light of those theological criteria from the Old Testament that are foundational and represent the priorities. To people who say that such critique is none of our business, I can only answer that such critique is part of the biblical tradition itself, that it has always been part of the history of biblical interpretation practiced programmatically or *de facto* without a single exception by everybody who has ever touched the Bible. The question is what our criteria are for a theological reading of the Bible, and not whether a critical assessment of its theologies is legitimate. The alternative to such assessment amounts to the abandonment of any theologically accountable reading of the scriptures.

theologies are subject to confrontation with the criteria decisive for all, neither a canonic nor a tradition-historical nor a thematic approach can in principle claim priority over the others.

The second task is important. For it is here, in the texts, where the meaning of it all becomes a matter of actual debate. The texts are not the criterion for their validity. But without them, Yahweh's relationship to reality would remain speechless and removed from human experience. Less pressing is the extent of exhaustive completeness requiring the inclusion of all exegetical details ever discovered. The chances for such completeness become more and more remote anyway. More important is that such completeness is not mandatory for the validity of the program. 〚46〛

Conclusion

This is not the place for suggesting the actual outline of an Old Testament theology based on the criteria just discussed. Instead I want to mention a number of points that highlight the different implications of the proposal presented here from arguments that have played a role in the discussion.

The need to discern kinds and degrees of quantitative and qualitative relationships among the Old Testament's theologies by asking which embraces or governs which indeed amounts to the recognition of an order of semantic priorities in which the place and function and therefore the validity of theological notions or messages can be determined.

Likewise, the need to discern the most fundamental theological aspect (Yahweh's universal dominion in justice and righteousness: the aspect expressing what talking about Yahweh and reality, Yahweh and Israel, Yahweh and people is ultimately all about) indeed amounts to the recognition of a theological aspect that is normative for all others. It amounts to the discernment of a canon in and for the canon.

Once these two principal heuristic guidelines for reading the Old Testament are identified, some differences come into focus.

Old Testament theology is not concerned with finding a unifying topic that replaces all others. Instead, it is concerned with criteria by which the various theologies can be correlated in terms of theological priorities including the ultimate priority governing all others. The need for the process of working out these priorities remains even if some of the substantive assumptions referred to in this paper should have to be updated or revised.

Old Testament theology is conceptually not based on traditionally assumed methodological antinomies such as 〚47〛 concept versus story, idea versus text, theology versus message, kerygma versus reflection. None of these categories substantiates per se the theological validity of what is said, or of an argument; nor are there any texts, small or large, that reflect the surface-structure only, the story-line only, and not also a conceptual depth structure. An Old Testament theology based on such antinomies overlooks the fact that all of these categories represent modes of transformation in the interaction between language and meaning. But neither these modes nor the constant process of which they are part constitutes per se theological validity. Old Testament theology must be based on the theological argument itself. It must be theology in the strict sense of the word.

Categories such as the Word of God, Revelation, Yahweh's Presence, Inspiration, etc., provide no basis for solving the theological problem of the Old Testament. They have their place in the interpretation of Israel's theological anthropology, of Israel's knowledge of Yahweh or her theological spirituality all of which are themselves subject to the substantive theological criteria.

The function of the Old Testament theologian is neither descriptive nor confessional. It is systematic. In one way or another, Old Testament theology is a systematic theology of the Old Testament, or an Old Testament theology in the singular is impossible. It systematizes the plurality of theologies analyzed by exegesis, and summarily described in the conclusions of or appendices to exegetical works, under theological priorities discerned from within the Old Testament, and it provides the criteria for the accountability of what ought to be confessed. It is the indispensable and distinct relay-station between exegesis and systematic theology or hermeneutics. In this place, the Old Testament theologian has to stand on the Old Testament's behalf. This task differs from the task of systematic [[48]] theology or biblical hermeneutic because its criteria and agenda are intrinsic to and drawn from the Old Testament. And it does not have to be unsystematic because dogmatic theology is systematic. The category "systematic" is not reserved for systematic theology.

The conceptual basis for the systematic theology of the Old Testament is neither the view of the evolution or continuity of a certain central or of several important motifs, or of the believing community, nor the prevalence of one setting or genre over others. The basis are the decisive theological arguments themselves regardless where, when, how, and by whom they are expressed. These arguments themselves, both in their relationship to one another and in light of Yahweh's universal dominion in justice and righteousness, represent the criteria for the theological validity of any continuity or discontinuity, including the theological validity of the history of the believing community. They also represent the criteria for the validity of the forms and settings of these messages, theologies, ideas, concepts, motifs, stories, kerygmata, as well.

The extent to which the socio-historically contingent theologies in the Old Testament have a potential for universalization in the horizon of Yahweh's universal dominion also marks the point of critical difference from methods of theological interpretation such as allegory, typology, spiritualization, midrash, or from interpretation based on the assumption of the multi-level nature or of the multivalency of the scriptures or of passages thereof. None of these methods guarantees as such that the semantic potential of a text is examined in light of the theological criterion of Yahweh's universal dominion and its priorities. And the establishment of this criterion does not depend on any of these methods, nor on the method of historical exegesis for that matter. As soon as this criterion becomes the basic [[49]] method for theological interpretation, and as soon as texts are read in light of it, the alternatives between the various methods of interpretation become relative. In fact, none of them is either valid or invalid by virtue of its methodological idiosyncrasy. Rather the validity or invalidity of each depends on whether in light of Yahweh's universal dominion and its priorities, it reveals the potential of a text to point to that dominion or its resistance to that potential.

Also, the fact of the history of the ongoing validity and effectivity of texts (der Wirkungsgeschichte von Texten) including the effectivity of Old Testament texts in the New Testament provides no theological vantage-point for an Old Testament theology. Nobody denies this fact. Yet this ongoing vitality and effectivity, this ever new adaptation, reinterpretation and new interpretation of texts proves only the dynamic self perpetuation of an institution in ever new facets—nothing more, nothing less. It does not demonstrate per se why any of its arguments is legitimate. For them to be considered legitimate by virtue of the fact that they are part of the process, especially of the process of the faith-community, is not good enough. The fact of every history of such ongoing vitality and effectivity is itself inescapably accountable to theological criteria that verify its legitimacy. Indeed, none should be recognized theologically until it has stood the test under the criterion of Yahweh's universal dominion in justice and righteousness, and its subsequent priorities. We have every reason to emphasize this point. There are too many vital and effective *Wirkungsgeschichten* around that have little if anything to do with the Bible's central perception of God's dominion.[13]

The same is true also for the so-called charismatic or pneumatic element in interpretation. Charismatic or pneumatic interpretation can be

13. For an example of the continuity of the vitality and effectivity of a stratum of biblical texts from ancient Israel to our times, basically sustained by the history of the believing community, and for the ambiguous quality of such a vitality, cp. the book by J. Ebach, *Das Erbe der Gewalt* (Gütersloh: Gütersloher Verlagshaus Gerd Mohn, 1980).

pluralistically heteronomous. ⟦50⟧ It can be true or false. It must be guided and controlled by theologically legitimate criteria. Whenever that is the case, however, interpretation, indeed every interpretation becomes a legitimate charismatic or pneumatic event. This type of charismatic event gives interpretation its freedom. In fact, it represents the most authentic type of interpretation.

The type of theological interpretation proposed for the Old Testament can also be proposed for the religions of the Ancient Near East. Ancient Israel's Yahweh-theology is part of the view of reality in the Ancient Near East. It is a religious phenomenon. It is not theological whereas they are only religious. Nor are they non-theological because theology is reserved for Israel or Christianity. Both their and Israel's religiosity have developed theologies all of which belong to the phenomenon and history of human religion. The theological task within this total religious environment would be to examine each theological system in its own right, and subsequently to compare the systems critically. Such a process will go a long way in demonstrating not only what they have in common and where they are different but also where they teach and validate each other and where not.

The task of Old Testament theology as defined in this paper should also provide a fresh basis for examining the relationship of the two testaments of the Christian Bible, including the role of Jesus Christ in this relationship. I do no longer believe that this relationship can be sufficiently explained on the basis of patterns such as Old and New, continuity in whatever form, promise and fulfillment in whatever form, of one or more Old Testament aspects ending up in the New Testament, or of quotations of Old Testament passages in the New, etc. Nor is the thesis sufficient that the Old Testament must be interpreted from Christ, or Christ from the Old Testament. What is true is that both, the Old and the New Testament including Christ ⟦51⟧ must be interpreted in view of what can be discerned in either testament and in the Jewish tradition as God's universal dominion over his world, and the world's response to this dominion, and the priorities subsequent to this aspect. Such a vantage point may also offer a basis for a fresh review of the relationship between the Jewish and the Christian communities. We are dealing with the problem of the horizon in view of which not only the varying but also the conflicting traditions in the Old-New Testament and in the Jewish-Christian relationship can be sifted and amalgamated.

Finally, Old Testament theological interpretation does not presuppose the production of comprehensive volumes. In order to be legitimate, it does not always have to say it all, but what it says must rest on a foundation that is applicable to all. Likewise, it can be applied to the interpretation of texts or traditions or corpora or themes. It can be thematic or homiletical. The choice of approach can be verifiable and circumstantial just as much as the selection of the point of access to the material. Here is freedom for true plurality and flexibility. Decisive for any of these approaches is the interpretation of the transparence of the chosen subject in light of Yahweh's universal dominion, and the interpretation of its place, function, and validity which it has in light of the discernible theological priorities. With these criteria in mind, I envision a thriving pluralism of teaching and preaching and, last but not least, of a specific genre of expertly executed theological essays, monographs, and dissertations.

Appendix

JOHANN P. GABLER

b. 1753   d. 1826

An Oration on the Proper Distinction between Biblical and Dogmatic Theology and the Specific Objectives of Each

Theological Synopsis

If philosophy is a series of footnotes to Plato, then Old Testament theology is a series of very expansive footnotes to Gabler. Johann Philipp Gabler was born in Frankfurt, Germany, in 1753. Having already attained a broad education in the humanities, especially philosophy and history, he studied theology at the University of Jena from 1772 to 1778; his dissertation was on Heb 3:3–6. Returning to Frankfurt, he occupied an ecclesiastical position and served as a preacher. Following further studies at the University of Göttingen, he was called, in 1785, to be professor of theology in the University of Altdorf, near Erlangen. From there he was called back to his *alma mater*, Jena, in 1804. Five years after his departure, the University of Altdorf was dissolved. Gabler continued at Jena until his death in 1826 (Saebø 1987: 2–4).

Gabler's contributions to biblical scholarship and theology were prodigious, and he undertook them while maintaining an active interest in the church and the preparation of its ministers. Those contributions and that interest have been largely forgotten, however. Gabler is remembered today for his inaugural lecture, on 30 March 1787—he was thirty-three years old—in the University of Altdorf. The lecture itself was brief and, in some of its parts, not especially clear (Morgan 1987: 165). Furthermore, the lecture was in Latin, and its translation into English (and German) is sometimes a matter of dispute (Sandys-Wunsch and Eldredge 1980). More than anything Gabler said in the lecture, it is its title that has proved influential in the history of biblical and Old Testament Theology: "The Proper Distinction between Biblical and Dogmatic Theology and the Specific Objectives of Each." Gabler came to be seen as the "father" of biblical theology because, it is claimed, he defined its independent status over against dogmatic (or systematic) theology. Whatever the merits of that status may be, Gabler would have been deeply troubled by any suggestion that biblical theology should be set loose from dogmatics. His intention was precisely to give dogmatic theology a firm and unchanging foundation, and this he saw as biblical theology's "specific objective" (Morgan 1987: 164).

Gabler began his career at the University of Altdorf profoundly aware of the issues confronting dogmatic theology and, thus, the church. He was also convinced of the possibilities that historical-critical study of the Bible offered in addressing and resolving these issues. His inaugural lecture meant to demonstrate this conviction and to point to the possibilities. The lecture is firmly rooted in its precarious intellectual context, between eighteenth-century rationalism and its deconstruction under Kant's critiques and the idealism they gave birth (Ollenburger 1985). Perhaps for that reason, neither Gabler nor anyone else carried out the program he sketched in his inaugural. Old Testament theologians have appealed to it as justification for a strictly historical definition of their task, and as a rationale for conducting it in isolation from dogmatic theology. Gabler's later work made clear, in case his inaugural lecture did not, that this falls very far short of his own intention (Merk 1972: 69–81). For that reason, the lecture here reprinted stands both as the foundation of Old Testament theology and as a continuing provocation to it.

                                                                        B.C.O.

Writings about Gabler

Merk, Otto
   1972   *Biblische Theologie des Neuen Testaments in ihrer Anfangszeit.* Marburg: Elwert.
Morgan, Robert
   1987   Gabler's Bicentenary. *Expository Times* 98:164–68.
Ollenburger, Ben C.
   1985   Biblical Theology: Situating the Discipline. Pp. 37–62 in *Understanding the Word: Essays in Honor of Bernhard W. Anderson.* Edited by James T. Butler, Edgar W. Conrad, and Ben C. Ollenburger. Journal for the Study of the Old Testament, Supplement Series 37. Sheffield: JSOT Press.

Saebø, Magne
  1987   Johann Philipp Gablers Bedeutung für die biblische Theologie. *Zeitschrift für Alttestamentliche Wissenschaft* 99:1–16.
Sandys-Wunsch, John, and Laurence Eldredge
  1980   J. P. Gabler and the Distinction between Biblical and Dogmatic Theology: Translation, Commentary, and Discussion of His Originality. *Scottish Journal of Theology* 33:133–58.

Johann P. Gabler on Biblical Theology

Excerpted with permission from John Sandys-Wunsch and Laurence Eldredge, "J. P. Gabler and the Distinction between Biblical and Dogmatic Theology: Translation, Commentary, and Discussion of His Originality," *Scottish Journal of Theology* 33 (1980) 133–44. Translated by John Sandys-Wunsch and Laurence Eldredge. The translators provide helpful commentary (pp. 148–58), which is not reprinted here.

Translators' Introduction

[[133]] Gabler's inaugural address *De justo discrimine theologiae biblicae et dogmaticae regundisque recte utriusque finibus* was written in a very complex, classically-based Latin, but the ideas he expressed were those of eighteenth-century Enlightenment theology. The responsibility for this translation was shared in that Dr Eldredge dealt with the philological and idiomatic sense of the Latin, and Dr Sandys-Wunsch filled in the theological background to Gabler's thought. Dr Sandys-Wunsch alone is responsible for the commentary and discussion.

There is evidence that the address was published in 1787, but this edition may no longer be extant. The text used in this translation is that given in the second volume of Gabler's *Kleinere Theologische Schriften* (Ulm: 1831), pp. 179–98, edited by his sons after his death. For convenience of reference we have indicated approximately the pagination from this volume in the body of our translation [[marked with a double slash followed by the page number; as throughout this book, page numbers of the reprint source are in double brackets]].

An excellent translation into German is found in Otto Merk, *Biblische Theologie des neuen Testaments in ihrer Anfangszeit* (Marburg: Elwert, 1972), pp. 273–84. We have, however, on occasion differed from him in matters falling into that grey area that lies between etymology and interpretation. There is also a partial translation into English in W. G. Kümmel, *The New Testament: The History of the Investigation of its Problems* (London: S.C.M., 1973), pp. 98–100.

Footnotes with Latin numerals are Gabler's; those with Arabic numerals are ours. Gabler's footnotes have been altered in two respects; they have been numbered consecutively [[134]] and the bibliographical details they contain have been enriched where possible.

Conventions referring to deceased scholars in the eighteenth century do not translate well into English. Faced with the choice between incon-

492

gruity and anachronism we have opted for the latter; for example, 'the late Professor Zachariae' instead of 'the blessed Zachariae'.

An Oration

ON THE PROPER DISTINCTION BETWEEN BIBLICAL AND DOGMATIC THEOLOGY AND THE SPECIFIC OBJECTIVES OF EACH

which was given on March 30, 1787, by Magister Johann Philipp Gabler as part of the inaugural duty of the Professor Ordinarius of Theology in Alma Altorfina

Magnificent Lord, Rector of the Academy;

Most Generous Lord, prefect of this town and surrounding area;

Most revered, learned, experienced and esteemed men;

Most excellent and most celebrated professors of all faculties;

Patrons of the college, united in your support;

and you, students, a select group with respect to your nobility of both virtue and family;

Most splendid and worthy audience of all faculties:

All who are devoted to the sacred faith of Christianity, most worthy listeners, profess with one united voice that the sacred books, especially of the New Testament, are the one clear source from which //180 all true knowledge of the Christian religion is drawn. And they profess too that these books are the only secure sanctuary to which we can flee in the face of the ambiguity and vicissitude of human knowledge, if we aspire to a solid understanding of divine matters and if we wish to obtain a firm and certain hope of salvation. Given this agreement of all these religious opinions, why then do these points of contention arise? Why these fatal discords of the various sects? Doubtless this dissension originates in part from the occasional [[135]] obscurity of the sacred Scriptures themselves; in part from that depraved custom of reading one's own opinions and judgments into the Bible, or from a servile manner of interpreting it. Doubtless the dissension also arises from the neglected distinction between religion and theology; and finally it arises from an inappropriate combination of the simplicity and ease of biblical theology with the subtlety and difficulty of dogmatic theology.

Surely it is the case that the sacred books, whether we look at the words alone or at the concepts they convey, are frequently and in many places veiled by a deep obscurity—and this is easily demonstrated; for one thing it is self-evident and for another a host of useless exegetical works proclaims it. The causes of this state of affairs are many: first the very nature and quality of the matters transmitted in these books; second, the unusualness of the individual words and of the mode of expression as a whole; third, the way of thinking behind times and customs very different from our own; fourth and finally, the ignorance of many people of the proper way of interpreting these books, whether it is due to the ancient characteristics of the text as a whole or to the language peculiar to each scriptural writer. //181 But before this audience it is of little importance to describe each and every one of these causes, since it is self-evident that the obscurity of the Holy Scriptures, whatever its source, must give rise to a great variety of opinion. Also one need not discuss at length that unfortunate fellow who heedlessly dared to attribute some of his own most insubstantial opinions to the sacred writers themselves—how he increased the unhappy fate of our religion! There may even be some like him who would like to solidify the frothiness of such opinions about the sacred authors; for it is certainly something to give a divine appearance to their human ideas. Those completely unable to interpret correctly must inevitably inflict violence upon the sacred books; truly we even notice that often the wisest and most skilled of interpreters goes astray, so much so that, disregarding the laws of correct interpretation, they indulge their own ingenuity for its own sake. And let us not think then that it is suitable and legitimate for those who use the sacred words to tear what pleases them from its context in the sacred Scriptures; for it happens again and again that, when they cling to the words and do not pay attention to the mode [[136]] of expression peculiar to the sacred writers, they express something other than the true sense of these authors. And if they continue to use metaphors when the context demands universal notions, then they may persuade themselves to say that some meaning which they brought to the sacred texts in the first place, actually comes from the sacred texts.[i]

//182 Another cause of discord, a most serious one, is the neglected distinction between religion and theology; for if some people apply to religion what is proper to theology, it is easy to understand that there would

i. The best things to read in this connexion are the observations truly and learnedly made by the late immortal J. A. Ernesti in his learned work *Pro grammatica interpretatione librorum sacrorum* and *De vanitate philosophantium in interpretatione librorum sacrorum*, in *Opuscula Philologica* (2nd ed.; Leiden, Luchtman, 1764) 219–32 and 233–51; and the very distinguished Morus in *Prolus. de discrimine sensus et significationis in interpretando* (Leipzig, 1777).

be enormous room for the sharpest differences of opinion, and these differences will be even more destructive because each party to the quarrel will only with great reluctance surrender what he considers to pertain to religion. However, after the work of Ernesti, Semler, Spalding, Toellner, and others, most recently the venerable Tittmann[ii] has shown us brilliantly that there is considerable difference between religion and theology. For, if I may quote this excellent scholar, religion is passed on by the doctrine in the Scriptures, teaching what each Christian ought to know and believe and do in order to secure happiness in this life and in the life to come. Religion then, is every-day, transparently clear knowledge; but theology is subtle, learned knowledge, surrounded by a retinue of many disciplines, and by the same token derived not only from the sacred Scripture but also from elsewhere, especially from the domain of philosophy and history. It is therefore a field elaborated by human discipline and ingenuity. It is also a field that is advanced by careful and discriminating observation //183 that experiences various changes along with other fields. Not only does theology deal with things proper to the Christian religion, but it also explains carefully and fully all connected matters; and finally it makes a place for them with the subtlety and rigor of logic. But religion for the common man has nothing to do with this abundance of literature and history.

[[137]] But this sad and unfortunate difference of opinion has always been and, alas, always will be associated with that readiness to mix completely diverse things, for instance the simplicity of what they call biblical theology with the subtlety of dogmatic theology; although it certainly seems to me that the one thing must be more sharply distinguished from the other than has been common practice up to now. And what I should like to establish here is the necessity of making this distinction and the method to be followed. This is what I have decided to expound in this brief speech of mine in so far as the weakness of my powers allows and in so far as it can be done. Therefore, most honored listeners of all faculties[1] I strongly beg your indulgence. Would you grant me open ears and minds and be so kind as to follow me as I venture to consider these increasingly important matters. I pray and ask each and every one of you for your attention as far as is necessary so that I may speak my mind as clearly as possible.

There is truly a biblical theology, of historical origin, conveying what the holy writers felt about divine matters; on the other hand there is a dogmatic theology //184 of didactic origin, teaching what each theologian

---

ii. C. C. Tittmann, *Progr(amm) de discrimine theologiae et religionis* (Wittemberg, 1782).

1. A.O.O.H. Presumably an abbreviation for *Auditores omnium ordinum honorabiles*.

philosophises rationally about divine things, according to the measure of his ability or of the times, age, place, sect, school, and other similar factors. Biblical theology, as is proper to historical argument, is always in accord with itself when considered by itself—although even biblical theology when elaborated by one of the disciplines may be fashioned in one way by some and in another way by others. But dogmatic theology is subject to a multiplicity of change along with the rest of the humane disciplines; constant and perpetual observation over many centuries shows this enough and to spare. How greatly the churches of the learned differ from the first beginnings of the Christian religion; how many systems the fathers attributed to each variety of era and setting![2] For history teaches that there is a chronology and a geography to theology itself. How much the scholastic theology of the Middle Ages, covered with the thick gloom of barbarity, differs from the discipline of the fathers! Even after the light [[138]] of the doctrine of salvation had emerged from these shadows, every point of difference in theology was endured even in the purified church, if I may refer to Socinian and Arminian factions. Or if I may refer to the Lutheran church alone, the teaching of Chemnitz and Gerhard is one thing, that of Calov another, that of Museus and Baier another, that of Budde another, that of Pfaff and Mosheim another, that of Baumgarten another, that of Carpov another, that of Michaelis and Heilmann another, that of Ernesti and Zachariae another, that of Teller another, that of Walch and Carpzov another, that of Semler another, and that of Doederlein finally another. But the sacred writers are surely not so changeable that they should in this fashion be able to assume these different types and forms of theological doctrine. What I do not wish to be said, however, //185 is that all things in theology should be considered uncertain or doubtful or that all things should be allowed according to human will alone. But let those things that have been said up to now be worth this much: that we distinguish carefully the divine from the human, that we establish some distinction between biblical and dogmatic theology, and after we have separated those things which in the sacred books refer most immediately to their own times and to the men of those times from those pure notions which divine providence wished to be characteristic of all times and places, let us then construct the foundation of our philosophy upon religion and let us designate with some care the objectives of divine and human wisdom. Exactly thus will our theology be made more certain and more firm, and there will be nothing further to be feared for it from the most savage attack from its

2. The translation here represents a conjectural emendation of the untranslatable Latin text. *Quanta* has been added before *Patres*.

enemies. The late Professor Zachariae did this very capably,[iii] but I hardly need to remind you of the fact that he left some things for others to emend, define more correctly, and amplify. However, everything comes to this, that on the one hand we hold firmly to a just method for cautiously giving shape to our interpretations of the sacred authors; and on the other that we rightly establish the use in dogmatics of these interpretations and dogmatics' own objectives.

The first task then in this most serious matter is to gather [[139]] carefully the sacred ideas and, if they are not expressed in the sacred Scriptures, let us fashion them ourselves from passages that we compare with each other. In order that the task proceed productively and that nothing is done fearfully or with partiality, //186 it is necessary to use complete caution and circumspection in all respects. Before all else, the following will have to be taken into account: in the sacred books are contained the opinions not of a single man nor of one and the same era or religion. Yet all the sacred writers are holy men and are armed with divine authority; but not all attest to the same form of religion; some are doctors of the Old Testament of the same elements that Paul himself designated with the name 'basic elements';[3] others are of the newer and better Christian Testament. And so the sacred authors, however much we must cherish them with equal reverence because of the divine authority that has been imprinted on their writings, cannot all be considered in the same category if we are referring to their use in dogmatics. I would certainly not suggest that a holy man's own native intelligence and his natural way of knowing things are destroyed altogether by inspiration. Finally since especially in this context it is next asked what each of these men felt about divine things (this can be understood not from any traditional appeal to divine authority but from their books) I should judge it sufficient in any event that we do not appear to concede anything which lacks some proof. I should also judge that when it is a case of the use in dogmatics of biblical ideas, then it is of no consequence under what authority these men wrote, but what they perceived this occasion of divine inspiration clearly transmitted and what they perceived it finally meant. That being the case it is necessary, unless we want to labour uselessly, to distinguish among each of the periods in the Old and New Testaments, each of the authors, and each of the manners of speaking //187 which each used as a reflection of time and place, whether these manners are historical or didactic or

iii. G. T. Zachariae in his noted work *Biblische Theologie* (5 vols.; Göttingen and Kiel, 1771, 1772, 1774, 1775, 1786).

3. The expression from Gal 4:9 is cited in Greek in Gabler's text. It is translated here as Gabler understood it but many modern commentators would interpret it otherwise.

poetic. If we abandon this straight road, even though it is troublesome and of little delight, it can only result in our wandering into some deviation or uncertainty. Therefore we ⟦140⟧ must carefully collect and classify each of the ideas of each patriarch—Moses, David, and Solomon, and of each prophet with special attention to Isaiah, Jeremiah, Ezekiel, Daniel, Hosea, Zachariah, Haggai, Malachi, and the rest; and for many reasons we ought to include the apocryphal books for this same purpose; also we should include the ideas from the epoch of the New Testament, those of Jesus, Paul, Peter, John, and James. Above all, this process is completed in two ways: the one is in the legitimate interpretation of passages pertinent to this procedure; the other is in the careful comparison of the ideas of all the sacred authors among themselves.

The first of these two involves many difficulties.[iv] For not only must we consider here the linguistic problem of the language then in use, which in the New Testament is both graeco-Hebrew and the vulgar Greek of the time; we must also consider that which is peculiar to each writer; that is, the uses of the meaning that a particular word may have in one certain place whether //188 that meaning be broader or narrower. Also we should add the reason for the divergence of these uses and explain, if possible, the common meaning in which several instances of the same word fall together.[v] But we must also investigate the power and reason of the meaning itself; what is the primary idea of the word, and what merely added to it. For the interpreter who is on his guard must not stop short at the primary idea in the word, but he must also press on to the secondary idea which has been added to it either through long use or through ingenuity or through scholarly use of the word, and in so doing one may certainly make the most egregious of blunders. Let us not by applying tropes[4] forge new dogmas about which the authors themselves never thought. Not only in prophetic or poetic books but also in the writings of the Apostles there are often improper uses of words which should be traced either to an abundance of genius or to the traditional usage of opponents, or to the

---

iv. The late Professor Ernesti warned us of this problem in his distinguished fashion in his two works *De difficultatibus N.T. recte interpretandi* and *De difficultate interpretationis grammatica N.T.*, in *Opuscula Philologica*, 198–218 and 252–87.

v. That excellent man S. F. N. Morus in his *Prolus. de nexu significationum eiusdem verbi* (Leipzig, 1776) has taught us what caution must be observed in interpreting the relationship amongst meanings of the same word.

4. This is a technical term referring to allegorical or similar methods of extracting a 'spiritual' meaning from a text.

use of words familiar to the first ⟦141⟧ readers.[vi] Up to now this is mostly done when we are comparing carefully many opinions of the same author, such as Paul; in comparing many things and words, //189 we reduce to one idea and thing the many passages which, although variously expressed, show the same meaning. Morus[vii] recently showed and illustrated all this in a distinguished fashion—a very great man whose reputation is his monument. Finally one must properly distinguish whether the Apostle is speaking his own words or those of others; whether he is moved only to describe some opinion or truly to prove it; and if he wants to do the latter, does he repeat the argument from the basic nature of the doctrine of salvation, or from the sayings of the books of the Old Testament, and even accommodating them to the sense of the first readers? For although the opinions of the Apostles deserve our trust, so that we may easily get along without some part of their argument, the first readers nonetheless wanted the proofs that were appropriate to their own sense and judgment. Therefore, it is of great interest whether the Apostle proposes some opinion as a part of Christian doctrine or some opinion that is shaped to the needs of the time, which must be considered merely premises, as the logicians call them. If we rightly hold on to all these things, then indeed we shall draw out the true sacred ideas typical of each author; certainly not all the ideas, for there is no place for everything in the books that have come down to us, but at least those ideas which the opportunity or the necessity for writing had shaped in their souls. Nonetheless, there is a sufficient number of ideas, and //190 usually of such a kind that those that have been omitted can then be inferred without difficulty, if they constitute a single principle of opinion expressly declared, or if they are connected to the ideas that are stated in some necessary fashion. This process, however, requires considerable caution.

At this point we must pass on to the other part of the task, namely to a careful and sober comparison of the various parts attributed to each testament. Then, with Morus, the best of men, as our guide, each single opinion must be examined for its ⟦142⟧ universal ideas, especially for those which are expressly read in this or that place in the Holy Scriptures, but according to this rule: that each of the ideas is consistent with its own era, its own testament, its own place of origin, and its own genius. Each one of these categories which is distinct in cause from the others should be kept separate. And if this cautionary note is disregarded, it may happen that the

---

vi. The distinguished J. A. Noesselt did this in his *Disp. de discernenda propria et tropica dictione* (Halle, 1762).

vii. That great man dealt with this first in his *Disp. de notionibus universis in Theologia* and then in his *Prog. de utilitate notionum universarum in Theologia* (Leipzig, 1782).

benefit from the universal ideas will give way to the worst sort of damage to the truth, and it will render useless and will destroy all the work which had been brought together in diligently isolating the opinions of each author. If, however, this comparison with the help of the universal notions is established in such a way that for each author his own work remains unimpaired, and it is clearly revealed wherein the separate authors agree in a friendly fashion, or differ among themselves; then finally there will be the happy appearance of biblical theology, pure and unmixed with foreign things, and we shall at last have the sort of system for biblical theology that Tiedemann elaborated with such distinction for Stoic philosophy.

When these opinions of the holy men //191 have been carefully collected from Holy Scripture and suitably digested, carefully referred to the universal notions, and cautiously compared among themselves, the question of their dogmatic use may then profitably be established, and the goals of both biblical and dogmatic theology correctly assigned. Under this heading one should investigate with great diligence which opinions have to do with the unchanging testament of Christian doctrine, and therefore pertain directly to us; and which are said only to men of some particular era or testament. For among other things it is evident that the universal argument within the holy books is not designed for men of every sort; but the great part of these books is rather restricted by God's own intention to a particular time, place, and sort of man. Who, I ask, would apply to our times the Mosaic rites which have been invalidated by Christ, or Paul's advice about women veiling themselves in church? Therefore the ideas of the Mosaic law have not been designated for any dogmatic use, neither by Jesus and his Apostles nor by reason itself. By the same token we must diligently investigate what in the books of the New Testament was said as an accommodation to the ideas or the ⟦143⟧ needs of the first Christians and what was said in reference to the unchanging idea of the doctrine of salvation; we must investigate what in the sayings of the Apostles is truly divine, and what perchance merely human. And at this point finally the question comes up most opportunely of the whys and wherefores of theopneustia.[5] This matter, to be sure very difficult, is, in my opinion at least, rather incorrectly inferred from the sayings of the Apostles, in which they make mention of a certain divine inspiration, since these individual passages are very obscure and ambiguous. //192 However, we must beware, if we wish to deal with these things with reason and not with fear or bias, not to press those meanings of the Apostles beyond their just limits, especially since only the effects of the inspirations and not their causes, are perceived by

5. This is a transcription of the term Gabler uses in Greek script. 'Theopneustia' was often used for 'inspiration' in the eighteenth-century debates on the subject.

the senses. But if I am judge of anything, everything must be accomplished by exegetical observation only, and that with constant care, and compared with the things spoken of and promised by our Saviour in this matter. In this way it may finally be established whether all the opinions of the Apostles, of every type and sort altogether, are truly divine, or rather whether some of them, which have no bearing on salvation, were left to their own ingenuity.

Thus, as soon as all these things have been properly observed and carefully arranged, at last a clear sacred Scripture will be selected with scarcely any doubtful readings, made up of passages which are appropriate to the Christian religion of all times. These passages will show with unambiguous words the form of faith that is truly divine; the *dicta classica*[6] properly so called, which can then be laid out as the fundamental basis for a more subtle dogmatic scrutiny. For only from these methods can those certain and undoubted universal ideas be singled out, those ideas which alone are useful in dogmatic theology. And if these universal notions are derived by a just interpretation from those *dicta classica*, and those notions that are derived are carefully compared, and those notions that are compared are [[144]] suitably arranged, each in its own place, so that the proper connexion and provable order of doctrines that are truly divine may stand revealed; truly when the result is biblical theology in the stricter sense of the word //193 which we know the late Zachariae to have pursued in the preparation of his well-known work.[7] And finally, unless we want to follow uncertain arguments, we must so build only upon these firmly established foundations of biblical theology, again taken in the stricter sense as above, a dogmatic theology adapted to our own times. However, the nature of our age urgently demands that we then teach accurately the harmony of divine dogmatics and the principles of human reason; then, by means of art and ingenuity by which this can happen, let us so elaborate each and every chapter of doctrine that no abundance is lacking in any part—neither subtlety, whether in proper arrangement of passages or the correct handling of arguments, nor elegance in all its glory, nor human wisdom, primarily philosophy and history. Thus the manner and form of dogmatic theology

6. This is a technical expression that refers to the standard collection of proof texts in the orthodox theology of the eighteenth century. G. T. Zachariae had been the first to challenge the usefulness of these lists of texts isolated from their context.

7. Here our translation differs from Merk's 'biblical theology in a stricter sense than Zachariae followed'. The Latin is ambiguous at this point, but in the next sentence the expression 'stricter sense' is used without any direct comparison. Furthermore, Gabler is very dependent on Zachariae here in his reference to the *dicta classica* and therefore he seems to be making this remark in connexion with rather than as a contrast to Zachariae's position. At all events there is no real difference between Gabler's and Zachariae's approach to biblical theology on this point.

should be varied, as Christian philosophy especially is,[viii] according to the variety both of philosophy and of every human point of view of that which is subtle, learned, suitable and appropriate, elegant and graceful; biblical theology itself remains the same, namely in that it deals only with those things which holy men perceived about matters pertinent to religion, and is not made to accommodate our point of view.[8]

viii. J. G. Toellner, *Theologische Untersuchungen* (Riga, 1772) 1.264ff.

8. The remainder of Gabler's address is not concerned with biblical theology but with the polite formalities of the occasion. Merk translates this section in his work.

SOURCES

The following books and articles are cited in the essays by the editors.

Albertz, Rainer, Hans-Peter Müller, Hans W. Wolff, and Walther Zimmerli (editors)
  1980   *Werden und Wirken des Alten Testaments: Festschrift für Claus Westermann zum 70. Geburtstag.* Göttingen: Vandenhoeck & Ruprecht/Neukirchen-Vluyn: Neukirchener Verlag.
von Ammon, Christoph F.
  1801–2 *Biblische Theologie.* 3 volumes. 2d edition. Erlangen: Palm.
Baab, Otto J.
  1949   *The Theology of the Old Testament.* New York: Abingdon-Cokesbury.
Baker, D. L.
  1976   *Two Testaments, One Bible: A Study of Some Modern Solutions to the Theological Problem of the Relationship between the Old and New Testaments.* Leicester/Downers Grove, Illinois: InterVarsity.
Barr, James
  1963   The Interpretation of Scripture, II: Revelation through History in the Old Testament and in Modern Theology. *Interpretation* 17:193–205.
  1988   The Theological Case against Biblical Theology. Pp. 3–19 in *Canon, Theology, and Old Testament Interpretation: Essays in Honor of Brevard S. Childs.* Edited by Gene M. Tucker, David L. Petersen, and Robert R. Wilson. Philadelphia: Fortress.
  1989   Are We Moving toward an Old Testament Theology, or Away from It? Paper read at the Annual Meeting of the Society of Biblical Literature, November 1989. Summary in *Abstracts of the American Academy of Religion [and the] Society of Biblical Literature 1989,* p. 20. Edited by James B. Wiggins and David J. Lull. Atlanta: Scholars Press.
Bauer, Bruno
  1838–39 *Kritik der Geschichte der Offenbarung: Die Religion des Alten Testaments in der geschichtlichen Entwicklung ihrer Principien.* 2 volumes. Berlin: Dümmler.
Bauer, Georg Lorenz
  1796   *Theologie des Alten Testaments; oder, Abriss der religiösen Begriffe der alten Hebräer von den ältesten Zeiten bis auf den Anfang der christlichen Epoche: Zum Gebrauch akademischer Vorlesungen.* Leipzig: Weygand.

Baumgarten-Crusius, Ludwig F. O.
  1828   *Grundzüge der biblischen Theologie.* Jena: Frommann.
Beecher, Willis J.
  1905   *The Prophets and the Promise.* New York: Crowell.
Benz, Ernst
  1983   *The Mystical Sources of German Romantic Philosophy.* Translated by Blair
          R. Reynolds and Eunice M. Paul. Pittsburgh Theological Monographs,
          n.s. 6. Allison Park, Pennsylvania: Pickwick.
Brömse, Michael
  1984   W. Vatkes philosophische Theologie im Streit der Polemik und Apol-
          ogie. Pp. 129–45 in *Vergessene Theologen des 19. und frühen 20. Jahrhun-
          derts: Studien zur Theologiegeschichte.* Edited by Eilert Herms and
          Joachim Ringleben. Göttinger theologische Arbeiten 32. Göttingen:
          Vandenhoeck & Ruprecht.
Brown, Raymond E.
  1989   The Contribution of Historical Biblical Criticism to Ecumenical
          Church Discussion. Pp. 24–49 in *Biblical Interpretation in Crisis: The
          Ratzinger Conference on Bible and Church.* Edited by Richard J. Neuhaus.
          Grand Rapids: Eerdmans.
Brueggeman, Walter
  1972   *In Man We Trust: The Neglected Side of Biblical Faith.* Richmond: John
          Knox.
  1977   *The Land: Place as Gift, Promise, and Challenge in Biblical Faith.* Overtures
          to Biblical Theology 1. Philadelphia: Fortress.
  1979   Trajectories in Old Testament Literature and the Sociology of Ancient
          Israel. *Journal of Biblical Literature* 98:161–85.
  1980   A Convergence in Recent Old Testament Theologies. *Journal for the
          Study of the Old Testament* 18:2–18.
  1984a   Futures in Old Testament Theology. *Horizons in Biblical Theology* 6/1:
          1–11.
  1984b   *The Message of the Psalms: A Theological Commentary.* Augsburg Old Tes-
          tament Studies. Minneapolis: Augsburg.
  1985   A Shape for Old Testament Theology, I: Structure Legitimation; II:
          Embrace of Pain. *Catholic Biblical Quarterly* 47:28–46, 395–415.
Bultmann, Rudolf
  1955   *Theology of the New Testament.* Volume 2. Translated by Kendrick Gro-
          bel. New York: Scribner.
Burrows, Millar
  1946   *An Outline of Biblical Theology.* Philadelphia: Westminster.
Childs, Brevard S.
  1960   *Myth and Reality in the Old Testament.* Studies in Biblical Theology 27.
          London: SCM/Naperville, Illinois: Allenson.
  1962   *Memory and Tradition in Israel.* Studies in Biblical Theology 37. Lon-
          don: SCM/Naperville, Illinois: Allenson.
  1967   *Isaiah and the Assyrian Crisis.* Studies in Biblical Theology 2/3. London:
          SCM/Naperville, Illinois: Allenson.

1970   *Biblical Theology in Crisis.* Philadelphia: Westminster.
1974   *The Book of Exodus: A Critical, Theological Commentary.* Old Testament Library. Philadelphia: Westminster/London: SCM.
1979   *Introduction to the Old Testament as Scripture.* Philadelphia: Fortress.
1984   *The New Testament as Canon: An Introduction.* Philadelphia: Fortress.
1986   *Old Testament Theology in a Canonical Context.* Philadelphia: Fortress.

Clements, Ronald E.
1969   *God's Chosen People: A Theological Interpretation of the Book of Deuteronomy.* Valley Forge, Pennsylvania: Judson/London: SCM.
1970   Theodorus C. Vriezen: *An Outline of Old Testament Theology.* Pp. 121–140 in *Contemporary Old Testament Theologians.* Edited by Robert B. Laurin. Valley Forge, Pennsylvania: Judson.
1976   *One Hundred Years of Old Testament Interpretation.* Philadelphia: Westminster. [British edition: *A Century of Old Testament Study* (Guildford/London: Lutterworth).]
1978   *Old Testament Theology: A Fresh Approach.* New Foundations Theological Library. Atlanta: John Knox/London: Marshall, Morgan & Scott.
1980   *Isaiah and the Deliverance of Jerusalem: A Study of the Interpretation of Prophecy in the Old Testament.* Journal for the Study of the Old Testament Supplement 13. Sheffield: JSOT Press.

Collins, John J.
1990   Is a Critical Biblical Theology Possible? Pp. 1–17 in *The Hebrew Bible and Its Interpreters.* Edited by William H. Propp, Baruch Halpern, and David N. Freedman. Winona Lake, Indiana: Eisenbrauns.

von Cölln, Daniel G. C.
1836   *Biblische Theologie.* Volume 1: *Die biblische Theologie des Alten Testaments.* Leipzig: Barth.

Crenshaw, James L.
1978   *Gerhard von Rad.* Makers of the Modern Theological Mind. Waco: Word.

Cross, Frank M., Werner E. Lemke, and Patrick D. Miller Jr. (editors)
1976   *Magnalia Dei, The Mighty Acts of God: Essays on the Bible and Archaeology in Memory of G. Ernest Wright.* Garden City, New York: Doubleday.

Davidson, Andrew B.
1904   *The Theology of the Old Testament.* Edited by S. D. F. Salmond. International Theological Library. Edinburgh: T. & T. Clark/New York: Scribner.

Davies, G. Henton
1970   Gerhard von Rad: *Old Testament Theology.* Pp. 63–89 in *Contemporary Old Testament Theologians.* Edited by Robert B. Laurin. Valley Forge, Pennsylvania: Judson.

Deissler, Alfons
1972   *Die Grundbotschaft des Alten Testaments: Ein theologischer Durchblick.* Freiburg im Breisgau: Herder.
1981   *Die Grundbotschaft des Alten Testaments.* 8th edition. Freiburg im Breisgau: Herder.

Dentan, Robert C.
1950   *Preface to Old Testament Theology.* Yale Studies in Religion 14. New Haven: Yale University Press.
1963   *Preface to Old Testament Theology.* Revised edition. New York: Seabury.
Diestel, Ludwig
1869   *Geschichte des Alten Testamentes in der christlichen Kirche.* Jena: Mauke.
Donahue, John R.
1989   The Changing Shape of New Testament Theology. *Theological Studies* 50:314–35.
Donner, Herbert, Robert Hanhart, and Rudolf Smend (editors)
1977   *Beiträge zur Alttestamentlichen Theologie: Festschrift für Walther Zimmerli zum 70. Geburtstag.* Göttingen: Vandenhoeck & Ruprecht.
Dreyfus, F.
1975   Exégèse en Sorbonne, Exégèse en Église. *Revue Biblique* 82:321–59.
Dyrness, William A.
1979   *Themes in Old Testament Theology.* Downers Grove, Illinois: InterVarsity.
Eichrodt, Walther
1929   Hat die Alttestamentliche Theologie noch selbständige Bedeutung innerhalb der Alttestamentlichen Wissenschaft? *Zeitschrift für die Alttestamentliche Wissenschaft* 47:83–91 [English translation on pp. 30–39 above].
1933   *Theologie des Alten Testaments.* Volume 1: *Gott und Volk.* Leipzig: Hinrichs.
1935   *Theologie des Alten Testaments.* Volume 2: *Gott und Welt.* Leipzig: Hinrichs.
1939   *Theologie des Alten Testaments.* Volume 3: *Gott und Mensch.* Leipzig: Hinrichs.
1959   *Theologie des Alten Testaments.* Volume 1: *Gott und Volk.* 6th edition. Stuttgart: Klotz/Göttingen: Vandenhoeck & Ruprecht.
1961   *Theology of the Old Testament.* Volume 1. Translated by John A. Baker. Philadelphia: Westminster/London: SCM.
1964   *Theologie des Alten Testaments.* Volume 2/3: *Gott und Welt/Gott und Mensch.* 5th edition. Stuttgart: Klotz/Göttingen: Vandenhoeck & Ruprecht.
1967   *Theology of the Old Testament.* Volume 2. Translated by John A. Baker. Philadelphia: Westminster/London: SCM.
1969   *Religionsgeschichte Israels.* Bern: Francke.
1970   *Ezekiel: A Commentary.* Old Testament Library. Translated by Cosslett Quin. Philadelphia: Westminster/London: SCM.
Eissfeldt, Otto
1926   Israelitisch-jüdische Religionsgeschichte und Alttestamentliche Theologie. *Zeitschrift für die Alttestamentliche Wissenschaft* 44:1–12 [English translation on pp. 20–29 above].
Flanagan, James W., and Anita W. Robinson (editors)
1975   *No Famine in the Land: Studies in Honor of John L. McKenzie.* Missoula: Scholars Press/Claremont: Institute for Antiquity and Christianity.

Fohrer, Georg

1972   *Theologische Grundstrukturen des Alten Testaments.* Theologische Bibliothek Töpelmann 24. Berlin: de Gruyter.

Fretheim, Terence E.

1984   *The Suffering God: An Old Testament Perspective.* Overtures to Biblical Theology 14. Philadelphia: Fortress.

Gabler, Johann P.

1980   An Oration on the Proper Distinction between Biblical and Dogmatic Theology and the Specific Objectives of Each. Translated by John Sandys-Wunsch and Laurence Eldredge. *Scottish Journal of Theology* 33:134–44 [reprinted on pp. 489–502 above].

Gaffin, Richard B., Jr.

1976   Systematic Theology and Biblical Theology. *Westminster Journal of Theology* 38:281–99.

Gammie, John G., Walter A. Brueggemann, W. Lee Humphreys, and James M. Ward (editors)

1978   *Israelite Wisdom: Theological and Literary Essays in Honor of Samuel Terrien.* New York: Scholars Press for Union Theological Seminary.

Garcia Cordero, Maximiliano

1970   *Teologia de la Biblia.* Volume 1: *Antiguo Testamento.* Madrid: Católica.

Gelin, Albert

1948   *Les Idées maîtresses de l'Ancien Testament.* Lectio Divina 2. Paris: Cerf.

1955   *The Key Concepts of the Old Testament.* Translated by George Lamb. New York: Sheed & Ward.

Gese, Hartmut

1957   *Der Verfassungsentwurf des Ezechiel (Kap. 40–48): Traditionsgeschichtliche Untersuchung.* Beiträge zur historischen Theologie 25. Tübingen: Mohr.

1958   *Lehre und Wirklichkeit in der Alten Weisheit: Studien zu den Sprüchen Salomos und zu dem Buche Hiob.* Tübingen: Mohr.

1974   *Vom Sinai zum Zion: Alttestamentliche Beiträge zur biblischen Theologie.* Munich: Kaiser.

1977a   Tradition and Biblical Theology. Pp. 301–26 in *Tradition and Theology in the Old Testament.* Edited by Douglas A. Knight. Philadelphia: Fortress.

1977b   *Zur biblischen Theologie: Alttestamentliche Vorträge.* Munich: Kaiser.

1981a   *Essays on Biblical Theology.* Translated by Keith Crim. Minneapolis: Augsburg.

1981b   Wisdom, Son of Man, and the Origins of Christology: The Consistent Development of Biblical Theology. *Horizons in Biblical Theology* 3:23–57.

1983   *Zur biblischen Theologie: Alttestamentliche Vorträge.* 2d edition. Munich: Kaiser.

Goldberg, Michael

1982   *Theology and Narrative: A Critical Introduction.* Nashville: Abingdon.

Goldingay, John
  1987   *Theological Diversity and the Authority of the Old Testament.* Grand Rapids:
          Eerdmans.
Goshen-Gottstein, Moshe H.
  1987   Tanakh Theology: The Religion of the Old Testament and the Place
          of Jewish Biblical Theology. Pp. 617–44 in *Ancient Israelite Religion:
          Essays in Honor of Frank Moore Cross.* Edited by Patrick D. Miller Jr.,
          Paul D. Hanson, and S. Dean McBride. Philadelphia: Fortress.
Gottwald, Norman K.
  1970   W. Eichrodt: *Theology of the Old Testament.* Pp. 23–62 in *Contemporary
          Old Testament Theologians.* Edited by Robert B. Laurin. Valley Forge,
          Pennsylvania: Judson.
  1985   *The Hebrew Bible—A Socio-Literary Introduction.* Philadelphia: Fortress.
Gramberg, Carl P. W.
  1829–30 *Kritische Geschichte der Religionsideen des Alten Testaments.* 2 volumes.
          Berlin: Duncker & Humblot.
Groves, Joseph W.
  1987   *Actualization and Interpretation in the Old Testament.* Society of Biblical
          Literature Dissertation Series 86. Atlanta: Scholars Press.
Gunkel, Hermann
  1913   *Reden und Aufsätze.* Göttingen: Vandenhoeck & Ruprecht.
  1926-27 The "Historical Movement" in the Study of Religion. *Expository Times*
          38:532–36.
Hanson, Paul D.
  1975   *The Dawn of Apocalyptic: The Historical and Sociological Roots of Jewish
          Apocalyptic Eschatology.* Philadelphia: Fortress.
  1978   *Dynamic Transcendence: The Correlation of Confessional Heritage and Con-
          temporary Experience in a Biblical Model of Divine Activity.* Philadelphia:
          Fortress.
  1980   The Responsibility of Biblical Theology to Communities of Faith. *The-
          ology Today* 37:39–50.
  1982   *The Diversity of Scripture: A Theological Interpretation.* Overtures to Bibli-
          cal Theology 11. Philadelphia: Fortress.
  1984   The Future of Biblical Theology. *Horizons in Biblical Theology* 6/1:13–
          24.
  1985   Theology, Old Testament. Pp. 1057–62 in *Harper's Bible Dictionary.*
          Edited by Paul J. Achtemeier. San Francisco: Harper & Row.
  1986   *The People Called: The Growth of Community in the Bible.* San Francisco:
          Harper & Row.
Hartlich, Christian, and Walter Sachs
  1952   *Der Ursprung des Mythosbegriffes in der modernen Bibelwissenschaft.* Tübin-
          gen: Mohr.
Hasel, Gerhard F.
  1972   *Old Testament Theology: Basic Issues in the Current Debate.* Grand Rapids:
          Eerdmans.

1974 The Problem of the Center in the OT Theology Debate. *Zeitschrift für die Alttestamentliche Wissenschaft* 86:65–82.

1975 *Old Testament Theology: Basic Issues in the Current Debate.* 2d edition. Grand Rapids: Eerdmans.

1978 *New Testament Theology: Basic Issues in the Current Debate.* Grand Rapids: Eerdmans.

1981 A Decade of Old Testament Theology: Retrospect and Prospect. *Zeitschrift für die Alttestamentliche Wissenschaft* 93:165–83.

1982a Biblical Theology: Then, Now, and Tomorrow. *Horizons in Biblical Theology* 4:61–93.

1982b *Old Testament Theology: Basic Issues in the Current Debate.* 3d edition. Grand Rapids: Eerdmans.

1984 The Relationship between Biblical Theology and Systematic Theology. *Trinity Journal,* n.s. 5:113–27.

1985 Major Recent Issues in Old Testament Theology, 1978–1983. *Journal for the Study of the Old Testament* 31:31–53.

1988 Old Testament Theology from 1978–1987. *Andrews University Seminary Studies* 26:133–57.

1991 *Old Testament Theology: Basic Issues in the Current Debate.* 4th edition. Grand Rapids: Eerdmans.

Hävernick, Heinrich A. C.

1848 *Vorlesungen über die Theologie des Alten Testaments.* Edited by Heinrich A. Hahn. Erlangen: Heyder.

1863 *Vorlesungen über die Theologie des Alten Testaments.* 2d edition. Edited by Hermann Schultz. Frankfurt: Heyder & Zimmer.

Hayes, John H., and Frederick C. Prussner

1985 *Old Testament Theology: Its History and Development.* Atlanta: John Knox/ London: SCM.

Heinisch, Paul

1940 *Theologie des Alten Testaments.* Bonn: Peter Hanstein.

1950 *Theology of the Old Testament.* Translated by William G. Heidt. Collegeville, Minnesota: Liturgical Press.

Heschel, Abraham J.

1962–65 *Theology of Ancient Judaism.* London/New York: Soncino [Hebrew].

Hinson, David F.

1976 *The Theology of the Old Testament.* Theological Education Fund Study Guides 15. London: SPCK.

von Hofmann, Johann C. K.

1841–44 *Weissagung und Erfüllung im Alten und im Neuen Testamente: Ein theologischer Versuch.* 2 volumes. Nördlingen: Beck.

1852–56 *Der Schriftbeweis: Ein theologischer Versuch.* 2 volumes. Nördlingen: Beck.

1879 *Encyclopädie der Theologie.* Edited by H. J. Bestmann. Nördlingen: Beck.

1880 *Biblische Hermeneutik.* Edited by W. Volk. Nördlingen: Beck.

1959 *Interpreting the Bible.* Translated by Christian Preus. Minneapolis: Augsburg.

Høgenhaven, Jesper
    1988   *Problems and Prospects of Old Testament Theology.* Biblical Seminar 6. Sheffield: JSOT Press.

van Imschoot, Paul
    1954–56 *Théologie de l'Ancien Testament.* 2 volumes. Tournai: Desclée & Cie.
    1965   *Theology of the Old Testament.* Volume 1: *God.* Translated by Kathryn Sullivan and Fidelis Buck. New York: Desclée.

Irwin, William A.
    1945   The Reviving Theology of the Old Testament. *Journal of Religion* 25:235–46.

Jacob, Edmond
    1955   *Théologie de l'Ancien Testament: Revue et augmentée.* Paris/Neuchâtel: Delachaux & Niestlé.
    1958   *Theology of the Old Testament.* Translated by Arthur W. Heathcote and Philip J. Allcock. New York: Harper/London: Hodder & Stoughton.
    1968   *Théologie de l'Ancien Testament: Revue et augmentée.* 2d edition. Paris/ Neuchâtel: Delachaux & Niestlé.
    1970   *Grundfragen Alttestamentlicher Theologie.* Franz Delitzsch–Vorlesungen 1965. Stuttgart: Kohlhammer.

Kaiser, Gottlieb P. C.
    1813–21 *Die biblische Theologie.* 3 volumes. Erlangen: Palm.

Kaiser, Walter C., Jr.
    1978   *Toward an Old Testament Theology.* Grand Rapids: Zondervan.
    1981   *Toward an Exegetical Theology: Biblical Exegesis for Preaching and Teaching.* Grand Rapids: Baker.
    1983   *Toward Old Testament Ethics.* Grand Rapids: Zondervan.
    1987   *Toward Rediscovering the Old Testament.* Grand Rapids: Zondervan.

Kayser, August
    1886   *Die Theologie des Alten Testaments in ihrer geschichtlichen Entwicklung dargestellt.* Edited by E. Reuss. Strassburg: Schmidt & Bull.

Kelsey, David H.
    1975   *The Use of Scripture in Recent Theology.* Philadelphia: Fortress/London: SCM.

Kittel, Rudolf
    1921   Die Zukunft der Alttestamentlichen Theologie. *Zeitschrift für die Alttestamentliche Wissenschaft* 39:84–99.

Klein, Ralph W.
    1979   *Israel in Exile: A Theological Interpretation.* Overtures to Biblical Theology 6. Philadelphia: Fortress.

Knierim, Rolf
    1971   Offenbarung im Alten Testament. Pp. 206–35 in *Probleme biblischer Theologie: Gerhard von Rad zum 70. Geburtstag.* Edited by Hans W. Wolff. Munich: Kaiser.
    1981   Cosmos and History in Israel's Theology. *Horizons in Biblical Theology* 3:59–123.

1984   The Task of Old Testament Theology. *Horizons in Biblical Theology* 6/ 1:25–57.

Knight, Douglas A.

1973   *Rediscovering the Traditions of Israel: The Development of the Traditio-Historical Research of the Old Testament, with Special Consideration of Scandinavian Contributions.* Society of Biblical Literature Dissertation Series 9. Missoula: University of Missoula.

Knight, George, A. F.

1959   *A Christian Theology of the Old Testament.* Richmond: John Knox/London: SCM.

Köberle, Justus

1906   Heilsgeschichtliche und religionsgeschichtliche Betrachtungsweise des Alten Testaments. *Neue kirchliche Zeitschrift* 17:200–22.

Köhler, Ludwig

1935   *Theologie des Alten Testaments.* Tübingen: Mohr (Siebeck).

1953   *Theologie des Alten Testaments.* 3d edition. Tübingen: Mohr.

1957   *Old Testament Theology.* Translated by A. S. Todd. Philadelphia: Westminster/London: Lutterworth.

Kort, Wesley A.

1988   *Story, Text, and Scripture: Literary Interests in Biblical Narrative.* University Park: Pennsylvania State University Press.

Kraus, Hans-Joachim

1977   Probleme und Perspektiven biblischer Theologie. Pp. 97–124 in *Biblische Theologie heute: Einführung, Beispiele, Kontroversen.* By Klaus Haacker et al. Biblisch-theologische Studien, n.s. 1. Neukirchen-Vluyn: Neukirchener Verlag.

Krentz, Edgar

1975   *The Historical-Critical Method.* Guides to Biblical Scholarship. Philadelphia: Fortress.

Laurin, Robert B. (editor)

1970a   *Contemporary Old Testament Theologians.* Valley Forge, Pennsylvania: Judson.

1970b   Edmond Jacob: *Theology of the Old Testament.* Pp. 141–69 in *Contemporary Old Testament Theologians.* Edited by Robert B. Laurin. Valley Forge, Pennsylvania: Judson.

Lehman, Chester K.

1971   *Biblical Theology.* Volume 1: *Old Testament.* Scottdale, Pennsylvania: Herald.

Levenson, Jon D.

1985   *Sinai and Zion: An Entry into the Jewish Bible.* Minneapolis: Winston.

1987   Why Jews Are Not Interested in Biblical Theology. Pp. 281–307 in *Judaic Perspectives on Ancient Israel.* Edited by Jacob Neusner, Baruch A. Levine, and Ernest S. Frerichs. Philadelphia: Fortress.

1988a   *Creation and the Persistence of Evil: The Jewish Drama of Divine Omnipotence.* San Francisco: Harper & Row.

1988b   The Eighth Principle of Judaism and the Literary Simultaneity of
           Scripture. *Journal of Religion* 68:205–25.
Lindbeck, George
1989   Scripture, Consensus, and Community. Pp. 74–101 in *Biblical Interpre-
           tation in Crisis: The Ratzinger Conference on Bible and Church.* Edited by
           Richard J. Neuhaus. Grand Rapids: Eerdmans.
McKenzie, John L.
1956   *The Two-Edged Sword: An Interpretation of the Old Testament.* Milwaukee:
           Bruce.
1965   *Dictionary of the Bible.* New York: Bruce/London: Collier-Macmillan.
1974   *A Theology of the Old Testament.* Garden City, New York: Doubleday.
Maier, Gerhard
1977   *The End of the Historical-Critical Method.* Translated by Edwin W. Lever-
           enz and Rudolph F. Norden. St. Louis: Concordia.
Martens, Elmer A.
1977   Tackling Old Testament Theology. *Journal of the Evangelical Theological
           Society* 20:123–32.
1981   *God's Design: A Focus on Old Testament Theology.* Grand Rapids: Baker.
           [British edition: *Plot and Purpose in the Old Testament* (Leicester: Inter-
           Varsity).]
1986   *Jeremiah.* Believers Church Bible Commentary. Scottdale: Herald.
Marti, Karl
1897   *Geschichte der israelitischen Religion.* 3d edition. Strassburg: Schmidt &
           Bull.
Mayo, S. M.
1982   *The Relevance of the Old Testament for the Christian Faith: Biblical Theology
           and Interpretative Methodology.* Washington, D.C.: University Press of
           America.
Mendenhall, George E.
1955   *Law and Covenant in Israel and the Ancient Near East.* Pittsburgh: Biblical
           Colloquium. Reprinted from *Biblical Archaeologist* 17 (1954): 26–46,
           50–76.
Merk, Otto
1972   *Biblische Theologie des Neuen Testaments in ihrer Anfangszeit.* Marburg:
           Elwert.
Möller, Wilhelm, and Hans Möller
1938   *Biblische Theologie des Alten Testaments in heilsgeschichtlicher Entwicklung.*
           Zwickau: Johannes Herrmann.
Morgan, Robert
1987   Gabler's Bicentenary. *Expository Times* 98:164–68.
Muilenburg, James
1961   *The Way of Israel: Biblical Faith and Ethics.* Religious Perspectives 5. New
           York: Harper & Row.
Munson, Thomas N.
1975   A Biographical Sketch of John L. McKenzie. Pp. 1–13 in *No Famine in
           the Land: Studies in Honor of John L. McKenzie.* Edited by James W. Flan-

agan and Anita W. Robinson. Missoula: Scholars Press/Claremont: Institute for Antiquity and Christianity.

Noack, Ludwig
1853   *Die biblische Theologie.* Halle: Pfeffer.

Oehler, Gustaf F.
1845   *Prolegomena zur Theologie des Alten Testaments.* Stuttgart: Leisching.
1873–74 *Die Theologie des Alten Testaments.* 2 volumes. Edited by Hermann Oehler. Tübingen: Heckenhauer.
1874–75 *Theology of the Old Testament.* 2 volumes. Translated by Ellen D. Smith and Sophia Taylor. Edinburgh: T. & T. Clark.
1883   *Theology of the Old Testament.* 2 volumes. 2d edition. Translated by Ellen D. Smith and Sophia Taylor. Edinburgh: T. & T. Clark/New York: Funk & Wagnalls.

Oeming, Manfred
1985   *Gesamtbiblische Theologien der Gegenwart: Das Verhältnis von AT und NT in der hermeneutischen Diskussion seit Gerhard von Rad.* Stuttgart: Kohlhammer.

Ollenburger, Ben C.
1985   Biblical Theology: Situating the Discipline. Pp. 37–62 in *Understanding the Word: Essays in Honor of Bernard W. Anderson.* Edited by James T. Butler, Edgar W. Conrad, and Ben C. Ollenburger. Journal for the Study of the Old Testament Supplement Series 37. Sheffield: JSOT Press.
1986   What Krister Stendahl "Meant"—A Normative Critique of "Descriptive Biblical Theology." *Horizons in Biblical Theology* 8:61–98.
1987   *Zion, the City of the Great King: A Theological Symbol of the Jerusalem Cult.* Journal for the Study of the Old Testament Supplement Series 41. Sheffield: JSOT Press.
1991   *So Wide a Sea: Essays on Biblical and Systematic Theology.* IMS Text Reader 4. Elkhart, Indiana: Institute of Mennonite Studies.

Payne, John Barton
1962   *The Theology of the Older Testament.* Grand Rapids: Zondervan.

Plümacher, Eckhard
1987   Wilhlem Martin Leberecht de Wette in Weimar (1819–1822): Fünf Briefe an Georg Andreas Reimer. Pp. 184–206 in *Altes Testament und christliche Verkündigung: Festschrift für Antonius H. J. Gunneweg zum 65. Geburtstag.* Edited by Manfred Oeming and Axel Graupner. Stuttgart: Kohlhammer.

Procksch, Otto
1950   *Theologie des Alten Testaments.* Gütersloh: Bertelsmann.

von Rad, Gerhard
1957   *Theologie des Alten Testaments.* Volume 1: *Die Theologie der geschichtlichen Überlieferungen Israels.* Munich: Kaiser.
1960   *Theologie des Alten Testaments.* Volume 2: *Die Theologie der prophetischen Überlieferungen Israels.* Munich: Kaiser.

1962   *Old Testament Theology.* Volume 1: *The Theology of Israel's Historical Traditions.* Translated by David M. G. Stalker. New York: Harper & Row/ Edinburgh: Oliver & Boyd.

1965   *Old Testament Theology.* Volume 2: *The Theology of Israel's Prophetic Traditions.* Translated by David M. G. Stalker. New York: Harper & Row/ Edinburgh: Oliver & Boyd.

1966   *The Problem of the Hexateuch and Other Essays.* Translated by E. W. T. Dickens. Edinburgh: Oliver & Boyd.

Ratzinger, Joseph

1989   Biblical Interpretation in Crisis: On the Question of the Foundations and Approaches of Exegesis Today. Pp. 1–23 in *Biblical Interpretation in Crisis: The Ratzinger Conference on Bible and Church.* Edited by Richard J. Neuhaus. Grand Rapids: Eerdmans.

Rendtorff, Rolf, and Klaus Koch (editors)

1961   *Studien zur Theologie der Alttestamentlichen Überlieferungen.* Neukirchen-Vluyn: Neukirchener Verlag.

Reventlow, Henning Graf

1982   *Hauptprobleme der Alttestamentlichen Theologie im 20. Jahrhundert.* Erträge der Forschung 173. Darmstadt: Wissenschaftliche Buchgesellschaft.

1983   *Hauptprobleme der biblische Theologie im 20. Jahrhundert.* Erträge der Forschung 203. Darmstadt: Wissenschaftliche Buchgesellschaft.

1985a   Die Entstehung der historisch-kritischen Bibelexegese auf dem Hintergrund von Aufklärung und neuzeitlicher Rationalität. Pp. 35–53 in *Die historisch-kritische Methode und die heutige Suche nach einem lebendigen Verständnis der Bibel.* Edited by Helmut Riedlinger. Munich/ Zurich: Schnell & Steiner.

1985b   *Problems of Old Testament Theology in the Twentieth Century.* Translated by John Bowden. Philadelpia: Fortress/London: SCM.

1986   *Problems of Biblical Theology in the Twentieth Century.* Translated by John Bowden. Philadelphia: Fortress/London: SCM.

1987   Zur Theologie des Alten Testaments. *Theologische Rundschau* 52:221–67.

Riehm, Eduard K. A.

1889   *Alttestamentliche Theologie.* Edited by Karl Pahncke. Halle: Strien.

Robinson, H. Wheeler

1946   *Inspiration and Revelation in the Old Testament.* Oxford: Clarendon.

Rogerson, John

1984   *Old Testament Criticism in the Nineteenth Century: England and Germany.* Philadelphia: Fortress/London: SPCK.

Rowley, Harold H.

1956   *The Faith of Israel: Aspects of Old Testament Thought.* Philadelphia: Westminster/London: SCM.

Saebø, Magne

1982   Eichrodt, Walther. Volume 9: pp. 371–73 in *Theologische Realenzyklopädie.* Berlin: de Gruyter.

1987   Johann Philipp Gablers Bedeutung für die biblische Theologie. *Zeitschrift für die Alttestamentliche Wissenschaft* 99:1–16.

Sakenfeld, Katharine Doob
  1982   Old Testament Perspectives: Methodological Issues. *Journal for the Study of the Old Testament* 22:13–20.

Sanders, James A.
  1978   Comparative Wisdom: L'Oeuvre Terrien. Pp. 3–14 in *Israelite Wisdom: Theological and Literary Essays in Honor of Samuel Terrien.* Edited by John G. Gammie, Walter A. Brueggemann, W. Lee Humphreys, and James M. Ward. New York: Scholars Press for Union Theological Seminary.
  1987   *From Sacred Story to Sacred Text: Canon as Paradigm.* Philadelphia: Fortress.

Sandys-Wunsch, John, and Laurence Eldredge
  1980   J. P. Gabler and the Distinction between Biblical and Dogmatic Theology: Translation, Commentary, and Discussion of His Originality. *Scottish Journal of Theology* 33:133–58.

Schmid, Hans Heinrich
  1977   Unterwegs zu einer neuen biblischen Theologie? Anfragen an die von H. Gese und P. Stuhlmacher vorgetragenen Entwürfe biblischer Theologie. Pp. 75–95 in *Biblische Theologie heute: Einführung, Beispiele, Kontroversen.* By Klaus Haacker et al. Biblisch-theologische Studien, n.s. 1. Neukirchen-Vluyn: Neukirchener Verlag.

Schmidt, Werner H.
  1968   *Alttestamentlicher Glaube in seiner Geschichte.* Neukirchener Studienbücher 6. Neukirchen-Vluyn: Neukirchener Verlag.
  1972   "Theologie des Alten Testaments" vor und nach Gerhard von Rad. *Verkündigung und Forschung* 17:1–25.
  1982   *Alttestamentlicher Glaube in seiner Geschichte.* 4th edition. Neukirchener Studienbücher 6. Neukirchen-Vluyn: Neukirchener Verlag.
  1983   *The Faith of the Old Testament: A History.* Translated by John Sturdy. Philadelphia: Westminster.

Schultz, Hermann
  1869   *Alttestamentliche Theologie: Die Offenbarungsreligion auf ihrer vorchristlichen Entwicklungstufe.* 2 volumes. Frankfurt am Main: Heyder & Zimmer.
  1878   *Alttestamentliche Theologie: Die Offenbarungsreligion auf ihrer vorchristlicher Entwicklungstufe.* 2d edition. Frankfurt: Heyder & Zimmer.
  1892   *Old Testament Theology: The Religion of Revelation in Its Pre-Christian Stage of Development.* 2 volumes. Translated by John A. Paterson. Edinburgh: T. & T. Clark.
  1895   *Old Testament Theology: The Religion of Revelation in Its Pre-Christian Stage of Development.* 2d edition. 2 volumes. Translated by John A. Paterson. Edinburgh: T. & T. Clark.
  1896   *Alttestamentliche Theologie: Die Offenbarungsreligion auf ihrer vorchristlicher Entwicklungstufe.* 5th edition. Frankfurt: Heyder & Zimmer.

Sellin, Ernst
  1933   *Alttestamentliche Theologie auf religionsgeschichtlicher Grundlage.* 2 volumes. Leipzig: Quelle & Meyer.

Shaffer, Elinor S.
1975   *"Kubla Khan" and the Fall of Jerusalem: The Mythological School in Biblical Criticism and Secular Literature, 1770–1880.* Cambridge: Cambridge University Press.

Smart, James D.
1943   The Death and Rebirth of Old Testament Theology. *Journal of Religion* 23:1–11, 125–36.

Snaith, Norman H.
1944   *The Distinctive Ideas of the Old Testament.* London: Epworth.

Spriggs, David G.
1974   *Two Old Testament Theologies: A Comparative Evaluation of the Contributions of Eichrodt and von Rad to Our Understanding of the Nature of Old Testament Theology.* Studies in Biblical Theology 2/30. London: SCM/ Naperville, Illinois: Allenson.

Stade, Bernhard
1899   Über die Aufgabe der biblischen Theologie des Alten Testaments. Pp. 77–96 in *Ausgewählte akademische Reden und Abhandlungen.* Giessen: Ricker. Reprinted from *Zeitschrift für Theologie und Kirche* 3 (1893) 31–51.

1905   *Biblische Theologie des Alten Testaments.* Volume 1: *Die Religion Israels und die Entstehung des Judentums.* Tübingen: Mohr (Siebeck).

Staerk, Willy
1923   Religionsgeschichte und Religionsphilosophie in ihrer Bedeutung für die biblische Theologie des Alten Testaments. *Zeitschrift für Theologie und Kirche* 31:289–300.

Stanton, Elizabeth Cady (editor)
1895–98 *The Woman's Bible.* 2 volumes. New York: European Publishing Co.

Stendahl, Krister
1984   Biblical Theology: A Program. Pp. 11–44 in *Meanings: The Bible as Document and as Guide.* Philadelphia: Fortress. Reprinted from "Biblical Theology, Contemporary" in *Interpreter's Dictionary of the Bible,* 1:418–32. Edited by Geogre A. Buttrick. Nashville: Abingdon, 1962.

Sternberg, Meir
1985   *The Poetics of Biblical Narrative: Ideological Literature and the Drama of Reading.* Bloomington: Indiana University Press.

Steudel, Johann C. F.
1840   *Vorlesungen über die Theologie des Alten Testaments.* Edited by Gustaf F. Oehler. Berlin: Reimer.

Steuernagel, Carl
1925   Alttestamentliche Theologie und Alttestamentliche Religionsgeschichte. Pp. 266–73 in *Vom Alten Testament: Karl Marti zum siebzigsten Geburtstage.* Edited by Karl Budde. Beiheft zur Zeitschrift für die Alttestamentliche Wissenschaft 41. Giessen: Töpelmann.

Stoebe, Hans J., Johann J. Stamm, and Ernst Jenni (editors)

1970   *Wort–Gebot–Glaube: Beiträge zur Theologie des Alten Testaments: Walther Eichrodt zum 80. Geburtstag.* Abhandlungen zur Theologie des Alten und Neuen Testaments 59. Zurich: Zwingli.

Strauss, David F.

1865   *Der Christus des Glaubens und der Jesus der Geschichte: Eine Kritik des Schleiermacher'schen Lebens Jesu.* Berlin: Franz Duncker.

1977   *The Christ of Faith and the Jesus of History: A Critique of Schleiermacher's "Life of Jesus."* Translated by Leander E. Keck. Philadelphia: Fortress.

Stuhlmacher, Peter

1977   *Historical Criticism and Theological Interpretation of Scripture: Toward a Hermeneutics of Consent.* Translated by Roy A. Harrisville. Philadelphia: Fortress.

1979   *Vom Verstehen des Neuen Testaments: Eine Hermeneutik.* Grundrisse zum Neuen Testament 6. Göttingen: Vandenhoeck & Ruprecht.

Terrien, Samuel L.

1978   *The Elusive Presence: Toward a New Biblical Theology.* Religious Perspectives 26. San Francisco: Harper & Row.

1981   The Play of Wisdom: Turning Point in Biblical Theology. *Horizons in Biblical Theology* 3:125–53.

Toews, John E.

1980   *Hegelianism: The Path toward Dialectical Humanism, 1805–1841.* Cambridge: Cambridge University Press.

Trible, Phyllis.

1978   *God and the Rhetoric of Sexuality.* Overtures to Biblical Theology 2. Philadelphia: Fortress.

1982   (guest editor) The Effects of Women's Studies on Biblical Studies. *Journal for the Study of the Old Testament* 22:3–71.

1984   *Texts of Terror: Literary-Feminist Readings of Biblical Narratives.* Overtures to Biblical Theology 13. Philadelphia: Fortress.

1989   Five Loaves and Two Fishes: Feminist Hermeneutics and Biblical Theology. *Theological Studies* 50:279–95.

Troeltsch, Ernst

1913   The Dogmatics of the "Religionsgeschichtliche Schule." *American Journal of Theology* 17:1–21.

Tsevat, Matitiahu

1986   Theology of the Old Testament—A Jewish View. *Horizons in Biblical Theology* 8/2:33–50.

Tucker, Gene M., David L. Petersen, and Robert R. Wilson (editors).

1988   *Canon, Theology, and Old Testament Interpretation: Essays in Honor of Brevard S. Childs.* Philadelphia: Fortress.

van Unnik, W. C., and A. S. van der Woude (editors)

1966   *Studia Biblica et Semitica: Theodoro Christiano Vriezen . . . Dedicata.* Wageningen: Veenman & Zonen.

Vatke, Johann K. W.

1835   *Die biblische Theologie wissenschaftlich dargestellt.* Volume 1: *Die Religion des Alten Testaments nach dem kanonischen Büchern entwickelt.* Berlin: Bethge.

Vischer, Wilhelm

1934–42 *Das Christuszeugnis des Alten Testaments.* 2 volumes. Zurich/Zollikon: Evangelischer Verlag.

1949   *The Witness of the Old Testament to Christ.* Volume 1: *The Pentateuch.* Translated by A. B. Crabtree. London: Lutterworth.

Vos, Geerhardus

1948   *Biblical Theology: Old and New Testaments.* Grand Rapids: Eerdmans.

Vriezen, Theodorus C.

1949   *Hoofdlijnen der Theologie van het Oude Testament.* Wageningen: Veenman & Zonen.

1954   *Hoofdlijnen der Theologie van het Oude Testament.* 2d edition. Wageningen: Veenman & Zonen.

1958   *An Outline of Old Testament Theology.* Translated by S. Neuijen. Boston: Branford/Oxford: Blackwell.

1966   *Hoofdlijnen der Theologie van het Oude Testament.* 3d edition. Wageningen: Veenman & Zonen.

1970   *An Outline of Old Testament Theology.* 2d edition. Translated by S. Neuijen. Newton, Massachusetts: Branford/Oxford: Blackwell.

Wall, James M.

1976   1976: "The Year of the Evangelical." *Christian Century* 93 (Dec. 29): 1165–66.

Westermann, Claus

1960   *Grundformen prophetischer Rede.* Beiträge zur evangelischen Theologie 31. Munich: Kaiser.

1964   *Forschung am Alten Testament: Gesammelte Studien.* Theologische Bücherei 24. Munich: Kaiser.

1966   *Das Buch Jesaia 40–66.* Das Alte Testament Deutsch 19. Göttingen: Vandenhoeck & Ruprecht.

1967   *Basic Forms of Prophetic Speech.* Translated by Hugh C. White. Philadelphia: Westminster.

1968   *Der Segen in der Bibel und im Handeln der Kirche.* Munich: Kaiser.

1969   *Isaiah 40–66: A Commentary.* Translated by David M. G. Stalker. Old Testament Library. Philadelpiha: Westminster/London: SCM.

1974   *Forschung am Alten Testament: Gesammelte Studien II.* Edited by Rainer Albertz and Eberhard Ruprecht. Theologische Bücherei 55. Munich: Kaiser.

1974–82 *Genesis.* 3 volumes. Biblischer Kommentar: Altes Testament 1. Neukirchen-Vluyn: Neukirchener Verlag.

1976   *Die Verheissungen an die Väter: Studien zur Vätergeschichte.* Forschungen zur Religion und Literatur des Alten und Neuen Testaments 116. Göttingen: Vandenhoeck & Ruprecht.

1977   *Der Aufbau des Buches Hiob.* 2d edition. Stuttgart: Calwer.

1978a   *Blessing: In the Bible and in the Life of the Church.* Translated by Keith Crim. Overtures to Biblical Theology 3. Philadelphia: Fortress.

1978b   *Theologie des Alten Testaments in Grundzügen.* Göttingen: Vandenhoeck & Ruprecht.

1979   *What Does the Old Testament Say about God?.* Edited by Friedemann W. Golka. Atlanta: John Knox/London: SCM.

1980a   *Promises to the Fathers: Studies on the Patriarchal Narratives.* Translated by David E. Green. Philadelphia: Fortress.

1980b   *The Psalms: Structure, Content, and Message.* Translated by Ralph D. Gehrke. Minneapolis: Augsburg.

1981   *The Structure of the Book of Job: A Form-Critical Analysis.* Translated by Charles A. Muenchow. Philadelphia: Fortress.

1982   *Elements of Old Testament Theology.* Translated by Douglas W. Stott. Atlanta: John Knox.

1984   *Erträge der Forschung am Alten Testament: Gesammelte Studien III.* Edited by Rainer Albertz. Theologische Bücherei 73. Munich: Kaiser.

1984–86 *Genesis: A Commentary.* 3 volumes. Translated by John J. Scullion. Minneapolis: Augsburg/London: SPCK.

1987   *Prophetische Heilsworte im Alten Testament.* Forschungen zur Religion und Literatur des Alten und Neuen Testaments 145. Göttingen: Vandenhoeck & Ruprecht.

de Wette, Wilhelm M. L.

1813   *Lehrbuch der christlichen Dogmatik.* Volume 1: *Biblische Dogmatik Alten und Neuen Testaments.* Berlin: Realschulbuchhandlung.

1831   *Lehrbuch der christlichen Dogmatik.* Volume 1: *Biblische Dogmatik Alten und Neuen Testaments.* 3d edition. Berlin: Reimer.

1846   *Die biblische Geschichte als Geschichte der Offenbarungen Gottes.* Berlin: Reimer.

Whybray, R. N.

1987   Old Testament Theology—A Non-Existent Beast? Pp. 168–80 in *Scripture: Meaning and Method: Essays Presented to Anthony T. Hanson for His Seventieth Birthday.* Edited by Barry P. Thompson. Hull: Hull University.

Wink, Walter

1973   *The Bible in Human Transformation: Toward a New Paradigm for Biblical Study.* Philadelphia: Fortress.

1980   *Transforming Bible Study: A Leader's Guide.* Nashville: Abingdon.

Wolff, Hans W. (editor)

1971   *Probleme biblischer Theologie: Gerhard von Rad zum 70. Geburtstag.* Munich: Kaiser.

Wrede, William

1973   The Task and Methods of "New Testament Theology." Pp. 68–116 in *The Nature of New Testament Theology: The Contribution of William Wrede and Adolf Schlatter.* Edited by Robert Morgan. Studies in Biblical Theology 2/25. London: SCM/Naperville, Illinois: Allenson.

Wright, G. Ernest
  1950   Review of *Preface to Old Testament Theology*, by Robert C. Dentan. *Journal of Biblical Literature* 69:393–97.
  1952   *God Who Acts: Biblical Theology as Recital*. Studies in Biblical Theology 8. London: SCM/Chicago: Regnery.
  1959   Review of *Old Testament Theology*, by Ludwig Köhler. *Religious Education* 54:386–87.
  1960   Review of *Theology of the Old Testament*, by Edmond Jacob. *Journal of Biblical Literature* 79:78–81.
  1969   *The Old Testament and Theology*. New York: Harper & Row.
Wright, G. Ernest, and Reginald H. Fuller
  1957   *The Book of the Acts of God: Contemporary Scholarship Interprets the Bible*. Garden City, New York: Doubleday.
Young, Edward J.
  1958   *The Study of Old Testament Theology Today*. London: James Clark.
Zimmerli, Walther
  1968   *Der Mensch und seine Hoffnung im Alten Testament*. Göttingen: Vandenhoeck & Ruprecht.
  1969   *Ezekiel*. 2 volumes. Biblischer Kommentar: Altes Testament 13. Neukirchen-Vluyn: Neukirchener Verlag.
  1971a   *Man and His Hope in the Old Testament*. Translated by G. W. Bowden. Studies in Biblical Theology 2/20. London: SCM/Naperville, Illinois: Allenson.
  1971b   *Die Weltlichkeit des Alten Testaments*. Göttingen: Vandenhoeck & Ruprecht.
  1972   *Grundriss der Alttestamentlichen Theologie*. Theologische Wissenschaft 3. Stuggart: Kohlhammer.
  1975   *Grundriss der Alttestamentlichen Theologie*. 2d edition. Theologische Wissenschaft 3. Stuggart: Kohlhammer.
  1976   *The Old Testament and the World*. Translated by John J. Scullion. Atlanta: John Knox.
  1978   *Old Testament Theology in Outline*. Translated by David E. Green. Atlanta: John Knox/Edinburgh: T. & T. Clark.
  1979–83   *Ezekiel: A Commentary on the Book of the Prophet Ezekiel*. 2 volumes. Translated by Ronald E. Clements and James D. Martin. Edited by Frank M. Cross, Klaus Baltzer, Leonard J. Greenspoon, and Paul D. Hanson. Hermeneia. Philadelphia: Fortress.
  1982a   *Grundriss der Alttestamentlichen Theologie*. 4th edition. Theologische Wissenschaft 3. Stuggart: Kohlhammer.
  1982b   *I am Yahweh*. Translated by Douglas W. Stott. Edited by Walter Brueggemann. Atlanta: John Knox.
  1985   *Grundriss der Alttestamentlichen Theologie*. 5th edition. Theologische Wissenschaft 3. Stuggart: Kohlhammer.

INDEX OF TOPICS

Since this is (naturally) an index only of the excerpts reprinted above, it should not be considered comprehensive relative to author or topic. Thus, one cannot assume that looking up every reference to, say, *covenant* or *canon* will reveal the totality of Eichrodt's thinking on covenant or Childs's thinking on canon. In line with the goal of this book and, indeed, this series, the purpose of this index is to push the reader further—back to the writings of the theologians discussed above.

INDEX OF AUTHORITIES

INDEX OF SCRIPTURE REFERENCES

Old Testament

Index of Scripture References

Deuterocanonical Books

New Testament